Rosemarie Tanzketli

Fall '92

The Market Revolution

The Market Revolution

JACKSONIAN AMERICA

1815–1846

Charles Sellers

New York   Oxford
OXFORD UNIVERSITY PRESS
1991

Oxford University Press

Oxford   New York   Toronto
Delhi   Bombay   Calcutta   Madras   Karachi
Petaling Jaya   Singapore   Hong Kong   Tokyo
Nairobi   Dar es Salaam   Cape Town
Melbourne   Auckland

and associated companies in
Berlin   Ibadan

Published by Oxford University Press, Inc.,
200 Madison Avenue, New York, New York 10016

Oxford is a registered trademark of Oxford University Press

Library of Congress Cataloging-in-Publication Data
Sellers, Charles Grier.
The market revolution: Jacksonian America, 1815–1846/ Charles Sellers.
p. cm.   Includes bibliographical references and index.
ISBN 0-19-503889-4
1. United States—Economic conditions—To 1865.   2. Capitalism—
Social aspects—United States—History—19th century.
3. Representative government and representation—United States—
History—19th century.   4. Democracy—History—19th century.
I. Title.
HC105.S38   1991   90-24188

2 4 6 8 9 7 5 3 1
Printed in the United States of America

In memory of

Giles Sellers
1892–1960

two-mule farmer
christian
democrat
southern gentle man

Contents

The Market Revolution

Chapter 1

Land and Market

1815 OPENED with the fate of the American republic—and worldwide republicanism—hanging in the balance. A pall of chill, ashes, and gloom lay over muddy little Washington. Burned out of the Capitol, congressmen found standing room in a patent office spared by British invaders' reverence for technology. Amid blackened rubble, they dreaded news from every direction.

Four days' travel to the north, the elders of New England were thought to be plotting secession behind closed doors at Hartford. A month away to the south, Sir Edward Pakenham's seasoned British army, fresh from victory over Napoleon Bonaparte, advanced through the swamps of the lower Mississippi toward New Orleans. Few thought it could be stopped by the raw western militia hastily assembling under Indian fighter Andrew Jackson.

Only forty years before, the American Revolution had loosed republicanism on the modern world. Within a generation the French Revolution and Bonaparte's legions broadcast the contagion across Europe. Through twenty years of unparalleled bloodshed, British-led coalitions of European autocracy made war on revolutionary Bonapartism. When the United States rashly joined the fray against the preoccupied British, it brought upon itself a train of left-handed humiliations even as the British right hand crushed Napoleon. And now Britain's mighty fleets and armies redeployed to choke off the republican infection at its New World source.

Americans' only hope lay in stalled peace negotiations at faraway Ghent in the European Low Countries. By last report, two months in transit, British negotiators were still dragging their heels, presumably awaiting a Pakenham victory to dismember the upstart republic.

After weeks of suspense, on February 5 glorious news arrived from below New Orleans. The invaders had been routed on January 8 by murderous fire from Jackson's hasty entrenchment behind the little Rodriguez Canal. With a loss of only thirteen men, the western citizen-soldiers cut down seven hundred Britons, including General Pakenham. Celebration climaxed eight days later, when the capital

3

learned that a treaty of peace had already been signed at Ghent on Christmas Eve, over two weeks before Jackson's stunning triumph.

Despite overwhelming military superiority, the war-weary, tax-ridden British agreed to leave the United States intact. With victory miraculously snatched from defeat, the republic was safe. As lumbering mail coaches spread rejoicing across the wide land, speeches, toasts, and schoolboy compositions celebrated the brilliant destiny of the most extensive republic the world had known.

Yet postwar boom ignited a generation of conflict over the republic's destiny. History's most revolutionary force, the capitalist market, was wresting the American future from history's most conservative force, the land. As market revolution stressed Americans into unparalleled mobilization, both spiritual and political, the Hero of New Orleans found another commanding role.

In the beginning was the land, immemorial provider of survival for the many and honor, riches, power, and independence for the few. When a New World to exploit galvanized an Old World swarming with too many people for too few acres, European mercantile capital reached across the seas for world dominion. A global division of labor drew Asian spices, enslaved African labor, and the New World's inexhaustible acreage into an intricate network of production for exchange, funneling back into Europe the capital that launched the industrial revolution. Wherever merchant capital reached, the market's irresistible commodities drew people into producing the commodities it demanded. As the division of labor rationalized and multiplied production, money value allocated natural resources and human energy. As traditional cultures gave way to a spreading market culture, new beliefs, behaviors, emotions, and interpersonal relations spurred work and consumption.

Where England's venturous capital met the New World's abundant acreage along the coast of temperate North America, a new kind of society developed. Reversal here of the Old World's person/land ratio opened a refuge for swarms of the needy and servile uprooted by the market from the European land. New World land—fertile, abundantly watered and wooded, and easily wrested at first from its aboriginal populace—elevated them to landowning security and respect.

Cheap land, virtually free at first, not only elevated the mass but imposed a limit on wealth by making labor expensive. With farm ownership readily attainable, Euro/Americans would not labor for others except briefly and at high wages. A few years of high wages financed enough cheap land to yield a comfort and independence inconceivable to poor Europeans. With wages too high for most farmers to pay, production was limited—no matter how much land they had—by the family labor available. While raising European immigrants to an exhilarating rural well-being, the person/land ratio inhibited further accumulation. The resulting society of roughly equal landowning families was the seedbed of American republicanism.

Yet from the beginning land and market pulled Euro/Americans toward diverging forms of New World opportunity. Along the seaboard, Virginia colonists quickly discovered a European market for tobacco, and New Englanders for fish. As colonials learned to venture in shipbuilding and transatlantic commerce, the possibilities of wealth began to transform coastal society. Settlers clustered around the best ports—Boston, New York, Philadelphia, and Charleston—and in the lower valleys of navigable rivers—the Connecticut, the Hudson, the Delaware, the maze of Chesapeake estuaries, the Savannah. Here cheap water transportation gave access to the world market for furs, timber, wheat and flour, livestock and salted meat, indigo, and rice. In the southern tidewater, planters broke through the high-wage barrier to wealth by exploiting the bound labor of indentured Europeans and enslaved Africans. Here and in the ports, wherever sea brought market, growing wealth concentrated in fewer hands, and status became steeply graded. Freed from Old World aristocracy, wealth conferred gentility, and law evolved a new conception of freely negotiable fee-simple property.

But New World land closed the interior to the market it galvanized at tidewater. Moving goods was infinitely more difficult across the thinly inhabited reaches of America than in densely populated Europe. Beyond water transportation, bulky farm products had to be wagoned over scarcely maintained and often impassable roads and trails. Hauling them more than thirty or forty miles cost more than they were worth. Consequently people who settled at any distance from navigable water mainly produced use values for subsistence rather than the market's commodity values for sale.

Profound cultural differences arose from these contrasting modes of production. The market fostered individualism and competitive pursuit of wealth by open-ended production of commodity values that could be accumulated as money. But rural production of use values stopped once bodies were sheltered and clothed and bellies provided for. Surplus produce had no abstract or money value, and wealth could not be accumulated. Therefore the subsistence culture fostered family obligation, communal cooperation, and reproduction over generations of a modest comfort.

During the eighteenth century a demographic explosion swelled this subsistence-farming sector into a major historical force. Low mortality and the fecundity of colonial mothers, combining with a new surge of immigrants displaced from the market's European core, sent population flooding into the interior. By the end of the century, a majority of free Americans lived in a distinctive subsistence culture remote from river navigation and the market world.

By 1815, however, a market revolution was surmounting the overland transportation barrier. While dissolving deeply rooted patterns of behavior and belief for competitive effort, it mobilized collective resources through government to fuel growth in countless ways, not least by providing the essential legal, financial, and transport infrastructures. Establishing capitalist hegemony over economy, politics, and culture, the market revolution created ourselves and most of the world we know.

The stressed and resistant Jacksonian majority has eluded or baffled our historiography of consensual, democratic capitalism. Despite contradictions of patriarchy, racism, and fee-simple property, they rallied around enduring human values of family, trust, cooperation, love, and equality. Understanding of both the world they lost and the world we have gained begins with understanding differences between the cultures of land and market.*

The New World's ancient immigrants, people of the land *par excellence*, throw into sharpest relief the cultural gulf separating land from market. Bark lodges in the eastern woodlands, tipis on the plains, pueblos in the arid southwest, and igloos on the Arctic ice typified Native Americans' ingenious adaptations to varied ecological niches. Through ancient human techniques of hunting, gathering, fishing, and planting, these mainly Indian peoples extracted their subsistence directly from the land. Their only domesticated animal was the dog until the European horse reached the plains, but they had brought their maize/vegetable polyculture to a high level of sophistication. Like other premarket ecological adaptations, the Indian mode of production furnished adequate subsistence without onerous labor.

From this mode of production a culture flowed. Intimately dependent on the natural order, Indians felt imbedded in its seamless animistic web. Religious taboos against overexploitation maintained the ecological balance on which survival depended. Native Americans lived in communal, cooperative, and egalitarian bands of related families. Indulgent rearing prepared children to emphasize sharing over individual accumulation. With roles allocated by sex, age, and kinship, people competed only to win honor through warrior valor or hunter/craft skill. Frequent moves minimized personal possessions, and goods were shared as needed. Self-interested calculation and bargaining were legitimate only in limited trading with other Indian groups. While hunting territories or planting fields might be period-

---

*For the profundity of capitalist transformation: Karl Polanyi, *The Great Transformation* (Boston, 1944); and Jean-Christophe Agnew, *Worlds Apart: The Market and the Theater in Anglo-American Thought* (Cambridge, England, 1986). As explained by Ian Tyrrell, *The Absent Marx: Class Analysis and Liberal History in Twentieth-Century America* (Westport, 1986), horror at Karl Marx's politics has blindered bourgeois historians to the most powerful conceptual tools for understanding Americans' central transformation.

But Marx's European analysis requires considerable adaptation to the special circumstances flowing from cheap American land—widespread property ownership, a farming populace oriented more to subsistence than profit, and a bourgeoisie massively reinforced by small enterprisers. Here the industrial capitalism of commodified wage labor was not possible until merchant capital pushed a market revolution across the countryside to transform economy, culture, and politics by commodifying the family labor of subsistence producers. "Market," in this capitalist sense, excludes local exchange for subsistence while including production for a competitive world market with commodified slave labor. Only on the battlefields of the Civil War did the progressive bourgeoisie of free-labor exploitation finally prevail over resistant farmers, workers, and the anachronistic planter bourgeoisie of slave-labor exploitation.

For scholarly debate over subsistence farming, see the bibliographical essay under "The Land: Subsistence Farming."

ically allocated to particular kinships, allocations were based on need, and the idea of private property hardly existed.

Traditional norms served so well to regulate Indian behavior that political institutions were rudimentary. Within each band a well-understood system of retributive justice substituted for laws, courts, and police. But conflict between tribes was only partly moderated by trade and conventions limiting the lethality of warfare. Weaker neighbors were terrorized by warlike Iroquois or marauding Navajo, and some tribes practiced torture and ritual execution of captives. The limited leadership necessitated by intertribal conflict fell to patriarchs, and sometimes matriarchs, in senior lineages. Leaders mainly negotiated consensus; and if they controlled an outsized share of communal produce, it relieved the needy, entertained visitors, and constituted the communal reserve against crop failure. Status and power were asserted, as in most premarket cultures, more by giving than accumulating; and rich fisheries along the northwest coast organized potlatch cultures around cutthroat competitive gift-giving.[1]

By 1815 Indians and their cultures were nearing extinction in the eastern United States. Wherever whites settled, Indians disappeared. Creeks and Cherokees still held western Georgia, and some five thousand of the once mighty Iroquois were herded onto reservations in upstate New York; but fewer than three thousand Indians survived in all New England, and they had almost vanished from the rest of the Atlantic seaboard.[2]

Native Americans were destroyed by lack of immunity to both the microbes and the market brought by whites. In the Carolina upcountry, after one smallpox epidemic wiped out five-sixths of the native populace, another left the woods so "offensive with the dead bodies of the Indians" that dogs, wolves, and vultures were "busy for months in banqueting on them."[3] Staggered everywhere by the white invaders' lethal pathogens, Indians came under cultural attack by the market's irresistible trade goods and insatiable demand for furs. Lacking textiles and iron, they wanted the greater comfort and labor savings of warm woolen blankets, guns, and such instantly indispensable metal utensils as fishhooks, needles, knives, hatchets, traps, and cookware.

As Indians stepped up their harvest of animal pelts to exchange, taboos broke down, and overkilling disrupted the Indian ecology. As they accumulated pelts for their commodity value, the ethic of sharing came under strain. As they bought articles formerly made, traditional crafts died out. Competition for scarcer furs provoked intertribal wars, rendered more bloody by the market's firearms. If these forces of cultural demoralization were not enough, the market was happy to supply all the firewater Indians could pay for.[4]

Native American cultures were already decimated and demoralized, therefore, when they encountered the decisive phase of the genocidal process, the inexorable advance of white settlement over Indian lands. By 1815, after two hundred years of this, the crisis of Indian survival was at hand.

Whites occasionally regretted the strange "disappearance" of the Native American, assuaging conscience by claims that they were Christianizing or "civilizing" him. Civilizing was more talked about as white society became more secular, while even religious folk who actually attempted to Christianize the Indian agreed that he had to be civilized first. Civilizing meant teaching him the market's blessings of private property, self-denial, and hard work in settled agriculture and handicrafts. And in the process of becoming civilized, he could surrender most of his hunting lands to civilized use by whites. The federal government from its inception purported to advance the Indian's civilization by demanding ever larger land cessions and taking them by military force when not yielded fast enough. As the tide of white occupation flooded over the Appalachian crest, federal troops had much hard fighting to clear Native Americans from the upper Ohio valley. While Indians' lands were steadily converted to civilized use, few Indians were converted to civilization. After two centuries of white profession and effort, the handful of converts drawn into the white man's schools, religion, or style of living were only too ready to revert to Indian ways at the first opportunity.

More striking was the ease with which whites converted to Indian ways. Colonial officials had constant problems with deserters to the Indians. Hundreds of white captives in the colonial wars were taken into Indian families and refused to return to their white families. Even when captives were persuaded to come back, as Benjamin Franklin reported, "in a Short time they become disgusted with our manner of life and the care and pains that are necessary to support it, and take the first good Opportunity of escaping again into the Woods, from whence there is no reclaiming them." Franklin blamed "the proneness of human Nature to a life of ease, of freedom from care and labour." The modern historian of these white Indians concludes, however, that they preferred Indian life for its "strong sense of community, abundant love, and uncommon integrity."⁵

Confrontation between white and Native American cultures presented in the starkest terms a contrast, and for some a choice, between the cultures of land and market. That Indians and whites who faced a choice so often chose Indian ways suggests something about the human costs of "civilization." It also suggests why so many whites clung to a more attenuated culture of the land.

Demoralized culturally by the market, Native Americans were displaced physically by Euro/American farm folk practicing a similar premarket mode of use-value production. White subsistence farmers adopted the Indian maize/vegetable horticulture to extract from the same resource base most of their caloric food values. But European livestock and short-fallow cultivation enabled whites to reproduce the permanent settlement of their peasant tradition. Where eastern woodland Indians cultivated with hoes and long fallows, periodically exhausting fields and moving their villages to fresh lands, Euro/Americans adapted to the Indian horticulture their more intensive cultivation by plough, while cultivating the same fields indefinitely on short rotation. The livestock that made ploughing possible supplied whites with the protein requirements that Indians procured through peripatetic hunting and fishing. Paradoxically European technology made white farmers more independent of the market. Fabricating tools from iron, spinning and weaving cloth, and distilling whiskey, they produced for themselves important use values that Indians had to buy.[6]

The white mode of subsistence production needed much less land to achieve permanent settlement and greater comfort. But it demanded more labor, which families supplied by having many children. Consequently the subsistence culture could not reproduce itself over generations without a constant abundance of cheap land to provide farms for its ever more numerous offspring. Irony compounded tragedy as a doomed white culture sustained itself a few generations longer—and cleared the American land for market domination—by sweeping away a more archaic Indian culture.

The subsistence culture enforced its heavier labor demands through a paternal authority inherited from European household production. The father controlled the labor of family members for most of their waking hours and made all major family decisions. He might not even consult his wife about uprooting the family and moving hundreds of miles. Patriarchy was further inflated by the rigors of immigration, farm making, and Indian fighting in a New World where civil institutions were too weak to provide security. Even in long settled rural areas, the law of the strong prevailed, and families relied on the brawn and courage of avenging fathers and brothers. Aggressive masculinity asserted the patriarchal "honor" on which the safety and prospects of women and children depended.

Cheap land, held absolutely under the seaboard market's capitalist conception of property, swelled patriarchal honor to heroic dimensions in rural America. The father's authority rested on his legal title to the family land. Where European peasant landholdings were usually encumbered with obligations to some elite, the American farmer held in fee simple. Supreme on his domain, he was beyond interference by any earthly power. Except for a modest tax and an occasional half day of neighborhood road work or carousing militia drill, he owed no obligations of labor, money, service, or (finally) religious fealty to any person or entity. Fee-simple land, the augmenting theater of the patriarchal persona, sustained his honor and untrammeled will. This extraordinary independence inflated American farmers' conception of their class far above peasantry. The hero of South Carolina's first play, *Independence* (by William Ioor, 1805), almost caricatured the prototype of the subsistence culture. "I am an independent farmer, don't owe five guineas in the world," he asserted. Owning a farm that yielded "every necessary comfort for me and mine," he disdained lawyers and planters, and was always "boasting of, his INDEPENDENCE, and declaring, that an honest farmer knows of no dependence, except on heaven."[7]

Cherishing patriarchal independence, the American farmer clung even more fiercely than his peasant forebears to the land that conferred it. Paradoxically the capitalist doctrine of private property was the juridical foundation for both the market's expansion and the farmer's resistance. The historical outcome turned on this contradiction, as commitment to property undermined and compromised rural resistance to capitalism and its culture.

The contradiction between capitalist property and use-value communalism was apparent in the cultural norms that controlled the actual use of land. New England towns (as Yankees called both rural and urban communities) donated communal lands to families in proportions determined by communal criteria of status and need. Throughout the South and West farm folk maintained (in some areas until the twentieth century) the principle of open range that many of their forebears had known in Ulster, Scotland, and Wales. Exclusive property rights attached only to land that was used, and the landowner was obliged to fence his cultivated fields to keep other people's livestock out. Even fee-simple ownership did not permit him to fence uncultivated land or bar others and their livestock from using it. In practice much of early rural America was a great forested commons, in which everybody freely hunted, fished, trapped, grazed livestock, and harvested firewood and lumber, roots and herbs, honey, nuts, and berries.[8]

Farm people's overriding priority was to maintain and reproduce the family's subsistence way of life. Like other premarket peoples, they practiced a hard-won folk wisdom about how to utilize their labor-power and technology to extract sufficient use values from their resource base. Experience taught American farmers that the optimum division of labor and scale of production could be achieved— with considerable variation for time and place—on as little as twenty improved acres, employing a labor force of father, mother, and six to eight surviving children out of eight or ten pregnancies. And like other premarket cultures, the American subsistence culture drew upon folk experience in controlling pregnancy to maintain this balance, through delayed marriage, extended lactation, and little-understood forms of premarital contraception, especially *coitus interruptus,* that accompanied the New England practice of "bundling" and its equivalents elsewhere.

The farm family moved through a life-cycle in which it first had the nuclear appearance of a conjugal pair with an increasingly crowded houseful of children. Marriage was delayed until enough land could be had to support a family, which usually meant the middle to late twenties for men and the early to middle twenties for women. Meanwhile young people enjoyed, amid a bawdy folk vernacular, considerable sexual freedom.

Upon marriage a couple put romance behind them for the rigors of farm-making and endless childbearing. In this joint enterprise they commonly developed a durable if undemonstrative loyalty and affection. Yet "the old woman" and her "Mr. So-and-so," as she usually addressed him, valued each other primarily for productive reliability in their respective spheres. The folk realism of an Ohio valley jingle warned newlyweds against romantic illusions:

> *First month, honey month,*
> *Next month like pie;*
> *Third month, you dirty bitch,*
> *Get out and work like I.*[9]

The family division of labor was along lines of sex and age. Women paid a heavy price in labor and motherhood for patriarchal afflatus. While constantly pregnant or nursing infants for fifteen or twenty years, wives were responsible for the domestic interior, cooking, extensive food preservation, gardens, poultry, dairy animals, and the endless textile processes of carding, spinning, weaving, fulling, dyeing, quilting, sewing, and mending. Husbands attended to field crops, livestock, buildings, firewood, and hunting and fishing, which afforded both recreation and additional animal proteins for the family diet. Daughters worked with mothers and boys with fathers at age-graded tasks. Probably it is going too far to say that childhood did not exist in the subsistence culture, that youngsters were in fact treated as the little adults portrayed by the self-trained folk limners who produced the earliest American family portraits. But certainly children were expected to labor as much as strength, skill, and attention span admitted. Shaming and physical punishment broke rebellious wills while enforcing prescribed behavior and labor.

The psychodynamics seem to have produced what was wanted: dutiful and reliable replicas of parents. Commonly the oldest child of each sex was named for its same-sex parent (and often, therefore, for its grandparent and great-grandparent as well); and if it died, the same name was often rebestowed on the next child of the same sex. Discouraging individuality and competitive striving, the subsistence culture socialized its young to a familism of all-for-one and one-for-all.

Demands on farmer and wife eased as maturing children's labor brought more acreage into production. In this middle phase of its life-cycle, the family needed a surplus to supply support for aging parents and farms for maturing sons. To this end it typically required children's labor well into adulthood. Holding title to the family property, the father could deny children a share of the patrimony until he permitted them to marry or withdraw their labor. Grown sons and daughters, chafing under long delays of marriage, often paid for the privilege of leaving home.

Patriarchal authority was not, of course, absolute. Premarital pregnancy often coerced parental approval of marriage; and even in straitlaced New England at times, more than one bride in three was pregnant on her wedding day. By way of compensation the subsistence culture presented young people with few identity crises, problems of career choice or entry, fears of failure, or uncertainties about their futures. To replicate the parents was to succeed. Sons who satisfied fathers ascended in due course to paternal authority themselves.

Although white subsistence folk worked harder and under stricter supervision than Indians, their premarket way of life was considerably less arduous than most market occupations.[10] So long as land was assured for the rising generation, accumulation was pointless and productive effort could be relaxed as soon as conventional standards of consumption were achieved. Work exercised varied skills and alternated with considerable leisure as dictated by season and weather. Often it was interwoven with family and neighborhood sociability.

The farm family entered the third phase of its life-cycle when it transferred property from one generation to the next. Now it became apparent that subsistence folk reproduced their way of life across generations by transmitting land through a "stem" type of extended family structure. The nuclear household was only a recurrent form in a lineal kinship system emphasizing generational continuity and cohesion. Fathers strove to accumulate enough land near the "old homeplace" to provide farms for sons, leaving daughters to look for land from families of prospective husbands. Consequently brides usually moved into the social sphere and often the neighborhood of the husband's family. Only the most successful fathers could provide land for daughters and thus bring sons-in-law within the family orbit.

The paternal homeplace was usually willed to the eldest son, or sometimes the youngest if he stayed home longer to care for aging parents. The favored heir often married and established his own household under the paternal roof before gaining title at his father's death. He also inherited his father's patriarchal responsibility for the widow and for the extended stem family's aged great-grandparents, orphaned children, and unattached women. Fathers' wills and laws governing intestate estates required adequate support for the widow and usually guaranteed her life use of part of the farm. During this phase the household often held three or four generations, one or both original parents, heir and spouse, and heir's children, along with several dependent relatives. Ubiquitous single aunts were casualties of hazardous sexuality, family exploitation, or male migration, mortality, or desertion.

This way of passing on property produced rural neighborhoods dominated by clanlike networks of related households and the patriarchs who led them. Even today certain surnames cluster in the least disturbed rural neighborhoodsthroughout the United States and in the surviving graveyards of rural churches. The once common family graveyards, lovingly maintained over many generations on patriarchal homeplaces, have almost vanished. In a world where other institutions were rudimentary, kinship was people's only source of protection and assistance.[11]

Subsistence families were not wholly self-sufficient. Much of their comfort and security derived from a neighborhood division of labor. Some farmers, as a sideline, furnished specialized skills to the community. During the winter months, when farm work was slack, the farmer/shoemaker carried his tools from house to house, supplying each family's yearly needs for footwear. Every Sunday the farmer/ preacher left his fields to dispense the Christian gospel. Other part-time farmers operated such essential community facilities as the grist mill, blacksmith's shop, tannery, and sawmill. All rendered their services, not to an impersonal market, but to meet immediate needs of lifelong neighbors, who usually furnished the raw materials and made return in farm produce or labor.

Moreover neighboring farm families balanced their varying productive capabilities, shortages, and surpluses by constantly exchanging labor and commodities. "Trade, barter, and exchange of commodities and swapping work in corn-planting and harvest time for work back in corn-husking and hay-making time was the only commerce known," recalled one man about his boyhood farming community. Through sociable communal labor, neighbors lightened each others' most onerous tasks—raising houses and barns, cutting logs and splitting rails, harvesting wheat, and shucking the corn crop. On such occasions, an Ohioan reported, "it was the custom always to send one from a family to help, so that you could claim like assistance in return."[12]

Expecting rough reciprocity in exchange, subsistence folk were rather less altruistic than Indians. The social realm of altruism—where altruistic exchange predominates over self-interested bargaining—encompassed the whole band or village among Indians but shrank to the small nuclear household in the market world. In the intermediate subsistence culture, altruism predominated throughout the extensive stem family, while exchanges among families were neither wholly self-interested nor wholly altruistic. On the other hand, "honest, faithful memory, discarding day book and ledger, held all accounts and recorded balances of money and labor due," as an Illinois man put it. But on the other hand, "merciful, charitable memory forgot all debts of debtors too poor to pay."[13]

Actually some farmers, especially the widely literate New Englanders, did keep day books recording in money values elaborate networks of mutual indebtedness with neighbors. But accounts were balanced by further exchanges rather than money payment, and deficits were thought due only when one could pay. Interest was rarely calculated because money was not a medium of exchange and accumulation. In the subsistence world, money was a specialized commodity, needed only for limited exchanges with the outside market world, for paying taxes or buying the few store goods that farm produce could not command.[14]

Rural neighbors depended upon each other for companionship almost as much as for economic assistance. When the men in a community were summoned to a house raising, according to a typical account,

> there was commonly some sort of mutual job laid out for women, such as quilting, sewing, or spinning up a lot of thread for some poor neighbor. This would bring

together a mixed party, and it was usually arranged that after supper there should be a dance, or, at least, plays, which would occupy a good part of the night, and wind up with the young fellows seeing the girls home in the short hours; or, if they went home early, sitting with them by the fire in that kind of interesting chat known as sparking.[15]

Youthful sociability provided escape from parental discipline and work demands, along with early introduction to the delights and perils of libido. But most adult sociability was sexually segregated. When men gathered, they competed in displaying the elements of male honor—strength, courage, storytelling boast and wit, and such manly skills as riding and shooting—accompanied by considerable cursing, whiskey-drinking, and fighting. Women, on the other hand, formed tight networks of neighbor and kin wives for friendship and mutual support. These networks gave women their only escape from the male-dominated world of the household and their only opportunity to value themselves by other than male standards. And through these networks women managed for each other the recurrent female trauma of childbirth. Neighborly sociability was an essential safety valve for the pressures generated in crowded cabins by the subsistence family's stern patriarchalism. No one expected the family to swathe its members in warmth and emotional intensity. The household was a practical institution of human production and reproduction, and people often found their most rewarding ties with kin and neighbors outside its confining walls.

These interdependent farm families were also roughly equal in condition. Differences were mainly ascribable to age and stage in the family life-cycle. When sons of the subsistence world looked back nostalgically from market success, they mainly professed to miss its egalitarian and cooperative quality. "Needs of mutual help bound old settlers in fraternal bonds of closest, tenderest ties," recalled one. "The dependence upon each other caused differences of education and station to disappear, and almost absolute social equality prevailed," wrote another; "hence every person felt that he or she was the social equal of every other person, each being ready and willing at all times to assist others to the extent of his or her power, the latch-string always hanging out." By the late nineteenth century, novelist William Dean Howells's father could "hardly realize how greatly things have changed." What had become almost inconceivable in a world of cutthroat competition was the subsistence world's "general dependence of all upon the neighborly kindness and good offices of others."[16]

While bartering crops and labor with neighbors, most farm families also secured a little money for taxes and high-utility purchases by selling some products to the market. The market's ambassador to the subsistence world was the country storekeeper. Except in the earliest period of settlement most farm folk lived within a day's ride of a store, around which there often developed a little village or county-seat town. Country stores dispensed a limited range of high-utility commodities and accepted in return farm products sufficiently valuable in proportion to bulk and weight to bear the cost of transportation to a distant market. Periodically the storekeeper wagoned collected produce to the nearest river port or seaport, where the proceeds replenished his stock of store goods.

From the perspective of economic historians, farm folk who bartered a few hams or a tub of cheese for a frying pan or piece of calico sometimes seem incorporated into the market. But from the perspective of the household devoting its labor overwhelmingly to subsistence, the market remained marginal. Directly measuring the cost of store goods in the additional labor required to obtain them, rural America found that transport made most prohibitively expensive.

Moreover production for market was inconsistent with rural culture's fundamental commitment to maintaining and reproducing the stem family. Unpredictably fluctuating market prices put at risk the family's hold on its land. A year or two of low prices or poor yields, or both, might leave them without enough to eat, forcing them to risk the farm by borrowing. The two great bugaboos of the subsistence world were debt and taxes, through which the market world could seize the farmer's land to enforce its demands for money.

Consequently the farm household labored first and foremost to insure its subsistence and its reproduction in the next generation. Only after these requirements were met was additional labor expended to produce a small "marketable surplus" of such high-value farm products as whiskey, maple sugar, potash, and salted beef and pork, or of livestock, which could be driven to market on the hoof. Modest sales provided enough money or store credits to pay taxes and procure such essential items as salt, powder and shot, cooking and eating utensils, and iron for tools. With a little additional labor the family could periodically enjoy tea, coffee, or refined sugar and gradually acquire a few such luxuries as crockery and window glass.

The market was less threatening and more easily entered when it offered high prices for the grains and livestock raised for subsistence. Prudent farmers planted more grain than needed as insurance against a poor yield, and the prudent surplus became a marketable surplus when grain prices rose sharply enough in the late eighteenth century to offset the high cost of wagoning from the interior. Now, without altering their pattern of production or endangering their subsistence or risking the family farm, rural households could acquire more store goods by expending more labor on their marketable surplus.

For some sixty-five years preceding 1820, Europe was unable to feed itself and relied increasingly upon American wheat, flour, beef, and pork. As wheat prices rose in response, more farmers at ever greater distances from the market discovered that they could profitably enlarge their marketable surplus despite the high cost of transportation. Between 1772 and 1819, the profitable wagoning distance for wheat doubled to over one hundred miles. A wheat exporting belt spread from the lower Connecticut to the lower James and inland to Virginia's lower Shenandoah valley.[17]

The wheat boom introduced many farm folk to the market or increased consumption of store goods. In highly accessible and fertile areas like Pennsylvania's Susquehanna valley, the marketable surplus may have reached a third of farm production, and some farmers were reorienting themselves to the market by hiring labor and buying more land and equipment. But even here cultural transition made slow headway against traditional commitments to family, use values, and communal obligation. The marketable surplus was not enough to push most of the Pennsylvania Dutch and their neighbors across the cultural divide into pursuit of wealth. As long as family labor was concentrated on necessities, store goods remained a secondary objective with painfully apparent labor costs.

Similarly, when a cotton boom pushed market production into the southern interior at the turn of the century, few farmers took the planter road to wealth. Producing a bale or two of cotton for taxes and store goods, most free southern families devoted most of their labor to raising corn and hogs for subsistence. This dual economy persisted throughout the antebellum period because accumulating capital to buy slaves and additional land was too difficult and borrowing too risky for farmers committed to the stem family and patriarchal independence.[18]

Migration was an essential feature of a culture combining farm ownership with large families. Every subsistence family confronted a dilemma after subdividing its land among a generation or two of multiplying sons and grandsons to the point where the remaining paternal farm could support only one heir. At the same time settlement thickened from natural increase and immigration, and land became too expensive to buy with the limited surplus of traditional production. Typically the son who got the shrunken farm was encumbered with years of compensating payments to landless siblings in worse plight. Only by working some years as tenant farmers or migrating to cheap frontier land could they get farms of their own; only in later years might they hope to accumulate enough acreage to support them in old age and give their children a start.

Many a far-sighted father preferred an alternative strategy that also fed the western migration, but without fragmenting the stem family and undermining patriarchal authority. Selling the family farm well in advance of the children's maturity, he used the proceeds to acquire a much larger tract of cheaper land farther west, on which the maturing children's labor could provide support for aging parents and farms for adult sons. Often many households of kin migrated as a clan, or related households followed a lead household in chain migration.

This folk migration spread the ethnocultural diversity of the Old World across the New. English genes and English ways predominated among seaboard whites, but only in New England were farmers homogeneously English. While rural Anglo/Yankees overflowed their nucleated peasant villages to crowd Dutch peasants in New York's Hudson valley, coastal English and Welsh filtered inland farther south and west, among communities of Germans and Scotch-Irish.

By the time Jackson's artillery rattled the fancy ironwork of New Orleans' French/Spanish/African Vieux Carre, folk migration had unrolled from the Hudson to the Mississippi a mosaic of ethnic styles and artifacts. The salt-box houses with attached ells that Yankees originally brought from East Anglia mingled in upstate New York with Dutch gable-ends. The Pennsylvania "Dutch" (*Deutsch* or German) introduced the notched-log construction that housed most of rural America; and even in the grain-exporting Susquehanna valley at the end of the eighteenth century, most people lived in small, one-story log cabins with few windows. As Germans graduated to stone houses and big, fancifully decorated, overhung "Switzer" barns, the Scotch-Irish adapted log construction to the Ulster rectangular form and spread it through the South and West. Here it met other cultural forms—the square English log house brought to the uplands by immigrants from the old coastal settlements and the double-pen "dogtrot" cabin with connecting breezeway that spread through the Southwest from Appalachia.[19]

The American subsistence culture's explosive expansion attested its vitality. While abundantly meeting human needs for security, sociability, and trust, however, it inflicted costs—in patriarchy, conformity, and circumscribed horizons— that left rural ways vulnerable to the market ways pushed inland by the wheat and cotton booms. In coping with this challenge, moreover, the rural world was hobbled by a simultaneous demographic crisis.

Adapted to a munificent person/land ratio, the subsistence culture was ultimately doomed by its own population dynamics. It could reproduce itself only so long as its exponentially multiplying offspring could find cheap land through periodic migration. As the cheap-land frontier receded west, however, the cost of migration and farm-making became prohibitive for the eastern landless. Consequently, by the mid-eighteenth century the oldest rural communities near the northeastern ports were feeling the first tremors of a rolling agrarian crisis. As the market assailed traditional ways, shrinking farms were spawning more people than they could feed.

Peaking agrarian crisis along the northeastern seaboard in the 1790s was exacerbated by a commercial boom pushing capitalist relations into the countryside. Here the first federal census revealed spiraling population densities. Compared with nine and sixteen persons per square mile in the interior states of Vermont and New Hampshire, Delaware County adjoining Philadelphia had fifty-three, Connecticut's Fairfield County fifty-seven, and Rhode Island as a whole sixty-six. Studies of older rural communities from Massachusetts to Delaware Bay reveal a pattern of demographic stress. Land prices had soared as farms contracted. Although residents were leaving in droves, enough remained to swell an increasingly insecure class of landless tenant farmers, laborers, and craftsmen.[20]

Demographic pressure was heaviest in southeastern New England, where farms had undergone subdivision longest. Moreover the proliferating Yankees were long walled off from the cheap western acreage that elsewhere enabled the subsistence culture to reproduce itself. West of the Connecticut valley, land-seekers encountered a belt of rugged terrain over which colonial New York claimed sovereignty. The next good land, the great north-south corridor of the Hudson valley, was already occupied by New Yorkers; and beyond the Hudson, Iroquois power astride the Mohawk corridor barred the way west until after the Revolution. With most of New England's arable acreage occupied, land-hungry Yankees swarmed over the steep Berkshire hills, pushed the New York boundary almost to the Hudson by riot and defiant occupation, seized Vermont through revolution, and embarked on the disastrous experiment of trying to wrest a living from the rocky coasts and frosty heights of northern New England.[21]

This desperate expansion onto marginal lands was not enough to relieve demographic stress in the old settlements. Here farms shrank to a third or less of their former size, averaging below fifty acres in coastal Chebaco and seventy-five in Lincoln farther inland. Population density exceeded forty persons per square mile in most of the old farming towns, reaching one hundred in some, and land values had doubled or trebled. A rich "loaner class" appeared, wealth became more polarized, sons fell below the status of their fathers, and the poor were poorer and more numerous. The agrarian crisis disrupted customary human relationships to produce a rising age of marriage, a declining birthrate, an increasing incidence of premarital pregnancy (reaching 41 percent of first births in some towns), and an erosion of patriarchal authority. Fathers with no patrimony to bestow had to let sons and daughters fend for themselves, and the general practice of naming first-born sons after fathers rapidly disappeared.

Uprooted from the extended stem family, the landless poor swarmed across the New England countryside in search of livelihood. A fourth of Concord's taxpayers departed every decade, and more than half of Andover's fourth-generation natives migrated. By the 1790s Yankee emigrants were flooding northern New York and leapfrogging the Hudson valley settlements to advance along the Mohawk corridor. Simultaneously the wages of a galvanized seaboard market drew a growing stream to the ports. But many of the landless poor simply drifted from town to town, never finding a stable maintenance.

Even landowners who stayed put often found their diminished farms encumbered with obligations to landless siblings and yielding a mean living. Attempting to meet the stem family's traditional responsibilities to kin, small farmers joined the landless in a scramble for supplementary income. As they intensified the traditional neighborhood division of labor by taking up part-time crafts and providing some specialized service or product, they found markets outside the neighborhood. Wives and daughters stepped up their household spinning and weaving to produce surplus yarn and cloth for sale. Wider markets for farmer/shoemakers encouraged concentrations of full-time shoemakers in Lynn and Bedford. Hadley farmers peddled far and wide the brooms they fashioned from their special broom corn. Putting-out systems reached into the countryside to engage part-time rural labor in producing shoes, cloth, straw hats, fans, wooden clocks, and all manner of utensils, which Yankee peddlers vended throughout rural America.[22]

Scrambling to sustain the traditional family, the dislocated rural populace of southeastern New England was experiencing the transition to capitalist production that would presently overtake most Americans. Under these pressures, Yankees won their reputation for sharp bargaining. Nothing tended so totally "to eradicate every moral feeling," wailed the Reverend Timothy Dwight, as the peddling resorted to by so many displaced young men. Their character "is exchanged for cunning," and they aspire "solely to the acquisition of petty gains," he complained. They "fasten upon this object; and forget every other" as "the only source of their pleasure, or their reputation." An Amherst schoolgirl noticed that people were becoming "generally avaricious" and "tight in their dealings." Traditional patterns of communal cooperation weakened, and agricultural reformers derided old-fashioned farmers "who cannot bear to work alone," who were always having to "call in a neighbour to change work." While it might be "very pleasant" to "have our neighbours at work with us," said advocates of the new capitalist order, "it tends to lounging and idleness, and neglect of business."[23]

Capitalist transformation invaded the southern and western interior when postwar boom galavanized the market culture into market revolution. Fittingly the first news of peace reached the New World shore in the heart of the American market. On the frigid evening of February 11, 1815, "tumultuous joy" swept from the East River docks through the hundred thousand souls inhabiting New York City. Within twenty minutes streets blazed with the torches of densely packed revelers, and candles glittered from every window. "Men of property," as their favorite newspaper exulted, had special cause to "felicitate themselves." The war had retarded "our growth" ten years, said the *Evening Post,* "and no place in the U. States will more experience the revived blessings of a peace."

"Our growth" was already a shibboleth to New Yorkers; and its resumption was such an exhilarating prospect that they suspended all business for a day of celebration. That evening horses and carriages were banned below Chambers Street so the populace could turn out to enjoy the general "illumination" of houses with candles, a spectacular fireworks display from Governor's Island, and elaborate "transparencies" adorning all public buildings and scores of gentlemen's mansions.

Painted on cloth and backlighted, these transparencies displayed—aside from the inevitable eagles, doves, and olive branches—a heavily economic iconography. Cornucopias abounded (one at the Mechanic's Bank discharging silver dollars and five-dollar gold eagles "in anticipation of the speedy recommencement of Specie payments"), and the streets swam with representations of loaded ships entering and leaving port. Tammany Hall's offering included a rising sun "as an emblem of the growing prosperity of our country," while the Union Bank featured "a female figure sitting on a Strong Box the Key in its hand, pointing to a Ship in full sail."

Only poetry could express for one citizen what peace meant to New Yorkers.

> *Commerce and Plenty, attendants in her train,*
> *Again shall flourish through our vast domain.*

"With Peace and Commerce," proclaimed another display, "America Prospers." The Bank of New York put all its candlepower behind a single glowing talisman, "PROSPERITY," while the politicians at City Hall squandered candles in their care to salute every sector of the anticipated resurgence: "Commerce unfettered, Industry encouraged, and the [mechanic] Arts revived." Celebrants could wind up the evening at the theater, passing under a transparency entitled "The Renewal of Commerce" to witness "the Patriotic Spectacle of the FESTIVAL OF PEACE, or, COMMERCE RESTORED."[24]

Impatient New Yorkers were about to lead the American market into its historic takeoff. Through the eighteenth century, the country's simple staple-exporting economy had grown only at the sluggish pace of about 0.4 percent a year, as measured in per capita goods and services. But following the War of 1812 the growth rate more than doubled to about 1 percent, then doubled again to 2 percent by midcentury, and eventually passed 3 percent. These deceptively modest figures registered such spectacular growth that by the middle of the twentieth century the American 6 percent of humanity would be producing and consuming a third of the world's goods and services.

Economic takeoff spread from the major ports as merchant capital and government-fostered transport pushed an accelerating division of labor across the interior. Hinterlands specialized to comparative advantage in producing agricultural and extractive commodities for Boston, New York, Philadelphia, and Baltimore. In exchange, urban manufacturers multiplied production for the countryside by subdividing tasks and exploiting labor more totally through wages and closely supervised central workshops. As surging trade set off surging productivity, capital began shifting from commerce to more profitable wage exploitation.

By the 1830s and 1840s, trade and specialization among the four port/hinterland regions were creating an integrated sectional market embracing the Northeast as a whole. Meanwhile commercial agriculture spread over the West and

South; and during the second half of the nineteenth century, the Northeast market reached out to incorporate these sections into an integrated national market. By midcentury, capital and technology were converting enough central workshops into mechanized factories to convert the market revolution into a staggeringly productive industrial revolution.[25]

The American economy's takeoff was fueled by the unusually feverish enterprise of its market sector. Colonial Americans pursued wealth more freely than Europeans because they were not overshadowed and hemmed in by aristocrats and postfeudal institutions. And they pursued wealth more avidly because it made them the American equivalents of aristocrats.

American merchants, planters, and large landowners, along with the lawyers and clergymen who served them, were accorded the exalted status of "gentlemen." Only gentlemen were addressed as "Mr." Cocked hats, periwigs, ruffled shirts, and lavish waistcoats asserted the superiority of this provincial gentry over men who wore leather aprons and worked with their hands. Gentlefolk lived in elegant townhouses or country mansions furnished like those of the British gentry and adorned with family portraits. Through indulgent affection and careful education, they shaped self-reliant children for venturesome enterprise, prudent hedonism, and dynastic marriage. They were waited upon by slaves and servants and vied with each other in ornateness of coaches and extravagance of entertainments. Above all they demanded deference from inferiors.

Especially daring and ingenious in pursuit of profit were the import-export merchants who dominated enterprise in the colonial ports. American exchanges of raw materials for British manufactures, southern European wines, African slaves, and West Indian sugar and molasses had to be conducted within the complex regulations of the British mercantile system. Moreover the British market had little use for the agricultural exports of the middle and northern colonies, so that credits to finance imports from the mother country had to be earned by trading somewhere else. With market information by sailing ship months out of date, success required keen intuition about trading opportunities in many far-flung parts of the globe. The gentility conferred by large profits could be snatched away by large risks.

To minimize risk, merchants diversified investments and shared the hazards of particular ventures. Six or eight might finance a single sailing, and all were constantly seeking alternative investments. The merchant was a general capitalist entrepreneur, not only sending out trading ventures but lending to local borrowers, financing retailers, speculating in urban real estate and interior lands, underwriting marine insurance, and engaging in privateering and military contracting during the recurrent colonial wars.

Urban wealth steadily concentrated in the hands of the successful. Because merchants required considerable capital to get started, the advantage went to those with inheritances or family connections. And because credit was the lifeblood of commerce in this capital-hungry economy, success depended upon trust among merchants within communities and between remote trading points. Consequently merchants relied upon networks of acquaintance based on family and class ties, dispatching as agents to distant ports relatives or young men whose fidelity to class values was certified by graduation from Harvard, Yale, Columbia (originally King's College), or the College of New Jersey at Princeton.

Traditionally the mercantile career had required neither strenuous exertion nor large-scale organization. The typical merchant needed only a warehouse and a counting room where, with a clerk or two, he conducted his correspondence and five or six transactions a day. Much of his time he spent "on change," gathering with other merchants at a favorite tavern to mix business deals with conviviality. His life had ample space for entertaining, weekly dining clubs, and politics.

The Revolution upset this leisurely mode of doing business. Some of the biggest merchants lost out by taking the Loyalist side, and all lost their privileged access to British and West Indian markets. In the pell-mell search for new trade, established houses fell and more venturous new men rose in their places. New Yorkers pioneered a flourishing trade with China, and a new generation of fiercely competitive Bostonians, many from the smaller outlying ports, discovered that Canton wanted sea otter furs from the northwest American coast and sandalwood from the Sandwich (Hawaiian) Islands. Nantucket and Salem ships braved Cape Horn for the whales of the Pacific and the spices of the East Indies.[26]

A fabulous commercial boom set the stage for market revolution when these avid enterprisers were fortuitously presented with almost unlimited opportunities for profit. The great wars that broke out in Europe following the French Revolution raged with brief interruptions from 1793 until 1815, as a British-led coalition struggled for world supremacy against a coalition headed by Revolutionary/ Napoleonic France. With their economies disrupted and their merchant ships liable to seizure on the high seas, both sides turned to American producers for foodstuffs and to American shipowners to carry their trade, particularly with their West Indian possessions. Under the rules observed by both sides at first, neutral Amercian shipping could carry goods without molestation between colonies and their mother countries, but only if they were landed in an American port en route and then reexported. Commercial boom swelled American exports from $20.2 million in 1790 to $108.3 million in 1807. Domestically produced exports more than doubled from $19.9 million to $48.7 million. American shipowners' share of American trade climbed from 59 percent to 92 percent, and their earnings from $5.9 million to $42.1 million. These enormous increases financed an almost fourfold jump in imports for domestic consumption.

Glittering profits fueled market revolution with new entrepreneurial energies, as a host of rising venturers swamped the exclusive mercantile gentry. "Our catalogue of merchants was swelled much beyond what it was entitled to be from the state of our population," observed pioneer statistician Adam Seybert, and "the most adventurous became the most wealthy." Two poor immigrants, Philadelphia's Stephen Girard and New York's John Jacob Astor, became the early republic's biggest money-makers by exemplifying Seybert's further observation that "the accumulated capital of our merchants enabled them to explore new sources of wealth,"[27] Girard in private banking and Far East trade, and Astor in organizing and monopolizing the fur trade of the Far West. Similarly Providence merchant Moses Brown launched the American textile industry, and Boston merchant Frederic Tudor began shipping New England ice southward as far as Havana, pioneering a trade that would transform the dietary habits of the modern world.

The torrent of profits swelled port populations and brought into being a host of specialized economic activities and institutions. Philadelphia, the largest city in 1790, increased its population 114 percent by 1810; but New York, with a growth of 191 percent during the two decades, passed it and neared the hundred-thousand mark. Although Boston, third in 1790, grew by 84 percent, it was passed by upstart Baltimore, whose 156 percent growth was fueled by a flood of Susquehanna and Chesapeake wheat, which the city manufactured into flour and exported. In all the port cities new banks and marine insurance companies sprouted, and more specialized marketing systems developed around brokers, auctioneers, wholesalers, and commission merchants.[28]

But the commercial boom collapsed in 1807, when the British banned the lucrative reexport trade and humiliatingly, at cannonpoint, boarded and seized sailors from an American naval vessel in Chesapeake Bay. The spectre of war drove President Thomas Jefferson into his most radical demonstration of his ultimate commitments. Sacrificing market for land, he pushed through Congress an Embargo Act forbidding American ships from leaving American waters.

This Draconian secession from the world market could not be sustained politically in the face of the resulting commercial devastation. But neither could war with Britain be long avoided once the Embargo was repealed, and again American commerce languished under embargo, this time British blockade. Only with peace could the march of enterprise resume.

While enriching many, commercial boom had made life more precarious for the nine out of ten urban dwellers who worked with their hands. Already about half of these working-class people were without skills or property. Laborers, sailors, cartmen, domestics, and small shopkeepers eked out a bare subsistence, constantly threatened with disaster by unemployment or illness. Most vulnerable were blacks and women, who bore the special burdens of racial and sexual discrimination.[29]

Insecurity was also overtaking the skilled half of the urban working class, the artisans or mechanics. These leather-apron workers were divided into dozens of different crafts, each manufacturing ("making by hand") in home workshops a different product. Every neighborhood had bakers and butchers, shoemakers and tailors, to supply its daily essentials. Buildings constructed by carpenters and masons were furnished by cabinetmakers, glaziers, pewterers, and chandlers; while the merchant fleets that sustained the urban economy were built and maintained by shipwrights, caulkers, cordage makers, sailmakers, blockmakers, and riggers. A mechanic learned the "art" or skill of his particular craft as an unpaid apprentice to a master mechanic. Then he typically worked a few years for wages as a journeyman, until he acquired the tools and capital needed to set up his own shop as a master. Once established he might take on several apprentices and a journeyman or two.

The mechanic culture shared much of the precapitalist quality of the subsistence culture. Skills, tools, and shop gave master mechanics something of the security and independence that land gave farmers, as well as a similar patriarchal control over their families, including apprentices and journeymen. In the moral economy of their European artisan tradition, they were not competing for wealth but providing essential services to the community in return for the right to a decent competence. Often they banded together by craft to enforce production standards and adequate prices. Working to order for individual customers and seeking repute from quality products, mechanics, like farmers, claimed dignity from the use-values their labor created. Chairmakers, according to the banner they carried in New York parades, saw their labor as furnishing "Rest for the Weary," while tailors marched under the legend "Naked Was I and Ye Clothed Me." Pride in meeting human needs sustained the mechanics' class conviction that honest labor was the only source of value.

Championing republicanism of a democratic cast in the Revolutionary crisis, mechanics had mustered class pride and influence against merchant elitism in the emerging party politics of the 1790s as Jeffersonian Republicans. In the major ports, united organizations of the various crafts mobilized "the mechanic interest" and proclaimed a mechanic ideology symbolized by an upraised arm wielding a hammer. To this emblem New York's General Society of Mechanics and Tradesmen attached the motto, "By Hammer and Hand All Arts Do Stand."[30] But commercial boom inaugurated a historic shattering of mechanics' unity by extending markets for their products beyond neighborhood and local customers. As widening markets intensified competition, cost-cutting masters with access to merchant capital in the major ports intensified the division of labor by subdividing work processes to exploit cheap, unskilled labor under close supervision in central workshops. Alternatively, to avoid the high cost of large workshops on expensive urban land, many of these mechanic/entrepreneurs paid unskilled workers low piece rates to complete at home single steps in the production process.

This "putting-out" system of preindustrial manufacturing flourished first in producing clothing and shoes, items of universal consumption that could be sold in large lots to southern slaveholders or to the "slop shops" that clothed the urban poor. Every effort was made to simplify work processes so the cheapest labor could be used. Shoe uppers were put-out to be sewn together, precut cloth to be sewn into garments, or semifinished garments to be provided with cuffs, collars, or button-holes. Soon cheap furniture, gloves, stockings, and hats were being mass-produced in this fashion.

Most of this tedious work was done by women and children, often the families of widows with no other means of support. Barred by social convention from most jobs outside the home, they had to work for so little, compared with males, that only constant toil yielded a bare living. Increasingly such work was put-out to labor contractors, who initiated a long-lived pattern of urban sweatshop produc-tion by crowding workers into strictly supervised garret workshops.

Journeymen in these trades found themselves pushed back to the level of unskilled wage workers and unable to acquire the skills that formerly gave them bargaining power with masters and the promise of becoming masters themselves. The increasing capital required to set up in competition with established masters was harder to get. Disparities of wealth between journeymen and masters widened; the average age of journeymen approached the average age of masters; and jour-neymen, once fewer than masters, began to outnumber them, from three-to-one in some trades up to eleven-to-one in printing. "Very few," complained journeyman printers facing the high cost of printing presses, "ever have it in their power to realize a capital sufficient to commence business on their own account."

Although many crafts were at first less affected, especially in smaller centers, commercial boom had inaugurated an irreversible proletarianization of the mechanic class. In many of the largest urban crafts, mechanic/entrepreneurs were becoming capitalist bosses who could survive intensifying competition in widening markets only by cutting labor costs. As apprenticeship decayed into an excuse for cheap labor, journeymen became permanently dependent on wages. Sharpening competition between white workers and blacks, both free and slave, intensified pressures in Baltimore and other southern centers. Fears of total destitution in hard times were borne out in the wake of the Embargo. In 1809 over a thousand men were incarcerated for debt in New York City alone, half for owing less than ten dollars, a week's wages.[31]

Journeyman mechanics, with their tradition of skills and craft pride, fought back. They began excluding masters from journeymen's societies organized in the various crafts to defend labor against capital. Isolated strikes by journeymen are recorded as far back as 1768. The first journeymen's society clearly designed to protect wages—the first labor union in the modern sense—was organized by Phil-adelphia shoemakers at the beginning of the commercial boom in 1794, and a surge of journeymen organizations and strikes filled the boom years. Employers eventually resorted to the courts. Hard times and the conviction of striking shoe-makers for conspiracy at Philadelphia in 1806 and New York in 1810 quelled worker militancy for a decade.[32]

Masters, too, felt threatened by capitalist relations of production. When "wealthy capitalists" built an enormous bakehouse in New York to mass-produce bread with wage labor, three hundred mechanics met to declare solidarity with besieged neighborhood bakers. The Bread Company's backers, charged "A Mechanic," intended to "monopolize by degrees all profitable mechanical branches." Their large capital would enable them to buy flour cheaper, or to forego profits temporarily, so as to undersell and drive out of business any "obstinate mechanics . . . unwilling to become servants." They would then hire hundreds of mechanics at miserly wages, reserving for themselves the extra profits. "They will screw down the wages to the last thread," this prophetic newspaper essayist asserted. "Next, the independent spirit, so distinguished at present in our mechanics, and so useful in republics, will be entirely annihilated. The workmen will be servants and slaves." This crisis was resolved by destruction of the bakehouse in a fire of undetermined origin.[33]

While deskilling and proletarianizing a majority of the urban working class, market growth opened unprecedented opportunities for a minority. Masters who commanded the capital to exploit more wage labor energized market revolution as nascent manufacturers. New York's tax assessments identify many of these successful masters. The potter Clarkson Crolius increased his taxable worth from $8,300 in 1808 to $22,400 in 1815, while the holdings of the baker Thomas Mercein rose from $2,600 to $11,100. The 1815 assessments included a tailor worth $15,900, a shoemaker worth $18,300, and two builders worth $49,500 and $9,100.

Success on an even greater scale enabled some masters to push through the status boundary into gentility. Particularly inspiring to the upwardly mobile was Stephen Allen, who began as a penniless apprentice sailmaker, had his own sailmaking partnership by the time he was twenty-one, and ended worth $32,000 and occupying the gentleman's position of mayor. Painter and glazier Jacob Sherred accumulated assets valued at $120,000. Tanner Jacob Lorrilard, beginning business with a $3,000 loan from wealthy relatives in 1800, owned $90,700 worth of property by 1815, including three houses, two leather stores, and forty acres of Manhattan real estate. Noah Brown, a "barefoot frontier boy" who began as an unknown journeyman shipwright, became a prominent shipbuilder. His activity in Republican politics eased his way upward, doubtless helping him obtain during the War of 1812 a $200,000 navy contract on which he employed over two hundred men. The famous cabinetmaker Duncan Phyfe almost went broke after he served his apprenticeship and opened a small shop. Saved by the patronage of John Jacob Astor's daughter, he developed a large shop and elegant salesroom and was eventually worth $500,000. Phyfe's elaborate display for the 1815 peace celebration won newspaper praise along with that of eminent gentlemen.

By example, precept, and shopfloor discipline, these successful mechanic/ entrepreneurs preached a new ethic of ascetic effort against the easygoing pace and free-drinking camaraderie of traditional workways. Eschewing such working-class entertainments as cockfights and bull baitings, Duncan Phyfe followed strict Calvinist work habits, while sailmaker/mayor Allen ascribed his prosperity to working fourteen hours a day, avoiding debt as much as possible, and "employing the utmost economy in all my concerns." Mechanics, said Allen, should labor with "industry and full attention to business."[34]

Through New York's General Society of Mechanics and Tradesmen, the mechanic elite established a school and a library for apprentices. "Who can tell how many Franklins may be among you?" society president Thomas Mercein asked apprentices at the library's dedication. Baker Mercein's $11,100 worth lent credibility to his assertion that "your opportunities are great and liberal." If, aided by the new library, they would shun "the alluring but fatal paths of vice and dissipation," he promised, "industry, ardour, sobriety and perseverance in your different pursuits, will lead to successful competition in the world."

Sharpening competition enforced the stricter discipline imposed by these exemplars of capitalist success. While most rank-and-file mechanics resisted, others embraced the ethic of "successful competition in the world" to avoid falling into the despised urban underclass of propertyless and demoralized laborers. Seeking ideological reinforcement through working-class churches and associations, some even embraced the dominant mythology, endlessly proclaimed by the successful, that opportunity was rife and that success or failure turned on effort and character alone.[35]

Commercial boom touched off industrialization, as expansive capital engrossed the desperate rural labor set adrift by the northeastern agrarian crisis. Large-scale production started with textiles and shoes, articles of potentially enormous demand that promised high returns to capital and entrepreneurship. When shoemakers in Lynn and other towns discovered distant markets for cheap, mass-produced shoes, the more resourceful masters, usually backed by merchant capital, began putting-out various steps of the process to rural families in the surrounding countryside. Increasingly they assembled unskilled labor in central workshops to perform the steps under supervision. Long before shoemaking machinery was developed, manufacturers in many Yankee towns were mass-producing cheap shoes for a national market through the putting-out and central-shop systems.[36]

Meanwhile cotton-spinning machinery had been developed by British inventor/entrepreneurs, and in 1791, at the onset of the commercial boom, the enterprising mechanic Samuel Slater carried his mastery of the latest technology to the United States. He found a backer in Moses Brown, a wealthy Quaker merchant of Providence. Together they built beside the Blackstone River falls at nearby Pawtucket the first little American factory using water-powered machinery to spin cotton fiber into thread. The thread was then put-out to rural households to be woven into cloth on hand looms.

Slater's mill was an instant success, and other capitalists joined the Brown/Slater interests in building little spinning mills on many streams in southeastern New England. Protected from English competition during the Embargo and the War of 1812, such mills spread widely, with a second concentration developing in the Delaware valley around Philadelphia. At water-power sites along Connecticut streams, little mills arose to fabricate from wood and metal all manner of products.

These early manufacturers succeeded by exploiting efficiently the most vulnerable workers forced into the labor market by agrarian crisis. To utilize the cheapest female and child labor, they hired large families, housing them in company-owned villages or compounds and feeding and clothing them from company stores. Hired by contract for terms up to a year, workers saw cash wages at the end of a term only if their earnings exceeded their charges at the company store. Constrained by debt peonage, repetitiously tending the relentless machinery twelve to fourteen hours a day, isolated from the surrounding rural culture, and frequently moving from mill to mill in search of better conditions, mill workers began to be regarded as a separate and inferior class.[37]

Soon the American textile industry was reaching for technological parity with the British. During the War of 1812 the wealthy Boston Associates shifted much of their mercantile capital to textile manufacturing, and their leader, Francis Cabot Lowell, brought back from England the jealously guarded operating principles of the new power looms. Working closely with Lowell, a gifted Massachusetts mechanic Paul Moody designed and built the necessary series of machines, some of them improvements on the British models, and in 1814 the Boston Associates began operating at suburban Waltham the country's first fully integrated cotton factory, placing under one roof all the processes required to convert raw cotton into finished fabrics.

Cheap manufactured cloth led the market's penetration of the subsistence culture. By 1817, when Lowell died at forty-two, the Waltham mill was producing fabulous profits, and within eight years dividends exceeded the original investment. Farm families were discovering they could save labor by purchasing their textiles. With a little more labor to increase their marketable surplus, they could save the far more onerous labor of raising and processing fiber, spinning thread, and weaving and dyeing cloth. "This transition from mother-and-daughter power to water-and-steam power," the Reverend Horace Bushnell told an audience of Connecticut farmers, carried "with it a complete revolution of domestic life."[38]

The capitalist revolution of life did not convert Americans overnight into the self-confident enterprisers of liberal mythology. Instead, as rural spinning wheels fell silent, a historic surge of religious fervor crested to nerve their stressful passage from resistance through evasion to accommodation. Only religious intensity could reconstitute intrapsychic/interpersonal life to the imperatives of competitive effort.

Our secular mythology renders almost incomprehensible the religious mythology that organized experience for early rural America. The gnostic cosmology and stoic resignation of peasant forebears, who likewise lived at the mercy of nature and invoked its fertility with daily labor, sacralized the behavioral norms demanded by the subsistence mode of production.

A vast repertoire of orally transmitted tales, ballads, jingles, and aphorisms— much of it now irrecoverable—resonated folk conviction that the fruitful earth and all natural objects were alive and filled with spirits and magical possibilities. Following the ancient belief that heavenly bodies influenced earthly events, farm folk scheduled planting and other tasks by the zodiac, and the astrological almanac was more likely than the Bible to be the only book they had. They located their wells by divination and practiced an herbal/magical medicine derived partly from the Indians. The spirits and demons that populated their landscape and awed their children they accommodated as angels, devils, and witches to the Christianity they formally professed.[39]

For centuries peasant animism had magicalized the patriarchal Christian God who reconciled Europeans to hazards of weather, terrors of plague, and exactions of fathers and rulers. The Protestant Reformation revitalized this magical patriarchalism to cope with the Old World market's initial surge. The awesome Jehovah proclaimed by Geneva's Protestant theologian John Calvin was brought to the New World by uprooted emigrants and preached from the Congregational meetinghouses of New England Puritans, the Presbyterian kirks of the Scotch-Irish, and the Reformed churches of Germans, Dutch, and French Huguenots. Calvinism's thrilling promise of divine encounter sacralized deep springs of animistic magic and mystery to arm rural Euro/Americans with invidious power against capricious fate. The more vividly they felt Jehovah's omnipotence, the safer they felt in a hazardous world. Paradoxically worship of an Absolute Patriarch stabilized this patriarchal society by restraining patriarchal abuse. Women found communal protection in a fellowship of intense piety that many men disdained. Where survival depended on the sexual division of labor, congregations enforced communal horror at marital infidelity and punished male drunkenness and violence. Shared fervor reinforced familial and neighborly altruism for isolated farmsteads dependent on cooperative work and mutual help.

But the farming interior's supernaturalism was threatened by the seaboard market's enterprising ethic. Holding these opposing impulses in tension, the Reformation had faced forward as well as backward. While revitalizing traditional piety against market corrosion, Calvinism also became the spiritual medium of capitalist transformation by sanctifying worldly work as religious duty and wealth as fruit of grace. Under the New World's person/land ratio, pious venturers found worldly success by equating Christian virtue with the market ethos of self-disciplined effort. As God seemed kindlier, the environment more manageable, and their fate more dependent on their own abilities, they could no longer see themselves as sinners helplessly dependent on the arbitrary salvation of an all-powerful God. Even in Puritan New England by the early eighteenth century, Boston's most fashionable pulpits echoed Dutch theologian Arminius in relating salvation to human capability and effort. Through "arminian" heresy, commercial/planter elites of ports and the tidewater South moved toward the cosmopolitan quasi-deism and capitalist moralism of Boston-bred Benjamin Franklin.[40]

Fed by the secular optimism of the European Enlightenment, arminianism foreshadowed a revolutionary mythology threatening Christianity itself. In the marketlike, self-regulating, mechanistic cosmos of Sir Isaac Newton and John Locke, rational empiricists could maximize hedonic income by manipulating inert matter. What made this promethean myth so congenial to entrepreneurial/intellectual hubris and so destructive to ages of human "superstition" was its radical new epistemological claim—that only its empirical science yielded truth.

Arminian heresy shocked the rural interior into the opposite, "antinomian" heresy that God visits ordinary people with the "New Light" of transfiguring grace and revelation. With the subsistence world's integrating mythology at stake, a Great Awakening blazed up in the 1730s and 1740s to forge evangelical Protestantism into the dominant form of American religious expression. Periodically for a hundred years, mounting market pressures reignited the wildfire of ecstatic revival—a New-Light Stir amid the Revolution's dislocations, a Great Revival amid commercial boom at the turn of the century, and a culminating Second Great Awakening amid market revolution in the Jacksonian era.[41]

Antinomian evangelicals insisted that the only basis for valid religious experience was the emotionally cataclysmic new birth of adult conversion. By preaching that the unconverted sinner is doomed to eternal damnation, they stoked anxiety for an ecstatic catharsis in which the New Light of divine grace flooded a "changed heart." Expressing rural culture's deep strain of pre-Christian animism in suitably Christian theological terms, antinomianism asserted the subsistence world's commitment to communal love against the market's competitive ethic.[42]

Direct access to divine grace and revelation, subordinating clerical learning to everyperson's reborn heart, vindicated the lowly reborn soul against hierarchy and authority, magistrates and clergy. Contention and schism broke the mold of ecclesiastical uniformity, splitting traditional churches, spawning plain-folk sects, and swelling upstart Baptists and Methodists into the largest American denominations. Bathed in the New Light of a living God, antinomians activated deepening social fissures to portend American democracy.[43]

Protestantism's antipodal heresies signified a far broader clash of cosmologies. Antinomian/arminian polarities in technical theology arrayed piety against moralism, the magical spirituality of a parochial and fatalist countryside against the self-reliant effort of a cosmopolitan and activist market. While arminian moralism sanctioned competitive individualism and the market's rewards of wealth and status, antinomian new birth recharged rural America's communal egalitarianism in resistance. A heresy of capitalist accommodation confronted a heresy of precapitalist cultural revitalization in a *Kulturkampf* that would decide American destiny on the private battlegrounds of every human relationship.[44]

Only after protracted spiritual mobilization did the antinomian farming majority resort haltingly to the distant abstractions, ambiguities, and power struggles of politics. Despite the rural equality and representative institutions fostered early by the American person/land ratio, colonial governments had become more oligarchic over time. An inherited European tradition of deference allowed politics to be largely monopolized by the emerging market elites who had most to gain.[45]

The Awakening had an ultimately profound political effect by undermining deference. As the New Light validated heart over intellect, unlettered evangelical fervor over learned authority, humble plainness over pride and luxury, antinomian rebellion overflowed into politics to foster the subsistence culture's most enduring legacy, political democracy. By the late eighteenth century the evangelical revolt had divided Americans into rival religious communities, one concentrated along the market-oriented seaboard and the other dominating the subsistence-oriented interior, but self-consciously demarcated as they overlapped in many areas. Evangelicals were themselves unaware of their political thrust. "We concern not ourselves with the government," protested Virginia Baptists in disclaiming "any attempts to alter the constitution of the kingdom to which as men we belong."[46]

The elite hysteria stirred up by this cultural rebellion is a better measure of its political as well as religious potential. An Anglican priest complained that evangelical missionaries were traversing the South Carolina upcountry "Poison[in]g the Mind of the People" with "Democratical and Common Weath Principles." It was no accident that North Carolina's Regulator movement, a massive farmers' uprising against elitist exploitation that ended in pitched battle in 1771, arose in an area recently swept by Baptist revivalism.[47]

Democracy emerged during the American Revolution as a new thing under the sun. The word *democrat* did not appear in the English or French languages until 1789. "Democracy," denoting in classical political theory the popular element in mixed governments, was consistently disparaged by the liberal Revolutionary gentry. Dreading democracy, they wanted instead a "republic" providing security of property, equal rights before the law, and a carefully restricted system of representation through which enterprising elites could shape the state to the market ambitions of capital.[48]

But genteel leaders found themselves dependent on farmers, workers, and shopkeepers inspired by the egalitarian implications of Revolutionary ideology. As the market undermined traditional communities, farming and working people were appropriating the "Mr./Mrs./Miss" (Master/Mistress) formerly reserved for the gentry. The democratic impulse was driven by feelings of insecurity and powerlessness as the market disrupted ordinary lives. Contrary to liberal mythology, democracy was born in tension with capitalism, and not as its natural and legitimizing political expression.

When independence forced reconstruction of the polity, therefore, the combined influence of subsistence farming areas and urban workers made the new state constitutions far more open to popular impulse than the gentry desired. In state after state, the evangelical countryside pressed for the most democratic features—manhood suffrage, secret ballot, annual elections, unicameral legislatures. In Pennsylvania, where colonial elites were most completely discredited by their opposition to independence and where farmers were joined by the radicalized laboring and artisan classes of Philadelphia, the popular coalition won a complete victory. Even where more limited concessions were wrung from Revolutionary elites, the new state governments were considerably more democratic than the colonial regimes. Given the social roots of these democratic reforms, it should not be surprising that their backers often demanded religious qualifications for officeholding.[49]

In the more open regimes, popular influence soon threatened elite interests with paper-money and debtor-relief laws. Alarmed by "this great upbearing of our masses," a coalition of commercial and planting elites brought off the constitutional coup of 1787. Essentially they shifted the locus of power from the unreliable states to a strong central government, buttressed it with special guarantees of capitalist property relations, and carefully insulated it as much from popular influence as they thought politically feasible. Then the brilliant leader of their commercial wing, Alexander Hamilton, charted for the new federal government a series of boldly conceived policies, capped by a national Bank, through which their dreams of empire and profit might be realized.

Commercial boom made government promotion of economic growth the central dynamic of American politics. Entrepreneurial elites needed the state to guarantee property; to enforce contracts; to provide juridical, financial, and transport infrastructures; to mobilize society's resources as investment capital; and to load the legal dice for enterprise in countless ways. Especially they strove for a powerful, gentry-led national state, through whose developmental policies they dreamed of rivaling British wealth and might.

The rural majority, by contrast, idealized the republic already at hand. Democracy promised farmers protection from intrusive government. Dreading taxes and meeting most of their social needs through their own institutions of family and church, they jealously resisted any enlargement of public functions or expense as threatening patriarchal independence. To preserve the independence and equality of a self-sufficient, self-governing citizenry, they wanted government weak, cheap, and close to home. By threatening this yeoman republic, market elites stirred up a powerful democratic counterforce seeking a tighter control over government by ordinary voters.

Thus the clashing perspectives of land and market focused early American politics on three tightly linked questions:

1. How democratic—how responsive to popular majorities—would government be?

2. Would government power be extensive and concentrated at the federal level or limited and diffused among the states?

3. To what extent and in what ways would government promote economic growth?

When commercial boom and Alexander Hamilton unveiled the developmental capitalist state, antinomian rebellion overflowed from Great Revival into political animus against his intrusive, aristocratic Federalism. The politicalization of the democratic majority began when Hamiltonian developmentalism was challenged by a disaffected wing of the elite, the tobacco-planting gentry of the Chesapeake region. Thomas Jefferson's Republican party, by presenting itself as vehicle for the rising democratic impulse, politicized enough farmers to oust the Federalists in "the revolution of 1800."

Republicans won overwhelming ascendancy by abandoning Hamilton's expensive developmentalism while symbolically affirming the civic worth of farmers and workers. But Republicanism was compromised by contradictions between opportunity and equality, while rural egalitarianism itself was compromised by farmers' commitment to private property and the patriarchy it sustained. The potential dangers of unlimited property rights under market conditions were obscured by Americans' premarket experience with private property under a person/land ratio sustaining family security and equality. On these contradictions would turn the postwar generation's climactic struggle over American destiny.

Chapter 2

Ambiguous Republicanism

THE NEWS of peace—reaching Washington on the evening of February 13, 1815, by "an express on its way to Alexandria for a speculation in flour"— sounded the knell of the whole system of politics pitting Federalists against Republicans. Federalism had heard its doom the evening before, when delegates bearing the Hartford Convention's demands to a beleaguered Congress were overtaken by the rumor at Baltimore. With convention and party condemned overnight to treasonable opprobrium, the delegates abandoned their mission, and Federalism abandoned the contest for national power. As Federalist politicians retreated, however, their policies were taken up by their triumphant opponents. The peace news found Republicans creating a new national Bank (herein capitalized to distinguish it from state-chartered banks), five times bigger than the Federalist original.

Republicanism had been ambiguous from the beginning. Gutted soils and glutted world tobacco markets had wrenched Virginia's planter patriciate into a remarkable role as midwife to democracy. Simultaneously beset during the Revolutionary crisis by British creditors and evangelical democracy, this proud, cultivated, pleasure-loving, child-indulging, slave-driving gentry had maintained its hegemony by Whig militancy and granting religious freedom. With chronic depression stifling enterprise and muting competition, both Chesapeake planters and their farmer neighbors cherished patriarchal independence and high commondity prices, and both abhorred debt, creditors, and taxes. In this unchallenging environment, a Yankee tutor found a "familiarity and frankness" quite unlike the "coldness and unfeelingness," the "avarice and ceremony," of "our Northern manners." The difference, thought young William Ellery Channing, was that Virginians "*love money less* than we do."[1] Therefore Virginia gentlemen were less threatened politically than the commercial gentry by lower-class discontent. With slavery muzzling their black labor force and racism solidifying their leadership of white farmers, the tobacco gentry followed the bold young liberals Thomas Jeffer-

34

son and James Madison, first into Revolution, then into religious freedom, and finally toward fraternization with democracy.[2]

Traumatized by debt, Virginians were especially susceptible to the Revolutionary ideology portraying Britain as corrupted by commercialization. They saw the challenge of both Revolution and republican politics as preserving from British corruption the virtue sustaining American republicanism. Commercialization was seen as threatening virtue by engendering luxury and self-indulgence among the rich while making the poor too vicious and too dependent on others to exercise republican citizenship.[3]

Accordingly the hard-pressed tobacco gentry took alarm when Hamilton threatened to promote commerce at the expense of agriculture. In the light of Revolutionary ideology, they saw in his national developmentalism the funded debt, national Bank, and chartered privileges that commercialized and corrupted Britain. Reaching out for allies against the mercantile gentry, they followed Jefferson in relying on farmers who had always followed planter leadership. Experience left Virginia gentlemen few qualms about shaping their appeal to the rising demand for a democratic dramaturgy. Only gradually did they realize what a powerful (and dangerous) energy they were tapping.

Capitalizing on the swelling egalitarian mood, the emerging Republican party presented itself as champion of democracy against the Hamiltonians' aristocratic Federalism. Jefferson's "great power over the mass of the people," as Chief Justice John Marshall unhappily observed, was "chiefly acquired by professions of democracy."[4] The Republicans were bound to triumph as soon as they managed to politicize enough of the potentially overwhelming democratic majority.

To Hamilton's political economy of promoting commercial and industrial development the Republicans countered a political economy of preserving republicanism by preserving the virtuous independence of American farmers and mechanics. The remarkable Jefferson was almost unique, even among the Virginia gentry, in his willingness to trust the political judgment of ordinary people. His radical conviction that "the earth belongs to the living" asserted every generation's right to reshape inherited institutions and property arrangements to its needs. Witnessing in Europe the squalor and demoralization that accompanied the highly developed capitalist market, Jefferson became convinced that the virtue of ordinary citizens would best preserve the republic from the market's corruption. For in America the mass of ordinary citizens were farmers, and his Virginia experience led him to regard "those who labour in the earth" as uniquely virtuous. These "chosen people of God," he said, looked "to their own soil and industry . . . for their subsistence," thus avoiding the "subservience and venality" of those depending on the market's "casualties and caprice of customers."

Jefferson understood, moreover, that political equality requires economic equality. He built his political economy on the hope that America's cheap and abundant lands would preserve a just and humane society within the existing system of capitalist property relations. His experience of small-farming Virginia suggested a more literal reading than John Locke intended of his famous justification of private property. "The earth is given as a common stock for man to labour and live on," as Jefferson put it. All persons had a natural right to enough land to produce their subsistence, as well as a right to the property produced by mixing their labor with the land. Living this theory sanctified private property for most free Americans.

Pragmatically Jefferson recognized that the country was not ready "yet" to let the landless appropriate enough uncultivated land to meet their needs. But "it is not too soon," he insisted, "to provide by every possible means that as few as possible shall be without a little portion of land." Accordingly he persuaded the Virginia legislature to abolish primogeniture and entail, the common-law provisions for handing down large estates intact over generations. As "another means of silently lessening the inequality of property," he suggested taxing large properties at progressively higher rates while exempting small properties. But the men of large property who filled legislatures were not ready for this suggestion, and he got nowhere with his more radical proposal that Virginia give fifty acres to every landless adult.[5]

Jefferson's election to the presidency in 1800 thus seemed to mean that the federal government would not be used to promote the "Englandization" of America. Instead the Louisiana Purchase—"an empire for liberty," he called it—promised indefinite perpetuation of the yeoman republic. Beyond this what the emerging majority wanted from the federal government was exactly what it got—low taxes, rigid economy, retirement of the Hamiltonian public debt, an ostentatious simplicity of official style, and no grandiose projects.

Jefferson and Madison spent most of their four presidential administrations trying to force their remaining objective of free trade on the warring European powers. Their willingness to resort to so Draconian a measure as the Embargo, full in the face of the entrepreneurial pressures generated by the commercial boom, attested the depth of their commitment to a minimally commercialized yeoman republic. This commitment was reflected, too, in the primitive circumstances of official life. The dilapidated, unfinished public buildings rising from the bogs along the Potomac mocked the grandeur of L'Enfant's imperial design and symbolized a rapid retreat from the pomp and ceremony of the Federalists' more splendidly conceived national state. Parsimonious Republican lawmakers would expend no more to make their squalid capital decently habitable than they did for the President's salary.

The poverty of the government's headquarters was matched by its poverty of function. Except in matters of diplomacy and war, its only direct services to citizens were the lightly used postal system, the federal courts, a National Road, and scattered lighthouses and navigational aids. Excluding Congress and the military, the entire government establishment at Washington, from President to door-keeper, numbered only 153 people at the beginning of Jefferson's administration and would increase to only 352 by 1829. In 1815 the President paid out of his own pocket the single secretary who assisted him; the Attorney General had neither clerk nor office; the Supreme Court convened for two months a year in a Capitol Hill boarding house; and during the summer only the clerks and bureau chiefs remained in the muggy capital to keep the wheels of state slowly turning.[6]

Meanwhile the Federalist/Republican struggle politicized much of the potential electorate, at least to the extent of voting. In Massachusetts, for which we have annual voter turnout figures back to the Revolution, only 10 to 12 percent of the adult white males voted in the first decade of independence. Even the bitter debtor/creditor battles surrounding Shays's Rebellion never brought more than 32 percent to the polls. What pushed Massachusetts turnout permanently over 50 percent was close competition between Federalists and Republicans in the late 1790s. And turnout climbed to a new plateau of 63 to 84 percent when party competition reached a new peak of intensity following the Embargo.

The less complete records of turnout for other states similarly show an initial peak around 1800 and a further surge in the Embargo years to impressive new plateaus. Orange County, North Carolina, managed to record over 100 percent of its adult white males as voting in 1808, as did Baltimore in 1812. Turnout was highest where the two parties were closely matched and intensely competitive, while politicians had least incentive to mobilize voters in one-sided states like Virginia where the minority party had no hope.[7]

A growing electorate meant growing Republican majorities, as a growing number of ordinary folk not only voted for Republican candidates but identified with the Republican party. Democratic-minded voters, lacking time and information to keep up with the baffling complexity of issues and candidates, could hold the aristocratic Federalists at bay by marching regularly to the polls under the Republican banner. In the mid-Atlantic states, where the struggle was fiercest, the Republicans quickly began to call themselves Democratic Republicans and soon simply Democrats.

Within a few years of Jefferson's election, most states came under almost continuous Republican control. Only the prostration inflicted by his Embargo produced a brief Federalist revival on the eve of the War of 1812. Thus, from the perspective of somnolent Washington, the country's miraculous escape from the war, coupled with Federalism's suicide in the seditious proceedings at Hartford, might suggest an indefinite perpetuation of the Jeffersonian yeoman republic.

Yet focus on Washington yields a misleading picture of the political economy. People's lives were far more affected by state and local governments. There entrepreneurial interests concentrated their political energies after they lost control of the federal government, bidding for control of Republicanism in the most commercial states. Ambitious politicians deserted federal office in droves—more senators resigned than failed of reelection—to pursue power on the more intensely contested battlegrounds of state politics. In the bitter struggle for New York, De Witt Clinton resigned from the Senate to become mayor of New York City, and subsequently Daniel P. Tompkins would have resigned the vice presidency if he had succeeded in his campaign against Clinton for governor. In these contests the market revolution was transforming Republicanism in ways that would soon become apparent at Washington.[8]

Republican ambiguity was rooted in the Constitution, which made American politics a zero-sum game by requiring an electoral majority to win the potent presidency. To win all executive power, as politicians quickly understood, they had to piece together a national majority from the diverse elements affected by politics in widely dissimilar states. The inherent dynamic was toward competition between two heterogeneous coalitions or parties, and this two-party system came to encompass every kind of state and local rivalry and division. Each party necessarily contained jarring elements of class, interest, and culture.[9]

Where Federalism paradoxically got much of its following from the threatened rural culture of New England, Republicanism got much of its leadership from entrepreneurial and often elitist elements that were excluded or otherwise alienated from local Federalist establishments. The Crowninshields, a rising merchant family in Salem, became Republican out of rivalry with the more established Federalist Derbys. The Federalist preference for the British trade made Republicans of many merchants trading elsewhere, especially in flour-shipping Baltimore, where much of the upstart commercial establishment, resenting domination by Maryland's Federalist planter class, followed merchant/politician Samuel Harrison Smith into the Republican ranks. In New York Clintons and Livingstons perpetuated the colonial politics of baronial family factions by allying as Republicans against the Federalist Schuylers, Jays, and Morrises—Alexander Hamilton being a Schuyler son-in-law. Everywhere the Republican party attracted such upwardly mobile outsiders as the foreign-born John Jacob Astor, Stephen Girard, Albert Gallatin, and Alexander J. Dallas; and everywhere ambitious young lawyers like Dallas in Philadelphia, James Sullivan in Boston, Joseph Story in Salem, and Aaron Burr in New York advanced themselves by organizing Republicans locally. Under the Republican banner of equal rights a recurrent paradigm of American politics emerged, as a democratic majority asserting equality empowered an aspiring elite asserting opportunity.

Thomas Jefferson was as remarkable for his pragmatism and political skill as for his ability to transcend the perspective of his class and imagine a democratic society. Fearing Federalist designs on republicanism itself, he mobilized in its defense whatever disaffected or aspiring elites were available. Pursuing the utopian goal of a yeoman democratic republic, Jefferson accommodated to entrepreneurial Republicanism as much as he thought necessary to maintain Republican ascendancy. No doubt he exaggerated the Federalist threat to republicanism itself, and perhaps he accommodated more than necessary.

Throughout his career he kept close to him as confidant and alter ego the very different James Madison. A rather insignificant-looking little man, especially alongside the gangling, red-haired Jefferson, Madison was notable for depth of knowledge, analytical clarity, and cautious judgment. A Princeton education and precocious leadership in the Revolutionary Congresses made him a committed nationalist. He so far absorbed the commercial perspective as to collaborate with Hamilton in organizing the movement for a constitutional convention (Jefferson being in France as American minister at the time), and the convention largely followed his impressive intellectual leadership. Madison's *Federalist* essays brilliantly advocated the new Constitution as meeting the needs of a market society by organizing politics on the market principle of competing economic interests.

Soon estranged from Hamilton by rivalry, by intimacy with Jefferson, and by the sentiments of his Virginia constituents, Madison came to share Jefferson's fear that the Hamiltonians were monarchists at heart. The crucial difference between the two friends was also the crucial ambiguity at the heart of Republicanism. Jefferson was anxious about the corrupting effect of the market on American farm families, while Madison saw farmers as incipient small entrepreneurs who were to be fulfilled by the market.

Both wanted to preserve the farmers' virtuous independence, and thus republicanism, first by guaranteeing enough cheap land to supply a growing population of roughly equal farm families, and second by maintaining the freest possible flow of trade with Europe. Free trade mattered to Jefferson because he wanted to import manufactures from Europe rather than see swarms of dependent factory workers in America. Madison wanted free trade on the rather different ground that American farmers would not work hard enough to be virtuous without the incentive of profitable export markets for their produce.

Madison's affinity for the market muffled Jefferson's affinity for the land, as a besieged landed gentry accommodated to the commercial boom's expansive capital under the imperatives of two-party politics. Their friendship melded agrarian radicalism with enough market liberalism to maintain Republican hegemony. The historical Jefferson would hardly have been possible without a Madison. By always acting under the influence of Madison's cautious realism, Jefferson could succeed as a politician while sustaining the visionary breadth of social sympathy that gave Republicanism its mass appeal.[10]

The Jeffersonian strategy succeeded for almost a generation in denying the federal government to market forces energized by commercial boom. Shifting their developmental demands to the states, where a democratic electorate was rejecting Federalism, they had no trouble finding entrepreneurial Republican advocates, especially in the most commercial states.

As men from the middling orders—the mechanic/entrepreneurs of the port towns, for example—responded to widening opportunities for profit, the Republican party became the political vehicle for their resentments against the exclusiv- ism and elitism of the Federalist commercial establishment. And as the Republican ~ty won control of more and more state governments, it increasingly attracted ~prisers who wanted government aid. Even small-farmer constituencies tended ~presented in times of political calm by county-seat lawyer/politicians sym- to a market-oriented minority.

,ates with rapidly growing economies—particularly Massachusetts, New ~, and Pennsylvania—government aid to enterprise became as much a Repub- ,can as a Federalist policy. Republican legislatures and governors outdid their Federalist predecessors in granting direct state loans to infant manufacturing enterprises. "Works of public importance deserve public encouragement," announced the preamble of a Pennsylvania act authorizing a state loan to a steel works; a New York act granting a loan to a manufacturer of earthenware similarly declared that "the establishment of useful manufactures is clearly connected with the public weal." The New York legislature authorized twenty-eight such loans in five years, between 1811 and 1816. In addition state governments authorized lotteries and tax exemptions in aid of countless private businesses, exempted certain manufacturers and their employees from jury duty and militia service, and conferred direct bounties or monopolies on favored enterprises.[11]

By 1815 the combined influence of Federalism and entrepreneurial Republicanism had completed an essential stage of the market revolution by committing the commercial states to the political economy of capitalism. This institutional transformation was most important where least visible, in the intricacies of law. Increasingly visible were the overtly developmental policies that also made the state governments indispensable engines of the market revolution.

Most dramatic was the use of state credit to amass the enormous capital for a transport network. Private capital markets could not have underwritten the mammoth state canal systems, even if they had promised enough profit to attract private investors.

The Empire City led the way. Natural advantages helped it pass Philadelphia and Boston in total volume of international trade during the commercial boom. Its harbor was unrivaled—large and deep, close to the ocean, relatively untroubled by fog or winter ice, and with miles of waterfront suitable for wharfage. The Hudson River and Long Island Sound gave it unparalleled access by cheap water transport to a far more populous hinterland than its rivals'. Between 1790 and 1810, as land-hungry Yankees flooded the Champlain country and Mohawk valley, the population of New York State grew 182 percent, compared with 86 percent for Philadelphia's Pennsylvania, 25 percent for Boston's Massachusetts, and 11 percent for Baltimore's Maryland.

New Yorkers exploited their advantages aggressively in reaching out to engross the rising exports of southern cotton. They bought cotton in Charleston, Savannah, Mobile, and New Orleans through resident agents called factors; their ships carried it to Liverpool, usually by way of New York; and the return cargoes guaranteed their dominance of the European import trade.

With this pattern established, British exporters concentrated their postwar dumping of cut-rate merchandise in New York. Instead of resisting this destructive competition with American manufactures, New York commercial interests jumped at the chance to sell British products at the lowest possible rate through their already established system for auctioning imports to the lowest bidder. In 1817 they persuaded the legislature to reinforce this cheap-goods policy by prohibiting goods from being withdrawn from auction, no matter how low the bidding. As retailers flocked in from all over the country to replenish their stocks at rock-bottom costs, New York established during the postwar boom the preeminence it would retain for a century as the great American entrepôt for European goods. Its commercial attractions increased in 1818 when the Black Ball line scheduled weekly departures of fast sailing ships between New York and Liverpool. Speed and reliability made this first transatlantic packet service irresistible to shippers and passengers, while guaranteeing New York first news of European markets.

New Yorkers were just as aggressive in pushing commerce into their hinterland. In response to market pressures for cheaper, faster, and more reliable water transport up the magnificent water highway of the Hudson, Robert Fulton developed in 1807 the world's first successful steamboat, the *Clermont*. By the time Fulton died, a few weeks after the news of peace arrived, steamboats had dramatically increased the speed and reliability of passenger travel between New York and Albany and were rapidly extending service on New York Bay and Long Island Sound.

At the inland limits of water carriage, New Yorkers pushed the market past the overland transport barrier by persuading the state to charter turnpike companies. Seeking a profit from tolls, these companies built scores of improved roads radiating out into the countryside from energized river ports. Over one thousand miles were completed by 1810 and four thousand by 1820, more than twice the mileage of any other state. These roads reduced wagon hauling rates some 50 percent, still too much for high-weight-to-value commodities such as grain except at very high prices, but opening the countryside to consumer goods that could now be brought at lower cost from the metropolis.[12]

Only one thing threatened New York's dream of becoming the Empire City of a vast American market. The rival ports of Philadelphia and Baltimore were closer to the trans-Appalachian West and dominated the burgeoning western trade by way of improved roads across the Appalachian Mountains to the upper Ohio. Philadelphia interests had promoted in the 1790s the country's first major turnpike, extending west to Lancaster. Subsequent extensions carried an improved wagon road all the way to the head of the Ohio at Pittsburgh. By the early 1820s about thirty thousand tons of freight moved over this route annually. Another ten thousand were hauled over the federally constructed National Road, which connected Baltimore with the Ohio at Wheeling, Virginia, a hundred miles downriver from Pittsburgh.

New York had a potential advantage, however, that more than outweighed its greater distance from the West. Only in upstate New York was there a break in the Appalachian mountain barrier that walled off the rest of the Atlantic seaborad from the interior. The Mohawk River, flowing from the west into the Hudson at the head of deepwater navigation near Albany, gave access to a relatively level transport corridor along the south shore of Lake Ontario all the way to Lake Erie, with a maximum elevation above sea level of 650 feet. Controlling this corridor, the Iroquois once dominated the trade for interior furs; the advantages of this vaunted "water level route to the West" would make the New York Central a giant of the railroad age; and in the age of the automobile the New York Thruway would funnel the country's heaviest East-West traffic along this historic thoroughfare.

For years some New Yorkers had dreamed of cheap water transportation from the Hudson to the Great Lakes, bringing the interior fully into the market by moving the bulky agricultural commodities that could not pay their way on the best roads. The most obvious route utilized the Mohawk to a point where a few miles of canal would connect with Oneida Lake, the Oswego River, and Lake Ontario. The failure of a state-backed canal company charging tolls demonstrated in the 1790s that state aid and private capital were inadequate and the short route too shallow and steep. Soon New Yorkers were hoping for federal aid to build a far more ambitious canal, independent of natural waterways, that would stretch 364 miles from the Hudson all the way to Lake Erie, bypassing Lake Ontario and the Niagara Falls barrier between Ontario and Erie. This seemed utterly visionary when the world had only one canal more than a tenth as long, and the United States only three canals more than two miles long, the longest twenty-seven miles and none profitable.

Deferred by Embargo and war, the Erie Canal project revived in the postwar boom as the focus of the city's bid for commercial supremacy. According to its chief proponent, Mayor De Witt Clinton, it would make New York "the great depot and warehouse of the western world," or "the greatest commercial city of the world." The inland surge of population and commodity production made intolerable the transport barriers that clogged the market's advance. Everywhere enterprising Americans turned to government to create the transport infrastructure required for a national market. And now that the market confronted the formidable Appalachian barrier, only the resources of the federal government would suffice. New York's mercantile gentry had long regarded government as an indispensable instrument of market growth. Their turnpikes were built under state-granted charters and rights of eminent domain; Fulton perfected the steamboat under a state-granted monopoly; and the state enforced their auction system. But the federal government had been less amenable to enterprise under the Virginia Republicans.

Too impatient to wait longer for federal funds, Governor De Witt Clinton in 1817 persuaded a Republican New York legislature to finance the Erie Canal itself. Completed in 1825 at a cost of some $7,000,000, the Grand Canal was an instant sensation. Tolls in the first year of full operation reached nearly $500,000, and soon paid off the entire cost of construction. More important, Clinton's big ditch cut shipping costs between Lake Erie and New York City from $100 to under $9 a ton, and eventually as low as $3 for some commodities. Within a few years it carried $15,000,000 worth of freight annually, twice the amount reaching New Orleans by the Mississippi River, and the figure would near $200,000,000 by midcentury.[13]

This bonanza generated a transportation revolution. Philadelphia fought back with a state canal across mountainous Pennsylvania to Pittsburgh on the Ohio; Baltimore seized on the latest technology to push the world's longest railroad up the Potomac and over the Appalachians to the western waters at Wheeling; and Boston tapped the Erie's western trade with a railroad to Albany.

Although none of these projects matched the Erie's profits or regained substantial western trade from New York, they did galvanize market revolution by dramatically extending the division of labor in each port/hinterland region. As transport gave areas comparative advantage in more specialized production, diverse manufactures developed around the port cities, the adjacent countryside specialized in perishable vegetables, fruits, and dairy products for urbanites, grain and livestock were produced at successively greater distances, and interior towns processed lumber, hides, and grain.

New York itself built connecting canals in every direction—between the Hudson and Lake Champlain, the Erie and Lake Ontario, the Erie and Pennsylvania waterways, and around Niagara Falls to link Lakes Ontario and Erie. An Ohio canal connecting Lake Erie with the Ohio-Mississippi river system extended the Grand Canal's reach of continuous water transport all the way to New Orleans. Then came a second Ohio connection, an Indiana connection, and eventually an Illinois canal connecting Lake Michigan with the upper Mississippi. By the 1840s, as a consequence, a northeastern sectional economy was integrating the port/hinterland economies and reaching out to create a national market.[14]

The transportation revolution that made market revolution possible was financed mainly at first by Republican-controlled governments. Public agencies, principally state governments, furnished some $41.2 million of the $58.6 million spent on canals before 1834 and, in the following decade, another $57.3 million of the $72.2 million spent on additional ambitious canal systems, notably those of Ohio, Indiana, and Illinois. Although public funds were a smaller proportion of total investment in other forms of transport, they were still substantial: some $5 million of the $30 million invested in turnpikes before 1830 and over a third of the $137.1 million invested in railroads before 1843. In addition New York encouraged development of the steamboat through its grant of monopoly privileges to the Fulton/Livingston interests.[15]

Local governments helped finance railways. Troy and Cincinnati built their own, while Baltimore contributed heavily to the Baltimore and Ohio, and Philadelphia to the Pennsylvania Railroad that eventually supplanted the Mainline Canal. Smaller towns often invested to avoid being bypassed in favor of rival towns, and the Oswego and Midland was described as zigzagging across upstate New York "in search of municipal bonds."[16]

Whereas canals were mainly built and operated directly by states, government usually supported turnpikes and railroads by subscribing capital to private enterprises. Only as the more costly and economically risky sections of the transportation network were completed—especially those surmounting the Appalachian barrier—and only as private capital markets developed the capacity to underwrite extensive undertakings did private capital gradually supplant government financing. But the very possibility of assembling private capital for large-scale enterprise was created by state policies fostering the corporate form of business organization.[17]

Virtually all businesses in colonial America were small-scale individual enterprises, and an ancient English legal tradition discouraged concentrations of private capital as threatening the sovereignty of the state. Individuals could pool their capital and spread risk in short-term enterprises like trading voyages through such legal forms as partnerships and joint-stock companies. But such forms were poorly adapted to enterprises of large scale or long duration. They could be disorganized by the death or withdrawal of any partner; they faced complex legal problems in owning and transferring property, suing, and being sued; and they left each participant fully liable for all debts a joint venture might incur. Corporations—entities of indefinite duration with the same legal rights as an individual—could be chartered only by special legislative act and were reserved for nonprofit agencies carrying out public purposes, such as town governments and colleges.

Independence freed American legislatures from the restraints of British law and enabled merchant/entrepreneurs to present profit-seeking ventures as serving a public purpose and thus deserving the advantages of corporate organization. Only seven private business corporations were chartered under the colonial regime, whereas the number climbed to forty in the first decade after the Revolution and passed three hundred during the commercial boom of the 1790s. The first corporations were chartered to enlist private capital for such public facilities as bridges, turnpikes, and urban water systems, with investors deriving their profits from tolls and user fees. Their public purpose also justified legislatures in granting them monopoly privileges as to route and location, as well as the right to seize private property under the state's power of eminent domain.

Yet the line between public purpose and private purpose proved elastic. Prominent among early corporations were marine insurance companies and banks, serving mainly the purposes of merchants, while manufacturing corporations multiplied after 1800. The country's first incorporated bank, the Bank of North America, was chartered at Philadelphia in 1781 by the Confederation Congress, ostensibly as a solution to a crisis in public finance. Actually "its directors wanted to make money," according to banking historian Bray Hammond, "and they succeeded, for the annual dividend averaged close to ten per cent for the first forty years of its existence." Inspired by this example, commercial interests in the rival ports of Boston, New York, and Baltimore within a few years persuaded their legislatures to charter banking corporations for their cities.

Banks' contribution to the takeoff of a capital-hungry economy can hardly be exaggerated. Most obviously, they pooled the limited capital available so it could be rationally allocated to the most productive purposes. But banks did much more. For the first time they provided, in place of chronically fugitive gold and silver coin, an ample circulating medium that made possible a new standard of punctuality in meeting business obligations. If banks did not, according to classical theory, actually increase the amount of real capital, they did increase the velocity with which money flowed from hand to hand and widen capital's availability. Thus they galvanized entrepreneurial energies to maximize exploitation of available opportunities for increased productivity.

Banks did all this by transcending the innocence of an age that regarded only gold and silver coin as real money. Only such "specie," guaranteed by its magical aura and inherent commodity value as a precious metal, was "legal tender" that a creditor had to accept in discharge of debt. Theoretically banks raised their capital by selling stock for specie and made their handsome profits by lending at interest the capital thus raised. Actually, instead of lending borrowers coin, they lent bank notes, or engraved certificates in varying denominations carrying a promise that the issuing bank would redeem them in specie upon demand at its counter.

So long as the public had confidence in a bank's soundness (ultimately the soundness of its loans), these bank notes circulated freely as the community's everyday form of money. And so long as public confidence was maintained, the bank could lend out far more than the actual specie in its vaults. Alternatively, instead of receiving bank notes, a borrower could be credited on the bank's books with a "deposit" in the amount of the loan, to be drawn upon by check. This, too, increased the community's total supply of money and capital. More wonderful still, even the "capital" of these early banks was often only nominally in the form of specie, purchases of stock being financed in part by loans from the banks themselves. In effect, early American entrepreneurs devised a mechanism for pulling themselves up by their economic bootstraps, raising the capital for productive investments by hypothecating, often extravagantly, the future productivity of the investments themselves.

Hugely profitable because they collected interest on loans considerably exceeding their real capital, banks seemed from the beginning threatening and fraudulent to the subsistence-oriented sector of American society; and the Pennsylvania legislature's "gentlemen from the country" almost strangled the prototype Bank of North America in its cradle. Similar anxieties were felt by some more habituated to market ways. Jefferson thought banks were created "to enrich swindlers at the expense of the honest and industrious"; while even the Federalist John Adams could declare, "Every dollar of a bank bill that is issued beyond the quantity of gold and silver in the vaults represents nothing and is therefore a cheat upon somebody."

The first banks met more potent opposition from those who coveted their benefits. Dominated by the commercial and mainly Federalist elites in the major ports, they confined themselves to loans of ninety days or less to merchants of established credit with goods in transit to market. But as the commercial boom of the 1790s opened new opportunities for profit, a host of rising master mechanics and would-be entrepreneurs clamored for the longer-term credit essential for realizing their aspirations, particularly in small-scale manufacturing. Rebuffed by the established banks, they channeled through Republican politics their demand for banks of their own.

In 1793 Albert Gallatin shepherded through a Republican Pennsylvania legislature a charter for the Bank of Pennsylvania, breaking the local monopoly of the Bank of North America. Six years later, capitalizing on New Yorkers' public-health concerns in the wake of a yellow-fever epidemic, Aaron Burr hoodwinked Hamilton and other prominent Federalists into supporting a charter for a much needed waterworks company, which utilized an obscure provision in its charter to become the Republican-controlled Bank of the Manhattan Company. As the commercial boom rolled on, Republican legislatures, often influenced by wholesale bribery, granted bank charters wholesale to capital-hungry entrepreneurs and communities. By 1815 the country had over two hundred state-chartered banks.[18]

Thus by the end of the War of 1812 countless legislative acts had thoroughly legitimized banks and other incorporated enterprises as instruments of private profit-seeking, now only tenuously tied to the original concept of public interest. Corporate charters were increasingly being granted for manufacturing, and several states had experimented with general incorporation laws allowing certain enterprises to secure the privileges of incorporation without special legislative action in each case. But corporations were only beginning to win two of their cardinal privileges, limited liability of stockholders for corporate debts and corporate freedom from interference by the state.

These privileges were won not in legislative halls but in the courts. Behind the facade of democratic decision-making in legislative bodies—as few contemporaries realized and as historians have only lately begun to discover—the decisive reshaping of the law to the demands of the market was being accomplished by lawyers and judges, both Federalist and Republican, in the state courts.[19]

Lawyers were the shock troops of capitalism. The bar mushroomed as the market proliferated contractual relationships. During the commercial boom, merchants abandoned informal arbitration and relied increasingly on lawyers and the courts to settle ever more disputes over ever larger sums. Even the criminal courts shifted from enforcing communal morality to enforcing the market's property relationships. In Massachusetts offenses against morality dwindled from a majority of prosecutions before the Revolution to 7 percent of the criminal calendar after 1800. They were replaced by offenses against property, with prosecutions for theft rising to over 40 percent of the cases.[20]

As specialists in advocacy, lawyers became the main purveyors of capitalist ideology. Most of them absorbed the commercial perspective by growing up in prosperous, market-oriented families that could supply the education and connections essential for success at the bar. Nearly three-fourths of the attorneys practicing in Massachusetts and Maine between 1760 and 1840 came from the tiny elite of college men, and after 1810 over half were sons of lawyers and judges.[21]

"Lawyers as a body," Alexis de Tocqueville concluded, "form the most powerful, if not the only, counterpoise to the democratic element." Being "secretly opposed to the instincts of democracy," this "American aristocracy" saw itself as defending the sacred rights of property against the propertyless. "When the American people are intoxicated by their passions or carried away by the impetuosity of their ideas," the astute Frenchman argued, "they are checked and stopped by the almost invisible influence of their legal counselors."[22]

The adversary system trained legal advocates to practice and to preach the market's emerging ethic—that the unbridled pursuit of self-interest is in the ultimate interest of all. Theoretically justice resulted when each competing attorney put the best possible face on his good, bad, or indifferent case. Of course, legal representation was itself an expensive market commodity sold to the highest bidder, and only the best-heeled clients could afford the superior representation provided by the most successful lawyers.

Adversary advocacy freed the bar, before most occupations, from traditional norms of truth and equity. "Indiscriminate defense of right or wrong," according to Virginia moralist John Randolph, dulled Chief Justice John Marshall's "perception . . . of truth or falsehood." But even in old-fashioned Virginia, a pioneer of the bar scorned "specious harangues concerning the Morality or Immorality of an Action that is to be determined by the Laws." Law had nothing to do with "the strict rules of natural Justice," he explained, for if ethical principles governed, "there could be no such Thing as buying and selling."[23]

As entrepreneurs sought to bend the state to their vision of the future, their legal advocates took over electoral and legislative politics. The American political system was tailor-made for the lawyers who largely designed it. Only the clergy, traditionally barred from public office, rivaled them in rhetorical skills, public exposure, and contact with local influentials. Few other occupations were flexible enough to combine with campaigning and legislative service, whereas lawyers profited from political exposure. Once elected, even a minority of lawyers could bend legislation to entrepreneurial interests. Nonlawyers, especially if unaccustomed to public speaking or rustic in discourse, were no match for articulate specialists in legal technicalities.

Thus lawyers in politics fell naturally into advocacy of bank charters and promotional legislation desired by their most influential constituents. Even the best of these lawyer/representatives, complained a physician/congressman in 1819, "seem to forget that they are not in court, charged with the interest of a client."[24]

Less than a third of the first Congress, lawyers moved into a majority after about 1813. In New Jersey two-thirds of the postwar generation's prominent politicians (of all parties) were lawyers, while nearly all prominent lawyers participated in politics.[25] As the market surged forward, its lawyer/advocates took control of the American state and pushed it into the developmental role demanded by entrepreneurs.

But lawyers' decisive contribution to the expanding market was accomplished outside the limelight of electoral politics and legislation. What entrepreneurs needed even more than developmental legislation was to change the rules of the game—the whole body of law through which the state's coercive power regulated economic relations. With impressive creativity and speed, the legal profession supplied a new law.

Not even the wiliest lawyer/politicians could have extracted the law required by expansive capital from legislatures vulnerable to a broad electorate still imbued with premarket values. But in the courts the lawyers' technical expertise could not be democratically challenged. By taking control of the state courts and asserting through them their right to shape the law to entrepreneurial ends, lawyer/judges during the first half of the nineteenth century fashioned a legal revolution.[26]

Their starting point was the English common law. English law had been shaped less by legislation than by an infinite series of judicial decisions stretching back into the dim mists of time. In theory generations of judges built up the body of the law by applying in a multitude of particular cases the immutable principles of natural justice. The tradition emphasized fidelity to the maze of judicial precedents thus established and to the intricately arbitrary forms for presenting cases called pleadings. A classic English treatise by Joseph Chitty expounded to lawyers such mind-boggling technicalities of common-law pleadings as the following:

> A traverse may be *too extensive,* and therefore defective, by being taken in the *conjunctive* instead of the *disjunctive,* where proof of the allegation in the conjunctive is not essential. Thus, in an action on a policy on ship and tackle, the defendant should not deny that the ship and tackle were lost, but that *neither* was lost.[27]

Few American lawyers had mastered the full intricacies of the common law. Only in the decade before the Revolution did Sir William Blackstone's celebrated *Commentaries on the Laws of England* make its mysteries available to the ordinary provincial practitioner. Blackstone's glorification of the common law as guardian of property against arbitrary power made it congenial with the Revolutionary cause. Moreover the legal profession had a vested interest in a system of law made by lawyer/judges and so abstruse as to demand legal expertise in large measure. Consequently most of the Revolutionary state governments, needing more law than the scant provincial statutes afforded, declared the common law in force in their courts.

Armed now with the argument that a complex body of law required professionally expert judges, lawyers replaced laymen on the bench. Only two lawyers had been among the eleven judges serving on the highest Massachusetts court in the fifteen years preceding the Revolution, while all but two who served during the next half century were lawyers. By the turn of the century lawyers filled nearly all state and federal judgeships above the lowest magistrates' courts.[28]

The new class of lawyer/judges lost little time in seizing power from juries. A complex body of law, made by judges and understood only by lawyers, was inconsistent with the right of colonial juries to rule on matters of law as well as fact. Lawyer/judges began instructing juries on points of law, arguing that not to do so would "render laws, which ought to be an uniform rule of conduct, uncertain, fluctuating with every change of passion and opinion of jurors, and impossible to be known till pronounced." By 1804 Massachusetts required judges to instruct juries on all points of law; by 1810 its highest court was accepting appeals where juries violated judges' instructions; and soon afterwards this tribunal began overturning decisions on the ground that juries, in attempting to evade judges' instructions on the law, had decided cases contrary to the weight of the evidence.[29]

Judges further weakened juries by declaring more questions to be matters of law. In addition lawyers persuaded some states to introduce equity proceedings, an arcane branch of English jurisprudence in which special judges called chancellors decided without a jury certain classes of cases, utilizing special rules and procedures almost as intricate as those of the common law. The jury, concludes a historian of these developments, "had ceased to be an adjunct of local communities which articulated into positive law the ethical standards of those communities."[30] Instead it was restricted to weighing competing testimony or assessing damages on the facts, in the service of an increasingly complex and standardized system of law that could be understood and influenced only by expert lawyers.

, As lawyer/judges brought adjudication under the control of their expert instructions on the law, they gave wider authority to their opinions by publishing them so they could be cited as precedents in other courts. Following the lead of Connecticut in 1784, the states began to require written opinions. By the turn of the century the decisions of appellate courts in the leading commercial states were regularly published, and by 1815 a half dozen states provided official court reporters. As judges in inferior courts turned increasingly for guidance on novel points to the published appellate decisions, especially those of the most commercial states, a rough uniformity of legal doctrine began to emerge.[31]

"Taught law is tough law," in Frederic William Maitland's aphorism; and publishing decisions was only one way legal luminaries taught law to a changing society in search of legal principles to cover a host of novel situations. Through private law schools, Jefferson's mentor George Wythe in Virginia and Judge Tapping Reeve (in partnership with James Gould) in Connecticut trained hundreds of rising attorneys and politicians.[32]

Even more influential were two legal scholars, Federalist James Kent of New York and Republican Joseph Story of Massachusetts. Their treatises not only systematized the American law emerging from diverse state laws and decisions but also toughened its commercial bias. The authority of Kent's four-volume *Commentaries on American Law* (1826–1830) was reinforced by his role in developing equity jurisdiction as chancellor of New York, and Story completed many of his treatises while commuting between his seat on the federal Supreme Court in Washington and the professorship he held after 1829 at Harvard's law school.

But the law being taught to the young republic and enforced in its courts was not the old English law. Once the common law empowered lawyer/judges to exploit the law-making potential of the courts, they stood Blackstone on his head. Continued adherence to ancient common-law principles, said one judge, would prevent "improvement in our commercial code." With growing confidence judges modified Blackstonian precedents to facilitate commercial ends. "Theoretical[ly] courts make no law," Judge Tapping Reeve taught by 1813, "but in point of fact they are legislators." By acquiescing in judge-made law, he added, elected legislatures obviated any theoretical difficulty.[33]

While judges ritually invoked the common law's immutable antiquity, they were in fact changing it in a thousand ways, largely beyond the ken of laypeople but of vast social portent. What common law had really come to mean was judge-made law, judicial legislation. The "true glory" of the common law, as Joseph

Story proclaimed the new principle in his inaugural lecture as Dane Professor of Law at Harvard in 1829, was that "it must for ever be in a state of progress, or change, to adapt itself to the exigencies and changes of society."[34]

Progress for Republican Justice Story, as for Federalist Chancellor Kent, meant adapting law to the needs of entrepreneurs. Both revered property as the spring of enterprise. By making property "inherent in the human breast," said Kent, God lifted men from sloth and stimulated "the various and exalted powers of the human mind." "The spirit of commerce," said Story, along with "ambition and enterprise, the love of wealth," supplied "comforts and enjoyments to all classes" and fostered "the best interests of humanity." Upon this inarticulate major premise, he overruled a jury for awarding such large damages that commercial plans "would be involved in utter uncertainty."

These American Justinians felt engaged in a desperate struggle to strengthen the law as a bulwark against envious democracy. "Without law," warned Story, "good men would be everywhere expelled from office and bad men under colour of some captivating delusions would seize the reins of power." Invasion of private property would be followed by anarchy and tyranny. With this perspective, Kent frankly designed his *Commentaries* to propagate nationally the commercially oriented law "as known and received at Boston, New York, Philadelphia, Baltimore, Charleston, etc." "I shall not much care," he confessed, "what the law is in Vermont or Delaware or Rhode Island, or many other states." In his pioneering development of equity, he said, with few precedents to restrict him, "I *most always found principles suited to my views of the case.*"[35]

The legal revolution fashioned by this generation of lawyer/judges in the state courts responded to a protoindustrial economy undergoing what Karl Marx called "primitive accumulation." Entrepreneurs generating intense pressure for capital demanded law that would ease the transfer of property from subsistence uses to the more profitable and productive uses of entrepreneurs and corporations. The law they required would not only protect property but promote its marketability.

Additionally entrepreneurs needed law sufficiently elaborated and uniform to make the consequences of business decisions highly predictable. They needed law that gave new and dynamic forms of property, particularly transportation and manufacturing facilities, priority over old and static forms of property, particularly agricultural land. They needed law that favored holders of capital, in their roles as sellers, lenders, and employers, over buyers, borrowers, and employees. And they needed law that facilitated the concentration and efficient management of capital for large enterprises, while protecting them from interference by the state.

American judges, Federalist and Republican, responded creatively to all these needs. Seeking to liberate property for development, they did not hesitate to undermine the most fundamental doctrine of the common law, the absolute right of the property owner to free use of his property without the slightest interference. The common law had evolved in medieval England to preserve over generations the distribution of agricultural land maintaining a static hierarchy. It allowed land-owners to entail lands so they could not be broken up or pass out of the family and made transfers of ownership complex and difficult. In cases of competing uses of a single resource, such as a stream passing through several properties, it gave preference first to "natural" (that is, agricultural) use, and then to priority of use. And it allowed landowners to recover damages for any actions by others that impaired their free use and enjoyment of their property.

American courts began modifying these doctrines as antidevelopmental. In conjunction with legislative actions, they abolished entails so as to make land a freely marketable commodity and simplified and standardized the process of trans-ferring ownership. It was "the wise policy of government, in this state," declared the highest Massachusetts court in 1811, "to facilitate the alienation of lands, and to encourage their cultivation."[36]

An important line of decisions gave entrepreneurs access to the waterpower on which early manufacturing depended. A "balancing test," first foreshadowed in an 1805 New York decision, weighed benefits to a dam builder against losses incurred by upstream owners whose property was flooded or downstream owners whose flow was interrupted. The new doctrine implied that ownership carried the right to develop property for business purposes. To clog such development with damage awards under traditional common-law doctrines, said the New York judge, would deprive the public of "the benefit which always attends competition and rivalry."[37]

Courts increasingly protected other business uses of property from suits by damaged adjacent property owners. Whether a man could operate a stable that disturbed his neighbors, Judge Tapping Reeve told his law students in 1813, would depend on whether "he could exercise his business in another place—for men must be allowed to carry on their business."[38] This line of judicial reasoning culminated in an 1839 Kentucky decision allowing a railroad to run its cinder-belching loco-motives into the heart of Louisville. So necessary were "agents of transportation in a populous and prospering country," said the court, that "private injury and personal damage . . . must be expected."

> The onward spirity of the age must, to a reasonable extent, have its way. The law is made for the times, and will be made or modified by them. The expanded and still expanding genius of the *common law* should adapt it here, as elsewhere to the improved and improving conditions of our country and our countrymen. And therefore, railroads and locomotive steamcars—the offsprings, as they will also be the parents, of progressive improvement—should not, in themselves, be considered as *nuisances*.[39]

So that the onward spirit of the age could have its way, common-law principles of liability were steadily eroded. To encourage men to take risks in the interest of productivity, American judges began to insist that injured parties demonstrate illegality or negligence by the person (or corporation) causing the injury. The new American law of damages "held that every man of mature age must take care of himself," according to its most influential interpreter. "He need not expect to be saved from himself by legal paternalism.... When he acted, he was held to have acted at his own risk with his eyes open, and he must abide the appointed consequences."[40]

Common-law property rights were further infringed under the doctrine of eminent domain, by which the state could seize private property, provided a public purpose was served and just compensation paid. The scope of eminent domain was vastly expanded when the states began condemning land for great canal systems and conferring the power of eminent domain on scores of private corporations chartered to build bridges, turnpikes, canals, waterworks, and railroads. By the 1830s some states were granting eminent domain to manufacturing corporations for waterpower sites and mining corporations for access routes. Courts consistently construed the rules of eminent domain in favor of invading enterprises. A landmark Massachusetts decision in 1823 limited compensation to property actually taken and ruled out damages inflicted on remaining adjacent property, forcing original owners to subsidize new enterprises. Furthermore the prior owner's compensation was reduced by any estimated appreciation in the value of his remaining property. Under this doctrine railroads often obtained their rights-of-way almost free. In Ohio court-appointed appraisers "uniformly found that the benefits from the great iron way ... equaled or exceeded the value of damages."[41]

When eminent domain enabled a manufacturing corporation to seize farms for a waterpower site or shielded a mining corporation from suit for damages inflicted on its neighbors, the question of public purpose was raised in stark form. Rather than confront directly the ancient doctrine that permitted corporate privileges and eminent domain only when a public purpose was served, the courts broadened the definition of public purpose almost to meaninglessness. "The ever varying condition of society is constantly presenting new objects of public importance and utility, "proclaimed a New Jersey court in 1832, "and what shall be considered a public use or benefit, must depend somewhat on the situation and wants of the community for the time being." Not until the eve of the Civil War did a Massachusetts court avow unambiguously what had long since become the controlling doctrine:

> It has never been deemed essential that the entire community or any considerable portion of it should directly enjoy or participate in an improvement or enterprise, in order to constitute a public use.... Everything which tends to enlarge the resources, increase the energies, and promote the productive power of any considerable number of the inhabitants of a section of the State, or which leads to the growth of towns and the creation of new sources of private capital and labor, indirectly contributes to the general welfare and to the prosperity of the whole community.[42]

With such a view of public purpose, it is small wonder that the jurists of the early republic loaded the dice in favor of beneficent enterprise in every possible context. A Massachusetts court in 1808 first limited the liability of stockholders for corporate debts. Everywhere judges labored to expedite remedies for creditors against debtors and to promote the negotiability of instruments of indebtedness ranging from municipal and corporate bonds to bills of exchange and certificates of deposit.

When the bulk of the mechanic class began sinking into a wage-dependent proletariat, the courts outlawed strikes with landmark conspiracy convictions at Philadelphia in 1806 and New York in 1810. As the introduction of steam engines and heavy machinery increased the hazards of the workplace, the Massachusetts courts led the judicial rush to protect employers and capitalists from the costs. An 1824 decision announced the doctrine of contributory negligence, freeing an employer from all liability for any injury to which the injured worker's negligence contributed. The courts extended this doctrine in 1842 with a fellow-servant rule relieving the employer of liability if a fellow employee's negligence contributed to the injury. What the judges claimed to be protecting was the worker's freedom to enter into a contract to perform dangerous work at wages theoretically commensurate with the risk.[43]

The judicial transformation of the common law of contracts reflects with particular clarity American judges' devotion to the idea of a free market in which no-holds-barred competition would generate maximum growth. Where the common law frowned on excessive profit-making, American law opened the door to usury. Where the common law enforced equity and fair value in contracts, the emerging American doctrine—absolute freedom of contract coupled with absolute enforcement of contract—came to mean "buyer beware." The common-law principle of implied warranty, said a Pennsylvania court in 1839, "would put a stop to commerce itself in driving everyone out of it by the terror of endless litigation." The person who could not guard his own interests in making a contract, the judge declared, "is not a fit subject of judicial guardianship."[44]

The impact of the silent juridical revolution effected by the state courts of the early republic can scarcely be exaggerated. "A society of well-ordered communities united in the pursuit of ethical ends" was undermined, according to one modern student of the development, by the new jurisprudence, which "assumed that a fluctuating marketplace was the central institution in the economy and left individuals free to manipulate its working so that they rather than their neighbors would most benefit from it." Inevitably the strong, the able, the ambitious, and the avaricious benefited most. The law had become "a tool by which those interest groups that had emerged victorious in the competition for control of law-making institutions could seize most of society's wealth for themselves and enforce their seizure upon the losers."[45]

The consequences of these allocational decisions became apparent with the full flowering of industrial capitalism following the Civil War. "There has hardly ever before been a community in which the weak have been so pitilessly pushed to the wall," marveled the legal historian Sir Henry Maine in 1885, "in which those who have succeeded have so uniformly been the strong, and in which in so short a time there has arisen so great an inequality of private fortune and domestic luxury." But Maine thought progress worth the social costs, and the New York Supreme Court agreed. The antebellum transformation of traditional law had been necessary, said the court, because "we must have factories, machinery, dams, canals, and railroads. They are demanded by the manifold wants of mankind, and lay [sic] at the basis of all our civilization."[46]

The legal revolution in the antebellum state courts was obscured for contemporaries and for historians alike by the more politicized controversy over the federal courts. In the 1790s a uniformly Federalist band of new federal judges fanned out across the land to assert the supremacy of the new Constitution over state powers and the instrumentality of the law in the expansion of the market. In the first of the widely publicized grand-jury charges through which the Federalist judiciary sought to instruct an unsound public mind, Chief Justice John Jay insisted that "our individual prosperity depends on our National prosperity," and "our National prosperity depends on a well-organized vigorous government, ruling by wise and equal laws, faithfully executed."[47]

By the time Federalist hegemony was broken in 1800, the federal courts had asserted their right to nullify legislation, both state and federal, that they deemed in conflict with the Constitution. And in doing so they began to apply the constitutional clause that became American capitalism's holiest writ: "No state . . . shall coin money; emit bills of credit; make any thing but gold and silver coin a tender in payment of debts; [or] pass any . . . law impairing the obligation of contracts." Federal judges overturned state debtor relief laws as impairing the obligation of contracts and compelled states to honor the federal government's treaty obligations to British creditors and claimants of confiscated Tory property. By 1802 the lower federal courts, in over twenty cases, had invalidated statutes of eleven of the fifteen states.[48]

Moreover federal judges, like state judges, lost little time in asserting broad powers under the common law. Struggling to enforce Federalist neutrality policy against Francophile Republicans, federal courts claimed the right to punish, under the common law or even under "international law," acts that neither Congress nor state legislatures had declared criminal. In 1799 Chief Justice Oliver Ellsworth instructed a grand jury to indict on these broad authorities not only acts violating American neutrality but also acts "opposing the existence of the National government or the efficient exercise of its legitimate powers." Such judges did not wait for the Sedition Act to indict Republican editors on common-law charges of sedition. Nor is it surprising that they enthusiastically enforced the act once passed, upheld its constitutionality, and defended it in their increasingly partisan grand-jury harangues, feeding the political reaction that brought the Republicans to power.[49]

Saddled with a militant judiciary, bloated in the last hours of Federalist rule with a whole set of new lifetime "midnight" judges, militant Republicans vowed to make it "bow before the strong arm of Legislative authority." The issue, as they saw it, was "whether men appointed for life or the immediate representatives of the people ... are to give laws to the community." Jefferson personally directed an attempt to rein in the judiciary by impeaching the most partisan judges.[50]

The impeachment drive stalled—entrepreneurial Republicans were too attached to judicial independence to remove judges from office—but it imparted caution to the leading midnight judge, the shrewd and engaging Virginia lawyer, Chief Justice John Marshall. Some Federalists had worried about Marshall's "strong attachment to popularity" and "disposition to feel the public pulse," for he was a politician to the toes of his often muddy boots. A product of the tobacco kingdom's commercial enclave centering in Richmond, he was also a dedicated nationalist, but with none of the condescending elitism that handicapped so many of his fellow Federalists.[51]

Marshall lost no time in giving notice of both his political commitments and his political skill. In *Marbury v. Madison* (1803) he managed to assert ringingly the judicial right to nullify acts of Congress on constitutional grounds, while cleverly evading any challenge by declaring that the Supreme Court's jurisdiction in this case had been unconstitutionally granted. Throughout the Republican assault on the judiciary he was notably cautious in dealing with cases that might excite Republican or popular sensibilities. He did firmly resist Republican efforts to convict Aaron Burr of treason on circumstantial evidence, but the early Marshall Court carefully avoided challenging the laws or judicial decisions of the states, except in one case where Pennsylvania forced the issue so egregiously as to shock many Republicans. The Chief Justice abandoned his formerly strong claim to a federal common-law jurisdiction; and as late as 1810 the Court refused an opportunity to rule on the constitutionality of the national Bank and the right of a state to tax it.

While Marshall patiently awaited a political climate in which the major constitutional issues could be decided correctly, his judicial restraint and what Jefferson called his "lax, lounging manners" converted the Supreme Court into a tight-knit band of brothers who lived together "with perfect harmony" in a Washington boarding house while in session and worked out their differences "in gay and frank conversation," often enabling Marshall to speak for a unanimous Court. A "born diplomatist" and "natural politician," the Chief Justice was described as

> a delightful companion ... fluent and facile in conversation ... full of sly, waggish humor, genial and convivial ... his patience almost inexhaustible, and his judgment cool, wary, and calculating.

When vacancies brought Republican appointees, they too succumbed to his "seductive personal magnetism" and judicial consensus.[52]

Doubtless encouraged to greater boldness by the temporary Federalist resurgence following the Embargo, the Marshall Court commenced in the 1810 case *Fletcher v. Peck* the militant assertion of contractual rights and national authority that was henceforth its hallmark. Georgia could not reclaim millions of acres of its rich Yazoo country, the Chief Justice declared for the Court, even though they had been fraudulently granted by a notoriously bribed legislature. Defining the corrupt grant as a binding contract, he insisted that the legislature's subsequent revocation of the grant violated the constitutional ban on state laws "impairing the obligation of contracts," including by Marshall's reading even fraudulent contracts entered into by the state itself. This gratuitous assault on state sovereignty was the first decision by the Supreme Court, as distinguished from lower federal courts, nullifying a state law on constitutional grounds.[53]

Marshall's decision followed the argument of one of the attorneys for the Yazoo purchasers (mainly Yankee entrepreneurial Republicans), the rising young legal scholar Joseph Story, just entering his thirties. After graduating from Harvard, Story learned his law from a Massachusetts attorney who thought the common law Americans' "noblest inheritance." Entering politics as a Republican protégé of Salem's princely merchant family the Crowninshields, he annoyed many Massachusetts Republicans by his efforts to strengthen the state judiciary through higher salaries for judges and the introduction of equity jurisdiction. "Though he is a man whom the Democrats support," commented High Federalist George Cabot in recommending Story to friends at Washington, "I have seldom if ever met with one of sounder mind on the principal points of national policy."[54]

Six months after the Yazoo decision the death of the senior Federalist justice opened the way for a Republican majority on the Supreme Court. The vacancy had to be filled from New England, and ex-President Jefferson barraged President Madison with warnings that only the firmest kind of Republican could resist Marshall's "twistifications of the law" as evidenced in "the late Yazoo case." Jefferson explicitly ruled out young Story, whom he had already denounced as a "pseudo-republican" for his prominent role in getting the Embargo repealed, and whom he now characterized as "unquestionably a tory." By "tory" the ex-President meant a devotee of Blackstone's common law as twisted to commercial ends by England's Lord Chief Justice Mansfield. The "honied Mansfieldism of Blackstone" had caused the legal profession, "the nursery of our Congress," to "slide into toryism," Jefferson complained, "and nearly all the young brood of lawyers now are of that hue."[55]

Thus warned, Madison offered the vacant judgeship to an irreproachable Republican so old and blind that he declined as expected, and then to another so abrasively radical that he was rejected by the Senate as expected. With these Jeffersonian gestures behind him, Madison moved in a more congenial direction by nominating ex-President Adams's son John Quincy Adams, who had broken with the Federalists on patriotic grounds over the Embargo. But Adams too declined, confessing to his father "some very heretical opinions upon the merits of the *common law,* so idolized by all English lawyers and by all who parrot their words in America." Only after these three rebuffs did Madison finally nominate, and the Senate confirm, Joseph Story.[56]

Marshall astutely welcomed the young attorney to the Court and relied heavily on his vast legal erudition. "We are all united as one," Story soon reported with satisfaction. ". . . We moot every question as we proceed, and by familiar conferences at our lodgings often come to a very quick, and I trust, a very accurate opinion." The Chief Justice confessed at one of these conferences that he had not "looked much into the books" but felt sure "our brother Story here" could "give us the cases from the twelve tables down to the latest reports." In fact the justices followed Story's views in an unusually complex case that was the first decided after his appointment. During his early years on the bench he found the docket "stuffed with all sorts of complicated questions" of admiralty and international law growing out of the War of 1812, and here Story's expertise was so indispensable that "as usual," he commented wryly, "the old maxim was verified—*Juniores ad labores.*"[57]

Story could not persuade Marshall to take up again the cause of federal common-law jurisdiction. But in other respects the Chief Justice gradually fell so much under the influence of the younger justice's legal philosophy as well as legal knowledge that Story bears equal responsibility for Marshall's most celebrated decisions on behalf of vested rights and national power. Rarely has scholarly prowess been deployed more consequentially.

Story epitomized the conversion of enterprise-minded Republicans in the market's northeastern core to the Federalist vision of an entrepreneurial destiny to be advanced by a powerful national state. "Let us extend the national authority over the whole extent of power given by the Constitution," he wrote to a friend shortly after news of peace reached the United States. "Let us have great military and naval schools; an adequate regular army; the broad foundations laid of a permanent navy; a National bank; a National system of bankruptcy; a great navigation act; a general survey of our ports, and appointments of port wardens and pilots; Judicial courts which shall embrace the whole constitutional powers; National notaries; public and National justices of the peace, for the commercial and national concerns of the United States."[58]

The Republican Story's infatuation with the very word *national*—he usually capitalized it—heralded a new political economy. His bipartisan judiciary, appropriating much of society's rule-making power through common law and judicial review, had already turned the republic decisively toward his entrepreneurial nationalism. The Marshall Court's major decisions were soon to come, and the next Congress would take up the legislative developmentalism pioneered by the most commercial states. By 1815 the market had sufficiently penetrated the American hinterland to produce scores of young Republican lawyer/politicians who shared Story's vision.

The peace news interrupted a historic confluence between the entrepreneurial Republicanism of the northeastern market core and a new "National" Republicanism of the cash-crop frontiers. Their joint project was a new national Bank. During the final desperate months of war, with treasury bare and public buildings in ashes, the government had submitted to an ultimatum from a "deliberate concert among the Capitalists." Only by agreeing to get a new Bank chartered did the Madison administration obtain the loans to avert collapse. Miraculous peace arrived just in time to relieve unhappy Republican congressman from duress to approve a charter.

The first Bank of the United States epitomized the elitist developmentalism that Republicans challenged in driving the Federalists from power, and a Republican Congress refused to renew its twenty-year charter in 1811. Yet more than duress now aligned many Republicans behind the proposed new Bank. Its promoters were the country's two wealthiest capitalists, John Jacob Astor of New York and Stephen Girard of Philadelphia, both Republicans. Running political interference for them were two of the party's senior leaders, Alexander J. Dallas and Albert Gallatin; and Dallas had succeeded Gallatin as Secretary of the Treasury to shepherd the project through Congress. The enterprise-minded Republicanism of men like these, developing mainly around the commercial centers, had so far been resisted by a Congress responsive to the rural majority.

They found new support from the southern and western interior, however, when Secretary Dallas recruited John C. Calhoun to push the Bank project through this Congress. Representing the heart of the cotton boom, Calhoun was articulating for younger Republicans from recently commercialized agricultural areas a new sense of the promise and the requirements of an emerging national market. Insisting on safeguards against undue profits for the Astor/Girard interests, Calhoun and his allies advocated a Bank like the Federalist original, which had provided, stably and efficiently, the national system of money and credit required to realize the market's promise.

As Dallas and his Pennsylvania confederate Gallatin led the older entrepreneurial Republicanism of the northeastern ports, so the Carolinian Calhoun and his Kentucky confederate Henry Clay led the newer National Republicanism of the commercializing interior. Through the intersecting careers of these four, remolded Republicanism bent the national state to the ends of expansive capital.[59]

Alexander J. Dallas demonstrated to a rising generation of lawyer/politicians the rewards of serving enterprise through Republican politics. Genteelly reared and educated in England but deprived of his anticipated inheritance, he migrated to Philadelphia after the Revolution to recoup his fortunes by practicing law. Resenting "the pride of Wealth and the Arrogance of Power" that barred outsiders like himself from the local Federalist establishment, he carried his considerable talents "to the best market"[60] and—with energy and ambition to match—became the chief organizer of the Republican opposition in Pennsylvania.

But Dallas was no leveler. Through untiring application to law and politics, he sought to win his way back to the wealth and status he thought he deserved by birth. While organizing Republicans he also led the movement to strengthen judicial influence by publishing judges' decisions. Only a single volume of Connecticut cases preceded Dallas's volumes reporting Pennsylvania decisions, and he was the first reporter of the federal Supreme Court's opinions. Commercial boom and international war swelled his fees from Philadelphia's leading merchants and financiers to a staggering twenty thousand dollars by 1814. Embracing their entrepreneurial/developmental élan, he speculated heavily in lands; helped organize the corporation that built the country's first extensive turnpike, connecting Philadelphia with Lancaster; and served as manager or director for several other turnpike and canal companies.

With this perspective, Dallas labored to keep gentlemen of sound principles in control of a Republican party whose voting strength was supplied by farmers and workers of doubtful reliability. Unhesitatingly he mobilized Pennsylvania troops to crush the Republican interior's rebellion against Hamilton's whiskey tax. In the process he befriended and rescued from association with the whiskey rebels another well-bred European émigré, the Genevan Albert Gallatin.[61]

Two years younger than Dallas, the orphaned Gallatin had brought to western Pennsylvania a Rousseauvian enthusiasm for the virtuous and democratic farmer of the American interior and a highly educated intelligence that recommended him as a representative for the farmer in the Pennsylvania legislature. He also brought a substantial patrimony, which he invested in thousands of western acres and a series of enterprises—a town promotion, a glassworks, a gun factory—employing nearly a hundred workers.

In fast friendship Dallas and Gallatin labored both to defeat Federalism and to align Republicanism with booming enterprise. Gallatin persuaded the lawmakers to retire Pennsylvania's paper money and to out-Hamilton Hamilton by paying the state's creditors higher interest than they received under Hamilton's federal assumption of state debts. Further echoing Hamilton, he led the legislature in chartering a Republican-controlled Bank of Pennsylvania, having a relationship with the state government similar to that of Hamilton's national Bank with the federal government. And he went beyond Hamilton's developmental vision as an author of Pennsylvania's policy of chartering and subsidizing corporations to build turnpikes and canals.

Gallatin soon moved into federal politics, giving what assistance he could from his position in Congress and then as Secretary of the Treasury in the Jefferson and Madison administrations, while Dallas took primary responsibility for party management in Pennsylvania. Only by insisting in 1799 that Jefferson's election and the national destiny of Republicanism depended on party unity in Pennsylvania did he force an unhappy party to accept as its gubernatorial nominee the conservative chief justice of the state supreme court, Thomas McKean.

Once McKean and Jefferson were elected, the intraparty tensions could no longer be restrained. Anxious for rapprochement with Federalist respectability, Dallas, Gallatin, and Governor McKean resisted demands by leaders of Philadelphia's working-class wards for a wholesale removal of Federalist officeholders. Soon labeled a "trimmer," Dallas was so zealous for judicial independence that he opposed Jefferson's efforts to abolish the new Federalist circuit courts and their midnight judges.[62]

The judiciary was becoming the major issue in American politics. The political ascendancy of lawyers allied with business elites aroused deep suspicions among farming and working people. Although laypeople could perceive only dimly the silent revolution going on in the courts, enough was visible to create widespread alarm. While Jefferson's drive to chasten the federal judiciary through impeachment stalled in Washington, bitter political struggles erupted over courts in the states. With Republicans coming to dominate most states, these struggles typically pitted business-oriented Republicans against representatives of Republican farming and working-class constituencies. In state after state the latter sought to stem the juridical revolution through such measures as elective judges, exclusion of the common law, and requiring most cases to be adjudicated by lay magistrates and referees without the intervention of lawyers.

In Pennsylvania only the most determined resistance by Dallas and Governor McKean thwarted the large legislative majorities that rallied behind this drive for judicial reform. Republican legislators forced the governor into repeated vetoes "to prevent their running riot." When the lower house impeached the Federalist majority of the state supreme court for imprisoning a litigant on a shaky extension of the common law of contempt, Dallas undertook the judges' defense before the senate. For six days he lauded the common law as the "birth-right and inheritance" of Pennsylvanians, barely preventing the two-thirds majority that would have removed the judges from office. Similarly his testimony at the congressional impeachment trial of federal Supreme Court Justice Samuel Chase helped blunt Jefferson's drive against the federal judiciary. ·

Outraged Republicans denied Governor McKean renomination in 1805, nominating instead the rural champion of judicial reform Simon Snyder, a former tanner's apprentice. Dallas then bolted the party to get McKean barely reelected through coalition with Federalists. But in 1808 the "clodhopper" Synder—

McKean had derided the judicial reformers as ignorant "clodhoppers"—could not be prevented from winning the governorship, and Dallas lost control of Pennsylvania politics to Snyder's Country Democrats.[63]

Meanwhile Dallas's ally Treasury Secretary Gallatin had been pressing, to the limits of President Jefferson's tolerance, a Hamiltonian use of government to promote economic development. In 1802 he convinced Congress to allocate land revenues from the new state of Ohio for a National Road connecting it with the Potomac via southwestern Pennsylvania, where his own investments were concentrated.

By 1805 mounting federal revenues helped Gallatin persuade Jefferson to declare that anticipated surpluses might be applied to "rivers, canals, roads, arts, manufactures, education, and other great objects"—but only, the President cagily insisted, after a politically impossible constitutional amendment. Nevertheless Gallatin recommended to Congress in 1808 a $20-million program for constructing a series of "great canals" affording protected inland navigation along the coast from Massachusetts to North Carolina; a "great turnpike road from Maine to Georgia"; improved navigation and parallel canals along four of the great rivers flowing into the Atlantic, with "firstrate turnpike roads" crossing the mountains from each of these rivers to the Mississippi valley; improved roads to Detroit, St. Louis, and New Orleans; and a series of smaller projects such as canals around the falls of the Ohio and the Niagara. The Embargo and approaching war dashed any immediate prospect for a national transportation system but did not deter the persistent Secretary from proposing in 1810 a $20-million federal loan fund to encourage manufacturing.[64]

Gallatin's sharpest difference with his President and party was over the national Bank. He had valued Hamilton's Bank from its beginning because it increased "the rapidity of the circulation of money" and facilitated the Treasury's operations; and upon assuming responsibility for federal finance, he lost no time in proposing "the most liberal spirit of accommodation" between Bank and Treasury. Consequently he stubbornly resisted Jefferson's plan to utilize instead a network of Republican-controlled state banks. "Now, while we are strong," the President remonstrated with his Treasury Secretary, "it is the greatest duty we owe to the safety of our Constitution to bring this powerful enemy to a perfect subordination." But Gallatin doggedly held his ground, even gaining Jefferson's assent to new branches of the Bank at Washington and New Orleans to facilitate the government's financial operations.

Thus it is not surprising that Gallatin wanted the Bank's twenty-year charter extended before its expiration in 1811. Waiting until Jefferson was leaving office, and with the tacit support of incoming President Madison, he organized a campaign to persuade Congress to recharter the Bank at a trebled capital of $30 million. But the recharter bill was stalled, not just by orthodox Jeffersonians and antidevelopmentalists but also by the politically influential stockholders, borrowers, and would-be borrowers who surrounded the growing host of Republican-chartered state banks.[65] The multiplying venturers spawned by the commercial boom wanted the profits from the large federal deposits that would be transferred to the state banks upon the national Bank's demise; they wanted the expanded loans these deposits would make possible; even more they wanted to escape the national Bank's power to restrain the state banks from overlending; and in all these ways they hoped to make the economy and their personal fortunes "go ahead."

The recharter bill was finally defeated in 1811 by the casting vote of Vice President George Clinton in an evenly divided Senate. The senile Clinton's remarks on this occasion were written for him by a representative of one of the new centers of market energy, brash young Senator Henry Clay, late director of the Bank of Kentucky. The darling of the Bluegrass gentry, Clay rejoiced with his leading constituents that state banks could now lend more freely.[66]

Clay represented the intensely enterprising spirit generated as the commercial boom extended cash-crop agriculture into subsistence-farming areas. As a beginning lawyer in Lexington, the West's largest town and hub of the hemp boom, this Virginia-born protégé of Jefferson's mentor George Wythe had audaciously challenged the local establishment. Siding with the subsistence-farming Green River section in a campaign for a constitutional convention to democratize the Bluegrass-dominated Kentucky government, he argued eloquently that the reforms should include the gradual abolition of slavery. Humiliating defeat as a candidate for convention delegate cured him permanently of such quixotism.

Clay's political sins were quickly forgiven because the gentry needed his remarkable gifts. An aggressive homegrown lawyer, Felix Grundy, was rallying the Green River country against the chief institutional props of the expanding market in Kentucky, the court system and Lexington's new bank. Clay was splendidly equipped to combat Grundy in the rough-and-tumble of Kentucky's oral political culture, for his boyhood hero and model was Patrick Henry. To colloquial fluency and political and legal shrewdness this "Cock of Kentucky" added an irresistible personal magnetism—a vibrant sense of fun, a warmth of male camaraderie, a gallant weakness for the long chance (he was an inveterate gambler and a reputed womanizer)—that made him an obvious comer in the masculine world of Kentucky politics.

Marriage into a leading family eased Clay into the Bluegrass establishment, and these hemp and tobacco planters, land speculators, merchants, distillers, and lawyers chose him to defend their interests against Grundy's assaults in the legislature. By the time he confronted the Green River democracy at the state capital, he was a stockholder in, and attorney for, the Kentucky Insurance Company, which—utilizing an obscure provision in its charter—had opened at Lexington the first bank west of the Appalachians.

The struggle between the subsistence world and the market world in Kentucky involved land titles and therefore the courts. A haphazard system of granting and surveying lands had created shaky titles and a paradise of litigation for ambitious young lawyers like Clay. Through such lawyers the Bluegrass gentry manipulated a highly centralized court system in support of their extensive land speculations. When the courts reinstated the speculators' previously invalidated claims to large tracts in the Green River country and elsewhere, Grundy rode the crest of a massive reaction by farmers whose titles were threatened.

Even Clay could not stem the tide of popular anger that carried Grundy's court reform bill through the legislature and over the governor's veto. Courts were now to be held in every county, and judges were to travel circuits, sitting in each county with two local laymen "not learned in the law" and submitting cases to local juries that would favor local farmers over nonresident speculators and creditors. In vain did Clay and his allies warn that this change would undermine credit and economic growth. "The man who lends,—the man who forms a contract," wailed one legislator, "has no confidence in the mode . . . provided for him to recover his property." When the reformers sought in addition to drive the common law from Kentucky courts, only Clay's most impassioned eloquence, evoking tears from his audience, forced an apparent compromise. British legal decisions rendered since American independence were not to be cited in Kentucky courts, but this left the great body of the common law in force.[67]

With the tide of resentment against the Bluegrass gentry still running strong, Grundy next proposed to repeal the Kentucky Insurance Company's banking privileges. Pointing to the bank's 18 percent dividends, he argued that its loans obviously far exceeded its real capital. Banks "tend to move the ballance of wealth out of the hands of the people," he charged; and the Lexington bank was raising up a "monied aristocracy" that controlled the whole circulating medium of the state. Clay answered—anticipating a momentous Supreme Court decision—that the corporation's charter was a contract, which the state could not subsequently modify. Mainly he argued that the old economy of barter and primitive exchange would no longer do, that Kentucky was shipping its produce to the four corners of the globe, and that banking was essential to continued growth. More consistently and more unambiguously than any other politician during his long and illustrious career, Clay would preach and practice a politics of market expansion.

This doctrine met strong resistance in the farmer-oriented Kentucky legislature. Only by a single vote, and only by agreeing that the bank's loans could not exceed its assets, was repeal averted. But Grundy was back at the next session with an implacable antibank majority that passed the repeal bill by wide margins in both houses. When the governor vetoed the measure, the house repassed it, and the senate was prevented from doing so only by a brilliant Clay maneuver. If the senate repassed the bank repeal bill, he suddenly threatened, he had the votes to enforce immediate payment from the many farmers in the Green River country who had bought their lands from the state on credit. To save their constituents' farms, enough Green River senators deserted Grundy, and the bank survived.

From these triumphs Clay moved on to represent the Bluegrass in Congress and to help slay Hamilton's national Bank in the name of sweet credit. His hopes for freer state banking were abundantly fulfilled. Within a few years the number of state-chartered banks swelled from 88 to 208, bank note circulation from $28 million to $68 million, and total loans including those represented by deposit credits even more. This staggering inflation intensified when Clay and similar young congressmen drove the country into a second war with Great Britain.[68]

Clay shared leadership of the War Hawks with John C. Calhoun. The Scotch-Irish Calhoun clan settled originally in Pennsylvania, moved on to western Virginia, and finally retreated from Indian hostility to the wilderness of upcountry South Carolina. There Patrick Calhoun, combining farming with surveying and taking a share of the surveyed land for his fees, accumulated property and influence. Amost continuously from 1769 until his death in 1796 he represented westernmost South Carolina in the colonial assemblies, Revolutionary congresses, and state legislatures. By 1790, when his youngest son John turned eight, this backwoods grandee owned a thousand acres, and his thirty-one slaves placed him among the handful of substantial slaveholders in the upcountry.

Instead of dedicating a promising son to the ministry, patriarchal families emerging from the subsistence culture to wealth and prominence often groomed him to advance their interests and honor through law and politics. To this end Patrick Calhoun and, after his death, his prospering brothers and older sons saw that young John was given every advantage. To equip him for a political arena in which a cotton-booming Republican upcountry was reaching accommodation with a Federalist lowcountry, he was sent all the way to Federalist Yale and trained under the eye of the redoubtable Timothy Dwight. Here he modeled himself on his cousin, a nominally Republican senator from South Carolina who "gained himself much honour in N. England," as young John noted proudly, by his "sperited" defense of the Federalist midnight judges against Jeffersonian assault. Tutored then in the Charleston office of South Carolina's leading attorney, the Federalist Henry W. De Saussure, he completed his mastery of the new, enterprise-oriented law in the Litchfield law school of the Federalist Tapping Reeve.

By the time this prepossessing young man came home to the South Carolina upcountry to open his own law office in 1808, he had an unusually cosmopolitan exposure to the best in style and intellect that his country could offer. Promptly he was sent to fill Patrick Calhoun's old seat in the legislature. Credentials of family, education, and prospects, not to mention conspicuous talents and ambition, qualified him to marry an heiress of the lordly lowcountry planter class. In doing so, he rejected the marriage settlement usually required by planting families, insisting that his bride's entire fortune in plantations and slaves be placed wholly at his disposal. Calhoun refused to leave the property under the control of his bride's widowed mother partly because religious scruples were preventing her from buying additional slaves to make the lands fully profitable.[69]

Profit was becoming an overriding commitment for cotton planters. As the industrial revolution swirled out from its vortex of whirring spindles and clattering looms in faroff Lancashire to transform the modern world, no spot on earth was more squarely in its path than upcountry South Carolina and Georgia, main suppliers of raw cotton for British mills. During the commercial boom, with cotton bringing over twenty cents a pound and reaching forty-four, good land trebled in value as planters doubled their profits every year.

Once again, like Chesapeake tobacco planters in the late seventeenth century and the Carolina lowcountry's rice and indigo planters in the eighteenth, white slave-drivers extracted baronial fortunes from black sweat. In 1804 upcountry representatives persuaded the South Carolina legislature to reopen the African slave trade; and before it was legally ended under a provision of the federal Constitution in 1808, nearly forty thousand African men, women, and children were sold from Charleston auction blocks. Many were driven in gangs to new upcountry plantations financed by lowcountry capital. White men mortgaged homes and lands to buy black men; and the more ambitious upcountry farmers in favored locations labored and scrimped to purchase a slave or two to grow more cotton to buy more slaves and land.

In this heady atmosphere of opportunity, Calhoun formed his conception of republican society. Ability was more likely to emerge from the middle and lower ranks, he would tell the Fourteenth Congress. "Rich men, being already at the top of the ladder, have no further motive to climb," he would explain, as contrasted with "that class of the community who find it necessary to strive for elevation." To encourage such rising venturers, he would insert in the charter of the new national Bank elaborate provisions ensuring, as he boasted, "the opportunity to every capitalist, however inconsiderable, to share in the capital of the Bank."[70] Calhoun's rhetoric expressed the enterprising ethos of the new class of cotton planters who, within two generations, would spread across the wilderness Southwest and lead the South out of the republic. Like venturers everywhere, they conceived the ideal republic as a social marketplace offering "opportunity" to "every capitalist, however inconsiderable," as "a motive to climb."

Although most free South Carolinians continued to own few or no slaves and grow little cotton for market, the farming majority in this agricultural society was still content to follow planter leadership. When the new class of Republican cotton planters began to dominate the upcountry, the Federalist lowcountry gentry in 1808 gracefully yielded a substantial share of state power to their upcountry brethren. Unanimously the legislature approved a state constitutional amendment basing representation half on population, in which the upcountry preponderated, and half on property taxes, in which the lowcountry preponderated because of its denser concentration of taxable slave property. As a freshman legislator at the next session, Calhoun helped consolidate this political unification. With planter control guaranteed by high property qualifications for election to the all-powerful legislature, the ruling class conciliated democratic sentiment by extending the suffrage to all free white males.

Carolina planters closed ranks just in time to confront the Embargo's devastation. Leading all states in per-capita value of exports, South Carolina was hardest hit. With American cotton exports falling in a single year from 66 million pounds to 12 million, planter capital was tied up in land and slaves, partly still to be paid for, and could not be shifted, like New England's mercantile capital, into manufacturing or other enterprises.

Adversity tested South Carolina Republicanism severely. While the tobacco economy had been depressed since the Revolution, no American elite had enjoyed such uninterrupted opulence as South Carolina planters. Rice and indigo generated steadily mounting profits in the Federalist lowcounty from the mid-eighteenth century, with sea-island cotton becoming profitable just in time to cushion the dislocations that accompanied the Revolution; and short-staple cotton then extended the protracted boom across the Republican upcountry.

Moreover this planter class was unusually munificent, cohesive, cosmopolitan, and commercial. More great fortunes had piled up in the lowcountry parishes than anywhere else in the country, perhaps the world. The wealthiest educated their sons in England or at Yale and summered in such budding elite resorts as Newport, where Calhoun first met his wife-to-be. Lowcountry families who did not travel farther congregated during the malarial months in their great townhouses along Charleston's breezy Battery, where they maintained intimate social and kinship ties with each other and with wealthy merchants who marketed their crops and often doubled as planters themselves.

In political as in personal style South Carolina planters betrayed a characteristic imperiousness, born of absolute mastery over other people, habituation to luxury, and unchallenged hegemony. Although Republican planters had come to dominate the state's politics, they agreed with the lowcountry's Federalist gentry that a flourishing commerce was essential to South Carolina's agricultural prosperity. When, therefore, the Embargo destroyed their profits by destroying commerce, they reacted with mounting impatience. If Republican administrations could answer British restrictions on American commerce only with more onerous American restrictions, they fumed, war was preferable. In 1810 they elected three new congressmen pledged to war, John C. Calhoun, William Lowndes, and Langdon Cheves.

In Washington the South Carolinians allied with Clay and other young congressmen to seize control of the House of Representatives by electing Clay Speaker.

Clay put the principal committees in the hands of these War Hawks—none coming within a dozen years of the average age of Congress—and eventually they forced war on a President Madison who had run out of alternatives.[71]

Treasury Secretary Gallatin faced a nightmarish struggle in financing the War of 1812. A British blockade prostrated the market sector and dried up imports, the main source of federal revenues, while military expenditures ballooned and the country's scarce specie drained into New England banks to pay for Yankees' mounting manufactures and smuggled European imports. Gallatin could have borrowed up to $18 million from the national Bank if he had gotten it rechartered, whereas the state banks had no aid to offer, in New England because they opposed the war and elsewhere because they were about to suspend specie payments. Consequently he had to compound inflation by issuing Treasury notes and hawking federal bonds around the country at enormous discounts. Even then he realized so little that he warned President Madison military operations might have to be curtailed.

In this crisis the Secretary of the Treasury repaired to Dallas's Philadelphia drawing room to negotiate national survival with the capitalists Astor and Girard and an associate representing European capital. Astor, an old friend through Gallatin's New York in-laws, subsequently offered the Secretary a lucrative partnership, set his sons up in business, and found him a sinecure in old age as president of a New York bank. Dallas served Girard as lawyer and lobbyist on many occasions, and as federal attorney was once overruled by superiors for undue favoritism toward him.

Now these four old associates—all of them, curiously, foreign-born—struck a bargain that preserved the American republic. In exchange for federal bonds promising a triple profit, the capitalists supplied enough millions to continue the war a little longer. Getting their bonds at a big discount while collecting regular interest, they insisted in addition on promise of a national Bank. By Hamiltonian precedent, their depreciated federal bonds could be exchanged at par value for Bank stock, which would quickly appreciate because of the handsome profits for which banks were notorious.

Yet Astor and Girard were taking large risks, and there was more to the Bank project than greed. Deeply interested in banking, both had fallen out with the old Bank and looked forward to controlling the country's currency and credit through a new Bank. They doubtless saw themselves, like later international bankers, as exercising a public responsibility by intervening to rescue and discipline the economy through a national Bank. As holders of the largest capitals, they represented the market's rationalizing thrust, and they aimed to impose monetary and credit restraints on the newer and smaller capitalists whose reckless greed endangered sustained growth.

The Bank project faltered after Gallatin was sent to Ghent for the all-important peace negotiations. When Pennsylvania's Country Democratic senators blocked President Madison's effort to replace him at the Treasury with their old foe Dallas, the capitalists turned off the financial spigot, and soon the government was again out of money. Only the burning of Washington and a Dallas-conveyed ultimatum from "a deliberate concert among the Capitalists" melted the Pennsylvania opposition. "Tell Doctor Madison," Senator Abner Laycock is reported to have said to the President's private secretary, "that we are now willing to submit to his Philadelphia lawyer for the head of the treasury. The public patient is so very sick that we must swallow anything the doctor prescribes however nauseous the bolus."[72] When peace allowed this last war Congress to adjourn without swallowing the bolus (nauseous pill) of national Bank—for that is what Dallas's appointment meant—a political epoch closed.

In the Fourteenth Congress, assembling in December, Calhoun and his new-style Republicans would not only charter a Bank but push national developmentalism far beyond anything envisioned by the parochial Federalism of port elites. Embracing the visions of enterprising Americans everywhere—southern and western staple producers, New York canal boosters, Ohio valley shippers and distillers, rising northeastern manufacturers—these National Republicans sought to turn the republic irrevocably toward its capitalist destiny.

All that stood in their way was the anticommercial animus of a democratic countryside. Aroused a generation before against Federalism, it had empowered an ambiguous Republicanism. Now, as entrepreneurs and National Republicans rushed to embrace the promise of postwar boom, they might have pondered more carefully the fate of their Federalist predecessors.

Chapter 3

"Let Us Conquer Space"

THE Fourteenth Congress, convening amid prosperous peace in December 1815, was filled with enterprise-minded lawyers elected amid wartime despair with a mandate for vigorous measures. Its youthful leaders had first come to Washington from the boom's interior beachheads to take up arms for threatened honor and interrupted bonanza. In saving the republic from the military ineptitude of penny-pinching, old-fogy Republicanism, they embraced the Northeast's entrepreneurial vision. To realize it, they were now anxious to exercise with wartime vigor the peacetime power of an activist capitalist state. Never has a Congress turned the United States more sharply in a new direction.

This new breed was slow to abandon the protective coloration of Republicanism by avowing the National Republican label. Claiming the Republican heritage for opportunity rather than equality, they celebrated equal rights as liberating the enterprise of free men to create a rich and powerful United States. "It is the spirit of a free country which animates and gives energy to its labor," insisted their favorite orator. Freedom, Edward Everett would exult in dedicating the amazing new cotton mill city of Lowell, "puts the mass in action, gives it motive and intensity, sends it off in new directions, subdues at its command all the powers of nature, and enlists in its service an army of machines that do all but think and talk."[1]

The National Republican moment of opportunity to legislate in this spirit was produced by the conjunction of renewed boom and Federalist collapse. Unlimited opportunities for money-making generated unusual political support for a developmentalism no longer tainted by Federalist hauteur. As pent-up demand galvanized commodity production, as masters of slaves and capital followed a flood of pioneer farming folk across the Appalachians into the heart of the continent, Americans first realized that they were indeed undergoing a market revolution. In place of staple-exporting dependence on Europe, the enterprising began to envision limitless growth through extension of the internal market across a continental domain.

Postwar boom dramatized sectional interdependence, as agricultural exports, cotton above all, flooded from South and West, to pay for a returning flood of European imports, and plantations bought more northeastern manufactures. The very landscape changed as peace released the commercial boom's pent-up capital and enterprise. "Everywhere," exulted Baltimore editor Hezekiah Niles,

> the sound of the axe is heard opening the forest to the sun, and claiming for agriculture the range of the buffalo. Our cities grow and towns rise up as by magic. . . . The busy hum of ten thousand wheels fills our seaports, and the sound of the spindle and the loom succeeds the yell of the savage or the screech of the night owl in the late wilderness of the interior.[2]

Under these circumstances a Republican President could summon a Republican Congress to promote economic growth in all the ways Federalism pioneered. The country's "flourishing condition," said President Madison in his state of the union message to the new Congress, was generating enough revenue to finance all kinds of "undertakings conducive to the wealth and individual comfort of our citizens"—a national university at Washington, protective tariffs to encourage manufacturing, a permanently enlarged army and navy, additional military academies, and "the roads and canals which can best be executed under the national authority." Any "defect of constitutionality" with regard to roads and canals, he added, could be supplied by a constitutional amendment. The most urgent task, the President insisted, was to create a stable infrastructure of money and credit by chartering a new national Bank.[3]

Again as in War Hawk days Clay, Calhoun, and company seized the House of Representatives by electing Clay Speaker, and again Clay gave them parliamentary control and friendly committees. Calhoun headed the committee responsible for a national Bank, and his bosom friend and fellow Carolinian William Lowndes—an aristocratic and amiable lowcountry planter who was the most widely respected of the National Republican leaders—headed Ways and Means, the committee responsible for revenue and tariff policies.

President Madison urged lawmakers to give their first attention to restoring a "uniform national currency." With the state banks still refusing to pay specie on their notes, each bank's notes were depreciated at different rates in different places, and the Treasury was hard put to move its funds from places of collection to places of payment. A national Bank was the proper remedy, Madison said without constitutional quibble, privately reassuring himself that any constitutional objection had been "precluded" as a result of "repeated recognitions" by the legislative, executive, and judicial branches and by "a concurrence of the general will of the nation."

Accompanying the President's message was a report from Secretary Dallas arguing that the federal government had the exclusive constitutional power and responsibility to provide a national currency and that a national Bank was "the best, and, perhaps, the only adequate resource to relieve the country and the Government from the present embarrassments." Calhoun had secured Dallas's agreement to the kind of Bank he insisted on at the previous session, and Dallas recommended to Congress a replica of the Hamiltonian Bank, except that the capital was more than trebled to $35 million (Dallas originally proposed $50 million).[4]

Little was said in debate about constitutionality, which had dominated the discussions in 1811. Chastened by the disastrous experiment in unrestrained state banking and glimpsing the possibilities of enterprise in a far-flung national market requiring a uniform and reliable national currency, spokesmen for business interests now accepted the necessity of controls over credit and the money supply. Speaker Clay left the chair to announce his conversion, but it was Calhoun who set the tone of the debate.

The fundamental problem, the Carolina nationalist argued, was that the states, by creating banks, had unsurped "the exclusive right of Congress to regulate the currency." Congress would be "deeply responsible," he insisted, if it allowed this constitutionally remediable evil to continue. For reasons not yet apparent, even Baltimore's Republican nabob General Samuel Smith seemed converted. This champion of the state banks against the old national Bank in 1811 now could find few "who in conversation did not appear favorable to the establishment of a Bank." The charter bill passed the House 80–71 and the Senate 22–12, with noes coming from an odd assortment of old-fashioned Republicans opposed on principle and surviving Federalists opposed on party grounds.[5]

Headquartered in Philadelphia, the second Bank of the United States could establish branch banks anywhere. The government subscribed for a fifth of the stock, appointed a fifth of the directors, and deposited its funds in the Bank; and the Bank's notes were receivable for sums due the government. The Bank's exclusive right to conduct banking on a nationwide basis and its privileged relationship with the Treasury—by far the largest transactor in the economy—were invaluable assets. In return the Bank transferred Treasury funds without charge and paid the government a bonus of $1.5 million.

As soon as the monetary problem was on its way to solution, Calhoun gave notice of the rest of the staggering National Republican agenda: a national transportation system, protective tariffs to encourage manufacturing, a bigger and more professional army, a navy capable of resisting British impositions on American commerce, and a massive system of coastal fortifications.

The South Carolinian functioned as visionary legislative architect for the market elites of his day as Alexander Hamilton had done for the narrower Federalist elite. Education and associations prepared him intellectually to mediate the older Federalist vision to the newer Republican elites. He would presently tell Hamilton's son that his father's policy was "the only true policy for this country";[6] and his purpose now was to reenact the Hamiltonian program on a broader scale. While Clay wielded a potent influence in the cloakrooms and Lowndes reassured the timid, the thirty-three-year-old Calhoun presented with lucidity and passion their series of great measures as articulated elements of a bold design for the republic. Insulated from normal constituency pressures by the elitist politics of South Carolina, he was freer than most of his colleagues to seek distinction as a disinterested and far-sighted champion of some great public cause. Cultivated, handsome, eloquent, highly intelligent, and supremely self-confident, this political Galahad was the decisively persuasive speaker on behalf of each of the principal National Republican measures.

When Calhoun forthrightly called on Congress to address first the problem of financing his expensive agenda, he challenged frontally a deep-rooted American tradition, sanctified by the Revolution, of resisting centralized power by resisting taxation. Nothing angered American farmers like taxes. Virginia congressman Daniel Sheffey tried to explain that most of his rural constituents "cannot bear taxes to any amount without great distress" because they had no way of obtaining the money to pay them. They "have the means of an independent subsistence," he said, "yet, owing to their distance from commerce, and the consequent difficulty of reducing the proceeds of their industry into money, which the tax gatherer wants and must have, their property must be put under the hammer and sold for what it will bring."[7]

Taxes had been a continual battleground for the competing American subcultures. In the face of a tax-hating rural majority, the federal government got its revenues mainly from import duties, which taxed consumers invisibly through higher prices for their purchases; while in many states banks were tolerated only because dividends on state-owned bank stock reduced and sometimes obviated the need for state taxes. In attempting to exact from the citizenry not only greater revenues but greater acquiescence in centralized authority, Alexander Hamilton designed his whiskey tax to make the weight of federal power palpable to interior farmers who otherwise fell outside its scope. To meet a threatened military emergency in 1798, Federalists imposed even more intrusive direct excise and property taxes requiring detailed reports from retailers and appraisals of every family's house and possessions. Repeatedly the subsistence culture answered taxes with violence. It was only thirty years since Daniel Shays and other Massachusetts farmers took up pitchforks and rifles against heavy taxes and debt collections. Then the whiskey tax spread rebellion through western Pennsylvania and as far as Kentucky. The direct taxes of 1798 provoked Pennsylvania German farmers into Fries's Rebellion and dogged Republicanism, locking Pennsylvania into place as the "keystone of the democratic arch" that insured the Republicans' national hegemony.[8]

Although the hated Federalist taxes were promptly repealed under Jefferson, thousands of farms were already foreclosed for unpaid arrears. So many were jeopardized in Kentucky that people were "all Cussing and Swearing about the Business"; Lexington was terrorized by a mob of Green River farmers threatening to burn the tax records and kill the collectors; "and it did appear Like we should have a little warr in the state."

Strict economy and low federal taxes were President Jefferson's most popular policies. Consequently when the War Hawks doubled import duties in 1812 to finance the military effort, they were warned that "no party, no administration that would impose a tax would stand three months"; and some of them blamed Jefferson's "empyrical phylosophy—his utopian politics" for "this disgusting, this frightful" resistance to taxation. In addition, to stave off national collapse in the darkest days of the war, they resurrected the direct taxes of 1798, including the hated whiskey tax, at higher rates more onerously enforced.[9]

Having induced the citizenry to accept heavy war taxes for national survival, the War Hawks were boldly attempting in the Fourteenth Congress to peg peacetime taxes near the wartime level. Secretary Dallas recommended partial continuance of the war taxes so as to produce an estimated annual revenue of $27 million, nearly three times the prewar level of federal expenditures. This was one of those rare moments in history, Calhoun told the House, when a nation's "fame, prosperity, and duration" were to be determined. Would they "go on in the old imbecile mode" and let the nation "travel downward," he implored, or would they "act on an enlarged policy" of promoting "the prosperity and greatness of the nation"?

Entranced like Hamilton with national wealth and power, Calhoun also betrayed a Hamiltonian impatience with the rural majority who contributed so little as taxpayers, producers, or consumers. Warning against "that fatal weakness of human nature" that would sacrifice the future to "present ease and pleasure," he called for "considerable sacrifices on the part of the people." He urged Americans—many of whom could obtain money for taxes only by working harder and becoming more enmeshed in the market—to choose "labor and virtue" over "ease and pleasure."

Calhoun thought the decision a momentous one because Providence had charged this Congress "not only with the happiness of this great and rising people, but in a considerable degree with that of the human race." The success of an American government "founded on the rights of man," he predicted, would inaugurate "a new era in human affairs." When Congress responded to Calhoun's appeal by continuing many of the war taxes, including a $3 million property tax, it was committing itself to a comprehensive program of national developmentalism.[10]

The most urgent item after the national Bank was protection for the host of newly arisen American manufacturers who were being driven to the wall by renewed peacetime competition from cheap British imports. Most operated small-scale shops, and many were Republicans of mechanic origin. Secretary Dallas recommended a tariff bill roughly doubling prewar rates. Imports competing with American products, particularly textiles and metals, were to be taxed at a rate high enough to make domestic producers competitive. Working closely with Francis Cabot Lowell, Dallas and Calhoun devised a "minimum principle" to disguise much higher rates for the cheap cottons that Lowell's big Waltham mill produced. Cheap cloth, imported at as low as six cents a yard, was to be taxed as worth at least twenty-five cents, enabling domestic producers to charge high prices for their goods without meeting foreign competition. Lowndes's Ways and Means Committee introduced a bill embodying the Secretary's principles and setting rates (somewhat lower than Dallas's) at 20 percent for most protected articles and 25 percent for textiles. There was much pulling and hauling as congressmen sought special treatment for interests in their districts, but the policy of protection was not challenged until the minimum principle came under discussion.

Only at this point, in defense of the provision upon which the country's most advanced industry relied, did Calhoun enter the debate. The long period of commercial restriction and war had convinced him that the country should no longer depend on others for its manufactures. Manufactures, commerce, and agriculture were all essential to prosperity, he argued. When European trade and manufactures were cut off, the economy stagnated, the government's revenue dried up, and the country could not defend itself. His long-range solution was to build a navy that would guarantee American trade with the rest of the world under all circumstances. But that would take years, and meanwhile the country should be making itself self-sufficient by fostering its manufactures and internal trade through tariff protection and roads and canals. Then, he said, "the farmer will find a ready market for his surplus produce; and, what is almost of equal consequence, a certain and cheap supply of all his wants."[11]

Calhoun's argument saved the minimum principle, and the Republican Fourteenth Congress went on to adopt the country's first tariff act avowedly designed to encourage manufacturing. In thus carrying out the recommendations of Alexander Hamilton's masterly Report on Manufactures of a quarter-century before, the Republicans were finally enacting the only major Hamiltonian policy that his Federalist colleagues, with their commitment to international trade, rejected.

The margin of victory came from the northeastern core of the market. The thirty-seven-vote majority in the delegations of New York, New Jersey, and Pennsylvania exceeded the thirty-one-vote margin by which the measure passed the House as a whole; while Massachusetts, still wavering between old commercial and new manufacturing interests, recorded seven yeas, four nays, and nine members unable to make up their minds. The bill's 24–10 margin in the delegations of South Carolina, Georgia, Kentucky, Tennessee, Ohio, and Vermont revealed that a new vision of wealth through national development was infecting hinterland elites.[12]

Meanwhile Calhoun and Lowndes were promoting a naval buildup. Jefferson had reversed the Federalist policy of naval strength, preferring to defend American harbors with cheap gunboats. But South Carolina Republicans became staunch navalists when British naval power destroyed their prosperity; and the war made the navy popular everywhere. American naval feats (often brilliant but strategically inconsequential victories by single ships) were the only bright spots in the long chronicle of military disaster preceding New Orleans; and the navy won new eclat at the end of the war by disciplining the piratical Barbary powers. "I am not ashamed, Mr. Chairman, to speak of national glory," declared a Virginia congressman in urging higher taxes to build up the navy. "I love national glory."[13]

By ample majorities Congress passed a naval construction act making an unprecedented advance commitment of $1 million annually for the next ten years. This financed nine seventy-four-gun ships of the line, the largest fighting ships of the time and the backbone of British naval power, as well as nine of the next largest class, frigates mounting forty-four guns. Particularly visionary was a provision for three steam batteries for coast defense, stemming from Robert Fulton's recent efforts, far ahead of their time, to build a steam-driven warship. Thus the United States committed itself to becoming a major naval power.[14]

Similarly this Congress appropriated $1 million to begin massive fortifications at such hitherto vulnerable points as the mouth of the Mississippi and Chesapeake and Delaware bays. To ensure the most up-to-date design and construction, the War Department was authorized to employ Napoleon's celebrated military engineer, General Simon Bernard. The Fourteenth Congress departed farthest from traditional Republican reliance on a citizen militia by authorizing a general staff at Washington for a professional standing army twice the size of the prewar establishment.[15]

Because of President Madison's constitutional doubts, the National Republicans postponed their most cherished project, transportation, until the second session of the Fourteenth Congress in the winter of 1816–1817. By then booming land sales, heavy importations, and continuing war taxes were pushing the year's revenues to an astonishing $40 million, leaving a surplus of $9 million even after large payments on the war debt. The President sounded less adamant about a constitutional amendment, and the inventive Calhoun's national Bank already offered a relatively painless source of capital.

The Carolinian's supra-Hamiltonian vision was fully unveiled when he now proposed to reserve for transportation the $1.5 million bonus from the Bank, plus the dividends of approximately $650,000 a year on the government's Bank stock. Months of poring over maps with friend Lowndes committed them to essentially Gallatin's blueprint—a series of canals and roads across the Appalachians, improvement of the Ohio-Mississippi river system, and a great road south through the Atlantic interior and around to New Orleans. Except for a single intervention by Speaker Clay, Calhoun carried the argument for his Bonus Bill almost single-handedly, boldly challenging President Madison's constitutional doubts.[16]

Ever since Hamilton and Jefferson's conflicting advice to President Washington about the first Bank, constitutional issues had dominated the debate over national developmentalism. Contention focused on the word *necessary* in the Constitution's clause empowering Congress to "make all laws which shall be necessary and proper for carrying into execution" a long list of specifically enumerated powers—among others, to lay taxes, declare war, regulate commerce among the states, and "establish" post offices and post roads. Was a Bank "necessary" for executing any of the enumerated powers?

"Necessary," Hamilton had advised Washington, meant "no more than *needful, requisite, incidental, useful,* or *conducive to.*" Accepted by Washington, Hamilton's doctrine of "implied powers" provided constitutional warrant for Bank and every developmental proposal since. "If the *end* be clearly comprehended within any of the specified powers," he maintained, "and if the measure have an obvious relation to that *end,* and is not forbidden by any particular provision of the Constitution, it may safely be deemed to come within the compass of the national authority."

Vainly Jefferson warned that broadening "necessary" to "convenient" removed all limits on congressional power. There was no measure, he argued, "which ingenuity may not torture into a *convenience, in some way or other, to some one* of so long a list of enumerated powers." Such loose construction would reduce the Constitution to a statement giving Congress the "power to do whatever would be for the good of the United States," he said prophetically; "and, as they would be the sole judges of the good or evil, it would be also a power to do whatever evil they pleased."[17]

The issue was fundamental. The very possibility of national developmentalism was at stake, and thus the pace and direction of the republic's actual development. The line between Hamilton's broad construction and Jefferson's strict construction was a line between rival subcultures projecting alternative visions of the American future. Hamilton, who never approved the diluted nationalism of the original constitutional bargain, made no bones about entering the Washington administration to "prop up this frail and worthless fabric" by broad interpretation and vigorous administration. Men like Jefferson, who had accepted the bargain of 1787 with opposite reservations, saw in Hamiltonian construction a constitutional revolution as fundamental as the original Constitution itself.

Calhoun hardly concealed his contempt for the tediousness into which the constitutional debate had descended over many years. He was "no advocate for refined arguments on the Constitution," he declared. "The instrument was not intended as a thesis for the logician to exercise his ingenuity on. It ought to be construed with plain, good sense." His plain, good sense saw few limits to congressional power. He thought building roads and canals plainly implied by the enumerated power to "establish" post roads—under which Congress had long practiced the lively patronage politics of mail contracts, post-office location, and postmaster appointments by designating mail routes over existing roads. While the Carolinian thought the post-roads clause a sufficient constitutional justification for the timid, he argued strenuously for a broader warrant of congressional authority. The Constitution's revenue clause, he maintained, by authorizing Congress to levy taxes "to pay the debts and provide for the common defence and general welfare," empowered Congress to appropriate public funds for anything it deemed conducive to the "general welfare."

Roads and canals were preeminently conducive to the general welfare, Calhoun explained, by extending the market. Making "the country price . . . approximate to that of the commercial towns," internal improvements extended "to the interior the advantages possessed by the parts most eligibly situated for trade," stimulated "every branch of national industry, Agricultural, Manufacturing, and Commercial," and diffused "universal opulence."

In addition Calhoun emphasized their military importance, not only for moving troops but also for sustaining the internal trade essential for financing a war. Beyond this he urged an even more important consideration, the difficulty of maintaining the unity of a republic stretched over such vast distances. "We are great, and rapidly," if not "fearfully, growing," he said, and this threatened "the greatest of all calamities, next to the loss of liberty, and even to that in its consequences—*disunion.*" "Let us then bind the Republic together with a perfect system of roads and canals," he implored. "Let us conquer space."

With almost evangelical fervor, the Carolinian appealed in conclusion for a patriotic nationalism that transcended selfish and sectional considerations. "In a country so extensive, and so various in its interests," he conceded, "what is necessary for the common good may apparently be opposed to the interest of particular sections." But that, he insisted, "must be submitted to as the condition of our greatness." Happily the moment was peculiarly propitious. At peace and "abounding in pecuniary means," Americans were submerging party and sectional feelings "in a liberal and enlightened regard to the general concerns of the nation." The current Congress, he congratulated his colleagues, had already done so much in this spirit that it "had never been excelled." Before them lay "a most splendid future." Only "a low, sordid, selfish, and sectional spirit" could prevent them from realizing it and lead them instead into disunion, misery, and despotism.[18]

Again the Fourteenth Congress followed Calhoun toward his most splendid future and passed the Bonus Bill, though by a scant two-vote margin in the House. Again the critical votes came from the northeastern centers of market energy, New York and Pennsylvania congressmen supporting the measure 42–6, in hope of federal funding for the ambitious canal projects envisioned by commercial interests in their states.

Their hopes were dashed. The day before the Fourteenth Congress and the Madison administration left office in March 1817, the President told Calhoun he was vetoing the Bonus Bill. As Jefferson's coadjutor in defining Republican orthodoxy, Madison had already strained his consistency by approving the national Bank. And as the Constitution's chief architect and expositor, he could not allow Calhoun's reliance on the revenue/general-welfare clause to pass unchallenged. Such a construction would give Congress "a general power of legislation instead of the defined and limited one hitherto understood to belong to them," the veto message warned. Moreover, because constitutional federal laws took precedence over state laws, Calhoun's construction would obliterate the boundary between federal and state powers. Nor, said Madison, did Congress have any "implied" power to build roads and canals. The President remained convinced of "the great importance" of internal improvements but hoped for a constitutional amendment.[19]

National developmentalism had crested, and for the moment the initiative in advancing the market through roads and waterways passed to the states. Within two weeks De Witt Clinton persuaded the New York legislature to proceed with the Erie Canal on its own.

On March 4, 1817, the day after Madison vetoed the Bonus Bill, the Fourteenth Congress assembled for the final time to inaugurate as his successor the last of the Virginia triumvirate around whom the Republican party formed. James Monroe's knee breeches and silk stockings bespoke a Revolutionary Republicanism already exotic to a Congress uniformed mainly in the businesslike trousers brought by the commercial boom.

As Jefferson's law student and devoted protégé, this ambitious son of the lesser tobacco gentry had worked his way up through county and legislative politics to the Confederation Congress, the Senate, and major diplomatic missions. Resenting the precedence Jefferson gave Madison, the slower-witted Monroe distrusted his rival's readiness to trim Republican principles to enterprising interests. In 1808, when Virginia's ideological purists were resisting Madison as Jefferson's successor, Monroe let himself be advanced as a rival presidential candidate, drawing back just in time to avoid an open break. Jefferson counted on Monroe's scrupulous integrity—"turn his soul wrong side outwards, and there is not a speck on it"—to preserve Republicanism from corruption as Madison's successor. Invited at Jefferson's urging to join Madison's lackluster Cabinet, Monroe brought much of the executive energy that enabled the country to survive the War of 1812. While the rest of the government crumbled in flight from the British invasion of Washington, Monroe coolly and energetically improvised such defense as was possible. Nominated in due course for President by the Republican caucus in the Fourteenth Congress, he ran almost unopposed, losing only the diehard Federalist strongholds Massachusetts, Connecticut, and Delaware.

In more than his antique garb the new President seemed to be reaching back to the pomp and elegance with which the Washington administration asserted national power. His Cabinet secretaries fought off the official livery he proposed they wear, but he uniformed American diplomats and prescribed European rules of formal etiquette for official society. As soon as a new coat of gleaming paint covered the British smokestains on the rebuilt presidential mansion—henceforth the White House—Monroe filled it with ornate French furniture and instituted lavish weekly receptions where Mrs. Monroe dazzled the ladies with her fifteen-hundred-dollar Parisian wardrobe. "Miserable pageantry," snorted Pennsylvania's Country Democrat Abner Laycock, just as his homespun senatorial predecessor William Maclay had snorted at Federalist extravagance a generation before.

But Monroe was not reviving the exclusivism of Federalist grandees. His administration represented instead the hegemony of a new and broader elite, the rising enterprisers who rallied around and flourished under the Republican banner. For a host of influentials spread across the land, the Monrovian style celebrated a national wealth and power that mirrored their personal success, as well as a sophisticated elegance that validated their newly claimed gentility.

Monroe, the purist Republican of 1808, was not a likely representative of this postwar ebullience. But his harrowing efforts to keep the war afloat convinced him that the national government had to be strengthened, and the disasters of wartime finance committed him to the Astor/Girard scheme for a national Bank. Claiming a place in history as the patriot statesman who led the republic back to consensus, the President was especially sensitive to the bitter estrangement of the increasingly weighty northeastern commercial interests. The national Bank, he explained to Madison in terms remarkably reminiscent of Hamilton, would "attach the commercial part of the community to a much greater degree to the Government." This, he said, "is the great desideratum of our system." Meanwhile he was falling thousands of dollars in debt to the Bank's chief promoter, John Jacob Astor, who regularly subsidized his habit of living far beyond his means; and he would soon be many thousands in debt to the Bank itself.[20]

Belying his archaic garb and purist reputation, therefore, Monroe shaped his administration to the National Republican vision of a powerful, activist national state. Although a mounting surplus induced him to accept repeal of the war taxes, he insisted repeatedly that they should be reimposed the moment they were needed to maintain the expanded federal functions mandated by the Fourteenth Congress.

The Monrovian political economy proceeded from the unquestioning assumption that a powerful government should promote the economy's growth in each of its three conventional sectors of agriculture, commerce, and manufactures. Manufactures, as the newest and most dynamic sector, commanded the President's special attention. In six of his eight annual messages he urged Congress to extend further encouragement to manufactures by raising the protective duties legislated by the Fourteenth Congress.

Picking up a Hamiltonian argument advanced by Calhoun in the 1816 debate, Monroe maintained that protective tariffs were the best means of aiding the agricultural sector also. A growing manufacturing population, he contended, would provide a "home market" to replace the shrinking overseas markets for the American farmer's grains and livestock products.

As for the commercial sector, national diplomacy had revolved from the beginning around trade opportunities for American shippers. With Europe now at peace for the first time in a generation, the American diplomatic establishment—especially its far-flung network of consular agents in ports around the world—became even more preoccupied with problem-solving for American merchants. And the expensive new navy, designed primarily to protect American commerce, was deployed as fast as it could be built, against Levantine pirates in the Mediterranean and raiders spawned by wars of independence in the Caribbean, and to foster a growing American commercial presence in the remote Pacific.

To promote all three sectors, the President made the Gallatin/Calhoun dream of "a perfect system of roads and canals" the keystone of his political economy. Captivated by the developmental vision and its brilliant young Carolina prophet, he appointed Calhoun his Secretary of War and absorbed his sophisticated argument for transportation as making possible both economic and territorial growth. Calhoun had full presidential support to design a new professional army for territorial expansion and consolidation. Through military roads and military engineers, he intended to make the War Department the fulcrum of the internal-improvement effort.

Monroe celebrated, as Calhoun had in the Fourteenth Congress, "a domestic market" based on "the difference of climate and industry" across the country's "vast territory." It would create "an active intercourse between the extremes and throughout every portion of our Union," as the President explained the market's magic, because different areas had different natural advantages for producing different crops, for manufacturing, or for commerce and fisheries. But none of these blessings of the division of labor could flow, Monroe emphasized, without transportation. Only through roads and canals could "distant lands . . . be made more valuable, and the industry of our fellow-citizens on every portion of our soil be better rewarded." And the lowered cost of transporting goods to market would far outweigh the cost of a national system.

In addition the President, like Calhoun, thought such a system essential to national unity. A territorial expansionist in the tradition of Jefferson and Madison, Monroe worried that the country's vastness threatened sectional conflict and disunion. But with roads and canals to extend and thicken the web of market relationships, he argued, "the parts would soon become so compacted and bound together that nothing could break it." With a comprehensive transportation system, the republic could safely expand into "a great" rather than "a small power." Moreover, Monroe insisted, the country's unmatched natural advantages—extensive coastlines, deep bays and estuaries, the Great Lakes, a labyrinth of navigable rivers—made such a network readily achievable. It would be "practicable and easy," he assured Congress, "to connect by canals the whole coast from its southern tip to its northern extremity in one continued inland navigation"; "to connect in like manner in many parts the Western lakes and rivers with each other"; and to connect the Atlantic coast with the Mississippi valley by roads linking the heads of improved rivers, and in some cases by canals. And the intervening territory could be intersected by good roads.

But to create the transportation infrastructure for a vast free market that would convert the republic into a great power, Monroe had to confront in constitutional terms the fundamental division in American society. With his great patron Jefferson looking on from Monticello, he had to find some way around Jeffersonian principles of strict construction. The problem far transcended his personal consistency. The President thought it his historic role to ease the old-fashioned Jeffersonian consciousness into the new world of the untrammeled market. To make the transition as painless as possible for the public as well as himself, he followed Jefferson and Madison in insisting on a constitutional amendment authorizing internal improvements. Where an amendment had been politically impossible in his predecessors' day, however, Monroe thought it attainable in the new political climate of National Republicanism. If Congress would initiate an amendment authorizing national roads and canals, he predicted in his first annual message, the "benign spirit of conciliation and harmony which now manifests itself throughout the Union" would produce a prompt ratification by the states. And while Congress was at it, he suggested, they might get national "seminaries of learning" authorized as well.[21]

Although embracing the new entrepreneurial vision of the republic's destiny, Monroe remained an eighteenth-century gentleman in his conception of politics. Gentlemen, both Republican and Federalist, still idealized a politics that selected society's best minds to discover and legislate the common good through rational deliberation. Gentlemen knew best the public good, and their professions of disinterestedness obscured, even for themselves, the personal and class interests they served.

Federalist collapse allowed Monroe to revive the ideal of united elite leadership after a generation of bitter party warfare. Deliberately he sought to undermine party and party spirit. The first President since Washington to make public appearances, he opened his administration with a goodwill tour to the Boston citadel of Federalism, where his "era of good feelings" was first hailed by a Federalist newspaper. Then he compounded the political confusion by refusing to groom a successor—as Jefferson had groomed Madison and Madison had groomed him—to be nominated by the congressional Republican caucus and duly elevated to the presidency by loyal Republican voters.

The younger Monroe had been an almost fanatical Republican partisan, believing that "in the present state of the world, not another republick in it, the safety of free government depends on the existence and exertions of the republican party." Because of the party's historic role as the world's only defender of republicanism, he argued that individual differences of opinion should be sacrificed to party unity; and the importance he attached to Republican unity explains his willingness to adjust his own views to the new National Republican consensus.

But like most of the republic's founding gentry, Monroe had always believed that "the existence of parties is not necessary to free government." Like Jefferson he regarded the Republican party as an emergency expedient to save the whole republican system from its Federalist enemies. He had long hoped that once Federalism was finally vanquished, the President would "cease to be the head of a party." Now Federalist demise allowed him to celebrate a "new epoch" in which "our government may go on and prosper without the existence of parties." The President's antipartyism sought to contain democracy. The perfection of American republicanism made parties unnecessary, he lectured the country, by retaining "the sovereignty in the people, while it avoids the tumult and disorder incident to the exercise of that power by the people themselves."[22]

With Monroe disdaining party leadership, uncontrolled rivalry stalled the national transportation system. Henry Clay, miffed at being passed over for Secretary of State and heir apparent, rebuffed an offer of the War Department and challenged the administration for leadership of the development movement. Resuming the powerful Speakership, Clay persuaded the House to reject the President's proposed constitutional amendment. An amendment would be defeated, he feared, because opponents of improvements would be joined by those who believed, as he did, that Congress already had the power to build roads and canals. Congress would not initiate an amendment, while without an amendment the President stood pledged to veto any improvement measure Congress passed.[23]

Especially frustrated by this impasse was the Secretary of War. Already Calhoun was at work to provide the engineers needed for a transportation system through the military academy at West Point, where the army had previously offered only elementary instruction to a trickle of engineers for its fortifications. Within a few years the Secretary created a new West Point, modeled on the world's most advanced military and engineering school, the French Ecole Polytechnique. The able Sylvanus Thayer was made superintendent, and trusted officers were dispatched to France to bring back a curriculum, a scientific library, and professors of science, engineering, and mathematics. A permanently enlarged cadet corps— soon including Jefferson Davis, Robert E. Lee, and fourteen other future Confederate generals—pursued a demanding four-year regimen of mathematics, French, and science, spiced with instruction by a celebrated Italian dancing master and culminating in a senior course in moral and political philosophy as expounded through Chancellor Kent's *Commentaries on American Law.*

The growing stream of graduates from the new West Point furnished the country's only supply of civilian engineers, as well as filling the elite corps of military and topographical engineers that Calhoun organized in the army. Even the army engineers were intended to serve broader purposes than overseeing the massive new fortifications. As his engineering manpower grew, Secretary Calhoun deployed it to exploring and mapping the frontiers, to surveying rivers and harbors, and increasingly to providing free engineering services for transportation improvements by the states or state-chartered corporations.[24]

By 1819 the Secretary was ready to assume public leadership of the internal-improvement effort by announcing an audacious new "general-survey" strategy. Eliciting a congressional inquiry about the military usefulness of roads and canals, he responded that a system meeting the most pressing military needs would be almost identical with a system designed for "the convenience of commerce." The grand system he sketched out as best meeting both needs was essentially Gallatin's vision of 1808. His most important recommendation was that a general survey of the whole system be made, and alternative routes and costs be assessed, before individual projects were undertaken. And his military engineers, he announced proudly, were ready and able to do the job.[25]

Meanwhile President Monroe was devoting all his free time to composing a twenty-five-thousand-word treatise on the constitutional problem. He proposed to lay this remarkable document before Congress the next time it forced him to veto an internal-improvements measure, and he obviously hoped to resolve the impasse by converting the opponents of amendment through sheer weight of argument. Four years would pass before this heavy ordnance could be unlimbered.

Stepping in to cut the gordian knot with a constitutional revolution was the branch most shielded from the "tumult and disorder" of democratic politics. As Congress and President embraced the political economy of capitalist development, the Supreme Court buttressed it constitutionally in a remarkable series of decisions between 1816 and 1819. Converging in purpose with Chief Justice Marshall and his brethren, the Fourteenth Congress increased their salaries and provided them a handsome new courtroom and an official reporter for their decisions. While national Bank and protective tariff were being enacted in 1816, elsewhere on Capitol Hill Justice Story delivered one of the first opinions published by the new reporter, the sweeping assertion of federal judicial supremacy in *Martin v. Hunter's Lessee.*

Virginia courts had defied a Supreme Court decision requiring the state to return the vast acreage it confiscated in Revolutionary days from the loyalist Lord

Fairfax and resold. With hundreds of land titles in jeopardy, an aroused Virginia Court of Appeals rejected this judgment on the ground that the Judiciary Act of 1789 violated the Constitution in authorizing appeals from state to federal courts. With Marshall abstaining because his land-speculating family was deeply interested in the Fairfax title, Virginia's defiance gave Story the opportunity to write an opinion expressing his bold conception of national preeminence.

Believing that "the Government of the United States is intrinsically too weak, and the powers of the State Governments too strong," the Republican Story resolved to make the most of his opportunity by frontally demolishing the Jeffersonian state-rights view of the Constitution as a compact among sovereign states. The Constitution, he declared for a Republican Court majority, "was ordained and established, not by the States in their sovereign capacities, but emphatically, as the preamble declares, by 'the people of the United States.'" This view, later elaborated in his three-volume *Commentaries on the Constitution of the United States* (1833), was the foundation of all subsequent nationalist theory.

The Supreme Court thus created by "the voice of the whole American people," Story proclaimed, was therefore "in many respects, national, and in all, supreme." Consequently Congress had not only the power but the constitutional obligation to vest the justices with the whole judicial power required to ensure uniformity respecting federal laws and treaties—most imperatively, appellate jurisdiction over state courts. Story's opinion in this case, according to constitutional historian Charles Warren, "has ever since been the keystone of the whole arch of Federal judicial power."[26]

The mood of American influentials as reflected in the Fourteenth Congress doubtless encouraged a Republican Court to follow Story in this bold proclamation of its constitutional supremacy. Convinced now that he could finally lay aside his political caution, Chief Justice Marshall waited for opportunities to exercise the Court's newly asserted supremacy. With a fusillade of momentous decisions in early 1819, the Court established the critical constitutional bulwarks required by the emerging capitalist order.[27]

The first concerned Dartmouth College. Royally chartered in 1769, endowed with public lands, and governed by self-perpetuating Federalist trustees, the college was appealing against an act of New Hampshire's Republican legislature amending its charter by adding politically appointed trustees and bringing it in some degree under state control. In arguing this case for his alma mater at the previous term, Daniel Webster first gained national fame as a lawyer and orator, particularly for his emotional peroration: Dartmouth was but "a small college . . . yet *there are those who love it.*"

Webster's love was reinforced by a thousand-dollar fee, and his good friend Justice Story long remembered "the fiery flashings of his eye, the darkness of his contracted brow, the sudden & flying flushes of his cheeks, the quivering &

scarcely manageable movements of his lips, in the deep guttural tones of his voice, in the struggle to suppress his own emotions, in the almost convulsive clenchings of his hands without a seeming consciousness of the act." Many of his hearers "were sinking under exhausting efforts to conceal their own emotions," Story recalled, and even Chief Justice Marshall was reduced to tears.[28]

However affecting to this audience the defense of a beleaguered little elite institution against an antielite legislature, there was much more at stake. The heart of Webster's argument was that all corporations, and "private rights" in general, must be protected from "the rise and fall of popular parties and the fluctuations of political opinions." Corporate charters, therefore, must be construed as irrevocable contracts and protected by the constitutional ban against state laws "impairing the obligation of contracts."[29]

Several Republican justices had doubts. Only once before, in the Yazoo lands case, had the Court invalidated a state law, and Marshall was anxious to have his brethren united in enunciating an important new principle. Accordingly he postponed further proceedings until the 1819 term, and meanwhile both sides circulated printed arguments and lobbied the justices assiduously. Webster's side enlisted Chancellor Kent, who had been hoping to establish the inviolability of corporate charters ever since the 1803 legislature amended the corporate charter of New York City to broaden the suffrage in local elections. Kent apparently helped win over two of the doubtful Republican justices, the South Carolinian William Johnson and the New Yorker Brockholst Livingston, perhaps with De Witt Clinton assisting in the latter case.

Justice Story, in his zeal for his friend Webster's cause, considerably overstepped the bounds of judicial propriety. He helped Webster get some new cases started in the lower courts so that additional arguments could be brought up to the Supreme Court; he circulated Webster's printed arguments among his colleagues; and he was the likely source of Webster's accurate knowledge about how the various justices stood. Story was anxious to base the inviolability of corporate charters not just on the contract clause but also on the common law, and he went so far as to urge Webster to prepare arguments on which such an opinion could be based. Webster's opponents, on the other hand, hoped to present newly discovered evidence for their contention that the college was a public institution and therefore subject to state regulation.[30]

But Marshall had his majority in hand and opened the 1819 term by pulling from his sleeve and reading an eighteen-page opinion upholding the college. One justice was absent, another dissented silently—a practice Marshall encouraged when dissent was unavoidable—and the other four justices concurred with the Chief Justice. Marshall's reasoning—not very clearly articulated in his politically vigorous and fluently argued opinion—would seem to have been this: (1) the essence of contracts is the inviolability of the property rights they specify; (2) corporations are chartered for the management of property; (3) corporate charters, because they affect property, are contracts and therefore inviolable by the states. The dizzying leap from point two to point three he accomplished mainly offstage, meanwhile diverting his audience with the American judiciary's first great apotheosis of the corporation.

A corporation was an "artificial being," said the Chief Justice, endowed by law with the advantage of "immortality and, if the expression be allowed, individuality." These advantages were conferred to enable it "to manage its own affairs, and to hold property without the perplexing intricacies, the hazardous and endless necessity, of perpetual conveyances for the purpose of transmitting it from hand to hand." As a result, he marveled, "a perpetual succession of individuals are capable of acting for the promotion of the particular object, like one immortal being." Dartmouth College was one of these marvelous and inviolable entities, "incorporated for the preservation of its property, and the perpetual application of that property to the objects of its creation." Its charter was thus a contract that could not be modified by the state. Story filed a concurring opinion reaching the same conclusion on common-law grounds.[31]

All parties recognized that this decision had more to do with the growing swarm of business corporations than with Dartmouth College. Webster viewed it as a "defence of vested rights against State Courts and Sovereignties," while his co-counsel, the Philadelphia Federalist Joseph Hopkinson, rejoiced that the Court had established "principles broad and deep and which secure corporations . . . from legislative despotism and party violence for the future." Story told Kent that the decision would protect "private rights" against "any undue encroachments . . . which the passions or the popular doctrines of the day may stimulate our State Legislatures to adopt"; and Kent himself called it the most important step in placing beyond popular reach the "literary, charitable, religious, and commercial institutions of our country."[32]

Two weeks after *Dartmouth,* the Court's decision in *Sturgis v. Crowninshield* brought the contract clause to bear on an even more fundamental question, bankruptcy and enforcement of debts. The Constitution's contract clause struck down state laws passed in the 1780s easing creditor pressure on small debtors. In some places, a third of the householders were still being hauled into court as defaulting debtors every year; and for those who could not pay, the penalty was jail. Although imprisonment for debt was alleviated by prison-bounds laws releasing debtors during the day to follow their occupations, and although most were held only briefly, thousands were still being arrested, often for small sums. In Boston 1,442 debtors went to jail in 1820, and horror stories abounded. George Riley spent six years in prison for owing less than fifty dollars, and a blind Bostonian with a dependent family was jailed for a six-dollar debt.

The Constitution's framers demonstrated their class bias most clearly by coupling the contract clause's inflexibility toward small debtors with a bankruptcy clause mandating relief for large debtors. When they authorized Congress to enact "uniform laws on the subject of bankruptcies throughout the United States," bankruptcy was understood as a process whereby large debtors were freed from their debts by surrendering their assets.

The rationale for bankruptcy laws was that entrepreneurship was socially beneficial. If a volatile economy plunged a risk-taking entrepreneur hopelessly into debt, the argument ran, his debts should be forgiven so that society could again enjoy the benefits of his enterprise. "Is it no object to a young country like ours," a South Carolina congressman asked, "to restore to society the labor which is now paralyzed—the enterprise which slumbers—the talent which is crushed—the virtue which is trampled in the dust?" Similarly the governor of Connecticut declared that leaving such enterprisers mired in debt would "render them unprofitable members of the community"; while in neighboring Massachusetts it was argued that such debtors were seldom able to pay their accumulated debts, so that requiring them to do so "is seldom of any advantage to the creditor, whilst it is injurious to the debtor, and to the community in which he resides."[33]

In 1800 a Federalist Congress passed a national bankruptcy act forgiving the debts of insolvent merchants and traders, but a Republican Congress promptly repealed it in 1803. While Webster and Hopkinson argued the Dartmouth case, they were simultaneously as congressmen leading a campaign for a new bankruptcy law, with technical support from Justice Story. Repeatedly over the next several years the measure was defeated. It was another manifestation of the current congressional tendency "to encourage everything," complained a Virginia opponent; "the manufacturer must be encouraged by duties; the merchant must be stimulated to mercantile enterprise by sponging his debts if he fails. And on whom do these encouragements operate as a burden? On the farmer and planter."[34]

As people of the small-debtor class swelled the electorate, Republican legislatures began to pass laws abolishing imprisonment for debt and making it possible for small debtors to discharge their obligations through bankruptcy proceedings. In *Sturgis v. Crowninshield* such a New York law was challenged, on the double grounds that the Constitution gave Congress the exclusive right to pass bankruptcy laws and that such laws by the states impaired "the obligation of contracts."

Marshall obtained a unanimous judgment against the New York law only by surrendering his own view that the bankruptcy clause preempted the field and prevented any state action on the subject even if Congress failed to exercise its bankruptcy powers. He also had to concede that the states could abolish imprisonment for debt. Thus he induced several justices to agree that the New York law impaired the obligation of contracts. Even then several justices remained convinced that states could pass laws relieving debts contracted subsequent to the legislation. The opinion the Chief Justice drafted for an ostensibly unanimous Court was ambiguous on this point, but it clearly forbade states to relieve debts already contracted.[35]

This decision had not yet penetrated the farther reaches of the country when Marshall, speaking for a unanimous Court in the celebrated case *McCulloch v. Maryland,* cut the ground out from under strict construction and state sovereignty with a ringing endorsement of the Hamiltonian doctrine of implied powers. The case involved the constitutionality of the new national Bank and a Maryland law levying a prohibitive tax against its Baltimore branch.

Webster and the Bank's two other attorneys went little beyond Hamilton's original argument to President Washington, and Marshall's opinion put the Supreme Court's imprimatur on the Hamiltonian interpretation. "Necessary," the Chief Justice declared, often means "no more than that one thing is convenient, or useful, or essential to another." Rephrasing Hamilton's principle, the Court concluded: "Let the end be legitimate, let it be within the scope of the constitution, and all means which are appropriate, which are plainly adapted to that end, which are not prohibited, but consist with the letter and spirit of the constitution, are constitutional." The Bank, being "plainly adapted" to such enumerated powers as collecting and expending revenues, was therefore constitutional.

Gratuitously Marshall elaborated the nationalist interpretation of the origin and nature of the federal union that Justice Story had enunciated in *Martin v. Hunter's Lessee.* The Constitution emanated from "the people," he insisted, and not "as an act of sovereign and independent States." For convenience the people had acted through ratifying conventions assembled in the several states, but their acts of ratification did not "on that account cease to be the measures of the people themselves, or become the measures of the state governments." The federal government, therefore, "(whatever may be the influence of this fact on the case), is emphatically and truly a government of the people" and not the states.

This "fact" had no necessary relation to the Court's further finding that Maryland had acted unconstitutionally in taxing the Baltimore branch. "The power to tax involves the power to destroy," Marshall declared in language from Webster's argument, and through it the states would be "capable of arresting all the measures of the government, and of prostrating it at the foot of the states." Therefore, to protect the constitutional "supremacy" of the federal government, the Court found that "the states have no power, by taxation or otherwise, to retard, impede, burden, or in any manner control, the operations" of constitutional federal laws.[36]

Thus within the space of six weeks in early 1819, a Supreme Court that had previously challenged only one state law struck down three. In the process it forbade the states to interfere with the chartered privileges of corporations, to relieve existing debts, or to impede in any fashion the constitutional functions or instrumentalities of the federal government. Moreover it asserted its own right to define the range of permitted federal functions so broadly as to include not only the national Bank but also by implication internal improvements, protective tariffs, and the rest of the developmental program. Indeed the justices soon took the extraordinary step of informing the President directly that they were "all of the opinion that the decision on the Bank question completely commits" them to upholding internal improvements as implied by the enumerated congressional power to establish post offices and post roads.[37]

Meanwhile, with Calhoun's "perfect system of roads and canals" stalemated, the Monroe administration was conquering space through territorial expansion. Monrovian expansion sought more than Jefferson's empire for yeoman liberty. Western farmers were being overtaken by masters of capital and slaves bent on market profit. Where Federalist nationalism, facing toward Europe, had feared the westward extension of a democratic farming populace, National Republicanism staked out a continental base for the most extensive free market the world had yet seen. Monrovians sought to create a "great" nation by pushing relentlessly against the territories of Indians, Spanish, and British.

The primary victims were Indians. During the war an unprecedented invasion of their treaty-guaranteed rights was set in motion by the military campaigns of General William Henry Harrison in the Old Northwest and General Andrew Jackson in the Old Southwest. Jackson's ferocious will and driving energy—here first exhibited to the American public—devastated American Indians. Implacable in his military annihilation of the Georgia-Alabama Creeks, he was equally implacable in his demands for vast land cessions, not only by the Creeks but by all the southwestern tribes whose lands were coveted by whites. A self-made frontier bigwig, Jackson shared the anti-Indian animus of a subsistence culture that required constant new supplies of cheap land to enable its numerous offspring to reproduce its ways. Like frontier farmers, he thought Indians were savage and warlike because they had too much land over which to pursue their "wandering habits of life." It would be better for Indians as well as whites, he argued, if most of their lands were taken from them so that "necessity would prompt them to industry and agriculture, as the only certain and lasting means of support."

The Madison administration yielded to such sentiment by appointing Jackson to replace the commissioners originally selected to negotiate a treaty with the defeated Creeks in 1814. When the hostile chiefs refused the general's summons to a parley, he bullied the chiefs who had sided with the whites against their fellow Creeks into ceding most of the best Creek lands, some 23 million acres comprising three-fifths of present Alabama and a fifth of Georgia. The "friendly" Creeks suffered most, being driven from the border of Spanish Florida into the hilly and infertile northeastern corner of Alabama, leaving for whites the rich lands across which the Cotton Kingdom soon spread.

Meanwhile Jackson's stunning victory over the British at New Orleans made it impossible for the administration to resist his views on the Indian question. The

Treaty of Ghent required the United States to restore to the Indians all their pre-war lands—which would have left an Indian buffer state between white settlements and Spanish Florida—and the Madison administration dutifully instructed Jackson to take steps toward fulfilling this national obligation. But the popular general went on expelling the Creeks, and no one dared say him nay.

The incoming President Monroe was bent on conciliating all elements and had little desire to antagonize the West or its hero. Nominally responsible for Indian affairs was Secretary of War Calhoun. Over the next few years, with Calhoun's full support, Jackson negotiated personally or through commissioners amenable to him treaties extorting from the Cherokees, Choctaws, and Chickasaws millions of acres in North Carolina, Georgia, Alabama, Mississippi, Tennessee, and Kentucky, including the western fifth of Tennessee, the fabulously fertile Yazoo delta country of west central Mississippi, and a broad corridor through northern Alabama connecting the Tennessee settlements with the Creek cession and the Gulf coast. In all these negotiations the usual method of bribing chiefs was followed, but such enormous cessions could not have been extorted without Jackson's chilling threats that all who resisted his demands would meet the fate of the savaged Creeks.

By 1820 there was opened to white appropriation a vast territory sweeping from mid-Georgia to the Mississippi and up through West Tennessee to Kentucky. Jackson's soldiers herded its former inhabitants into confined enclaves of the least desirable lands—the Cherokees mainly in northwest Georgia, the Creeks in northeast Alabama, and the Choctaws and Chickasaws in northern Mississippi. Already the Cotton Kingdom was being established on the rich soils they vacated.

Andrew Jackson still was not satisfied. He was willing that individual Indians should keep enough land to farm. But tribal lands and tribal jurisdictions were intolerable to him, and like other frontier whites he wanted a "final solution" that would remove the bulk of the Indian population. So he seized upon the precedent of an earlier treaty that granted some Cherokees new lands across the Mississippi in exchange for their old territory. In his negotiations with the Cherokees and Choctaws he insisted that the Indians move from the lands to be ceded and take up new lands on the edge of the Great Plains along the Arkansas and Red rivers, a country thought so desolate that it was labelled on maps as "the Great American Desert." The Indians' new lands were, as usual, guaranteed to them "forever." When some of the new Choctaw lands turned out to have valuable salt springs, however, they were quickly taken back through another "treaty." Meanwhile, in the Choctaws' ancestral homeland, the whites' new state of Mississippi named its capital Jackson. Backed by frontier sentiment, the Tennessee general forced the removal policy on the administration. By 1824 President Monroe was calling for eventual removal of all Indians beyond the Mississippi.[38]

Simultaneously Secretary Calhoun was extracting land cessions from the weaker northwestern tribes almost as aggressively as Jackson in the Southwest. In addition he pushed the line of frontier military posts up to the head of navigation on the Mississippi and to the falls of the St. Mary's between Lakes Huron and Superior. He dispatched an expedition to build a string of forts eighteen hundred miles up the Missouri to the mouth of the Yellowstone, and by 1819 the first post was garrisoned at Council Bluffs in present Iowa. He sent a botanist, a zoologist, a geologist, a painter, and mapmakers on Major Stephen H. Long's scientific expedition to survey the Great Plains and the Rocky Mountain front between the South Platte and Arkansas rivers. And he pushed to completion a system of military roads connecting the Ohio settlements with the Michigan frontier and Tennessee with the Gulf coast at New Orleans and Mobile.[39]

These measures were designed to overawe the tribes and expedite the westward march of the white fontier. President Monroe argued that the Indians' scattered hunting population should "of right" give way "to the more dense and compact form and greater force of civilized population." "The earth was given to mankind to support the greatest number of which it is capable," as he explained this early version of the market's doctrine of highest use, "and no tribe or people have a right to withhold from the wants of others more than is necessary for their own support and comfort." Accordingly he celebrated the "rapid and gigantic" expansion of white settlement into Indian territory, "which the rights of nature demand and nothing can prevent."

But the President had to be sensitive to the many religious groups with a humanitarian concern for Indians, and he justified the Jacksonian policies as the best possible way to preserve the Native Americans. Only through removal, extinction of tribal jurisdictions, and complete government control over tribal life, he argued, could they be saved from extermination. His administration's policy was presented as a humane one of "civilizing" the Indians, particularly by training for "the acquisition and culture of land."[40]

Therefore Secretary Calhoun's management of Indians had a paternalist cast. "By a proper combination of force and persuasion," he said, "they ought to be brought within the pales of law and civilization." Applying this combination, he told a Cherokee delegation: "You see that the Great Spirit has made our form of society stronger than yours and you must submit to adopt ours if you wish to be happy by pleasing him."[41] To this end, Calhoun instructed Jackson to include in his Choctaw treaty a reservation of public lands to be sold for the support of missionary-operated Choctaw schools; and he secured from Congress an annual appropriation of ten thousand dollars for similar schooling in agriculture and handicrafts among other tribes. To oversee this program he established in the War Department an Office of Indian Affairs headed by Thomas L. McKenney, a professedly humanitarian paternalist.

By this time trappers representing St. Louis firms and John Jacob Astor's American Fur Company were fanning out across the Rockies in search of beaver pelts. Calhoun sought to protect American trappers from competition by the British Hudson's Bay Company while at the same time protecting the Indians from exploitation by unscrupulous trappers and traders. Congress rejected his proposal for a government monopoly of the fur trade. But he managed to defend against private traders the existing government-operated trading houses, called factories, while strengthening the system of allowing private trade with the Indians only under expensive licenses forbidding the sale of firearms or whiskey. The administration legitimized its policy of Jacksonian aggression against Indians with the gloss of a "civilizing" mission.

The Monroe administration pursued its expansionism as aggressively against the powerful British as against the helpless Indians. Fundamental to its diplomatic triumphs was a shift in British foreign policy that first showed itself in the negotiations at Ghent to end the War of 1812. Weary from the sacrifices, debts, and taxes of a generation of warfare on the European continent, and threatened by new conflicts with their victorious anti-Napoleonic allies, the British decided they had little to gain from pressing their military advantage against their rebellious former colonists. Substantially they agreed to restore the prewar boundaries and relations between the two countries. The skill and tenacity of the American negotiators—John Quincy Adams, James A. Bayard, Henry Clay, Albert Gallatin, and Jonathan Russell—extracted all the British were willing to yield. Again, as with the Louisiana Purchase, the United States profited from the vicissitudes of European power politics.

Yet the Treaty of Ghent seemed at first a mere truce, leaving so many threatening issues to be quarreled over that it prompted the postwar American military/naval buildup. Only gradually would it become apparent that the War of 1812 had in fact been a "Second War for American Independence" and that Britain was now, for the first time, ready to recognize and deal with the United States as a permanent and substantial power, indeed as the dominant power in the Western Hemisphere.

Anglo-American relations were transformed by economic developments. The industrial revolution was making Britain the central dynamo of an expanding world market, and its wealth and might depended increasingly on customers for its rising flood of manufactured exports. British leaders were beginning to understand that the growing American economy provided their best market as well as the best source for the raw cotton required by their leading industry.

Doubtless these realists were also pushed toward rapprochement by Jackson's quite effectual victory at New Orleans and by the National Republicans' taxation-backed military/naval/fortification buildup. At any rate, the British Prime Minister was soon declaring that everyone "who wishes prosperity to England must wish prosperity to America." So it turned out that the British navy, supreme on the world's oceans, would for a century to come protect the United States from European interference, conferring on Americans the boon, unexampled among modern nations, of a century of free military security in which to develop without outside molestation.

Britain's Foreign Secretary, Robert Stewart, Viscount Castlereagh, set all this in train by his conciliatory stance in the delicate postwar adjustment of the remaining differences between the two nations. His American counterpart was John Quincy Adams, who moved from the Ghent negotiations to London as American minister and then to Washington as Monroe's Secretary of State. Adams's contribution was to push Castlereagh to the limit of the concessions he was willing to make.[42]

Balding and growing corpulent as he neared the age of fifty, Adams had been assiduously trained for statesmanship by his father, the Revolutionary diplomat and Federalist President John Adams, and had spent much of his life at European courts, first as his father's secretary and then as American minister in his own right. Like his father he was too rooted in traditional Yankee morality to be comfortable with the politics of Boston's State Street capitalists. Feeling "abhorrence and contempt of simple democracy," he had nevertheless at first opposed the Constitution on the ground that it would "increase the power, influence, and wealth of those who have any already." Trained for the bar by a major architect of the new enterprise-oriented jurisprudence, he fled from legal practice, derided the lawyers' veneration of the common law, and refused a seat on the Supreme Court.

Adams's family heritage and long residence at Europe's condescending courts made him above all an American nationalist. In a single Senate term, this young Federalist maverick from Massachusetts took up the visionary cause of a national transportation system. He shocked New England more by supporting the Louisiana Purchase. Finally he went over to the Republicans out of disgust at what seemed to him the Federalists' unpatriotic opposition to the Embargo. Monroe appointed him Secretary of State partly because he was the country's most experienced diplomat and partly to conciliate estranged New England. The State Department had become a stepping stone to the presidency, and Adams's appointment soothed rising exasperation at Virginians' occupancy of the presidency for twenty-four of the twenty-eight years it had existed.[43]

The fervor of Adams's nationalism had deep personal sources in the conflict between an intensely ardent temperament, exemplified by his robust sexuality, and the repressive self-discipline required to realize his father's expectations of political and intellectual distinction. At the age of fourteen and for seven years afterwards Adams dreamed about a young actress he saw on the stage in Paris, an experience that left him with a "very extravagant fondness" for the theater for the rest of his life. In middle age he confessed to his wife that for nearly two years he was "tortured with the desire" for this young actress. "Of all the ungratified longings that I ever suffered," he said, this was "the most intense." Later, as a law student at Newburyport, he fell so deliriously in love with another young woman that "all my hopes in life, center in the possession of that girl"; and he remembered to the end of his days the delights of bundling, "muffled up in furs, in the open air, with the thermometer at Zero."

But Adams subdued his passions. The lesson he learned from the French actress was that of "never forming an acquaintance with an actress[,] to which I have since invariably adhered, and which I would lay as an injunction upon all my sons." And he finally declined to marry the Newburyport girl for "prudential and family reasons." When he did eventually decide to marry at age thirty, his redoubtable mother Abigail suspected a flight from passion. What about the girl back in Newburyport? she asked, unsatisfied by her son's assurance that "the enthusiasm of youth has subsided."[44]

The personal costs were considerable. The mature Adams described himself as "a man of reserved, cold, austere, and forbidding manners." "With a knowledge of the actual defect in my character," he added, "I have not the pliability to reform it." His hypochondriac wife, who thought he married her in part for a £5,000 dowry, fell into depression and wrote a history of what she regarded as the failure of her marriage.

He pushed his three sons even harder than his father pushed him, and certainly with less affection and support. Pressed relentlessly by Adams to finish at the top of his Harvard class—otherwise "I could feel nothing but sorrow and shame in your presence"—middle son John got himself expelled, failed at the practice of law, and died young and alcoholic. Eldest son George Washington Adams did better at Harvard and seemed on the threshold of a promising political career in Boston when he suddenly went to pieces and, summoned to Washington by his father, jumped to his death from a steamboat in Long Island Sound.

The senior Adams seemingly learned little from this tragedy. Even while mourning his eldest, he sat his youngest son, Charles, down for a lecture on "family pride." "I am the only one who remains to keep the name and the family . . . from destruction," the young man reflected that evening in the diary his father instructed him to maintain. "I feel at times depressed by it, for now the dependence upon me is perfectly prominent." Under this pressure, Charles Francis Adams managed to carry into a third generation—and prepare his sons to carry into a fourth (where the suicide was Mrs. Henry Adams)—the public distinction and private trauma of the most accomplished elite family in American history.[45]

The Adamses epitomized both the fruits and the human costs of the self-repressive effort exacted by capitalist transformation. The sublimation of psychic energy that fueled the country's astonishing surge of production also generated the emotional intensity that John Quincy Adams displaced onto his beloved republic. The result was the most brilliant and consequential chapter in the history of American diplomacy.

Adams launched this diplomacy by his vigorous assertion of American interests in resolving with Lord Castlereagh the remaining Anglo-American disputes. As American minister in London and then as Secretary of State in Washington, he won substantial concessions through a series of negotiations. An 1815 agreement not to discriminate against each other's shipping gave Americans a near monopoly of the north Atlantic carrying trade. The Rush-Bagot agreement of 1817 (so called after its nominal signers) forswore naval armaments on the Great Lakes, laying the basis for that spectacular monument to Anglo-American detente, the undefended border between the United States and Canada. Resolving many remaining differences, the Convention of 1818 extended American fishing and onshore curing privileges along the coasts of British Canada; compensated American owners for several thousand American slaves carried away by the British at the end of the war; abrogated the right of British citizens to navigate the Mississippi and trade with the Indians; and (in generous recognition of the Louisiana Purchase) conceded a boundary across the northern plains along the 49th parallel.

Beyond the Rockies agreement broke down. Adams maintained a claim going back to Captain Robert Gray's "discovery" in 1792 of the great river that he named for his Boston-based trading ship *Columbia*. The British countered with an older claim going back to Captain James Cook's explorations farther north around Vancouver Island in 1778, while the Spanish had sailed this coast even earlier. Jefferson's overland explorers Lewis and Clark wintered at the mouth of the Columbia in 1805–1806; and in 1811 John Jacob Astor's fur traders beat out rival British fur interests to briefly maintain a fort there. Meanwhile ships of many nations were attracted to the northwest coast by its abundant sea otter, much prized for the China trade, and British traders in beaver pelts ranged the upper reaches of the Columbia.

Therefore it seemed to the British negotiators in 1818 reasonable to compromise on the Columbia as a boundary. Adams refused, holding out for at least an extension along the 49th parallel to include all of present Washington state, especially the magnificent harbors of Puget Sound. With Adams adamant for a weak case, the negotiators could agree only to leave this Oregon country, as it was coming to be called, open to citizens of both nations for the next ten years.

Adams's devotion to the market made one difference uncompromisable. American shipowners had lost privileged access to British West Indian ports upon secession from the British empire, and the Secretary saw any restriction on free trade as an "enormous outrage upon the rights of human nature, and upon the first principles of the Rights of Nations." Because the "pursuit of happiness is a natural right of man," he argued on another occasion, "commerce is then among the natural rights and duties of men." For commerce "leads to the division of labour," and "there is no other way by which men can so much contribute to the comfort and well-being of one another." Holding out, therefore, for complete equality in the West Indian trade, he precipitated a mutually costly embargo that lasted until the United States accepted in 1830 substantially the concessions Castlereagh offered originally.[46]

The West Indian quarrel did not disturb the Anglo-American rapprochement.

Particularly important was Castlereagh's refusal to insist on the Ghent stipulation that the United States restore the Indians' prewar territories. The American government fulfilled its treaty obligation, his Foreign Office told complaining Indians, if it permitted them "to return to their former Situation for a week or a month"; and Castlereagh did not inquire too closely whether Andrew Jackson granted the Creeks even a day on the ancestral lands from which he expelled them.

This was the first indication that Great Britain would no longer resist the expansion of its bumptious former colonies. "We might as well suppose that a race of barbarians would be permitted to exist in Cornwall or Yorkshire, with independent rights and privileges," declared the London newspaper closest to the government, "as that the Indian tribes should oppose a barrier to the westward march of American civilization."[47]

The "westward march of American civilization" became an increasingly exhilarating vision to Secretary Adams. As he asserted against the oddly complaisant British lion the American claim to the Oregon country, he began to perceive that the simultaneous negotiations with Spain over Florida might also be used to buttress a frontage on the distant Pacific for a continental republic.

The Napoleonic wars delivered a fatal shock to the decaying Spanish empire, and throughout Central and South America its colonies were in revolt. Every Republican administration schemed for Spanish Florida; and the Madison administration—alleging a tenuous claim under the Louisiana Purchase—took advantage of Spain's wartime helplessness to seize West Florida, comprising the Gulf coast westward from the present state of Florida to the Mississippi.

Now Secretary Adams was demanding East Florida (the present state) as well, in compensation for Spain's wartime seizures of American shipping. Although the Spanish government was resigned to losing the rest of Florida eventually, its minister Don Luis de Onís dragged out the negotiations in an effort to get as much as possible in return. The Spanish wanted a promise that the United States would not aid or recognize the independence of their rebellious colonies; but all Adams would promise was present neutrality.

Madrid was even more anxious to protect Spanish Mexico from the Yankee advance by agreement on a boundary—the undefined southwestern limit of the Louisiana Purchase—as close to the Mississippi as possible. Retreating from the absurd American contention that the Louisiana Purchase included all of Texas west to the Rio Grande, Adams proposed a boundary along the Colorado River in central Texas. But Onís stubbornly held out for a line fifty miles inside the western boundary of the state of Louisiana and running north to the Missouri River, so as to restore to Spain most of the Louisiana Purchase.

Meanwhile Major General Andrew Jackson, commanding the southern division of the army from his Tennessee plantation, the Hermitage, impatiently eyed the crumbling Spanish position in Florida. During the war Jackson had invaded East Florida without authorization and stormed the Spanish capital, Pensacola, to drive out British forces based there. Now, as the Adams-Onís negotiations dragged on into the winter of 1817–1818, a border incident gave the administration an opportunity to break the diplomatic impasse by unleashing the general again.

When a band of Seminole Indians resisted removal from their ancestral lands just north of the boundary and massacred a party of whites, Jackson was ordered to pursue them into Florida if necessary. Although his orders cautioned him to respect Spanish authority, he was given broad power "to adopt the necessary measures to terminate" the border troubles. In view of the general's earlier flouting of Spanish authority and his well-known passion for expelling the Spaniards, the administration must have understood and intended the probable consequences of dispatching such a man on such a mission.

Even so, Jackson gave them considerably more than they bargained for. His immediate response to his orders was a counterproposal to the President that "the whole of East Florida [be] seized and held as an indemnity for the outrages of Spain upon the property of our citizens." This could be accomplished in sixty days "without implicating the Government," he wrote, if he received assurance through a certain Tennessee congressman that it was desired. Monroe later claimed that illness prevented him from seeing this extraordinary letter, while Jackson claimed, almost certainly erroneously, that he received the necessary assurance through the designated congressman.

In any event, the general rounded up unauthorized reinforcements and crossed the international boundary with some five thousand men, killing and capturing any and all Indians wherever he could. When most of the Indian population fled into the trackless swamps, he contented himself with burning their towns and crops and hanging the chiefs he captured. He also executed two British citizens he found among the Indians, one of them a seventy-year-old trader whose fair dealings had won their trust and who was protesting to the British government against their abandonment.

Having inflicted demoralizing starvation on the Indians, Jackson marched on Pensacola and overwhelmed the token Spanish garrison. Running up the American flag, installing an American government, and imposing American customs duties, he informed President Monroe that he now held all the places "essential to the peace and security of our frontier." With an additional regiment, he added, he could capture the remaining Spanish post of St. Augustine on the Atlantic coast, and with one frigate "will insure you Cuba in a few days." His conquest was essential to the security of the southern frontier and "to the growing greatness of our nation," he told the President. "I . . . hope the government will never yield it."[48]

The administration was thunderstruck, both by Jackson's egregiousness and by the international brouhaha it stirred up. The French minister joined Onís in furiously protesting this military assault on a friendly nation. The British Parliament was so angry, Castlereagh sternly told the American minister, that he could get a nearly unanimous vote for war "BY HOLDING UP A FINGER." Jackson's nominal superior, Secretary of War Calhoun, already smarting from several encounters with the general's temper and insubordination, now insisted that he be reprimanded and his actions disavowed—a stance that eventually proved fateful for Calhoun's career. Only Adams defended Jackson through the long Cabinet debates and contended for holding on to his conquest.

Monroe quickly decided that Florida had to be returned to Spain for the moment—the diplomatic and political risks of keeping it were too great. But Adams's strenuous arguments persuaded the President that there should be no disavowal of Jackson or apology to Spain. Instead the Secretary won Monroe's permission to tell Onís that Spain was to blame for not fulfilling an earlier treaty obligation to restrain the Florida Indians. Adams's truculent defense of Jackson's hammer blow paralyzed the Spanish will for further resistance. Fearful of losing Florida without getting anything in return, and dreading a further assault on Cuba by the American "Napoleon of the woods," Madrid instructed Onís to settle for the best terms he could get.

Now Adams raised the ante. The southwestern boundary, he informed Onís, would have to be extended from the Gulf of Mexico all the way to the Pacific, ceding to the United States the Oregon country north of California. Thus the weak American claim to the northwest coast would be reinforced against the stronger British claim by the Spanish claim, which was the strongest of all three on the traditional ground of prior European "discovery."

The Secretary warned Spain through the French minister that the President would ask Congress for authority to seize Florida if it were not ceded. "Spain," he declared in a widely circulated statement of the American position, "must immediately make her election, either to place a force in Florida adequate . . . to the fulfillment of her engagements, or cede to the United States a province, of which she retains nothing but the nominal possession, but which is, in fact, a derelict, open to the occupancy of every enemy, civilized or savage, of the United States, and serving no other earthly purpose than as a post of annoyance to them."

Under this ultimatum Onís finally signed in February 1819 what Adams proudly called his Transcontinental Treaty. In return for Florida, the United States would pay the claims of its citizens against Spain up to $5 million. The southwestern boundary with Spanish Texas and Mexico ran north from the Gulf up the Sabine River along the western border of present Louisiana to the Red River, then northwestward along the Red and Arkansas rivers and the Rocky Mountain crest to the 42nd parallel of north latitude in present southern Wyoming, and thence west along the present northern borders of Utah, Nevada, and California to the Pacific. Monroe had persuaded a reluctant Adams to retreat from the Colorado

River east to the Sabine as the boundary's starting point on the Gulf, and even Jackson, intent on Florida, approved this concession of the absurd American claim to Texas. "The acknowledgment of a definite line of boundary to the South Sea," Adams exulted, "forms a great epocha in our history." His biographer has justly called this "the greatest diplomatic victory won by any single individual in the history of the United States."

The Transcontinental Treaty aroused in Adams a grander territorial aspiration. When a Cabinet colleague expressed worry over the European impression that Americans were "an ambitious and encroaching people," Adams retorted that Europe would have to get used to "the idea of considering the continent of North America as our proper dominion." He thought it "a physical, moral, and political absurdity" for possessions of distant European monarchies "to exist permanently adjoining a great, powerful, enterprising, and rapidly growing nation." Assuming as "a settled geographical principle that the United States and North America are identical," he shaped his diplomacy around the abiding conviction that "the remainder of the continent should ultimately be ours." In addition he instructed the American minister to Spain that its colonies Cuba and Puerto Rico were "natural appendages to the North American continent" and that eventually "the annexation of Cuba to our federal republic will be indispensable."

The substantial British contribution to Adams's triumph over Spain did not deter him from coveting British territory. Lord Castlereagh had refused to support Spanish resistance to the American demands or to complain about Jackson's high-handed execution of two British citizens in Florida. When the Spanish delayed ratification of the Transcontinental Treaty almost two years, hoping to delay American recognition of their rebellious colonies, Castlereagh prodded them into ratifying.

But none of these considerations prevented an angry Adams outburst when the British minister in Washington had the temerity to inquire about a rumored American settlement on the Columbia. "There would be neither policy nor profit," sputtered the Secretary more candidly than wisely, "in cavilling with us about territory on this North American continent." Shocked, the minister asked if the United States had designs on Canada. "No," Adams retorted, realizing he had gone too far. ". . . Keep what is yours, but leave the rest of the Continent to us."[49]

Adams's Transcontinental Treaty, Calhoun's general-survey plan, and Marshall's judicial salvos brought National Republicanism to its apogee in early 1819. With American productivity soaring, with the world clamoring for American commodities, with American sails blossoming on every ocean, the entrepreneurial vision seemed well on its way to realization.

All this owed much to purposeful leaders acting through the organized power of the state. A Federalist/National-Republican jurisprudence intensified the acquisitive energy that drove the market's expansion by loading the dice in favor of entrepreneurs while protecting their enterprises and gains from democratic interference. Entrepreneurial Republicans elaborated transport, monetary, and corporate infrastructures in the states. National Republican diplomacy rounded out the southeastern domain for a continental republic and staked its unshakable claim on the Pacific. Within this continental theater, National Republican policies promised to stabilize money and credit, subsidize manufacturers, and—as soon as the constitutional obstacle was overcome—provide a perfect system of roads and canals.

Rarely has a generation of leaders so visibly done so much to shape the future they envisioned. And rarely has a presidential administration effected such a fundamental shift in national direction with so little apparent political difficulty, at least by the most obvious indicator. Only a single eccentric electoral vote was cast against Monroe's reelection in 1820.

The dramatic reversal of Republican tradition bewildered many. Republicans, President Madison explained, had become "reconciled to certain measures and arrangements which may be as proper now as they were premature or suspicious when urged by the champions of Federalism." Younger Republicans like Calhoun and Story, who never embraced the party's original antidevelopmentalism, did not need to justify themselves. And Philadelphia's gifted young Federalist, Nicholas Biddle, now found it safe to join the Republicans because they had finally "outgrown many of the childish notions with which they began their career twenty years since."

Inveterate Federalists were at a loss. "The Party now in Power seems disposed to do all that federal men ever wished," mused old Gouverneur Morris, "and will, I fear, do more than is good to strengthen and consolidate the federal government." A Federalist editor explained that his party's congressional rearguard often opposed this neo-Federalism to keep the Republicans "from carrying their measures to a length far beyond what was ever contemplated by the federal administration." Less wonder then that old-fashioned Republicans were alarmed. One who entered the House under Washington protested in the Fourteenth Congress that he had "no wild notions about conquests and national energy, and military glory, and all that mischievous trumpery that entered so much into the character of gentlemen's policy in these new days." Clay, Calhoun, and Lowndes, he complained, "were actually taking a somerset over the heads of the Federalists and running on far beyond them."[50] Such voices were drowned out. As party lines blurred, a common economic vision effected a rapprochement among most sectors of a flourishing market elite. To American influentials the postwar boom years were indeed an Era of Good Feelings. Around the policies of the Fourteenth Congress, the Monroe administration, and the Marshall Court, it seemed to them, a new national consensus had emerged.

Yet class euphoria blinded the National Republican gentry to a gathering crisis that was about to shatter their dreams. Monroe, the last Revolutionary worthy, instead of being elevated to the American pantheon for skillfully easing a grateful republic's turn toward its capitalist destiny, would retire from office a forgotten has-been. Jackson and Adams would compete two elections hence in the most scurrilous presidential campaign in American history. Calhoun would assume his commanding historical role as the great naysayer to the political economy that he, more than anyone, conceived and nurtured. And the rhetorical defense of the nationalist vision would pass to that hired gun of wealth and power, Webster.

Chapter 4

The Crisis of 1819

MONROE's first Congress was elected by a premonitory tremor of crisis and adjourned on March 4, 1819, to its full eruption. Voter anger at the Fourteenth Congress had sent so many new members bent on "retrenchment and reform" that "a new party" was rumored "about to be organized, within the very bosom of the republican party." The President found them "very querulous" about taxes, and Secretary Adams grew querulous about "a great mass of desire to be in opposition." Congress ignored the presidential recommendation for higher tariff protection, while the big New York delegation deserted federal internal improvements when their state had to go it alone on the Erie Canal.[1]

As this Congress wound down in early 1819, Old Republican revival was making Treasury Secretary William H. Crawford the frontrunner to succeed President Monroe in 1824. With Crawford's backers and Speaker Clay's whipping up reformist zeal against their potential rivals Secretary Adams and Secretary Calhoun, Congress scrutinized appropriations as in Jeffersonian days, and Cabinet Secretaries and their clerks worked overtime to supply the endless reports demanded by congressional investigating committees. The main target was Calhoun's expensive War Department, where investigators uncovered some costly and indefensible concessions to influential contractors.[2]

The antiadministration campaign peaked in an assault on General Jackson's shocking invasion of Spanish Florida. Both houses ordered formal investigations, and the irascible general, preternaturally sensitive about his honor, hastened from Tennessee to defend himself. For a month Washington belles filled the Capitol galleries as the longest and most publicized congressional debate in memory rumbled to a rhetorical climax in Clay's three-day philippic against military despotism.

The outcome was anticlimactic. Although the investigating committees spread before the public a full and seemingly damning record of the general's transgressions, a majority could not be found to censure him. The attack on Jackson provoked a portentous outpouring of popular enthusiasm for the hero of New

Orleans; and while Congress pondered his case, he was being engulfed by public acclaim on a triumphal tour of the eastern cities. Neither Clay nor Crawford realized, as they joined Jackson's hate list, what a formidable rival they had stirred up.[3]

While the country was still applauding Old Hickory, slaveholding Missouri's application for statehood suddenly arrayed free-state representatives overwhelmingly against any further extension of slave territory. The republic could no longer evade its great contradiction. A fire had been kindled, warned a prophetic Georgian, that "seas of blood can only extinguish."[4] Two days after Congress broke up in angry deadlock, Chief Justice Marshall's constitutional revolution culminated in *McCulloch*. Americans barely had time to absorb the disturbing news brought by homecoming congressmen when they were engulfed by economic disaster.

In the crisis of 1819, the market's explosive growth forced its multiple contradictions—economic, political, constitutional, and moral—simultaneously to a head. Staggered by boom/bust catastrophe, resurgent Old Republicanism, and the wrenching dilemma of slavery, National Republicans were slow to recognize the threat of democratic insurgency. Jackson's popularity was dismissed as military infatuation, just as electoral repudiation of the Fourteenth Congress had been dismissed as a minor contretemps over congressional salaries.

Ever since the first Congress, senators and representatives had been paid six dollars per day of attendance, averaging some nine hundred dollars per annual session, plus mileage to and from Washington. But inflation so eroded this once handsome sum that government clerks now got more. Under the per diem system, critics charged, sessions were prolonged to stretch members' pay. Accordingly, in the spring of 1816, the Fourteenth Congress passed a Salary Act approximately doubling congressional pay, at the flat rate of fifteen hundred dollars a year.

Instantly a volcano of public indignation erupted, the greatest ever known according to many observers. Protest meetings resolved, legislatures instructed, citizens petitioned, grand juries indicted, and newspapers clamored. Georgians burned their representatives in effigy; and everywhere on the Fourth of July the Salary Act was "toasted till it was black." Protest caught up "many who had seldom if ever been seen before on the political theatre," and "inspired those with eloquence who never spake before." Congress was betraying "the simple habits of republicanism" in order to grasp "the emoluments of power," complained a North Carolina meeting; and Americans would be left, warned a Pennsylvania meeting, to "sigh over the extinguished embers of republican simplicity and republican manners."

Public wrath, searing nine congressmen into immediate resignation, slaughtered incumbents as never before in the elections of late 1816. At least half (twenty from New York alone) prudently declined to stand for reelection. Leading Old Federalist Timothy Pickering retired rather than even consider whether the Salary Act "would be popular or unpopular." Leading young Federalist Daniel Webster withdrew carping at "the lowest democracy" that had no respect for talents, services, character, or *feelings.*" A Georgia congressman declined "to course through the country in pursuit of votes; to fawn and creep, and wriggle into favor, and to insure temporary caresses by deserving permanent contempt."

John Randolph, whose gentleman's proviso excluding the enacting Congress did not reconcile constituents to his vote for a gentleman's salary, pleaded ill health. He was amazed that the people—this "great Leviathan, which slept under" a foolish war, a swollen national debt, and a presidential election preempted by caucus—"should be roused into action by the Fifteen Hundred Dollar Law."

Incumbents who dared stand for reelection went down in droves. Two-thirds of the House and half the Senate were replaced, and not one old member came back from Ohio, Delaware, and Vermont. Only fifteen of the Salary Act's eighty-one supporters survived. In Kentucky, where every office-seeker from constable to Congress had to denounce salaries, Clay saved himself only by a stumping tour to apologize to his constituents. Baltimore's usually invincible war hero General Smith had to promise repeal; and Calhoun was challenged by three opponents. Even some who voted against the obnoxious legislation were punished for accepting (or not returning) corrupt salaries. "I have been dismissed for voting for the bill," complained a New Jersey congressman; "one of my colleagues for voting against it, and another one for not voting at all on either side."[5]

The Salary Act roused the Leviathan by translating into vivid terms of personal extravagance and corruption the menace of a whole line of policy inflicting heavy taxes. Abandoning Republican parsimony to resurrect an activist national state far surpassing the Hamiltonian model, the Fourteenth Congress trebled peacetime spending and saddled people indefinitely with odious Federalist taxes that Republicans had dared impose only in dire emergency. The Salary Act provided familiar personal targets for rural anger over congressional extravagance and onerous taxation.

To rural folk invoking "the simple habits of republicanism," the Salary Act was another tentacle of an alien market world that threatened them through taxes, money, credit, banks, and courts. Farmers' twin nemeses, taxes and debts, as a western Virginia congressman explained, enabled the "few who have money and are inclined to speculate on the distresses of the country to monopolize the property of their fellow citizens, and constitute them '*hewers of wood and drawers of water.*'" Tax sales and mortgage foreclosures of farms threatened livelihood, familial culture, and patriarchal independence and honor.[6]

Congressional salaries—"emoluments of power" requiring menacing taxes— were especially irritating because the security of a guaranteed income was available outside government to only a handful of Americans. Farm folk might not see fifteen hundred dollars in a lifetime. In the Revolutionary tradition, "salary" still reeked of official sinecure and British corruption.

Thus the congressional election of 1816 revealed a gulf between the country's market-oriented leadership and small-farming majority. If interior farmers could see only greed and corruption in congressmen contending with inflation and expensive living at Washington, the National Republicans saw civic malingering in opponents of taxes that were payable with moderate sacrifice by most people living in the market economy. Lulled by the exhilarating consensus among elites, the country's impatient young leaders did not recognize the cultural chasm yawning between them and their constituents.

When the lame-duck Fourteenth Congress reconvened in the wake of the electoral revolt of 1816, it hastened to repeal the obnoxious act. But National Republicans misread the electoral rebuke as involving congressional salaries alone and did not let it shake their belief that they knew what was best for the people. Most myopic was Calhoun, who urged Congress to defy the voters' verdict. Reelected handily while advocating an even higher salary of twenty-five hundred dollars, he stoutly though vainly opposed repeal. Americans were "greatly distinguished" by a "love of gain" that was "founded on the Purest virtue," he argued, and the ablest would not serve in Congress "unless duly rewarded." But he found the congressional ear "sealed against truth and reason" by the clamor of public opinion. "Well, then, has it come to this?" he demanded. "Have the people of this country snatched the power of deliberation from this body?" Scorning "the mere trimmer, the political weathercock," Calhoun insisted that just because "the law is unpopular" was no reason for members to repeal it "in opposition to their conscience and reason."

Repeal passed handily because most congressmen felt compelled by the voters to affirm, like the Salary Act's author, Richard M. Johnson of Kentucky, "*vox populi vox Dei.*" Even if the people were "carried away by a momentary impulse," said this popular war hero, "... the presumption is, that the people are always right." Yet they were able to dismiss this remarkable ebullition of democratic insurgency as "a momentary impulse," appeased by repeal, while blithely assuming public acquiescence in the vastly more expensive developmental program to which they had committed a tax-weary citizenry. Political business resumed as usual, and this signally repudiated Congress went on to the massive further commitment for a national transportation system entailed by Calhoun's Bonus Bill.[7]

But Thomas Jefferson was not so sure the electoral revolt was over. He was alarmed by a Republican Congress "at a loss for objects whereon to throw away the supposed fathomless funds of the treasury." Soon he would conclude that these younger National Republicans have "nothing in them of the feelings or principles of '76." They wanted a "single and splendid government of an aristocracy, founded on banking institutions, and moneyed incorporations," he complained, through which the few would soon be "riding and ruling over the plundered ploughman and beggared yeomanry." Therefore he was immensely heartened by the uprising against the Fourteenth Congress. It demonstrated, he rejoiced, "the innate good sense, the vigilance, and the determination of the people to act for themselves."[8]

Democracy still had a long way to go. Majority rule, even for white males, was just becoming theoretically possible. The constitutional barriers insisted on by Revolutionary elites had first come under attack in the states as the commercial boom energized the democratic impulse that carried the Republicans to power. Where the gentry were less entrenched institutionally and farmers predominated, elite factions competed for popular support by conceding piecemeal reforms. Gradually, in twelve of the eighteen states, this process opened the polls to nearly all adult white males, in half through a modest taxpaying requirement. Written ballots freed voters from intimidation in all but five states, and convenient local polling places were provided in all but three. Several states abolished and several others reduced property requirements for officeholders. The formerly appointive municipal governments in New York and Philadelphia were made elective; and the choice of local officials was given to the voters in a number of states.

By 1815 this process had produced relatively democratic constitutional structures—for white males—in half the states: New Hampshire, Vermont, and Massachusetts in northern New England; the mid-Atlantic states New Jersey, Pennsylvania, and Delaware; and the newer western states except Louisiana. The presence of slavery inhibited democracy even for whites. Among the old south Atlantic slave states, only Georgia approached the degree of white male democracy in the more advanced free states, while west of the Appalachians slaveholding Kentucky and Tennessee were somewhat less amenable to democratic influences than free Ohio. But in the remaining half of the states, where elites were most strongly entrenched behind institutional barricades, the democratic impulse met fierce resistance. A third of the states continued to disfranchise large numbers of white males through property and taxpaying requirements, perhaps 60 percent in Louisiana (80 percent in New Orleans), 50 percent in Rhode Island and Virginia, and a lesser proportion in Connecticut. New York's property qualifications excluded three-fourths of the adult males from voting for governor and state senators and a third for assemblymen and congressmen, while North Carolina barred half from voting for state senators.

Even a broad suffrage did not make popular control possible. In South Carolina and Maryland, planter elites had conciliated democratic sentiment by opening the polls to all white males while neutralizing popular voting power through other means. South Carolina allowed its democratic electorate to choose as legislators only wealthy men owning five hundred acres or £1,000 in personal property, while Maryland fortified wealth in a state senate chosen by an electoral college.

In all the south Atlantic states the older, smaller, planter-dominated counties along the coast were grossly overrepresented in comparison with the more populous small-farmer counties of the interior. Jefferson calculated that a voter in Virginia's little tidewater county of Warwick had twenty-two times the political weight of a voter in populous interior Loudoun. The 53 voters in South Carolina's tiniest lowcountry parish elected one state senator, as did the 3,749 voters in the most populous upcountry district. Seven of Maryland's old tobacco counties, containing fewer people than Baltimore, had sixteen times the city's legislative representation. Through similar means the French Creole sugar parishes in southwestern Louisiana ruled increasingly Anglo-American New Orleans and northwest Louisiana, and Rhode Island's static agricultural towns maintained their sway over the swelling populations of Providence and the textile-manufacturing Blackstone valley.

Popular influence was weakest where elite control at the local level was mutually reinforcing with elite control at the state level. Local officials were mainly appointed by state authorities in Rhode Island, New York, Maryland, and South Carolina; and New York's Council of Appointment regularly replaced thousands of local officials with every change of state administration. In Virginia and North Carolina, and in diluted form in their offshoots Tennessee and Kentucky, all-powerful county courts were made up of justices of the peace appointed for life and filling vacancies in their own ranks. In all these states, local officeholding oligarchies controlled the election of legislators, who in turn controlled the appointments that maintained the local oligarchies in office.[9]

Thus at the return of peace more than half the American people lived in states—the two most populous, New York and Virginia, being among the most restrictive—where democracy (even for white males) was not yet institutionally possible. Federal politics could be no more democratic than the politics of the states. States decided who could vote for congressmen, and congressional elections could be no more democratic than state elections. State legislatures chose federal senators, and half reserved the choice of presidential electors to themselves.

As the postwar boom again accelerated the disruption of traditional communities and ways of living, pressure again mounted for democratic controls over a political economy that was getting out of hand. Hard on the heels of the electoral revolt against the Fourteenth Congress, Connecticut voters in 1817 toppled the last bastion of Federalist oligarchy and went on to adopt a new state constitution giving the vote to virtually all adult white males. Between 1816 and 1820 six new states entered the union—Indiana, Mississippi, Illinois, Alabama, Missouri, and Maine—with constitutions that were ultrademocratic by prevailing standards. Significantly most of these new constitutions placed special restrictions on banking. More important, in the great state of New York the democratic impulse was finding an organizational form for breaching elitist barricades.

Nowhere had market relationships evolved more fully than in New York. Only Pennsylvania rivaled the Empire State in diversity of topographies and settlement patterns, of ethnicities and faiths, of classes and conditions, of occupations and economic interests—of all the elements that influence political attitudes and figure in political coalition-building. Nowhere had the market's explosive expansion made people so conscious of the linkage between public policy and economic consequences. Nowhere had economic consequences undermined traditional cultural norms more ruthlessly or made life more competitive and uncertain. And nowhere, therefore, had the democratic impulse developed faster or found such precocious organizational form.

New York's elitist constitution perpetuated the colonial politics of competition between shifting coalitions of baronial family factions, each using the Council of Appointment in victory to reward its supporting army of officeholders and would-be officeholders. But the Byzantine complexity of these fluid alignments among patrician leaders should not obscure the underlying stability of the antagonistic social forces from which they derived their electoral support and policies. The driving force in New York politics was the determination of commercial elites centering in New York City to wield state power in the service of their entrepreneurial interests and visions. Their zeal and resources always shaped one of the rival coalitions to their purposes. Invariably the competing coalition relied on the even stronger counterforce of antielitism, appealing to interior farmers threatened by the market, to democratic-minded urban workers, and to smaller enterprisers and would-be enterprisers. So strong was the democratic impulse in the New York electorate that each succeeding elitist/entrepreneurial coalition was defeated and driven from contention by its more popular rival.

Hamilton led the Federalist coalition of Schuylers (his in-laws), Jays, and Morrises, while the rival Republican coalition of Clintons and Livingstons, with Burr in tow, followed the popular perennial governor George Clinton. The Republicans drove the Federalists into a small minority after 1800 by branding them as aristocrats. Again wielding the issue of democracy, the Old Clintonians (as these original Republicans might be called to distinguish them from a later brand of Clintonians) dispersed a new coalition between Federalists and entrepreneurial Republicans. The "honied and cordial" manners of the Old Clintonian "Farmer's Boy," Daniel D. Tompkins, won him four consecutive gubernatorial elections before he retired bibulously to the Monrovian Vice Presidency. Astonishing turnouts of 88 to 95 percent attest the eligible voters' deep engagement in these ceremonial reaffirmations of democracy.[10]

Again exiled from power, New York's elitist/entrepreneurial interests found their next political champion in Governor Clinton's nephew and heir apparent. City-bred and Columbia-educated, the imposing and ambitious De Witt Clinton was appointed mayor by the Clintonian Council of Appointment. Hobnobbing with the Federalist gentry, he cultivated their graces and causes, from literature to science to abolition, and made himself during the commerical boom the prophet of New York's flamboyantly envisaged commercial destiny. Meanwhile he nurtured with Old Federalist Gouverneur Morris the dream of an Erie Canal that would presently make the reality as flamboyant as the vision.

As the younger Clinton gradually took over Republican leadership from his aging uncle, he blurred party distinctions by frequently supporting Federalist measures and appointees. With an ambition as extravagant as his conceptions, this "Magnus Apollo" offered his patrician leadership to entrepreneurial Republicans and to the Northeast's predominantly Federalist commercial elite as well. Federalist magnates, representing the country's wealth and economic destiny, regarded themselves as its rightful leaders and deeply resented their exclusion from national power, even before they were further embittered by the Embargo and enraged by the war. Repeatedly Federalists had attempted to enlist dissident New York Republicans in a New York–New England alliance that could throw off the yoke of "Virginia rule." Should that fail, some were ready for the commercial Northeast to secede.

De Witt Clinton began to see that a New York–New England alliance of the country's weightiest interests could make him President. When the Embargo inflamed the commercial gentry, he associated himself with their attacks on Republican foreign policy. Deploring party distinctions, he ran for President against Madison in 1812 as virtually the Federalist candidate. He further affronted Republican sensibilities by supporting a notorious bank charter obtained by Federalists through legislative bribery.

A more tactful leader might have managed in traditional patrician style to carry his followers in whatever direction served his personal ambitions. But Clinton's "cold repulsive manner" worried even his friends, and one bluntly warned him that "you have not the jovial, social, Democratical-Republican-how-do-you-do Suavity." The city Democrats (as urban Republicans called themselves) were the first to revolt. Aroused in defense of Jefferson's Embargo, patriotic and anti-Federalist mechanics—some shielded by the Embargo from foreign competition with their products—backed anti-Clintonians in taking over the city Republican organization. Thereafter Tammany Hall, the party headquarters maintained by the closely allied Society of St. Tammany, was a bastion of anti-Clintonian loyalty to the Republican cause nationally.[11]

The revolt spread upstate as Clinton's autocratic political management alienated the growing cadres of ambitious activists who sought elective and appointive office through the governing party of the country's wealthiest state. Skilled in disciplined factional politics but motivated more by career ambitions than by the traditional loyalty to a family or a leader, these younger party workers chafed increasingly under Clinton's arbitrariness, particularly in appointment matters. The wartime resurgence of Federalism intensified their ideological Republicanism while making Clinton's tolerance for Federalists more suspect. Following the war these Bucktails—so called after the ceremonial adornments worn by their Tammany allies in the city—boldly challenged Clinton's leadership.

The Bucktails found a new kind of leader in auburn-haired, meticulous little Martin Van Buren. Sprung from six generations of Dutch Calvinist farmers in the Hudson valley and handicapped by lack of a genteel education, Van Buren made himself a successful country lawyer by defending tenants and small landowners against the inflated land claims of the valley's manor lords. Affronted by the hauteur of the local Federalist establishment, he embraced Old Clintonian Republicanism not only for the career it offered but also out of commitment to the equality and free opportunity it symbolized. Avoiding the limelight, unflappably amiable to friend and foe, marshaling allies through tactful persuasion, the "Red Fox of Kinderhook" recruited a formidable force to purge the perfidious De Witt and restore New York Republicanism to its Old Clintonian purity.

The modern form of American party politics was born when the Bucktails challenged on democratic grounds the whole system of family and personal factions that Clinton epitomized. A political party, they argued, should be an internally democratic association run by its members and responsible to its constituency. Their "cardinal maxim" was "always to seek for, and when ascertained, always to follow the will of the majority." Only through such a party, experience had taught them, could the majority unite to prevail against elites. According to Van Buren, the Republican party represented "the democratical spirit" that sought to "resist the encroachments and limit the extent of executive authority."[12]

This democratic rationale the Bucktails exploited with a new level of political organization, skill, and professional élan. Far from rejecting the political discipline they had learned in the Clintonian school, they celebrated the technically proficient political party. Like middle managers in an old-fashioned family firm, they scorned the bungling and inconsistent leadership of showy patricians like Clinton, preferring careful technicians of party consensus and loyal servants of party interests like Van Buren. Once a decision was democratically reached in party caucus, the Bucktails denounced breaking ranks as the blackest political sin. "Tell them they are safe if they face the enemy," was the message Silas Wright, Jr., sent to his Bucktail allies in one crisis, "but that the first man we see *step to the rear*, we *cut down*."[13]

The Bucktails got most of their votes from the most democratic and least business-oriented New Yorkers—Tammany's working-class following in the city, the Yankee farmers swarming into northern and western New York, and small farmers, shopkeepers, and mechanics in the old Dutch counties along the middle Hudson, where landlord-tenant conflict kept class awareness keen. But in a capitalist democracy, as New York politics was precociously demonstrating, votes do not equate with effective political force. The realistic Bucktails quickly learned that a coalition broad enough to gain power must accommodate to the superior resources and political involvement of business interests.

Consequently Van Buren and his friends displayed considerable ambivalence toward the powerful forces of market expansion. They reflected the bias of their voting majority by ending the state policy of exempting manufacturers from taxation and their workers from militia duty or jury service. They at first opposed the Erie Canal. But after Clinton came back from his first defeat by brilliantly marshaling around his grand project all the latent entrepreneurial energies in the state, the Bucktails were persuaded by the pragmatic Van Buren that they had to support it. Although Van Buren consistently opposed bank charters as a legislator (save one to help Buffalo recover from a disaster), his associates were siding with upstate banks against the big banks in New York City. Their Tammany wing was led by rising entrepreneurs, and en route to power the Van Burenites even cooperated with Rufus King's faction of "high-minded" anti-Clintonian Federalists, who had patriotically supported the war effort.

The Bucktails brought Clinton down at the height of his comeback by persuading a troubled electorate that majority rule depended on absolute loyalty to "regular nominations" in democratically conducted party caucuses. They became invincible when Clinton flouted democracy not only by defying Republican caucus decisions favorable to the Bucktails, but also by resisting their demands for a constitutional convention to democratize the state's politics. They were "identified with the people," as genteel Clintonians sneeringly conceded, because they had "neither property, talent, character or any other thing to set them up as objects of suspicion." By 1820 a democratic electorate had entrenched Van Buren and his friends so firmly in the state capital that they were beginning to be called the Albany Regency.[14]

The victorious Regency's first priority was to call a constitutional convention in 1821. There an overwhelming Bucktail majority laid an axe to the main institutional props of aristocracy. Led by Van Buren, they abolished the hated Council of Revision, through which Chancellor Kent and the other lifetime Federalist judges of the state's highest courts exercised a veto over the elected legislature. They abolished the increasingly unpopular Council of Appointment, whose fifteen thousand placemen sustained Clintonian autocracy, and transferred choice of most local officials to the voters. And they forbade future bank charters except by a two-thirds vote of the legislature.

Characteristically, however, Van Buren devoted his energies in the convention mainly to retaining party appointment of the several thousand sheriffs and justices of the peace who were the backbone of the Bucktails' local cadres. By dint of party discipline, he carried a complicated plan that maintained Regency control over the justices, but he had to yield local election of sheriffs.

Van Buren met resistance from a vociferously democratic wing of the Bucktails. The convention was elected without the usual property qualifications for voters, and the ultrademocratic northern and western sections, ablaze with the New Light of antinomian revival, sent more farmers than lawyers as delegates. The ultrademocrats opposed Van Buren's efforts to consolidate the Bucktail victory by leading his heterogeneous coalition back toward the political center. Above all they demanded universal white male suffrage.

Ultrademocrats evoked hysterical reactions from the minority of crusty elitists led by Chancellor Kent. This was the last generation of American gentlemen who could publicly avow their horror at the "evil genius of democracy." The Chancellor expressed their shock that "this great moral pestilence" had so suddenly infected the country and was "now running a triumphant career from Maine to Louisiana." Ten years ago, he marveled, the broadened suffrage the convention was considering "would have struck the public mind with astonishment and terror." For elitists like Kent democracy meant "inflammatory appeals to the worst passions of the worst men in society," producing "fierce and vindictive majorities" through which the poor would plunder the rich. Within a century, the Chancellor predicted, rapidly growing New York City's "motley" populace would "govern this state." Warning that a broadened suffrage "never can be recalled or checked, but by the strength of the bayonet," he implored the convention to pause "on the brink of fate, on the very edge of the precipice," and reserve at least the senate to those who owned enough property to make them "free and independent lords of the soil."

The convention's big Bucktail majority rejected Kent's proposal; but the consternation of his wealthy and powerful class warned Van Buren to stop short of universal suffrage. Intent on holding his coalition together, he insisted that "we are hazarding everything by going to such lengths." The convention only approximated universal white male suffrage by extending the vote to all who paid a tax, served in the militia, or worked on the roads.[15]

Bucktails of all stripes represented popular white racism and had no trouble agreeing that blacks (who voted Clintonian/Federalist) should be virtually disfranchised. "We feel an insurmountable repugnance to mix and associate with them as equals," the Regency newspaper declared.[16] Over conservative opposition, the convention barred blacks from the polls unless they paid taxes on $250 worth of property.

So irresistible was the demand for white male democracy in New York that within four years the ultrademocrats would win the main points they lost in the convention. Through a further constitutional amendment the Regency yielded justices of the peace to popular election and removed the mainly cosmetic restrictions on universal white male suffrage. With New York refashioned to their notion of democracy, the Bucktails' next priority was to bid for national power by reviving the Jeffersonian (and Old Clintonian) alliance between New York and Virginia. Once again, they hoped, the Old Republicanism of southern planters might unite with the resurgent democracy of northern "plain republicans" to contain the aggressive forces of market expansion.

Virginia, too, felt the postwar resurgence of the democratic impulse. While voters everywhere were turning out incumbent congressmen in the summer of 1816, delegates from thirty-five western Virginia counties convened at Staunton demanding a convention to democratize the Old Dominion's constitution. The wheat boom had infected western Virginia's village notables and political leaders with market ambitions, but the legislature repeatedly rebuffed their pleas for the banks and transportation improvements required to realize them.[17] Angered by the unfair apportionment that allowed an eastern planter minority to dominate the legislature and frustrate their hopes, western gentlemen organized the constitutional-reform movement to change the apportionment. They were especially indignant that only four of the twenty-four state senators came from west of the Blue Ridge, where nearly half the free population resided.

Suddenly in 1816 broad popular support developed for the constitutional-reform movement, and with it came a more radically democratic emphasis. Opponents of Virginia's highly restricted suffrage took over the Staunton meeting, voting down by a large majority the organizers' effort to restrict reform to the apportionment of representation. Although the original organizers were demanding reapportionment on democratic grounds, they were as fearful as Chancellor Kent of the actual democracy threatened by a broader suffrage. If "the idle and vicious & worthless" were allowed to vote, one of these conservative reformers predicted, candidates of property and talents would be rejected, and "the rights then of those who own the country will be invaded by those who have no part of it." Accordingly they warned the state political leadership "with Horror" that if the senate were not reformed, the movement for a broader suffrage would be unstoppable. "The public feeling on this subject has become too strong to be resisted," their spokesman insisted; "the people appear determined that the minority in the state shall not continue to hold the reins of government."[18]

Ex-President Jefferson, by contrast, enthusiastically welcomed the reform movement and encouraged its most democratic demands. Unconstrained now by the responsibilities and compromises of party and national leadership, he again gave free rein to his vision of a democratic republic, and again he found it imperiled. The developmental capitalist state he had thwarted in 1800 was rising from the ashes of Federalism in the Fourteenth Congress. In facing this new menace, as when facing the earlier Hamiltonian menace, the ex-President relied upon the democratic impulse among farmers and mechanics, the "determination of the people to act for themselves." Consequently he threw his formidable influence behind radical democratic reform in Virginia.

Experience was imparting a toughened democratic realism to Jefferson's conception of republicanism. The prewar and postwar booms had stimulated entrepreneurial energies too strong for the democratic energies he counted on to control them. Now he began to measure republicanism itself by a realistic democratic standard: "the control of the people over the organs of their government." A government was truly republican, he now insisted, only if "every member" had "his equal voice in directing its concerns" through "representatives chosen by himself, and responsible to him at short periods." And by this standard of democracy (for white males), he maintained, "our governments have much less of republicanism than ought to have been expected." In a letter designed for publication, the ex-President—who otherwise avoided pronouncing on public issues—called on Virginia to "let every man who pays taxes or serves in the militia" vote for governor, legislature, and judges "at short intervals."

Yet Jefferson had come to realize that a broad suffrage and frequent elections were not enough to ensure democracy. Through most of his career he had assumed that gentlemen would lead, and his commitment to democracy merely trusted the voters to choose the best gentlemen. Now he had come to understand how democracy was frustrated in Virginia by "the vicious constitution of our county courts" and by genteel politicians who professed Republicanism but served elite interests. Now the objective "nearest my heart," he said, was to encourage a vital democratic political life in every neighborhood of the Virginia countryside. Inspired by the New England town, he proposed to divide each county into self-governing wards, "pure and elementary republics," each electing a justice and a constable and each having charge of its own militia company, school, poor relief, public roads, jury selection, and all voting. By thus "constituting the people, in their wards, a regularly organized power," he thought, they would be enabled "to crush, regularly and peaceably, the usurpations of their unfaithful agents."[19]

For generations the self-perpetuating county-court squirearchy had ruled Virginia through its legislature. Some two-thirds of the legislators were justices of the peace or people with the same surnames as justices in their counties. The legislature was ruled, in turn, by an inner elite of senior members who perpetuated themselves by co-opting the ablest, best connected, and most congenial of the younger legislators.[20] The young Jefferson found this political system impervious to democratic reform; and he and Madison made Virginia Republican by rising to the top of this oligarchic structure through the conventional means of talents and connections. When they moved on to national leadership, they left Virginia politics in the hands of this traditional ruling group, now calling itself Republican and headed by Jefferson's patrician friend Wilson Cary Nicholas.

A "central committee," organized to ensure Virginia's entire electoral vote for Republican presidential candidates, developed into an informal "Richmond Junto" of leaders living near the capital who dominated party and legislative policy. Nicholas shared leadership with a group of newer recruits headed by Spencer Roane, an attorney from the languishing tidewater tobacco county of Essex. "Distinguished for intellectual vigor, profound legal knowledge, strong passions, and morose manners," Roane might have been Chief Justice in John Marshall's place if the vacancy had been delayed a few months until Jefferson became President. Instead Judge Roane gave leadership to Virginia's highest court, the Court of Appeals, where he maintained the old-fashioned doctrine that corporations should only be chartered "in consideration of services to be rendered to the public" and never "if their object is merely *private* or selfish."[21]

Meanwhile the judge was filling the Junto with his relatives and friends from Essex. One of these, his cousin Thomas Ritchie, established at Richmond in 1804 a newspaper that for forty years would mold Virginia political opinion—"the Enquirer and the Enquirer only is taken everywhere & almost in every cabin in the State," complained an opponent—while circulating far beyond the Old Dominion as the voice of Republican orthodoxy.[22]

The Junto was not altogether immune to the allure of enterprise. In response to developmental pressures generated by the wheat boom, the Junto-led legislature introduced banks to Virginia, but in a special Virginia fashion. Banking was confined to two carefully regulated institutions and their branches. To prevent them from falling under the control of would-be borrowers, they were partly owned by the state and cautiously managed by trusted Junto men. Dr. John Brockenbrough, an Essex cousin of both Roane and Ritchie, presided for years over the Bank of Virginia, while an unsatisfactory president of the Farmers' Bank was forced out and replaced by Nicholas's younger brother. When the second national Bank was chartered, Nicholas kept things in the family by himself obtaining the presidency of its Richmond branch.

Controlling the politics, credit, and currency of the state, the Junto managed its banks with a notable aversion to speculative excess, strenuously resisting any increase in banks or banking capital. Dr. Brockenbrough would eventually shock the enterprise-minded with his radical deflationary proposal for an "Independent Treasury," through which the federal government would boycott banks and bank notes in managing its finances.[23] The Junto also acceded cautiously to market pressures by supporting a modest state fund to assist transportation projects; and on the eve of the Fourteenth Congress, Nicholas had no objection to federal internal improvements. Above all, the Junto men labored to keep their party united, so that Virginia's decisive block of electoral votes could be delivered intact to the Republican presidential candidate every four years; and this caused them increasingly to value party loyalty and party regularity.

The first threat to the Junto's strategy arose from strident Republican purists who criticized the party's accommodations to the commercial spirit, both nationally and in Virginia. When John Randolph of Roanoke led Virginia purists into the "Tertium Quid" revolt against the Jefferson/Madison leadership, the Junto capitalized on his tactlessness and ineptitude to drive him temporarily from Congress; and they easily brushed aside Monroe's challenge to Madison in 1808.

Democracy gave the Virginia gentry more difficulty. With the economic foundation of their traditional hegemony crumbling beneath them—Nicholas would die bankrupt, and Ritchie would eventually be reduced to teaching school for a living—they were increasingly assailed by the pressures from below that other American elites encountered earlier. When a Baptist preacher got elected to the legislature from Jefferson's county by calling himself "the poor man's candidate" and proclaiming a "difference of interest between the poor and the rich," Jefferson's son-in-law had to head off a move by the local gentry to bar him from his seat. "I have seen enough of the temper of the people in this election," Thomas Mann Randolph warned, to think it would be "inflamed into downright hatred" by any effort to exclude the popular preacher.

The more old-fashioned Virginia gentlemen who inclined to purist views refused even symbolic assent to this rising democratic impulse. Boasting in the Fourteenth Congress of his "contempt for grovelling, for all that is mean, popular, and eleemosynary," John Randolph of Roanoke declared that "I have never flattered the people, and so help me God I never will." His friend John Taylor of Caroline, the purists' intellectual leader, refused to run for Congress, exclaiming that he would not engage in the necessary courtship of the voters "for a seat in heaven."

But the Junto men were more practical. Knowing that their awesome power rested ultimately on popular consent, they cultivated the voters assiduously and were attentive to their views. When Dr. Brockenbrough's brother Judge William Brockenbrough was first elected to the legislature from Essex, he had to spend two months traversing every part of the tiny county, becoming acquainted "with almost the whole of the people" and "observing the state of their manners, and sentiments." Spurning the common practice of treating the voters with whiskey, Brockenbrough thought he had been elected by the "neighborhood influence" of the "extremely independent, and intelligent." Others required courting, he admitted, while still others were suspicious of him as a lawyer, "taking it for granted that a lawyer was interested in multiplying the laws and making them more complex."[24]

In 1816 the Junto's sensitivity to popular mood led Ritchie's *Enquirer* to endorse the democratic reforms demanded by the West. But on this question, and this question alone, Virginia's ruling class was not yet ready to heed the authoritative voice of the Richmond Junto. The lawmakers would agree only to increase the West's share of the senate, extorting in return a law shifting more of the tax burden to the West. No wonder, then, that Jefferson took consolation in the voters' revolt against the Fourteenth Congress. "I am not among those who fear the people," he wrote. "They, and not the rich, are our dependence for continued freedom."[25]

The postwar boom threw the Virginia gentry on the defensive. While most of the country hummed with enterprise, the old tobacco kingdom languished. In 1816, as exploding market energy again imperiled the planter/yeoman republic, as the Fourteenth Congress threatened local autonomy with national power, the Supreme Court's Fairfax lands decision threw down the nationalist gauntlet at the feet of Spencer Roane's Court of Appeals.

The Old Dominion's congressional delegation led a stiffening opposition to National Republican measures. Senator Philip P. Barbour, who voted for the Tariff of 1816, opposed all subsequent tariffs on the ground that manufacturing divided society into classes and concentrated wealth in the hands of a few. There was something dishonest, he said, about the way manufacturers borrowed "fictitious" capital to build factories and hired others to do the work while they sat in their offices counting their paper profits. Virginians led the opposition that defeated a federal bankruptcy law in 1818 and again in 1821, on the ground, as one of them told his constituents, that it would "encourage that gambling commerce, which, if it enriches a few, makes many poor."[26]

Such rhetoric announced revival of the anticapitalist Republicanism kept alive by John Randolph of Roanoke, John Taylor of Caroline, and North Carolina's Nathanial Macon. Social anomaly fueled the purists' political fervor. They were the most intensely ideological leaders of a decaying aristocracy caught between Revolutionary liberalism and the slaves who sustained their increasingly threadbare gentility. Troubled by slavery, which they could neither justify, abandon, nor publicly discuss, they displaced a compulsive moralism onto the rest of politics. Nervousness about the democratic farmers and small planters on whom they had to rely sharpened their polemic against the common capitalist foe.

Randolph was the most brilliant anachronism of his anachronistic class. Isolated early by family deaths and demasculinized by illness, he asserted himself through aristocratic hauteur, wide learning, ideological rectitude, and the most cutting invective of his generation. Henry Clay "shines and stinks," shrilled this verbal bully on one occasion, "he stinks and he shines, like a dead mackerel in the moonlight." Carried by his gifts to leadership of the House of Representatives under Jefferson, he quickly rebelled in outrage against the President's pragmatic accommodations. His eccentricity frustrated efforts at organized opposition, but admiring constituents kept him almost continuously in the House to maintain a slashing critique of all deviations from purist Republicanism.

Nathaniel Macon typified a less aristocratic purism. In Congress since 1791, he had, after Randolph's desertion, managed the House for Jefferson as Speaker. The tobacco depression attuned this master of many slaves to the subsistence orientation of his farmer constituents. He wore homespun in protest against protective tariffs, lived in a tiny two-room house on his Buck Spring plantation, and worked in the fields with his slaves. His "poor and stony" soil, he said, would "not raise much for sale, & buy less," but what it did produce "is honestly made, enough to have full bellies and warm clothes for any time of the year."[27]

Demanding of government the Baptist asceticism he practiced personally, the Speaker was notorious for always voting against claims and new appropriations. John Quincy Adams thought him "a man of small parts and mean education"— Macon was a College of New Jersey graduate—"but of rigid integrity." Marveling at the electoral longevity of this "political Walter Shandy," Adams sadly acknowledged that "nothing takes with the people like this stubborn opposition to expense."[28]

The North Carolina that kept Macon in Congress for thirty-seven years was immunized against enterprise by a shoaling coastline that limited access to the market. Populated overwhelmingly by landlocked subsistence farmers and led politically by a class of unambitious small to middling planters in the fertile river valleys of its middle eastern section, the Old North State was coming to be known as the Rip Van Winkle of the republic.

This environment sustained Macon's deep distrust of paper money and credit. He regarded banks as "gaming shops" and thought that "every kind of negotiable paper adds to the evil." Credit, he complained, enabled cunning "projectors," as he called entrepreneurs, "to live on the labor of others." He was appalled by the grand projects of the National Republicans and expressed contempt for Calhoun's "fashionable & favorite expression to conquer Space" through internal improvements. Warning a young colleague against being "led astray" by "love of improvements or a thirst for glory ... grand notions or magnificent opinions," Macon reminded him that "you belong to a meek state and just people, who want nothing but to enjoy the fruits of their labor honestly and to lay out their profits in their own way."[29]

Although Macon's voice was drowned out in the Fourteenth Congress, similar reactions were rising wherever the booming market invaded traditional countrysides. In the electoral revolt of 1816 the South Carolina upcountry sent to the Senate the irascible and dedicated Jeffersonian purist "Judge" William Smith, whose supporters were challenging Calhoun's nationalist faction for control of the state. "The republic is in danger," exclaimed an Ohio editor, from the "new era in ... policy" inaugurated by the Fourteenth Congress. By 1819 acquisitive frenzy was evoking Maconian sentiments even in the northeastern market core. The "undue relish for speculation and trade" was undermining "personal industry" and producing "a deterioration of the public morals," a New Jersey congressman exhorted his constituents. "We can abridge our wants without lessening our happiness," he advised. "Let us do it."[30]

The theoretician of Old Republican revival was the Revolutionary veteran, lawyer, planter, agricultural improver, and occasional Republican Senator John Taylor. Taylor "of Caroline," as he was called to distinguish him from John Taylors in other counties, had been the leading polemicist against Hamiltonian developmentalism, charging that it would produce "a peasantry, wretchedly poor, and an aristocracy luxuriously rich and arrogantly proud." He had pushed through the Virginia legislature the classic statement of Republican constitutional doctrine, the famous resolutions of 1798 against the Alien and Sedition Acts. Having contributed so prominently to Jeffersonian hegemony, he was dismayed to find the Hamiltonian drift of the political economy continuing. To explain why, he published in 1814 *An Inquiry into the Principles and Policy of the Government of the United States.*[31]

In this old-fashioned country gentleman, late preindustrial capitalism met its most penetrating critic. When Virginia sent Taylor back to the Senate late in the Monroe administration, he personified a revival and analytical toughening of the original Republican challenge to the political economy of the market. In his broad-brimmed beaver hat and suit of antique "London brown," he impressed a younger colleague as "the ideal of a republican statesman . . . plain and solid . . . innately republican—modest, courteous, benevolent, hospitable—a skilful, practical farmer, giving his time to his farm and his books, when not called by an emergency to the public service—and returning to his books and his farm when the emergency was over." Taylor's quaint attire, predicted his ally Randolph, "will be rather nearer the fashion of the day than his principles."[32]

Taylor's principles arose from his hard-headed economic realism in trying to understand why his class and his world were crumbling. As Karl Marx would analyze capitalist exploitation of European industrial labor, the Virginian explained capitalist exploitation of American agricultural labor. Both men cherished human labor as the source of economic value. "Labour is in fact the great fund for human subsistence," said the Virginian; "—a surplus of this subsistence is wealth." Labor's "degree of safety" was for him the "barometer of good government."

Also like Marx, the Virginian thought labor "the object which tyranny invariably attacks." The American Revolution had no sooner guaranteed the republic's labor against the ancient extortions of European aristocracies and priesthoods, he argued, than a new and even more oppressive "aristocracy of paper and patronage" arose. Taylor calculated that "this legal faction of capitalists" was extorting 40 percent of the proceeds of agricultural labor. Writing just as wage labor galvanized capitalist exploitation, he anticipated Marx in sensing that capital "will, in the case of mechanics, soon appropriate the whole of their labour to its use, beyond a bare subsistence."

This doomed aristocrat, elaborating the labor theory of value while slave labor supplied his every want, epitomized the contradictions of capitalist transformation. His radical class politics called on planters to contain the lesser threat of democracy by rallying the democratic masses against the greater threat of capitalism. Latent in his tory radicalism, as in the original Jeffersonian planter/farmer alliance, was another function. As slavery came under capitalist assault, antinationalism in defense of rural liberty would become state rights in defense of human bondage.

In staking out common ground with the farming majority, Taylor cherished not only labor but land, "the mother of men" and the source of their subsistence. Therefore he accorded a unique moral legitimacy to the agricultural labor of extracting human subsistence directly from the earth. He thought it singularly free of temptations and "the best architect of a complete man."

Yet agriculture languished, Taylor argued, because the capitalists had seized government to enact a "paper system" embodying "indirect laws of confiscation." By paper system he meant the ramifying web of bank notes, bonds, mortgages, promissory notes, bills of exchange, and corporate stocks. Because law gave a fictitious value to these paper representations of capital, Taylor maintained, their holders grew wealthy through legalized extortion of the labor of mechanics and agriculturalists.

The Virginian's focus on the paper system astutely emphasized credit and government developmentalism as instruments of capitalist exploitation on the eve of industrialization. If he sometimes seemed to regard all interest on capital as fraud, it was because the "capital" of his day seemed so heavily derived from insider manipulation and legal privilege rather than real production and saving. Property so accumulated Taylor regarded as "artificial" and illegitimate. "Natural" and legitimate property, by contrast, was "fairly gained by talents and industry." Under the republic's benign person/land ratio, he seems to have believed, large fortunes and great inequalities of wealth could not have arisen naturally. Only artificial intervention could subvert such a natural and happy social order. What he did not sufficiently appreciate was the effect of differential access to capital, however accumulated.

Experience had taught the Virginian that the problem could not be solved by an elitist politics in which "the weight of talents will follow leisure and wealth." The Republicans and even Jefferson had disappointed him. Aristocracy "takes refuge under the one and then the other of our parties, because it cannot stand alone," he complained; "but whilst it is fondling first one and then the other of its nurses, it is sucking both into a consumption and itself towards maturity."

So it was with some desperation that Taylor fell back on the democratic masses to save his own class. "We farmers and mechanics," wrote this master of scores of bondsmen, were usually "political slaves . . . because we are political fools," easily duped by the high-sounding principles behind which the capitalists concealed their depredations. This rustic Virginian had a prescient understanding of the hegemonic power of capitalist ideology. Where ancient aristocracies deluded the oppressed "by exclaiming, the Gods! the temples! the sacred oracles! divine Vengeance! the Elysian fields!" he said, the modern aristocracy "of paper and patronage exclaims, national faith! sacred charters! disorganization! and security of property!" Through such means the capitalists—"whose object it is to monopolize the sweets of life, which we sweat for"—persuaded farmers and mechanics that politics would be a "ridiculous affectation" for them.

On the contrary, Taylor insisted, "agriculture must be a politician." Planters must lead farmers in electing legislatures and a Congress that would strip artificial property of its unjust privileges. "All societies," he asserted, "have exercised the right of abolishing privileged, stipendiary, or factitious property, whenever they became detrimental to them."

Taylor's seemingly anachronistic distinction between natural and artificial property marked, in fact, the crossroads for his society. As a planter he shared with most free Americans a deep devotion to private property, which seemed thus far in their experience to have produced both personal independence and social equity. Taylor was warning against two threats to private property: "the first, by which the poor plunder the rich, is sudden and violent; the second, by which the rich plunder the poor, slow and legal."

Taylor blamed both threats on the capitalists. Only "the indignation inspired by the fraudulent legal modes for acquiring wealth," he thought, gave rise to the "pernicious and impracticable idea of equalizing property by law." Having aroused this opposition to property, Taylor complained, the capitalists sought to defend their artificial and illegitimate property by allying with the natural and legitimate property produced by the labor of agriculturists and mechanics, "just as a good man and bad man would unite against an assassin, indifferently determined to murder them both."

The Virginian's desperate efforts to rally a political movement around the distinction between natural and artificial property arose from his perception that expansive capitalism was making private property inconsistent with a humane and equitable society. He foresaw that a capitalist coalition in which natural property legitimized artificial property would be unstoppable. It would mean, he predicted, the total triumph of "a legal faction . . . pretending to no religion, to no morality, to no patriotism, except to the religion, morality and patriotism of making itself daily richer, which it says will enrich the nation."

While Old Republicanism revived in the countryside, the paper system came under sustained attack in the crowded working-class districts surrounding central Philadelphia, where people felt most sharply the stress of intensifying market relationships. Here the "dangerous incendiary" William Duane linked this new political consciousness to the radically democratic working-class politics of Jeffersonian days. Back in the 1790s this Irish-born storm-petrel of Pennsylvania politics had brought the passionate antielitism and slashing polemical style of British artisan radicalism to the editorship of the Republicans' semiofficial national newspaper. His Philadelphia *Aurora,* Jefferson testified, was "our comfort in the gloomiest days" and "the rallying point for the Orthodox of the whole union."

Believing that only "a continued roiling of the democratic waters" could prevent them from stagnating into "a pestilential pool of monarchy, aristocracy, or priestcraft," Duane had long been the nemesis of the entrepreneurial Republican gentry. Promoting incessantly busy party organizations in working-class neighborhoods, he and his allies generated hundreds of activists and immense Republican majorities. After ensuring Jefferson's election and an irreversible Republican ascendancy in Pennsylvania, Duane's City Democrats, as they called themselves, capped a long struggle by uniting with Country Democrats demanding judicial reform to elect Simon Snyder governor and drive the Dallas-Gallatin-McKean coterie from power. "The immediate agency of the people," they hoped, would now be "perpetually necessary to every executive, legislative, and judicial purpose."

Instead—while a rural majority still remote from the market made Governor Snyder an unbeatable symbol of democracy through three terms—the City Democrats were fragmented and overwhelmed by the prewar commercial boom. As markets widened, household shops and independent master mechanics were squeezed out by larger and more mechanized shops requiring greater capital. A swelling class of journeymen and low-skilled laborers were becoming wage dependents of a minority of successful mechanic/manufacturers and merchant-backed putters-out. Class realignment shattered traditional working-class culture, and ethnic tensions broke up the City Democrats' carefully fostered alliance between Irish and German workers. With their class base demoralized, the Duaneites were powerless to resist the political energy of avid enterprisers.

Hungry for capital or credit to expand shops and hire more wage labor, upwardly mobile master mechanics joined forces with genteel Republicans of the old Dallas clique. Ousting the Duaneites from leadership of Philadelphia Republicanism, these New School Democrats, as they called themselves, cut deals in the legislature with the more opportunistic of Governor Snyder's Country Democrats to get several mechanic-oriented banks chartered for the city. In 1814 state treasurer William Findlay helped the New Schoolers logroll through both houses and over Governor Snyder's veto the "mammoth" banking act chartering forty-two new banks all over the state. At the height of the postwar boom three years later, with Snyder ineligible for another term, the New School men and the intensely enterprising forces they represented—now led by Alexander J. Dallas's son George—took power by electing Findlay governor.

Meanwhile the Old School Democrats, as Duane and his working-class following now called themselves, were being educated as well as shattered by the onrushing market. The democratic radicalism of Anglo-American workers—as voiced in the previous generation by Duane's predecessor Thomas Paine—had been friendly to economic development. On this ground the mechanic class supported the Constitution; for this reason working people increasingly favored encouragement of manufacturing through protective tariffs; and Duane himself had been equivocal about banks. Differences over such matters repeatedly disrupted the democratic coalition between Pennsylvania workers and farmers.

But now, as working people began to see, an expansive capitalism threatened the traditional moral economy that promised them a decent competence, ultimate independence, and the civic equality and respect of republican citizenship. They were Democrats of the Old School because orthodox Jeffersonianism relied on the independence and virtue of mechanics as well as farmers to realize and sustain the vision of a democratic republic. Consequently they saw in the "den of sordid speculation" brought by the commercial boom both class injustice and moral decay.

The people's "useful industry and frugal habits" were being corrupted, the *Aurora* complained.

With a sharpened understanding of the role of capital, credit, and the state, Duane followed John Taylor of Caroline in identifying the paper system as the point for attack. "*Paper*, which has worked so many wonders," predicted the *Aurora*, "will be so plenty presently that no man, but one who feels qualms of conscience, or 'that damn'd starving quality called *honesty*,' need be without an estate."

Old Schoolers had also learned like Taylor that party labels were not to be trusted, that a broadly democratic coalition like the Republican party could carry to power a new elite as oppressive as the one it displaced. The democratic *"mass"* no sooner displaced the Federalist *"few"* in 1800, Duane complained, than "there arose *another few* amongst the *old mass.*" Just as the Hamiltonians disguised their antirepublicanism under the name of Federalism, he lamented, "in the present times the name of *democrat* is used to cover *shaving* and *peculating* and cheating the public." Alienated by the new national Bank and the National Republicanism of the Fourteenth Congress and the Monroe administration, the Old Schoolers denounced the Republican caucus system as undemocratic and in their frustration even flirted with Federalists as allies against the New Schoolers.

The postwar boom confirmed and sharpened the Old School critique of banking. Leading the attack in the *Aurora* was Duane's young protégé Stephen Simpson, signing himself "Brutus." Simpson had gained an acute understanding of banking abuses from his father, cashier of both the first national Bank and the private Bank of Stephen Girard that took over its business and imposing headquarters. Idealistically casting his lot with the Old School, the younger Simpson would soon be the leading theoretician of Philadelphia's radical Workingmen's Party. Now as Brutus he was subjecting banking and its class effects to a cogent and unsparing critique, and he was the first to alert the country to the national Bank's irresponsible inflation.[33]

By early 1819 the Old Republican revival had gained such momentum that it threatened to control the presidential succession. Most of the aspirants to succeed Monroe after his traditional two terms in 1824 were committed to National Republicanism. Secretary of State John Quincy Adams was pursuing a nationalist diplomacy in the office through which every Republican President had advanced, and he offered preeminently the traditional qualifications of ability and experience. Speaker Henry Clay had long since staked his claim as a stronger advocate of developmental nationalism than the administration. Waiting offstage were War Secretary John C. Calhoun, New York's Governor De Witt Clinton, and perhaps others.

But the candidate most popular with congressmen was the imposing and affable Treasury Secretary William H. Crawford. This "giant of a man" had been such a formidable presidential contender in the 1816 caucus that he might have defeated Monroe if he had not voluntarily withdrawn, calculating that this would make his claims for the succession irresistible. Accordingly Monroe felt obliged to give him a prominent Cabinet position. But if Crawford was in the administration, he was not of it.

The Treasury Secretary owed much of his strength to pragmatic shrewdness. Born in Virginia, he learned his politics in a middle Georgia being transformed by a booming cotton-slave economy. Georgia had a more democratic polity than Calhoun's similar bailiwick across the Savannah River in South Carolina. In leading a proplanter faction embattled with a rival faction appealing to interior farmers, Crawford mastered early a more popular style of politics than had developed in many states. Rising into the Republican national leadership, he was picked by Gallatin to manage the fight for recharter of the Hamiltonian national Bank in 1811—as Dallas later recruited Calhoun to renew the struggle.

Though hardly an antidevelopmental ideologue, Crawford was now counting on the big delegation from his native Virginia to ensure his caucus nomination, and he was correspondingly alert to Virginia's growing antidevelopmentalism. In his own Georgia, moreover, the Salary Act had aroused tax-hating democracy into an almost clean sweep of congressional incumbents. Consequently Crawford was the only Monrovian notable to take seriously the reaction against National Republicanism. Carefully distancing himself from the administration's developmental nationalism, he was regarded with growing suspicion by his colleagues.

As the Treasury Secretary positioned himself at the head of resurgent Old Republicanism, his supporters led the congressional campaign for retrenchment and reform. They announced their root-and-branch seriousness by taking the name Radicals—from Great Britain's ultrademocratic reformers—and the Crawford following would be known as the Radical party. Radicals threatened to replay the Jeffersonian script by uniting planters with democratic farmers as advocated by John Taylor of Caroline. Resurrecting under Crawford's banner the historic Republican alliance between New York and Virginia, the Richmond Junto and the Bucktails' Albany Regency could unite the American majority against the market's aggressive advance.

Suddenly, in early 1819, all political calculations were upset when the portentous issue of slavery forced its way onto the national stage. The market's postwar surge, entrenching slavery, intensifying antislavery liberalism, and pushing both slave and free population across the Mississippi into Missouri, made the question no longer avoidable. Responding to an unexpected proposal from a New York congressman, an overwhelming majority of free-state representatives turned out to be adamant against admitting another slave state to the republic.

Slavery was becoming a profound contradiction for capitalism. Never have so many been enslaved as when the European market dragooned Africans into subduing the New World to commodity production. With abundant American acreage offering independence and security to the landless, only the lash could compel enough disciplined exertion to meet capital's demands. Human enslavement energized the market's global conquest.

But as slave labor extended the market and multiplied capital, wage labor became more profitable. Liberalism arose to motivate entrepreneurs, reconcile workers, and bend the state to market ends by idealizing competition among free and juridically equal individuals. As free, self-motivated labor energized growth, bound labor both offended liberal morality and impeded capitalist progress.[34]

When Thomas Jefferson led the Revolutionary gentry in proclaiming that "all men are created equal," they honored their liberal ideology to the extent of abolishing slavery where slaves were few and of little profit (north of Delaware and Maryland), manumitting some of them where they were numerous but unprofitable (the old tobacco kingdom), and importing more to drive as hard as ever where they were both numerous and profitable (the rice and cotton country of South Carolina and Georgia). Only the Constitution's compromises sanctioning human bondage made a united republic possible.

This clash between principle and practice was more tolerable in the early republic because slavery seemed in retreat. While liberalism drove it from the North, tobacco depression was multiplying manumissions in the upper South. Most politicians tried to suppress an issue that could split their fragile new republic and their new national parties, and they thought it better left to the processes of time.

Slavery's dramatic rejuvenation by the cotton boom and lightning advance across the Gulf plains after the war intensified the ideological strain on the republic's liberal elites. Organization of the American Colonization Society in 1817 gave them a safe way of assuming a liberal posture toward slavery. The Society's project of colonizing freed blacks in Africa could be promoted among southern slaveholders as removing a population dangerous to slavery and among antislavery northerners as reducing bondage through gradual manumission and deportation. The slaveholding Clay was a leading organizer of the Colonization Society, and the capital of its colony Liberia on the west coast of Africa was named Monrovia for the slaveholding American President who provided the essential diplomatic and naval support.

The racism to which colonization appealed was endemic in white society. Legal freedom did not free blacks from being reviled, shunned, and exploited by whites, everywhere north and south. By 1820 the United States contained over a quarter million of these free or quasi-free "Negroes," persons of African or part-African ancestry. Over half remained in the midst of slavery, principally in the depressed upper South where voluntary manumissions had been common. These "slaves without masters" had to register with local authorities—North Carolina required those in towns to wear a shoulder patch ironically inscribed FREE—and they lived under constant threat of being kidnapped back into slavery or bound out by local authorities for idleness. Any white could mistreat them with impunity, for they were forbidden to testify against whites in court. Only marginally better off were the hundred thousand free blacks in the ostensibly free states, who were crowded into urban ghettoes and also subjected to various civil disabilities.

Ironically both free and slave states responded to a broadened and politicized white male electorate by disfranchising free blacks. New York's disfranchisement of most blacks in 1821 was part of a national movement. New Jersey emphasized that this was a white man's country by eliminating in 1807 both black voting and a loophole through which some women were briefly allowed to vote. Maryland banned black voting in 1810, Connecticut in 1811. Aside from the minuscule black population in northern New England and the few well-to-do blacks allowed to vote in New York, the legal possibility of free black suffrage survived a little longer only in Rhode Island (until 1822), North Carolina (until 1835), and Pennsylvania (until 1837).[35]

In the face of this pervasive racism, the most extensive opposition to human bondage arose in the subsistence culture of the upper South, where the ascetic egalitarianism of evangelical farming folk competed for cultural hegemony with slaveholding opulence. Here well into the nineteenth century nearly all Quakers, many Methodists and Baptists, and a good many Presbyterians supported a sustained agitation against slavery. As late as 1827 this area reported 106 antislavery societies with over five thousand members, four or five times as many as could be found in the free states. By the 1820s, however, this premarket abolitionism was in headlong retreat before a resurgent slavery. As it became clear that "the slave power was and would be the dominant influence in the future," a North Carolina Quaker recalled, ". . . the spirit of emigration took possession of whole neighborhoods."[36]

Most Quakers left the South for free soil north of the Ohio, and so did thousands of Methodist, Baptist, and Presbyterian families. North Carolina's Benjamin S. Hedrick saw nearly half his rural boyhood neighbors and kin depart "to seek homes in the free West, knowing, as they did, that free and slave labor could not both exist and prosper in the same community." Later fired from the state university faculty for antislavery views, Hedrick may have wished he had gone with them; while a Kentucky Presbyterian did not care where he went so long as "I may only get where every man I see is as free as myself." Similar considerations may have influenced the antislavery Baptist Tom Lincoln to move his family, including son Abe, from his hardscrabble Kentucky farm across the Ohio to free Indiana.[37]

As the market drove antislavery farmers into retreat before its advancing cotton planters, it was generating at the polar extremity of American society its own version of antislavery. In the top echelon of market elites, among the Federalist/Clintonian merchants, lawyers, and financiers in the northeastern cities, Protestant piety meshed with liberalism to engender the antislavery animus of a fully articulated capitalist culture. John Jay organized the New York Manumission Society in 1785; Alexander Hamilton succeeded him as its president; and Jay's son Peter was an even more dedicated antislavery crusader. Soon there were similar societies under similar leadership in most of the northeastern cities.

Here at the core of the market, successful businessmen were most fully committed to the liberal ideology. Competitive self-seeking among juridically equal individuals, they believed, rewarded character, ability, and effort, while mobilizing human energy for maximum production and the ultimate benefit of all. Equating poverty with depravity and laziness, they had little sympathy for the fractious mechanics and rustics who resisted their efforts to mold a disciplined labor force.

Such harshly competitive values jarred with a Protestant heritage that condemned egoistic materialism even as it sanctified the striving that produced capitalist success. The most devout entrepreneurs were often the most successful, and such men eased their way into the market mentality through a new kind of piety emphasizing benevolence as evidence of spiritual grace. By the 1790s Great Revival was propelling devout commercial gentlemen into a wide range of good works. To the needy next door—the dubiously worthy working-class poor of liberal doctrine—they extended only grudging relief along with generous doses of religious instruction and moral uplift. Entrepreneurial benevolence found far more appealing beneficiaries in oppressed blacks and Indians who could not be blamed for their plight.

Abolitionism attracted the most pious of successful businessmen. Wealthy Quakers, who notoriously "did well by doing good," were the driving force of antislavery in every major city from Baltimore to Moses Brown's Providence, and their stronghold, Philadelphia, became the center of the movement. They found allies in pious Episcopalians like the Jays in New York and pious Presbyterians like Elias Boudinot in New Jersey. Through the traditional elitist politics of mobilizing notables, the abolition societies led the protracted campaign to rid the North of slavery and to protect the rights of the many blacks not yet freed under gradual emancipation plans.

Abolitionism did more for benevolent entrepreneurs than endow them with virtue. It was "a highly selective response to labor exploitation," as historian David Brion Davis argues. By making chattel slavery the uniquely immoral form of human exploitation, abolitionism undercut the mounting working-class complaints about wage slavery and beatifed the capitalist order. These abolitionists hated slavery not just for its inhumanity but also for impeding their vision of a capitalist society of free individuals whose labor could be freely exploited.

Benevolent businessmen sought moreover to elevate free labor, white and black, into self-disciplined productivity, reliability, and docility. Capitalism required workers to extort more labor from themselves than slavery could extort by the lash. "Freedom required the internalization of moral precepts in the place of external coercion," as Davis puts it. Emancipation, as these enterprising abolitionists saw it, "did not mean freedom to live as one chose, but rather freedom to become a diligent, sober, dependable worker who gratefully accepted his position in society."³⁸

Accordingly the abolitionist gentry subjected free blacks to the same paternalist supervision they had imposed as their masters in slavery. In 1808 the New York Manumission Society viewed "with regret the looseness of manners & depravity of conduct in many of the Persons of Colour in this city" and sought some means "for promoting a reformation." The next year the society scolded blacks for a parade they were planning to celebrate abolition of the foreign slave trade, fearing it would "cause reflections to be made on this Society." But the blacks stood their ground, telling the white abolitionists that "they could not think of relinquishing their proposed method of Celebrating the day."³⁹

Yet urban gentlemen deplored—and where possible shielded their clients from—the virulent racism of insecure working-class whites who competed with blacks for society's crumbs. These alignments of caste and class found expression in politics, where blacks voted solidly with their Federalist patrons. Concentrated in critical Manhattan wards, black votes in 1813 tipped the New York state election to Federalism. A disgruntled Bucktail expressed alarm that "a few hundred Negroes of the city of New York, following the train of those . . . whose shoes and boots they had so often blacked," could "change the political condition of the whole state"; and the next Bucktail legislature put special restrictions on black voters.⁴⁰

Slavery's resurgence deeply alarmed not only abolitionists but the whole northeastern commercial elite to which they belonged. The cotton boom closed the door on further abolition through state action by providing a profitable market for the upper South's masses of economically redundant slaves. And slavery's postwar rush to the Mississippi intensified the old Federalist/Clintonian fear of domination by a hostile South and West. In 1819 Missouri's application for admission as a slaveholding state intensified the commercial gentry's fears. Abolitionist gentlemen brought to the Missouri question both humane concern for oppressed blacks and calculations of political power.

Overriding Jefferson's early dream of a slave-free West, an implicit intersectional compact had barred slavery from the Old Northwest while allowing it in the Old Southwest. New states were admitted alternately from each region, keeping the Union, and incidentally the Senate, evenly balanced between free and slave states. With the postwar westward rush filling the original national territory up to the Mississippi—only Michigan and Wisconsin awaited statehood—the Missouri decision was expected to determine whether slavery would be confined where it was or allowed to spread over the entire Louisiana Purchase. The earlier fears of Federalist/Clintonian gentlemen were already confirmed by a solid phalanx of new Republican states in the West. Now they could envisage a further solid phalanx of new slave states, hemming the free states into one corner of a slave-driving nation. They would be barred forever from national power, and their entrepreneurial vision of the republic's destiny would be doomed.

In New York the Federalist/Clintonians had for years complained that their commercial interests were being sacrificed, through the three-fifths representation of slaves, "to the domineering aristocracy of Virginia." When Madison's veto of the Bonus Bill dashed hopes of federal funding for the Erie Canal, Clinton was furious that the President, "after swallowing the national Bank and the Cumberland Road &c., ... would strain at Canals." Nor could these embittered New Yorkers see in Monroe, who endorsed Madison's veto, more than another instance of "Virginia dictation." A Clintonian legislator refused to attend a special session for choosing Monroe presidential electors in 1820 because he was "unwilling to poach through the mud 225 miles to perpetuate the slavery of the north."[41]

Meanwhile, in the struggle for New York, the Bucktails were impelled by their principles of party regularity and political economy to support the Virginia Presidents and the Republican caucus system for choosing them. When the Clintonians discovered that they could win votes by denouncing the Bucktails as proslavery, they and their Federalist/New England allies glimpsed the possibility of coming back to power nationally by uniting the North against the South.

At this political juncture, early in 1819, New York's Clintonian congressman James Tallmadge, Jr., introduced his antislavery amendments to the Missouri statehood bill. No further slaves should be admitted to Missouri, he proposed as a conditon of statehood, and those present should be freed when they reached the age of twenty-five.

The political motives for restricting slavery were frankly avowed by the leading advocate of Tallmadge's amendments in the Senate, New York's Rufus King. A widely respected Federalist and framer of the federal Constitution, King had been elevated to the Senate by the margin of the Manhattan black vote in 1813 and kept there only by a Bucktail/Clintonian stalemate in the New York legislature. He told senators that he was concerned about slavery "solely in its bearing and effects upon great political interests, and upon the just and equal rights of the freemen of the nation." He was trying to block any further extension of the "disproportionate power" that the slave states derived from the three-fifths clause— twenty extra representatives and twenty presidential electors, he calculated, seven from Virginia alone. The question "settles forever the Dominion of the Union," he explained to his son. "If decided against us, ... Old Mr. Adams, as he is the first, will ... be the last President from a free state." King was especially worried about losing also that capitalist bastion the Supreme Court, and with it "some of the most important" of the "political Rights" that John Marshall was just enunciating.

Never before had there been broad northern support for halting the spread of slavery. Now free-state congressmen backed the Tallmadge amendments by sufficiently overwhelming margins (84–10 and 80–14) to pass them despite nearly unanimous opposition from slave-state representatives (1–66 and 2–64). In the upper house, where the new Alabama senators would restore the customary balance between slave and free states, a solid phalanx of slave-state men found five free-state allies to reject the crucial Tallmadge amendment. Against all pressure the House insisted on it (78–76); and in March 1819 a deadlocked Congress broke up, leaving the republic's fate to the new Congress that would assemble in December.[42]

Tallmadge's proposition "disclosed a secret," John Quincy Adams observed, that was not anticipated "even by those who brought it forward." It was a fateful revelation: the North could be united almost solidly against any further expansion of slavery. The debate "revealed the basis for a new organization of parties," as Adams put it in his diary. ". . . Here was a new party ready formed, . . . terrible to the whole Union, but portentously terrible to the South—threatening in its progress the emancipation of all their slaves, threatening in its immediate effect that Southern domination which has swayed the Union for the last twenty years, and threatening that political ascendancy of Virginia, upon which Clay and Crawford both had fastened their principal hopes of personal aggrandizement."[43]

The solid free-state vote for the Tallmadge amendments revealed also that a widening market was disseminating to centers of enterprise throughout the North the capitalist culture and antislavery perspective of the old urban elite. Amid economic prostration, slavery affronted capitalist benevolence while the capitalist design for the republic was challenged both by slavery and by a formidable Radicalism.

Sharpening political/moral contradictions were brought to a head in the crisis of 1819 by the economic contradiction between established wealth and aspiring enterprise. Rising venturers, winning the tug-of-war with entrenched capital for control of the monetary system, were whirling it into capitalism's cycle of boom-and-bust. Entrepreneurial extravagance both fed National Republican hubris and threatened economic disaster.

Spectacular real growth underlay speculative excess. Fueled by the productivity gains of an intensifying division of labor in the northeastern core, the economy was taking off both quantitatively and spatially. As pioneer farmers flooded trans-Appalachian lands swept clear of Indians during the war, steamboats and cotton brought the market hard on their heels. With federal land sales jumping from a little over a half million acres in 1813 to nearly four million in 1818, the West produced five new states in rapid succession—Indiana 1816, Mississippi 1817, Illinois 1818, Alabama 1819, and, fatefully, Missouri 1820.

The market could not gain headway along the Mississippi-Ohio river system as long as the farmer's products had to be rafted hundreds of miles down to New Orleans and the store goods laboriously rowed back upriver in keelboats. But at the end of the war a steamboat first demonstrated upriver feasibility. By 1820 sixty-nine of these vessels were operating on western waters, and within a decade there were hundreds.

In order to penetrate far up such tributaries as the Cumberland, Wabash, and Monongahela, the western steamboat's multitiered superstructure was built on a shallow raft and driven by paddlewheels churning the surface. Western rivermen boasted that their vessels could run on a heavy dew; and one, at least, carried forty tons of freight and eighty passengers in two feet of water.

. The three or four months required by flatboats and keelboats moving between New Orleans and Louisville was cut by steamboats to about a week, a little less downriver and a little more upriver. They transformed the West, including the cotton Southwest, by carrying freight downriver for a fourth of the flatboat cost and upriver for 5 to 10 percent of the keelboat cost. Villages and towns grew up at landings as outposts of the market culture. Their stores offered a tempting array of goods in exchange for the farmer's grain and livestock; their gristmills, tanneries, and distilleries processed his products into more marketable form; their blacksmiths, coopers, shoemakers, tailors, doctors, and lawyers offered more specialized skills and services than the rural neighborhood could supply.

As steamboat transportation spread production for market along the river system, regional markets radiated out from the more important trading centers. By 1820 Cincinnati had more than nine thousand people, Pittsburgh more than seven thousand, and Louisville more than four thousand. The populations of all more than doubled in the next decade, Cincinnati reaching nearly twenty-five thousand as a meat-packing and flour-milling center.[44]

Solid prosperity was turned into speculative saturnalia by postwar abnormalities in the world market. For four years—as Europe dumped its backlog of exports on American docks at cut rates and paid fancy prices for American staples— money-making opportunities surged across the American landscape. The postwar boom fed on expectation. Entrepreneurial hopes stimulated public investment, and public investment multiplied opportunities for private profit. Turnpike construction peaked, New York began the Erie Canal, and the military/naval/fortifications buildup pushed federal construction expenditures from $700,000 in 1816 past $14,000,000 in 1818.[45]

Public monetary policy had even greater effects. Glittering investment opportunities created insatiable demands for capital. Chronically short of capital, venturesome Americans knew how to manufacture the next best thing, credit, through the marvelous device of banking. Now there was an explosion of bank charters and bank notes. "Like a dropsical man calling out for water, water," Jefferson lamented in 1816, "our citizens are clamoring for more banks, more banks." A bank seemed to be demanded "wherever there is a 'church, a blacksmith's shop and a tavern,'" commented the country's first news weekly. The number of state-chartered banks passed 200 in 1815 and nearly doubled, to 392, in the next three years. Kentucky chartered 46 at the single legislative session of

1817–1818; and even the Virginia legislature yielded to clamor from the bankless western half of the state by creating 2 new banks.

The delusion that "legerdemain tricks upon paper can produce as solid wealth as hard labor in the earth," complained Jefferson, made it impossible to "reason Bedlam to rights." "Confidence is already on the totter," he worried as the inflationary spiral swirled out of control, "and every one now handles this paper as if playing at Robin's alive," a contemporary game of chance. Early in 1819, with the denouement at hand, he wrote that the speculative frenzy had produced "a general demoralization of the nation, a filching from industry its honest earnings, wherewith to build up palaces, and raise gambling stock for swindlers and shavers, who are to close their career of piracies by fraudulent bankruptcies."[46]

The new banks of which Jefferson complained were not created by capital seeking investment nor to meet the financial needs of established enterprises. Instead, as Treasury Secretary William H. Crawford explained, they were created because "men without active capital wanted the means of obtaining loans, which their standing in the community would not command from banks or indiviuals having real capital and established credit."[47]

These newer entrepreneurs and their banks suffused a new spirit through economic life. They were experimenting with the possibilities of a system that even established bankers did not yet understand very well. From transactions in real commodities, they were shifting to transactions in the more spectral values represented by paper instruments—bank notes, bills of exchange, and corporate stocks. Corporate charters were multiplying in manufacturing and transportation as well as banking; and by 1817 the brokers who traded stocks and bonds on the curbs of Manhattan's Wall Street found business so flourishing that they organized a formal stock exchange and moved indoors. Real money (specie) was giving way to paper promises to pay money (bank notes). And, *mirable dictu,* these promises to pay could apparently be multiplied far beyond the amount of specie that existed to satisfy them. "If a promise was as good as a deed in some instances," comments banking historian Bray Hammond, "it was unapparent why everything might not be left to promise." On this ethically foggy terrain, sound business practice shaded imperceptibly into irrresponsibility, and irresponsibility into chicanery, while the crime of embezzlement had not even been defined.

Thus it is not surprising that the state banks, most having suspended specie payments during the war, were reluctant to resume redeeming their notes in gold or silver coin on demand. With specie payments suspended, new banks could open on no other capital than stock loans and a little borrowed specie, and then force their notes into circulation by lending freely. Established banks could earn dividends of 12 to 20 percent by extending loans and note issues far beyond their specie reserves. The resulting uncontrolled inflation threatened sound growth, and it was primarily to reform the currency by forcing the state banks to resume specie payments that Congress chartered the Second Bank of the United States.[48]

But the national Bank itself succumbed to the get-rich mood. Astor and Girard were double-crossed in the election of directors by their erstwhile confederate, the outgoing Treasury Secretary Dallas. Falling in with the speculative state banking interests led by General Samuel Smith, Dallas had already alienated his old friend Gallatin by refusing to press them hard enough through the Treasury for resumption of specie payments. Now, as his last official act, Dallas threw the Madison administration's support in the election of Bank directors to a speculative cabal centering around the Smith-Buchanan interests in Baltimore. Gallatin never spoke to him again.

The Bank's charter assigned one vote to each share of stock, with Calhoun's democratic proviso that no shareholder could have more than thirty votes. This rendered the huge, bond-derived Astor/Girard stockholdings unavailing against the Baltimoreans' tactic of paying for large stock purchases with loans from the Bank and then fictitiously dividing ownership to maximize their voting power. One Baltimore man voted, ostensibly as attorney, 1,172 shares registered as belonging to 1,172 different individuals. The directors elected by these votes chose as president Captain William Jones, a failed Philadelphia merchant, Republican politician, and longtime Dallas associate, who served briefly and ingloriously in the Madison Cabinet. Thus the second national Bank began its career, according to its later president Nicholas Biddle, as "a monied institution governed by those who had no money, . . . a mere colony of the Baltimore adventurers."[49]

Prodded by incoming Treasury Secretary Crawford, Captain Jones and his directors arranged with the leading state banks a nominal resumption of specie payments in February 1817. But the resumption was never more than nominal. The national Bank was designed to force the state banks to reduce their vastly inflated loans and note issues by regularly presenting for specie redemption the state bank notes it received as the federal government's despository. Instead Jones and company sought to appease the demand for credit while maximizing the Bank's profits by extravagant lending, particulary at the Bank's branches in the booming West. This put so many of its notes into circulation that it could no longer press the state banks for specie without being equally pressed in return. Thus the national Bank not only threw away its ability to restrain inflation but redoubled inflationary pressures.

The Baltimore branch, center of the interests backing Jones, did a bigger business than the main office at Philadelphia. The prewar commercial boom made Baltimore the fastest growing Atlantic port. "There is not a city in the Union which has had so much apparent prosperity," commented John Quincy Adams, "or within which there has been such complication of profligacy." Like the Bank's western branches, the Baltimore branch was lending far more than its share of the institution's capital; and through Jones the Baltimore men enforced a policy that made the other branches responsible for redeeming the notes it and the western branches issued so profusely in making loans. The Baltimore directors and other insiders got many of these loans without collateral. Half a million went to the propertyless cashier James W. McCulloch, ironically the protagonist on whose behalf Chief Justice Marshall vindicated both Bank and capitalist state. Within two years the branch was looted of $3 million, half of it never recovered.[50]

The country's inflationary binge meshed ruinously with postwar readjustments in the Europe-centered world economy. Pent-up civilian demand and high prices encouraged American entrepreneurs to borrow extravagantly to expand production. Once expanded production satisfied abnormal world demand, the jerrybuilt pyramid of American credit was threatened by collapse of the inflated prices on which it was predicated.

Even after nominal resumption of specie payments, the shakiness of American banks made specie unavailable except at a premium. Only a tacit public conspiracy not to demand specie maintained apparent specie convertibility. "The whole of our population are either stockholders of banks or in debt to them," a Philadelphian explained to the puzzled English economist David Ricardo. "It is not the *interest* of the first to press the banks and the rest are *afraid*." If the banks were pressed for specie, they would have to protect their specie reserves by pressing their debtors for immediate payment.

Their debtors were extremely vulnerable. Bank loans were usually made for no longer than ninety days. While the older and more conservative banks confined their loans to short-term commercial ventures that could be liquidated within the loan period, the newer banks made short-term loans for long-term investment with the expectation that they would be renewed indefinitely, "Our numerous banks have sometimes stretched their loans to the utmost" in financing lands, houses, and factories, a Carolinian recalled several years later. "We wanted to take short cuts to fortune."

Both banks and borrowers were gambling on the indefinite continuance of high commodity prices and speculative profits. Most of these investments would require years to yield enough profit to repay the loans. Moreover many of these loans were guaranteed not by tangible collateral but by the credit of co-signers, whose own property was liable for repayment. Therefore "everyone is afraid of bursting the bubble," reported a traveler from the Northwest. Anyone who demanded specie from the banks, said Ricardo's Philadelphia informant, "would have been persecuted as an enemy of society." Indeed one demander of coin from an Ohio bank was stabbed to death by the infuriated cashier.[51]

The inflationary policies of the new national Bank put the final critical pressure on the shaky monetary structure. As the flood of notes from the Bank's Baltimore and western branches flowed with the course of trade into the northeastern branches for redemption, the Bank's specie reserves drained away. Finally, in the summer and fall of 1818, at the last possible moment to save itself, the Bank began to retrench, calling in loans, demanding settlement of its heavy balances against state banks, and requiring each branch to redeem its own notes. Early in 1819 the frightened stockholders, marshaled by Astor, Girard, and Secretary Crawford, elected new directors who ousted Captain Jones and replaced him as president with Calhoun's austere War Hawk colleague from South Carolina, Langdon Cheves. Ruthlessly Cheves pressed the contraction, reducing the Bank's demand liabilities over the next several years from $22 million to $10 million and its circulating notes from $10 million to $3 million, while building its specie reserves from about $2.5 million to $8 million.

This brutal deflation saved the national Bank by sacrificing not only its debtors but the state banks and their hordes of debtors as well, which is to say, most of the market economy. Suddenly in the spring of 1819, as the Bank's pressure was intensified by a similar financial crisis in Britain, world commodity prices collapsed. Cotton fell from a recent high of 33¢ a pound to 14¢, tobacco from 40¢ to 4¢. A price index of export staples for the whole country plummeted from 169 in August 1818 to 77 in June 1819. Nor did prices quickly recover. Philadelphia wheat, peaking at $2.41 a bushel in 1817 and breaking sharply in 1819, did not stop falling until it reached 88¢ in 1821. New York cotton, averaging 24¢ to 30¢ during the boom years, did not hit bottom at 11¢ until 1823.[52]

Coming on top of the national Bank's drastic contraction, the collapse of agricultural prices made it impossible for state banks to collect from borrowers or meet obligations to the national Bank. When most state banks suspended the pretense of specie redemption, a flood of business failures and personal liquidations plunged Americans into their first experience of general and devastating economic prostration.

Chapter 5

Hard Times, Hard Feelings,
Hard Money

THE Panic of 1819 was a traumatic awakening to the capitalist reality of boom-and-bust. Not until the postwar boom had the market spread far enough to inflict general prostration in bust. Suddenly everyone committed to the money economy was in peril, as bank notes depreciated in their pockets.

Distress was most acute in the cities, where the insecurity of the growing new class of wage laborers was now fully demonstrated. As customers stopped buying and businesses failed, an estimated half million workers were left without means of support, fifty thousand in New York, Philadelphia, and Baltimore. In Philadelphia three out of four workers were reported idle, and 1,808 were jailed for unpaid debts. Philanthropic groups distributed soup to the starving and passed out recipes for a "cheap, wholesome, and savoury" concoction of rice and mutton suet gravy that could feed a family of six for three cents. The eight thousand public paupers who alarmed other New Yorkers in 1819 swelled in a year to nearly thirteen thousand. Everywhere the traditional mechanic dream of owning a modest home was shattered as missed mortgage payments triggered a wave of foreclosures. Even the smaller towns faced "the prospect of families naked—children freezing in the winter's storm—and the fathers without coats and shoes to enable them" to work. And everywhere the cities and towns lost population as the destitute fled back to kin in the countryside for subsistence.

Distress was not confined to the working classes. Wherever the market extended, the remorseless process of debt liquidation chastened not only modest venturers but also the apparently wealthy who had plunged and borrowed most recklessly. Specie to satisfy their creditors could not be had. Even if they owned ample property, it could not be sold except at vastly depreciated rates because no one had money to buy it. The result was a devastating wave of business failures and sheriffs' sales of property to satisfy debts or taxes. Over five hundred suits for debt were brought at a single term of the county court in Nashville, Tennessee, and nearly fifteen thousand were commenced in Pennsylvania during 1819. Jefferson heard of Virginia sheriffs auctioning off debtors' farms for a year's rent; likewise he reported—with his society's shocking nonchalance about human property—"good slaves selling for one hundred dollars, good horses for five dollars, and the sheriffs generally the purchasers." It was "an entire revolution of fortune," he said, and "I fear local insurrections against these horrible sacrifices of property."[1]

Baltimore's leading commercial house, Smith and Buchanan, "failed with a crash which staggered the whole city" and toppled within three months over a hundred leading merchants. "Gone distracted" and "confined dangerously ill in bed" was General Samuel Smith, the city's economic and political sachem for a generation.[2]

Another conspicuous business failure was Smith's kinsman Wilson Cary Nicholas, longtime leader of Virginia Republicanism and president of the national Bank's Richmond branch. Dragged down with Nicholas was Thomas Jefferson. Under the code of Virginia gentlemen, Jefferson had felt obligated to co-sign for the debt of his longstanding and loyal friend, particularly since Nicholas had rescued him with a national-Bank loan after he lost his crops in the frigid summer of "1816-and-froze-to-death." As a result the aged ex-President spent his last years struggling to save Monticello from his and Nicholas's creditors.[3]

New England, where specie-strong banks and renewed competition from cheap foreign manufactures restrained the postwar boom, escaped the worst. Elsewhere distress was keenly felt. Never "in the recollection of our oldest merchants," said the New York *Gazette,* had there been such "mercantile *embarrassment.*" "Go where you will," wrote a New Jersey farmer, "your ears are continually saluted with the cry of *hard times! hard times!*" A "deeper gloom" was reported from Kentucky "than was ever witnessed by the oldest man." The "Scarcity of money," according to a Mississippian, was "beyond any thing of the like Since my first remembrance."

The liquidation of property was most severe in the West, where the national Bank had lavished credit. "All the flourishing cities of the West are mortgaged to this money power," complained Missouri Senator Thomas Hart Benton. "They are in the jaws of the monster! A lump of butter in the mouth of a dog! One gulp, one swallow, and all is gone!" The most valuable property in Benton's St. Louis was pledged for bank debts that could not be repaid. With Henry Clay as its well-rewarded supervising attorney, the national Bank was indeed ruthlessly stripping its western debtors of their property. Most of Cincinnati fell into its hands.[4]

Hard times shattered Monrovian consensus to inaugurate an era of hard feelings. Conventional federal politics were embittered and sectionalized by slavery and by geographically polarized interests struggling for survival over National Republicanism's developmental bounties. Simultaneously the shock of boom/bust intensified market disruption of traditional ways to ignite antinomian insurgency in religion and a new class politics in the states.

In national politics, insurgent democracy and resurgent Old Republicanism threatened to replay the Jeffersonian scenario. But the Missouri tocsin transfixed slaveholding Virginia gentlemen as they unfurled the Radical banner for farmers and workers to follow. The spectre of a united antislavery North shattered tobacco planters' Jeffersonian equanimity toward a democratic impulse now demanding a real share of power. By resisting democracy at home and focusing Radicalism abroad on defense of slavery, the siege mentality of this doomed aristocracy aborted a promising political movement. Waiting in the wings was Andrew Jackson.

While depression spread anxiety and suffering across the land, abolitionists and Federalist/Clintonian politicians joined forces to capitalize on the northern antislavery sentiment revealed by the Tallmadge amendments. For three months before a new Congress met in December 1819 to decide the Missouri question, they mounted a vociferous public campaign against any further extension of slavery. Imposing arrays of local notables turned out in every sizeable town in the free states to applaud antislavery speeches and pass antislavery resolutions. The principal organizers were a coterie of Federalist/Clintonian politicians led by Webster and his nominally Republican friend Justice Story. Also involved were Senator King, Webster's frequent co-counsel Joseph Hopkinson of Philadelphia, and Timothy Dwight's brother Theodore, who had been secretary of the Hartford Convention and whose New York *Daily Advertiser* led the antislavery chorus of the Federalist/Clintonian press.

The passions unleashed by the congressional debate over Missouri during the depression winter of 1819–1820 frightened most participants. Threats of disunion were freely exchanged, and southerners were particularly agitated. A Virginian fainted while speaking, and a dying Kentuckian expired before friends could carry him to the Capitol for the crucial vote.

Slavery in Missouri mattered mainly to Missouri slaves, slaveholders, and would-be slaveholders. Most politicians, southern and northern, were contending for sectional power. But the debate distressed southerners acutely by forcing them to contend also for self-respect. Ever since the Revolution they had been able to maintain their republican integrity by deploring slavery while disclaiming responsibility for its introduction and arguing the impossibility of its eradication. Compelled now to defend their brutal system of labor exploitation, they found such liberal pretensions more difficult. The leading orator on the southern side of the Missouri question was rebutted by his earlier liberal pronouncements. Back in the heyday of post-Revolutionary liberalism, William Pinkney had called on his state of Maryland to "blush at the very name of Freedom" for holding in bondage blacks who were "in all respects our equal by nature." It would not do, he had insisted in words that now came back to haunt him, "to be perpetually sermonizing it with liberty for our text, and actual oppression for our commentary."[5]

Yet except for a handful of Radicals—Virginia's John Randolph, North Carolina's Nathaniel Macon, and South Carolina's William Smith—southerners adhered to their liberal pretensions in the Missouri debate by declining to justify slavery in principle. A Georgian even professed to look forward to the "most glorious" day when blacks would attain "the high eminence of equal rights."

Now, however, such liberal sermonizing was mocked by the proslavery "buts" that invariably followed. "We protest in our own name, and that of so many others, that we do not vindicate servitude," declared Thomas Ritchie's Richmond *Enquirer,* in a classic statement of the liberal slaveholders' dilemma. "We wish no slave had touched our soil; we wish it could be terminated. As republicans, we frankly declare before our God and our country, that we abhor its institution." "But," he added, "does not every man, unless he be a fanatic, conceive how difficult it is for us to be rid of it, in a manner consistent with our future peace and tranquility?"[6]

Southern congressmen were also dismayed by the implacability of the unexpected antislavery majorities in the House. It had become "political suicide," a New Hampshire congressman explained to his son, for a free-state representative "to tolerate slavery beyond its present limits."[7] Consequently a House majority could not be obtained to admit Missouri as a slave state without a sharp restriction on the further advance of slavery.

The formula for compromise was offered by a slaveholding senator from free but culturally southern Illinois, Jesse Thomas. While admitting slaveholding Missouri, Thomas proposed, Congress should bar slavery "forever" from all the remaining Louisiana Purchase except that small part (expected eventually to become the state of Arkansas) lying south of Missouri's southern boundary in latitude 36°30'. In addition, Missouri would have to be balanced by admitting to statehood free Maine, heretofore the detached eastern district of Massachusetts.

Even with assurance of Maine and the Thomas Proviso restricting slavery, free-state congressmen voted 87–14 against admitting a slaveholding Missouri. Only unanimous southern support and Henry Clay's adroit tactics eked out a three-vote margin for this most closely contested element of the compromise. The Proviso itself won comfortably with the backing of a bare majority of southerners and an almost unanimous North. In the Senate the compromise passed as a package 24–20, with the North opposed 4–18 and the South in favor 20–2. The two southern dissenters were the Radicals Macon and Smith. Macon explained that the Thomas Proviso acknowledged "the right of Congress to interfere and to legislate on the subject," and "this would be acknowledging too much."

A relieved President Monroe properly credited the compromise to "the patriotic devotion" of the fourteen northerners "who preferr'd the sacrifice of themselves at home to . . . the risk of the Union." Except the Maine men, who won statehood for their constituents, these northern congressmen who voted to admit slaveholding Missouri were bitterly attacked back home, and most of them were defeated for reelection. They got little thanks from slaveholders. John Randolph of Roanoke had only scorn for "these men, *whose conscience, and morality, and religion, extend to 'thirty-six degrees and thirty minutes north latitude.'"* They "were scared at their own dough faces," he sneered, "—yes, *they were scared at their own dough faces!"* For the next forty years American politics would echo with Randolph's taunt at northern "dough faces" who blanched at the threat of disunion and yielded to southern demands.[8]

The Missouri debate shocked Americans by revealing a resurgent slavery on a collision course with an aroused antislavery North. "This momentous question, like a fire bell in the night, awakened and filled me with terror," said Jefferson. "I considered it at once as the knell of the Union." No compromise could last, he predicted, for "a geographical line, coinciding with a marked principle, moral and political, once conceived and held up to the angry passions of men, will never be obliterated; and every new irritation will mark it deeper and deeper." The only "good effect" he saw was that people were awakening to "the necessity of some plan of general emancipation and deportation"; and he doubtless influenced his son-in-law, Governor Thomas Mann Randolph, to recommend such a plan to the 1820 Virginia legislature. But the lawmakers refused to act, and Jeffersonian liberalism was itself deeply tainted with white society's racism. Governor Randolph advocated ridding Virginia of blacks because they were degraded "by slavery, if not by nature." When criticizing slavery Jefferson always insisted that emancipated blacks must be deported. "To the mixture of colour here," he said, "I have great aversion."

Jefferson claimed that giving up his slave property was "a bagatelle which would not cost me a second thought, if, in that way, a general emancipation and *expatriation* could be effected." But with the spectre of Santo Domingo's bloody black revolution before him, he feared that the Missouri Compromise would lead eventually to emancipation without deportation, "in which case all the whites south of the Potomac and Ohio must evacuate their States, and most fortunate those who can do it first." Thus "we have the wolf by the ears, and we can neither hold him, nor safely let him go," he said. "Justice is in one scale, and self-preservation in the other."[9]

Some northerners, by contrast, could not help thrilling to the Missouri fire bell's omen. John Quincy Adams, as the only northern presidential candidate, would be the chief political beneficiary of heightened sectional feelings. But in the privacy of his diary he looked far beyond the presidential election to the slave rebellion and civil war that could purge slavery "from this whole continent." Such an Armageddon would be "calamitous and desolating," Adams confessed, but "so glorious would be its final issue, that, as God shall judge me, I dare not say that it is not to be desired." A life devoted to such a "sublime and beautiful" cause, he mused, "would be nobly spent or sacrificed."[10]

Most southern whites were much less excited than their congressmen. With their liberal honor not so directly challenged, they greeted the Compromise with relief. In the border slave states some voices were even raised for restricting slavery, and throughout the economically prostrated Southwest editors complained that the Missouri debate diverted attention from really important matters like relief for defaulting buyers of federal land.

In South Carolina and wherever else Calhoun's influence extended, slaveholders were reassured by his insistence that few northerners "look to emancipation." Hostile southern reactions, he warned, would lead "directly to disunion with all its horrors." Instead he urged continued adherence to a National Republican politics that sought "without a regard to sections . . . to advance the general interest." At the same time he maintained that "the genius of the age is equality" and urged stronger American support for the liberal revolutions in Europe.[11]

But the Compromise threw southern Radicals into an uproar and inaugurated a two-generation campaign to unite the white South in defense of slavery. Where other slave-state congressmen supported the Proviso restricting slavery 33–15, the delegations from Radical Virginia and Georgia opposed it 6–24. The legislatures of both states resolved against congressional restriction of slavery; and the Virginia legislative caucus refused to endorse Monroe for reelection until he misleadingly fostered the impression that he would veto the Compromise.

The Virginia gentry, after ruling the republic for a generation, suddenly saw their power evaporating. The panic, converting chronic depression into wholesale bankruptcies and emigration, suggested that the downward slide of the whole Chesapeake planting class was irreversible. Simultaneously they were confronted by a united antislavery North in the Missouri controversy and by the Marshall Court's alarming decisions in *Darmouth, Sturgis,* and *McCulloch.* It had already occurred to Radicals like Nathaniel Macon that "if Congress can make canals, they can with more propriety emancipate."[12] In the Missouri crisis, strict constitutional construction—heretofore the first line of defense for the humane Jeffersonian vision of the republic—became also the first line of defense for slavery. Now Virginia's anxious gentlemen fused both struggles with the struggle to maintain their power against the threatening sectional alliance and the threatening constitutional doctrines effected by their Federalist/Clintonian foes.

The Richmond Junto wheeled up its heaviest artillery to bombard the broad constructionism of Marshall's *McCulloch.* The Virginia legislature entered a "most solemn protest" and proposed a new tribunal for adjudicating federal-state conflicts. Judge Roane wrote for the *Enquirer* under the signature "Hampden" a series of essays powerfully criticizing the Hamilton/Story/Marshall line of constitutional reasoning. John Taylor of Caroline set feverishly to composing an elaborate exegesis of the Virginia doctrine of strict construction and state rights. Published in 1820, his *Construction Construed and Constitutions Vindicated* took as its primary targets *McCulloch* and the Missouri restrictionists. Ritchie's widely circulated *Enquirer* blazed away at the same targets, claiming that it was defending state rights and not slavery, "an evil" to be sure, but—the inevitable but—one "we know not how to get rid of."

Although Jefferson resisted Roane's efforts to draw him publicly into the fray, he approved "every tittle" of Hampden's argument and thought the states should present a copy of *Construction Construed* "as a standing instruction" to every representative they elected. Once again it seemed to the ex-President that the federal judiciary, "working like gravity, without intermission, is to press us at last into one consolidated mass." He particularly resented the Supreme Court's "crafty chief judge," whose "lazy or timid" associates allowed him to deliver, as if unanimous, opinions "huddled up in conclave, perhaps by a majority of one." Jefferson thought the earlier Republican failure to impeach notoriously partisan judges had made the judiciary indifferent to public opinion. Unawed by the shibboleth of judicial independence, he insisted that in a republican government, "independence of the will of the nation is a solecism."[13]

Radicals and National Republicans grappled most fiercely in South Carolina, where the forces led by Senator William Smith were stepping up their attack on Calhoun's nationalism. "Calhoun is the author of all the measures we condemn," railed Smith's ally Dr. Thomas Cooper, a radical democrat in his native England, a Jeffersonian martyr to the Sedition Act, and now president of the state college at Columbia. Calhoun "was the adviser of that fool Monroe," Cooper fumed; "he is a national-internal-improvements man; he is fortification mad; he spends the money of the South to buy up influence in the north." Eventually driven from the college presidency in retaliation for his attacks on religion, the squat, bald "Old Coot," as Cooper's students called him, found the prepossessing Calhoun "active, showy, fluent, superficial & conceited."[14]

Nevertheless, according to one of Calhoun's lieutenants, nineteen-twentieths of the South Carolina citizenry backed his loose constructionist nationalism. A majority of the state's congressmen supported the Proviso restricting slavery, and the Charleston *Patriot* praised "that spirit of diffusive patriotism that takes in the welfare of the Union, in opposition to the strength of local attachments." The lower house of the 1820 legislature denounced the Radicals for appealing "to the states as *distinct and independent sovereignties . . .* to exercise a control *over* the general government"; and in 1822 a Calhounite legislature defeated the Radical Senator Smith for reelection, on the ground that he should not be rewarded for opposing the Compromise and thus risking the horrors of disunion.

But in that year the vastly outnumbered white population of the lowcountry was terrified by Denmark Vesey's extensively organized and barely thwarted slave insurrection. Meanwhile upcountry planters were devastated by the depression, and the red clay hills they had ruthlessly mined for cotton during the boom were washing away in the often torrential rains. Unable to compete at low prices with the level, black loams of the lately opened Southwest, they and their slaves were departing by the thousands for cotton's new promised land.

The Radicals, already strong in South Carolina's northeastern region of sandy soils, small slaveholdings, and numerous nonslaveholding farmers, now found a growing audience in the big-plantation regions. The relief legislation needed by distressed planters and farmers, they argued, was relief from the confiscatory and unconstitutional taxation of Calhoun's protective tariff. Why should southern agriculturalists be taxed to subsidize northerners and to pay for Calhoun's roads, canals, fortifications, and army, they asked, especially when northern attacks on slavery were inspiring slaves to insurrection? A loose construction that authorized Congress to levy tariffs and build canals, they warned, would authorize Congress to interfere with slavery. Such arguments were powerfully appealing to a long-invincible ruling class suddenly threatened from so many directions.

What is impressive under the circumstances is the conviction with which Calhoun's closest South Carolina associates so long sustained their nationalism. "There was something in the picture of a magnificent government, invincible in war, beneficent in peace," one of them recalled later, that was "well calculated to fascinate the imagination." As late as 1824 Calhounites believed, in the language of a legislative committee, "that the People have conferred no power upon their state legislature to impugn the Acts of the Federal Government or the decisions of the Supreme Court of the United States," and "that any exercise of such power by this state would be an act of usurpation." Yet within a few years these men, with Calhoun at their head, appeared at the opposite extremity of the constitutional spectrum as the high command of nullification.[15]

The most violent nationalist among them, as he would be the most violent nullifier, was Calhoun's emotional protégé George McDuffie. The states were not "sentinels upon the watchtowers of freedom, or in any respect more worthy of confidence than the general government," he would tell Congress in 1824.

Outraged by a Radical state-rights argument in a Georgia newspaper, McDuffie uncompromisingly rested South Carolina nationalism on the Story/Marshall doctrine of the union. The Constitution was not established by the states but by "*the people of the United States,*" he argued in reply, and "*the people*" reserved "to *themselves,*" not to the states, "the *immediate control* over the whole mass of delegated powers." In fact, he went on, "the states, as political bodies have no original inherent rights." He could "neither understand nor regard" the "imaginary rights" claimed for the states. "They are mere sounds," he said, "used by misguided or designing men for the advancement of their popularity in particular sections of the Union." McDuffie could conceive no greater "climax of political heresies" than the Radical contention that the states, as original parties to the Constitution, were the proper judges of whether it had been violated. This "licentious principle" would enable every state to destroy every delegated power of the federal government, he warned. It would reduce politics to physical force and usher in "anarchy and blood."

With marvelously ironic prescience, McDuffie portrayed the dangerously absurd consequences of a state's declaring a federal revenue law unconstitutional and forbidding its enforcement: "You might, then, behold a revenue officer of the United States confined in a state dungeon for obeying the revenue laws of Congress." Unless there was "some *one* supreme power" in government, he insisted, "force must be the inevitable consequence"; and he maintained that the Constitution located that power in the national judiciary as its final interpreter. The whole-souled McDuffie—who would presently be supporting a South Carolina army to defy federal revenue laws—argued in 1821 that the Constitution authorized calling out the militia to enforce federal laws against a recalcitrant state. "But I sincerely hope," he concluded in a parting shot at his Radical opponents, "that your licentious doctrines will never have the effect of misleading the state authorities so far as to render this terrible resort unavoidable." This acerbic attack on Radicalism involved McDuffie in two duels, and he carried away bullets in his elbow and against his spine that eventually crippled him.[16]

Radical outrage mounted as the Supreme Court resumed the offensive. Chief Justice Marshall blamed "the great Lama of the mountains" at Monticello for the "coarseness and malignity" of the Virginia assault on the judiciary. Encouraged no doubt by the demonstration of antisouthern strength in the Missouri crisis, the Chief Justice resolved to press home his judicial offensive against "the powerful and violent party in Virginia" whose "deep design" it was "to convert our government into a mere league of States."[17] In 1821 the Marshall Court accepted an appeal from two Virginians who had been convicted at Norfolk for violating a Virginia law forbidding the sale of lottery tickets. This unprecedented review of a state criminal conviction was justified on the ground that Congress had authorized the federal city of Washington to establish the lottery in question.

When the incensed Virginia legislature, disputing the Court's jurisdiction, forbade the state's lawyers to argue the merits of the case, Marshall resorted to his *Marbury* tactic. In *Cohens v. Virginia* he ruled for Virginia on the merits by concluding that Congress did not intend to authorize sale of lottery tickets outside the District of Columbia. Thus he avoided any further challenge to his sweeping jurisdictional ruling that the Court was final arbiter for any matter remotely involving interpretation of a federal law. All this was embedded in an eloquent *obiter dictum* on the inherent necessity for federal power, which left open the implication that Congress might have forced lottery tickets into Virginia if it had wanted to.

Again the *Enquirer* thundered. Again Judge Roane fulminated in a series of newspaper essays, this time signing himself "Algernon Sidney" and now advocating repeal of the law (the twenty-fifth section of the Judiciary Act of 1789) authorizing appeals from state courts to the Supreme Court. Again John Taylor scribbled furiously, as though the consolidationists might overwhelm the republic before he completed his massive line of theoretical fortifications. In *Tyranny Unmasked* (1822) he made state rights his bulwark, not only against the federal judiciary but also against such congressional oppression as protective tariffs transferring wealth from agriculture to manufacturers. Completing in 1823 a final state-rights polemic, *New Views of the Constitution,* Taylor spent the last two years of his life personifying in the Senate the political platform he had elaborated for Virginia and a spreading Radicalism.

Meanwhile the Marshall Court stirred up opposition in other states. In *Green v. Biddle* (1821) it plunged Kentucky land titles into chaos by siding with the big speculators to strike down state laws protecting occupying claimants whose titles were challenged. Simultaneously it was bringing to heel the state of Ohio, which forcibly collected a prohibitive tax on the national Bank in defiance of *McCulloch v. Maryland.* The federal circuit court imprisoned an Ohio official for flouting its injunction and seizing over a hundred thousand dollars from the Bank; and in *Osborn v. Bank of the U.S.* (1824) the Supreme Court forced the state to submit. By 1825 the Marshall Court had struck down laws of ten states, and every session of Congress was hearing new proposals for curtailing its powers.[18]

But rising opposition did not deter the Chief Justice. With his brethren now well in hand, Marshall resolved to add the capstone to his edifice of constitutional buttresses for a capitalist republic. As local and regional markets intermeshed into an emergent national market lawyers had begun to glimpse the latent possibilities in the enumerated congressional power to "regulate Commerce . . . among the several States." Through creative construction of the commerce clause, the Court could consolidate federal power and guarantee against local interference the freedom of an American market now being projected to continental dimensions. In 1824 the opportunity Marshall awaited reached the Supreme Court in *Gibbons v. Ogden.*

The case involved a substantial impediment to the free growth of the American market. A New York law had conferred a monopoly of steamboat navigation in the state's waters on the steamboat's inventor, Robert Fulton, in partnership with his longtime patron Robert R. Livingston of the politically powerful Republican family. When the partners gained similar monopolistic privileges from Louisiana, free competition was threatened on the increasingly vital Mississippi-Ohio river system. Other states fought back, New Jersey and Connecticut barring the monopoly's steamboats from their waters. The case arose when a competing steamboat line, in which the aggressive entrepreneur Cornelius Vanderbilt was getting his start, defied the monopoly in the profitable short run across New York harbor from New Jersey to Manhattan.

With public opinion strongly against the monopoly, Marshall no doubt realized that an antimonopoly decision could push federal power under the commerce clause much further than would otherwise be politically feasible. Daniel Webster, the leading attorney on the antimonopoly side of the case, provided the Court with an ample arsenal of arguments for this purpose. He defined the fundamental problem as the economic cost of state jurisdiction over commerce, exemplified here by the collision between the New York monopoly and the retaliatory legislation of other states. The remedy was a proper application of the commerce clause, under which the power of Congress was "complete and entire, and to a certain extent, necessarily exclusive." The monopoly, being a state attempt to exercise a power of regulation lodged exclusively in Congress, was therefore unconstitutional.

Webster observed with satisfaction that the Chief Justice was accepting his argument "as a baby takes in its mother's milk"; and when Marshall pronounced for a unanimous Court, it was Webster's logic he followed. By "commerce," he said, the Constitution meant not just a mere traffic in goods but "every species of intercourse," the broader term *intercourse* implying the carrying of passengers as well as goods and certainly including the vessels or other conveyances on which they were carried. Because such commerce "cannot stop at the external boundary-line of each state," he argued next, the congressional regulatory power "must be exercised within the territorial jurisdiction of the several states."

But the Chief Justice hesitated to base the decision on Webster's contention that the federal regulatory power over commerce was exclusive, barring any state regulation whatever. "There is great force in this argument," he declared, "and the court is not satisfied that it has been refuted." The problem was to avoid challenging the mass of state legislation affecting commerce with regard to such matters as pilots, health, quarantine, ferries, turnpikes, and bridges, which Webster had disposed of as "regulations of police" rather than regulations of commerce. But this distinction would involve the court in endless litigation defining the two classes of regulation, and Marshall preferred to leave to state regulation purely local commerce that "does not extend to or affect other States."

For this reason Marshall's far-reaching exposition of the commerce clause ended up a mere *obiter dictum,* technically irrelevant to the immediate decision. Instead he decided the case on a secondary argument of Webster's, an extremely strained contention that the federal act licensing coastal vessels conferred on them the right of navigating "freely the waters of the United States." Therefore the New York law contravening this federal law was unconstitutional.

The decision won immediate applause on antimonopoly grounds. The monopoly's rivals sent their steamboats into New York harbor festooned with banners and firing salutes, to the cheers of Manhattanites massed on the docks. Within a year the number of steamboats serving the city rose from six to forty-three, while competition reduced fares on the New Haven run from five dollars to three dollars. At the same time the Supreme Court was vehemently denounced by people who asked if the extension of federal power, pushed now into the very centers of the supposedly sovereign states, could ever be stopped at any point. With commerce defined as "intercourse" subject to federal regulation within the states, said a North Carolinian, "I shall soon expect to learn that our fornication laws are unconstitutional."[19]

Virginians were especially outraged that the Court had again extended federal power by proclaiming broad principles unnecessary for deciding the case at hand. They were further annoyed by Marshall's gratuitous attack on strict construction as "that narrow construction, which would cripple the government"; nor were they mollified by his explanation that his lecture was "unavoidable" because "powerful and ingenious minds" were trying to "explain away the constitution of our country and leave it a magnificent structure indeed, to look at, but totally unfit for use."

To the chief target of Marshall's lecture, the eighty-two-year-old Jefferson, *Gibbons* was the last straw. It culminated, he complained, "the rapid strides with which the Federal branch of our Government is advancing towards the usurpation of all the rights reserved to the States, and the consolidation in itself of all powers, foreign and domestic; and that too by constructions which, if legitmate, leave no limits to their power."[20]

Everywhere bitterness like Jefferson's eroded the generous nationalism of the postwar boom years. Taught by National Republicanism that prosperity depended on public policy, each stricken interest group focused on government its hopes for survival. Never, said an Indiana representative, had "the solicitudes of the nation ... been so much directed towards Congress—their interests so generally presented, and ardently pressed."[21] All were quick to feel injury from measures aiding others. And because clashing interests were concentrated in different sections, these conflicts polarized conventional federal politics sectionally.

The loudest and best organized demands for congressional assistance arose from the host of prostrated manufacturers. Mostly masters of small shops rather than factories, many had risen from mechanic origins. Concentrated in the Northeast, they were most numerous in Philadelphia, New York, and Baltimore, and their enterprises had also come to dominate the economic life of many smaller places—Lynn, Troy, Newark, Paterson, Wilmington, Pittsburgh, Cincinnati, and Lexington—while their iron works and textile mills were scattered widely across the northeastern countryside. Where the prosperity of whole communities depended on such enterprises, imperiled workers and the neighboring farmers who supplied them supported the manufacturers' demands for a sharp increase in tarriff protection.

Congressmen were, of course, responsive to such interests in their districts; and in the middle of the Missouri crisis, Representative Henry Baldwin of Pittsburgh (an Old School Democrat) had Speaker Clay's full support in pushing through the House, 91–78, a bill raising import duties on various articles anywhere from 20 percent to 100 percent. Free-state representatives voted 80–18 for the Baldwin bill, while slave-state congressmen opposed it 11–60. Hard-pressed southern planters and farmers were beginning to ask why money should be taken from their pockets, through higher prices for their purchases, to enrich manufacturers. But each section had a dissenting minority. The commercial interests of the northeastern ports, opposing restrictions on the flow of international trade, could still muster Massachusetts congressmen 10–7 against the Baldwin bill, while the border slave-state delegations of industrializing Delaware and hemp-growing Kentucky voted for it 2–0 and 4–3.

The pattern was similar in the Senate, but here the South was strong enough to defeat the bill by a single vote. This frustrating southern preponderance in the Senate would be perpetuated by the Missouri Compromise, complained a Pennsylvania newspaper. "The misery entailed upon the black population to the south, is accompanied by the impoverishment and distress of the white population of the other parts of the union." Similarly the South was mainly responsible for the repeated defeats of a federal bankruptcy act, now urged more desperately than ever by stricken northeastern commercial interests.

This Congress also faced demands from the many thousands who could not complete payment for public lands bought on credit during the great land boom. Under relief legislation recommended by Treasury Secretary Crawford, they were allowed to retain the proportion of land for which they had already paid, or get a substantial discount for cast payment, or extend the payment period free of interest charges. To prevent recurrence of this problem, the Land Act of 1820 abolished credit in federal land sales while reducing the minimum price from $2.00 an acre to $1.25 and the minimum amount that could be purchased from 160 acres to 80. Now a farm could be had for a hundred dollars.

The most important form of congressional relief was relief from taxation. "I want a cheap government," as a Pennsylvanian expressed the widespread sentiment. That was "the real, true democracy," he added, as opposed to "this new-fangled democracy, which seems to be made for nothing but noise and extravagance." The unpopular direct taxes had been repealed in the wake of the electoral revolt against the Fourteenth Congress, but the depression cut so deeply into other federal revenues that existing programs could be funded only by reimposing the direct taxes. Instead Radicals led Congress in applying a meat-axe to the most expensive programs, ending the naval buildup, drastically scaling down the fortifications program, and cutting the army almost in half.[22]

Hard times made the economic stimulus promised by roads and canals particularly attractive, infusing the internal-improvements debate with close calculations of sectional benefits and costs. In 1822 an almost unanimous West found enough support from Middle Atlantic representatives to push through Congress an act authorizing tolls to finance repairs on the National Road. As last, in vetoing this measure, President Monroe had a chance to fire off his twenty-five-thousand-word constitutional disquisition. Through unanswerable argument he hoped to convince the country that a national transportation system was indispensable, that it could not be created under existing constitutional authority, and, therefore, that the Constitution must be amended.

At the last minute, however, Monroe held up his dissertation a day to insert a hurried addendum before sending it to Congress. Deep in the President's interminable critique of the various implied powers, and after he had rejected on orthodox Jeffersonian grounds a broad construction of the revenue and general-welfare clause, his prose and logic abruptly became almost unintelligible.

Here and there were islands of clarity. At one point he plainly said he had recently changed his mind about the revenue/general-welfare clause which empowered Congress to "collect taxes ... to pay the debts and provide for the common defence and general welfare." At another he declared that the congressional power to appropriate money under this clause was "restricted only by the duty to appropriate it to purposes of common defense and of general, not local, national, not State, benefit." And finally, at another point he announced that he could therefore see no constitutional objection to appropriations for roads and canals "carried to a certain extent," particularly if they were useful for military defense, or expedited the mails, or enhanced the value of public lands.

Only the persevering reader would finally realize that this incongruous and not very logical addendum reversed Monroe's position. Despite all his Jeffersonian camouflage about the inadequacy of the enumerated powers and the need for a constitutional amendment, the President now supported congressional appropriations for national roads and canals built with the permission and cooperation of the states through which they passed.[23]

The obvious influence was Calhoun's. The premier champion of roads and canals doubtless warned that if the National Road bill were vetoed without leaving some other way to finance repairs, Monroe would be blamed for abandoning this great national work. Above all the President's favorite Cabinet adviser offered, and no doubt persistently argued for, a constitutional interpretation that could be seen as reconciling roads and canals with Jeffersonian opposition to implied powers.

Monroe reached back to the debate over the Bonus Bill for Calhoun's audacious contention that the Constitution's framers intended to empower Congress to appropriate money for any worthy national purposes, such as roads and canals. The best authority on the framers' intent was ex-President Madison, and he went out of his way in vetoing the Bonus Bill to express shock at Calhoun's contention. But through an ingeniously drawn series of resolutions in 1818, Calhoun's confederate Lowndes demonstrated that more congressmen were willing to justify internal improvements by the revenue clause than by any of the implied powers.[24]

Monroe finally accepted Calhoun's doctrine for the same reason that recommended it to many Republican congressmen—it was the only one in sight that preserved the letter of Jeffersonian orthodoxy on implied powers while in fact opening the way for roads and canals. Monroe professed to believe, *contra* Madison, that state sovereignty was less liable to invasion under a broad power of appropriation than under a broad construction of the enumerated powers. In any event he discovered and propounded a Republican reading of "general welfare" that would serve almost as well as the Federalist reading of "necessary and proper" to sanction a virtually unlimited federal role in the political economy of a market-organized society.

If the President's opaque addendum hid his real meaning so successfully that many contemporaries missed it, he was muffling it from that part of himself and of the populace over which Mr. Jefferson's consciousness still held sway. Yet the moment Monroe yielded to Calhoun's arguments the transformation of Republicanism was completed. Caught between two worlds and conceiving it his historic role to unite the country around the National Republican vision of wealth and power, he grasped the nettle, however awkwardly, and made the decision that placed the federal government fully at the service of the republic's capitalist destiny.

Jefferson was appalled. With "deepest affliction" he charged that all three branches of the federal government "are in combination to strip their colleagues, the State authorities, of the powers reserved to them." Under the power to regulate commerce, he said, they take the earnings of agriculture "and put them into the pockets of" manufacturers. Under the power of establishing post roads, "they claim that of cutting down mountains for the construction of roads, of digging canals." And "aided by a little sophistry on the words 'general welfare,'" they claim the right to do "whatsoever they shall think or pretend will be for the general welfare."[25]

The politicians did not miss Monroe's meaning. Coupled with Calhoun's general-survey proposal, as they quickly understood, the President's turnaround meant that a national transportation system could be built by piecemeal appropriations for different segments, with the general survey defining each local segment as part of a potential national system and thus meeting Monroe's new constitutional test of national importance. At the very next session Congress passed with the President's advance approval a direct appropriation for repairing the National Road, as well as the first general appropriation bill for harbor improvements. After Monroe recommended using army engineers to survey a canal connecting the Potomac with the Ohio, as well as canals connecting the Ohio with Lake Erie, Congress finally passed in 1824 (and Monroe signed) the General Survey Act, authorizing Calhoun's military engineers to prepare surveys, plans, and estimates for whatever canals and roads the President deemed of national importance. While awaiting surveys and the political support for various projects that the surveys could be expected to generate, Congress contented itself with authorizing extension of the National Road westward from Wheeling across Ohio and projecting its eventual extension all the way across the Mississippi to the capital of Missouri.

Secretary Calhoun established a Board of Engineers for Internal Improvements in the War Department and laid down for it priorities of national importance, in terms of the commercial, military, and postal utility of proposed projects. Of highest national importance, he decided, were the President's favorite canal projects to connect the Potomac with the Ohio and the Ohio with Lake Erie, including navigation improvements on the Ohio and Mississippi and canals around the falls at Louisville and Muscle Shoals. Next he ranked the great inland waterway along the Atlantic, and after that a durable road from Washington to New Orleans. Under these guidelines the Board's surveying brigades, each with a half dozen engineers, fanned out across the land. By 1828 eleven brigades were continuously in the field; the engineers had surveyed almost a hundred projects, including thirty-four canals, eighteen roads, and forty-four river and harbor improvements; and they were about to undertake their first railroad survey.

Calhoun's general-survey strategy for achieving a national transportation system encompassed, like Alexander Hamilton's most creative proposals, a decided political thrust. It was not just that the Secretary boosted his presidential prospects among Pennsylvanians by his eagerness to provide them with engineers at the height of their canal mania. More significant were the developmental hopes generated in every locality through which an alternative route was surveyed, and the rising support for internal improvements that resulted.

The strategy was ingeniously calculated to mobilize and politicize the latent entrepreneurial energies scattered through the American hinterland. Already hearing rumbles of opposition from his own South Carolina, Calhoun made sure that the engineers themselves understood the political thrust of their activities. Because southerners seemed to have doubts about supporting the system, he instructed the Board, surveys on the Washington–New Orleans road should be expedited. It was desirable, he explained, for doubters to "not only see, but feel some of the immediate benefits which will result from a system of internal improvement." He did not yet recognize the popular upheaval that was dooming not only his "perfect system of roads and canals," but his whole developmental design for "a most splendid future."[26]

Popular upheaval in both religion and politics registered widely experienced stresses of capitalist transformation, as thrust inland by the postwar boom and sharpened by hard times. This was the first American generation to push or be pushed in large numbers across one of history's great divides. They were passing from a use-value world permeated by familial/communal ties and God's everyday presence to a market world that takes the competitive ego for human nature and rationality for revelation.

Radically new imperatives confronted people when they were lured or pushed from modest subsistence into open-ended market production. By the 1820s rapidly spreading channels of trade were replacing an unpressured security of rude comfort with an insecurity goaded by hope of opulence and fear of failure. Within a generation in every new area the market invaded, competition undermined neighborly cooperation and family equality. Ancestral ways and parental example no longer worked. Increasingly individuals had to chart their own chancy courses.

The carrot-and-stick of wealth/poverty and the lash of competition enforced a new intensity of effort. More labor was required to survive respectably, let alone succeed. Holders of much or little capital mined their own energies as well as the energies of people lacking capital. Manufacturing workers labored twelve to fourteen hours a day six days a week, averaging three thousand hours a year, half again today's two thousand. These deceptively simple figures tell economic historians that "lost leisure" and "more work per laborer" paid for much of the economy's apparent income growth. And today's market world, they also mean, still exacts more labor from most people than did the premarket world. Average hours of farm labor stayed below today's industrial two thousand throughout the nineteenth century, as farmers clinging to easy-going subsistence outweighed those working harder for the market.[27]

Moreover the capitalist market exacted alienated labor. Where traditional workways had been relaxed, varied, geared to felt needs, and interwoven with sociability and family life, competition compelled people to objectify themselves and others as abstract labor-power. Objectified labor-power could be almost totally exploited in producing abstract commodity values, leaving people barely enough waking hours and vitality to reproduce themselves through family life. With labor increasingly deskilled, routinized, and supervised into a drudgery segregated from what was left of life, more and more Americans sank into Henry Thoreau's "lives of quiet desperation."[28]

Success required not only unremitting effort but a habit of rational calculation, beginning with measurement and counting of labor-time, capital, commodities, and money. By the dismal decade's close, foreign travelers along the main market corridors were encountering, as the Englishman Thomas Hamilton reported, a "guessing, reckoning, expecting and calculating people." The Frenchman Alexis de Tocqueville was equally struck by Americans' propensity for "definite calculations." Statistics, first compiled to measure and celebrate the commercial boom, now proliferated on every subject. Most businessmen finally adopted the double-entry system of bookkeeping to measure profit margins closely and continuously. Demand for numerical skills inspired new teaching methods and textbooks, making arithmetic considerably easier to learn. "You must calculate," young men were told by a new advice literature. Embarking now on uncertain "careers," they were exhorted to perfect their quantitative competence in "every circumstance . . . where reckoning is required."[29]

Life by reckoning alienated people not only from their labor but from the organic matrix of the natural world. With experience no longer patterned mainly by kinship and the revolutions of the heavens, competition imposed on perception a grid of time and space calibrated in quantitative increments. The land itself became units of capital. People fled failure for success by strenuously converting countable time-units of alienated labor (their own or others') into countable money-units of capital. Thus one became "worth" so many dollars. The most worthy were those quickest to adjust perception and effort to the new calculus.

Human energy, the most elastic factor in the capitalist equation, required the closest reckoning. Self-exploiting calculation of labor-time became habitual and unconscious. By the 1820s public clocks—adding a second pointer to measure minutes as well as hours—were spreading to inland centers of trade. Hourly or quarter-hourly their bells reminded townspeople and the nearby countryside that "time is money."

To meet the demand for measured time—and to exploit the cheap labor of distressed rural Connecticut—the highly skilled mechanic art of clockmaking was "systematized in the most perfect manner and conducted on a large scale," as manufacturer Chauncey Jerome boasted. With his workers alone producing reliable wooden clocks in lots of ten thousand—his aptly numerical measure of his worth—the price fell from five dollars to fifty cents. By 1840 cheap household clocks had penetrated the backwoods. "In every dell in Arkansas," a traveler reported, "and in cabins where there was not a chair to sit on, there was sure to be a Connecticut clock." Soon Americans reared by the zodiac would be carrying pocket "watches" as ever-present monitors of their alienated labor.[30]

People's initial responses to the market are harder to recapture than its ultimate consequences for their lives. Certainly its opportunities and its discipline were embraced eagerly by hustlers with access to capital like Chauncey Jerome, whose memoirs gloried in his "splendid" clock factories, all "effected through my untiring efforts."[31] Because historical records were left mainly by this successful minority, liberal historiography all too easily sees them as typical. Although a new labor history is recovering the complex responses of urban working people, written sources only occasionally reveal much about the interface between the market and the oral culture of the farming majority.

Fetishism of commodities can be seen in Thurlow Weed's memoirs of his farm boyhood in upstate New York. The editor/politician recalled that the first store, seven or eight miles down the river, was "all the talk" for several weeks, while families pooled resources to send a wagonful of wives reconnoitering. They came home "rejoicing" over "fragrant bohea [tea] for themselves, plug tobacco for their husbands, flashy calico for the children, gay ribbons for the girls, jack-knives for the boys, crockery for the cupboard, and snuff for 'Grannie.'" Yet "staring eyes and open mouths" registered their cultural distance from "the wonders of the 'new store.'" "The merchant and his clerk were criticized in their deportment, manners, and dress," Weed remembered. "The former wore shiny boots with tassels—the latter a ruffle shirt—and both smelt of pomatum!"[32]

The pull of store goods was more complicated in an Illinois family visited by Methodist circuit rider Peter Cartwright in the 1820s. The husband was saving money to pay for the farm, and the furnishings were especially primitive—a hole in a dirt hearth for cooking, rough lumber beds and table, sharpened pieces of cane for forks, and a single broken chair. "The old sister kept up a constant apology," and Cartwright admonished the husband. "Now, brother," he said, "do . . . go to town and get you a set of chairs, knives and forks, cups and saucers, and get you a couple of plain bedsteads and bed-cords. Give your wife and daughters a chance. These girls, sir, are smart enough to marry well, if you will fix them up a little."

The husband resented the preacher's interference, but Cartwright found on his next visit that all his suggestions had been followed. Moreover "the women all had new calico dresses, and looked very neat." They "had taken my lecture to the old brother for a text, and they had preached successfully to him." This old brother was drawn into the market by more than commodity fetishism or even the utility of store goods. Intrafamilial pressures enforced the communal standards Preacher Cartwright invoked.[33]

By the late 1820s many a reluctant Illinois patriarch felt such pressures, as neighborhood after neighborhood abandoned buckskin, homespun, and moccasins in favor of cloth coats, calico dresses, and shoes. Churchgoing by young people, in Governor Thomas Ford's opinion, promoted the change. "The young ladies," he explained, instead of walking barefoot to church, "now came forth arrayed complete in all the pride of dress, mounted on fine horses and attended by their male admirers." If church attendance "effected no better end," Ford thought, at least it taught young men as well as women "to admire and wish to be admired. Each one wanted to make as good a figure as he could." The older people, by contrast, "would have been better contented to live in their old log cabins, go bare-footed, and eat hog and hominy." They complained "that the spinningwheel and the loom were neglected and that all the earnings of the young people were expended in the purchase of finery." The important point to Governor Ford, a self-made man and champion of progress, was that "those who adopted the new habits were more industrious and thrifty than those were who held on to the old ones." The younger people's desire for finery "created in them a will to exert more than the old measure of industry; and taught them new notions of economy and ingenuity in business, to get the means of gratifying their pride." These "settled habits of enterprise" caused "a thriftiness unknown to their fathers and mothers."[34]

Female attire is a curiously prominent issue in these and similar accounts, representing a new anxiety about status. Patriarchal honor made the subsistence culture peculiarly susceptible to the emulative consumption stirred up by the market's open-ended production. As in other patriarchal cultures, women and their adornments became tokens of family honor. Once the first farmer in a neighborhood increased his marketable surplus to buy calico for his women to wear to church, everyone else had to match the new standard of honorific display or forfeit the claim to patriarchal equality. Loss of honor carried the rural world's ultimate emotional penalty, shame. "The women desire dress," explained the English visitor Harriet Martineau, "not only because it is becoming, but because they revolt from sinking, even outwardly, into a lower station of life than they once held." To maintain equality, patriarchal families had to keep up with the Joneses. Women's dress became the critical marker of a new kind of status graded by family levels of commodity consumption.

Store-bought clothing translated into the moral vocabulary of rural America as "luxury," with overtones of sinful lapse from ancestral virtue. Martineau found farm folk full of "declamation against luxury." This "painful sensibility," swelling to a national litany of *mea culpa* after the panic, was evoked by a competitive materialism that many could neither condone nor resist. In long-stressed Massachusetts, Martineau observed that the "old-fashioned" farmer, even while denouncing luxury, all too often mortgaged his already inadequate land "in order that his wife and daughters may dress like the ladies of Boston." And all too often, she added, "loss or ruin ensues" because "the great Insurance Company at Boston . . . will not wait a day for the interest."

The evil, this hard-headed liberal concluded, "is not in the dress; it is rather in his clinging to a mode of life which does not enable him to pay his debts." Farmers "must either go down with their farm, for the love of it, and the ways which belong to it," she insisted, "or they must make a better living in some other manner." And with the market's tempting luxuries "growing before their eyes," it seemed "pretty clear which they will choose."[35]

Subsistence farmers eventually faced the additional pressure of agrarian crisis—too little land for too many children—that had long intensified the pressure of neighborhood emulation in rural Massachusetts. Unless they shifted to commodity production, they found themselves producing children for the market instead. Fathers were forced into the market in an often losing effort to provide children the traditional patrimony of land or an alternative start in life. Direct economic pressure reinforced all these social pressures. As the state's power of eminent domain extended cash-crop production inexorably along turnpikes, canals, and railroads, land values rose, and with them the farmer's taxes. If one generation hung on by working harder in the old way, ever-rising taxes eventually forced a succeeding generation to produce for market or sell out.

Yet American farm families, far from embracing the market, yielded grudgingly to its potent pressures. A widespread disposition "to go down with their farm, for the love of it, and the ways which belong to it," persisted far into the twentieth century. Constantly the market's agricultural reformers complained about the "invincible *inertium*" of the farmer "who condemns new things because they are new," who "knows how to conduct a farm only by imitation," who is satisfied with low yields and profits "so long as he departs from no established usage." If few adhered wholly to subsistence ways, few converted overnight to the market calculus. Although spreading transport committed ever more farmers to substantial commodity production, most continued to produce most of their subsistence needs, while working harder for enough market commodities to meet a slowly rising neighborhood standard of respectability.[36]

In fact the main brake on American economic growth was farmers' bemusing refusal to behave with market rationality by maximizing return on capital. Led to this conclusion by "relatively low farm income and modest increases in farmland values," economic historians have had to recognize that "agriculturalists responded to more than economic incentives."[37] What governed rural behavior— more than the labor costs of store goods—was attachment to a use-value way of life now under heavy assault.

Market disruption of the household economy, peaking in the 1820s, disrupted traditional sex roles and intergenerational ties. Patriarchal authority eroded; women's responsibilities and validations shrank; children grew burdensome; and customary rearing ill prepared them for chancy careers. When the cultural break came, it was mainly generational. Sons and daughters, sometimes with discreet maternal support, took up new ways that fathers resisted. Resenting a paternal authority that seemed less reasonable as it became less functional, many departing children leapt into the capitalist race with the zeal of converts. Thus market pressures, felt especially through competitive consumption, activated the fault lines of generation and gender along which a doomed culture fractured.

The pressures of postwar boom-and-bust brought spiritual/political insurgency to a peak. The antinomian fervor that had fueled the democratic impulse against Revolutionary elites in the New-Light Stir, and Jeffersonian democracy against Federalist hauteur and commercial boom in the Great Revival, now plunged the Jacksonian generation into a Second Great Awakening and democratic revolution. As the magical New Light validated everyperson's heart against authority in church and state, plebeian evangelicalism became the predominant form of American Christianity.[38]

Since the New-Light Stir, millennial fantasy had impelled the most disaffected evangelicals to "come out" of a secular world corrupted by market egotism. Yearning like ages of stressed and powerless Christians for the Biblically promised Millennium when an avenging Christ would return to destroy evil and inaugurate a thousand-year Kingdom of God on earth, Come-outers perfected themsleves for the Glorious Day in church communities of pure righteousness and love. They sought, in the words of New-Stir evangelist Henry Alline, "a spiritual assurance which rejected and transcended the tribulations of the secular world."

The market world's most painful tribulations inspired radical innovation. Imbued with the primitive communism of New-Testament Christians, a host of little Come-outer cults, many led by women, found ecstatic assurance of spiritual perfection by purging themselves of egoistic possessiveness in relations of sex and property. In luxuriantly various ways, they reconstructed the most basic human relationships around the antinomian values of love, community, and equality. Many were rightly suspected of trampling on "the bonds of matrimony, the separate rights of property, and the laws of civil society."

The most durable of the radical Come-outer sects combined communism with celibacy. Followers of Rhode Island's electrifying Publick Universal Friend, Jemima Wilkinson, fled the world for a flourishing New Jerusalem in the wilds of New York's Genesee valley, where they perfected themselves for the Kingdom of God in loving sexual equality. Mother Ann Lee's United Society of Believers in Christ's Second Appearing inventively displaced eroticism from carnal intercourse to sexually segregated spiritual ritual. Taking their common name from ecstatic dances where catharsis charged life with loving intensity, these Shakers scattered their handsome, productive communities across the stressed New England hills, and every ebullition of the New Light brought a new harvest of recruits.

Less desperate Come-outers from the old-line denominations rejected college-educated clerical elites for the unpretentious fervor of Baptist and Methodist exhorters. With direct infusion of the New Light furnishing the spiritual intensity formerly inspired by Calvin's awesome doctrine of divine sovereignty, many egalitarian evangelicals challenged orthodoxy for confining salvation to a God-chosen elite. Loving antinomianism was particularly affronted by the Calvinists' grim consignment of babies dying unsaved to the fires of Hell. Free-Will Baptists and Universalists arose in rural New England to promise salvation for all. Farther south Methodists preached that the lowliest sinner had only to "believe" to be saved. Winning followers in droves, they became the main bearers of antinomian universalism. Methodists would pass the one million mark in 1844 to become the largest American religious body, with Baptists close behind.[39]

Baptists embodied most fully the Come-outer traditionalism of rural America. Their dramatic conversion ritual immersed the newly reborn in the cleansing waters of the nearest stream to wash away the sins of "the world." Baptists were admonished against "an inordinate desire of earthly things, or what belongs to our neighbours, and a dissatisfaction with what we have, an overanxious care about the things of this world, a rapacity in obtaining wealth, and a tenaciousness in keeping it." A North Carolina Baptist association denied that "false titles of industry and frugality" justified a covetous sinner "on account of his riches." The market's competitive ethic defied the Biblical injunction to *"love thy neighbor as thyself,"* the association warned, and *"if ye bite and devour one another, take heed that ye be not consumed, one of another."*[40]

This antinomian Come-outerism led rural Quakers to secede from their urban and increasingly secular co-religionists. Their leader Elias Hicks, opposing all improvements, taught that if God had wanted the Erie Canal, he would have put a waterway there. "Happy is the man who has a good farm clear of debt, and is therewith content and does not know how to write his name!" preached Hicks. "I say to those who have been brought up in the country, stay there." Even Presbyterians were exhorted "to live within your incomes" and "contract no extravagant debts." Transfiguring encounter with Almightly God called the reborn out of the world of calculating ego to a separated church community of holy love.[41]

Evangelicals dramatized their rejection of the world in countless ways. Against the world's pride of intellect, they asserted the heartfelt emotion of rustic preachers and believers. Rejecting the world's pride of rank and dress, they practiced congregational democracy, accorded women and slaves a more equal role, and condemned "superfluity of apparel." More fervent male Baptists cropped their hair "like Cromwell's round-headed chaplains, and the women cast away all their superfluities so that they were distinguished from others."[42] Baptists required their part-time preachers to share the common lot of farming for a living, and Methodists kept their full-time bishops and circuit riders on the road in search of lay hospitality by paying them only sixty-four dollars a year.

Baptists institutionalized most fully the egalitarian localism of the subsistence culture. Against both state and wider church, they defended fiercely the independence of their democratic congregations. The only donominational organization they could tolerate was voluntary regional associations. Churches so inclined dispatched "messengers" to association meetings with congregationally approved "letters" and occasional "queries." These festivals of revival preaching, deliberating at first without a moderator and requiring unanimity for decision, rarely ventured more than cautious "advice."

Baptists dramatized evangelical flight from the world's estranging competition by seizing upon every Biblical precedent to sacralize intimacy and touching. Imitating New-Testament Christian rites as literally as possible in adult baptism and weekly celebration of the Lord's Supper, they also practiced "laying-on of hands," "foot washing," "feasts of charity," "anointing the sick," and "devoting children." Ritual confession bared souls to a caring community, and "holy affection" made credible the charge that more souls were bred than saved at camp meetings.

The New Light's intensification of communal bonds was perhaps its essence. Most evangelicals called each other "Brother" and "Sister" and joined Baptists in such Biblical practices as embracing in prayer and meeting with the "kiss of charity." At streamside immersions of converts, hymn-singing Baptists exchanged the "right hand of fellowship," often "melted in tears" because "the act seemed so friendly, the ministers appeared so loving." This scriptural rite, soon secularized to invoke godly integrity in sealing market contracts, swept through a populace anxiously shoring up human ties to become the perfunctory modern handshake.

The born-again relied on the "watchful care" of their intense, lifelong, Come-outer communities to sustain their newborn resistance to temptation. Baptist and Methodist churches maintained constant vigilance against family-threatening adultery; and temptations of the flesh figured prominently in the "conviction" of sinfulness that propelled young people to the new birth. Bishop William

McKendree, who led the Methodist conquest of the West, recalled luridly his struggles against a "lascivious love" who "spreads her temptations" with limbs "soft and delicate; her attire loose & inviting, wantonness sparkles in her eyes." "Fly every temptation that leads to her banquet," he implored, "as you would the devil himself."[43]

Entire congregations participated in bringing offenders to repentance and reformation. Suspension or excommunication was a last resort, and the door was always open for the contrite sinner to return. Watchful care extended also to the patriarchal vices of drinking, swearing, gambling, and fighting, or any dishonesty or slander that threatened communal harmony. The minutely elaborated Methodist *Discipline* forbade haggling, usury, and fraud and required members to submit disputes to a deacon before taking them to a secular court.

The Come-outerism of these tight communities erupted at whitest heat in millennial fantasy. "Fully persuaded that the glorious Millennial Day had commenced," ecstatic converts anticipated Christ's imminent return to revolutionize the world. The New Light "was not sent to RE-FORM the churches," proclaimed one enthusiast, but "to prepare the way for that kingdom of God, in which all things are new."

Millennial hopes for rapid Christianization of the world redoubled evangelical efforts to spread the New Light. "Ride on, blessed Redeemer," exulted Methodism's remarkable field marshal Francis Asbury at the peak of the Great Revival, "until all states and nations of the earth are subdued unto thy sacred sway." No one rode on in the Redeemer's cause more indefatigably than Bishop Asbury and his Methodist cavalry. Baptists were outdistanced, despite their deeper roots in rural culture, by Methodism's superb horseback organization for gathering in the harvest ripened by the New Light.[44]

Founder John Wesley had designed his missionary enterprise for efficiency in rechristianizing Britain's demoralized working classes. Where Baptist congregations multiplied by licensing farmer/preachers to nourish nearby offshoots into independent churches, American Methodists adapted to their vast vineyard Wesley's centrally directed cadre of full-time evangelists. Bishops supervised regional conferences and licensed earnest, strong-voiced young converts to travel around circuits of up to two hundred miles, preaching in houses, barns, or churches wherever people were willing to hear them. The circuit rider organized converts into neighborhood classes and appointed the most fervent as lay class leaders to oversee services and church discipline between his visits. As fast as class leaders could be groomed into circuit riders, bishops pushed them into new territories.

Measuring their stewardship by numbers of converts, these Methodist horsemen were proverbial for humble devotion. "There is nothing out today," country people said in bad weather, "but crows and Methodist preachers."[45] Circuits shortened as classes thickened into neighboring churches, three or four of which could jointly support a circuit rider retiring to rear a family as a rotating local minister.

Bishops periodically reassigned both circuit riders and local ministers to new appointments, keeping them freer of lay control than most Protestant ministers. Conferences were subdivided into districts with superintendents for more efficient supervision.

Methodists disarmed democratic opposition to their military hierarchy by explicit appeal to the poor and downtrodden. Only a secession of Republican Methodists dissuaded Asbury from replacing the quadrennial General Conference of ministers with a council of bishops as the church's highest authority. But he gloried in the humble origin of his cadres, who both personified and proclaimed the Biblical assurance that "God is no respecter of persons."

Especially appealing was the democratic thrust of their theology. Although their doctrine of free grace to all believers technically preserved divine sovereignty by arguing that God enabled the newborn to believe, circuit riders were far more interested in the practical business of saving souls than in theological elegance. Taking over the camp meetings, shouting Methodists embraced every bizarre impulse of the reborn antinomian heart.

The spelled-out dos and don'ts of Wesley's *Methodist Discipline* provided a clear road map for the born-again life. Under the watchful eye of clergy, congregation, and neighborhood class, Methodists were expected to backslide occasionally while striving continually toward the attainable Christian perfection of "sanctification." This ethical athleticism, imposed by Wesley's British experience but eclipsed at first by New-Light antinomianism, left Methodists more susceptible to capitalist imperatives than the atavistic Baptists. Eventually capitalist transformation would obliterate from the memory of both great popular denominations their origins in a massive cultural mobilization against the market and its ways.

Spiritual Come-outerism from the market world peaked during the era of hard feelings to sustain political insurgency against market encroachment. While competing interests polarized federal politics sectionally, a new class politics surged up in the states. People experienced hard times most painfully through state-enforced debt collection and through the depreciated notes of state-chartered banks. Hence state politics first felt the intense popular reaction that would presently transform federal politics as well.

For the host of Americans newly caught up in the paper system, the panic of 1819 was a devastating introduction to the hazards of the developed capitalist market. Within a generation, and especially since the war, the market had lured multitudes from the traditional rural values of patient industry, economy, and limited expectations. Essayist "Lycurgus" in Ritchie's *Enquirer* spoke for many a venturer awakened by disaster to

the influence of money, in the control of his actions. Its advances are so gradual, as at first to escape the eye. By degrees, however, it grows upon us from little to little, until, at length, we become intoxicated by its influence, and indulge in all its vices, insensible to our real situation.

Now debtors faced loss of their all. Wage workers, if not discharged, were paid in the most depreciated bank notes to be found. Everywhere people's savings and cash on hand evaporated as bank notes depreciated. Who had done this to them?

Hard times, answered New York's Tammany Society from the heart of the market, were "an Act of Providence to arrest our hasty strides to national destruction." Pulpit, press, and platform agreed. "Let us turn from the wickedness of our ways, "advised a Maryland editor. In a widely copied series of articles on "Domestic Economy" in his New York *National Advocate,* Tammany stalwart Mordecai M. Noah called for a return to the industry and economy of an earlier day. Luxuries and conspicuous consumption by the rich, he argued, stimulated yearnings for cashmere shawls and leghorn hats among all classes. Many male commentators followed Noah in picturing women as particularly susceptible to this demoralizing fetishism of commodities. Also widely condemned were the Yankee peddlers who had fanned out across the countryside during the boom to tempt American matrons with their glittering wares; and North Carolina sought to tax these market outriders from its borders.

But preachments of universal guilt could not ward off an outpouring of anger from the depression's innocent victims. Anger also relieved the guilt of those who had allowed themselves to be inveigled into the mysterious paper system and then felt corrupted and somehow robbed. The obvious villains were the bankers, who had urged men to borrow and now showed no mercy. "Like the candle in the night," said the *Enquirer*'s Lycurgus, banking "drew around its blaze all those insects of avarice, and beetles of ambition that are eternally on the buzz for some new adventure—some change of fortune"; and "many will be the wings that will be singed."

Bankers' "inordinate solicitude for the dividend," charged North Carolina's Radical governor John Branch, "led the citizens of our once happy country into the wilds and mazes of speculative life." He was particularly indignant that they could repudiate their debts by suspending specie payments and still draw their "eight, ten, or twelve per cent interest," while an indebted individual was "degraded and stripped even to the last cow that gives sustenance to his family, to meet the demands of his creditors."[46]

A distressed public awakened to the concentration of wealth and power around the banks. Bank directors in country towns "are apt to encircle round them a kind of monied aristocracy," a New Jersey congressman warned, "who hold in their hands in too great a degree the destinies of the adjacent country." These directorates could become "virtual dictatorships," he said, "—so potent is money even in the shape of bank notes." The directors of a local bank decided, in fact, who got credit in the whole surrounding area, and typically a community's wealthiest entrepreneurs were not only the bank's stockholders and directors but also its biggest borrowers.[47]

Suspension of specie payments was essentially debtor relief for banking/entrepreneurial elites. Under suspension a bank did not have to enforce payment from favored borrowers in order to meet demands for coin. It could maintain or even expand its profitable business and handsome dividends. True, its notes were no longer good for payment outside the area except at great discount, and their depreciation grievously taxed the whole community. But to local elites this seemed a small price for avoiding "an entire revolution of fortune." And the states could not compel the banks to meet their legal obligations without risking a general liquidation and universal ruin.

Frustrated and angry, a populace that had ignored entrepreneurs and their little-understood projects in times of piping prosperity moved into political revolt. In community after community people began to blame their distress not only on bankers but also on the ingratiating Republican lawyer/politicians who regularly flattered democratic sentiment at election time and who, come to think of it, got the banks chartered. Now politicians began to discover that they had to appease the surging tide of antibank anger or risk defeat by a new breed of ambitious office-seekers who were volunteering to champion "the people" against "the aristocrats."

In Pennsylvania the panic of 1819 and the corruption of Governor Findlay's New School administration awakened the rural majority to the dangers of the paper system that Stephen Simpson had been flaying in the Old School's Philadelphia *Aurora*. Popular opinion rallied behind Brutus' call for "the total prostration of the *banking* and *funding* system" through the abrogation of "*all bank charters.*" William J. Duane, son of the Old School bellwether and *Aurora* editor, led the legislature in resolving against the national Bank and shutting down the forty-two village banks of 1814—"that great hot-bed of aristocracy"—by imposing on them the impossible requirement of resuming specie payments. Meanwhile the Old Schoolers had organized against the governor a diverse coalition of all the state's dissident elements. When he obstructed enforcement of the specie-resumption law, a surge of new voters to the polls drove him from office in 1820.[48]

Elsewhere in the East, Vermont forced all its banks to close by requiring them to resume specie payments; and the Delaware legislature came within a few votes of adopting the same policy. Other eastern states moved in this direction by forbidding suspending banks to pay dividends or by exacting an interest penalty on their notes. Some eastern states required their banks to publish balance sheets, and still others forbade them to issue notes in small denominations or in larger amounts than their real capital. Debtor-relief laws were passed in Vermont and Maryland and had substantial support in New York, New Jersey, Delaware, Virginia, and

North Carolina; while New York and Rhode Island eased pressure on debtors in lesser ways.[49]

While anger at the paper system arrayed eastern farmers, workers, and many petty enterprisers against business elites, it was convulsing every western state except Louisiana and Mississippi. Beyond the Appalachians, where the most reckless abuse of bank credit galvanized the most democratically responsive political systems, debtor relief played a larger role in the class realignment of politics. Debtor-relief laws were ingeniously contrived to circumvent the federal Consititution's prohibition against impairing the obligation of contracts. In various ways they denied the state's debt-enforcement machinery to creditors: postponing execution on the debtor's property up to two years, or allowing execution only if the sheriff's sale brought two-thirds of the property's value as estimated by a jury of the debtor's neighbors, or encumbering foreclosed property with the debtor's right to reclaim it upon payment of the debt.

But relief laws could be drawn to favor different classes. In most states the first debtor legislation afforded relief only if creditors refused to accept in full payment the depreciated notes of the suspended state banks. This conservative form of debtor relief sanctioned suspension of specie payments and mainly propped up the banks and the imperiled market elites who were their stockholders and biggest borrowers.

Such favoritism toward the perpetrators of the general misery provoked massive political uprisings in many western states. Legislatures expressing popular outrage abolished banking entirely and/or reversed the class thrust of relief legislation. The more radical form of debtor relief was to lend small debtors state-issued paper money (which usually depreciated more than bank notes) and then impede creditors who refused to accept it in full payment. Where the original conservative form of relief protected banks and large debtors, radical relief protected small debtors against banks as well as other creditors, while driving bank notes from circulation through the competition of state-issued paper money.

Eventually the judiciary—which never challenged the patently illegal suspension of specie payments—struck down all forms of debtor relief and state paper money as patently unconstitutional. By then, however, they had served their emergency purpose. Once shielded through the crisis, chastened small debtors quickly abandoned state paper money. Like William Duane's eastern working-class following, western farm folk were turning against the whole paper system for the stability and equity of hard money, gold and silver coin, with its magical resonance of treasure from the earth.

The western upheavals of the 1820s brought the democratic impulse to critical mass. Periodically since the Revolution, the gentry's hauteur and class legislation had aroused the "determination of the people to act for themselves" that Jefferson celebrated in the revolt against the Salary Act. Energized by the spasmodic anger of outraged traditional morality, "this great upbearing of our masses" fumbled for political constraints on American elites.

An evangelical folk translated the interest politics of self-serving calculation into the intensely personal/moral terms of their face-to-face culture. Farmers and workers experienced politics as a search for good men who could be trusted to defeat the selfish stratagems of market elites. Politicians who engaged popular trust in these terms—New York's George Clinton, Pennsylvania's Simon Snyder, North Carolina's Nathaniel Macon—became unbeatable. Around such avatars Republican party identification rationalized a remote and chaotic political reality for most rural Americans. So long as developmentalism affected them only prospectively, they were fitfully aroused only by such egregious affronts as the Salary Act.

The banking/debtor crisis evoked an ultimately irrepressible demand for plebiscitory democracy by dramatizing the Republican gentry's treachery to traditional values. While Thomas Jefferson dreamed of a radical neighborhood democracy that could empower the people to "crush, regularly and peaceably, the usurpations of their unfaithful agents," democratic insurgency blazed with the New Light of antinomian revival to new heights across the West. The whole style of western politics was transformed by an aroused public encouraging a new breed of politicians, men of humble origin who challenged genteel officeholders by courting voters assiduously in the oral style of rural vernacular. To compete with these political innovators, a Tennesseean reported, candidates had to "live on their horses" for six months and "do little else but electioneer."[50]

Insurgent democracy was aggressively egalitarian in style and antidevelopmental in substance. The lieutenant governor of Illinois promised an unintrusive, folksy state in running against college-educated Governor Ninian Edwards:

> I do not pretend to be a man of extraordinary talents; nor do I claim to be equal to Julius Caesar or Napoleon Bonaparte, nor yet to be as great a man as my opponent, Governor Edwards. Nevertheless, I think I can govern you pretty well. I do not think that it will require a very extraordinary smart man to govern you; for to tell you the truth, fellow-citizens, I do not think you will be very hard to govern no how.[51]

Yet democratic politicians proved even more susceptible to the market's rewards than their genteel predecessors. The prototype was Felix Grundy, who demonstrated in Kentucky's Green River country how wit, sensitivity to audience, and a flow of homespun rhetoric could carry a poor boy to prominence by way of law and politics. Grundy was no doubt sincere in riding a wave of farmer anger at Bluegrass aristocrats; but once political power introduced him to the market world, he could not resist its enticements or its perspective. Having led farmers against the first bank in the West, he was soon cooperating with Bluegrass entrepreneurs in organizing a bigger one. Moving to Nashville for a fresh political start under new colors, he was presently Clay's respected War Hawk colleague in Congress. Then he left Congress to get rich as the most celebrated criminal lawyer in the West. Legally unsophisticated—Jackson thought him a "quack"—Grundy had such remarkable powers over juries that he was reputed never to have lost a capital case.[52]

The panic of 1819 drew Grundy back into politics, for no one knew better how to exploit the popular emotion it provoked. Championing conservative debtor relief until Tennessee voters rose in rebellion, he shifted to radical relief while unobtrusively undermining it to allay elite outrage. Nimbly accommodating popular mood while inconspicuously serving banking and land speculating interests, he became Tennessee's most powerful political broker, and his ultimate reward was the attorney generalship of the United States.

Democratic politicians like Grundy cannot be dismissed as opportunistic, any more than magnates, pundits, and historians can be blamed for the class interests and perspectives they inherit or achieve. Nor can the new politicians be dismissed as demagogues without denigrating democracy. By focusing popular anger against threatening change on polemicized banks and aristorcrats, the Grundys gave an egalitarian majority its only leverage on a calculating politics.

Shouldering aside gentleman amateurs, such ambitious young country lawyers were making democratic politics a profession requiring special skills. Their ability to mediate between popular mood and other forces in the political environment has given the American political system whatever democratic content it has possessed. Majority rule is frustrated not by the venality of politicians but by the political advantages of elites—wealth, influence, intellectual resources, control of public media, and sleepless involvement—to which office-seekers learn to accommodate.

Grundy and his kind succeeded by adopting the style demanded by an aroused democratic public. Old-fashioned politicians had to conform or retire. "I have assumed the style of our western popular declaimers," the college-educated Tennessee Congressman William B. Campbell confided to a friend. "Without having any regard to the substance, I attempt to excite the feelings of my audience by wild, ranting declamation and indeed such speaking succeeds finely, the people say that it is a fine speech and they hollow *hurrah* for *Campbell*."[53]

Some could not or would not make the transition. When challenged for reelection by the folksy Davy Crockett, a genteel Tennessee legislator withdrew from the race. "The practice of *electioneering* has become so exceedingly disgraceful on the part of some candidates, that I cannot condescend to the little arts and contemptible contrivances which are frequently adopted," he announced to the public. To "go up creeks, down valleys, over hills, and into dales for the purpose of collecting votes," and to "buy up freemen's votes with a half pint of white face CORN WHISKEY," he complained, was "so far descending beneath the . . . independence of a correct politician" that "I would not condescend to such an act of degradation to be President of the United States."

Elected as "the poor man's friend," nonlawyer Crockett was an unusual democratic politician because success did not shake his fidelity to his class and culture. In the legislature he assailed banking as "a species of swindling on a large scale"; whereupon his pleased constituents in newly settled West Tennessee sent him to Congress to defend their farms against Tennessee's land-speculating elite. When Washington dealt with his naive incorruptibility by exploiting him as a caricature of his culture, he fled the market world to die heroically at the Alamo.[54]

Banking "aristocracies" penetrated the western states in different degrees to provoke three different patterns of political convulsion. In Ohio, where market influences were strongest and where debtors were already protected by a relief law adopted in pioneer days, general antibank passions were swallowed up in a sensational campaign against the national Bank.

Ohioans rehearsed a drama, verging on both farce and tragedy, soon to be acted nationally. Here hard-money foes of the inflationary paper system first experienced the frustration of having to confront the state and national banks simultaneously. In the contest between deflationary and inflationary forces, the national Bank occupied an anomalous position. To farmers angry at banks in general, it seemed the worst because the biggest. But Ohio entrepreneurs also resented the big Bank for opposite reasons—its competition with their inflationary state banks and its deflationary capability to restrain them.

Nowhere had state-banking elites entered more extravagantly into the speculative frenzy of the boom years, and nowhere had they been more thoroughly prostrated when the Bank of the United States belatedly called them to account. A public prostrated along with them turned in fury on banks in general.

In Cincinnati, the vortex of Ohio's entrepreneurial excesses, voters expelled local officeholders connected with the state banks, and a Fourth of July celebration degenerated into an antibank riot so violent that local editors suppressed all news of it and many prominent citizens fled the city. Here General William Henry Harrison, popular hero of Tippecanoe, bank director, and longtime grandee, was hard run for the state senate by an upstart radical lawyer and hero of the city's working class. The general won by declaring that he would like to see all banks destroyed, if it were constitutionally possible, and their paper money replaced with gold and silver coin.

Yet Harrison shrewdly emphasized his opposition to the national Bank. The big Bank's prepanic excesses and the unusually devastating impact of its ruthless contraction in Ohio made it a natural lightning rod for popular wrath against the paper system in general. Launching a sensational campaign to tax the national Bank out of the state, in defiance of the Supreme Court's *McCulloch* decision, Harrison and other entrepreneurial politicians deflected the public fury that was destroying state banks elsewhere.

The Cleveland *Register* illustrated the success of this strategy. Its editor excoriated banks in general. They enabled the "moneyed speculator" to seize the "hard earnings" of "honest and industrious farmers," he charged; they built up "monied aristorcracies"; they introduced luxury, "the bane of republics"; and they caused morals "to depreciate with bank paper." Yet he and other Ohioans could not resist concentrating their fire on that "monster of iniquity" the national Bank. Thus the even more culpable state banks got off scot free, and fundamental class differences between entrepreneurial and antientrepreneurial elements were papered over.[55]

The newer western states, by contrast, were one-sided against all banking. Here entrepreneurial interests were too weak to defend the banks originally chartered by territorial officials against the farming majorities recently empowered by statehood. In reaction against the excesses of the boom years, the constitutions adopted between 1816 and 1820 by Indiana, Illinois, Missouri, and Alabama each permitted only a single bank to be chartered in the future, and it was to be partly owned and controlled by the state. In addition the Indiana and Illinois constitutions sought to keep out the national Bank by forbidding any bank not chartered by the state.

In all these states the panic so intensified antibanking sentiment that the constitutionally authorized single-bank projects were abandoned, while the territorially chartered banks were forced out of business. Under the new constitutions, as an Indiana newcomer observed, elected officials found the "sovereign people" to be "most uncompromising task masters." Under insurgent attack from the rustic lieutenant governor of Illinois, the typically entrepreneurial territorial governor Ninian Edwards survived popular election only by resigning his bank directorship and going with the antibank tide.

Indiana, Illinois, and Missouri enacted debtor-relief laws, while Illinois, Missouri, and Alabama issued state paper money for the particular benefit of small debtors. To evade the constitutional prohibition against state bills of credit, these state-paper loan offices were usually camouflaged as "banks" in which the faith and credit of the state governments substituted for a specie capital.[56]

Alabama had the most explosive political reaction because it was more tightly controlled by a bank-linked entrepreneurial elite than the other new states. Hard on the heels of the expelled Indians, a group of wealthy cotton planters from the Broad River valley of middle Georgia moved into Alabama with the first rush of pioneer farmers. Inspired by boom prices for cotton, they bid in at federal land auctions the richest acreage along the Tennessee River in the northern end of the state, the first center of settlement, and later along the Alabama River in the fabulously fertile Black Belt farther south.

Several generations before, the much-intermarried Broad River people had migrated as a group from Virginia to Georgia, where they prospered from slave-grown cotton and where one of their number, William H. Crawford, led the planter-based faction that contested the state with a farmer-based faction. As prominent Broad River men migrated to Alabama—among them the two Georgia senators expelled over the Salary Act—Crawford became a power in Washington. Federal patronage and the prospect that their Washington connections could win statehood for Alabama gave them control of the territorial government and at first of the new state government.

Thus the Broad River gentry were able to finance their land purchases by chartering for themselves a bank at Huntsville, the main settlement in north Alabama; and they enhanced their banking profits by repealing the law limiting interest on loans to 8 percent. When the panic broke, the state government propped up their hopelessly overextended bank by accepting its depreciated notes for taxes at par and by issuing state notes to guarantee them.

The reaction from an enraged farming populace carried a south Alabama politician, Israel Pickens, into the governorship over the Broad River candidate, and Pickens's antibank policies made him unbeatable as long as he lived. Annulling the Huntsville bank's charter because it could not resume specie payments, the Pickens forces established a state-operated loan-office "bank," which apportioned small loans of state paper among the counties according to their legislative representation. Thereafter, as politicians and editors quickly learned, popular favor had to be won in Alabama by opposing the evil machinations of the "royal party."[57]

The oldest western states, Kentucky and Tennessee, had extensive entrepreneurial/banking interests like Ohio's, but their banks were linked to tighter political elites. Here the first relief laws were drawn to favor banking/large-debtor interests, and here the outcome was a deep and lasting polarization between entrepreneurial and antientrepreneurial constituencies.

The sale of Kentucky's lands under the laws of its parent state enabled Virginia gentlemen to establish themselves on the best Bluegrass acreage and to control the new state politically, despite constant challenges from subsistence farming areas. Drawn into the market during the prewar commercial boom, the Bluegrass gentry fended off Felix Grundy's farmer-backed attack on their original Lexington bank and then, co-opting Grundy, replaced it with a larger Bank of Kentucky having branches in the principal towns. During the renewed entrepreneurial surge that followed the war, they yielded to the demands of a host of village entrepreneurs by chartering forty-six new banks.

At the onset of the panic the governor advocated a constitutional amendment outlawing banks from the whole country, but the legislature hastened to prop up the established entrepreneurial/banking interests. Appeasing antibank sentiment by repealing the charters of the new and already failing village banks, it enacted over the governor's veto a large-debtor relief law impeding creditors who refused to accept the depreciated notes of the suspended statewide Bank of Kentucky. Kentucky farmers exploded with such anger against this class legislation that many established politicians took the antibank side. General John Adair, Kentucky's hero of the battle of New Orleans and a leader of the Green River farming country, won the governorship on a platform of radical relief for small debtors. By large majorities the legislature abolished the Bank of Kentucky and established a state paper-money loan office called the Bank of the Commonwealth of Kentucky. Without any capital except the state's credit, it was authorized to issue up to $3 million in loans of two hundred dollars or less; and creditors were impeded if they refused to accept these state notes at par from their debtors.

The Bluegrass gentry mounted a ferocious resistance to this popular uprising, and their allies on the state Court of Appeals declared the relief law unconstitutional. Backed resoundingly by voters in an intervening election, the legislature abolished the court and established a new one in its place. When the old court refused to give way, Kentucky was plunged into a bitter struggle between an Old Court party and a New Court party. So tenacious were the political attachments thus formed that even after the pressure on debtors eased and the old court was restored, the same alignment of political forces carried over into the new party system emerging nationally.[58]

Tennessee was even more tightly controlled by a ruling elite based on the most fabulous land grab in American history. Speculators associated with the territorial governor William Blount obtained from the parent state North Carolina land claims sufficient to cover most of Tennessee. Intent on making good these claims, the Blount men had governed the new state almost continuously. Led after Blount's death by the wealthy John Overton, they embraced the new entrepreneurial opportunities brought by the postwar boom and controlled the state's two banks headquartered at Nashville and Knoxville. It was to protect their banking interests that Tennessee levied in 1817 a fifty-thousand-dollar prohibitory tax to keep the national Bank from establishing a branch in the state.

As in Kentucky, the first legislative response to the panic was a conservative relief law protecting the banks and large debtors by impeding creditors who would not accept bank notes. And again as in Kentucky this provoked a massive public outcry, which was marshaled by the Radical faction opposed to the Blount/Overton group. "While the balance of the community feel so much distress," the leading Radical newspaper asked, why did "bank directors, with few exceptions feel none of it?" Bankers, the editor complained, "are the horse-leeches of the country who have cried out Give! Give! until they have drained every drop of blood they could suck from a suffering community." They "have ruined the country to build up towns," he charged, and "produced a monied aristocracy which makes the rich more rich—& the poor more poor." Similarly a Radical congressman called banking "a rank fraud upon the laboring and industrious part of society," a scheme "to make idleness productive and filch from industry, the hard produce of its earnings."

Bowing to popular outrage, the legislature again followed the Kentucky pattern by establishing a loan-office "bank" to lend state paper money to poor debtors and revising the relief law to impede creditors who refused the new notes. With voters "in a perfect ferment," the Blount/Overton candidate for governor in 1821 was trounced 4–1 by Radical-backed William Carroll, another hero of the battle of New Orleans, who blamed the depression on the banks and wished he "had never seen one in the state." Carroll's supporters in the legislature—among them Davy Crockett—drove the old banks out of business by requiring them to resume specie payments. Politically invincible, Carroll would hold the governorship fourteen years except for a two-year interim required by the state constitution.

The brief flirtations with fiat money in Tennessee and other states did not signify a mass conversion to the blessings of paper and enterprise. They were instead emergency expedients of class defense against a paper system rigged in favor of market elites. As soon as the debt crisis eased, farming and working people reverted to their preference for the stability and equity represented by hard money, gold and silver coin. "The farmer and labourer," said their leader Governor Carroll in recommending abolition of Tennessee's loan office, ". . . are the last in society who can bring up their services to the standard of a depreciated currency." Here and elsewhere, magical gold increasingly symbolized the determination of the people to act for themselves against entrepreneurial elites and the whole mentality of the market.[59]

Chapter 6

"A General Mass
of Disaffection"

THE POLITICAL firestorm sweeping the states alarmed contenders for the 1824 presidential succession. With "enormous numbers of persons utterly ruined" and "multitudes in deep distress," Secretary Calhoun warned Secretary Adams late in 1820, there was "a general mass of disaffection to the government, not concentrated in any particular direction, but ready to seize upon any event and looking out anywhere for a leader."[1] A leader for the democratic conquest of presidential politics emerged in a curious fashion from the Tennessee relief struggle.

Governor Carroll's 1821 landslide left the defeated Blount/Overton men desperate to regain power. At stake were both their banks (ultimately forced by the Carrollites to close) and their land speculations (recently jeopardized by the state supreme court). Blount's son-in-law Pleasant M. Miller suggested to Overton that only Andrew Jackson could defeat Carroll for reelection in 1823. The hero's popularity would ensure a legislature that would save the banks and pack the supreme court with friendly judges. A friendly legislature could also replace Jackson's personal enemy, Radical Senator John Williams, with his friend, Pleasant Miller.

Although Jackson had long since eschewed politics and the speculative enterprises of the Blount/Overton men, he and Overton had been close friends since first entering public life under Blount's aegis back in territorial days. Moreover the general had quarreled violently with several of the now triumphant Radicals and detested their presidential candidate Crawford, whose congressional supporters attacked his invasion of Spanish Florida. Apparently he now rejected the idea of running for governor, for Overton countered Miller's suggestion with the idea that much the same purposes could be served by nominating Jackson for President. Tennesseans would then defeat the hero's enemies for the legislature and the Senate. Miller immediately fell in with Overton's counterproposal, arguing that the Radicals "must be held in check & this is all the hold we have—in a state of excitement publick opinion will keep them down."

Some of Jackson's politically inconsequential friends had entertained the presidential fantasy, but no experienced politician anywhere took it seriously, for only long and distinguished service in Congress, diplomacy, and Cabinet conferred presidential eligibility. Jackson himself favored Adams or, as a longer shot, Calhoun, for he thought they had defended his Florida exploits; and the would-be Senator Pleasant Miller, who also favored Adams, argued that Jackson's candidacy would help Adams by denying Tennessee and perhaps other southwestern states to Crawford or Clay.

Early in 1822 the Blount/Overton newspapers began puffing Jackson as a presidential candidate, and that summer the legislature formally nominated him. None of the Tennessee politicians who hatched Jackson's nomination thought he could be a serious contender nationally, and most of them thought his candidacy could be dropped once this became evident and once it served its local purposes.

Clay appears to have been Overton's real choice for the presidency, and the Kentuckian was also attractive as a westerner to such disparate politicians as Governor Carroll and Felix Grundy. Overton's nephew promised Clay Tennessee's ultimate support; and the Kentuckian was assured by Governor Carroll and various other politicians that the Tennessee nomination was "nothing but a diversion in favor of Adams"; that Pleasant Miller had "played off this manoeuvre to bring Jacksons name to bear, & make a point in the election of Senator"; that "so soon as the election of Senator is over, we shall hear no more of a Tenn. candidate for the office of President"; and that Grundy had promised, if Jackson faded as expected, to get Clay nominated by the next session of the Tennessee legislature.

But the politicians were in for a shock. In response to the Tennessee nomination a "contagion" of popular enthusiasm for Jackson broke out, not only in the southwestern states but also in such unexpected places as North Carolina and New Jersey, reaching such stunning proportions in Pennsylvania that it blocked the expected nomination of Calhoun by the Republican state convention.

And no sooner had Overton's old friend emerged as a formidable presidential candidate than he revealed dangerous proclivities. Jackson was outraged when Overton, Miller, and Grundy induced the legislature that nominated him to pack the state supreme court with judges who would favor the land speculators. Joining the hue and cry against the speculator/banking interests, he "put Judge Overton in a great state of fretfulness." Soon he was egging on a Nashville editor and legislative candidate who advocated returning "to those days that are past when we lived happy without banks." Old Hickory was telling all who would listen, in fact, that he opposed all banks on principle.

Overton and his closest associates moved in alarm to contain the menacing genie they had unloosed. So quietly that Jackson did not learn for years of their activities, they began lining up legislators to reelect their old foe Senator Williams. Because Williams was also a notorious foe of Jackson and a Crawford supporter, his reelection would demonstrate the general's unpopularity in his own state and nip his presidential candidacy in the bud.

Jackson's inexperienced advisers did not perceive the threat until they reached tiny Murfreesborough for the 1823 session of the legislature. Strangely, neither Pleasant Miller nor any of several other candidates they backed could muster a majority against Senator Williams; and Jackson repeatedly refused their entreaties to come and lend his personal influence. Williams's Radicalism was attractive to many Tennesseeans. Among the evangelical and often antislavery populace of subsistence farmers in mountainous East Tennessee, he represented a tradition of resistance to land barons and Nashville Basin planters that went back to the Revolutionary hero, Indian fighter, and Blount foe "Nolachucky Jack" Sevier. He also appealed to antibank, antispeculator legislators from all sections, such as the semiliterate but unabashed West Tennesseean Davy Crockett, who had been swept into office with Governor Carroll. Senator Williams had ridden tirelessly across the state securing advance commitments, and the secret support of the usually hostile Overton men made him all but unbeatable.

Finally, in despair of saving Jackson's presidential candidacy any other way, his supporters sent a message to the Hermitage that they were proposing the general himself for senator. With honor at stake, he galloped posthaste for Murfreesborough, arriving the evening before the ballot. Even in the imposing presence of Tennessee's hero, Crockett and twenty-four others stubbornly stood by Williams, and Jackson was elected senator by a margin of only ten votes. Once the decision was made, however, Overton's confederate Grundy led a rush to the Jackson bandwagon by getting the legislature to resolve against the congressional nominating caucus. Unable to stop the hero, Overton and company sought to control him by gradually taking over from his Hermitage coterie the main burden of campaign correspondence, public meetings, and newspaper essays.[2]

The first presidential candidate of nongentry origin, Old Hickory was superbly shaped by experience and temperament to appeal to the country's beleaguered common folk. His subsistence-farming family had reached the Carolina backcountry in 1765 with the latest wave of Scotch-Irish immigrants moving south from the Delaware River ports. As part of a typical clan migration the elder Andrew Jackson and his wife, Elizabeth, left Ireland to join her five married sisters and their Crawford in-laws. These poor but land-hungry immigrants were drawn to the gently rolling Waxhaw country along the disputed boundary between the two Carolinas—as earlier Scotch-Irish were drawn to the disputed Pennsylvania/Maryland boundary—by the ease of squatting on unoccupied lands where all titles were in doubt. There Andrew was killed by a falling log while clearing a farm to which the family did not gain title for some years.

The younger Andrew Jackson was born to insecurity at an in-law's cabin while the family was still mourning the father he would never know. Whether his birthplace was in North or South Carolina depends on which sister the expectant widow resorted to for her confinement. Jackson himself thought he was born at

Aunt Jane Crawford's on the South Carolina side of the line. Her husband, James Crawford, prosperous senior patriarch of the clan, had led the families of his brothers and many sisters-in-law from Pennsylvania to the Waxhaws. Now the Crawford household took in the widowed Elizabeth Jackson, with her infant and two other small sons, and here the outsider Andrew struggled through boyhood to hold his own against ten older siblings and cousins.[3]

The Presbyterianism of the Scotch-Irish required educated ministers—the Waxhaw settlement obtained one of the first in the backcountry—and in both Scotland and Ireland education for the ministry had been the main avenue to prominence for poor boys. With a piety deepened by vicissitude, the Widow Jackson dedicated her youngest son to the Lord and scrimped to give him far more schooling than most country boys got. From backwoods teachers Andrew learned to read, to cipher, to write crudely, and to spout a few tags of Latin. A precocious reader, he was soon being called on to read to assembled neighbors the occasional newspaper that reached the backcountry.

But the elementary schooling that made Jackson's later career possible did not immediately take. Establishing his manhood was more urgent business for the fatherless youngster, and when he was thirteen the Revolutionary War reached the Carolina backcountry to thrust precocious manhood on him. With uncles, brothers, and cousins he joined in hazardous guerrilla warfare against the hated British, historic oppressors of their people in Scotland and Ireland. One brother died early in the struggle, and Andrew was eventually captured along with his remaining brother. Permanently scarred by the sword of a British officer whose boots they refused to clean, the Jackson boys were crowded with other prisoners into the fetid little jail at Camden and there contracted smallpox. Just in time to save Andrew's life, his mother arranged her sons' release in exchange for British soldiers captured by the Americans. His brother died two days after reaching home, and Andrew recovered only after weeks of delirium. By then Widow Jackson was off to Charleston to nurse two of the Crawford boys incarcerated aboard the notorious British prison ships, and there she was struck down by cholera and disappeared into an unmarked grave.

"I felt utterly alone," said Jackson, recalling many years later the pain of the orphaned fourteen-year-old. "Homeless and friendless," as he remembered it, he quarreled his way from one kin household to another. Riding down to Charleston to collect a substantial legacy from his Irish grandfather, he searched unavailingly for his mother's grave and then fell into a spasm of extravagance and debauchery that mocked her memory. Arraying himself as a gentleman with a fine horse, a brace of pistols, and a gold watch, he gambled, caroused, and raced horses with the young bloods of the lowcountry gentry. Only when his last penny was gone did he crawl back to his disapproving kin in the Waxhaws.[4]

Abundant symptoms suggest that Jackson's adult character was shaped by the traumas of his boyhood. A youthful "slobbering" impediment when he was excited ripened into an adult inability to speak in public "on account of the rashness of his feelings." "I have seen him attempt it repeatedly," said Jefferson, who witnessed his brief service in the Senate, "and as often to choke with rage." His "terrible" passions, as Jefferson characterized them, appeared also in his extreme touchiness, in the sanguinary violence of his rhetoric about his personal enemies, and in his implacable pursuit of Indians, Spanish, British, and the Bank of the United States.[5]

The psychodynamic sources of this enduring rage can only be guessed. Did anger arise in the lonely boy against the father he never knew, against the brothers and cousins—surrogate brothers—who took precedence over him, or primarily (as Freudians might infer from his oral difficulties) against the mother, his only source of security, who abandoned him in illness for his cousins and then left him alone in a hostile world?

Whatever the psychodynamics, the young Jackson managed his emotional pressures through the cultural categories available to him in a patriarchal society where males vied for honor. He carried to an extreme the aggressive masculinity through which men earned each other's respect. Younger and smaller in boyhood than his companions, he sacrificed book learning to excelling at running, jumping, and horse racing. Displaying a mean temper at the slightest affront, he swore like a trooper and brawled with a fury that daunted stronger opponents. Even the gambling, drinking, swearing, horse racing, and, no doubt, wenching of his Charleston binge were modes of displaying the socially prescribed maleness.

Like other rural mothers, the Widow Jackson inculcated in her sons this patriarchal code. Only girls cried, she reputedly told little Andrew, while boys were made to fight. Whenever he spoke of her in later years, he remembered the final advice she gave him before her ill-fated departure for Charleston. "Sustain your manhood always," she said. "Never bring a suit at law for assault and battery or for defamation. The law affords no remedy for such outrages that can satisfy the feelings of a true man."[6]

But Elizabeth Jackson coupled this bellicose advice with admonitions to treat others honestly and respectfully, for patriarchal honor involved more than anarchic egotism. It flourished because families relied upon male brawn and courage for security against Indians and lawless whites. Retributive justice executed by avenging fathers and brothers substituted for more formal institutions of social control. To restrain the resulting propensity to violence and bloody family feuds, patriarchal society imposed strict obligations of honesty and respect among males. Shame was the ultimate sanction against the man who would not or could not physically defend his honor against breaches of this code, and a shamed man meant a shamed and vulnerable family. Family honor, undergirding the safety and prospects of women and children, depended on male honor.

Just as Jackson exaggerated the aggressive component of male honor, so he also exaggerated its contrasting component of patriarchal family obligation. Channeling anxiety and rage into reproducing on a heroic scale the idealized father whose protection he was denied, he was fiercely protective toward women, toward the soldiers he commanded, and toward the surrogate sons he constantly collected. His anger could be honorably unleashed on behalf of those who claimed his paternal protection and accepted his paternal authority.[7]

Jackson's turning point seems to have been the Charleston spree. The taste of genteel panache for which he squandered his inheritance proved irresistible. The Waxhaws kin found the homecoming prodigal more purposeful. He enrolled again in school while accumulating a small stake by teaching and working for a saddler. A knack for reading was his only visible asset, and he knew that the law was surpassing the ministry as a way for poor country boys to rise. At age seventeen he turned his back on his kin, never to contact them again, and rode up into North Carolina.

Rebuffed as a student-clerk by a prominent attorney, he learned enough from obscure village lawyers to meet the standards of a rustic bar. His sprees and escapades were legendary by the time a well-connected drinking companion got him a little-sought appointment as the first public prosecutor in the wilds of newly settled middle Tennessee. En route to his post, he claimed the status of gentleman by fighting his first duel, a bloodless one, and purchasing his first slave, a young woman of eighteen or twenty.

As one of Tennessee's first lawyers, Jackson quickly became a prominent member of the backwoods oligarchy spawned by William Blount's vast land speculation. He began living with another man's estranged wife, marrying her only after a belated divorce; and Rachel's extensive pioneer clan of Donelsons, closing ranks around family honor, helped elect him to Tennessee's constitutional convention at age twenty-nine and then as the state's first congressman. Aligning himself during his single session of service with Nathaniel Macon's purist Republicanism, he opposed the Federalist direct taxes and a resolution commending the retiring President Washington. But he was quickly frustrated with political life. Elevated to the Senate, he resigned before his first session was over and abandoned politics after a few years on the state supreme court.

Meanwhile Jackson tried his hand at planting, land speculation, and merchandising, only to be wiped out by defective land titles and the bankruptcy of an associate whose notes he endorsed. Losing his plantation, he retreated to a log cabin on another tract, where he labored for years to sustain his honor by acquiring slaves to produce cotton to pay his debts. Although high cotton prices during the commerical boom restored his prosperity, the experience left him with a lifelong abhorrence of debt and the paper system.

Jackson's real passion during these years was for Indian fighting and military command. Arriving on the Cumberland while the doomed Indians were sporadically raiding the invading white settlements, he seized the first chance to join a retaliatory expedition and earned a reputation for being *"mad upon his enemies."*

The goal of his political career was the commanding generalship of the Tennessee militia, and he lost interest in politics once he attained it in 1801.[8]

Against Indians Jackson could vent his rage as patriarchal avenger of "our beloved wives and little prattling infants, butchered, mangled, murdered, and torn to pieces by savage bloodhounds, and wallowing in their gore." And toward his troops he could fulfill his patriarchal duty as "a father to his family," winning from them the soubriquet "Old Hickory" by defying government orders to discharge them far from home and sharing with them the hardships of a long, hungry march back to Tennessee. His soldiers' duty, he told them, was "strict subordination"; and he would not hesitate to exact the ultimate penalty of death from those who defied his authority.

Jackson's theatrical proclamations to his troops echoed the celebrated general who was currently corrupting the liberal revolution even as he spread it across Europe. "The conquering army of Bonaparte," exulted Old Hickory, was restoring "the rights of man" to "millions of distressed people"; and even after the Emperor Napoleon went down to defeat, Jackson insisted that he still "reigns in the affection of the soldiers."[9]

But for over a decade after Jackson assumed command of the Tennessee militia, he was restrained from leading them to Napoleonic victory over the Indians and Spanish by what he considered the pusillanimity of the political authorities. Meanwhile his rage boiled over into countless private quarrels and affrays. Hypersensitivity about his adulterous beginning with Rachel involved him in a fatal duel. His crackshot twenty-seven-year-old opponent got off the first fire, splintering several of the general's ribs. After the reeling Jackson's pistol stopped once at half-cock, he recocked, aimed deliberately at his helpless victim, and squeezed off the fatal shot. "I should have hit him," said the general as the young man lay bleeding to death, "if he had shot me through the brain." The War of 1812 transmuted this rage into heroism, enabling the Napoleon of the woods within a few years to humble the mighty British, seize the Southwest from the Indians, and drive the Spanish from the Gulf Coast.

The hero of New Orleans, his history and character well advertised through an 1817 biography written by two of his surrogate sons, was particularly irresistible to American farmers. Popular myth mistakenly attributed his New Orleans victory to the accurate rifle fire of untrained farmer-militiamen rather than to the well-drilled regular artillery. Under Jackson's leadership, rural America believed, "the *American Husbandman*, fresh from his plough," was "triumphantly victorious over the conquerors of Europe." This mythology, emphasizing that Jackson's "untrained militia" humbled "regular troops, the best disciplined and most veteran of Europe," echoed the claims to moral preeminence that unschooled antinomians had been asserting against cosmopolitan elites since the Great Awakening. Jackson himself contrasted "the untutored courage of the American militia" with "the habits, which are created by wealth" in "opulent and commercial" New Orleans.

Jackson identified himself with this mythology by claiming to be "a plain cultivator of the soil"; and his admirers appropriated classical legend by calling him the "American Cincinnatus." Like Rome's republican hero, he was seen as preferring to remain "upon his farm and at his plough" until summoned to his country's service. Thus the hero of New Orleans came to symbolize American farmers' claims to republican preeminence, not only against the barbarism of Indians and uncultivated wilderness, but even more against the menacing economic and cultural pretensions of the North Atlantic market world.[10]

Jackson's relationship with his public gained intensity from the emotional needs it satisfied in both. Just when hard-pressed farming and working people were ripening for political rebellion, victory on all fronts left Jackson without an adequate public arena for his overblown patriarchalism. A munificent salary as major general commanding the southern half of the army enabled him to maintain his headquarters on his Hermitage plantation near Nashville and to replace his log house with a pillared brick mansion. Here he lavished his paternalism on a band of junior staff officers and orphaned nieces and nephews whom the childless Jacksons had adopted as wards. With regard to his numerous "family" of slaves, he insisted that "subordination must be obtained first"; but he also insisted on "good treatment" and guarded them against overwork, "as far as lenity can be extended to these unfortunate creatures."[11]

Attacks on his Florida invasion drew him inevitably into national politics, and a physical constitution shattered by exposure, dysentery, and bullet wounds sharpened his rage, particularly against Crawford. When Crawford's Radical supporters in Congress cut the army in half, forcing Jackson's resignation as the junior of the two major generals, the hero concluded that, except for Adams and Calhoun, the administration was "corrupt to the core." Reluctantly he accepted in 1821 the sop President Monroe threw him, the governorship of the new territory of Florida.

Violent quarrels in Florida with departing Spanish officials who resisted his imperious demands introduced Jackson to a new patriarchal role as champion of the oppressed. Rushing to the defense of a lowly family he thought defrauded by the Spanish grandees, he saw himself as protecting "the poor and humble from the Tyranny of wealth and power." He extended the vote to all free males and boasted that his territorial administration made "no distinction between the rich and poor."

This impulse to champion the humble found a wider field when, after eleven stormy weeks, Jackson resigned his Florida post and, in the unaccustomed role of private citizen, returned to a Tennessee wracked by conflict over banking and debtor relief. Seemingly he at first took the elitist side by backing for governor the Overton candidate who was so thoroughly drubbed in the popular uprising that elected William Carroll. He did so partly on traditional grounds of friendship for a neighbor and partly out of opposition to the state-issued paper money briefly favored by bank-hating small debtors supporting Carroll. This state paper he opposed on the ground that it "is not worth 50/100 to the dollar and this depreciation falls upon the laborer." He equally opposed the bank-sustaining relief for large debtors advocated by the overextended plungers of the Overton elite. His hard-money stance was already separating him from the Tennessee gentry, while Governor Carroll and his farmer following quickly reverted to Old Hickory's hard-money fundamentalism.

Despite Jackson's military and expansionist nationalism, his disastrous market fling had pushed him in other respects back toward the localist, democratic, and hard-money bent of his native subsistence culture. His political creed "was formed in the old republican school," he said. "Every one that knows me," he claimed a few years later, "does know that I have been always opposed to the U. States Bank, nay all Banks." He asserted in 1820 the Virginia purist doctrine that the Constitution "prohibits the establishment of Banks in every State"; and he opposed state-issued paper money on the ground that "the imprudent speculator may be enabled to extricate himself from his pecuniary embarrassments but the burthen must ultimately fall upon the honest farmer and industrious tradesman."[12]

Jackson's inflated patriarchalism accelerated his deviation from the perspective of his gentry class. Identifying popular disaffection with his personal animus against his critics and President Monroe, the displaced general began to see himself as champion of a virtuous populace against a corrupting and exploitative market elite. Virtue, he fumed, was "to be found amongst the farmers of the country alone, not about courts, where courtiers dwell." Presently he would risk his oldest friendships to uphold justice for ordinary folk against Tennessee bankers and land speculators. Republicanism was in danger, he had decided, "and the people alone by their Virtue, and independent exercise of their free suffrage can make it perpetual."

Simultaneously Old Hickory was beginning to evoke in the beleaguered patriarchy of angry farmers the fantasy of a just paternal power that could drive the money-changers from the republican temple. In early 1822 a Virginia admirer assured him that a party was silently gathering—"as powerful as it wou'd be unexpected" though "as yet without a head"—to return "this grand republic" to "old republican principles" and thus "preserve the original simplicity of our institutions." To this end, he added pointedly, Presidents should be chosen "not for the splendour of their manners, but their simplicity and plainness—not for the eloquence of their haranguing, but the soundness of their judgment and their decision of character."

At this juncture local political maneuvers produced Jackson's presidential nomination by the Tennessee legislature. Demonstrating a sounder intuitive grasp of popular mood than conventional elitist politicians, he was both willing and confident. "Let the people do as it seemeth good unto them," he said.[13]

While the Jackson storm gathered, the historic Jeffersonian coalition between Virginia and New York was being revived to implement the planter/farmer alliance long advocated by John Taylor of Caroline. With New York's Bucktails "in full and almost unquestioned possession of the State Government in all its branches," their chieftain Martin Van Buren went to Monroe's Washington in 1821 as a senator, resolved "to realize similar results in the enlarged sphere of action to which I was called." His aim was to ally the "plain republicans" of the North with the planters of the South.

Convinced by his New York experience that only a renewal of the old party distinctions could unite a democratic majority against National Republicanism, Van Buren declared war on "Monroe's fusion policy." His first move was to organize Bucktail congressmen to elect a Virginian as Speaker over the incumbent New Yorker, who had been too Clintonian back home. His next move was to raise a furor over Monroe's appointment of a Federalist to the postmastership at Albany. As soon as Congress adjourned, he hastened to Richmond to cement an alliance with the Virginia gentlemen who were leading the attack on the consolidationists.

It was time "to commence the work of a *general resuscitation* of the *old democratic party,*" he proclaimed on his return to Washington, so as to produce "a *radical reform* in the political feelings of this place."[14] Crawford's Radical candidacy for President would be the rallying point, as John Quincy Adams observed, and "Democracy, Economy, and Reform" would be the watchwords.[15] Aided by the Treasury Secretary's extensive patronage, the big Virginia and New York delegations, with Georgia and North Carolina in tow, would ensure his nomination by the congressional Republican caucus; and as the "regular" Republican candidate he would be carried into the White House by the swelling tide of democratic and anti–National Republican sentiment.

Crawford's most formidable rival was Secretary Adams, who was bringing his brilliant diplomatic achievements to a peak in a duel with the British to fill the power vacuum left by the collapse of the Spanish empire and to make the United States preeminent in the entire Western Hemisphere. Although the Monroe administration had remained technically neutral between Spain and her rebellious colonies until Florida was safely in hand, American citizens gave substantial support to the rebels, particularly by fitting out privateers.

Henry Clay challenged the administration in Congress by agitating for diplomatic recognition of the revolutionary states. "Let us become real and true Americans," he argued, "and place ourselves at the head of the American system." As soon as the Transcontinental Treaty was ratified, the administration swung over to Clay's politically popular position. In 1822 the United States recognized five of the new republics—Chile, Colombia, Mexico, Peru, and the United Provinces of the Plata—being the first outside nation to so legitimate the Spanish American revolutionary cause.

The British, while eager for the trade opened to them by the Spanish American revolutions, were constrained by their European commitments. Since Napoleon's defeat they had been cooperating with the reactionary continental monarchies to prevent a resurgence of Bonapartism. But they declined to join the continental powers in the Holy Alliance, which sought to crush by armed force any spark of liberalism that appeared in Europe. Because the Holy Allies also threatened to help Spain's King Ferdinand VII reconquer his American colonies—and because they would not dare challenge the British navy—Adams tried unsuccessfully to persuade Britain to join the United States in recognizing the rebel states.

The European situation was transformed in 1822 when a French army representing the Holy Alliance invaded Spain to defend Ferdinand against a liberal constitutionalist uprising. George Canning, Castlereagh's successor as British Foreign Secretary, took alarm lest Britain's ancient rival upset the balance of power. Publicly he warned France against any continuing involvement in Spain or assistance to Ferdinand in America.

Having thus broken with the more reactionary policies of the Holy Alliance, Canning now inquired confidentially of the American minister in London whether their two countries might not issue a joint declaration against European intervention in America. For a time the Foreign Secretary courted Americans so assiduously that he seemed carried away—his colleagues thought him a bit enthusiastic—by the sensation of a dramatic rapprochement between the world's two liberal nations, united, as he aptly put it, "by a common language, a common spirit of commercial enterprise, and a common regard for well-regulated liberty."

President Monroe, excited by the prospect of attracting Britain away from the Holy Allies and into a virtual alliance to protect the republican Americas, asked the advice of his Republican predecessors in the White House. Both Jefferson and Madison advised accepting Canning's confidential overture. Jefferson thought this "the most momentous question that had arisen" since the decision for independence. "Great Britain is the nation which can do us the most harm of any one, or all on earth," he wrote to Monroe, "and with her on our side we need not fear the whole world."

But there were problems. Under pressure from conservatives in the British government, Canning still was not ready to recognize the revolutionary republics and wanted the proposed Anglo-American declaration to leave the way open for Spain itself to reconquer its colonies if it could do so without the aid of other powers. More seriously, he wanted Britain and the United States to renounce any future acquisitions themselves in Spanish America. The two countries had recently suspected each other of designs on Cuba; and although they tacitly agreed to leave it for the present in the hands of Spain, John Quincy Adams for one balked at renouncing future hopes for the strategic island. And some Americans already had their eyes on Texas.

Problems with Russia suggested an alternative course to the Secretary. In support of trading operations in Russian Alaska, the Czar had issued a ukase claiming the American northwest coast down to the 51st parallel and forbidding foreign ships within a hundred miles of shore. Britain and the United States both protested, and they were now separately negotiating agreements (concluded in 1824 and 1825) for a Russian pullback to present Alaska. Moreover the Czar's minister had recently presented Adams with an elaborate defense of the Holy Alliance's crusade against liberal governments in both Europe and the Americas.

Putting all these developments together, Adams shrewdly concluded that Canning's confidential overture, coming on top of his public warning to France, meant that the British navy was already committed against European interference in the Americas. Therefore the United States had nothing further to gain from the joint declaration proposed by Canning, and much to gain from declaring unilaterally principles that the British navy could be counted on to enforce. Such unilateral declarations, announced in notes to Britain, Russia, and other powers, would enable the United States to define on its own terms, and without disclaiming future acquisitions in Spanish America, the relationship between the Old World and the New. "It would be more candid, as well as more dignified to avow our principles explicitly," the Secretary argued in the extensive Cabinet debates, ". . . than to come in as a cock-boat in the wake of the British man-of-war."

Americans did not know that France had by now promised Canning to stay out of the Western Hemisphere; and President Monroe and Secretary Calhoun clung to the proposed joint declaration as necessary for protection against the Holy Allies. Only gradually did the persistent Adams win them to a bolder course. First he got permission to tell the Russians and British that, once the quarrel over the Russian ukase was settled, "the American continents, henceforth, will be no longer subjects of colonization." Only then did he win permission to inform the Russians in addition that the United States dissented from the political principles of the Holy Alliance, and

> while disclaiming . . . all interference with the political affairs of Europe, to declare our expectation and hope that the European powers will equally abstain from the attempt to spread their principles in the American hemisphere, or to subjugate by force any part of these continents to their will.

The discussion awakened President Monroe's Revolutionary/Jeffersonian fervor to a historic opportunity, and he ended up not only embracing but amplifying his Secretary's bold initiative. The United States, he decided, as birthplace of a rising republicanism now everywhere under attack, must step forth as its champion. In fulfillment of this republican responsibility, Monroe himself proclaimed Adams's principles to the world in his annual message of December 1823.

The President, backed by Calhoun, had wanted to embrace not only Spanish American revolutionaries but also beleaguered constitutionalists in Spain itself, and especially Greeks who were fighting desperately for freedom from heathen Turks under the banner of an American-style constitution. But Adams's insistent realism finally persuaded him to couple European nonintervention in the New World with American nonintervention in the Old.

The Monroe Doctrine thus evolved proclaimed three principles that would eventually rescue this conscientious President from historical oblivion. First, in reporting on relations with Russia, he laid down what diplomatic historians have called the principle of noncolonization: "that the American Continents, by the free and independent position which they have assumed and maintain, are henceforth not to be considered as subjects for future colonization by any European power." Then, late in the message, he expressed sympathy for the Greek and Spanish liberals, but only in the context of Adams's principle of abstention: "In the wars of the European powers, in matters relating to themselves, we have never taken any part, nor does it comport with our policy, so to do."

Only then did he turn to Spanish American affairs to declare the principle of noninterference. To the Holy Allies he announced that "any attempt on their part to extend their system to any portions of this Hemisphere" would be regarded by the United States "as dangerous to our peace and safety." With respect to the revolutionary Spanish American states, he continued, "any interposition for the purpose of oppressing them, or controuling in any other manner, their destiny, by any European power," would be viewed "as the manifestation of an unfriendly disposition towards the United States."

Blandly Adams conveyed Monroe's message to the British as a substantial compliance with Canning's overture, which he hoped they would reciprocate by proceeding promptly to recognize the Spanish American republics. Canning's public response was to take credit for the nonintervention doctrine, arguing that "the ultra-liberalism of our Yankee co-operators" gave him "just the balance that I wanted" against the Holy Allies.

Privately the Foreign Secretary was appalled by the ardent republicanism of Monroe's rhetoric, shocked by the doctrine of noncolonziation (he considered a formal protest), and angered by the crass Americans' underhanded use of his confidential overture to score a diplomatic triumph. With critics taunting him for "following in the wake of the United States," Canning might have revised Adams's vivid metaphor. For the American cock-boat sheltered, in fact, behind the stout walls of His Britannic Majesty's men-of-war to fire its manifesto at a menacing Europe.[16]

Within less than a decade National Republican diplomacy had brought the country from the brink of dissolution to a position of unchallenged dominance in the American half of the world. Henceforth other nations were to stay out of the Western Hemisphere, and save British North America, they were to "leave the rest of the Continent to us."

Obviously this stunning achievement owed much to the military/diplomatic aggressiveness of Jackson and Adams, while Monroe deserves more credit than he has received for backing his combative lieutenants, always after deliberate consideration, with the responsibility of decision. Yet the most important role was played by Castlereagh and Canning in extricating Britain from its European entanglements and stationing the royal navy to quarantine the New World politically from the Old. The implicit Anglo-American bargain gave Britain free access to New World markets, while the United States got a century of free military security, a good share of the world's carrying trade, a voracious market for its cotton and presently wheat, the freedom to expand territorially at the expense of its vulnerable neighbors Spain and later Mexico, and the opportunity for such gratifying posturing as the Monroe Doctrine.

Secretary Adams's diplomatic triumphs reinforced his advantages as the only northern and nonslaveholding candidate in a presidential race sectionalized by depression and the Missouri controversy. Therefore his popularity with fellow New Englanders dashed Radical hopes of garnering Yankee votes from loyalty to Republican caucus nominations. Moreover the thousands of New Englanders pouring west along the line of the Erie Canal made Adams formidable in New York and beyond.

Similarly Henry Clay relied on the solid support of his section, the rapidly growing West. He sought additional support in the Northeast by championing Bank, protective tariff, and internal improvements as an integrated "American System" for national development. The plethora of candidates, he hoped, would deny anyone a majority in the electoral college, leaving the choice to the House of Representatives where his commanding personal influence could give him victory.

A late entry was the least sectional candidate. Secretary Calhoun's expensive War Department had been the primary target of the Radical economizers in Congress. As they cut his army almost in half, decimated his fortifications program, undermined his paternalist management of Indian affairs, tried to abolish his military academy, and blocked his internal-improvement projects, he dedicated himself to thwarting the Radicals' effort to "tamper with the high destiny of this country."[17] Moreover they were challenging him for control of South Carolina itself, and their candidate, Crawford, was his competitor for the southeastern sectional base on which his national career seemed to depend. Consequently Calhoun at first supported his Cabinet colleague Adams as the strongest anti-Crawford candidate. The administration's two archnationalists had come to admire and confide in each other. "Calhoun has no petty scruples about constructive powers and state rights," Adams enthused. "[He is] above all sectional and factional prejudices more than any other statesman of this Union with whom I ever acted."[18]

But the Missouri controversy dashed hopes for Adams electoral votes in South Carolina and other slaveholding states, while the rise of the Bucktails seemed to deny him New York. About this time Calhoun vacationed in electorally powerful Pennsylvania, which he now thought Adams had to win to stop Crawford. He returned to Washington convinced that Adams could not win Pennsylvania, but that he, Calhoun, could. Obsessed through the rest of his long career by presidential ambitions, he was not hard to convince. Certainly his decisive support for Pennsylvania's national Bank, numerous manufacturers, and ambitious canal projects won him enthusiastic backing from the enterprising New School Democrats who controlled the state's politics. Their leader George M. Dallas, son of Calhoun's collaborator in establishing the national Bank, promised him Pennsylvania's big electoral vote; while his formal nomination by a group of congressmen in late 1821 was engineered by the New School Congressman Samuel D. Ingham, an archprotectionist manufacturer from Bucks County near Philadelphia.

Calhoun's nomination appears to have been hastily improvised in anticipation of news arriving several days later that would have forestalled it—the South Carolina legislature, to save the state from Radicalism, had nominated his best friend William Lowndes as a favorite-son candidate for President. Calhoun had already tried to get the senior and more popular Lowndes appointed minister to France, perhaps to obviate his nomination; and despite it he now insisted on running himself. Fatally ill, Lowndes declined to press his own candidacy and was dead within six months. Adams, the only other man on intimate terms with Calhoun, was unconvinced by his claim that he had entered the race as an ally in defending the great cause of National Republicanism and saw only another ambitious rival.[19]

Outside South Carolina the only slave states where Calhoun had any support were North Carolina and Maryland. His campaign was pitched mainly at the northeastern heartland of National Republicanism. "His education had been northern, his politics, his feelings, his views, & his sympathies were all northern," a New England congressman reported him as saying. He defended the Marshall Court and let it be known that he shared the Chief Justice's contempt for strict construction, under which, he said, "the powers of the Union would be reduced almost to nothing." In the style of traditional elitist politics, he based his hopes on recruiting notables—his three noncandidate colleagues in the Cabinet, Monroe's sons-in law (he seems to have been the President's favorite), Yale classmates, and the far-flung network of army officers. He was particularly appealing to Federalists.

Educated by Federalists and personifying the fusion between South Carolina's lowcountry Federalist and upcounty Republican elites, Calhoun presented himself to politically homeless Federalists as a clearcut alternative to Radicalism. "The line between the [National] Republicans and the Radicals will finally be distinctly drawn," he said in welcoming Federalist wealth and power back to national politics, "and they will become national parties, *where sides may be selected by all.*" He assured Alexander Hamilton's son that his father's policy was "the only true policy for this country"; he won the enthusiastic backing of the leading younger Federalist Daniel Webster, with whom he had collaborated in reestablishing a Hamiltonian national Bank; and his support in Maryland was mainly Federalist.[20]

While appealing to market elites, Calhoun also exploited the democratic impulse. With the congressional caucus nomination sewed up by the big Virginia and New York delegations for Crawford, Calhoun newspapers in Washington, Philadelphia, and New York struck a popular chord by tirelessly denouncing the caucus for usurping the people's right to choose their President. In North Carolina, Pennsylvania, and New York, Calhoun's supporters called themselves the People's Ticket or the People's Party.

Like the Jeffersonian Virginia elite, Calhoun could align himself with the democratic impulse because farmers in his society still felt enough affinity with planters to defer to elite leadership. But where the archaic Chesapeake slavocracy sought democratic support to resist the capitalist market, Calhoun, representing an entrepreneurial slavocracy, was the first in a long line of presidential candidates to shape his politics to the beguiling chimera of a democratic capitalism.

Calhoun was the first victim of the Jackson enthusiasm. No one was greatly surprised when a "contagion" of small-farmer Jacksonism forced planter-oriented politicians to abandon their preference for Adams in Alabama and Mississippi, new states that owed their existence to the hero.[21] What staggered Calhounites and stunned politicians everywhere were developments in vastly different Pennsylvania.

Here William Duane's resurgent Old School Democracy needed a presidential candidate around whom to rally against the New School's favorite Calhoun. Adams was identified with the scorned Monroe administration and Clay with its anti-Republican policies, while Crawford relied on a caucus Old Schoolers reviled for undemocratically saddling the country with Madison and Monroe. For a time Duane even considered De Witt Clinton, mainly for his antiadministration, anti-caucus posture, and partly because Clinton had long catered to the ethnic loyalties of Duane's fellow Irish-Americans. But the New Yorker's chances were destroyed when he lost his state to the Bucktails.

Another presidential possibility was suggested by the Old School's antibank polemicist Stephen Simpson, who had idolized Andrew Jackson since serving under him at New Orleans. No doubt Simpson inspired the trial-balloon squib launched by Duane's *Aurora* in January 1822, months before Old Hickory's nomination by the Tennessee legislature: "If a choice of Clinton or Jackson could be made, then our country would prosper." Several months later, while the Jackson agitation was beginning in Tennessee, debts forced the aging Duane to abandon the *Aurora*. As its successor Stephen Simpson established the Philadelphia *Columbian Observer*, which was soon combining praise of Jackson with denunciation of the paper system.

Simpson's seed fell on fertile soil, and promptly Jackson meetings, editorials, and committees sprang up in rural countries where farmers were in revolt against the village banks of 1814 and in the largest interior cities, Harrisburg and Pittsburgh, where working people suffered severely from the depression. These areas were supporting the Old School's war on banking, and most of this budding Jackson movement originated with people already involved in Old School politics: Pittsburgh's Old School Congressman Henry Baldwin, who denounced the national Bank and led the fight for the tariff bill of 1820 as a relief measure for working people; the antibanking legislators and congressman from rural Westmoreland County; and the tavern keeper and the unemployed journalist who organized a Jackson committee in Harrisburg.

What confounded the New School Calhounites was the spontaneous public enthusiasm for the Old School's Jackson campaign. Considering themselves "the genteelest and most respectable" Democrats, the New Schoolers seriously underestimated a movement arising from the "grog shop politicians of the villages & the rabble of Philadelphia & Pittsburgh." The Jackson committees springing up everywhere, they sneered, were filled with "misguided youths," "giddy young men," "a new set, either wholly unknown or known only for their obliquities and disaffection."

In March 1823 these genteel Calhounites were rudely awakened at the Harrisburg state convention of the Democratic party—by now Pennsylvania Republicans of all Schools called themselves Democrats. Expecting an overwhelming endorsement of Calhoun, they encountered instead such enthusiasm for Jackson that they barely managed to postpone the presidential question until the 1824 convention.

Through the fall and winter of 1823–1824 the upstart Jacksonians agitated and organized to control the selection of delegates to the March 1824 Harrisburg convention. Inviting mass participation in their meetings and rallies, they shocked genteel politicians with their "noise and bustle," "confusion and tumult," "violence & audacity." "The Great Augean Stable at Washington wants cleansing," they proclaimed, "and we know of no other Hercules." The political gentry soon realized that Jackson's "excessive popularity" and the "unceasing perseverance" of his supporters were "running away with the public feeling," and they were helpless to "oppose the phrenzy."

The crucial struggle was in Philadelphia, where Stephen Simpson—denounced as "a *leveller,* a would-be destroyer of almost everything fixed, and stable, and valuable"—mobilized the Old School working-class forces to wrest the party machinery from the New Schoolers. Asserting the "sacred right" of "the people" to "select our own candidate for the presidency of the United States, independent of all interference" from "a self constituted aristocracy," they lauded Jackson as "a uniform and consistent democrat" and "a friend to the *rights of man* and *universal suffrage.*"

The "Catastrophe" for Calhoun came when the Philadelphia Jacksonians made themselves "masters of the wards" by winning ten of the fourteen ward committee elections, and thus gained control of the general ward committee that would choose the city's big delegation to the Harrisburg convention. At the delegate selection meeting on February 18, a desperate George M. Dallas "struck Calhoun's flag" and saved the New Schoolers from certain defeat by announcing their conversion to the Jackson cause. As a result "a host of enthusiasts," many of them "boys of a day's growth," gathered at Harrisburg to endorse Jackson by a vote of 124–1. "The good men were panic struck" with "fears of losing popularity," said the lone holdout, so that "when it came to the pinch every man went over" but himself. All the New School could garner was an endorsement of Calhoun for Vice President.

In one of the country's most diverse and populous states, a general mass of disaffection had mobilized around Jackson's standard an apparently invincible coalition of farming and working-class people. Old Hickory, they seemed to believe, would "effect a *radical* change" by a "thorough overhauling of affairs at Washington City." Exactly what this portended was not yet clear, mused the Harrisburg holdout, for "we know not how far the moonstruck madness may reach." But somehow, he was certain, there "must be a new order of things."[22]

Simultaneously in the very different state of North Carolina, Jackson's startling popularity was reversing Crawford's momentum while administering the coup de grace to Calhoun. Politically North Carolina was a kind of poor man's Virginia—"a valley of humility between two mountains of conceit," as residents saw it—ruled through a malapportioned legislature by a modest planter class centering in its overrepresented middle eastern counties. The dominant Radical politicians around Nathaniel Macon were accustomed to following Virginia and anticipated no difficulty in delivering their state for Crawford.

But revolt was brewing in the interior. The postwar boom carried entrepreneurial hopes to landlocked trading villages, where leading citizens, like their western Virginia counterparts, resented the refusal of a Radical-controlled legislature to provide the roads and river improvements that would bring them the market's largesse. The panic enabled these village elites to stir up embittered interior farmers in a campaign for democratic reform of the state constitution. This agitation culminated in a reform convention at Raleigh in 1823, just as the presidential campaign was heating up. In opposition to the Radicals' candidate Crawford, the reformers rallied around John C. Calhoun.

Calhoun was particularly appealing to the enterprising elites of the democratic interior as the great champion of internal improvements. Since touring the state's shoaling coastline with President Monroe in 1819, he had encouraged their hopes for federal aid in opening a deep-water outlet to the world market. His 1819 blueprint for a national transportation system promised a protected inland waterway along the coast, and his engineers were about to survey alternative routes through the interior villages for his proposed national road from Washington to New Orleans.

To ensure a united anti-Crawford effort, the North Carolina Calhounites joined forces with less numerous Adams backers (concentrated in Quaker counties, commercial towns, and the northeastern sound region) to organize an electoral ticket mainly composed of Calhoun men but nominally pledged to whichever anti-Crawford candidate proved stronger. Appealing to the swelling democratic impulse by attacking caucuses, they called their ticket the People's Ticket.

Jackson had no organized following in North Carolina until the end of 1823, when a few unaffiliated politicians, personally recruited by the general's Tennessee cronies, distributed pamphlets advocating his candidacy. These produced "an effect beyond calculation." Suddenly startled politicians realized that "a great change has taken place in the popular sentiment." "General Jackson is decid[ed]-ly the choice of the people," came the report from county after county, especially among "the more common and illiterate class."

Soon Calhoun's managers were being overwhelmed by the democratic genie whose escape they had abetted. "A Great Majority are in favour of Genl. Jackson," they were compelled to acknowledge. Only by pledging the People's Ticket to Jackson, they realized, could they avert defeat by a separate Jackson ticket. At this point news of Calhoun's Pennsylvania debacle forced his North Carolina backers into the surrender that was already inevitable. Following the example of their routed Pennsylvania allies, they converted their People's Ticket into a Jackson ticket and demoted Calhoun to candidate for Vice President.

In rejecting Calhoun for Jackson, ordinary folk also rejected the traditional leaders who were exploiting democratic sentiment for entrepreneurial purposes. The class consciousness of this voter uprising was most evident in commercial Fayetteville. The local gentry, smugly characterizing themselves as the "reading and reflecting" part of the community, favored Calhoun's People's Ticket ally Adams and expected to carry the town their way as usual. They were rudely shocked when an upstart "retailer of whiskey and onions" ran for the legislature as a Jackson man. He won by urging "such of my friends as can read the newspapers" to recommend him "to their neighbor who can't read, particularly to the mechanic and laboring man, and to the friend of General Jackson."[23]

With the presidential race reduced to two contenders, the North Carolina Crawfordites found it "very difficult to electioneeer successfully against Genl. Jackson." Only his character and services were the kind the voters seemed to "appreciate and feel," complained one. A grand jury explained that he was "the favorite of the people" because "he belongs to them; he has been raised with them; he has served them both in peace and war; they feel grateful to him, and will take a pride in honoring him."

Never before had the state seen such popular interest in a presidential election. New modes of mass participation had much of the countryside "in a buble for Jackson." The Jacksonians held scores of public meetings and capitalized on their candidate's popularity by taking straw votes at militia musters and other gatherings. Ruefully the Crawfordites tried to explain why "the result was always in favor of Jackson." "In almost every Captain's company the drums were beating and fifes whistling for the hero of New Orleans," reported one. "The officers would treat their men, make them drunk and then raise the war whoop for General Jackson." A single cup of *"generous whiskey,"* said another, "produces more military ardor than can be allayed by a month of reflection and sober reason."[24]

The swelling Jackson enthusiasm in North Carolina revealed the Radicals' inability to revive the Jeffersonian planter/farmer alliance. Here and elsewhere, planters threatened by hard times and the assault on slavery could see only an additional threat in farmers demanding the substance as well as the forms of democracy. In Virginia, Alabama, Georgia, and North Carolina, Radical planting elites had arrayed themselves against democratic reform or popular discontent. Only in Tennessee did Radicals take the popular side; and there, too, they were being overwhelmed by Jackson's popular appeal.

In some uncanny way General Jackson was reading the national mood better than anyone else. His only advisers at first were the hangers-on who congregated at the Hermitage, especially Major John H. Eaton and Major William B. Lewis. Now widowed, the two majors had entered the Hermitage entourage as brothers-in-law by marrying orphaned sisters who were nieces and wards of the Jacksons. As Jackson's biographer and protégé, the amiable Major Eaton sat in the federal Senate and linked the Hermitage to national politics.

Jackson's only national organization was provided by the busy pen of Major Lewis. The imposing Lewis earned his military title (unlike the peacetime militia titles flaunted by most Tennessee gentlemen) as quartermaster in Jackson's wartime campaigns; and now he rode over frequently from his neighboring plantation to perform similar staff services in his commander's political campaign. Through correspondence with the little-known leaders thrown up in various states by the Jackson excitement, Lewis set the campaign's tone and broadcast the encouraging news that soon poured in.

Old Hickory was showing the surprising insight and empathy that made him a superb democratic politician. Presidential candidates were expected to remain above the battle, or appear to do so. While the principled, ambitious Adams fought fiercely and often successfully against the temptation to advance his own cause, and while Crawford, Calhoun, and Clay were obviously directing their supporters' feverish electioneering, Jackson seized the high ground that the office should seek the man. Finding a loophole in the electoral etiquette, he managed to announce his availability while simultaneously dramatizing his lofty detachment and invoking democracy. An obscure tavernkeeper in Harrisburg, Pennsylvania, had written to ask whether the general would accept the presidency. Knowing that his reply would be published, Jackson answered that his "undeviating rule" was "neither to seek or decline public invitations to office." Just as the presidency should not be sought, he added to make his meaning unmistakable, it "cannot, with propriety, be declined." Therefore he left the matter "to the American people," who "have alone the right to decide." Jackson timed his reply to reach Harrisburg on the eve of the March 1823 state Democratic convention, where it helped block Calhoun's expected nomination.

Flooded with letters from admirers and subscribing to eighteen newspapers, the general had picked up the first tremors of the popular groundswell that surfaced at Harrisburg. It confirmed his special rapport with "the people," and he gave the Pennsylvania Jacksonians his full support. The Philadelphia "madman" Stephen Simpson frequently received warm and encouraging letters from his and the nation's hero, and Jackson defended him against genteel critics of his slashing and radically democratic style. "Follow the example of Pennsylvania," the general told supporters everywhere.

The only problem in Pennsylvania was Calhoun's appeal as champion of protective tariffs. Tariff protection—originally advocated by mechanics and opposed by lordly importers—had been a favorite measure of working-class Pennsylvanians for two generations. Stricken by hard times, Pennsylvania might well suspect Jackson of agreeing with the southern congressmen who denied them the tariff relief promised by the Baldwin bill of 1820. Hoping to elicit a protariff response from the general, one of his Pennsylvania supporters sent Mrs. Jackson a locally produced hat, suggesting it be worn "as an encouragement to *domestic manufacturers.*" Promptly the general wrote back that the hat exhibited "the perfection which our domestic manufactures may hereafter acquire, if properly fostered and protected." This statement quickly made the rounds of the national press, along with Jackson's pronouncement that American independence rested on "the success of our manufactures, as the handmaiden of agriculture and commerce."[25]

Just as Jackson's candidacy was gaining momentum in Pennsylvania, he found himself unexpectedly in the Senate during the winter and spring of 1824. Astutely he concentrated on allaying his reputation for violence and crudity. Patching up old quarrels, he charmed friend and foe alike at Secretary Adams's splendid ball in his honor on the January 8 anniversary of his victory at New Orleans. Daniel Webster thought his manners "more presidential" than any other candidate's, and Mrs. Webster was "decidedly for him."

Cheering political developments bolstered the general's determination to combine "*suaviter in modo*" with "*fortiter in re,*" as a favorite (Chesterfieldian!) aphorism advised. Clay was making little headway outside the Ohio Valley, and in

February Calhoun's candidacy crashed in Pennsylvania, delivering to Jackson his considerable following in New Jersey, Maryland, and the Carolinas. Crawford's early lead was melting as a democratic public applauded the combined assault on the caucus by all the other candidates and their newspapers; and Crawford himself had been felled by a massive stroke.

Since September the big Georgian had been lying behind the shutters of his Washington home, guarded from visitors and often paralyzed, blind, and dumb. Grimly cracking the whip of party discipline over the demoralized Radicals, Senator Van Buren could assemble only a fourth of the senators and representatives (nearly half of them New Yorkers and Virginians) in the February caucus to nominate Crawford. The institution that had given the country its three Republican Presidents would never meet again. All these auspicious developments made it easy for Jackson to preside convivially over a dinner party for his healthy rivals Adams, Calhoun, and Clay.

The general avoided political discussions and rarely opened his mouth in the Senate, but he missed few roll calls on the tough political questions of tariff and internal improvements. Election-eve constituency pressures produced congressional majorities for the first substantial increase in protective duties since 1816; and (now that President Monroe had broken the constitutional logjam) Calhoun's plan for initiating a national transportation system through a general survey was finally enacted. Sensitized by Pennsylvania to a national constituency, Jackson supported both as essential for national defense. Now his North Carolina backers pressed him for some antitariff statement to deflect Radical criticism. Again Jackson resorted to the device of a sure-to-be-published letter to make his only policy declaration of the campaign. Replying to an inquiry about his tariff views from a Dr. Coleman, he justified this mode of reaching the public on the democratic ground that it was his duty, as one being considered for the presidency, "when asked, frankly to declare my opinion upon any political national question." He declared, therefore, that he favored a "judicious" tariff.

"Well, by God, I am in favor of an *in*judicious tariff!" Clay is supposed to have exclaimed when Jackson's Coleman letter promptly reached the newspapers. Actually Jackson was cannily explicit in specifying Pennsylvania's iron and the Ohio valley's hemp and wool (but not New England's cotton textiles) as "the grand materials of our national defence" requiring duties high enough to make American producers competitive with Europeans. The tariff should also be high enough to pay off the national debt, he added, for a debt was "a curse to a republic" that would "raise around the administration a monied aristocracy, dangerous to the liberties of the country."

If the eclectic Jackson could echo John Taylor in one breath, in the next he could extol the market as the farmer's salvation. The farmer suffered from low prices, he maintained, because "there is too much labor employed in agriculture." If tariff protection diverted six hundred thousand people from agriculture, he predicted, "you will at once give a home market for more bread-stuffs than all Europe now furnishes us." These views, Jackson defiantly told his antitariff addressee, "I would not barter for any office."[26]

A Tennesseean who had known the general for years warned Henry Clay not to be deceived by his apparent commitment to tariffs and internal improvements. "Your favourite the American system the people of Tennessee is opposed to," he wrote, "also the Hero if he had no concealment." Grappling with unfamiliar national issues and never much concerned with ideological consistency, Jackson was sensitive by experience to the national-defense argument and determined to carry Pennsylvania. But his new patriarchal role as democratic tribune was pulling him away from the Tennessee gentry and Monrovian nationalism; and his ultimate position would depend on the farming and working Americans whose leader he was becoming. And "the commonality," according to another Tennesseean, thought Jackson "the only man" who could "revise what they thought a corrupt system of government, Meaning the caucus—the treasury and Bank influences."[27]

With Congress in recess during the summer and fall of 1824, Jackson waited out the final months of the campaign in dignified public silence at the Hermitage. Meanwhile the anticaucus din mounted and the stricken Crawford's once triumphant cause wilted. As the Jackson enthusiasm shut the Radical standard bearer out of the whole Southwest and invaded even his southeastern stronghold, another adverse current of popular feeling met him in the free states.

Although many old-fashioned northern Republican politicians favored Crawford, little of the anticipated support developed outside New York. Slavery's advance into Missouri had deeply shocked northern opinion and heightened northern resentment of southern domination and slaveholding candidates. North of New York both Federalists and Republicans rallied so unanimously around their nonslaveholding fellow New Englander Adams that no other candidate had a chance. West of New York fierce competition from Adams, Clay, and Jackson prevented a Crawford ticket in any northwestern state. And the middle Atlantic and border states south of New York were an unpromising battleground with Adams and Jackson.

All that kept Radical hopes alive was the smashing victory of Crawford's Bucktail supporters in the country's most populous state. By 1822 Martin Van Buren's Albany Regency had driven all but a handful of its foes from the New York legislature, which traditionally chose the state's big block of thirty-six presidential electors, one-seventh of the electoral college. Theoretically the democratic Bucktails favored popular choice of presidential electors. But controlling the legislature so totally, they could not resist the temptation to insure New York for Crawford by keeping the presidential choice in the legislature's hands for one more election. National power and the national destiny were at stake.[28]

With the Clintonian/Federalists shattered, the state's powerful entrepreneurial interests quickly found a new political channel. John C. Calhoun unwittingly initiated an astonishing counterrevolution in the spring of 1823, when he persuaded his coterie of able supporters in New York City to launch a public campaign on his behalf. They followed the classic Calhoun strategy of appealing to business interests, in this case the Clintonian/Federalists, while attracting democratic support by attacking caucuses. Announcing formation of an anti-Crawford People's Party, the Calhounites established a well-edited newspaper and began hammering on the only theme that gave them any chance for New York electoral votes. In the name of democracy, they demanded that the Regency's Crawfordite legislature let the voters choose presidential electors.

Most Clintonian/Federalists were already committed to the nonslaveholder Adams; but the instant popularity of the Calhounite agitation for popular election of the President excited their hopes for a comeback by turning the issue of democracy against the Regency. "We must be democratic, we must be on the side of the people," they began telling each other; "if our adversaries are republicans, we must be democratic; if they are democratic, we must be jacobin[ic]al." Moving into the People's Party, the Clintonian/Federalists took it over after Calhoun's candidacy crumbled in Pennsylvania. "All power emanates from the people," these jacobinical grandees proclaimed, and the people "alone can be trusted with its exercise." Catching the still rising tide of democratic sentiment, they generated enormous public pressure on the Bucktail legislature to pass an Electoral Bill transferring choice of presidential electors to the voters.[29]

The popular response to the People's Party left the Albany Regency between a rock and a hard place. Wary all along about entrusting their slaveholding southern candidate to the manifestly antislavery New York electorate, they now faced a greater danger. The popular enthusiasm stirred up by the People's Party could undo their years of struggle by reviving politically their bête noire Clinton.

Clinton was devoting himself in defeat to his unpaid duties as head of the Canal Board, and his Grand Canal excited an almost religious awe as he pushed it rapidly, efficiently, and profitably toward completion. The Erie, moreover, projected the market into the ultrademocratic Bucktail country of western New York and made Clinton a hero to bustling entrepreneurs and lawyers in the towns and villages springing to life along its banks. Elsewhere even those who distrusted him politically had to admire the vision and skill with which this "Magnus Apollo" conceived and managed the most stupendous engineering feat Americans had ever undertaken.

Now the Regency had good reason to fear that allowing the people to vote for electors would make Clinton President. If a Clinton ticket were offered, New Yorkers would certainly prefer a native son to Crawford and probably to Adams. And with New York in his pocket, Clinton would be an instant front-runner nationally. To avoid this supreme calamity the Bucktail legislators had to violate the democratic gospel that brought them to power. Professing to approve the Electoral Bill in principle, they voted to postpone it until the day after the legislature was scheduled to choose electors.

Once the reputed wizards of the Albany Regency blundered into this impasse, their internal divisions pushed them into an even more incredible blunder. To hold the party line against the Electoral Bill it was necessary to propitiate the ultrademocratic Bucktails, who hated the Clintonians with special fury and who had been repeatedly frustrated by Van Buren's moderating influence on the party. He had diluted their democratic reforms in the constitutional convention, and over his opposition they won only the single victory of persuading the convention to remove the despised lifetime high-court judges. Then Van Buren passed over the ultrademocratic leaders to bestow the governorship on the conservative Bucktail Joseph Yates; and straightaway Governor Yates shocked all Bucktails by reappointing the old judges to their lifetime positions.

Robbed of revenge against the judges and called on now to violate their democratic principles by opposing the Electoral Bill, the ultrademocrats demanded retribution against Clinton himself. Without warning, on the last day of the legislative session, the disciplined Bucktail majority stripped the feckless Clinton of his post as head of the Canal Board. Some Regency luminaries—an appalled Van Buren was out of reach in Washington—foolishly expected this public humiliation to finish the Magnus Apollo politically.

Instead Clinton became an instant martyr and hero. The People's Party was galvanized into furious activity, and like the Jackson campaign elsewhere was soon evoking mass participation in its meetings and rallies. The governorship and legislature were at stake in the October state election, just before the November presidential vote. Denouncing the Bucktails' legislative caucus as undemocratic, the People's Party countered with a state convention of delegates from the counties and nominated Clinton for governor.

Governor Yates's final contribution to the Bucktail comedy of political errors was to call the legislature into special session in August 1824 to reconsider the Electoral Bill. On the eve of facing the voters, the Bucktail legislators were compelled once again to affront democratic sentiment by rejecting the bill. Burdened in addition with an unpopular and incapacitated presidential candidate, the Regency was swept from power in October by a tide of votes for Clinton and People's Party legislators. Barely hanging on to the state senate, only part of which faced election each year, the inept Regency was outfoxed a few weeks later in Machiavellian legislative maneuvering over the presidential vote. Crawford got only five of New York's thirty-six electors, with most of the rest going to Adams.

The Bucktails fell by departing from the "cardinal maxim" that brought them to power—"always to seek for, and when ascertained, always to follow the will of the majority." With the democratic impulse surging to new heights across the country, they let themselves be caught on the less democratic side of an issue. Diverted through the channel of the People's Party in New York, this determination of the people to act for themselves was simultaneously fueling antibank and debtor-relief campaigns while pushing Andrew Jackson to the front of the presidential race.

The Bucktails were the first American politicians to succeed by giving some sustained effect to this widespread yearning for democratic control over a society suddenly grown threatening. What defeated them and doomed Radicalism was slavery. By challenging slavery in Missouri, developmental nationalism doomed the Jeffersonian alliance between New York "plain republicans" and Virginia planters. The barrage of state-rights polemics from Richmond identified Radicalism not with yeoman democracy but with human bondage. Called upon to do the impossible, the Bucktails loyally went down to defeat trying to mobilize the democratic impulse behind a slavery-tainted Radicalism. Thus passed Jeffersonian politics.

The democratic tide that rolled over the Regency was simultaneously sweeping away traditional presidential politics in a flood of ballots for Jackson. Returns from the eighteen states that allowed voters to choose presidential electors put the popular hero far ahead of all the conventional candidates. A sectional breakdown reveals the national breadth of Jackson's appeal.

	Jackson	Adams	Crawford	Clay
NEW ENGLAND (Me., N.H., Mass., R.I., Conn.)		84%	16%	
MID-ATLANTIC (N.J., Pa.)	63%	25%	9%	0.3%
NORTHWEST Ohio, Ind., Ill., Ky., Mo.)	33%	16%	2%	41%
SOUTHEAST (Md., Va., N.C.)	45%	21%	33%	1%
SOUTHWEST (Tenn., Ala., Miss.)	84%	11%	5%	0.2%
TOTAL	42%	33%	13%	13%

Jackson carried the southwestern states and Pennsylvania by overwhelming margins. In the East he also edged out Adams in New Jersey, barely trailed him in Maryland, and took North Carolina by a good margin from Crawford. In the Northwest he triumphed handily over Clay and Adams in Indiana and Illinois, ran close behind Clay in Ohio and Missouri, and got a respectable vote in Clay's Kentucky.

Old Hickory was shut out only in New England, where Adams's majorities were as overwhelming as Jackson's in the Southwest. Adams's traditional qualifications earned him conservative support everywhere—he got 44 percent of the vote even in slaveholding Maryland—and the westward swarming "universal Yankee nation" carried his appeal through upstate New York and along the shores of the Great Lakes all the way to northern Illinois. Neither Clay nor the crippled Crawford could hold his own section against the combined assault of Jackson and Adams, much less generate strength beyond.

But Jackson's commanding popularity did not yield the constitutionally required majority of presidential electors. Legislatures still chose electors in a fourth of the states. Vermont and New York gave most of their votes to Adams; Georgia was Crawford's; Calhoun delivered South Carolina for Jackson; and Delaware and Louisiana split their handful of votes. The final electoral result was as follows, with no candidate receiving the 131 votes needed for a majority:

Jackson	99
Adams	84
Crawford	41
Clay	37

In the absence of an electoral majority, the Constitution directed that the House of Representatives choose among the highest three, each of the twenty-four state delegations having one vote. With Clay eliminated and Crawford still disabled, Jackson had won eleven states in the electoral college and Adams seven. In all three Clay states (Kentucky, Missouri, and Ohio) Jackson had been the runner-up, and the Kentucky legislature was now urging its congressmen to support Jackson. If congressmen followed opinion in their states, the Jackson and Clay states were more than enough to sustain the manifest will of the majority.

Henry Clay thwarted the popular verdict by throwing his weighty influence in the House to Adams. In a world turned topsy-turvy by Napoleon Bonaparte, he genuinely feared to trust republicanism to the willful Napoleon of the woods. Reinforcing this high-minded objection was the pragmatic consideration that a Kentuckian was more likely to reach the presidency in succession to an easterner than another westerner. He well knew, moreover, that his decision would realign the building blocks of national politics. By casting his lot with Adams, he was opting for a political economy allying the newer northwestern centers of market energy with the market's dynamic northeastern core to realize the developmental program he was calling his American System. He was positioning himself to lead the republic into its capitalist destiny.

Insulated in the world of elite opinion, neither Adams nor Clay comprehended the general mass of disaffection welling up in the Jackson movement. Several weeks before the House presidential vote, the two conferred and reached an understanding. Probably neither was so indelicate as to mention what both knew, that Clay would be Adams's Secretary of State and heir apparent.

The Kentuckian's influence transferred to Adams not only the three Clay states but also the Jackson state of Louisiana. Jackson lost in addition three other states he had carried in the electoral vote—Maryland's contingent of ex-Federalist congressmen succumbed to Webster's missionary work on behalf of Adams; North Carolina's intransigent Radicals adhered to Crawford; and Illinois was delivered to Adams by a personal friend who was its lone congressman. Thus, excluding closely divided Maryland, six delegations were defying their constituents' known preference for Jackson. Consequently Adams entered the House voting on 9 February 1825 with twelve states, one short of a majority, to seven for Jackson and four doggedly for Crawford. New York held the balance, and the thirty-four New York congressmen were split down the middle, with seventeen for Adams—one short of the majority that would give him New York and the presidency—fourteen disciplined Bucktails holding out for Crawford, two mavericks for Jackson, and the unpredictable General Stephen Van Rensselaer. Hoping to salvage something from a deadlock, Senator Van Buren was struggling to deny Adams the one more New York vote he needed.

Everything finally came to depend on the aged, pious, and indecisive Patroon of Rensselaerwyck, largest landholder in the East, whose hundreds of tenants regularly sustained his seigneurial claim on the Albany district's congressional seat. If General Van Rensselaer held out against Adams, the two Jackson men would also, and Adams would fail. The Patroon, as a patriotic but unsuccessful commander in the War of 1812, admired Jackson; but as an anti-Clintonian "high-minded" Federalist, he was allied politically with the Bucktails. Van Buren courted him assiduously, lived with him in Washington, and thought he had promised to vote for Crawford.

But the Adams men played on the Patroon's class fears of anarchy if the election were deadlocked. Still in a frenzy of indecision as the ballot box came around, he bent over for a final invocation of divine aid and saw a providential Adams ballot on the floor. Impulsively he thrust it into the ballot box, and thus John Quincy Adams was elected sixth President of the United States.

Straightaway Adams designated Clay his Secretary of State. The Jacksonians had already accused Clay of bartering away the presidency for a promise of the State Department, and the "Bargain and Corruption" now seemed confirmed. Branding Clay "the *Judas of the West*," Jackson fumed publicly that *"Corruptions and intrigues at Washington . . . defeated the will of the people."* Much of the country took up the cry, opening a four-year campaign to vindicate popular sovereignty by placing Old Hickory triumphantly in the White House.[30]

For the first time, in 1824 presidential aspirants were required to run the gauntlet of a broad national electorate. Most states had long been so lopsidedly

Republican that they were rarely presidential battlegrounds. Even in the great Republican victory of 1800, legislatures chose presidential electors for two-thirds of the states; and as late as 1812 the voters were allowed to choose in only half. In the Northeast in 1808 and 1812, Federalist revival had produced state voter turnouts ranging from 35 percent to 75 percent; but in the two elections since, Monroe had run almost unopposed. Although American voters were by now turning out in large numbers for state elections, they were not accustomed to voting for Presidents.

In 1824 the institutional possibility of broad voter participation coincided with "a general mass of disaffection to the government." Since the war the rising democratic impulse had opened the presidential election to voters in the old states of North Carolina, New Jersey, Massachusetts, and Connecticut and all six new states. A farmer/worker populace victimized by the market's chaotic expansion and "looking out anywhere for a leader" found in Andrew Jackson more than military charisma. To an electorate fed up with conventionally qualified politicians, Jackson's primary qualifications was his very popularity. By insisting on the nonpolitician they most admired, ordinary Americans mustered democracy against the paper system and its new aristocracy of enterprise. In an election sometimes called devoid of issues, a majority was claiming control over a government that had been mainly responsive to elites.

The mobilization of democratic discontent only began in 1824. This first flood of the Jackson tide carried only to the southern border of New York, and nationwide only one in four adult white males voted. Because there was little incentive to vote in the many one-sided states where the result was a foregone conclusion, turnout was below 20 percent in Pennsylvania (76 percent Jackson) and most of New England (84 percent Adams) and registered only 11.5 percent in Virginia (57 percent Crawford, 21 percent Adams, 19 percent Jackson), where property qualifications further restricted the electorate. By contrast, 54 percent of the adult white males turned out in the most closely contested state, Maryland (Adams 44 percent, Jackson 43.7 percent); while turnouts of 42 to 52 percent in the one-sided Jackson states of Mississippi, North Carolina, and Alabama registered extraordinary enthusiasm for the hero.

Even this partial invasion of presidential politics by a democratic electorate was both unprecedented and irreversible. Modern presidential politics originated with the majority that claimed a democratic victory for Jackson in 1824. By robbing the majority of its victory, Adams and Clay crippled themselves politically and made Jackson the unmistakable symbol of an irresistible demand for majority rule.

Jackson would be swept into the White House in 1828 by a turnout of 56.3 percent, more than double 1824's. After 1828 only South Carolina would deny its voters a voice in the presidential choice. Henceforth Presidents (and the general parameters of national policy) would have to be ratified quadrennially by a broad electorate. State and local politics would increasingly attune their alignments to the absorbing presidential contests. Skilled career politicians, scrambling to shape democratic energies to the realities of the political environment, would gradually create a new two-party system. By the 1840s close competition in nearly every state between Jacksonian Democrats and anti-Jacksonian Whigs would regularly turn out for presidential elections over 70 percent of the qualified voters.

Yet while the people's hero waited to test the efficacy of a more democratic federal politics, the people were ever more stressed by market imperatives. Under political threat, market forces were mounting a religious and cultural offensive to ease traditional ways into the self-disciplined striving required by the capitalist mode of production. The republic's destiny would be decided on battlegrounds of religion and culture as well as politics.[31]

Chapter 7

God and Mammon

U<small>NDER</small> peaking market pressures in the 1820s and 1830s, Americans found religious salvation more compelling than political salvation. With a Second Great Awakening doubling the 1800 rate of church affiliation, diaries and letters of ordinary folk breathed an everyday spiritual preoccupation that politics interrupted only sporadically. Hope for God's grace and a better world to come sustained them through this world's tribulations. Only by headlong flight into domesticity, benevolence, and feeling could they tolerate the market's calculating egotism. Their pessimistic piety belies our historical mythology of capitalist transformation as human fulfillment.[1]

Unitarianism reshaped Christianity most fully to the market mentality. Emerging around Boston, where Puritan rationality had long fused Calvinist calling with arminian effort, it engaged the new Brahmin elite of intermarried Cabots, Lowells, Appletons, and Perkinses. Having risen from the outports by rational calculation, these enterprising merchant princes no longer found credible the trinitarian Christian God who mystically blended a divine Son with Father and Holy Ghost. Amid commercial boom and nascent industrialization at the turn of the century, the most fashionable urban congregations were taken over by believers in a unitary, remote, and benign creator-God. Their God endowed people with enough rationality and prudential morality to win for themselves—if they tried— the salvation of earthly happiness. Moreover the Unitarian God, according to the Reverend John T. Kirkland, "secures the rich from rapacity, no less than the poor from oppression; the high from envy, no less than the low from contempt." Yankees who got rich by trying found this Unitarian God irresistible.

Installing the right-thinking Kirkland as president of Harvard, Unitarians increasingly dominated Yankee elite culture; and their wealthy congregations overshadowed orthodox congregations in a widening arc of port and market towns fanning out from Boston. By clothing the market cosmology in the forms of Puritan tradition, Unitarianism enabled Yankee Brahmins—with fewer qualms and firmer conviction than entrepreneurial elites elsewhere—to abandon rural piety for the market's Newtonian/Lockean myth. Unitarianism was the quitessentially "liberal religion."[2]

But few Americans were sufficiently liberated from traditional values to embrace the Cold Light of Unitarian rationality. Consequently while the New Light mobilized the majority in Methodist/Baptist Come-outerism, market necessity generated for the more enterprising a Moderate Light tenuously blending the self-discipline of arminian effort with antinomian love.

This mainline American religion of the future was shaped by mainline Congregational clerics in lower New England, where traditional culture was hardest pressed by market stress, agrarian crisis, and the dawning industrial revolution. The Awakening had demonstrated from the start Christianity's protean adaptability to divergent needs. While the New Light revitalized traditional folkways and vindicated the lowly against their betters, it also eased venturers into worldly self-seeking. Relieving anxiety over departures from communal norms and paternal authority, spiritual rebirth reinforced the disciplined striving required for success.

In the Connecticut valley, where all these needs met, the Awakening had taken a moderate form. Commercial influences were sufficiently threatening to ignite the New Light but not strong enough either to radicalize it or to prevent it from sweeping over many established Congregational churches. Here regular pulpits were often filled by born-again young men of humble rural origin who followed the Awakening's brilliant herald of a new consciousness, the preacher/theologian/philosopher Jonathan Edwards.

This provincial Yankee parson challenged the arminian/capitalist mentality more fundamentally than any American or European of his time. To the urgent task of understanding his own mystically transfiguring new birth, he brought a dazzling philosophical virtuosity and the anti-Boston perspective of the family-farming interior. Appropriating Newton and Locke, in Puritan confidence that the latest findings of reason and science could never contradict divine revelation, he turned their latently atheistic system inside-out to the glory of God.

Edwards shrewdly attacked the market mythology at its most vulnerable point, Newtonian/Lockean epistemology. Mental conceptions, he argued in anticipation of romantic metaphysics, are all that can be known of external reality, and reality must therefore be "ideal." Resurrecting the omnipotent, omnipresent Puritan Jehovah as constant projector and sustainer of an immaterial reality of divine ideas poorly perceived by sinful humans, he validated the New Light as a divine emanation enabling the born-again to perceive God's beauty and holiness in everything. As a Yale-trained scion of the local River Gods, however, Edwards distrusted the fatalist millennial fantasy in which folk pain found surcease. To yearn for a cataclysmic Millennium, he feared, inspired delusions and suspect passions that were too often confused with the divine transport of the new birth. In place of the "pre-millennial" view that Christ would return to inaugurate the Kingdom of God by a cataclysmic destruction of evil, he drew from the Biblical prophecies a "post-millennial" view that Christ would return only after a Millennium of gradual victory over evil. Where the cataclysmic Millennium of the powerless left everything to Christ, Edwards's gradualist Millennium impelled human effort by making the born-again God's soldiers in the final conquest of evil.

Edwards electrified Yankee farm folk by declaring Millennium imminent. But they found his esthetic vision of the born-again state as "consent to Being in general" too mystical to attest the authenticity of the new birth as they experienced it. As a generation of disciples translated Edwards's theology into the everyday idiom of the New England countryside during the second half of the eighteenth century, a moderately antinomian "New Divinity" issued from rural pulpits.

The New Divinity's main codifier was Edwards's favorite student, confidant, and literary executor, Samuel Hopkins. Farm rearing and twenty-five years in an isolated rural pastorate left Hopkins with a "country style" that cost him the presidency of the Presbyterian New Lights' College of New Jersey at Princeton. Similarly the New Divinity's celebrated preacher Joseph Bellamy of western Connecticut was judged "not polite enough" for a Manhattan pulpit. "I may possibly do to be a minister out in the woods," Bellamy lamented, "but am not fit for the city."

In the Awakening's free religious marketplace, their "upstart divinity" won a following by meeting popular needs. People's "greatest need," Edwards had insisted, was "to have their hearts touched"; and he recommended the "kind of preaching that has the greatest tendency to do this." Preachers above all, his disciples shaped doctrine to touch hearts. Invoking against the competitive capitalist ego the more altruistic ethic of the stem family and subsistence community, these "Farmer Metaphysicians" told rural Yankees that in practice Edwards's "consent to Being in general" meant "love to God and our neighbour." Energizing the animistic substratum of Yankee feeling, the New Divinity's "disinterested benevolence" revitalized loving communities against encroaching market egotism. After several transformations, it would tenuously reconcile the anxious antinomian majority to a capitalist world.[3]

In 1793, just in time to arm rural Yankees against the combined assault of commercial boom, industrial revolution, and Unitarian heresy, the Reverend Samuel Hopkins published a definitive exposition of the New Divinity. Edwards's disciples, while modulating his theology to rural idiom, had always defended his middle ground between radical antinomians "turned enthusiasts and heretics" and the complacent orthodox and proto-Unitarians "fallen away to carnal security." Now another great "outpouring of the Spirit" enabled Hopkins to rejoice that "Edwardean sentiments" were about to "silence all opposition." By the turn of the century the Great Revival was making the New Divinity "the popular theology of New England."[4]

Hopkins's 1793 treatise was specially attuned to people stressed by sharpening capitalist relations. Late in his career he had left the remote valleys beyond the Connecticut for Newport, Rhode Island, where wealthy merchants distilled rum to trade for human merchandise on the coast of Africa. In Newport the New Divinity effected a historic junction with market-dislocated women. Hopkins was called to this hive of brutal enterprise by a "religious female society" that had for years kept the New Light alive among the humble members of the struggling little First Congregational Church. In calling Hopkins they challenged the arminianism of the flourishing Second Congregational Church, where the Reverend Dr. Ezra Stiles groomed himself for the presidency of Yale by feeding the complacency of Newport's rich and powerful.

The New-Light women's prophetic leader Sarah Osborn knew market vicissitude firsthand. Impoverished once by the death of her first husband at sea and again by the debts and business incapacity of her second, she supported her large family by teaching school and taking in boarders. Against the male egotism of market relations, she and her Newport sisters were defending the altruism that validated their nurturant role in the traditional family and community. They were also reaching, as the market thrust women into new roles, for greater autonomy, community, and leadership outside the all-encompassing patriarchy of the stem family. With rural prophetesses simultaneously challenging male dominance on chiliastic battlegrounds of sex and property, women everywhere felt most painfully capitalism's pressures on the affective fabric of family and communal life.

Osborn exercised her remarkable leadership in the only way open to women, by exemplifying through incessant love and benevolence a life lived constantly in the incandescence of the New Light. In her parlor, the sisterhood mobilized the spiritual energies that brought Hopkins to Newport by igniting a revival. Hundreds thronged her house for weekly jubilees, and every night except Saturday she hosted spiritual exercises for special groups—young women, young men, children, Baptists, and blacks.

Because Osborn's abilities inevitably challenged the male monopoly of spiritual leadership, she could proceed only by constant professions of Christian and womanly humility and only by cultivating a sympathetic New-Light minister, the Reverend Joseph Fisk, to monitor and endorse her activities. But Fisk faltered when revival focused patriarchal alarm on her spiritual power and ecumenical outreach. Hoping she was not "Moving beyond my Line," Osborn nevertheless defended her activities stoutly against his cautious admonitions, insisting especially that "my family do not Suffer thro My Neglect." She would serve "with all my Might within my *Proper Sphere,*" she declared, but did not think she should be asked "to shut up my Mouth and doors and creep into obscurity." Until Hopkins arrived, she proceeded without clerical sanction in reaching out to blacks against considerable criticism. Women like Osborn could not defend traditional altruism without eroding traditional patriarchy.[5]

Urban, female antinomianism embraced the New Divinity's rural altruism for support against the arminian market. Once the Newport Women secured Hopkins, they showered him with an adulation few ministers could still command; and Hopkins reciprocated by publishing a biography holding up Osborn as a model for the Christian life. The antinomian fervor of urban women confirmed for him the power of the New Light, and he prayed with a similar society of New-Light women every time he visited Boston. For a generation to come his male disciples proclaimed the spiritual superiority of women, protected by "retired circumstances" from "the numerous schemes for the acquisition of wealth, the offices of distinction," that left few males "truly religious."[6]

Vindicating rural/female altruism against a Newport "built up by the blood of the poor Africans,"[7] Hopkins sharpened the New Divinity's anticapitalist polemic. Newport deemed slavers and distillers moral if they were commercially honest, free of scandal, and faithful in attending Dr. Stiles's sermons. To penetrate this shocking moral complacency, Hopkins assailed frontally the market's emerging ethic of enlightened self-interest. Even Edwards had conceded that an inferior, self-serving kind of natural morality made civil life possible, while Adam Smith was proclaiming the general pursuit of self-interest to be the only practical altruism.

The New Divinity, as finally formulated under the stress of Hopkins's Newport experience, rejected all self-love, branding as sinful any act that did not arise from the "disinterested benevolence" of the truly born-again. Even to seek salvation out of self-concern he considered suspect. Revulsion against Newport's capitalist egotism drove Hopkins to his notorious test of true selflessness—a willingness to be damned for the glory of God.

Radical altruism transformed the Puritans' patriarchal God of will, power, and judgment into a God of maternal love. Hopkins's total rejection of self-love in humans made a self-loving God inconceivable to him. In a breathtaking reversal of the whole Calvinist tradition, he insisted that love—"disinterested benevolence"—was the essence of God's moral nature. The Puritan God who required humans to meet his arbitrary demands was transmogrified into a God whose benevolence required him to promote human welfare and happiness. "The Holiness of God primarily consists in LOVE, or Benevolence," Hopkins finally maintained, which "seeks the Good of the UNIVERSE, as comprehending both Creator and Creatures."[8]

By making love the moral essence of God and his reborn people, the New Divinity released a surge of eleemosynary energy in search of appropriate objects. Back in the Berkshire hills, Hopkins had joined Edwards in devoted service to remnant Indian communities. Now Newport's brutal everyday commerce in chained black human beings epitomized for him the evil of the market's self-love. Promptly he joined the early abolitionists and for twenty years figured prominently in anti-slavery appeals to Rhode Island legislatures, Continental Congresses, and finally the Constitutional Convention. Meanwhile he organized an African mission society to drum up lay support for Christianizing Africa through a colony of American black missionaries.

Remodeling Edwards's New Divinity for the second time, Osborn and Hopkins cast long shadows down the American future. Channeling benevolent and missionary zeal through voluntary lay association, they found a formula for eventual cultural hegemony. Osborn's leadership was prophetic of women who would again and again mobilize antinomian love through spiritual and benevolent associations like Newport's. And Hopkins's millennial fantasy of the Kingdom of God marshaled the chiliasm of the dislocated behind the New Divinity for cultural conquest.

Taught by Edwards that the climax of history was approaching, Hopkins saw in the commercial frenzy and party strife of the 1790s the Biblically predicted time of rampant discord and worldliness that would immediately precede Millennium. Christians now living, he announced, might share the triumph that would inaugurate the Kingdom of God during the just-dawning nineteenth century. The born-again, he exhorted, must "prepare the way" for Millennium and "promote its coming in proper time" through evangelism and disinterested benevolence. Hopkins published Osborn's devotional diaries to illustrate the obsessional selflessness expected of God's born-again at the end of time. Only an intensely pressured populace could have accepted her frenetic piety as a model.[9]

For intensely pressured Yankees, the New Divinity's apocalyptic utopia was an irresistible fantasy of surcease from market pressures. Amid "universal peace, love, and general and cordial friendship," Hopkins promised, no "unrighteous persons" would "invade the rights and property of others." Invoking one of the subsistence culture's favorite Biblical images, he declared that "every one shall securely sit under his own vine and fig-tree, and there shall be none to make him afraid." Lawsuits, luxury, and waste would cease. There would be "such benevolence and fervent charity" that "all worldly things will be in a great degree common, so as not to be withheld from any who may want them."

Yet amid Newport's wealth, the gradualist millennialism that Hopkins derived from Edwards could all too easily blend spiritual fantasy of escape from market pressures into secular fantasy of market abundance. Hopkins was as fascinated by the market's technology as he was appalled by its egotism. An undistinguished preacher who reached his public mainly through print, he dreamed of a Millennium in which edifying books spewed from high-speed presses by the hundreds of thousands. In Hopkins's Kingdom of God, technology married the lion of production to the lamb of loving equality.

"Convenience and comfort in this life" would be enhanced, he predicted, by "great advances ... in all arts and sciences." Necessary articles would be "made in a better manner and with much less labor." Two or three hours of work a day would create "worldly prosperity for all"; a "greatly advanced" agriculture would yield "perhaps an hundred fold more"; and even the endless rocks that frustrated Yankee farmers would be processed into new commodities. More enthralling still were countless "utterly incredible and impossible" inventions "beyond our present conception."[10]

Thus the New Divinity projected the American future. Hopkins's radical anticapitalism was undercut, even as it crystallized, by the market's seductive productivity. His gradualist millennialism resolved a widely experienced tension by summoning Yankees to achieve within history a Christian utopia of boundless production mystically purged of capitalist self-love. Insensibly pursuit of boundless love would sacralize pursuit of boundless wealth.

The gradualist vision of a Kingdom of God achieved through Christian effort appealed everywhere to more conservative evangelicals, especially Presbyterians, townspeople, and the well-to-do. At the height of the spiritual firestorm in 1802, the Fourth of July inspired a Charleston Baptist minister to predict a major American role "in the fulfillment of those sacred prophesies which have foretold the glory of Messiah's kingdom." In this citadel of cotton capitalism, even Baptists conceived the Kingdom of God in secular terms. The Reverend Richard Furman could hardly have selected a litany of scriptural prophecies that more clearly hailed an advancing market. "'God shall build the cities,' and 'cause them to be spread abroad,'" he assured his congregation. "'Righteousness shall dwell in the fruitful field, and the wilderness shall rejoice and blossom as the rose.'"[11]

Disinterested benevolence and gradualist millennialism would sanction capitalist striving, just as women's commitment to antinomian love would justify men's commitment to an unloving market. Like the New Divinity and the new women's consciousness, every popular cultural or political movement in the early republic arose originally against the market. Yet under the daily pressure of competitive imperatives on participants' lives, every such movement eventually became a mode of accommodating to capitalist necessity.

Hopkins shared leadership of the campaign against Rhode Island slavers and slavery with Moses Brown, the Quaker who was introducing the industrial revolution to the New World at nearby Pawtucket. Quakers followed an antinomian Inner Light akin to the New Light, and Hopkins's benevolence was as compelling for the Quaker capitalist as were Brown's clattering machines for the Congregational theologian. For pious magnates like Brown, benevolence bridged the contradiction between ancestral ethics and marketplace behavior. When Hopkins's precapitalist evangelism converged with Brown's capitalism on the platform of benevolence, an evangelical capitalist culture was in prospect.

The market's power to bend oppositional forces to its ends became fully evident as Hopkins's theology spread with the New Light across southeastern New

England. The New Divinity's appeal to stressed rural folk made it irresistible also to an orthodox clergy struggling to bolster its sagging authority.

A majority of Congregational ministers—deferred to as gentry in stable farming towns little disturbed by either market or New Light—had so far resisted both the arminian heresy that eventuated in Unitarianism/deism and the antinomian heresy that the Edwardeans tamed into the New Divinity. But New England's tight ruling order of ministers and godly magistrates was crumbling. *Kulturkampf* between market and New Light undermined clerical authority along with communal consensus, and public officials were becoming more devoted to enterprise than to a holy commonwealth.[12]

Suddenly in the 1790s the shaky standing order was assailed by the shock waves of the French Revolution. Vermont's Ethan Allen and Matthew Lyon flaunted the polemical anti-Christian deism of Thomas Paine in the heart of New England. Homegrown jacobins, backed by dissenters resisting church taxes, threatened to bring down the ecclesiastical/political establishment. With status and authority at stake, the orthodox clergy clung to the Federalist magistracy in an almost hysterical campaign to unite Yankees against "French infidelity" and the Republicanism of Paine's endorser, the free-thinking Thomas Jefferson.

The standing order triumphed by co-opting a New Divinity now radiating too successfully to be any longer resisted. Moreover it was demonstrating a remarkable capacity to mobilize Yankees under clerical leadership. Merging New-Divinity revivalism with the politics of market-oriented magistrates, the mainline clergy summoned New Englanders to a millennial Armageddon with satanic Republicanism. Thus they froze much of rural Yankeedom into political identification with the Federalist party. A stressed countryside, rallied around anticommercial orthodoxy by a beleaguered clergy, empowered arminian/Unitarian elites intent on commercial/industrial growth. The class needs of clergy and entrepreneurs meshed to build the cultural base for a capitalist political economy.[13]

Yet this Federalist mésalliance won only a temporary reprieve for the standing order, isolating New England for a generation from national power, while the tax-supported Congregational establishment came under mounting attack and market-oriented magistrates became steadily less amenable to the clergy. As their formal power eroded, ministers increasingly relied on the appeal of the New Divinity to sustain their influence. For a generation after 1800, a crypto-New-Light clergy carried on a campaign of revivalism, millennial expectation, and lay mobilization to rally a newborn army into battle for a Christian America.

Leadership centered in Connecticut, where magistrates were tightly linked with presbyterial ministerial associations. The orthodox army found its general when it retook Yale from the liberals in 1795 and replaced Jefferson's friend President Stiles with a celebrated critic of French infidelity, Jonathan Edwards's energetic grandson the Reverend Timothy Dwight. Utilizing the New Divinity's revivalism and much of its theology, Dwight swiftly reduced Yale's freethinking and libertine students to a spectacular state of evangelical piety. The approach that worked so well at Yale he then urged so vigorously on his clerical colleagues that most of them were soon wielding the New Divinity to save the standing order from infidelity and Republicanism.

"Pope" Dwight barely sustained Connecticut's Federalist standing order until his death in 1817, when it yielded to a Republican/anti-church-tax majority. By this time, however, the New Divinity had mobilized so much voluntary support that the clergy surrendered state support without much of a fight. Indeed the tireless field commander who inherited Dwight's mantle already saw that disestablishment could increase ministers' influence. "By voluntary efforts, societies, missions, and revivals," said the Reverend Lyman Beecher, "they exert a deeper influence than ever they could by queues, and shoe buckles, and cocked hats, and gold-headed canes."

No one did more than Lyman Beecher to deepen clerical influence. This blunt, farmer-looking organizer and agitator readily sacrificed theological niceties to pragmatic results. Assuming clerical leadership of the New Divinity's original heartland surrounding his church at Litchfield and working through the ministerial associations, he soon had most Connecticut ministers riding regularly on preaching circuits through each other's towns to promote revivals. Fascinated like Hopkins with the evangelical potential of the printing press, Beecher pioneered the mass distribution of religious tracts, established a magazine to spread the crypto-New-Light gospel, and recruited writers for an incessant pamphlet warfare on Unitarians, Episcopalians, and other foes.

While Beecher organized and agitated, his bosom friend and fellow Dwight protégé the Reverend Nathaniel W. Taylor was overhauling the New Divinity yet again. Where Hopkins maternalized the Edwardean theology, the first Dwight Professor of Didactic Theology at Yale's new Divinity School arminianized it by making salvation a matter of human effort. Taylor's "New Haven Theology" muffled the dangerously antinomian conception of the new birth as mystical transformation, insisting instead that salvation must be won by good works and assiduous use of such divinely appointed "means of grace" as prayer, Bible study, and clerical teaching. Widening revivalism's market by virtually promising salvation to those making the requisite effort, the crypto-New-Light clergy bolstered their influence as ethical arbiters by equating good works with self-repressive capitalist effort.[14]

Embracing the New Light out of necessity, Dwight, Beecher, and Taylor shuttered it into a Moderate Light of capitalist accommodation. Purged of antinomian excess, revivals were institutionalized as periodic occasions for the resident minister to recruit a rising generation to church membership. The Osborn/Hopkins device of voluntary association for benevolent ends was turned to new purposes. Although Hopkinsians enlisted prominent Moderate-Light ministers and laymen in a Connecticut antislavery society, women were excluded, and the society soon died of inaction.[15] Instead benevolent energies poured into missionary and moral societies propagating, along with the Moderate Light, the repressive moral conformity required by the capitalist mode of production.

The dangerously antinomian/democratic tide of uprooted Yankees threatened both clerical authority and capitalist discipline. "Whatever was not punishable by law," shrilled Timothy Dwight, "multitudes considered as rectitude." Viewing capitalist transformation and its casualties from the class perspective of boomtime enterprisers, the Connecticut Pope thought any industrious, thrifty man could "live almost as he pleases." Equating Christian grace with capitalist effort, poverty with sinful self-indulgence, he viewed laborers as "shiftless, diseased, or vicious." Moral defects also explained for him the multitudes driven to cheap frontier lands by "the pressure of poverty, the fear of the gaol, and consciousness of public contempt." They were "too idle, too talkative, too passionate, too prodigal, and too shiftless," he thought, "to acquire either property and character" or "live in regular society." These hapless emigrants, "impatient of the restraints of law, religion, and morality," were especially threatening because they "grumble about the taxes by which the Rulers, Ministers, and Schoolmasters are supported."[16]

Dwight had begun the evangelical campaign at Yale by organizing young Lyman Beecher and other student protégés into a Moral Society to police the college against profanity, gambling, and card playing. By threatening to report "a number of the most vicious" students to Dwight, the Moral Society enforced a "reformation." Upon graduating to the pastorate, Beecher adopted the Osborn/Hopkins system of voluntary association to promote moral societies in his and neighboring churches. "It was a new thing in that day for the clergy and laymen to meet on the same level and cooperate," Beecher testified, for the ministers were "all politicians" who "had always managed things for themselves." In 1813 he was able to organize a Connecticut Moral Society with nearly thirty local branches and several thousand members.

The moral societies' local campaigns against profanity and desecration of the Sabbath soon made Sunday travel impossible in Connecticut and, when news of peace reached New Haven on a Sunday morning in 1815, prevented the libertine "from publicly breaking the Sabbath by the ringing of bells & the firing of cannon." In these campaigns evangelical Protestants first targeted alcohol as epitomizing the self-indulgence that the market would no longer tolerate. Freely imbibed by ministers and laypeople alike, it was the medium through which rural culture most conspicuously sanctioned pleasure and instinctual liberation.[17]

Sanctifying entrepreneurial visions of a disciplined capitalist society, the mainline clergy channeled the Moderate Light's gradualist millennialism into a cultural imperialism that would create a Christian capitalist republic. To this end Dwight and company promoted a united front of respectable Protestants. They supported orthodox Massachusetts Congregationalists in establishing a seminary at Andover to challenge Unitarian Harvard in training ministers, and Beecher eventually moved to a Boston pulpit to lead personally the orthodox counterattack.

In the other direction, Connecticut Congregationalists had long worked closely with the "New Side" Presbyterians of New York and New Jersey. The New Siders shared the revival tradition going back to Jonathan Edwards, who had ended his career as president of their college at Princeton, and they were much influenced by Hopkins's New Divinity. In 1801 the two groups negotiated in Timothy Dwight's parlor a Plan of Union for a joint campaign to carry evangelical ministers, churches, and culture to the mainly Yankee populace that was flooding upstate New York and northern New England. Infected with the New Divinity's millennial expectations, these "Presbygationalists" established missionary magazines and missionary societies to enlist lay support and funds. Soon they were dispatching pious young graduates of Yale, Andover, and Princeton as missionaries to establish Presbygational churches and moral standards wherever Yankees migrated.

Governor John Treadwell, last of the old-fashioned godly magistrates, was first president of the statewide Connecticut Missionary Society that spearheaded the campaign. Over the next three decades the Connecticut and Massachusetts societies employed more than a thousand missionaries, trained or training for the ministry, to evangelize through new settlements or locate there as ministers of new congregations. Effort redoubled after a team of investigators published a sensational exposé in 1813 on the spiritual destitution of westering Yankees.

Although the missionary societies called for a united Christian front and gave token seats on their governing boards to other denominations, they recruited mainly for Presbygationalism. Under Timothy Dwight's Plan of Union, Moderate-Light missionaries gathered transplanted Yankees into Congregational churches in northern New England, while in western New York new churches joined the Presbyterians' more centralized denominational structure.[18]

Increasingly this cultural offensive was energized by lay commitment, wealth, and organizing skills. With godly magistrates disappearing, the Moderate-Light clergy turned to the new class of evangelical businessmen produced by the conjuncture of commercial boom and Great Revival in the northeastern ports. The first missionary society was organized by New York businessmen and clergymen in 1796. But reborn businessmen were soon inspired by another model of voluntary association reaching American ports with the flood of commodities from the market's British core.

The market linked the world's two most keenly entrepreneurial classes in transforming culture as well as economic life. On both fronts and on both sides of the Atlantic, deeply Christian businessmen were the cutting edge. Along with British goods, reborn American merchants imported more appealing agencies for evangelical zeal than clergy-dominated missionary societies. Through Bible, tract, and Sunday-school societies, devout British businessmen were turning to evangelical ends the market's most advanced technology and organization for mass communication and distribution.

Philadelphia merchant Robert Ralston was at least as alert as Samuel Hopkins or Lyman Beecher to the evangelical potential of technological progress in printing. When stereotyped printing plates minimized laborious hand composition, making books and pamphlets cheapest in the largest quantities, Ralston helped introduce in 1808 a new vehicle for evangelism. With a subsidy from the prototype British and Foreign Bible Society, Philadelphia laymen and clergy established a local society to broadcast Bibles wholesale. Within two years prominent laymen joined clergymen to organize state Bible societies in Massachusetts and Connecticut and local societies in New York and other cities. By 1815—aided despite the war by £5,000 in subsidies from the British society—there were over a hundred.

Similarly tract societies sprang up in American centers of the Moderate Light to reprint the cheap tales of sentimental piety being broadcast by London's Religious Tract Society. Extolling devout acceptance of poverty, these staples of evangelical indoctrination illustrate better than anything else the social sources and class thrust of the transatlantic Moderate Light. Heavily subsidized in enormous runs, cut-rate tracts drove much secular literature off the market through price competition, capturing for piety a mass readership hungry for otherwise expensive print.

Increasingly besieged by the unruly armies of the poor, urban evangelicals likewise embraced the British fad for Sunday schools. Wherever the Moderate Light glowed, particularly in churches around New York and Philadelphia, societies of lay volunteers imparted elementary literacy and saving grace on Sundays to thousands of unschooled poor children.

Gradually the Presbygational center of gravity shifted from Connecticut's clerical hierarchs to the seaboard cities, where voluntary association magically tapped the greatest riches and most anxious piety. New Englanders meanwhile adhered to their clergy-led missionary societies and followed British precedents cautiously. Yankee clerics sanctioned organizational innovation mainly to reinforce the missionary effort. Pushing their moral societies outward from Connecticut, they formed education societies to subsidize poor boys for the ministry and in 1810 established the American Board of Commissioners for Foreign Missions to send to India the first American overseas missionaries.

Beecher himself expressed best the cultural imperialism sealing the clerical alliance with Christian businessmen. Religion, he trumpeted from alienatd New England on the eve of peace, was "the central attraction" holding a dangerously fragmented society together. "The integrity of the Union," he insisted, depended on "the prevalence of pious, intelligent, enterprising ministers through the nation" and "institutions of homogeneous influence" to "produce a sameness of views, and feelings, and interests." Beecher's formula for a Christian capitalist republic was

"A Bible for every family, a school for every district, and a pastor for every thousand souls."

The Moderate Light's repressive ethical imperialism fed on needs beyond clerical authority and capitalist discipline. Most Yankees needed to reaffirm traditional altruism, and many needed fantasies of selflessness and exercises in benevolence to sanction their pursuit of capitalist wealth. The unreconstructed Hopkinsian "Father" Nathanael Emmons, whose colonial tricorn symbolized ministerial authority in rural Franklin, Massachusetts, for half a century after the Revolution, denounced the Moderate Lights for pandering to a spreading desire "to amass property, and become great, magnificent and prodigal."[19]

But the Moderate-Light clergy's obsessive moralism and growing phobia against alcohol were responsive to a wider need. All along the northeastern littoral, wherever commercial boom met agrarian crisis, masses of people were being ejected from the security of traditional modes of production. Confronting capitalism's hazards of landlessness and wage dependence, most struggled against traditional indulgence in ease and pleasure for threadbare respectability.

The Moderate Light evolved to mobilize stressed rural Yankees emotionally for a profound and inescapable transformation of personality and behavior. To avert demoralizing poverty, as the prudent quickly learned from multiplying examples of failure, the market required a new level of instinctual repression and disciplined effort. The godly community, including employers eager to force their heroic work ethic on others, would keep the born-again on the "strait and narrow path" to respectability, or at least survival. Mustering antinomian love against antinomian impulse, Yankees and eastern urbanites rehearsed in the Great Revival the ordeal of capitalist transformation that convulsed Andrew Jackson's generation in the Second Great Awakening.

Clerical fears of lay wealth and energy combined with Philadelphia–New York rivalry to impede national integration of the Moderate Light's forces. In vain British evangelicals urged Americans to follow their example by federating the local Bible societies. Resistance was overcome only when the postwar vision of a national market inspired all evangelicals with the postmillennial mission of national conversion. While the Fourteenth Congress legislated a national market, impatient Presbygational laymen—reinforced by promise of £500 from the British and Foreign Bible Society—convened clerical and lay representatives of the Bible societies in New York City on May 8, 1816. Leading this bold coup was New Jersey Presbyterian Elias Boudinot, a lawyer/entrepreneur long active in Federalist benevolence toward slaves and Indians and well connected in both Philadelphia and New York. A director of Hamilton's national Bank, he often cited it as inspiring his faith in national federation.

In the New York convocation, Boudinot and his confederate William Jay (evangelical Episcopalian, Federalist, and antislavery stalwart) neutralized the last clerical resistance to national federation by modifying the British precedent barring clergymen from the proposed board of managers. Their ingenious concession was sweeping in appearance but meaningless in practice and intent—the American board would consist of thirty lay managers plus any or all clergymen wishing to attend. "Thank God! Thank God!" sobbed a weeping chairman when Beecher and his fellow clergymen acquiesced in lesser roles as counselors to the lay leadership of an American Bible Society. Under its aegis Christian men of affairs first mustered the national evangelical army.

Prominent New Yorkers among its original managers included millionaire city landlord Henry Rutgers, Federalist attorney and former mayor Richard Varick, merchant Divie Bethune, the President-making "Old Patroon" Stephen Van Rensselaer, and Governor De Witt Clinton. Within four years the society distributed from its handsome Bible House on Nassau Street over one hundred thousand Bibles. Henceforth the Bible Society's annual "anniversary meetings" in New York on the May 8 date of its founding regularly brought together much of the overlapping leadership of the Moderate-Light societies for missions, tracts, Sunday schools, ministerial education, and morality.[20]

The Moderate Light's organizational and financial resources swelled into a formidable apparatus when the Second Awakening threatened antinomian rebellion while giving reality to the hope of a Christianized nation. In 1824 veteran lay leaders Ralston, Varick, and Bethune united Sunday-school societies claiming fifty thousand students into the American Sunday-School Union—with a constitution flatly barring clergymen from office. In 1825 the New England Tract Society, itself a federation of local societies with 167 titles in circulation, federated with similar societies in New York and other cities as the American Tract Society—also excluding clerical officers. From a handsome Manhattan Tract House, donated by merchant Arthur Tappan and banker Moses Allen, the latest steam presses poured out in ten years, through agents and depositories in every state, thirty million tracts, nearly a million *Christian Almanacs,* and over two million other publications. A prophetic irony made these spiritual missives the first standardized, mass-produced commodities to be distributed and promoted for the entire national market at the lowest possible price.

Thus in remarkably parallel ways Christian businessmen on both sides of the Atlantic energized, captured, and organized the swelling current of the Moderate Light. Lacking personal or institutional ties and despite war between their countries, the most aggressive entrepreneurs in Britain and America nevertheless integrated their parallel evangelical efforts almost automatically by responding to the functional imperatives of parallel class situations.

Class imperatives were experienced culturally and psychologically. British and American businessmen found in the Moderate Light more than the discipline that brought success. Especially for the growing number reared in devout families, evangelical zeal held at bay intolerable anxieties about their goodness as they made the difficult transition from traditional ethics to tough-minded capitalist egotism. Paradoxically and explosively, this anxious evangelicalism coincided with a new sense of personal power, of entrepreneurial ability to affect distant persons and remote events. Christian businessmen and their allied lawyers were pioneers of antislavery and other humanitarian reforms partly because their market perspective and heightened sense of potency made them the first to feel responsible for a broader range of evil wrought or good left undone. Thriving by scrupulous fidelity to business commitments, moreover, these revolutionaries brought a new scrupulosity to newborn moral commitments.

While the Moderate Light satisfied the most pressing psychic needs of Christian entrepreneurs, it also served their class need for cultural hegemony over the democratic antinomianism of the masses. Therefore businessmen who sold ever more commodities in an ever larger market found their special skills irresistibly challenged by the gradualist millennial mission of national conversion. From their radical new commitment to life by calculation, they brought to the evangelical movement their unique experience in projecting, organizing, and managing large schemes to yield large results over long periods. More concretely than the clergy, they could conceive of national evangelism as doable.

The Second Awakening so intensified the need to exercise disinterested benevolence that Christian businessmen began organizing societies with benevolent aims beyond evangelism. During the 1820s new societies proliferated through Moderate-Light territory—to aid and uplift the poor, promote peace, rescue prostitutes, reform prisons, stop drunkenness. Soon a society was being organized wherever alert benevolent gentlemen and their clerical counselors descried a new human problem. Even the American Colonization Society presumed fellowship with this swelling Benevolent Empire.

National organization culminated in 1826, just as De Witt Clinton's water highway linked the inland empire to the emerging evangelical headquarters in the Empire City. Societies supporting ministerial education merged as the American Education Society, which aided hundreds of divinity students. The major missionary groups finally united as the American Home Missionary Society, whose 169 missionaries would increase in eight years to 719. The Moderate Light's most absorbing cause organized nationally as the American Society for the Promotion of Temperance, whose traveling agents and lecturers were soon enlisting thousands of members in hundreds of local societies associated with Moderate-Light churches.

Urban wealth maintained for each society, usually in New York, a central bureaucracy headed by a clergyman secretary presiding over a corps of itinerating agents and lecturers, usually born-again ministerial students. Agents mobilized support and funds for their various causes by promoting local societies, and many a Presbygational community maintained three or four—depending on local enthusiasms or which agent arrived first—all with much the same membership and much the same clerical/businessman leadership. By 1830 the annual income of the thirteen leading societies exceeded half a million dollars. Proudly they compared the $2,813,550.02 raised during their brief life with the $3,585,534.67 spent by the federal government for internal improvements since its beginning.

Every year during the Anniversary Week of May 8, most of the societies convened their interlocking directorates and thousands of their overlapping followers in Manhattan. Many evangelicals moved on for an immediately succeeding Ecclesiastical Week in Philadelphia, whose loyalists controlled a few societies meeting there along with the national governing bodies of the Presbyterians, Episcopalians, and those Moderate-Light Baptists (mainly northeastern) who could tolerate national organization.

As the gloomy twenties closed, alarm grew at these "immense institutions spreading over the country, combining hosts," with "revenues such as kings might envy." *"The priest of fanaticism,"* shrilled Episcopalian Calvin Colton, was mounted on *"a tiger."* Even the temperate Unitarian William Ellery Channing was frightened by this "gigantic religious power, systematized, compact in its organization, with a polity and a government entirely its own." It was, he feared, "independent of all control."[21]

Both strategy and geography aimed the Moderate Light's awesome armament for cultural conquest at western New York, where the Erie Canal was bringing the American *Kulturkampf* to a climax. With unexampled force and rapidity, Clinton's big ditch thrust capitalist imperatives inland—to Utica on the upper Mohawk by 1820, past the Finger Lakes to Rochester at the foot of the fertile Genesee valley by 1823, and to the western waters at Buffalo by 1825. Invading a populace already shaken by boom and bust and converging with the volatility of uprooted Yankees, the Grand Canal ignited an antinomian/democratic wildfire. While ultrademocratic upstate farmers carried the Bucktails to power and leveled aristocratic institutions in the 1821 constitutional convention, the New Light blazed repeatedly across the Ontario plain.

The Plan-of-Union missionary societies had claimed western New York for the Moderate Light a generation before, with the first wave of Yankee settlers; and Yorkers had been engulfed by swarming refugees from New England's agrarian crisis and market stress. In most communities, subsidized Yankee Presbyterians had the oldest and strongest church, often the only one.

Now, in this "burnt-over" district, as its famous evangelist Charles Grandison Finney called it, the New Light of the lowly challenged the Moderate Light of the Presbygational establishment. "The unusual excitement about religion," as Joseph Smith, Jr., recalled his rebirth to Mormon prophecy, "commenced with the Methodists, but soon became general among all the sects." While "great multitudes united themselves to the different religious parties," the Baptists and Methodists swelled here, too, into the largest denominations. But not even they could satisfy the Come-outerism of Universalists, communists, and hosts of "Nothingarians."

By the mid-twenties Presbygationalists were mobilizing nationally to counter-attack antinomian rebellion in the burnt-over district. Here labored 120 of the 169 ministers employed by the missionary societies when they federated in 1826. Here during the next eight years the American Home Missionary Society expended forty thousand dollars and four hundred years of clerical effort to nurture more than two hundred churches. Allied education societies sustained a theological sem-inary at Auburn, whose students recruited thousands into Sunday schools by can-vassing the whole region house-to-house. Tracts sold at Sunday services reached four million pages in two years. Numerous societies pursued Beecher's goal of "a *Bible for every family*"; and the Rochester society exceeded it by distributing twelve hundred Bibles following a survey that, according to critics, exaggerated the need.

As the rural New Light contended in upstate New York with the market's Moderate Light for the soul of the universal Yankee nation, creative empathy sculpted multiform Christian piety to crosscutting stresses of gender, generation, and class. Already Jemima Wilkinson and Ann Lee had led the most revolutionary into loving celibate communism. Now the tall, magnetic Yankee Nothingarians Finney and Smith, both reborn in their twenties to Yorker prophecy, opened new channels for the less desperate Come-outerism of the antinomian majority.

Mormon Prophet Smith and his kin personified the popular antinomianism generated by capitalist stress and agrarian crisis. His roots went back to the first Puritan settlers along the Yankee coast. Both his grandfathers, born there to sub-stantial families falling on hard times, were forced to migrate to the inland hills.

A youngest son left landless, Grandfather Asael Smith eventually managed—through classic patriarchal migration to Vermont and then to New York's St. Lawrence frontier—to provide farms for most of his eleven children. Maternal grandfather Solomon Mack—indentured until twenty-one to an avaricious mas-ter to pay the debts of his father's failure in trade—spent most of his adulthood crisscrossing northern New England in pursuit of one failing speculation after another. Having "worried and toiled until an old age to try to lay up treasures in this world," he was reborn at age seventy-nine in the Great Revival and thereafter devoted himself to preaching, instead, pursuit of the treasures "that no man can take away."

Grandfather Mack reformed too late to save son-in-law Joseph Smith, Sr., from his lifelong example. Promptly the Prophet's father staked the farm provided by Grandfather Smith (as well as bride Lucy's dowry) on a speculation in the local ginseng root—much prized in China as an elixir of virility—and lost all. There-after Joseph led his growing family from tenant farm to tenant farm in Vermont and New Hampshire, eking out a living by wage labor, teaching school, and painting put-out oilcloths. Almost prostrated by a typhoid epidemic that left Joseph, Jr., limping for life, the Smiths were finally driven from the northern hills with thousands of others by the famine-threatening summer snows of "1816-and-froze-to-death." Uprooted from the stem-family matrix that had sustained them in repeated crises, they came to rest near Palmyra, New York, in the heart of the soon-burnt-over district.

Here total family effort at odd jobs, hiring-out by the season, peddling, maple sugaring, and treasure hunting eventually scraped together the down payment for a little farm. At last the labor of nine maturing children enabled the Smiths to build a two-room log house of their own. Then "as is quite natural," the Prophet's mother remembered, "we redoubled our diligence" with a view to "assisting our children" and providing for "the decline of life." But the advancing market, forcing them to buy at a land-boom price anticipating the Grand Canal, burdened them with such heavy mortgage payments that they would soon lose this farm too.

The Prophet's people survived capitalist transformation through intense familism. In preparation for death, Grandfather Asael Smith composed a solemn appeal to his eleven children to "live together in an undivided bond of love." "If you join together as one man," he urged, "you need not want anything." In the unconsciously Biblical cadences of Yankee vernacular, he implored them to "comfort, counsel, relieve, succor, help and admonish one another." They must visit whenever possible and gather at their mother's or eldest brother's at least once a year. "And when you have neither mother nor father left," this patriarchal valetudinarian admonished, "be so many fathers and mothers to each other." For multitudes like the Smiths and Macks, the hazards of a disordered world redoubled kinship's traditional obligations of all-for-one and one-for-all.

The pale emanations of the Moderate Light could not satisfy the antinomian yearnings of such Yankees. Indeed they were repelled by elitist, intellectual Presbygational clerics who reinforced the wordly order by saddling the disinherited with guilt for failure and shuttering the glorious Light sent to deliver them. Adversity soured three generations of Smith/Mack men on churches while infecting them with the New-Light hopes espoused by churchgoing mothers and wives. Divine apparitions spoke to Joseph Smith, Sr., in dreams and trances; and Uncle Jason Mack gave up storekeeping at age twenty for a lifetime of free-lance faith healing. The widespread Vermont fantasy that "immense treasures lie concealed upon our Green Mountains" caught up both Josephs in a craze for "money digging" guided by magical divination. Methodists and Baptists were insufficiently revolutionary to satisfy the apocalyptic imaginations of Come-outer Nothingarians like the Prophet's clan.[22]

Radical sects flowed with Yankees into the burnt-over district, and a new flood of converts from the Second Awakening carried Shakerism to Sodus Bay, near the Joseph Smith farm. From this seedbed of chiliasm, watered by the folk pain of cap-

belief that christ will personally reign during the millennium italist transformation, grew the most compelling new religious dispensation in American history. Its roots went back to a corner of the Green Mountains where, as the new century opened, a diviner of buried treasure (eventually exposed as a counterfeiter) beguiled a cult of New Israelites preaching Mosaic diet and imminent Millennium. With this Wingate or Winchell, as he was variously known, pointing them to hidden treasures and prophecies with a sacred Rod of St. John, apocalyptic money digging eventuated in excited preparations for Christ's return on 14 January 1801.

But the militia mustered needlessly, and Millennium was still to come when a rodsman of New Israelite parentage, Oliver Cowdery, turned up in the late twenties at Palmyra, New York, for a historic encounter with two other transplanted Vermont money diggers, the senior and junior Joseph Smiths. Turning up about the same time from Sodus Bay to excite a burst of gold hunting was a conjurer named Walters—or Wingate or Winchell?—who claimed to have found an ancient Indian record revealing hidden treasures. Out of this welter of pain and fantasy, the Gold Bible of Mormonism emerged.

Several years before, as the arriving Erie convulsed Palmyra, seventeen-year-old Joseph had electrified his vision-prone family. An angel, he announced, had directed him to a set of curiously inscribed golden plates buried on the neighborhood's most commanding eminence—"Hill Cumorah," he called it. This unschooled, dreamy youth with his fantastic stories and plausible clairvoyance was a familiar social type to neighbors straining between magical fantasy and Yankee-peddler trickery. His reputed ability to find lost articles by gazing, hat over face, into a curiously shaped and colored "peepstone" inspired the same mixture of suspicion and credulous longing as the professional conjurer Walters. Soon Joseph's fame got him hired by a seeker of buried Spanish treasure in Pennsylvania, where he was hauled into court and pronounced an imposter.

But in young Smith, trickster was so mixed with mystic that neither he nor posterity could tell where one gave way to the other. Methodist revival had plunged him into his first visionary trance; and he and the family became increasingly convinced, as Joseph, Sr., testified at his trial, that God had given him a "marvelous power" for some great purpose. The golden plates of Cumorah doubtless originated in the mystic's vision; but the trickster's theatricality pretended them real, so exciting his apocalyptic family that he could not retreat. For four years young Joseph sustained the fantasy only by vision-directed annual visits to inspect the plates on Hill Cumorah. When the hard-working oldest brother and chief family provider died, and mortgage payments could not be met, both Josephs were caught up in the Walters-inspired frenzy for hunting the ancients' buried treasures. Not until the Smiths lost their hard-won farm in 1827 did newly married Joseph, Jr., reach for the mantle of prophecy, partly no doubt in a desperate effort to rescue the demoralized family.

Following visionary instructions—he told the family—he had been allowed to retrieve the plates from Hill Cumorah, and along with them Urim and Thummim, a pair of "seer stones" set in silver spectacle frames that would enable him to translate the inscriptions. For two years substantial farmers supported twenty-three-year-old Joseph while he translated. Sitting behind a curtain or with a napkin covering the plates, often face in hat, he dictated mainly to his bride and twenty-two-year-old Oliver Cowdery. In 1830 a Palmyra printer published the *Book of Mormon*.

Joseph was a resourceful trickster. Family and neighbors were allowed to heft the plates in their chest or feel them through a cloth, but he warned that God would strike down anyone who peeped. When daring neighbors broke open the hidden chest and found it empty, he serenely revealed that he had providentially rehidden the plates in a pile of flax. Once translated, he reported, they were reclaimed by the angel, along with Urim and Thummim.

The trickster's resourcefulness was fully tested by the wife of his main financial backer. To allay Mrs. Martin Harris's suspicion that her husband was being bilked of their prosperous farm, Joseph gave him a copied page of inscriptions to authenticate with experts. The plates had been inscribed in "reformed Egyptian," he explained, to conserve scarce gold. By reforming the notoriously untranslatable hieroglyphs, he protected their plausibility against the philological breakthrough soon prompted by the Rosetta Stone.

Fortunately the Prophet had a further line of defense, for Harris doggedly tracked down a knowledgeable Columbia professor who pronounced the Gold Bible an untranslatable hoax. When the crestfallen Harris reported this result, Joseph banished all doubt by triumphantly reading a prophecy from Isaiah 25: "the words of a book that is sealed" would be delivered to "one that is learned, saying Read this, I pray thee: and he saith, I cannot for it is sealed: And the book is delivered to him that is not learned, saying Read this." Harris was so overwhelmed by his personal fulfillment of Biblical prophecy that he even recalled the professor saying, "I cannot read a sealed book."

Mrs. Harris was not impressed. In a final effort at persuasion, her husband borrowed to show her the first 116 pages of the miraculous revelation flowing from the lips of the "not learned" Joseph. She promptly stole the only copy, taunting the Prophet to retranslate the section exactly or be exposed as a fraud. Providentially additional plates turned up that could be translated to cover the missing part of the story from a different perspective. Contritely Harris, with Joseph playing relentlessly on his guilt, sacrificed farm and wife to finance publication of the *Book of Mormon*.

Perhaps the Prophet had the conflicted "imposter" identity described by psychiatry, in which a "strongly assertive imposturous" self maintains dominance over the "crude and poorly knit one from which the imposter has emerged" by

finding believers in its fantasy. "Extraordinarily immediate keenness and respon-
siveness, especially in the area of the imposture," as Dr. Phyllis Greenacre explains
the type, "is ordinarily associated with 'formal' awareness that the claims are
false."

Yet Mormonism was created by neither imposture nor visions, in whatever
proportion they were mixed. It was secular frustration, antinomian yearning, and
Biblical anthropology—woven by the Prophet into enthralling fantasy—that
induced eleven witnesses to "see" the plates and thousands more to believe their
testimony. Joseph himself was seized by his prophetic calling. Transcending treas-
ure-hunting trickery without altogether renouncing its techniques, he made himself the marvelously creative medium through whom a desperate culture shaped a
revolutionary mythology.

His *Book of Mormon* was cast, rather woodenly, in the form and rhetoric of
the King James Version. Where the Biblical Moses, Isaiah, and Matthew recorded
God's dealings with humanity in the Old World, Smith's Nephi, Mormon, and
Moroni revealed even more important developments in the New. A Jewish clan
populating America in Old-Testament times had fallen into fratricidal strife
between the more God-fearing, light-skinned Nephites and the barbarous, dark-
skinned Amanites, forebears of the "red Israelite" Indians. Christ appeared redeem-
ingly in both hemispheres; and in both, salvation was thwarted by human apostasy.
Where the old Bible of Palestinian Jews rooted cosmic history in the Old World,
the Gold Bible of American Jewish Nephites promised millennial culmination in
the New. Moroni, lone Nephite survivor of the final Amanite assault on Hill
Cumorah, had buried there the golden plates of a new revelation. And there, "in
the fullness of time," as foretold in Nephi II, the angel Moroni commissioned
Prophet Joseph Smith, Jr., to mobilize the faithful for an American Millennium.

The Prophet remagicalized life by wrapping Christian mythology in the local
mythology of his animistic culture. Legends of lost civilizations, titanic battles, and
spirit-guarded treasures surrounded the enormous burial mounds strewn across the
burnt-over district by the Indians' remote ancestors. More than one farmer
ploughed up the kind of copper breastplate that Joseph claimed he found with
Urim and Thummim. The spirits of the land validated a Mormon mythology
whose Biblical chronology and Jewish Indians were still plausible even to the
learned.[23]

When Joseph Smith tapped the animistic bedrock of his culture, he released a
gusher of Come-outer longing for an apocalyptic New Jerusalem. Fortified by frequent visions and announcing further revelations for every new contingency, he
proclaimed that the "latter days" were at hand—the Biblically predicted time of
great troubles just before the Jews were all converted to usher in Millennium. As
the Prophet of God's final revelation, he summoned sinners into one true church

of "Latter-Day Saints." Their mission, he announced, was to build on the western Indian border a holy city of Zion, where converted red Israelites would join them in welcoming the returning Christ to reign over the millennial Kingdom of God. Before his church had a hundred members, he deputed Oliver Cowdery to lead a party to western Missouri to select a site and proclaim the new gospel to the Indians.

Mormonism was the most successful of a multitude of antinomian sects struggling toward a millennial utopia modeled on primitive Christianity. All were repelled by the babble of Presbygational/Methodist/Baptist contention over the Biblically correct road to heaven. In rejecting all other churches as apostate, Mormons capitalized on their critical advantage. A charismatic Prophet, invoking the Gold Bible's mythology, provided them with fresh revelations of the Almighty's will on all doubtful points. Joseph Smith, Jr., had brewed a compelling spiritual potion. Within days of departing for the West, Cowdery's missionaries converted, at Kirtland in northern Ohio's Western Reserve, a whole community of radical Come-outer Baptists led by the celebrated preacher Sidney Rigdon.

While Cowdery's advance party went on to prepare the future holy city near Independence, Missouri, jumping-off point for the Indian plains, the Prophet concentrated his followers at Kirtland to develop the utopian communalism that Zion would exemplify. The Rigdonite converts already "considered from reading the scriptures that what belonged to one brother, belonged to any of the brethren." To avert jealousies over slothfulness, this primitive communism was modified by a revelation declaring "the law of consecration and stewardship." Brethren deeded their farms and other property to the church, receiving back as "stewards" management of enough to support a family and hopefully return a surplus to the communal storehouse. Surpluses bought "livings" for the propertyless, relieved the distressed, financed the western venture, and constructed at Kirtland the first temple.

As earnest Mormon missionaries spread through the countryside—promising that people who read the Gold Bible prayerfully would receive divine assurance of its authenticity—convinced farmers sold out, loaded families into wagons, and headed for Kirtland or the Missouri Zion. First by hundreds and then by thousands they came, despite disappointments, disasters, and apostasies.

Unfortunately the red Israelites proved indifferent to the cosmic role assigned them by the Gold Bible; and the slaveholding Missouri frontier erupted in violence against inundation by strange Yankees with communist ways, suspected abolitionist proclivities, and ambitions for political takeover. Murder, arson, and savage mobs drove them from Zion and then from their next holy city, Far West, in a neighboring county. Meanwhile the Prophet plunged the Kirtland Saints so recklessly into the land-speculating, paper-banking extravagance of another boom that the Panic of 1837 shattered the community with bankruptcies, lawsuits, and recriminations. Constant crisis broke down the system of "consecration and stewardship"; and the Prophet accommodated to capitalist reality by demanding only a voluntary contribution of each Saint's surplus, soon conventionally defined as a "tithe" or tenth of his production.

Yet persecution and hard times swelled the flood of desperate converts. Where Zion had twelve hundred Saints by the time it was destroyed, and Far West reached five thousand, the Prophet soon summoned twelve thousand to a greater holy city on the Illinois bank of the Mississippi. Outgrowing boom-town Chicago, Smith's Nauvoo reigned briefly as the metropolis of Illinois until mob violence erupted again in 1844 to level it, assassinate the Prophet, and expel these latter-day Israelites to wander across the American wilderness to a refuge in the savage remoteness of the Great Basin desert. With conversions outweighing defections, some thirty thousand Americans are estimated to have committed their all during these years to the Prophet of the Gold Bible.

Mormonism's remarkable appeal was more social than theological. What drew the disoriented was not its conventional evangelical doctrines of repentance and salvation but its Come-outer vision of a communal utopia. The pleasure-loving Prophet's sharpest departure from orthodoxy was a naive metaphysical material-ism that freed sexuality and pleasure from sinful association and inhibition. Church discipline was seldom exercised against sexual offenses. The Prophet him-self routinely transgressed the now canonical test of Mormon fidelity, the "Word of Wisdom" he reluctantly issued—as divine advice rather than command—against alcohol, tobacco, and hot drinks. While other Christians were succumbing to a repressive moralism, the Latter-Day Saints retreated grudgingly from the more relaxed expressiveness of traditional rural life.

Yet Mormonism's mainly male interpreters, critics, and apologists have been strangely oblivious to its most striking feature, a pervasive and egregious patriar-chalism. Males led families to the Gold Bible, reversing the usual female prepon-derance in religious movements. Most were scantily educated small farmers still in their twenties. They and the smattering of older, more prosperous, better educated farmers and mechanics were overwhelmingly of Yankee antecedents, although fre-quently born in New York and sometimes in Ohio.

Few wives battled the Gold Bible for husband and family so ferociously as Mrs. Martin Harris, but the pattern of conversion reveals a widespread female reluc-tance. Almost never converting first, wives frequently joined the Saints only months or years after their husbands; and even the Prophet's wife held out for a month against a special revelation commanding her conversion. While many women no doubt found Mormon communalism satisfying, the writings of the most loyal convey an undertone of resentment. A daughter complained that her father devoted so much of the family's resources to the church that "we were in very poor circumstances." Similarly a wife complained that her husband's gener-osity, "as long as we had a crust of bread to divide," stripped her of "my own personal clothing" and often left the family hungry.[24]

With women bearing the brunt of sacrificial consecration, men reveled in mystical apotheosis of patriarchy. The Prophet's theological fantasy absolutized paternal authority and equated male philoprogenitiveness with holiness, eventually to legitimize polygamy. In the Mormon heaven, where the Saints would enjoy their natural bodies and pleasures more fully, men attained different degrees of godhood depending on how many descendants issued from their loins. To males demoralized by powerlessness and failure, the Mormon Zion offered in addition a hierarchy of gratifying offices and roles in a spiritual army destined for cosmic victory. Male converts were immediately appointed teachers, deacons, or missionaries and soon ordained to the priesthood, which enabled them to preach, baptize, and ordain. Women, by contrast, were not even eligible for conversion unless married or related to a male Saint.

This patriarchal utopia arose from male panic. The manhood of a generation of young fathers was threatened by inability to meet traditional family obligations. A Prophet who rescued his father from jail for a fourteen-dollar debt wove a compelling fantasy from the shame and desperation of lost paternal honor and eroding paternal authority. In the face of the market, Mormon patriarchy was as atavistic as the communal familism that legitimized it. Only by coming out of the world—embracing polygamy and enforting themselves behind the Rocky Mountains—did the Saints resist capitalism's homogenizing pressures longer than other Americans. Eventually their attachment to fee-simple property as patriarchal domain—transmuting the primitive communism of the Rigdonites into the Mormon tithe—eased them into market ways.[25]

The stresses that drove Latter-Day Saints into the wilderness pushed many like them down a very different road to the future. Family by family, cultural destiny was fought out along the fault line of gender. While fathers led thousands to the Prophet of the Gold Bible, far more followed mothers inspired by Charles Grandison Finney.

Prophet Smith and evangelist Finney drew from opposite ends of the broad antinomian spectrum. The down-and-out rustic blended enough capitalist patriarchy with Mormonism's communal love to attract Come-outer fathers clinging for family security and paternal authority to fee-simple property. The rising village attorney, by contrast, infused the Moderate Light's repressive moralism with enough love to attract antinomian mothers and young people disoriented by capitalist transformation—and ultimately businessman husbands and fathers beset by ethical anxiety and working-class disorder.

Few individuals have left as deep a mark on American culture as Finney. In the burnt-over district he met head-on the climactic antinomian challenge to the culture of capitalist accommodation. Appropriating Come-outer enthusiasm, he blended it with enough Presbygational moralism and benevolence to make capitalism and an antinomian populace safe for each other. Thus he refocused the

Moderate Light into a pansectarian national faith that could sustain a Christian/ capitalist republic. Finney brought to this herculean task superb qualifications of intellectual confidence, fluency, and theological naïveté—he had never attended preaching regularly or even read the Bible until just before his shattering new birth. Burning with reborn zeal to save others, he told the first client he encountered, "I have a retainer from the Lord Jesus Christ to plead his cause, and I cannot plead yours."

Coming "right forth from the law office to the pulpit," Finney stumbled blithely into a theological revolution by demanding from the unconverted the immediate decisions he was accustomed to getting from juries. When his spiritual juries were too often hung by the "cannot-ism" of Calvinists waiting for an all-powerful God to flood them with grace, Finney boldly rejected Calvinism, and theological training along with it. Lawyers "would not gain a case," he maintained, if they argued like most ministers that God had to do everything.

Studying and interpreting the Bible for himself, "as I would have understood the same or like passages in a law book," Finney adjudged that "in a court of law" not one of the scriptural passages cited by Calvinists "would have been considered at all conclusive." Christ's sacrificial crucifixion, he decided, enabled God "to proclaim a universal amnesty inviting all men to repent, to believe in Christ, and to accept salvation." Making sinners responsible for their own salvation and demanding immediate decisions, he interpreted the resulting flood of conversions as indicating "that the Spirit of God had blessed my views." Stretched emotions were voting in a new theology.

Thus Finney began to refocus the Moderate Light by appropriating the antinomian universalism of Methodists, Free-Will Baptists, and Universalists. The village lawyer read juries too well to entertain the Presbygational delusion that this burnt-over sectarian populace still required proper conversion. Instead he saw that only a radicalized Moderate Light could compete with "the ignorant Methodist preachers, and the earnest Baptist preachers [who] produced so much more effect than our most learned theologians and divines."

Bypassing New Haven's crypto–New Light, Finney further recharged the Moderate Light by blending antinomian universalism with the antinomian benevolence of Edwards, Osborn, and Hopkins. Unrepetant sinners still deserved eternal torment, he preached, but a loving God freely embraced all who evidenced sincere repentance through assiduous morality and benevolence.[26]

Like Hopkins, Finney took his cues especially from female antinomianism. Female restiveness had been spreading for several generations from a lower New England undergoing capitalist transformation. As socially valued commodity production drew male labor from the household, women lost their traditional status and authority as skilled producers of a vital half or more of family livelihood. With families shrinking, children departing, textile machinery replacing their extensive household production, women found themselves relegated to the reproductive roles—uncompensated and altruistic—of childbearing, daily family subsistence, and child nurture and socialization. Simultaneously communal love, cooperation, and generosity were being driven from the male world of market ego to find their last refuge within the female world of family reproduction. Threatened with servile confinement in a suffocating patriarchy, women increasingly sought validation as religious avatars of embattled altruism.

Religion had long appealed more strongly to women as their main defense against patriarchal abuse. Insisting that Christianity "prevents our being treated like beasts of burden . . . and shut out from the society of lordly *man* . . . as drudges of domineering masters," a Connecticut minister's wife called on each woman to "ask herself, how much do I owe?" for "the elevated stations of wives and mothers." But as capitalism enforced a radical new division of psychosocial labor, arraying female love against male ego, home against market, women embraced revival even more disproportionately as a medium for enforcing their altruism upon children, husbands, and the market itself. *Kulturkampf* became intrafamilial.

The new gender consciousness produced a sharp rise in Yankee female literacy as advantaged young women began holding summer schools for their educationally neglected neighborhood sisters. During the Great Revival women adopted Sarah Osborn's principle of voluntary association to form local prayer groups throughout Moderate-Light territory. Although denied public roles in the missionary societies, they were allowed to contribute their egg money and home manufactures to the evangelical cause through "cent" societies, and to organize charitable societies to aid widows and other distressed women, or maternal associations to promote the nurture and salvation of children.[27]

Finney's Newport was Oneida County, where Yankee settlement first concentrated in the burnt-over district and the Erie Canal first disrupted traditional relationships. Alarmed by a female Baptist evangelist and a female pamphleteer for female preaching, local Presbygationalism defended patriarchal authority against sectarian subversion. Methodists seduced youth from the faith of the fathers, while Baptists attacked the rite of infant baptism that sacralized parental responsibility. The threat came closer to home. Oneida's restive Presbygational women, reborn in the Great Revival, were among the first anywhere to assert independence of the male evangelical establishment. Reconstituting their Female Charitable Society as the Oneida Female Missionary Society, they became Finney's first and most devoted supporters.

From Oneida's bustling river/canal port Utica, newly leisured and servanted wives of downtown merchants and lawyers reached out to "beloved sisters" on isolated farms through auxiliary missionary societies and "heartfelt communications of hope, joy, and gratitude." Most rural husbands were indifferent to religion, an Oneida minister discovered in farm-to-farm visits, while most wives expressed frustrated religious hopes and many were forbidden church attendance or membership. Again and again women told him, "I am dead to the world"; "I try to worship God in secret"; "I endeavor to bring my children for the Lord"; "I maintain secret prayer." Beleaguered women like these, born again in the Second Awakening, found autonomous voluntary association so appealing that in 1824 the Oneida society, claiming some seventy auxiliary societies, renamed itself the Female Missionary Society of the Western District. "We mutually look up to you as our parent society," a growing sisterhood gratefully assured the Oneida founders.

At the same time, rather more militant maternal associations spread through the rural sisterhood from booming Utica, led by wives from mechanic/entrepreneur households where paternal authority over workers was crumbling. Anxious over children facing the unpredictable hazards and temptations of market and city, mothers were learning from each other to implant a guilt-driven Christian conscience by lavishing and withholding love. Yorker women who flocked to the maternal associations pledged themselves to attend meetings semimonthly, read systematically on Christian education, set a pious example at all times, pray for each child daily, renew its baptismal covenant regularly, and spend its birthdays in fasting and prayer for its salvation.

Finney's revivals began with antinomian stirrings among these women and among young people like himself, uprooted from traditional families and finding adult identities as clerks and workers in the strange new ambience of Utica's boarding houses or the factory village at nearby New York Mills. Many youthful converts were responding to the example and entreaty of mothers who reported their rebirths in triumph to rejoicing maternal associations. Finney himself was pushed to conversion by his Oneida fiancée.

Promptly the sisterhood raised a salary for the six-foot-two, sandy-haired young bridegroom and sent him barnstorming with sonorous voice and piercing blue eyes along their network of rural outposts. His "disregard of the distinctions of age or station" soon alarmed the local Presbygational clergy. Complaining that youthful converts sneered at "this old hypocrite" and "that old apostate," these defenders of patriarchy were most upset by the Finney-condoned practices of "females praying in the presence of men and praying for [unconverted male] individuals by name." But the local clergy could no longer argue against success after the young evangelist took Utica by storm during the winter of 1825–1826.[28]

Here and in Rome, the next boom town along the Grand Canal, Finney's "new measures" for urban mass evangelism stirred national controversy. Like working-class Methodists in the eastern cities, he adapted camp-meeting techniques to an urban setting. Daily for weeks on end, he preached and held prayer meetings and personal inquiry meetings, while female supporters invaded patriarchal households to pray with pious wives whose unregenerate husbands were away at work. Appealing directly to the unconverted, he summoned them to the spiritual pressure cooker of an "anxious seat" in front of the congregation.

Other ministers complained "that I let down the dignity of the pulpit," the evangelist admitted; "that I was a disgrace to the ministerial profession; that I talked like a lawyer at the bar; that I talked to the people in a colloquial manner; that I said 'you,' instead of 'they;' that I said 'hell,' and with such an emphasis as often to shock the people." Finney pled guilty to addressing farmers and mechanics "in the language of the common people," to drawing illustrations from their life, to expressing himself "in few words, and in words that were in common use." To all objections he had one conclusive answer: "the results justify my methods."

The Moderate Light's Yankee hierarchs saw in the upstart evangelist only a dangerous eruption of antinomianism's "universal misrule and moral desolation." Vainly they tried to silence him with hysterical alarums of social disorder. By treating all sinners alike "without respect to age or station in society," they warned, the Finneyites threatened "a levelling of all distinctions of society." Like the mobs of the French Revolution, the "impudent young men" converted in the western revivals would be "poured out as from the hives of the North to obliterate civilization and roll back the wheels of time to semi-barbarism." Perhaps worst of all, complained strategist Beecher, Finneyism would wreck "the great evangelical assimilation which is forming in the United States."

In 1827 Beecher and other weighty Yankee clerics imperiously summoned Finney and his supporters to a conference at New Lebanon, New York, to be corrected. "I know your plan and you know I do," the hierarch stormed when the rebel proved unrepentant. "You mean to come into Connecticut, and carry a streak of fire to Boston. But if you attempt it, as the Lord liveth, I'll meet you at the State line, and call out all the artillery-men, and fight every inch of the way to Boston, and I'll fight you there." He would soon eat his words.[29]

Finney shocked clerical hierarchs by demonstrating how much antinomian enthusiasm they had to appropriate to remain competitive. Gradually he demonstrated also how antinomian rebellion could be channeled through benevolence into capitalist discipline. Eventually Dr. Beecher recognized the ardent young evangelist as the Moderate Light's savior. "I have felt the beating of his great warm heart before God," he would acknowledge when arraigned by orthodox Presbyterians for Finneyite heresy.

Although an instinctive Methodist by immersion of theological innocence in Come-outer Awakening, Finney had been reared on the Moderate-Light side of the tracks to disdain "ignorant Methodist exhorters." Soundly schooled in a Yankee academy and marked for success along village main streets, he was especially sensitive to the stresses of rising entrepreneurs. Swept into mushrooming canal towns on a tide of rural/female antinomianism, he silenced the Yankee hierarchs by inspiring Christian businessmen to heroic piety.

The merchants, lawyers, millers, and assorted entrepreneurs rising to affluence along the Grand Canal were typically canny Yankees who accumulated the capital to get started from stem-family networks and felt keenly the conflict between communal and market values. Assailed on one side by Finneyite wives, mothers, and children, they were dismayed on the other by social disorder. Transient laborers and roistering boatmen brought brothels and tippling houses to staid Presbygational villages. Communal controls dissolved as wage workers escaped the family discipline of patriarchal masters to crowd into their own rowdy districts, while the new elite withdrew to neighborhoods of quiet elegance. And Bucktail democracy defeated all efforts to stem a flood of drunkenness, cursing, and Sabbath desecration.

Finney offered businessmen who surrendered to maternal altruism both domestic and social tranquility. He promised to Christianize a fractious populace through antinomian universalism while defusing antinomian rebellion by making individual conversion the only means of social improvement. What sealed his alliance with businessmen and carried the refocused Moderate Light to hegemony was his unconscious equation of Christian virtue with their capitalist asceticism. Prescribing a heavy dose of New Haven's repressive moralism, he preached self-discipline to the working class.

"A self-indulgent Christian is a contradiction," the evangelist insisted. "You might just as well write on your clothes 'NO TRUTH IN RELIGION,'" he warned women, for their ribbons and ornaments proclaimed "GIVE ME DRESS, GIVE ME FASHION, GIVE ME FLATTERY, AND I AM HAPPY." He could not "believe that a person who has ever known the love of God can relish a secular novel" or give shelf room to "Byron, Scott, Shakespeare, and a host of triflers and blasphemers of God." At Oberlin College he lectured students " on the duty of keeping their nails clean and their clothes dry, of sitting straight in their chairs," and he joined faculty colleagues in banning meat, tea, coffee, and pastries from the dining hall. The only true reformers, he declared, were those "honestly endeavoring to reform mankind and denying their appetites."

But Finney offered businessmen more than capitalist discipline. By demanding total commitment to Hopkinsian benevolence, he assuaged their ethical distress. "Christians are by no means to conform to the business maxims of the world," he taught. Explicitly he warned against the market's basic maxim: "to buy as cheap as you can and sell as dear as you can, to look out for number one." Condemning debt and "the whole credit system" as dangerous "if not absolutely sinful," he called on the Christian businessman to follow Jesus' example "of self-denial, of benevolence, of sacrificing himself to do good to others." Wealth and capital were "tools with which he serves God and his generation."

The evangelist was powerfully drawn to the many businessmen along the Erie who professed this radical commitment. They attested the divine authenticity of his refocused Moderate Light, and he summoned them to the gradualist millennial mission of revolutionizing "the world" by converting individuals to discipline and benevolence. "Only make it your invariable principle to do right and do business upon principle," he told them, "and you can control the market." If all Christians did so, he insisted, they "would soon do the business of the world" and demonstrate "the power of the church to regulate the commerce of the world." Thus they could usher in a Hopkinsian Kingdom of God combining disciplined capitalist production with communal love.

Finney's reborn businessmen immediately seized local evangelical leadership by organizing a Western Domestic Missionary Society. When their wives, despite protests from rural affiliates, meekly allowed the independent Female Society to be swallowed up, the banner of gender passed to the flourishing maternal associations. Meanwhile the national furor over the evangelist's new measures attracted the attention of Christian businessmen worried by growing armies of the unruly poor in eastern cities. Sponsored by enthusiastic laymen, he was soon igniting revivals in Lancaster, Reading, Wilmington, Philadelphia, and New York; and all too quickly Beecher had to welcome him to Boston.[30]

Finney was invited to his greatest triumph by a Rochester businessman so totally committed that he went broke stubbornly maintaining along the busy Erie his Sabbath-keeping, nonalcoholic Pioneer Line. Overwhelmed by seven-day stage and packet lines, Josiah Bissell rejoiced at the seven-day Finneyite evangelism that engulfed the flour-milling city for six winter months in 1830–1831. Growing spiritual excitement finally brought all business to a halt as relays of ministers assisted Finney in a five-day, sunrise-to-midnight Protracted Meeting. So many eager hearers packed the gallery of the First Presbyterian Church that the walls gave way.

Doubling local church rolls and exciting contagious hopes for a general blaze of grace, Rochester's epiphany ignited a wildfire of revival across the northern states. Connecticut churches swelled a third in a year, Vermont's almost as much, and Presbyterians by sixty thousand nationally in three years. Finney claimed that the spark he struck at Rochester brought a hundred thousand people into the churches by 1835. It was, the awed and adaptable Beecher conceded, "the greatest work of God, and the greatest revival of religion, that the world has ever seen."[31]

Finney's "portentous union between the New Divinity and the New Measures" was especially impressive to the Christian businessmen who directed and financed the Moderate Light's cultural offensive from the Empire City. Confronting an uncontrolled working class, merchant Lewis Tappan was convinced that "this city must be converted or the nation is lost." He was looking for "ardent and practical men" rather than theologians and controversialists. There was "too much 'theology' in the church now, and too little of the Gospel," he thought.

Four Tappan brothers epitomized the desperately pious wealth that Finney challenged to new levels of benevolent commitment. They had been reared (preternaturally, in Jonathan Edwards's old house at Northampton) by an easygoing storekeeper father and a pious mother—"no ordinary woman" in "the energy of her moral character"—who thought her children, like herself, "woefully polluted with indwelling sin." Even when Providence appeared to have "thus far restrained them from vice, or at least shielded them from infamy," she knew "by woful experience, that by nature they are totally depraved."

Of six sons, the oldest, Benjamin, fled rebelliously into freethinking, antibank radicalism in Ohio; a second drank himself to death; and the other four became obsessive Boston entrepreneurs. Attracted despite maternal prayers to Unitarianism in the first flush of business success, the younger brothers were driven back to obsessive orthodoxy by guilt about wealth. Two stayed in Boston to support Dr. Beecher's campaign, while Arthur and Lewis moved to New York to become the leading angels of the Benevolent Empire. Insulating themselves profitably from the market's haggling and chicanery by fixed cash prices, low markup, and high turnover, they made a great fortune as the country's leading silk importers.

Dour Arthur, tormented into irascibility by excruciating headaches, kept no chair to encourage visits in the cubicle from which he supervised his clerks, lunched on a cracker and water, and passed out tracts wherever he went. But "Arthur Tappan's heart was as large as all New York," Finney thought, for he devoted himself to stimulating and channeling benevolent effort by enormous anonymous gifts. No doubt he enjoyed his unseen power and enormous reputation for pious benevolence, but Finney found him unfailingly ready to attack every new evil that appeared and totally dedicated to each new moral commitment, no matter what the opposition or expense. Arthur, said younger brother Lewis, loved "unpopular causes: the more unpopular they were the more they secured his patronage."

The tireless, efficient Lewis managed the silk business as well as the finances of the leading societies. "Believing that the accumulation of property for selfish purposes is repugnant to the gospel; that every person is a steward," the Tappan brothers led their circle of devout philanthropists into "a solemn engagement not to lay up any property we may hereafter acquire." Instead they pledged "the whole of it to the Lord, deducting sufficient to supply ourselves and families, in a decent manner, as becomes those professing Godliness." Much of this wealth went into subsidizing churches for the urban poor.[32]

In 1832 these Christian gentlemen smote Satan a mighty blow. Taking over New York's largest and most notorious theater, they converted it into the Second Free Presbyterian Church, threw it open without the customary pew rents to the poor of its degraded Chatham Street neighborhood, and installed Finney as pastor. Here every May the evangelical armies mustered for their anniversary meetings. Here every Sunday the Tappan brothers and a few other devout gentlemen conspicuously dotted Finney's swelling congregation of working-class people. Soon his "praying, working" Christians, women especially, were pursuing converts "into the highways and hedges," and free churches were spun off throughout the city, all readily subsidized by affluent "brethren."

Within a few years, lay wealth and enthusiasm built a new temple to the evangelist's power. Finney himself insisted on a radical design for the Broadway Tabernacle, an enormous rotunda with tiers of pews rising steeply from a central pulpit so as to focus all attention on the preacher while carrying his voice to the largest possible crowd. Amplified from this imposing forum by a Tappan-subsidized weekly, the New York *Evangelist,* he addressed a national audience with greater effect than any cleric since the touring George Whitefield ignited the intercolonial First Awakening.

But success plunged the evangelist into doubt and eventual despair. He was too honest to ignore friends' warnings against making revivals "a sort of trade, to be worked at so many hours a day"; and at first, floods of converts and a vivid sense of empowering grace kept him from "running into *formality.*" Amid the Empire City's full-blown capitalist reality, however, he began to worry about "the great weakness of Christians." Older church members, he fretted, "were making very little progress in grace" and would "fall back from a revival state, even sooner than young converts."

Still more disturbing was "my own want of stability in faith and love." Increasingly he spent his days in "fasting and prayer" to regain "the divine strength, that would enable me efficiently to labor for the promotion of revivals of religion." Most shattering was his discovery, while planning the Broadway Tabernacle, that the refocused Moderate Light could not usher in the Kingdom of God by converting businessmen generally into Bissells and Tappans. This became clear when antinomian benevolence carried him inevitably, like Hopkins, to the premier American evil of slavery.

Finney had always made benevolent action the critical test of rebirth. At his call enthusiastic converts cleansed Rochester (briefly) of alcohol and social disorder. But when he pointed in New York to slavery, certainly no less appalling, only the Tappans and a few others followed. Indeed Christian businessmen led a riotous assault on the Tappans for their antislavery views. Shortly thereafter, in January 1834, the evangelist broke down physically and spiritually. Seeking recovery on a Mediterranean voyage no doubt financed by generous brethren, the disillusioned Finney suffered "utter agony" over his failing powers and fears that revivals "would decline throughout the country." Finally "a day of unspeakable wrestling and agony in my soul" brought assurance that God would enable him to carry his evangelical mission to completion.

Back on shore the way opened when *Evangelist* editor Joshua Leavitt suggested a series of extemporaneous lectures on revivals. The bright young Yale graduate took them down for serial publication, building circulation and making Finney's spectacularly successful theology of revival available to evangelicals everywhere. An extemporaneous thinker, the evangelist had never articulated his whole system even to himself. Reviewing Leavitt's condensed and clarified notes to build each lecture on its predecessors, he now expressed himself more systematically than he had ever done. Just as politicians "get up meetings, circulate handbills and pamphlets, blaze away in the newspapers" to elect their candidates, Finney maintained, ministers must adopt the best means of persuading people to "vote in the Lord Jesus Christ as the governor of the Universe." Success required only "the right exercise" of "the ordinary powers of nature." Through multiplied example and explicit precept, he taught revivalists to be "theatrical" and address "animal feelings." If the church offered only "sanctimonious starch," he argued, "theatres will be thronged every night," for "the common-sense people *will be* entertained."

Finney's *Lectures on Revivals of Religion* became the standard manual of revival theology for several generations of Anglo-American evangelicals. Frequently reprinted in America and Britain and translated into French, German, and Welsh, they temporarily reassured him by inspiring "revivals of religion, in multitudes of places throughout the country." *Lectures* and the Broadway Tabernacle brought the forty-two-year-old lawyer/preacher to a dizzying pinnacle of fame and influence and the hundred-year Awakening to an apparently triumphant culmination. Christian profession was becoming a criterion of good repute, periodically reaffirmed in the four-day Protracted Meetings he recommended. "If the church will do her duty," he preached, "the millenium [*sic*] may come in three years."

But in 1835 Finney abruptly resigned the country's leading pulpit. Retiring to a clearing in the woods of northern Ohio, he joined a band of zealots erecting rough shelters for a new outpost of Yankee culture. Here he immured himself for life in the loving communal evangelicalism of Oberlin College, first as professor of theology, then president. This spiritual Quixote came out of a world he could no longer square with his antinomian millennialism. Perhaps the extravagance of the Broadway Tabernacle brought home to him the perils of ego. Perhaps he recognized the crassness of his instrumentalism when he saw it fully laid out in cold print. Critics were beginning to complain that Almighty God no longer dispensed his awesome New Light mystically. Instead revivals were "gotten up," they charged. Souls were reborn through "a system of operations set in motion by human contrivance." In capitalist culture, Finney may have begun to perceive, "human calculation" saved immortal souls through "the arithmetic of faith." Certainly he was vulnerable to the charge of teaching "practical skill in the art of bringing about an excitement" as "a particular branch of professional work"—on the market principle that "perfection in art is compassed by the division of labor." Probably he already sensed, as he would acknowledge within a decade, that revivals were "gradually becoming more and more superficial," with "so much policy and machinery, so much dependence upon means and measures, so much of man and so little of God" as to convince him that "I erred in manner and spirit."[33]

His doubts had crystallized around slavery. While he was wrestling with the Lord at sea, antiabolitionists burned the almost completed Broadway Tabernacle, forcing deep-pocketed brethren to rebuild it. For true believers like Finney and the Tappans, slavery became the acid test of spiritual authenticity. Dismayed by the angry outburst of racism and social conservatism that their first timid antislavery gestures evoked, they despaired of the world and fell back on their Yankee antinomian roots. Increasingly the philanthropists lavished their wealth on winning for benevolent, perfectionist spirituality the universal Yankee nation now flooding through northern Ohio's Western Reserve. Finney left New York with Arthur Tappan's confidential pledge to Oberlin (soon annulled by the Panic of 1837) of "my entire income, except what I need to provide for my family, till you are beyond pecuniary want."

Finney did not repudiate his evangelical mission. Disillusioned by converts too embedded in capitalist culture for the total commitment he demanded, he embarked in his last New York sermons on a radical new theological quest. Drawn to the "sanctification" claimed by "our Methodist brethren," he devoted the rest of a long life to developing the "perfectionist" argument that "an altogether higher and more stable form of Christian life was attainable," in which the truly reborn could "live without known sin."

When Finney and the Tappans moved on to antislavery perfectionism, they left leadership of a compromised Moderate Light to pragmatists. The issue had been clear ever since Beecher interrupted Finney's first appeal to wealthy Bostonians for total commitment. "You need not be afraid to give up all to Christ, your property and all, for he will give it right back to you," the hierarch reassured his constituency, throwing the evangelist into "an agony" to correct this "false impression." The Lord, Finney insisted, "did require them to renounce ownership" of their property and "to use themselves and everything else as belonging to him." Lewis Tappan eventually concluded that Beecher "believed in the doctrine of expedience to a criminal excess."[34]

The Yankee hierarch precipitated the final break after moving to Cincinnati as president of the new Lane Seminary, which the Tappans were backing to save the West by training young Finney converts for the ministry. When Beecher expelled students whose antislavery agitation was outraging local elites, the Tappans shifted their backing to Oberlin, and soon Beecher was attacking Finney for perfectionist heresy. Meanwhile he trained a houseful of talented children—home economist Catharine Beecher, sentimental antislavery novelist Harriet Beecher Stowe, and the Reverends William, Edward, George, Charles, and Henry Ward Beecher—to exemplify the cultural schizophrenia of a sentimentalized and triumphant Moderate Light.

Thus Edwards's revolutionary New Light, as finally modulated to the stresses of capitalist accommodation by Finney's genius, nerved Americans for the personal transformation required by a competitive market. But the remarkably effulgent Moderate Light did not, as the brash Yorker evangelist hoped, suffuse the market with love. Instead, and at fearful cost, it bifurcated the consciousness of cross-pressured Americans. Women and ministers ended up sustaining an illusory world of powerless love—actualized only in the female world of altruistic domesticity—that immunized and sanctified men for the segregated market world of calculating ego. From the fires of Moderate-Light revival, a "middle-class" culture emerged.

Chapter 8

Ethos vs. Eros

THE SEMICENTENNIAL of American independence was a more than symbolic watershed. During the jubilee year that peaked on the Fourth of July 1826, returning prosperity set off the decisive phase of market revolution, cultural as well as economic. While Finneyism blazed with the first flood of commerce along the Grand Canal, the Benevolent Empire's major societies federated nationally for cultural conquest and a national temperance movement surged up to school a spreading "middle class' in self-disciplined effort.

The so-called middle class was constituted not by mode and relations of production but by ideology. Where nobilities and priesthoods left folk cultures little disturbed, capital feeding on human effort claimed hegemony over all classes. A numerous and dispersed bourgeoisie of small-scale enterprisers pushed both themselves and their workers to staggering effort by mythologizing class as a moral category. Scorning both the handful of idle rich and the multitude of dissolute poor, they apotheosized a virtuous middle class of the effortful. The "business man"— originally a man conspicuously busy—became the archetype of a culture of busyness.

Atomizing society into a marketplace rewarding each according to effort, middle-class mythology both fueled and justified success to quell rising anger over the class reality of bourgeois exploitation. It appealed especially to a growing new class of "white-collar" clerks, salesmen, and bookkeepers aspiring to bourgeois enterprise. But it appealed also to farmers entering the market, to master mechanics becoming capitalist bosses, and to manual workers mustering effort against the disgrace of fading respectability. A middle class of consciousness encompassed people of whatever class who sustained precarious honor and sometimes prospered by embracing the bourgeoisie's self-repressive norms, competitive consumption, and middle-class mythology.[1]

237

Appropriately Henry Clay introduced the term *middle class* to public discourse, and his campaign biographer gave classic formulation to the middle-class mythology. "Ours is a country where men start from an humble origin, and from small beginnings rise gradually in the world, as the reward of merit and industry," proclaimed the Reverend Calvin Colton. "... One has as good a chance as another, according to his talents, prudence, and personal exertions." Because "this is a country of *self-made men,*" Colton argued, "work is held in the highest respect," while "the idle, lazy, poor man gets little pity in his poverty." For Colton and the bourgeoisie, "nothing better could be said of any state of society."[2]

But the reality lately discovered by historians belies the middle-class myth. Actually the generation of 1820 and its children experienced American history's sharpest rise in the "permanent inequality of conditions and aristocracy" feared by Alexis de Tocqueville. A new wage-exploiting aristocracy, "one of the harshest that ever existed," the Frenchman thought, was in fact widening dramatically the gap between wealth and poverty. According to the best estimates, the share of national wealth held by the richest 10 percent jumped, mainly after 1820, from the 49.6 percent of 1774 to reach 73 percent by 1860. The richest 1 percent more than doubled their share from 12.6 percent to 29 percent.

Under capitalism's primitive accumulation, the lion's share of swelling productivity gains went to capital, entrepreneurship, and to some extent labor, in the most progressive, wage-exploiting sectors fostered by technological innovation and the capitalist state. Average wages lagged far behind profits; but even the slowly rising average conceals many workers who actually lost ground because of deskilling and a sharply rising differential between skilled and unskilled wages. Capitalist development widened inequality in consumption as well as income. While the conveniences and luxuries of the well-to-do became cheaper and better under increasing applications of capital and technology, poor people's labor-intensive necessities of food, clothing, firewood, and shelter became relatively more expensive.[3]

These processes produced by 1840 an American plutocracy rivaling the world's most opulent, the upper British nobility. When room and board at New York's sumptuous Astor House could be had for only $1.20 a day, there were already some sixty American millionaires. Wealth was most concentrated in the cities. By 1828, 40 percent of the Empire City's assessed property was owned by 1 percent of its citizens. Every community touched by the market had its lesser business elite, and even in the rural North the wealthiest 10 percent owned 40 percent of the property.

Nor were the wealthy self-made. Overwhelmingly they were sons of rich and/or eminent families. The nearly two thousand wealthiest citizens of four northeastern cities, 1828–1848, break down as follows by family origin.

	Rich/Eminent	Middling	Humble
New York City	95%	3%	2%
Brooklyn	61%	16%	3%
Philadelphia	92%	6%	2%
Boston	94%	4%	2%

Upward mobility was somewhat greater in booming smaller places and among mechanic/manufacturers; and many workers climbed from rags to threadbare respectability. But general mobility was limited. The rise from rags to riches was statistically mythical, at least as crudely measured by Philadelphians' changes in status of occupation and neighborhood. Few moved more than one rung up a multirunged social ladder, many fell from wealth, and more into poverty.[4]

Across the North in the 1820s these sharpening realities of class coincided with middle-class mythology to threaten patriarchal families with shame of failure. Economic vicissitude, widely experienced and exemplified, made all classes susceptible to the cultural imperialism of the bourgeoisie. Pulpit, schoolroom, and a rising tide of print—drowning out radical antinomians, democrats, and laborites—dinned in middle-class myth and ethic. Many a dislocated worker or farmer, getting "little pity in his poverty," struggled for middle-class status as the only socially available strategy for saving patriarchal honor. While middle-class effort propelled some into bourgeois success, and a few to opulence, most managed only a precarious respectability while giving their all to capitalist production.

In the crucible of the middle-class family, a culture mobilizing effort forged itself for instinctual repression. While a militant temperance movement publicly demanded self-discipline, impulse was privately fought at its deepest springs in gender and libido.

The task fell to families under demographic stress. As never before, young adults and nuclear households were forsaking kin and neighborhood to wander from place to place. Population changes identify two great migratory tides, one flowing from East to West and the other from country to town or city. But a far greater tide of to-and-fro migration was required to produce the impressive net changes. In the best-studied example, less than half the Bostonians counted by the census of 1830 were still there ten years later. The 1836 city directory expunged 24 percent of the households listed the previous year. Some died, of course, but the vast majority moved on. An amazing 3,325,000 people passed through Boston between 1830 and 1890 to produce a net population growth of 387,000.

Less exact evidence suggests similar turnover in smaller towns and rural areas. The movers were mainly the poor in search of a better livelihood, and they often moved considerable distances. In this great uprooting, the peripatetic dispersal of Prophet Joseph Smith's clan was all too typical.[5]

The uprooted, insular household found children no longer an asset but an impediment to survival. Their labor on shrunken farms no longer earned their keep; they challenged a paternal authority that could no longer provide them with farms or livelihood; and they required a more rigorous socialization for market competition. Under these pressures Americans inaugurated history's most dramatic and sustained repression of human fertility. For more than a century, births per 1,000 whites declined, from 55.0 in 1800 to 43.3 by 1850 and 20.6 by 1930. The number of children born per married woman fell from 6.4 in 1800 to 4.9 by 1850 and 2.8 by 1880.

This revolutionary "demographic transition" eventually spread with industrialization and urbanization across the North Atlantic world and then to Japan and other countries. But only in the United States, where the birth rate noticeably declined first and farthest, did the demographic transition spread through a mainly rural people before a sharp mortality decline and before large-scale industrialization/urbanization. Only here was it so clearly associated (as ever more sophisticated tests confirm) with the rising price of land.

The transatlantic contrast arose from contrasting person/land ratios. Fertility was eroded at very different rates in the Old and New Worlds, first by land scarcity and then by industrial/urban imperatives. The land-scarcity stage occurred gradually and inconspicuously over several centuries in crowded, commercializing western Europe; and only in the late nineteenth century did the industrial/urban stage bring the conspicuous further downturn of the demographic transition. By contrast, North American cheap land kept births high until the market revolution surmounted the transport barrier and forced Americans to cope overnight with stresses that Europeans experienced over centuries. The American demographic transition telescoped the land-scarcity stage of fertility decline into a generation or two before merging imperceptibly into the industrial/urban stage.

Births declined first in the Moderate Light's southeastern New England heartland in the last quarter of the eighteenth century, and then across the countryside as local land became too expensive to provide farms for numerous offspring and cheap land receded beyond easy reach with western settlement and rising farm-making costs. Threatened by shame of paternal failure, a straitened patriarchy constrained itself. The land-scarcity stage of fertility control penetrated the South and West as the Northeast entered the industrial/urban stage. New England's fertility reduction of 1800 reached the upper South in 1820 and remote Michigan and Wisconsin in 1850. By then births in still more remote Arkansas and Oregon were falling to the somewhat higher 1800 level of the Middle Atlantic states. Meanwhile Massachusetts was entering the industrial/urban stage as education and the calculating rationality of bourgeois culture began to exert greater pressure on fertility than land scarcity.[6]

Fertility control was nothing new. Most cultures have tried either to limit or increase births. But until the demographic transition, Americans did so by restricting occasions for sex rather than its actual practice. The subsistence culture kept its large families within bounds by late marriage, which shortened women's child-bearing years, and by late weaning of children from the breast, which inhibited ovulation to prolong the interval between births.

Within these marital bounds, libido expressed itself without conscious constraint, an elemental force as compelling as hunger and as fructifying as the bountiful earth. Women were thought as lustful and as fulfilled by sexuality as men—or more so, in male fears and fantasies—and folk belief sustained against all experience a conviction that conception could not occur without female orgasm. Unsegregated nudity, casually exposed genitalia, and the sounds and smells of coition were commonplace in crowded cabins.

Rural culture affirmed sexuality most tellingly by covertly legitimizing sexual expression for its post-pubescent children awaiting marriage, so long as conception was avoided. Ritual condemnation of premarital sex enabled young women's parents to regulate it in practice. So many people "Confessed Fornication"before marriage when they joined the church in Groton, Massachusetts—sixty-six out of two hundred in the fifteen years before the Revolution, and nine of sixteen couples joining between 1789 and 1791—that the notation was abbreviated "C.F." on the church record. It was customary "in that part of the county," a New York judge noted in an 1804 paternity case, "for young people who are courting, to sleep together." As late as 1846 respectable rural matrons testified in another New York case that such "bundling" was "the universal custom of the country."[7]

The taboo against conception cramped premarital exuberance only moderately, for a fetus could be aborted without ethical or legal qualm until it made its life felt at "quickening," and a wide repertoire of abortive substances, devices, and techniques were disseminated through grandmothers, midwives, doctors, newspapers, and advice books. Babies were neither named nor sentimentalized until they survived the hazards of infant mortality; and infanticide may have been commoner than supposed. All else failing, premarital pregnancy was usually rewarded with the familial independence and freedom from contraceptive constraint of early marriage.

Of course, by formally condemning a libido it licensed as irresistible, folk culture demanded a price. The conviction of sin thus implanted could be expiated only by a religious conversion sealing fidelity to marital bonds and communal values. This religious restraint on sexuality fluctuated to the demographic imperatives of arminian market and antinomian land. Puritan antieroticism first crystallized under commercializing stress in Reformation England, then eased under the New World's person/land ratio, only to harden again into the repressive rigor of the Moderate Light when the market broke the transport barrier.[8]

While market competition uprooted families, curbed fertility, and demanded a new level of effort, it was driving the kin-and-neighbor cooperation of use-value production from community back to a final refuge in the isolated nuclear household. Consequently a shrunken family had to mobilize human effort for capitalist production while also satisfying the human needs for love and trust formerly met in a wider net of communal/kin relationships.

Through indulgent affection and careful education, the gentry were already shaping self-reliant children for venturesome enterprise, prudent hedonism, and dynastic marriage. But without the security of inherited wealth, the individualizing style of the gentry family was unavailable to most Americans. Children of farm and workshop were ill prepared for the market's hazards by the patriarchal will-breaking and communal conformity of household production.

In a signal demonstration of humanity's capacity for survival through social adaption, the traditional stem family transformed society by transforming itself into the middle-class, nuclear family. The middle-class family evoked maximum effort by combining the individualizing acculturation of the gentry family with the intense piety of the stem family. Maternal love activated filial guilt to internalize norms of self-repressive effort in carefully educated sons. Spreading from urban venturers to the susceptible of whatever class, the middle-class family's psychodynamics surged with the Moderate Light from lower New England across the North to reweave the fabric of human personality and relationships.[9]

This middle-class revolution, forged in the domestic pain and conflict of one generation, was typically carried to completion by the youthful adaptability of its children in the next. Capitalism fractured families along fault lines of gender and generation by demanding for market production the male labor traditionally devoted to family subsistence and reproduction. Thus it created a male public world of competitive production sundered from a female domestic world of altruistic reproduction. Women deprived of their autonomous sphere of authority and respect in household production were called upon to provide the love, tranquility, and socially invisible domestic labor needed by men pushing themselves to the limit of effort.

With demographic imperatives simultaneously easing the female hazards and burdens of constant childbearing, women found in the new needs of men an opportunity to push against a patriarchal oppression assuming new middle-class forms. Under the banner of altruism they claimed hegemony over home and children. But more than demographic imperatives carried this transformation of middle-class life to deep levels of gender and libido. Through a new sexual politics of erotic guilt and asexual love, families reconstructed themselves for self-repressive effort.

During the 1820s and 1830s, a radical redefinition of gender and an unprecedented denigration of eroticism accompanied an unexampled mobilization of human effort. A middle-class ideology of domesticity overflowed with cheap print from Moderate-Light tracts into advice books, home medical manuals, sentimental novels, and the tales, verses, and engravings of women's magazines and decorative gift books for the parlor. Written mainly by clergymen, physicians, and an upwelling host of "scribbling women" (as Nathaniel Hawthorne called them), our first popular literature grounded human relationships in a conception of True Womanhood as weak, selfless, and pure.

Male scribblers emphasized women's biological destiny of devotion to husbands and children. Woman is "a moral, a sexual, a germiferous, gestative and parturient creature," declared Philadelphia's eminent gynecologist Dr. Charles D. Meigs. Her head is "almost too small for intellect but just big enough for love." This "weak and timid" creature "needs a protector," male commentators insisted, and "is willing to repay it all by the surrender of the full measure of her affections." The True Woman must be "the solace, the aid, the counsellor" of her husband, "for whose sake alone the world is of any consequence to her." Scribbling women agreed that "true feminine genius" was "ever timid, doubtful and clingingly dependent, a perpetual childhood." They too urged the True Woman to "watch well the first moments when your will conflicts with his to whom God and society have given the control." She must "reverence his wishes even when you do not his *opinions*"; "stop (right or wrong) in the midst of self-defense, in gentle submission"; and "if he is abusive, never retort."

Yet female authors' language of love converted the doctrine of female abasement into a sexual politics of female hegemony over home and family. By conceding that "the man bears rule over his wife's person and conduct," the True Woman could "rule over his inclinations." With "no arms other than gentleness," she could immure market-hardened husband and threatened children in her "empire of softness." "Her commands are caresses, her menaces are tears," the scribbling women taught, but her ultimate armament was female purity—"the everlasting barrier against which the tides of man's sensual nature surge."[10]

Female antinomians—the Shakers' Mother Ann Lee and Publick Universal Friend Jemima Wilkinson—had first raised the banner of chastity against a philoprogenitive patriarchy inflicting on women the perils and burdens of endless motherhood. Meanwhile decay of the protective patriarchal family left women at the mercy of male initiative in choosing marriage partners. By the late 1820s the Moderate Light was crystallizing a phobic antieroticism from female sexual resentment, demographic necessity, and male needs for self-controlled effort.[11]

An organized purity movement arose when women's benevolent societies, while leading Moderate-Light men into engagement with the New York City poor, discovered prostitution as a paradigmatic evil that seemed to be increasing at an alarming rate. Male philanthropists, claiming their usual public leadership of a new cause, soon gave way under criticism to more militant women.

Both male and female reformers were inspired by evangelist Finney's first New York City revival in the winter of 1829–1830. Millennial hopes and Arthur Tappan's cash-backed organizational enthusiasm mobilized the local tract society to saturate the working class with middle-class evangelism. The city was divided into districts of sixty families, and five hundred solid citizens—half women and doubling to a thousand in Finney's second revival of 1834–1835—took spiritual responsibility for a district by visiting each family monthly with tracts, prayer, and proselytizing. John R. McDowall, a divinity student assigned in this campaign to the notorious cellar slums and jails of swampy Five Points, a few blocks north of City Hall, became absorbed in converting imprisoned women, mostly prostitutes. Reborn middle-class women took up his cause of rescuing prostitutes, and in 1831 the Tappan coterie provided male sponsorship by organizing a New York Magdalen Society, with McDowall as paid missionary. But McDowall's first published report painted such a lurid picture of urban vice that it became a pornographic sensation, and male leaders disbanded the society under a storm of righteous outrage and prurient derision.

Yet McDowall persisted, and his female supporters regrouped through moral societies in their neighborhood churches. In 1834 these women convened at Finney's church to organize the New York Female Moral Reform Society and elect the evangelist's wife, Lydia Andrews Finney, their first directress. As prostitutes proved resistant to reform, the society poured female anger into a national campaign against "honorable men" who "basely and treacherously" seduced and ruined trusting women. Too many men were "so passingly mean, so utterly contemptible," proclaimed the society's monthly *Advocate for Moral Reform,* as to "plunge into degradation, misery, and ruin, those whom they profess to love. O let them not be trusted." Branding male licentiousness as "a regular crusade against the sex," the lady editors called on "the virtuous daughters of America" to "rise in their own defense."

Women rose with impressive fervor as the *Advocate* and shockingly unchaperoned female agents spread the society's message through Moderate-Light territory. Reorganized in 1839 as the American Female Moral Society, the purity movement claimed 555 auxiliaries and the *Advocate* twenty thousand readers. Subscribing the society's oath to shun profligate men, militant women across the North harassed brothels with "active visiting" and prayer meetings; exposed brothel patrons, adulterers, and seducers by name in the *Advocate;* sued seducers for civil damages; and petitioned and agitated for state laws—won by New York reformers in 1848—making seduction a criminal offense.

Prostitution, seduction, and adultery epitomized for women the sexual double standard and the "despotism" of "lordly man," who "rules his trembling subjects with a rod of iron, conscious of entire impunity, and exalting in his fancied superiority." Repelling male notions of woman as madonna/whore who "must exist in spotless innocence, or else in hopeless vice," female reformers cast back on man "the shame and wretched consequences of his criminal conduct" that "have hitherto been heaped upon" the woman. Where even John McDowall blamed prostitutes for "voluntary vice" and thought their "suffering self-inflicted," women blamed "the treachery of man" and insisted that "very few" of these betrayed unfortunates "have sought their wretched calling."

Around the banner of sexual purity, middle-class women rallied "as a band of sisters, affectionately united" against domestic isolation and male domination. They found new autonomy and scope for their abilities in a movement led by women and hiring women as its editors, organizers, typesetters, and finally even its financial managers. Above all the purity crusade endowed them with moral superiority and real power over male behavior. No wonder the Female Society spurned a proposal by male evangelicals to swallow it up as an auxiliary to their belatedly organized American Seventh Commandment ("Thou shalt not commit adultery") Society. The women's executive committee replied that they were pledged to "a large portion of our sex" to occupy "ground which none but women could so appropriately or efficiently fill."

Beyond the implicit feminism of moral reform, abolitionism was just enabling vanguard middle-class women to glimpse capitalism's liberal promise of equal rights for interchangeable human beings. But most of the moral sisterhood was shocked when the *Advocate* published an equal-rights appeal by the notorious Sarah Grimké. Most True Women still clung instead to the rights sustaining their newfound domestic power:

> *The right to love whom others scorn,*
> *The right to comfort and to mourn,*
> *The right to shed new joy on earth,*
> *The right to feel the soul's high worth.*[12]

Yet female power was won at the cost of female as well as male libido. Many middle-class women accepted the male medical doctrine that "the majority of women (happily for them) are not very much troubled with sexual feelings of any kind." Dr. William Acton's *Functions and Disorders of the Reproductive System* taught that "love of home, children, and domestic duties are the only passions they feel." Harriet Beecher Stowe agreed. "What terrible temptations lie in the way of your sex," she exclaimed to her husband. "Tho I did love you with an almost insane love before I married you," she maintained, "I never knew yet or felt the pulsation which showed me that I could be tempted in that way. I loved you as I now love God."[13]

Moreover the female power of sexual purity rested on the female abasement of True Womanhood. In the face of overwhelming male power, woman could exercise domestic power only by meeting male needs. Even the True Woman's ego-defending anger was channeled not against the male-imposed wrenching of gender that provoked it but against a male libido that men themselves were struggling to master. True Men needed all the help they could get.

The market appropriated male libido to capitalist production by both repressing sexuality and plunging gender into confusion. With the traditional patriarchy of household production shattered, sons had to compete for elusive manhood in the market rather than grow into secure manhood by replicating fathers. Where many could never attain the self-made manhood of success, middle-class masculinity pushed egotism to extremes of aggression, calculation, self-control, and unremitting effort.

True Men could sustain this gender-wrenching only by wrenching True Women to opposite extremes of altruism and submission. Buffeted by the world's fierce competition, they could brook no competition at home. A masculinity tested daily by competing males required a domestic domain of unquestioned mastery. "The man will be manlier, that he has a true womanly wife," said the Reverend Horace Bushnell. "The power we ... get on our masculine character," he explained, "is not so much from what women do to us, as from what we do to them." True Manhood could realize itself only against the foil of antipodal True Womanhood. Without female claimants of male "concession and protection and courtesy," worried New York diarist George Templeton Strong, "manhood is gone too."

The True Woman's purity was critical. With male libido threatening self-controlled effort, men's fears of their own sexuality exacerbated their fears of female sexuality. Female libido threatened precarious middle-class manhood with intolerable anxieties of inadequacy, jealousy, and distraction from effort. A culture shaped by male power to male insecurities insisted that "a passionate woman is a disgrace to her sex." The woman who "entices the male of ardent passions," male moralists thundered, who "exposes publicly what prudence should conceal," commits "the crime of sentimental fornication."[14]

Most threatened by sentimental fornication were the swelling hosts of self-making young men who could not marry until they got ahead in the competitive race. Their firsthand experience of the libidinal threat was targeted in the 1830s by clerical and medical advisers rising from their ranks. A male crusade against masturbation coincided with the female purity crusade in an antierotic phobia that deepened throughout the nineteenth century.

Two self-making Yankee clerics opened the war on masturbation. The Reverend John Todd and the Reverend Sylvester Graham had surmounted remarkably similar childhood vicissitudes. Both were the youngest of many siblings in once prominent families falling on hard times. Both were born to mothers going insane; both soon lost their fathers as well; and both struggled through youth against chronic illness. Both suffered a classic adolescent ordeal of guilt (mirrored almost indecently in adult polemic against masturbation), precipitating a classic Moderate-Light rebirth.

An aspiring minister could no longer expect a congregation to take him "for better or for worse, until death do us part." Graham's father and grandfather had preached the Edwardean New Divinity to the same Connecticut valley congregations for fifty years. Now, however, newly affluent congregations were competing for converts by competing for the best preachers, and preachers were competing for wealthy urban churches offering the highest salaries and status. Clerical authority, no longer flowing from clerical office, had to be self-made in the ecclesiastical marketplace.

John Todd, vowing from infancy "to rise above my circumstances," won the manhood of clerical success by sheer effort. Working his way through Yale against all advice and trained in Moderate-Light revivalism at Andover Seminary, he moved rapidly from revival success at Groton to a more prestigious Northampton pastorate to (by his mid thirties, at doubled salary) Philadelphia's "most beautiful" Clinton Street Church, "the largest in the city." An honorary degree certified success, and his Moderate-Light keenness for the miraculous new medium of cheap print was already making "Dr. Todd" a household name.

In 1835 he published *The Student's Manual* that guided a whole generation of young men through self-making. This "great work of my life," exhausting seven editions in two years and at least annual reprintings for several decades thereafter, enabled him to retire from Philadelphia's fierce denominational strife to a Pittsfield pastorate. Here he reigned for thirty years as a "kind of bishop" over the peaceful Berkshire hills, plying the self-making middle class with fifteen books and countless sermons and tracts of hard-won advice.

The Student's Manual addressed the first large wave of young American men to brave the stresses of self-making in boarding houses and dormitories far removed from parental influence. The driven Todd (who boasted of reading 124 books in six months) advised them to follow his workaholic example. "SUCCESS," he exhorted, "fixes the eye" of the True Man, and religion enables him to "call forth the highest efforts." He encouraged rivalry as "a mark of health" and praised successful businessmen for "disciplined and concentrated mind" and "an energy that can surmount any obstacle." But "in order to compete with those around him," Dr. Todd warned, "a man must give his time, and thoughts, and life to it." Success required "an intensity that knows no diversion, and a concentration of thought that excludes everything else."

Todd's *Manual* touched the rawest middle-class nerve and won his middle-class audience by assailing libido as the "diversion" draining the "intensity" and "concentration" of True Manhood. A section provocatively set off in small-print Latin identified the threat in its most menacing form. Through tantalized schoolboy Latinists a generation learned, on Dr. Todd's high authority, that the "vicious act" of masturbation destroyed mind, body, and soul. His warning reverberated in the generational consciousness: "You who do this thing" would be "hunted down by the resentment and wrath of God," whose "eye, always vigilant, observes you."[15]

Todd's coy Latinity was already old-fashioned. Sylvester Graham had broken the taboo against this "delicate subject" a year before by publishing a sensationally explicit *Lecture to Young Men, on Chastity,* also often and long reprinted. Todd's

Manual and Graham's *Lecture* were the most influential of a sudden spate of publications inaugurating in the mid-1830s, a century-long middle-class polemic against libido in general and male masturbation in particular.

While Dr. Todd rapidly mounted the new career ladder of clerical success, the more troubled Graham had been struggling for its bottom rung. Instead of being groomed for Yale like his first-born father, seventeenth child Sylvester was virtually an orphan at birth. Shunted from foster-family to foster-family, he worked at various menial jobs when health permitted until age twenty-three. He found his road to manhood when he surmounted "one of those peculiar trials which young men too seldom have the courage to endure." Beset by friends to be a good fellow and share a glass of whiskey—which he hated as allergic to his frail constitution—he won their respect by standing on temperance in principle.

The incident "gave a direction to the whole course of my life," he said, launching him into temperance lecturing and preparation for the ministry. Expelled from a college-preparatory academy over some contretemps with his younger schoolmates, he learned enough from his local minister by age thirty-two to be licensed by the unreconstructed Hopkinsians of the Mendon Association. But the rural congregations willing to try him found his phobia against alcohol excessive. Rebuffed by rural congregations, Graham found an eager audience in 1830 among Philadelphia's young men as lecturer for the Pennsylvania Temperance Society. Moved by their "entreaties, and importunities, and . . . heart-rending appeals"— and emboldened perhaps by his easy victory over alcohol—he dared to challenge a far more familiar and intransigent foe of self-making young men. His lecture openly discussing the perils of sexuality was a sensation; and until he finally published it in 1834, popular demand kept him on the lucrative lecture circuit through the northeastern cities. Drawing two thousand New Yorkers on one occasion, he was mobbed on another in Portland for besmirching the purity of a female audience and mobbed twice more by Boston butchers for denouncing meat as sexually exciting.

Everywhere he warned that the "filthy vice" of masturbation was polluting young manhood. He estimated that 60 to 70 percent of twelve- and thirteen-year-old schoolboys were being "almost completely ruined in health and constitution by this destructive practice." It plunged the "miserable transgressor" into self-loathing; withered physical, mental, and moral powers; and often ended in suicide, insanity, or death. The masturbator, Graham admonished self-making young men, surrendered "his nobleness, dignity, honor and manhood." He was "no longer bold, resolute, determined, aspiring, dignified" but "disheartened, uncertain in his plans." He was "a drone to himself and society," a failure. True Manhood depended on mastery of libido.[16]

Graham and Todd distilled antieroticism from unusually severe experiences of widely experienced self-making stress. The threatening libido that resonated autobiographically through their polemic was the instantly recognizable nemesis of many a young man struggling for the total self-control of self-made manhood.

Todd made no bones about speaking from bitter experience. Warning against the sexual excitation of such "bad books" as Byron, Cooper, and Scott—"the most awful scourge with which a righteous God ever visited our world"—he admitted having "read them with too much care." He knew "every rock and every quicksand." Bad books, "secreted in the rooms of students," excited "those rovings of the imagination, by which the mind is at once enfeebled, and the heart and feelings debased and polluted." Masturbation, as Dr. Todd well knew, was "almost inseparable from the habit of reverie." Therefore beware of imagination, he implored, "of permitting the thoughts to wander when alone," lest evils slip in "which want a name, to convey any conception of their enormity."[17]

Dirty thoughts, "those LASCIVIOUS DAY-DREAMS, and amorous reveries," were the main problem for Graham also. But where the more traditional Todd could only invoke divine retribution, the sickly Graham's "Science of Life" promised effortful health by quelling libido through dietary restraint. His ideology of ascetic health crystallized when the temperance movement introduced his dyspepsia to Philadelphia's prestigious medical establishment, just being energized by the new medical ideas flowing from Paris. The most up-to-date medical science, he discovered, saw the body as a system of vital energies liable to the disruption of disease through debilitating excitements. Soon he was preaching, by the highest scientific authority and at first with impressive professional support, that human health and effort were threatened by sexuality and such exciting foods as meat, sweets, coffee, alcohol, and white bread.

The new medicine offered a way of dealing with those dirty thoughts that tormented Graham's struggle for True Manhood. The nervous system was seen as carrying debilitating excitation to the critical digestive tract, while excited viscera could in turn excite the nervous system. The key to health and effort, he preached, was avoiding sexual arousal. This *"peculiar excitement of the nervous system,"* he taught, "rapidly exhausts the vital properties of the tissues." True Manhood required stamping out dirty thoughts and eschewing the gross foods that could excite them. Accordingly Graham thought masturbation "the worst form of sexual indulgence" because it epitomized the "mental action, and power of imagination" operating "on the genital organs."

Graham's self-making obsession with human energy radicalized his antieroticism. While excessive masturbation had sporadically been criticized as impairing the healthy sexuality of marriage, he proclaimed sexuality too dangerous to be indulged in any form until the body fully matured in the late twenties. Even the mature and married, he warned, must avoid "venereal excess." The robust should indulge no more than once a month, the sickly and sedentary seldom or never. Prudent eaters could easily "subdue their sexual propensities . . . for several months in succession," he maintained, and "health does not absolutely require that there should ever be an emission of semen from puberty to death." Graham thought adultery and promiscuity only slightly less dangerous than masturbation because imagination was similarly "wrought up and presents lewd and exciting images." He condoned marital sex, by contrast, precisely because he thought it the dullest form of sexuality, least charged with anticipation and fantasy, least exciting to the fragile system of human energy on which precarious health and effort depended. Husband and wife "become accustomed to each other's body, and their parts no longer excite an impure imagination," he explained. Therefore their "sexual intercourse is the result of the more natural and instinctive excitements of the organs themselves"—which fortunately happens "very seldom." This quenching of libido by marital boredom was so essential to human health and survival, he taught, that monogamy was "founded in the constitutional nature of things."[18]

Both Graham and Todd seem to have found refuge in marriage from a masturbatory libido undermining effort and precluding True Manhood. In opposite ways, their marriages demonstrated how much True Men needed True Women.

"Mr. and Mrs. Todd," according to their son, always addressed each other by these "formal and distant" titles. "Demonstrations of affection" were "very few"; and "their many and different duties" did not "permit them to enjoy much of each other's society." Yet the younger Todd thought his mother a "wonderful woman" upon whom his father was "very dependent for his success." She "cheerfully sacrificed great beauty, brilliant powers of mind, and unusual social gifts, to the . . . work of helping forward her husband's success, keeping herself in the background, and toiling day and night the servant to all." Dr. Todd himself extolled her as "swallowed up in my success" and willing to "wear out that others might profit by my labors."

Mrs. Graham, by contrast, rejected her husband's doctrines and undermined his resolve by spreading their table with exciting foods. Unmanned at home—by female libido?—Sylvester Graham suffered a nervous breakdown and forfeited leadership of a swelling health movement that swept on without him. Backsliding to meat and whiskey in a final desperate effort to save his failing health, he died memorialized only by the "Graham crackers" descended from his coarse brown bread.

John Todd exemplified personal costs far more widely inflicted by self-making. "Pursuits of ambition," he confessed on one occasion, "are a succession of jealous disquietudes, of corroding fears, of high hopes, of restless desires, and of bitter disappointments." His frenetic effort alternated with illness and "nervous exhaustion." Constantly complaining of tiredness and indolence, he experienced life as a constant struggle to generate effort. "I never rise in the morning," he despaired, "without feeling that I *cannot* do what I must during the day." In the idiom of True Manhood's masturbatory anxieties, he lamented that he could "never acquire or create that unconquerable, unquenchable fire which is so necessary to prevent life from running through the fingers."

Like other self-making men, Todd could let no misgiving show through the mask of confident affability he presented to a competitive world. An "inexhaustible store" of anecdotes, his son recalled, gave him such "immense power" in company that "whoever came off second-best, it was not Dr. Todd." Yet unknown to his "multitude of friends," he led a "secret inner life" of "melancholy pathos" and "turns of depression." Only "his family were familiar with them, and their letters from him were almost uniformly sad."

The pathos of True Men arose, as Alexis de Tocqueville saw, from their "habit of always considering themselves as standing alone." The self-making man's self-repressive egotism—both taught and exemplified by the clerical prophets of American middle-class sexuality—"separates his contemporaries from him," as Tocqueville put it. "It throws him back upon himself alone, and threatens in the end to confine him entirely within the solitude of his own heart."[19]

Sharpening sexual politics exposed deep linkages among gender, sexuality, and capital's primitive accumulation of human effort. Dr. Todd lived to see True Men's deepest fears excited by "strong minded women, who clamor and disgust their sex and ours in demanding 'women's rights.'" Strong-minded women—belying True Genderhood's humanity-wrenching extremities of "feminine" altruistic dependence and "masculine" egoistic mastery—did more than shake the male prop of True Womanhood. These "moral Camillas," by confusing male "head" and female "heart," stirred up True Men's lurking fears of the feminine humanity they had to repress in themselves. The notorious Amelia Bloomer, claiming women's right to wear pants, frightened Dr. Todd by implying the corollary that "*men* have a natural right to wear petticoats, dress with low necks, short sleeves, wear pink slippers with paper soles."[20]

Fears of "effeminacy" fed the phobia against male masturbation, which masked another phobia so deep that it was almost repressed from public consciousness. Sylvester Graham violated taboo most egregiously by charging that many schoolboys and college students were not only masturbating but going "to the still more loathsome and criminal extent of an unnatural commerce with each other!"

Male homosexuality, when it could not be ignored, stirred shaky True Manhood into horrified denial. John C. Calhoun refused to see a friend, "nor do I wish to do so," who appealed to him when "blasted forever" by exposure of "the odious habit." By letter, as the Carolina statesman assured his mother-in-law, he advised the sodomite "to leave the country, and fly to some remote part; to give up all ideas of happiness in this life, and, by a life of contrition, to make his peace with heaven." This was "the first instance of that crime ever heard of in this part of the world," Calhoun insisted, assuming that his erstwhile friend fell into it "while a sailor in the West Indies." For weeks he could not "force it out of my mind."[21]

Compulsive denial of male homosexuality was institutionalized when the distinguished jurist Edward Livingston omitted from his model penal code for Louisiana "another species of offence" that could not even be named without inflicting "the most disgusting images" and "a lasting wound" on the public. "Although it certainly prevailed among most of the ancient nations, and is said to be frequently committed in some of the modern," he declared, it "cannot operate here" because of "the repugnance, disgust, and even horror, which the very idea inspires." Bringing a single offender to trial, he feared "would do more injury to the morals of the people than the secret, and therefore always uncertain, commission of the offense."[22]

Strong-minded women increasingly agitated male gender anxieties as the century wore on. While a historic proliferation of whiskers and beards protected True Men from suspicion of effeminacy or exposure of weakness, Dr. Todd broadcast male alarm over *Serpents in the Dove's Nest*. Most threatened by female libido escaping its biological destiny, he could only flail blindly at the female "rebellion" of contraception and the "direct war against human society" of abortion.[23]

As the Reverend Sylvester Graham had learned, another marginal profession was better equipped than the old-fashioned clergy to cope with libido. The market's spreading faith in human mastery through science enabled rising doctors to challenge the declining clergy's tutelary monopoly. But orthodox medicine, still ignorant of infection, antisepsis, and anesthesia, could not produce the scientific results to establish its authority. Its "heroic" bleedings and purgatives probably killed more patients than they cured.

Self-making doctors bolstered their credibility by medicalizing all of life. Weaving speculative physiological models to make sense of baffling somatic ills, they inevitably patterned medical mythology to the bourgeoisie's more treatable ills of self and society. The father of American heroic medicine, Philadelphia's Revolutionary patriot/physician Benjamin Rush, sought to make it "as much the business of a physician as it is now of a divine to reclaim mankind from vice." As disciples interpreted his teachings at the country's leading medical school, "disease is a habit of wrong action," and "all habits of injurious tendency are diseases."

Dr. Rush drew from his self-making experience a new emphasis on the nervous system as moral/somatic nexus. Driven by guilt over adultery into Moderate-Light rebirth and "a life of constant labor and self-denial," he ascribed most disease to idleness and instinctual appetites. While heroically purging the viscera of inflammation, he prescribed heroic moral discipline for the ganglia.

To test the therapeutic limits of nervous/moral discipline, Rush specialized in treating the insane through such barbaric inventions as his totally immobilizing "tranquilizer" chair. Experimenting on his own children, he preached to parents that a day or two of solitary confinement would internalize self-control through guilt-driven conscience. His favorite son, who in childhood "begged me to flog him in preference to confining him," was an apparent casualty of this paradigmatic middle-class character formation. Turning anger on guilty self, John Rush spent adulthood in his father's ward for the insane.

Meanwhile Dr. Rush provided the medical rationale for a new institutional reformation of the poor and deviant through disciplinary workhouses, prisons, and asylums; and his new penology inspired Pennsylvania and other progressive states to build great solitary-confinement "penitentiaries" in the 1820s and 1830s. At Philadelphia's celebrated Eastern State Penitentiary, penitents were immured for years in silent isolation. Known by number rather than name and forbidden speech, visitors, and letters, they were masked in black hoods and shod in noiseless felt when taken from their cells for solitary exercise. Visitor Charles Dickens recoiled from "the immense amount of torture and agony" inflicted by "this dreadful punishment, prolonged for years," and thought "this slow and daily tampering with the mysteries of the brain to be immeasurably worse than any torture of the body." A rival "congregate" system of reformation was practiced at New York's Auburn Penitentiary, where prisoners worked in gangs under a rule of absolute silence enforced by summary flogging.

Fusing medicine, self-making, and Moderate Light, the father of this progressive penology was also the first major American critic of both alcohol and masturbation. Rush thought the "secret vice" the worst form of "inordinate sexual appetite." His cures for this "disease of both the body and the mind" included "constant employment in bodily labour," "close application of the mind to business," and "marriage; but where this is not practicable, the society of chaste and modest women."[24] Rush's moralistic emphasis on the nervous system made Philadelphia's vanguard medical establishment receptive to the Parisian focus on excited nerves as "the strongest support to sound morality."

Teetotaling doctors, preempting in Pennsylvania the usual clerical leadership of the temperance movement, employed Sylvester Graham, introduced him to the new medicine, and launched the popular-health movement of which he became the prophet. Two of them established in 1829 the first popular *Journal of Health,* preaching "temperance, pure air, exercise, and the subjection of the animal passions."

Self-making middle-class obsession with health made medicine a cultural battleground. While a host of upstarts—hydropaths, homeopaths, and patent-medicine impresarios—competed with "regular" physicians, a Vermont country doctor, Samuel Thomson, mobilized around folk herbalism a broad antinomian resistance to professional authority and its mechanistic assumptions. At the other end of the cultural spectrum, Sylvester Graham's popular health movement spawned a journal, Graham clubs in colleges, and Graham boarding houses where spartan diet, cold water, four A.M. calisthenics, and ten P.M. curfew honed urban young men to self-making effort.

The total self-control of ascetic health was a secular response to the same repressive imperatives that generated the Moderate Light to sustain middle-class effort generally. Arthur Tappan attested their affinity by frequenting the Grahamites' New York boarding house. The manager of Boston's boarding house was hired to install the Graham system at Oberlin, where evangelist Finney himself taught that reforming humanity meant "denying their appetites." Because Oberlin daringly admitted as many women as men, Finney was especially anxious for dietary restraint on "so fierce and overpowering a source of temptation" as the young male body.[25]

American medical orthodoxy, otherwise dependent on Europe for ideas, responded to competition by developing boldly innovative specialties—psychiatry, obstetrics/gynecology, and especially gynecological surgery—to treat the gender/sexual maladies of self-making. The *American Journal of Insanity* and a journal of obstetrics were the country's first specialized medical publications. The new medical specialties carried to crescendo an antierotic phobia that focused increasingly on female libido. With True Manhood in flight from the female incitement of sentimental fornication, self-making doctors purged True Womanhood—finally by surgical knife—of any sexuality beyond reproduction.

Specialists in "nervous disorders" (not yet calling themselves psychiatrists) arose amid alarm over an apparent epidemic of insanity. With New York and Massachusetts leading the way in the 1830s, states followed Dr. Rush's principles in establishing public insane asylums. These monumental therapeutic barracks removed the afflicted from everyday excitements and decisions to rural quiet and a discipline of military regularity. The doctors superintending them organized the first association of psychiatrists.

Contemporary impressions are our only clue to the incidence and etiology of ill-defined psychic maladies. Doctors treating the afflicted agreed that insanity, increasing "at a rate unparalleled in any former period," was "more prevalent here, than it is in other countries." Immersion in psychic misery provoked these first psychiatrists into the first searching analysis of the costs of self-making. With remarkable unanimity they agreed that the "constant and wearing anxiety of what we call *bettering* our condition" threatened American manhood with insanity. "The demon of unrest, the luckless offspring of ambition, haunts us all," said Dr. William Sweetser. More concretely Dr. Samuel Woodward ascribed male insanity to "overtrading, debt, bankruptcy, disappointed hopes."

Some of these pioneer psychiatrists blamed the self-making mythology of opportunity itself. "Persons even in humble life cherish hopes which can never be realized," said Dr. William Rockwell. Similarly Dr. Edward Jarvis argued that "where all are invited to join the strife," many are encouraged "to aim at that which they cannot reach." American schools, he charged, "led their pupils to form schemes . . . which their talents, or education, or habits of business, or station in the world, will not obtain for them." Dr. Pliny Earle even allowed himself to wonder "whether the condition of highest culture in society is worth the penalties which it costs."

With male "melancholia" shaking middle-class mythology, self-making psychiatrists hastened to reaffirm their orthodoxy by ascribing the rest of insanity mainly to sexuality. Males were frequently diagnosed as suffering "masturbatory insanity," in which the victim "passes from one degree of imbecility to another, till all the powers of the system, mental, physical, and moral, are blotted out forever." Female insanity, by contrast, was ascribed almost wholly to a hysteria rooted in libidinal emotionality.[26]

While tyro psychiatrists treated the ravages of self-making sexuality, obstetricians confined True Women's threatening libido to male-managed reproduction. For centuries women had coped with the pains and perils of childbirth by making it a sociable rite of female solidarity, with woman friends and relatives assisting an experienced midwife in cheering, distracting, and comfortably positioning the mother. New York midwives had to swear they would not reveal "any matter Appertaining to your Office in the presence of any Man."

Technology enabled male doctors to force their way into this jealously guarded female domain. Late in the eighteenth century, British-trained physicians gained access to parturient bourgeois women through the new obstetrical forceps, which greatly decreased the hazards of difficult births. Called in at first to assist midwives with complications, doctors gradually displaced them at urban middle-class births. Self-making doctors found they could build up practices by delivering babies, thus ensuring, as Boston's Dr. Walter Channing acknowledged, "the permanency and security of all their other business."

Physicians protected this lucrative new bread-and-butter practice by refusing to train midwives in the new methods. Women's "feelings of sympathy are too powerful for the cool exercise of judgment" in medical emergencies, Dr. Channing opined; "they do not have the power of action, nor the active power of mind which is essential." During the four postwar boom years, 1815–1819, midwives listed in Philadelphia city directories dwindled from twenty-one to thirteen, while male obstetricians multiplied from twenty-three to forty-two; and five years later only six midwives were left. Although the male power of action that doctors derived from technological monopoly made birthing somewhat safer, it also medicalized the experience into a solemn and private ordeal of disease, hardly eased by the doctor's prim groping under sheets while communicating with his patient on delicate subjects through an elderly female intermediary.[27]

The father of American obstetrics, Rush's protégé Dr. William P. Dewees, articulated the repressive moralism of the medical profession in treatises on obstetrics, pediatrics, and *Diseases of Females*. This professor of midwifery at the University of Pennsylvania first treated parturient women with copious bloodletting. Advocating early toilet training for strictly disciplined children, he held up for emulation a baby who "had not worn a diaper since it was a month old." Parents mustn't let children lie late abed, he warned, for "warmth, the accumulation of urine and feces, and the exercise of the imagination, but too often leads to the precocious development of the sexual instinct."[28]

A new specialty, gynecology, emerged from obstetrics in the 1830s to target middle-class antieroticism on female sexual instinct. Gynecologists asserted male medical authority over a wide range of "female complaints" ascribed to "a sexual, a germiferous, gestative, and parturient creature." By the 1840s they were launching a campaign to make abortion illegal. Both male aggression against female libido and American medical innovation reached their apogee in the subspecialty of gynecological surgery, as pioneered by the Alabama country doctor J. Marion Sims.

A self-making sometime physician, sometime storekeeper, Sims was "ready, at any time and at any moment, to take up anything that held out an inducement of fortune, because I knew I could never make a fortune out of medicine." Especially irked by the chore of delivering babies, he confessed that "if there was anything I hated, it was investigating the organs of the female pelvis." Dr. Sims found his road to True Manhood when he adventurously discovered a facility with the surgical knife by operating successfully on a young woman's harelip. Hubris over this feat, perhaps reinforced by fascinated aversion, carried him to a technically similar malady of the vagina.

Surgeons had been unable to repair without infection the childbirth tearing of vesico-vaginal fistula, which tormented victims' lives with constant seepage of urine through the vagina. Sims solved this problem and self-made his success by scouring the countryside for afflicted slave women helpless to resist his experimental surgery. When owners demurred, he bought human guinea pigs for his backyard cabin/hospital. For four years, ignorant as yet of recently developed anesthesia, Dr. Sims cut and sutured without success on traumatized black women. One unsung heroine of scientific progress endured thirty operations. With patients unable to resist his demands, he introduced the knife to gynecological surgery and developed the speculum, which afforded doctors their first view of the vaginal interior. "I saw everything as no man had ever seen before," he said, "I felt like an explorer in medicine who first views a new and important territory." He finally conquered fistula by resorting to silver sutures.

Success carried Sims first to a flourishing practice in the state capital Montgomery, and by the 1850s to New York City. Backed by the medical and social establishment and a ten-thousand-dollar state grant, he established a Women's Hospital to treat poor women free. Thus he gained access to white patients on whom he perfected the techniques that brought fame and fat fees from bourgeois women. One Irish indigent matched her black Alabama sister by undergoing thirty operations in three years. On the suffering of the most defenseless women, Sims rose to the pinnacle of self-making success as an international celebrity surgeon and lion of high society.

As usual, True Manhood required True Womanhood. Mrs. Sims was "a true helpmeet," according to friends, and for her husband's "impulsive nature, her placid disposition was as essential as the flywheel in an engine." His gynecological surgery, condoning female sexuality only for reproduction, exposed True Genderhood's roots in male anxiety to master threatening female libido. Warning couples against " too frequent sexual indulgence," he refused to operate on one matron's painful affliction until she surrendered her objection to having more children. Her sacrifice was for naught. The operation "produced no good effect," as Sims had to admit, except that within a month she was pregnant again. This was success enough for Dr. Sims, who conceived his professional mission as surgical engineering to promote pregnancy. "It is only necessary to get the semen into the proper place at the proper time," he taught. Assuming male orgasm, he was implicitly hostile to female orgasm. "It makes no difference whether the copulative act be performed with great vigour and intense erethism, or whether it be done feebly, quickly and unsatisfactorily." Fortunately the uterus was of all organs, he thought, "the most subservient to the laws of physical exploration." He frankly "laid down the ideal of what a womb should be." Open to impregnation in its "normal conceptive state," it had—by contrast with "the sterile unimpregnated uterus"— a "gaping graceful form."

Constantly inventing such new instruments as a "uterine guillotine" to amputate the cervix, Sims eventually carried male aggression against female libido to a surgical climax in the deliberate sexual mayhem of clitoridectomy and female castration. American physicians, prescribing Sims's brutal procedures for a wide range of female complaints ascribed to libido, increasingly sentenced the middle-class woman's ovaries and/or clitoris to the surgical knife.[29]

Self-making doctors registered with peculiar sensitivity the linkage of gender and sexuality with race in middle-class anxiety. While Sims carved success from the bodies of black Alabama women, in nearby Mobile Dr. Josiah Nott was propounding a racist "science" of white superiority that was soon being elaborated by doctors North and South. The deepest middle-class phobias merged at midcentury, when student protest at the Harvard Medical School forced the faculty to back down from conditionally admitting three black men and a white woman—the blacks were to practice in Africa, while twelve-year practitioner Harriot Hunt was not to expect a degree.

Most obviously, black and female competition threatened the white male monopoly of a profession already fiercely competitive (three leading doctors of the day went insane over losing credit for anesthesia to a fourth). A faculty spokesman warned this Harvard class at entrance that the "success" of a "large practice" and "large income" had to be won in a field "always filled with eager and aspiring competitors." Self-making medical students saw their head start threatened if a Harvard degree were cheapened by the *"amalgamation of sexes and races."* Still more threateningly, the amalgamation of black men and strong-minded women stirred up the gender/sexual anxieties that True Womanhood and white racism barely quelled for True Men. Hunt complained publicly that the American Revolution gave freedom to the "white man only."

A boyhood encounter with strong-minded womanhood had prepared Dean Oliver Wendell Holmes to sympathize with the protesting students. Recalling his humiliation at not knowing the word *trite* as used by his brilliant schoolmate Margaret Fuller, he still smarted over "such a crushing discovery of her superiority." Fleeing smart women, Dr. Holmes married "the kindest, gentlest, and tenderest of women." A *"helpmate* the most useful, whose abilities seemed to have been arranged by happy foresight for the express purpose of supplying his wants," Mrs. Holmes "took care of him and gave him every day the fullest and freest chance to be always at his best, always able to do his work amid cheerful surroundings." Disclaiming "wit or literary or critical capacities," she was "an ideal wife."

True Women like Mrs. Holmes provided self-making men with "a place of quiet, and some quiet minds which the din of our public war never embroils," as the Reverend Horace Bushnell put the middle-class ideal. "God made woman to be a help for man, not to be a wrestler with him." Harriot Hunt was a particularly threatening wrestler because she confronted the deeper gender/sexual hostility behind medical students' fear of female competition. "If we could follow those young men into life," she commented bitterly, "and see them subjecting women to examinations too often unnecessary—could we penetrate their secret feelings, should we not find in some that female practitioners are needed?"[30]

Of course, bourgeois medical science did not—and cannot—penetrate the deep dynamics of human gender and libido. The scientific mythology that empowered the bourgeoisie to galvanize capitalist production implicitly denies a humanity inscrutable to its mechanistic assumptions. Although what happened in the well-curtained carnal bed is necessarily speculative, our only remote barometer of sexual activity confirms the erotic scarring indicated by cultural phobia and middle-class personal documents. Sampled rates of bridal pregnancy—which demographers have found to fluctuate with illegitimacy and premarital coitus—fell sharply, from 33 percent of first births during the last four decades of the eighteenth century to 23.7 percent for the first four decades of the nineteenth, and 12.6 percent in the next four decades. Human energy was capped and channeled to market production at its deepest springs in gender and libido.

The premarital sexuality of traditional culture seems to have trained the married for the contraceptive rigor of the demographic transition. Certainly many young women had long resorted to spermicides, sponges, douches, and menstrual cycles—usually misadvised by experts about the "safe" period—while many (most?) young men learned the self-manipulative (and masturbatory) constraint of coitus interruptus. Repressing this premarital sexuality, a self-making middle class pushed premarital contraceptive techniques to new extremes in marriage. Necessarily sexuality became more contrived, anxious, constrained. After midcentury the vulcanized rubber condom and diaphragm seem to have accelerated the industrial/urban stage of fertility decline, erotic privation, and staggering production.

Yet libidinal repression went far beyond demographic necessity and contraceptive contrivance. Capital conscripting human labor to productive manipulation of inert matter declared war on the vitality of both human and external nature. To a bourgeoisie leveling the wilderness, fighting off alcohol, fleeing dirt, and draping its carnivorous animality in ceremonial table manners, sexuality epitomized the uncontrolled nature they had to subdue. Between the hammer of demographic necessity and the anvil of capitalist discipline, human libido was wrought into anxious constraint. A middle-class society still fleeing its species-nature has yet to count the costs of this primitive accumulation of human energy.[31]

In the wake of the 1826 jubilee, as the competitive imperatives of another accelerating boom enforced bourgeois example and precept, middle-class culture crystallized in a new kind of collective repression. While struggling for effort on private battlegrounds of libido, self-making Northerners transformed themselves publicly by banding together to purge self and society of alcohol. Through "collective power," as Tocqueville perceived, temperance crusaders found "aid in resisting what is most intimate and personal to each man, his own inclinations." Through collective repression—arising periodically ever since against intoxicants, drugs, and the varied guises of sexuality—middle-class society disciplined recalcitrant inclinations to capitalist effort.

Alcohol was the obvious first target. Disrupting traditional drinking patterns, the market had by 1830 driven up estimated annual consumption of hard liquor to 9.5 gallons for every American over 14—plus 30.3 gallons of hard cider and other intoxicants to total 7.1 gallons of absolute alcohol. An epidemic of alcoholism precipitated a collective repression so powerful that consumption fell almost three-fourths in fifteen years. Radical shifts in drinking behavior registered the wrenching severity of capitalist transformation.

Traditionally Euro/Americans had esteemed "the good creature" as wholesome nutrition and washed down meals with apple cider (peach brandy in the South). Frequent drams in field or shop fortified them for bursts of heavy labor in cold or heat. Through alcoholic elixirs folk culture sanctioned—in settings that affirmed communal solidarity—the freest expressions of impulse, both aggressive and altruistic. Neighborhood sociability centered on taverns; and strong waters cheered funerals, ministerial ordinations, militia musters, elections, corn huskings, and house raisings. As long as elites could regulate taverns and punish drunkenness, gross intoxication and chronic alcoholics were infrequent.

But the market's competitive stress whetted appetites for its cheaper and stronger spirits, and rum consumption rose steadily around the colonial ports.

After the Revolution cut off this bargain by-product of the West Indian sugar boom, the commercial boom at the turn of the century caught up the even more potent whiskey that Scotch-Irish farmers distilled from ubiquitous American corn. Perfecting the technology of large-scale distilling, venturous capital flooded ever cheaper whiskey along the spreading channels of trade. The postwar boom brought it down to 25 cents a gallon, less by the drink than tea or coffee. Annual consumption—estimated below in gallons per person over fourteen—rose steadily with the rum trade until the Revolution and then took off from this high plateau into a historic national whiskey binge between 1790 and 1830.

Against this background the dramatic decline that accompanied the temperance movement between 1830 and 1845 registers a profound behavioral change.

	Hard Liquor	Cider	Absolute Alcohol, All Beverages
1710	3.8	34	5.1
1790	5.1	34	5.8
1830	9.5	27	7.1
1840	5.5	4	3.1
1845	3.7	0	1.8

As Americans drank more and harder liquor, they drank more compulsively in different settings. Moderate drams, which conditioned against intoxication, gave way to more frequent and more drunken communal binges. Men fell increasingly into solitary binges, followed by hangover and a week or month of remorseful sobriety until the next binge. Many solitary topers—especially, perhaps, young men of the best families—became hopeless alcoholics. Consumption estimates and family records lend credence to the temperance crusaders' warnings that America was "becoming a nation of drunkards." Most of the prominent families studied by historians, from business Tappans to clerical Beechers to presidential Adamses, seem to have had one or more victims.

Cross-culture studies ascribe this pattern of hard drinking to the anxiety of frustrated ambition. The successful, by contrast, drank wine, while rural cider (and later working-class beer) registered the contentment or resignation of the unambitious. The great American whiskey binge was fed primarily by the anxiety of self-making men.[32]

The psychodynamics are most evident in sons of successful fathers. When the national temperance crusade opened in the jubilee year, the country's two highest executive officials were suffering a remarkably similar anguish over their two oldest sons. While President Adams grieved over an alcoholic and an incipient suicide, Secretary Clay despaired of an alcoholic and a lunatic. Both fathers concentrated on a third boy the pressures for success that had broken their first- and second-born.

Like Charles Francis Adams, Henry Clay, Jr., was driven by an illustrious sire's insistence that "on you my hopes are chiefly centered." Sent to West Point under paternal injunction to devote himself *"steadily and constantly"* to his studies and "win the first honor if possible," he managed to graduate second. At his father's wish—trusting "not to my immature judgment, but to your knowledge and experience"—young Henry studied law under his father's supervision and established a modestly successful practice. Even modest success cost this dutiful son more than great effort. Paternal warnings—whether his life would be "happy or wretched depends mainly on yourself"—evoked self-making anxiety as well as self-making effort. "Like all young men of ambitious and aspiring temperaments," the junior Clay confessed, "the mere possibility of ill success keeps alive in me a thousand unnecessary and annoying fears." Containing his fears without resort to alcohol left him "so jealous and irritable in his temper," according to visitor Harriet Martineau, "that there is no living with him."[33]

Psychic disorders or opium addiction often cropped up along with alcoholism in self-making families. Opium and its derivative laudanum were widely disseminated by doctors' prescriptions and patent medicines to ease middle-class anxiety. Ebenezer Breed, who pioneered the Lynn shoe trade, spent his last years an opium addict in the local poorhouse. James K. Polk's father died with "his mind not being rite . . . under the influence of lodnam"; four of this driven politician's brothers died young (most or all alcoholic), one of them not long after "a spell of drinking" that "had like to a killed him"; and a sister's tantrums were so violent that relatives urged her husband "to lock her up and conquer her by force." The talented brood that grew up under the stern eye of temperance prophet Lyman Beecher evaded alcohol only at the cost of other maladies. Two sons went insane and committed suicide, three daughters took the water cure for nervous disorders, son Henry Ward suffered migraine headaches and a sensational adultery scandal, and daughter Harriet Beecher Stowe mourned an alcoholic son.[34]

Disrupting traditional behavior, the market revolution evoked collective repression by impelling the stressed into seeming epidemics of escapist addiction, insanity, suicide, and prostitution. As dislocated young men flocked to city boardinghouses and western clearings, imbalanced sex ratios, delayed marriage, and instinctual repression intensified the self-making anxiety that many could not sustain. With casualties mounting under sharpening competition, self-making Americans mobilized publicly for effortful survival, if not capitalist success. Through collective repression of alcohol, the middle class forged itself by conquering its "own inclinations."

Collective repression was set in motion by failure of elite repression. In response to an 1811 Presbyterian manifesto, the male clerics and notables of some two hundred northeastern communities (especially in New England) organized themselves into moral societies against a rising tide of profanity, Sabbath-breaking, and drunkenness. Reasserting the crumbling formal authority of Moderate-Light establishments by informing on offenders and upholding magistrates in stricter laws and enforcement, the moral societies revived traditional punishments for impiety to meet a growing secular threat: taverns and grog shops were multiplying out of official control, and magistrates' penalties no longer shamed multiplying topers into a penitence that restored deferential community.

Moral societies brought Puritan asceticism to a new pitch in the first concerted campaign against alcohol. Reformation fears of impulse, although long accommodated to traditional drinking in the rural New World, had flared up sporadically against alcohol around the commercializing ports. When the rum trade first disrupted Boston's deferential order in the early eighteenth century, the Reverend Cotton Mather organized a moral society against drunkards and the impious Hell-Fire Club. Even the Hell-Fire printer's apprentice Ben Franklin learned self-making temperance from the working-class demoralization of London's gin mills and the prudential prosperity of Philadelphia's Quakers. By the late eighteenth century Quakers were proscribing alcohol, and Methodists were imbibing Wesley's British anti-alcoholism although rejecting his rule of abstinence.

The moral societies fused the recharged Puritan asceticism of the Moderate Light with a more secular critique of alcohol. In Massachusetts, where genteel Unitarians scorned the sabbatarianism of orthodox notables, the warring elites could not unite on the comprehensive repression of Lyman Beecher's Connecticut Society for the Promotion of Good Morals. Instead their shared class fear of secular disorder drove them to find common ground in the first state Society for the Suppression of Intemperance.

Prominent in its ranks were physician-disciples of alcohol's main American critic, Dr. Benjamin Rush of the Quaker City. Condemning alcohol in secular terms as a quarantinable disease of body and society, he reached a popular audience with his broadside graphing beverages against a Moral Thermometer of "Health, Wealth." Water and milk registered the sunniest temperatures, with wine and beer ranked next for "Cheerfulness, Strength, and Nourishment, when taken only at meals, and in moderate quantities." Hard liquors, by contrast, descended the frigid degrees of vice (from idleness to suicide), disease (from "puking" to death), and punishment (from debt through black eyes, poorhouse, and jail to gallows). Dr. Rush advocated a special court of physicians and magistrates to commit drunkards—"more hurtful to society than most of the deranged patients of a common hospital would be if they were set at liberty"—to a disciplinary "Sober House."

As Rush's distinctions suggest, elite repression sanctioned the gentry's temperate drinking while repressing popular drinking. Emphasizing the economic costs of alcohol, the moral societies opposed tavern licenses, customary drinking at work, customary spirits on public occasions, and all drunkenness. The "grand healing measure," Massachusetts reformers preached, was for *"all hirers of labor, not to furnish ardent spirits to their laborers."*

But elite repression was overwhelmed during the postwar boom by a flood of cheap whiskey and democratic resentment. Moral societies had "almost wholly failed," the Reverend John Chester told one of the last survivors at Albany in 1821. When "armed with statutes and followed by officers," moral reform was too often seen as "intended to abridge the liberties and destroy the rights of the community." Chester concluded that "you can not coerce a free people that are jealous to fastidiousness of their rights." People would have to be persuaded.

Lyman Beecher laid down the new strategy in 1825. "Our Fathers could enforce morality by law, but the times are changed," argued his widely disseminated *Six Sermons on Intemperance,* "and unless we can regulate public sentiment, and secure morality in some other way, WE ARE UNDONE." As the only available substitute for elite repression, he recommended stirring up "A CORRECT AND EFFICIENT PUBLIC SENTIMENT." He had "lived to see that a new moral power must be applied by Sabbath-schools, revivals of religion, and Bible, tract, and missionary societies, before immoralities in a popular government can be replaced by law." Astutely the Moderate Light's bellwether proposed to radicalize and broaden the temperance movement as the secular cutting edge of cultural conquest. Declaring war on the elitist moderation of the Massachusetts temperance society, he preached that "THE DAILY USE OF ARDENT SPIRITS, IN ANY FORM, OR IN ANY DEGREE" was sinful.

Dr. Beecher's new banner—total abstinence from hard liquor—was soon unfurled at Boston orthodoxy's Brimstone Corner. In February 1826, shortly before he arrived to direct a sharpening orthodox offensive against Unitarian laxity, sixteen leading activists in missionary, Bible, and tract societies met at Park Street Church. Underscoring their differences with the Massachusetts Society for the Suppression of Intemperance, these Andover clerics and wealthy local businessmen (the Tappans contributed Boston brother John) announced themselves as the American Society for the Promotion of Temperance—soon renamed the American Temperance Society (ATS). "We have a new idea," they declared, "to induce *all temperate people to continue temperate* by practising total abstinence."

Their new idea met such a wide and desperate need that the ATS mushroomed overnight into the largest mass organization the country had known. Providentially the market revolution was fostering a new mode of social control, even as it undermined the old. By the late twenties, high-speed presses and mass organization were sweeping the collective repression of the Moderate-Light Second Awakening through a self-making northeastern populace. Endorsed by the Moderate-Light denominations, total-abstinence affiliates sprang up everywhere, spilling over from Presbygationalists to Methodists and Baptists, and from Northeast, with 77 percent of the societies (New England 38 percent, New York 34 percent), to South with 14 percent and West with 9 percent. Within five years twenty-two hundred local societies affiliated with the ATS. By 1833 a million members pledged total abstinence through more than six thousand local affiliates and statewide organizations in all but four states. The largest local society claimed a third of New York City's adults.

The ATS's Yankee founders capitalized on this surprisingly eager market by pushing to a new level the innovative techniques of the tract movement. They had taken up temperance, as a more focused tractarianism, when displaced from leadership of the American Tract Society by Arthur Tappan's twenty-five-thousand-dollar subsidy for a New York headquarters. Relying at first on the tractarian strategy of salvation through cheap print, the ATS achieved economies of high technology and scale by using the Tract Society's New York printer Daniel Fanshaw, who first introduced high-speed steam presses to American book publishing.

The Tract Society itself published more pamphlets on temperance than any other secular subject, thirteen in editions over a hundred thousand and totaling (by 1851) almost five million copies. Together these two great fountains of the Graphic Light led middle-class culture in largely preempting—against all competition except newspaper politics—the spreading perceptual realm of cheap print. Through a middle class defining itself in collective repression, capitalism forged its potent new medium of cross-class cultural hegemony.

Similarly the ATS's national network of agents, printing houses, and state and local affiliates blazed an organizational/marketing trail for the capitalist market to follow. Aggressively recruiting women, whom the moral societies shunned, the temperance movement generated much local energy from the sexual politics of True Women threatened or victimized by alcoholic menfolk. Special affiliates targeted such hard-to-reach market sectors as young men, apprentices, and congressmen.

The crusade against hard liquor was increasingly financed and led by a national coterie of zealous and wealthy businessmen. Most active was Edward Delavan of Albany, a repentant onetime wine merchant who made a fortune in hardware and retired at age thirty-four to become secretary of the state temperance society. His most spectacular coup was securing endorsements of abstinence from Presidents Madison, Adams, and Jackson. With Delavan's wealth subsidizing a free circulation of six hundred thousand, the New York society's Albany *Temperance Recorder* became the movement's national organ. Delavan/New York publications rose in two years to 1,303,000 and tripled in 1834 with purchase of the latest Napier presses. The hardware tycoon mailed one appeal to every household in the state, and his fellow activist, the "Old Patroon" Stephen Van Rensselaer, mailed a temperance broadside for display to each of the country's thousands of neighborhood post offices.

This torrent of print, far in advance of the market's advertising, first exploited new techniques for influencing a mass national audience beyond politics. Larger type, more open layout, simpler and more colloquial prose, and the first extensive wood-block illustrations limned reality unerringly to a middle-class market's sentimentality on the one hand and calculation on the other. While cautionary tales regaled female hearts with victimized True Women and starving babes the arguments addressed to male heads were strikingly secular, economic, and quantitative.

Americans were first habituated to statistics by the Benevolent Empire's bourgeois passion for enumerating souls saved, money raised, Bibles circulated, tracts printed, missionary years expended. Endlessly temperance reformers calculated the dollar costs of alcohol, including crime, pauperism, and lost labor. The $94,425,000 total of one tally would "buy up all the houses, lands, and slaves in the United States every five years."

But the clinching appeal was personal. Asking why one person succeeded when another with like advantages failed, Delavan's *Temperance Recorder* drove home the compelling point: "The enterprise of this country is so great, and competition so eager in every branch of business . . . that profit can only result from . . . *temperance.*"

Total abstinence mobilized a new kind of mass movement by assuaging self-making anxiety. Evangelical temperance focussed the millennial fervor of total self-purification on a manageable behavioral change certifying total self-control. The ATS pledge at first abjured only hard liquor. The aim was not to reform drunkards, explained national secretary Justin Edwards, but "to induce those that are now temperate to continue so." Society would be purified by heading off potential drunkards and mobilizing them "in a visible, organized union," said the Reverend Mr. Edwards. "Then, as all who are *intemperate* will soon be dead, the earth will be rid of an amazing evil." Instead of imposing elite repression on the lower classes, the Moderate-Light temperance crusade called on the swelling bourgeois/middle classes first to repress themselves—and then to impose their collective repression on the rest of society.[35]

The psychodynamics of personal transformation increasingly demanded a teetotal purification that radicalized and politicized collective repression. The ATS pledge came under attack for tacitly permitting the elite's wine drinking. Temperance leadership passed to teetotalers who felt most keenly the need for both personal and social discipline—self-making businessmen like Edward Delavan, commercial farmers and landlords like upstate New Yorker Gerrit Smith, and labor-exploiting mechanic/manufacturers. Teetotal pledges were demanded by young men's temperance societies, employer-fostered mechanic and apprentice societies, and the physician-led Pennsylvania state society. Alcohol was inherently poisonous and sinful, teetotalers argued. The least indulgence threatened fatal addiction and lured others into danger.

Spreading in the thirties, the teetotal spirit pressured churches to abandon Biblically sanctioned sacramental wine and expel dealers in any alcoholic beverage. Many a distiller and publican found another occupation, at least temporarily; and many an apple orchard was axed as cider consumption (per American over fourteen) plummeted from twenty-eight gallons in 1825 to fifteen in 1835 and four in 1840. Teetotalers took over the ATS in 1836 and, with Lyman Beecher's blessing, reorganized it as the American Temperance Union, requiring a teetotal pledge. By 1839 in New York state, a majority of the doctors and 85 percent of the ministers were claimed as subscribers.

With Moderate Light mobilizing millennial teetotalism against Demon Rum, demands for legal prohibition spread from lower New England. Campaigns against tavern licenses realigned Massachusetts politics in the thirties, escalating from towns to force election of county commissioners and culminating briefly in statewide prohibition. Taverns were driven by 1835 from all six southeastern counties and numerous towns in the other eight. The reformers' class bias became all too transparent when the 1838 legislature prohibited alcohol sales under fifteen gallons. Popular rebellion promptly empowered the hitherto feckless Democrats to repeal the obnoxious act, and statewide prohibition was temporarily discredited.

Yet teetotalism continued to spread with middle-class cultural transformation. Prohibitionism, falling back to local option in the forties to build a broader base for statewide purification, drove taverns from most of Massachusetts and expanded through Moderate-Light territory from Maine to the shores of Lake Michigan. Once Maine enacted total statewide prohibition in 1851, "Maine laws" swept the North. Within five years every free state restricted alcohol, and most adopted total prohibition. But estimated annual consumption of absolute alcohol (per American over fourteen) had already reached its nineteenth-century nadir, falling from 7.1 gallons in 1830 to 1.8 in 1845. Legal repression barely held the ground largely won by collective repression.[36]

As Moderate-Light teetotalism brought *Kulturkampf* to climax on countless local battlegrounds across the North, the struggle over prohibition politicized a deeper struggle of class and culture. Competitive necessity, reinforcing the economic and cultural pressures of a driven bourgeoisie, propelled many workers and farmers into middle-class mythology and collective repression. Pious employers banned drinking and hired only the sober. Churchgoing business elites rewarded churchgoing, teetotaling mechanics, clerks, and shopkeepers with the patronage that made success possible—advice, recommendation, contracts, customers, above all credit and capital. The churches became gatekeepers of opportunity, and the teetotal pledge a badge of deserving middle-class respectability.

Middle-class mythology powerfully reinforced economic imperatives—but more by phobic denigration of failure than by fable of success. The poor man got "little pity in his poverty" because businessmen demanding total effort from self and workers equated poverty with depravity. The psychodynamics of self-making self-discipline embittered bourgeois/middle-class resentment of traditional easygoing ways and instinctual freedom to sharpen demands for labor discipline. As never before the poor were stigmatized as lazy and vicious. Moderate-Light pundits insisted that *"vice* is almost the sole cause of pauperism." Moral indictment of the poor linked temperance reform with reform of poor relief in a wider collective repression that shamed a traditional folk into capitalist effort. Benevolence ought "not to bestow alms, but labour," said New York merchant/reformer John Pintard, "so that there shall be no pretext for idleness." By making poor relief contingent on collective repression, his pioneering Society for the Prevention of Pauperism in the City of New York sought "to expel the drones from society."

Welfare reform consigned paupers to society's ultimate degradation short of slavery, the local workhouse or poor farm. Benevolent morality made these institutions as grimly penal as possible, and inmates' cadavers were donated to medical schools. Ascribing opprobrious poverty mainly to alcohol, Lynn's teetotaling physicians refused to treat any family headed by a drinker. Widely experienced shame and disgrace, like that of Prophet Joseph Smith's clan, made collective repression a compelling alternative.[37]

The religious motivation and sincere benevolence of the vast missionary/benevolent enterprise and its bourgeois leadership can hardly be gainsaid. Neither, however, can their repressive cultural imperialism. Mobilized spiritually for self-repressive effort, Christian businessmen lavished market-frustrated human altruism on bringing to others the middle-class salvation of collective repression. Class needs for work discipline, social order, and cultural hegemony concentrated Moderate-Light altruism on temperance reform. Teetotalism blazed highest in manufacturing centers.

Antinomian democracy and the Old Adam resisted. At first only the most striving sector of the old working class, especially mechanic/manufacturers, embraced middle-class myth and ethic, some through indigenous working-class Methodism, some under middle-class Presbygational patronage. Collective repression did not penetrate the working class deeply, especially in the cities, until another downturn of the capitalist cycle in 1837 created mass desperation. The working-class Washingtonian movement, by contrast with middle-class temperance, organized drinkers fraternally to conquer addiction in the confessional style of Alcoholics Anonymous. Penetrating resistant classes, the temperance crusade was the public face of a pervasive new form of class domination. Through pious benevolence, bourgeois needs energized collective repression to shape a middle-class society.

The class/cultural dynamics of capitalist transformation centered in Arthur and Lewis Tappan, merchant-prince patrons of revivals, Bibles, tracts, free churches, purity, Grahamism, teetotalism, and abolition. To infuse business with Christian morality, they founded not only the New York *Journal of Commerce* but also the first national credit-rating agency, now Dun and Bradstreet, Inc. Recruiting local credit investigators from the Benevolent Empire's clerics and reformers, their Mercantile Agency evaluated individual creditworthiness for New York wholesalers and lenders. With growing efficiency the Mercantile Agency's make-or-break credit ratings enforced collective repression on aspiring venturers wherever the Empire City's potent capital reached.[38] Middle-class mythology and ethos take on flesh and blood in the credit reports of the Mercantile Agency. In awarding opportunity, American capitalism's Moderate-Light gatekeepers looked beyond birth, net worth, and liquidity to "character." Credit was denied "a rich man's son who . . . never was educated to economy" while recommended for "industrious young men, formerly clerks," the "careful small businessman," the man of "small capital, good character."

In certifying good character, the Tappans' credit reporters especially scrutinized the instinctual danger zones, alcohol and sexuality. Ambitions were routinely frustrated by such notations as "intemperate habits," "likes to drink too much," "leads a sporting life." Lenders were warned against all who "run after the women" or "got mixed up with a bad woman." Therefore marriage was essential to good credit—a young venturer "has been pretty wild but has recently married and will probably be more steady now." But even marriage had its career hazards, for in this era of erotic repression and demographic transition a "large and expensive family" or *"too many little Dutchmen"* impaired credit.[39]

The Moderate-Light benevolence that wrenched Old Adam into capitalist discipline is seen by liberal historiography as a great upsurge of humane "reform" seeking with boundless optimism to eradicate all human ills. Yet the only true reformers, insisted Finney himself, were those "honestly endeavoring to reform mankind" by "denying their appetites." By mystifying the relations of class, power, and culture, our historical mythology of consensual capitalism renders incomprehensible the massive resistance that rallied around Andrew Jackson. While collective repression pushed bourgeois hegemony across the North, antinomian democracy—and racist slavery—empowered the patriarchal Hero of New Orleans to bring *Kulturkampf* to a showdown in national politics.

Chapter 9

Politicians "Reapply Principles"

THE DECISIVE struggle over American destiny took shape in the semicentennial year, as the temperance movement rose to spearhead the market's cultural offensive while rising democracy threatened the political economy of capitalist development. At the 1826 jubilee of the Declaration of Independence, its aged co-authors proclaimed the clashing fears and hopes of a dividing republic. Clinging to life for the Fourth of July, John Adams, ninety, and Thomas Jefferson, eighty-three, poured their last energies into scrawled valedictories.

The sitting President's sire, refusing to retract or amplify, warned his Quincy neighbors that abuse could make the Declaration "the blackest" instead of "the brightest" page in history. Jefferson's still vibrant prose, by contrast, echoing at noon through the Capitol Rotunda, hailed imminent victory for "the rights of man." At last, he exulted, all eyes were opening to "the palpable truth, that the mass of mankind has not been born with saddles on their backs, nor a favored few, booted and spurred, ready to ride them, by the grace of God." A few hours later, across the Virginia hills at Monticello, the father of American democracy, whispering "Is it the Fourth?" peacefully surrendered to the people his tutelage of the republic. Before midnight, in distant Quincy, Adams too slipped away, murmuring—or muttering—"Thomas Jefferson survives." He was not altogether mistaken. Jefferson's democracy was already engulfing presidential politics, and for a generation to come, his name and ideals would be invoked more than any other founder's.[1]

Jefferson's deathbed faith overcame deep misgivings. Ascendant democracy was rallying behind a "dangerous man" of "terrible" passions and "little respect for constitutions." Yet despite alarm "at the prospect of seeing General Jackson President" in 1824, the sage of Monticello had reaffirmed his ultimate allegiance. Men divide naturally into two parties, "aristocrats and democrats," he wrote. On one side stood "those who fear and distrust the people, and wish to draw all powers from them into the hands of the higher classes"; on the other stood "those who identify themselves with the people, have confidence in them, cherish and consider them as the most honest & safe, altho' not the most wise depository of the public interests."[2]

Now, in the wake of Adams/Clay "bargain and corruption," Andrew Jackson stood even more palpably on the side of the people. On the other side stood an undisguised National Republicanism and an unconstrained capitalist state. While the Moderate Light consolidated the infrastructure projecting middle-class cultural hegemony across the North, the extravagant national developmentalism of a second Yankee Adams solidified the white South in cultural/political opposition. Amid jubilee vindicating the durability of republics, Americans were insensibly beginning to slide toward civil war.

Midway through the jubilee year, in December 1825, John Quincy Adams had summoned Congress to National Republicanism's millennial mission. Because "liberty is power," declared the new President, the republic's "gigantic growth" should make it proportionately "the most powerful nation upon earth." But power, he warned, carried the "sacred and indispensible duty" of using it for "ends of beneficence." Rejoicing that "the spirit of improvement is abroad upon the earth," he called on Congress to exercise its powers fully for "improvement of agriculture, commerce, and manufactures."

Roads and canals, said the President, were the improvements for which "unborn millions" would be most grateful. Submitting the army engineers' first surveys under the General Survey Act, he invited Congress to implement at last the Gallatin/Calhoun dream of a national transportation system by embarking on its first major segments, the Potomac canal to the Ohio and the national road from Washington to New Orleans. Once the national debt was paid, said the country's premier continentalist, "the swelling tide of wealth" from public land sales would provide "unfailing streams of improvement from the Atlantic to the Pacific Ocean." In addition he urged federal regulation of the state militias, a new Interior Department to handle multiplying federal responsibilities, and a bankruptcy law.

This manifesto of National Republicanism at full flood announced an enlarged vision of the capitalist state. With Yankee sensitivity to cultural infrastructure, Adams called for an "enlarged" conception of "internal improvement" to include "moral, political, intellectual improvement." Reciting the whole constitutional litany of federal powers as ample authority, he advocated "the cultivation and encouragement of the mechanic and of the elegant arts, the advancement of literature, and the progress of sciences, ornamental and profound." Specifically he recommended a national university, a naval academy, exploring expeditions, perfection of weights and measures, better patent protection for inventors, and a national astronomical observatory to rival the Old World's "lighthouses of the skies."

Unfurling the capitalist vision of a magnificent republic in the teeth of Jacksonian rebellion, the President added insult to menace. "It would be unworthy of a great and generous nation," he lectured the tax-hating rural majority, "to take a second thought" about the costs. And congressmen, he admonished, must not be "palsied by the will of our constituents." Privately Adams held even more shocking views of executive power. He believed that declaring war was "strictly an Executive act"; and he padded the federal budgets he proposed to Congress, on the ground that "if some superfluity be not given them to lop off, they will cut into the very flesh of the public necessities."

No American notable was less qualified by experience, conviction, and temperament to cope with surging democracy. From youthful repudiation of Federalism to postpresidential jeremiad against the slave power, this cosmopolitan diplomat displayed a characterological incapacity for popularity. By disdaining political advantage for principled duty, he stifled guilty yearnings for applause and excused in advance, perhaps, any failure to meet his father's daunting expectations.

While Adams acknowledged "the will of the people" as the source of government "and the happiness of the people the end," he insisted on a "confederated representative democracy" in which gentlemen defined the public happiness. Now that "the most discordant elements of public opinion" were "blended into harmony," he had congratulated a distracted citizenry at his inauguration, leadership could be restored "to talents and virtue alone." His opening manifesto to Congress defied his advisers' warnings. "The perilous experiment must be made," he said. "Let me make it with full deliberation, and be prepared for the consequences."

In the face of political chaos, the new President was determined to "break up the remnant of old party distinctions and bring the whole people together in sentiment as much as possible." Incredibly he attempted to abolish politics by uniting in his administration all the warring factional leaders. Designating Clay his successor at the State Department and sounding out Jackson to succeed Vice President Calhoun at War, he proposed to retain Crawford at the Treasury and Monroe's remaining appointees (originally Calhoun supporters) as Navy Secretary, Attorney General, and Postmaster General. When Crawford and Jackson spurned his quixotic overtures, he filled out his administration of all talents with a Pennsylvania New Schooler and an unusually flexible Virginian. To Clay's despair, the President ruled out political considerations in making lesser appointments as well and allowed Postmaster General John McLean to lavish his potent patronage on Jacksonians.[3]

Yet more than Adams's singularity arrayed the unalloyed capitalist vision against popular rebellion. Once again a galvanized market was exciting the enterprising with National Republican projects, and once again the class consensus of business elites persuaded the political gentry that insurgency had subsided. "We have put down the Military mania," said strategist Clay. "Reason and Mind have prevailed over phrenz[y] and idolatry." The President's manifesto "will be very popular," he predicted, and "I do not apprehend any serious opposition."[4]

Even Calhoun, putative organizer of the Jacksonian opposition, promised to support the administration so long as it adhered to the "enlightened system of measures" that "I had contributed in part to establish"—Bank, protective tariffs, and internal improvements. "I rejoice to think," he said, that "they will be considered as fixed in our system." They were "too popular to be attacked"; and "instead of opposition, the struggle appears to be who shall evince the greatest zeal in favor."

But the Carolinian was trying to ride two horses. By casting his lot with Jackson when his own presidential hopes collapsed, he both garnered the Vice Presidency and froze himself out of the Adams administration. While supporting the administration's developmental nationalism, he condemned its subversion of "the voice [of] the people." This "folly" doomed Adams at the outset, he was convinced, while Clay—"I pitty him"—"is not only fallen, but fallen under circumstances, as will make him miserable for life." Claiming primacy as both architect of National Republicanism and as foe of "the caucus, the choice of electors by State legislatures, the control of Juntos, or political leaders," Calhoun was confident of riding his chimerical democratic capitalism to power as Jackson's mentor and heir apparent.

Consequently the Vice President's letters and speeches harped at first on the theme that "I am with the people, and shall remain so." "It is with me an old course," he said. "The real, effective ascendancy of the people, has ever been my most sacred principle, from which I shall never depart; and to preserve which, I am ready to make any sacrifice." He even thought his anomalous position gave him "one great advantage." "Acting, as I always have, on fixed principles," he said ". . . I am never embarrassed in my course." His course was, of course, soon greatly embarrassed.

While blending democracy with developmental nationalism in speeches across South Carolina during the summer of 1825, Calhoun discovered that his old enemies, the "mad and wicked" Radicals, were blending "the Slave with the Indian question, in order, if possible, to consolidate the whole South." Across the Savannah, Radical Governor George M. Troup was consolidating planter leadership of land-hungry farmers by a crusade to seize Georgia's extensive Indian territory in defiance of federal treaty guarantees and Calhoun's paternalist "civilizing" policy. Still more disturbingly, the Vice President's Radical bête noire William Smith mobilized a stunning majority of South Carolina legislators behind resolutions denouncing protective tariffs and internal improvements on strict constructionist grounds.

President Adams's manifesto to Congress in December whipped this reaction into a "might[y] political revolution," as the Vice President soon realized. By the eve of the republic's fiftieth birthday, Calhoun thought its situation "more critical and perilous, than any I have ever seen." Never, he confided to his retired chief Monroe, had there been "so complete an anarchy." Every public figure was compelled to "reexamine his new position and reapply principles."

In fact, this paragon of fixed principles was being forced into the most radical reversal of principle in the history of American politics. Only by stealing the thunder of the mad and wicked Radicals could he hold his Carolina base and try to shape the Jackson movement. Already he was warning Virginians that the Adams administration threatened a "renewal of the Missouri question." A "reaction in favour of liberty," he insisted, must "come from the slave holding States, headed by Virginia." Virginia must "yield her prejudices" against Jackson, for he "is certainly the man."

Never again would Calhoun point the republic toward a most splendid future. No longer could he deplore his constituents' slaveholding and racist fears. Now this champion of sister republics took alarm at the mere suggestion of diplomatic recognition for independent black Haiti. "What would be our social relations with a Black minister at Washington?" he demanded. "Must he be received or excluded from our dinners, our dances and our parties, and must his daughters and sons participate in the society of our daughters and sons?" These considerations, he warned a confidant in the Adams Cabinet, "involve the peace and perhaps the union of this nation."[5]

A mighty political revolution—the first historic realignment of American politics—was indeed under way to expel Calhoun from national leadership. Around a white South uniting against developmental nationalism, the imperatives of two-party politics were marshaling the dissident farmers and workers of the North. Political realignment registered both the politicizing of slavery and the sectionalizing of culture. Subsistence folkways, while under heavy assault in the North, flourished little disturbed alongside the South's plantation slavery. As progressive capital's Moderate Light swept middle-class culture across the North, Adams's program became the whipping boy for politicians reapplying principles to democratic insurgency and slaveholder fears. Adolescent democracy—nursed through infancy by tobacco's decaying slavocracy—was falling into the arms of an aggressive cottonocracy. The slide toward civil war had begun; and democracy's slaveholding hero did not seem a likely candidate to arrest it.

In this political realignment, the "Old South" of Confederate rebellion was born. Hard times had sharpened the slaveholder alarm excited by the Missouri tocsin. While strict-constructionist/state-rights stridency masked proslavery fears in the Chesapeake tidewater, an unblushing defense of human bondage arose prophetically from the moss-hung swamps centering on Charleston harbor.

Nowhere was American slavery more brutal or more fabulously profitable than in the South Carolina lowcountry. Here slightly acculturated, Gullah-speaking Africans outnumbered whites as much as eight to one in healthy months, far more when planter families fled summer's often fatal miasma. Here blacks—more susceptible to malaria than whites admitted—were consigned to the mercies of swarming mosquitos and fevered overseers. While other American slaves multiplied gratifyingly enough to cushion hard times for planters of tobacco and upland cotton, the blacks who sweated rice from lowcountry muck had to be replenished by constant slave importations.

Consequently African tribal solidarity had persisted here for a century, stoking periodic outbursts of black violence and white brutality. When black rebels along the Stono murdered thirty whites, forty black lives were taken in retribution. Fifty blacks were hanged for another insurrectionary plot; still another set of conspirators were burned alive; and the visiting St. John de Crèvecoeur was horrified by the dying moans of a slave hung caged in a tree as flapping vultures pecked out his eyes and rended his flesh. This man had killed his overseer, and Crèvecoeur's planter hosts betrayed no Virginia squeamishness in defending slavery's barbarities by "the laws of self-preservation."[6]

A Charleston-centered life of dinner parties, balls, horse races, drinking, gambling, and dueling distanced lowcountry planters from their dangerous chattels. Describing a gifted Heyward as "lounging away his mornings" and "drinking away his afternoons," a lordly Manigault confessed that "Dissipation—or to speak more correctly—Idleness is the order of the day here." Abruptly in 1820 the Missouri crisis awakened this ruling class from self-indulgence to dread of insurrection. Any debates about slavery "threaten our safety," the governor warned. Promptly the legislature forbade manumissions, barred free blacks from entering the state, and prescribed severe punishment for circulating "incendiary" papers.

Slaveholder fears were soon realized. Inspired in part by the Missouri debates, a proud and charismatic free black carpenter, Denmark Vesey, recruited a formidable force of Charleston's black mechanics and trusted house slaves to ignite the overwhelmingly black countryside by seizing the city at midnight on June 17, 1822. At the last minute—with six black brigades poised for simultaneous assault on guardhouses, arsenals, and stables, with black cavalry organized to sweep the streets, with black assassins assigned to intercept fleeing whites in townhouse gardens—the plot was betrayed and the white militia mobilized. Vesey and thirty-four other blacks went to the gallows refusing to betray their fellow rebels, and thirty-seven more were banished from the state on suspicion, leaving the extent of the barely thwarted conspiracy to the imagination of panicked whites.

For a decade the black anger tapped by Denmark Vesey deepened white desperation. Lynch mobs roamed Charleston streets after an eighty-thousand-dollar fire on Christmas Eve 1825 inaugurated six months of almost nightly arson, culminating in a hundred-thousand-dollar conflagration. Three years later frightened authorities suppressed news of an insurrection scare at Georgetown and hanged so many suspects that a Charlestonian warned them "to save Negroes enough for the rice crop." Nat Turner's bloody Virginia uprising in 1831 brought white despair to a climax in the Carolina lowcountry. "Ah, why," brooded a Legare, "should such a happy state of things—a society so charming and so accomplished—be doomed to end so soon, and perhaps, so terribly!"[7]

With hard times simultaneously depriving many planter sons of a genteel inheritance, this decade of racial crisis nurtured a generation of proslavery firebrands. Heretofore most American slaveholders had maintained their claim to Revolutionary liberalism by deploring slavery as a necessary evil. Virginians burdened by redundant slaves had branded the "base" South Carolinians with "indelible disgrace" in 1804 for reviving that "most detestable of all iniquities," the foreign slave trade. This "horrid thirst for African blood," John Randolph railed, deserved "dreadful retribution."[8] Even many Carolinans had "exulted in what they termed the progress of liberal ideas" about bondage. "Slavery, in the abstract, I condemn and abhor," Charleston's William Drayton told Congress in 1828; and "all men would recoil with horror" from an African slave ship, "unless the vilest lust of lucre had steeled their hearts against every feeling of humanity."

By this time back in South Carolina, however, Denmark Vesey's plot had steeled white hearts against blacks as *"Jacobins," "anarchists,"* "the domestic enemy," "barbarians who would, IF THEY COULD, become the DESTROYERS of *our race.*" The arch-Jacobin was hardly cold in his grave before Charleston presses began emitting the first sustained American proslavery polemic—with opening salvos by Edwin Holland in 1822, the Reverends Frederick Dalcho and Richard Furman in 1823, Whitemarsh Seabrook in 1825, and Edward Brown in 1826. By the jubilee year of the Declaration of Independence, its liberal premises were being challenged on all the grounds an aggressive slavocracy would elaborate en route to civil war. A new orthodoxy insisted that human bondage was an ancient institution, "the step-ladder by which civilized countries have passed from barbarism to civilization," and Biblically certified as "lawful and right." Slavery, proclaimed Governor Stephen D. Miller in 1829, was *"not a national evil"* but "a *national benefit,"* about which Carolinians must not *"speak in a whisper, betray fear, or feign philanthropy."*

Yet liberalism was so endemic in this bourgeois slavocracy that even its polemical vanguard could not help feigning philanthropy. Holland conceded that "the curse" of slavery was "felt and acknowledged by every enlightened man in the Slave-holding States." The Reverends Dalcho and Furman both hoped that slaves could eventually be freed. Southerners "detested" slavery's "fatal effects," said Seabrook. "We abhor, we deplore it ourselves with all the pity of humanity." Even Brown, who considered equality "but another name for barbarism," thought slavery "alien to the feelings and principles of the human mind."

Thus proslavery southern whites revealed, at the onset of their Great Reaction, the ambivalence that would fuel their mounting stridency and drive them eventually into a bloody resolution. Every slaveholder confronted every day the dilemma described by Frederick Law Olmsted: "It is difficult to handle simply as property, a creature possessing human passions and human feelings, while, on the other hand, the absolute necessity of dealing with property as a thing, greatly embarrasses a man in any attempt to treat it as a person."

The Vesey conspiracy drove this dilemma home by demonstrating that "indulgent masters were the first sacrificed." Even hardened lowcountry planters were uncomfortable with the corollary that "great severity is the surest means of keeping slaves in due subjection" and found it difficult "to govern them on the only principle that can maintain slavery, the principle of fear." "God forbid that such a principle be adopted!" one pamphleteer exclaimed. "Humanity forbids it." The Charleston city council established a public treadmill in 1825 so that masters too squeamish to whip slaves adequately would, "without doing violence to their feelings, be able to break their idle habits."

The new proslavery orthodoxy was aimed primarily at southern white misgivings that could no longer be safely—or profitably—indulged. Polemicists warned that blacks were made dangerous by the "relaxed, sentimental, *covert abolitionist*," who "first begins by spoiling his slaves, next becomes severe." A prominent Beaufort planter confessed "scruples of conscience about slavery" because he "whips in a passion & half the time unjustly" out of fear his slaves would "gain ascendancy over him." The Reverend Furman designed his Biblical justification as "relief" for such "embarrassed" slaveholders. Even a lowcountry moderate was appalled by the "womanish qualms of conscience which we so often witness." Every planter, he exhorted, must "brace up his mind by every possible information on this subject."

Bracing up their minds against intractable blacks and a potentially antislavery national government, lowcountry planters could no longer tolerate any questioning of slavery. To quarantine slaves from dangerous ideas in the wake of the Vesey conspiracy, the South Carolina legislature ordered free black seamen jailed as long as their ships remained in Charleston harbor. When Great Britain protested this law as violating treaty-guaranteed rights of its seafaring citizens, leading lowcountry planters formed a South Carolina Association to insist on enforcement. Auxiliary societies throughout the lowcountry saw to rigid enforcement of the Black Codes, and the Association's Charleston annual meeting remained a great occasion of lowcountry life until the Civil War.

When the black seamen law was ruled unconstitutional by the federal Attorney General and a South Carolina justice of the federal Supreme Court—because the Constitution made federal treaties the "supreme law of the land"—the state first took the road to nullification by defiantly continuing to imprison black seamen. The duty "to guard against insubordination or insurrection . . . is paramount to all *laws,* all *treaties,* all *constitutions,*" declared the state senate. "It arises from the supreme and permanent law of . . . self-preservation, and will never, by this state, be renounced, compromised, controlled, or participated with any power whatever."

In launching the proslavery polemic, the Reverand Dalcho had suggested that if the free states would buy out plantations and send the slaves to Africa, few planters "would hesitate one moment, to get rid of both, even at something below their value." Yet when Ohio proposed such a plan in 1824, South Carolina minds had been braced up to reject it out of hand. Any discussion did "more harm than good" by stirring up "commotions and disturbance," said a legislative committee; and the governor recommended "a firm determination to resist, at the threshold, every invasion of our domestic tranquility."

The lowcountry's slaveholder alarm fused with antitariff bitterness in the upcountry, where slaves were fewer, planters harder hit by depression, and farmers phobic about taxes. Amid general conflict over National Republican bounties, southern producers for a free world market clamored against import duties, while northern producers for a protected internal market clamored to raise them. The hidden tax of higher prices for protected articles was indeed forcing southern consumers to subsidize northern industrial growth. Without protective duties, accounting for an estimated three-fourths of textile manufacturing's value-added, half the New England industrial sector would have gone bankrupt.[10] Even Carolina nationalists succumbed to the post-panic politics of sectional calculation, barely enabling southerners to defeat the Baldwin bill of 1820. But with congressional reapportionment registering faster northern population growth, this decision was reversed by the tariff increases of 1824.

Southern fears were promptly confirmed during the jubilee year 1825–1826 by a sectional divergence of the boom-bust cycle. As the reviving profits of a protected internal market launched the North into another gathering boom, the hazards of a free world market mired the South deeper in depression. Cotton prices, which had recovered from 11¢ a pound in 1823 to 19¢ in 1825, collapsed again to 12¢ in 1826, bottomed a year later at 9¢, and did not rise above 10¢ until 1833.[11]

Yet more than economics focused southern alarm on protectionism. The economic crisis was also a political crisis. A Yankee President simultaneously inflating federal power to ends of beneficence plunged planter capitalists into forebodings of abolition. In a liberal republic they no longer controlled, imperiled degraders of slaves discovered a special horror of political slavery. Fleeing the spectres of Denmark Vesey and John Quincy Adams, planters awoke to their political dependence on the farmer majority.

They awoke just in time, for contradictions between planter capitalism and farmer democracy were sharpening dangerously. Slave labor had pushed farmers off the most fertile acreage when plantations surged into the southeastern upcountry during the commercial boom and then across the Gulf plains during the postwar boom. Farmers were affronted both by slavery and by planter hauteur, extravagance, and materialism. Hard times in the 1820s swelled the democratic impulse;

and beyond the Atlantic seaboard, farmer democracy wreaked havoc on a vulnerable planter elite's banks, courts, and land speculations.

With planters struggling for leadership of a dividing white South in the mid-1820s, manifest sectional unfairness made the tariff issue ideal for drawing antitax farmers into a white political rapprochement ensuring black slavery. To the same end planters all across the South had to embrace (often unhappily) the popular enthusiasm for Andrew Jackson. But simple antitariff Jacksonism was not enough to maintain planter hegemony. Planter regimes succumbed to insurgency in the Southwest and were pushed to extremes to maintain themselves in the old southeastern plantation regions where slaves were most numerous and constitutions buttressed an aristocratic politics.

The Virginia gentry's Old Republican polemic grew shrill in diverting farmer resentment from local oligarchy to national developmentalism. Even so it failed to stave off popular demand for democratic reform. An endangered ruling class saved itself in the constitutional convention of 1829 only by mustering its entire galaxy of stars, from ex-Presidents Madison and Monroe to future President John Tyler, from Chief Justice Marshall to Randolph of Roanoke. Blocking universal suffrage—that "*ignis fatuus* of French politics and French irreligion"—and other substantial reforms, they saved Virginia from rule by the "potboilers of the towns" and "the peasantry of the West."[12]

South Carolina, where slavery was most pervasive, was harangued toward nullifying frenzy. Deserting Calhoun's nationalism, the legislature passed William Smith's Radical strict-constructionist resolutions in late 1825 and in 1826 sent Smith himself to confront the presiding Vice President in the Senate. There, to Smith's consternation, a chastened Calhoun "treated me with so much kindness and consideration that I could not hate him as I wished to do." Soon the country's archnationalist would be secretly elaborating against tariffs the radical new antinationalism of nullification.[13]

A harder pressed Georgia gentry whipped farmer hunger for Indian lands into defiance of federal authority. Georgia's Radical planter faction had been driven from power in the panic year 1819 by farmers backing Indian fighter John Clark in conflicts over banks and debtor relief. In a close vote of the 1823 legislature, George M. Troup rewon the governorship for Radicals by advocating aggressive expropriation of Indian lands. But the Clarkites threatened this planter comeback by getting the gubernatorial election transferred to the voters and supporting Jackson for President against the Radical native son Crawford. Governor Troup won reelection and consolidated Radical hegemony by defying federal treaty guarantees to the Georgia Indians.

Back in 1802, when Georgia surrendered its claim to the Gulf Southwest, the federal government promised to extinguish as soon as possible the Indians' claims to much of the state's remaining territory. Repeated federal treaties had extorted large tracts as fast as white settlement advanced, pushing the Cherokees back to northwest Georgia and crowding the Creeks into their last valley towns against the Alabama boundary. By the 1820s both tribes were adamant against further cessions—the Creeks decreed death for any local chief assenting to such a treaty—and President Monroe's War Secretary Calhoun would not force them. In 1824 Governor Troup broke the impasse by finagling a cession of the Georgia Creeks' entire homeland from his half-breed Creek cousin William McIntosh and a few confederates—who were promptly assassinated by their outraged tribesmen—and this "treaty" was hustled through the Senate in the confusion of President Adams's inauguration.

When Adams suspended this cession upon learning of its circumstances, Governor Troup provoked a crisis by insisting on surveying it anyhow for free distribution by lottery. In anxious Cabinet deliberations, President Adams found "too much foundation" for Clay's opinion that the Indians "were destined to extinction" and "as a race, not worth preserving." Considering them "essentially inferior to the Anglo-Saxon race" and "not an improvable breed," the Secretary thought "their disappearance from the human family would be no great loss." With these views, it is not surprising that the administration backed down under Troup's challenge, coercing the Creeks into a second treaty that surrendered all but a face-saving sliver of the domain originally ceded by McIntosh.

Now the triumphant Troup pressed his advantage by insisting on the original McIntosh treaty, defiantly ordering his surveyors into the disputed sliver, and alerting the state militia "to repel any hostile invasion of the territory of this State" by federal forces. Again the federal government backed down, forcing the Creeks into another "treaty" surrendering the last acres of their Georgia homeland. Troup then turned his succsssful strategy for nullifying federal authority against the Cherokees; and in 1828 the Troupites and Clarkites offered rival slates of Jackson electors to the Georgia voters.[14]

Thus, throughout the South, the contradictions of black slavery and progressive northern capital forced planter capital into Jacksonian alliance with the less threatening contradiction of white farmer democracy. This class reality has long been shrouded in the moonlight-and-magnolia haze of a mythical planter aristocracy. Actually, across most of the South, planters were a small minority, undistinguished in pedigree, fiercely entrepreneurial rather than seigneurial in values and style, and politically vulnerable to a precapitalist farmer majority. Not one in a hundred white southern families could claim planter status by the conventional standard of owning twenty or more slaves. At the peculiar institution's apogee in 1860, only 19 percent of the southern people belonged to families owning any human property, while 42 percent were free nonslaveholders, and 37 percent were enslaved. And most of the slaveholding minority were small farmers, half owning five slaves or fewer and three-fourths fewer than ten.

Beyond the old seaboard areas of eroding gentility, the planter minority typically lived in ramshackle houses of logs or unpainted siding, sacrificed amenities to the single-minded accumulation of land and slaves, moved often for greater profit, and socialized, worshiped, and intermarried with farmer kin and neighbors. With slaveholders increasing 70 percent between 1830 and 1860, many were newly risen from farmer origins. Planters in Alabama's Black Belt were uneducated "money-getters," said Harriet Martineau, and "few but money-getting qualifications are to be looked for in them." Rather than dominating poor whites, this planter-capitalist minority could defend its brutal labor system only by yielding to the antidevelopmental democracy of the precapitalist farmer majority.[15]

Farmers in turn either yielded to slavery or fled it. Early in the century the southeastern cotton boom had set off a massive farmer exodus. While one lengthening caravan of emigrant wagons rolled north to the free soil of Ohio, Indiana, and Illinois, another rolled west to populate the Gulf plains thickly with farmers before many plantations overtook them. Once the cotton boom swept the Old Southwest, a stream of southwesterners joined southeasterners bound for free soil. This northward migration of southern folk, as population scholars have lately discovered, was exceeded only by the better known westward movement. In the antebellum Northwest, families from the slave states outnumbered northern settlers, who more often arrived as young males. Southerners made up 44 percent of Indiana's 1850 population as well as a majority of the 31 percent arriving by way of Ohio, while only 17 percent came from New York and Pennsylvania and 3 percent directly from New England.[16]

The southern subsistence culture's extension across the lower Northwest strengthened it at home. Evangelical farmers' flight to free soil both relieved demographic pressure and drew off the white South's most conscious opponents of slavery. Quaker/Baptist/Methodist/Presbyterian abolitionism waned as the most antinomian departed and the least antinomian were caught up in the advancing cotton boom.

Thus folk emigration facilitated a symbiotic relationship between the Old South's dual farm/plantation modes of production. Plantation capital did not impinge so harshly on farm folkways as progressive northern capital. Plantation stores, cotton gins, and skilled slave artisans supplied farmers with services and outlets for their marketable surplus, while farmers supplied the overseers, slave patrols, and political support that guaranteed the plantation labor system. The Old South of Confederate rebellion crystallized politically in the 1820s as farmers accommodated to slavery and planters accommodated to antidevelopmental, antitax democracy.

This tenuous accommodation—periodically shaken in flush times by planter elitism and planter desires for banks and tax-threatening transportation projects—was stabilized by an increasingly virulent white racism. With black degradation underwriting the formal equality of white farmers and planters, a southern fireater struck John Quincy Adams in 1844 as a "compound of wild democracy and iron bound slavery." Ten years later a Mississippi senator invited northerners to his state "to see the specimen of that equality spoken of by Jefferson in the Declaration of Independence." In the South as nowhere else, "all men are equal," said Albert G. Brown. "I mean of course, white men; negroes are not men, within the meaning of the Declaration."[17]

Religious accommodation undergirded political accommodation. The Second Awakening transformed southern evangelicalism, as antinomian farmers (some acquiring slaves and a few en route to planterhood) met an influx of arminian planters anxious over slave-driving materialism. The popular churches filled and a new southern orthodoxy developed because the southern sin of slavery was both too egregious for New-Light sensibilities and too profitable for exposure to Moderate-Light benevolence. Sin-obsessed southern whites learned to live with the intractable sin of slavery by compartmentalizing sin. Old-South orthodoxy focused all anxiety inward on a narrow range of personal sins affecting salvation for a world to come, while defining all other sins of this world as divine afflictions to be patiently borne. Only through the divine grace of personal salvation could sin be vanquished, and this was all that mattered.[18]

Where a secular Millennium of benevolently repressive production energized northern evangelicals for the here and now, slavery drove southern evangelicals into fatalist escapism. Increasingly the confident activism of a progressive capitalist culture challenged the contradictions of an otherworldly folk/slavery culture.

While straitened planter capital deferred to southern Jacksonian farmers, progressive capital's reinvigoration stirred up northeastern strife. Most striking to European observers was a newly strident assertion of equality. All whites insisted on being referred to as "gentlemen" or "ladies." Dress was no longer a clue to class. "Helps" resented being called servants, presumed to dine with their employers, and seemed either "impudent" or "independent" according to the observer's bias. "Strong, indeed, must be the love of equality in an English breast if it can survive a tour through the Union," concluded English author Frances Trollope after a stay in Cincinnati. Equality was not so palatable as it might seem in theory "when it presents itself in the shape of a hard, greasy paw, and is claimed in accents that breathe less of freedom than of onions and whiskey."[19]

Anxiety for equality welled up most flamboyantly in the Antimasonic excitement that spread with other agitations from New York's burnt-over district. The Ancient Order of Free and Accepted Masons, claiming descent from the builders of King Solomon's temple, had arisen in eighteenth-century London and spread with the market revolution to every considerable American town and many a trading village. New York state had almost 350 lodges by 1825, with some twenty thousand members, and five years later New England had 388.

Masonry's exclusivism, fraternity, and cosmopolitanism were irresistible to mobile self-makers. Once admitted by unanimous consent, "brothers" could claim mutual aid and fraternal welcome wherever they went. Members were ritually obligated to employ, do business with, and perhaps even vote for brothers "before any other person in the same circumstances."[20]

Moreover their ceremonial participation in cornerstone layings and other civic events asserted new lines of precedence in communities where traditional status was eroding. Behind the guarded doors of imposing Masonic halls, leading businessmen, professionals, and officeholders consolidated local elites through oath-bound secrecy, arcane rituals and regalia, and elaborate hierarchy of degrees and offices.

Masons themselves boasted that they were "POWERFUL." "In almost every place where power is important," wrote a Connecticut brother in 1825, the order united "men of rank, wealth, office, and talent." The distress and dislocations of the 1820s made such secretly exercised power especially suspect, for Masons typically dominated the bank directorates and public agencies most blamed. Female suspicions were deepened by husbands escaping domesticity for Masonry's secret male revels, and antinomian suspicions by its blandly ethical quasi-deism.[21]

In 1826 latent suspicion blazed into popular outrage around Batavia, New York, when an apostate Mason was presumably murdered for publishing the order's secret rituals. Stonecutter William Morgan disappeared forever after being harassed, jailed, and finally kidnapped by prominent Masons in concert with public officials. Obstruction of justice for the perpetrators by Masonic sheriffs, judges, jurors, and witnesses swelled local excitement into a national agitation that forced most lodges to disband. An Antimasonic political party surged up across the Northeast to wage a "struggle of republican equality against an odious aristocracy." Mobilizing the democratic impulse among those northerners least amenable to the slaveholding Jackson, Antimasons won Vermont and held the balance of power for some years in New York, Pennsylvania, and several New England states. In 1831 they introduced the presidential nominating convention to national politics.[23]

While Antimasonry agitated the rural North, class lines sharpened among a swelling urban populace. The old "walking city," where counting rooms, merchant townhouses, and mechanic home/workshops mingled in compact familiarity around the docks, fractured outward in a mosaic of class neighborhoods. Gentry mansions withdrew to exclusive enclaves bordering the commercial centers—Boston's Beacon Hill, New York's Greenwich Village, Philadelphia's Rittenhouse Square, and Baltimore's St. Charles Square. Soaring land values (up nearly 750 percent in Manhattan in thirty years) drove small tradesmen and mechanics out of homeownership into multifamily tenements and boardinghouses provided by speculative builders and landloards on the cheaper land of the urban periphery. Maritime workers clustered around New York shipyards at Corlear's Hook and textile workers around Philadelphia cotton mills at Manayunk. Laborers and blacks crowded into the slum cellars and garrets of South Philadelphia, East Baltimore, Boston's North End, and New York's Five Points.[23]

Conflict broke out all along the class lines shaping urban geography. In shopfront chapels and fields, "Mechanick Preachers" gave fleeting public expression to the anger of the unskilled and deskilled who staved off the hunger of winter layoffs, recession, or sickness by laboring up to 16 hours a day for perhaps two hundred dollars a year. At Potter Field on the jubilee Fourth of July, while celebrants elsewhere applauded the valedictories of Jefferson and Adams, Manhattan workers heard a gardener invoke divine wrath against "robbery by law." A "pretty set" were aping "King John the First," cried David Whitehead in the second year of the second John Adams, to intimidate workingmen with "threats of sedition and blasphemy" while wresting away their property and privileges.

Most urban labor was employed by master mechanics becoming capitalist bosses, and new class antagonisms were breaking through the mounting contradictions of mechanic tradition. Most masters were small operators. Few bossed more than a dozen workers, and only three had one hundred in Boston, New York, and Baltimore combined. Although compelled by hard times and sharpening competition to cut labor costs or go under, many still clung to the moral economy of mechanic tradition. Having "never read Adam Smith," an English immigrant complained, these small masters were "all alike" in resisting division of labor for increased production. "This, sir, is a free country," a drug maker told him. "We want no one person over another which would be the case if you divided the labor." Similarly a substantial master coachmaster condemned the competitive, cost-cutting producer of shoddy goods as "an Evil to the labouring part of Society" who forfeited "his reputation as a Mechanic" by denying his workers "a fair and honest price."[24]

Resenting genteel disparagement of manual labor,[25] moreover, many masters still wore leather aprons and found common ground with their workers against gentry rule and merchant interests. A new urban politics was forced on municipal gentries in the early twenties by "discord" among "the different classes of citizens." In New York and Philadelphia, the democratic/Jacksonian professions of Tammany/Old-School Democrats staved off the most radical eruptions until the late twenties. Meanwhile the oligarchies led by Brahmin Federalist Harrison Gray Otis in Boston and Republican merchant prince Samuel Smith in Baltimore were toppled by insurgent mechanics and small tradesmen protesting high taxes. While Baltimore dissidents blocked merchant/miller projects for expensive canals north to the Susquehanna granary of the flour trade, Boston's "Middling Interest" warred on superfluous offices and unfair assessments whereby "the richer classes are not proportionately taxed with those of small property."

The Boston gentry were further assailed for suppressing brothels, grog shops, and the import auction rooms that circumvented consignment merchants to insure rockbottom prices at the "Cheap Shops" of the poor. When the victorious Middling Interest went on to repeal a fire law prohibiting wooden buildings, so as to "aid the middling and poorer classes by reducing rents"—to say nothing of the building trades—Brahmins despaired at "the triumph of the revolutionary movement."

Insurgency culminated in a new Boston charter, replacing elections in town meeting with voting by wards. The "most respectable persons" had prevailed in town meetings because they "have been habituated to act together" and "the old leaders have learnt the art of giving a salutary impulse to the whole body when collected together." Now ward elections, escaping gentry management and intimidation, broadened class representation on the governing Board of Selectmen by allocating seats to neighborhoods, where workingmen could "step in with our leathern aprons on" and "choose a man of our own sentiments—one who we know." Boston, grieved Otis, "will be revolutionized to a certainty."

Yet the Middling Interest turned out to be animated by its own less than revolutionary "MONEY CONCERNS." Shunned by the poorest wards, it installed the compromising Brahmin Josiah Quincy as mayor; and this promoter of municipal efficiency for economic growth was presently succeeded by Otis himself. The similar middling insurgents who won Baltimore soon alienated a broader public by anti-Catholic bigotry and their own expensive transport projects to open western markets for mechanic manufactures. In 1824 their mayoral candidate was defeated two to one by carpenter/house builder Jacob Small, who was repeatedly reelected as "a sound, honest, practical, industrious and persevering mechanic" promising "the strictest economy."[26]

The middling politics of enterprising masters was doomed by working-class alarm over proletarian degradation, as the easygoing camaraderie of master/journeyman tradition was driven from more trades. While religious revival mustered for some the self-discipline of middle-class respectability, many more embraced militant unions and radical class politics.

Religion was most compelling to self-making masters like New York hatter Joseph Brewster, who extorted effort from both self and workers through Moderate-Light rebirth, temperance reform, and middle-class identity. Converted around 1822, he joined Arthur Tappan in broadcasting tracts and serving (along with six other prominent master mechanics) on the first board of the city temperance society. Total abstinence increased profits 25 percent, Brewster argued, through harder and more disciplined work. To inculcate these truths, the zealous hatter joined a master bookbinder in founding an Association for the Moral Improvement of Young Mechanics. The mechanic elite's General Society of Mechanics and Tradesmen, which had long toasted "Religion and Morality," inculcated similar truths in its Apprentices' School. The two hundred pupils taught each other through the "Lancastrian" system for mass-producing rote learning and paraded in celebration of the Erie Canal under a banner emblazoned with the Bible and the *Life of Franklin.*

Successful masters and ambitious journeymen, gravitating since the Great Revival to middle-class Presbyterian respectability, filled the free churches of Finneyite revival. But the rising Methodists best reflected indigenous working-class values and accommodations. Organized by and almost wholly composed of the laboring poor, Methodist societies introduced to the city the emotional style of revivalism developed in the interior. Urban stress converted the antinomian ecstasy of Methodist conversion into the arminian effort of capitalist discipline, and a "changed heart" was most clearly evidenced by the capitalist virtues. Spiritual intensity functioned to motivate and sustain the personal transformations required for survival under intensifying market relations.[27]

But the religious response to worker stress was drowned out by a historic explosion of working-class militancy. Spasmodic turnouts defied not only bosses but courts and legislatures that punished employee concert to raise wages while condoning employer concert to lower wages. As economic revival dried up the pool of desperate potential strikebreakers in the mid-1820s, New York stonecutters struck for higher wages, and in Boston nearly six hundred journeymen carpenters turned out for a ten-hour day. Soon anger over survival wages and dawn-to-dusk hours engulfed every major city and many smaller ones in turnouts by hatters, stonecutters, cotton mill workers, tailors, ship carpenters, house painters, riggers, hand loom weavers, cabinetmakers, and laborers. With escape from wage dependence fading, deskilled journeymen in many crafts rejected traditional leadership by barring masters from associations that began to be called unions. As a growing proletariat discovered itself in these struggles, the modern labor movement was born.

Only sporadically successful, these pioneers of capitalist class struggle relied on intimidation backed by public opinion to enforce traditional notions of moral economy. A thousand dock workers, white and black, shut down the port of New York by parading the streets to the chant "Leave off work." The police had no sooner dispersed this menacing demonstration than social order was further shaken by the first all-woman strike. Tailoresses hired cheap to undercut male wages in "slopwork" production turned out against a further reduction. Editorial exclamations of "What next?" were answered in 1828 by a violent weavers' strike for wages. Nonstrikers had their fabrics destroyed, and the biggest employer was assaulted following a crudely lettered warning from "The Black Cat" to "either Quit the Business Or else pay the price you ought to for if you dont you will be fixed."[28]

Working-class anger radicalized the mechanic tradition of anticlericalism, democratic militancy, and use-value pride enunciated by Thomas Paine and kept alive by Philadelphia's Old School. A vigorous free-thought movement mobilized militant resistance to the bourgeois cultural imperialism of the Moderate Light, spawning newspapers in both New York and Philadelphia, along with debating societies, Universalist churches, weekly lectures attracting hundreds, celebrations of Paine's birthday, a New York Temple of Arts, and schools conducted on the progressive principles of Swiss educator Pestalozzi. In this "movement culture" middle-class dismay at the decay of communal values found common ground with self-taught mechanic/intellectuals for a radical critique of capitalist exploitation.

Native radicalism was sharpened by immigrants and ideas from the British core of the market. The anticapitalist communitarianism of the maverick Scottish manufacturer Robert Owen, long touted by William Duane's *Aurora,* impelled middle-class malcontents into organizing short-lived rural communes imitating Owen's model of voluntary communism at New Harmony, Indiana.

This anticlerical communalism, as voiced by a doctor falling back on his rural Quaker origins, arose from antinomian dismay that "labour is cheated of its true reward" and "men's interests are now opposed to each other, in such a manner that only a little sympathy can exist." Complaining that capitalist property made selfishness "the root of all national vices," Dr. Cornelius Blatchly advocated redistribution of every person's property at death. An alternative scheme for ensuring equality by rearing all children from infancy in state boarding schools was touted by New York's most notorious free thinkers, flamboyant feminist Frances Wright and Robert Dale Owen, son of the Scottish reformer.[29]

Working-class radicals were more inspired by the labor theory of value that the elder Owen and British laborites derived from economist David Ricardo to explain capitalist exploitation. In 1826 Langton Byllesby, a printer who worked for wages in New York's largest shop after failing as a master, drew out the radical implications of Ricardo's theory for *The Sources and Effects of Unequal Wealth.* Defining wealth as "only an excess of the Products of Labour," he asked why the "products of labour belong to almost any other than the producer, who generally obtains from the application of his power no more than a bare subsistence?" Through money and private property, this journeyman charged, capitalists had destroyed fair exchange and plunged the producing majority into "resourceless distress, and intense misery."

Byllesby scorned the communalist effort "to show how a more agreeable condition of mankind might exist, without enlarging on the intolerable nature of the prevailing one." Moral appeals were useless. "History does not furnish an instance," he insisted, "wherein the depository of power voluntarily abrogated its prerogatives." Workers had to unite in defending themselves. Byllesby advocated producer cooperatives conducting exchange through labor notes graduated in worker hours.[30]

The labor theory of value galvanized working-class militancy. When six hundred Philadelphia carpenters struck for the ten-hour day in 1827, British-born shoemaker/socialist William Heighton inspired an unprecedented upsurge of unionism in many trades by preaching that "capitalists" or "non-producers" were robbing laboring "producers" of the "full product of their labor." Establishing the *Mechanics' Free Press,* he provided both intellectual and organizational leadership for a Mechanics' Free Library, the world's first citywide labor federation, and an independent Workingman's Party to force radical working-class demands into politics.[31]

The contagion spread to New York in 1829, when machinist Thomas Skidmore inspired demonstrators for the ten-hour day to organize a Workingman's Party. "As long as property is . . . so enormously unequal," he preached, ". . . those who possess it *will* live on the labor of others." Scorning "the cause of a Clay or a Jackson," Skidmore's *The Rights of Man to Property!* exhorted the poor to force an equal division of property and inheritance through a democratized political process. In his patriarchal utopia of free and independent producers, there would be "no lenders, no borrowers; no landlords, no tenants; no masters, no journeymen; no Wealth, no Want."

For a brief radical moment, Workeyism offered the demoralized poor enough hope to rally thousands of New Yorkers behind Skidmore's call for "a civil revolution" that would eventually assure "every human being AN EQUAL AMOUNT OF PROPERTY ON ARRIVING AT THE AGE OF MATURITY, and previous thereto, EQUAL FOOD, CLOTHING, AND INSTRUCTION AT THE PUBLIC EXPENSE." Workey candidates almost upset Tammany by promising, as a start, to abolish all banks and chartered monopolies, which Skidmore targeted as prime agencies of capitalist expropriation.[32]

A wildfire of strikes and Workingmen's Associations swept through dozens of northeastern towns, meeting in long-stressed lower New England a backfire of rural Workingmen's Associations spreading from the mortgage-ridden Berkshire hills. Workingmen fostered unions, strikes for wages and the ten-hour day, citywide labor federations, workingmen's political parties, and a score of labor newspapers edited by such self-taught mechanic/intellectuals as Philadelphia's shoemaker Heighton and printer George Henry Evans of the New York *Working Man's Advocate.*

Workingmen's parties reached beyond traditional worker concerns—mechanic liens, imprisonment for debt, convict labor, the auction system, militia duty—for more fundamental remedies to save the republican promise of patriarchal equality. Led by middling mechanics fearful of slipping into the ignominious penury of the unskilled urban majority, Workeys felt keenly that "the laboring classes" and "the worth and respectability of *manual labor*" were "sinking in the scale of public estimation." What they most often demanded was free and equal public schools to give their children a better chance. Most often denounced were the "chartered monopolies" that enriched a favored few while disrupting honest industry and flooding society with the "rag money" paid by cheating bosses.

But middle-class alarm enabled mechanic/manufacturers to seize the New York party, and workingmen's parties elsewhere soon found—with Democrats co-opting their rhetoric and leaders while satisfying a few demands—that the American two-party system made an independent radical politics almost impossible to sustain. Instead class anger flowed into radicalizing both Democratic politics and a more militant unionism that crested in the mid-1830s.[33]

Organized resistance came more slowly to the textile mills where the unskilled were first disciplined en masse to the dehumanizing monotony of tending relentless machinery. Mill owners appropriated the patriarchal relations of rural labor to undercut worker resistance. Fathers contracting the labor of large families supervised their wives and children in the mills. Nevertheless worker resentment soon generated enough sabotage and arson to dictate fireproof stone construction of new mills.

Mill worker resistance first reached a critical level beside Rhode Island's Pawtucket Falls, where the first American factory and five others had grown up amid a flourishing culture of small mechanic enterprises. In 1824 mechanic sympathy enabled striking mill workers to defeat a concerted wage rollback. Nor was class resentment quelled by the employers' cultural counterattack through revivals, Sunday schools, and temperance societies. Collectively in 1830 Pawtucket workers erected a town clock to enforce honest time on the cheating mill bells that extorted their labor.[34]

Meanwhile the ultimate rigors of proletarian exploitation were just becoming visible at Merrimack Falls north of Boston. Here old Federalist commercial wealth, shifting to the large-scale textile manufacturing pioneered at Waltham by Francis Cabot Lowell, raised a fitting monument to the architect of the modern factory. Channeling the torrential runoff from the White Mountains into a millrace that could drive thousands of spindles and looms, the Boston Associates erected along its banks a series of humming granite fortresses. The rural village of Chelmsford, with two hundred souls in 1822, was transformed by 1830 into the industrial city of Lowell with nearly seven thousand. While Lowell's population mushroomed during the next decade to twenty-one thousand, similar great factories rose at Chicopee, Holyoke, Lawrence, Manchester, and Saco.

The first American factory city, much touted as realizing the bourgeois dream of a benign industrial future, reproduced on a heroic scale the ingenious fusion of economic, social, and moral elements that its namesake had perfected at Waltham. This "Waltham system" was only one part heavy application of capital and technology for economies of specialization and scale. Equally important was discovery of rural young women as a new source of cheap, dependable, and tractable labor. With agrarian crisis and capitalist transformation delaying marriage, skewing sex ratios, and reducing houshold textile production, straitened Yankee farm families needed mill wages more than the domestic labor of unmarried daughters. Young farm women accumulating dowry for a more competitive marriage market, or helping pay off the family mortgage, or contributing to a brother's education or aged parents' support, could be hired much cheaper than men because the patriarchal conventions enforcing a dual labor market barred them from so many occupations. Traditionally subject to male authority, moreover, such women submitted to machine discipline with less complaint because they expected to leave the factory after a few years for marriage.

Total institutional control—the final element of the Waltham system—both disciplined labor and eased parental fears of trusting rural daughters to independent urban living. Respectable matrons maintained an intimidating atmosphere of moral uplift in the long rows of company boardinghouses facing the mills, where young women lived six or eight to a room. The graceful spires of the many company-endowed churches they were required to attend promised that the ancient verities would undergird the industrial future.

For some years the Waltham system yielded factory owners both enormous profits and a gratifying sense of ethical stewardship. But gradually the capitalist logic of lower wages, longer hours, and a faster pace at the ceaselessly clattering machines stripped illusion from a dual labor market's ruthless exploitation of women. As Lowell "mill girls" rebelled in the 1830s and 1840s, the capitalists turned increasingly to another defenseless class, the rising tide of peasant refugees from starving Ireland.[35]

Accelerating labor exploitation accelerated northern capital's demands on government. While self-interested factory owners and mechanic/manufacturers embroiled Congress in logrolling for higher tariffs, a school of dedicated publicists—Philadelphia's Mathew Carey, Baltimore's Daniel Raymond, and editor Hezekiah Niles of the *Weekly Register*—translated Henry Clay's American System into a sophisticated political economy of federally fostered national wealth. Southern opposition, having barely defeated the Baldwin tariff in 1820, was both weakened and made desperate by congressional reapportionment pursuant to the census of that year. With southern farmers migrating to free soil and foreign immigrants shunning slave soil, the North gained twenty House seats to the South's eleven.

In 1824 strengthened protectionists obtained a substantial increase in tariffs by promising commercial farmers both a bigger home market for foodstuffs and the tangible bounty of duties on hemp and raw wool. Thus they carried Clay's rapidly growing Ohio valley (including slaveholding Kentucky and Missouri) 29–0. But wool duties for farmers raised costs for manufacturers of woolen cloth; and Massachusetts, where woolens mills were growing fastest and commercial interests still resisted protection, voted 1–11 against the tariff of 1824.

Consequently protectionists launched a campaign to make their coalition irresistible by raising duties on both wool and woolens. In 1827 Daniel Webster registered the shift of Massachusetts merchant capital to industry by abandoning free trade to maneuver a Woolens Bill through the House of Representatives. This arrant logrolling stirred South Carolina's antiprotectionism into frenzy and left Vice President Calhoun no choice when the Senate divided evenly over the Woolens Bill. As presiding officer, the father of National Republican protectionism cast the deciding vote against further protection. Within months he was secretly perfecting the nullification doctrine broached by Carolina hotspurs in the furor over the Woolens Bill, while Massachusetts joined an unprecedented public campaign to push tariffs to unprecedented levels.

The logrolling genius of Clay's American System linked protectionism with internal improvements. Northwestern entrepreneurs backed high tariffs to provide revenue for roads and canals, while northeastern manufacturers supported transportation appropriations to sop up surplus revenues that might force tariff reductions. The Ohio valley states opened the constitutional floodgate in 1824 by voting unanimously for the General Survey Act as well as the tariff. Promptly Carolina's quondam nationalists turned against internal improvements, but the loss was more than made up by increasing support from New England.

Although Vice President Calhoun's tiebreaking vote defeated several projects, the Adams Congresses appropriated more than twice as much for conquering space as all their predecessors combined. Extensions of the National Road were generously funded, along with various roads and river and harbor improvements. Stock was subscribed in four canal companies, $1 million worth to push the Chesapeake and Ohio over the mountains by way of the Potomac valley. Massive grants of public lands subsidized the ambitious canal projects of Ohio, Indiana, Illinois, and Alabama.[36]

As the army engineers stepped up their surveys for future links in a national transportation system, notably the projected national roads from Washington to New Orleans and Buffalo, multiple surveys of alternate routes stirred up so much local anticipation that a Tennessee Jacksonian congressman felt momentarily compelled to endorse internal improvements to get reelected. Once "the delusion passed off," a repentant James K. Polk complained that the voters had been "carried away with the prospect of having millions of public money expended among them." There was to be "a main route and cross routes intersecting the district in every direction," he recalled. A national road "was to run down every creek, and pass through almost every neighborhood."[37]

Meanwhile Clay and the enterprise-minded congressmen aligning the Ohio valley with the Northeast behind his American System were being challenged for western leadership. A rising Missourian, Thomas Hart Benton, had opportunely transcended his self-made mastery of the old politics of market interests to bring western insurgency to the national arena.

Expelled from the University of North Carolina for stealing, Benton moved west to recoup honor as a lawyer, first in Tennessee and then—after a bloody barroom brawl with local hero Andrew Jackson—in St. Louis. He reached the Missouri gateway to the Far West just as steamboats brought the postwar boom. With town lots soaring from thirty dollars an acre to two thousand dollars, with Astor capital and St. Louis enterprise deploying trappers through the Rockies and ever larger fortunes in beaver pelts floating down the Missouri, the ambitious young newcomer prospered as contentious lawyer/politician/editor for the territorial regime of old-line French fur magnates and Governor William Clark, Jefferson's transcontinental pathfinder.

Lawyer Benton defended his patrons' vast Spanish land grants; politician Benton orated and maneuvered for their candidates and causes; and editor Benton made their entrepreneurial visions compelling to "small capitalists" as well. Dreaming that a Pacific trade along the line of the Missouri would reward "all that useful class of traders 'whose enterprise is greater than their capital,'" he denounced the Monroe administration for accepting joint British occupation of Oregon in 1818. A year later, anticipating the Missouri wagon trains that soon rolled across the southwestern plains to Santa Fe, he also denounced the surrender of the American claim to Texas in the Transcontinental Treaty. When Missouri became a state in 1820, he was rewarded with a seat in the federal Senate.

Haunted as a senator for the next thirty years by the youthful disgrace that cost him a genteel education, Benton bristled at slights, buried bursts of florid eloquence in tiresome parades of autodidact learning, and abjured presidential prospects lest his past be dragged up. Championing at first the interests of his most influential constituents in fur trading, land grants, lead mining, territorial expansion, and internal improvements, he supported their favorite Henry Clay (who had married his cousin) in the presidential election of 1824. By this time, however, Benton was catching the beat of a different drum that kept him from following Clay into the Adams coalition. His bombastic facade shielded the sensitivities of a disgraced outsider; and the crisis of 1819 undermined his entrepreneurial orthodoxy to prepare him for a democratic politics. Already alarmed by the boomtime saturnalia of paper, he was mired in debt by the panic and a failing St. Louis bank. When the panic also aroused Missouri farmers, now empowered by statehood, to overthrow the territorial establishment, the new Senator became keenly attentive to "those who own and cultivate the soil." The "Old Bullion" of Jackson's Bank War emerged as Benton found support among these "chosen of God" for his dreams of a gold and silver currency, under which "the price of everything is reasonable, and a dollar stands for a dollar."

In the Senate the Missourian was drawn to the Old Republican purists Macon, Randolph, and Taylor of Caroline. Randolph became his confidant, and he increasingly viewed the conflict of sectional interests through the lens of Taylor's class analysis. His commitment to a new politics crystallized in 1824, when his "graduation/donation" bill placed the western popular demand for cheap or free land on the national agenda. Where most western politicians wanted the public lands donated to the states as capital for developmental/speculative projects, Benton "made himself amazingly popular," complained John Quincy Adams, by preaching "The lands belong to the people!" Rising migration costs to more distant frontiers had made the West's public lands too expensive for many refugees from eastern hard times, and the Missouri Senator stimulated "all the people of the Western country to madness" by advocating drastic "graduation" of land prices. After five years on the market, he proposed, the minimum auction price of $1.25 per acre would fall, by annual 25¢ increments, to a mere 25¢. Moreover, eighty acres would be donated to any settler after three years' residence on lands remaining unsold.

At the same time Benton proposed a constitutional amendment for direct popular election of Presidents. And he patched up his quarrel with the popular favorite Jackson, then briefly in the Senate. Once his kinsman Clay was counted out in the electoral college, he backed Jackson in the House showdown against Adams/Clay "bargain and corruption" and then for vindication in 1828. Old Hickory, cheap land, and hard money were so appealing to farmers that Benton became unbeatable in Missouri.[38]

Like Benton, Polk, Webster, and Calhoun, most politicians had to "reapply principles" as a cresting politics of fiercely competing interests and localities met the cresting democracy evoked by Andrew Jackson. The "original Jackson men," except for Tennesseeans and the prescient but now deceased John Taylor of Caroline, had been politically obscure. National and congressional leadership of the Jackson movement fell to Calhoun's experienced "eleventh-hour men" (mostly Carolinians and Pennsylvania New Schoolers) who enlisted late in the campaign of 1824.

In Adams's first Congress, therefore, Calhounites joined forces with Tennesseeans to launch the campaign for Jackson's vindication in 1828 by vilifying and obstructing the administration. Together they backed Missouri Calhounite Duff Green in establishing the Washington *United States Telegraph* to broadcast their fulminations against the "bargain and corruption" of Adams and Clay. Four days into the session, the Jacksonian bellwether George McDuffie denounced Clay as the "skulking manager" of a "bold and daring, and shameless coalition, setting at defiance the will of the nation and neglecting even the external decencies of political morality." The Carolina hotspur escaped a duel only because Clay's Kentucky defender insisted on ungentlemanly rifles; but John Randolph's searing invective against the coalition of "the puritan with the black-leg" evoked a challenge from Clay himself. At their encounter beside the Potomac, Randolph took a bullet through the coat while chivalrously firing into the air. "I will never make a widow & orphans," the bachelor Virginian declared. "It is agt. my principles."[39]

Randolph's fellow Radicals were far more hesitant about joining the Jacksonian assault, even after Adams's manifesto left them nowhere else to go. Southern Radicals had long distrusted both the headstrong general and his newfound champion Calhoun, while their northern Bucktail allies dared not offend pro-Adams sentiment in New York until they recovered from their 1824 debacle. Bucktail chieftain Van Buren was playing the deepest game for the highest stakes of his long and adroit career. While maneuvering in Washington to shape a Jackson coalition to Radical ends, the Red Fox of Kinderhook schemed in Albany against a triumphant Governor Clinton at his peak of adulation upon completion of the Grand Canal.

Clinton both complicated the Bucktails' problem and suggested a solution by endorsing Jackson as a stalking horse for his own intoxicating presidential prospects. Astutely they set out to drive a wedge between the Magnus Apollo and his pro-Adams following. Hiding their Jacksonian intentions, they quietly marshaled their disciplined cadres to rewin the legislature while lulling the overconfident governor with private overtures of Jacksonian coalition, with legislative confirmation of his appointees, and with deliberate choice of a weak candidate to oppose his reelection in 1826. Their master stroke was to choose an Adams supporter as sacrificial lamb in the gubernatorial election. This stratagem so alienated Adamsites from the nominally Jacksonian Clinton that he was barely reelected with a strongly Bucktail legislature, which overwhelmingly reelected Van Buren to the Senate. Only then did the again entrenched Bucktails unveil their Jackson campaign.

Senator Van Buren could not join the assault on "bargain and corruption" in the first Adams Congress without giving away the game in New York. Carefully choosing less blatantly partisan ground on which to align with the Jacksonians, he concerted with Calhoun to prevent the administration from riding Clay's popular hobbyhorse of friendship with revolutionary Latin America. When the President nominated delegates to claim United States leadership of the Western Hemisphere under the Monroe Doctrine at a congress of the new republics in Panama, the Jacksonians responded with outcries against "entangling alliances" and racist fears of association with blacks from Haiti. Obstruction of the delegates' confirmation by the Senate and funding by the House so delayed their departure that the congress adjourned in failure before they reached Panama.

While unobtrusively establishing his Jacksonian bona fides on the Panama question, the Little Magician prepared to draw the southern Radicals into the Jackson coalition and ultimately to displace Calhoun from its leadership. Proclaiming strict constructionism in speeches against internal improvements and a bankruptcy law, he ducked the issue of protective tariffs, which were popular even with many Bucktails in New York. His absence on a visit to the congressional cemetery forced Vice President Calhoun to declare himself in the tiebreaking vote against the Woolens Bill.

Once the Bucktails regained ascendancy in New York, Van Buren reached boldly for national leadership. As the aptest pupil in the country's most advanced political school, he had learned that party was the best instrument for protecting a democratic citizenry from the socially disruptive demands of capitalist elites. After gambling disastrously on Crawford to save the first national party system from Monrovian "amalgamation," and then exerting all his legerdemain for another chance, he now set out to fashion from Jackson's popularity a second national party system.

Astutely the Little Magician began by extracting consent from Calhoun. Driven from amalgamation by slaveholder exigency, the Carolinian could no longer resist the Radical strategy of blending democracy with defense of slavery. At a sociable gathering on a Virginia plantation over the Christmas holiday of 1826, he approved a letter that Van Buren proposed to address to the Richmond Junto through Thomas Ritchie. This notable manifesto, enlisting southern Radicals to make the Jackson coalition a "substantial reorganization of the Old Republican Party," was the blueprint for a second party system that would hold a fracturing republic together for another thirty years.

Jackson should not be elected merely for his popularity and "military services, without reference to party," Van Buren told Ritchie, but by "a political party, holding in the main, to certain tenets." Regarding political divisions as inevitable, he thought the "the old ones are the best of which the nature of the case admits." The "most natural & beneficial" combination was the old one "between the planters of the South and the plain Republicans of the north," he argued. "The country has once flourished under a party thus constituted & may again."

Having appealed so successfully to democratic New Yorkers through the talisman of Republicanism, the Little Magician anticipated political science by a century in understanding the power of party identification. "It would take longer than our lives (even if it were practicable) to create new party feelings to keep those masses together," he insisted. By instead "combining Genl Jackson's personal popularity with the portion of old party feeling yet remaining," it would be possible to substitute "*party principle* for *personal preference.*"

A Jacksonian Republicanism would do more than maintain proper principles in the North. Van Buren emphasized to his slaveholding allies in the South that it would also repress the threatening "prejudices between free and slave holding states."

> Party attachment in former times furnished a complete antidote for sectional prejudices by producing counteracting feelings. It was not until that defence had been broken down that the clamour agt. Southern Influence and African Slavery could be made effectual in the North. . . . Formerly, attacks upon Southern Republicans were regarded by those of the north as assaults upon political brethren & resented accordingly. This all powerful sympathy has been much weakened, if not, destroyed by the amalgamating policy. . . . It can & ought to be revived. . . . Instead of the question being between a northern and Southern man, it would be whether or not the ties, which have hitherto bound together a great political party should be severed.

Federalist/Clintonians had long denounced Van Buren's unfolding strategy as perpetuating slavery. Because "the inveteracy of party feelings" protected free-state Republicans from attack at home, argued Rufus King in leading the Missouri agitation, they succumbed to "hopes of influence and distinction by taking part in favor of the slave states." Thus the slave states would maintain "their dispropor-tionate, I might say exclusive, dominance over the Union."

King's class politics neutralized his sectional prophecy for Bucktail Republi-cans, who saw his capitalist developmentalism as forcing northern democracy into defensive alliance with southern slavocracy. Federalist/Clintonians had mounted the Missouri assault from "motives rather political than philanthropical," Van Buren believed, to subvert popular Republicanism. Because they "can never tri-umph when they meet the democracy of the country, openly," as his Bucktail edi-tor at Albany put it, they sought to "abrogate the old party distinctions" and "organize new ones, founded in the territorial prejudices of the people."

The proslavery import of Van Buren's strategy was obscured for a time by its brilliant success in carrying the Jacksonians to power and establishing a durable new party system. Proslavery intent was the more deniable because his leading southern allies still professed a Jeffersonian aversion to human bondage. Ritchie regularly denied that he was defending slavery and would shortly support an ear-nest effort to drive it from Virginia. Nearly a generation would pass before an embittered Little Magician began to understand how progressive capital had crip-pled democracy by driving it into the racist embrace of slave capital.

When Congress adjourned in March 1827, therefore, Van Buren hastened south to consolidate the new alignment. Soon after he passed through Richmond, Ritchie's *Enquirer* ran up the Jackson flag. Conferring with the politicians at every stop and royally entertained by the Calhounites in Charleston, he pressed on to the Georgia plantation of the Radicals' 1824 standard-bearer. Still disabled, Crawford surrendered his objections to Jackson but insisted that Calhoun be dropped as the general's vice-presidential running mate. Although Van Buren expediently rejected such an immediate move against his rival for Jacksonian leadership, he obtained the information that ensured his ultimate ascendancy. In the 1818 delib-erations of Monroe's Cabinet, as Crawford was only too happy to reveal, Calhoun had advocated punishing the general for his Florida incursion.

With southern front and future prospects secured, the Little Magician hurried back to New York to deal with the Jackson party's most threatening problem. Pro-tectionists, blaming him for loss of the Woolens Bill, were mounting the most extensive campaign of pressure on Congress since the Missouri agitation. Across the North local and state conventions of manufacturers, publicists, and politicians were passing resolutions and selecting delegates to a national protectionist con-vention at Harrisburg. In a carefully contrived address to the preliminary conven-tion at Albany, Van Buren insinuated that the convention movement "proceeded more from the closet of the politician than the workshop of the manufacturer," while trying to leave the impression that he favored a "temperate" and "salutary" tariff, especially for wool-growing farmers. "That was a very able speech!" exclaimed one listener, adding after a moment, "On which side of the Tariff question was it?"[40]

Clinton's unexpected death some months later removed the Bucktails' old threat just as Antimasonry presented a new one so ominous that Van Buren himself had to run for governor in 1828 to ensure a Jackson majority. Meanwhile, with the tariff question blurred, the elections of 1827 had favored Jackson's supporters in New York and elsewhere, portending presidential victory and producing Jackson majorities in the second Adams Congress.

The Jacksonians chose a Richmond Junto man as Speaker of the House and bestowed the lucrative printing contracts of both chambers on Duff Green's *Telegraph*. But they could no longer evade the tariff issue under the intense pressure for a general increase generated by the Harrisburg Convention movement. To avoid alienating either northern or southern supporters on the eve of presidential voting, they resorted to a desperate expedient. Both northern and southern Jacksonians supported amendments loading the tariff bill with prohibitive duties on the raw materials used by New England manufacturers, shipbuilders, and rum distillers—wool, iron, hemp, and molasses. While ingratiating themselves with sheep-raising farmers, Pennsylvania iron makers, Kentucky hemp growers, and Ohio valley whiskey distillers, they would force pro-Adams Yankee protectionists to kill the whole package.

Thus politics brought the fierce competition of interests and localities to a climax. Senator Josiah Johnston, Louisiana's champion of sugar duties, described the bitter struggle:

> Maine complains of the Iron & the hemp [duties]—New England of the molasses[,] the South of every thing—Penna. insists on the Iron[,] Ky on the hemp—N. York on the woolens—Penna. agrees to ease Maine on the Molasses—if she will take the Iron. . . . Maine implores & is obstinate—N England sickens with the Molasses & hesitates—The South tell them, it is a Naucious Medium, but will do them good, & will work-off the Tariff fever.[41]

But the Jacksonians were caught in their own trap when the Yankees wangled just enough concessions to vote for and pass the bill. Consequently, on election eve, a Jacksonian Congress found itself responsible for the "Tariff of Abominations." With grim satisfaction the Boston cotton-mill magnate Abbott Lawrence told Webster it would "keep the South and West in debt to New England the next hundred years."[42]

Seething South Carolinians had already begun to "calculate the value of the Union," in the words of Dr. Thomas Cooper; and Calhoun was secretly drafting for a legislative committee an Exposition and Protest claiming that the state could forbid enforcement of the tariff as constitutionally null and void. Only the hope of early relief by a Calhoun-guided Jackson administration restrained the forces of revolutionary resistance.

American plebiscitory democracy crystallized in the election of 1828. With voter turnout more than doubling—from 26.5 percent in 1824 to 54.3 percent and soon to reach 78 percent—presidential aspirants became subject to a broad spectrum of the white male populace. Yet the limits of majority rule were implicit in its Jacksonian advent. Farmers and workers were baffled as well as threatened by the abstraction and complexity of the interests and issues that engaged calculating elites. Trusting only face-to-face relations, an antinomian majority could rally in anxiety and hope around Old Hickory only through politicians and a party system of arminian proclivity.

Jackson's charisma froze voters into a pattern of party identifications favoring his entourage of pragmatic Democrats. Henceforth most votes were determined by party loyalties that passed from fathers to sons. As anti-Jacksonians mastered the new techniques of popular appeal, this second party system moved toward two-party parity, adjusted to the demographic tides of urbanization and immigration, and survived in considerable measure even the upheaval of civil war and reconstruction.[43]

The historic significance of the 1828 election has been obscured by the personal scurrilities that dominated it. Although the Jackson campaign was directed by genteel congressmen obsessed with the peaking issue-politics of competing interests, it reached a mass electorate attuned to personality through nongentry politicians and editors spawned by the class politics of the twenties. In recognition of this broadening base, Van Buren proposed a national nominating convention as "more in unison with the spirit of the times" than the discredited congressional caucus.[44] But instead the Jackson leaders, fearing a public dispute with diehard Radicalism over their plan to nominate Calhoun for Vice President, relied on gentry allies in legislatures to form electoral tickets. Less genteel politicians entered the campaign through county, town, and ward committees that erected "hickory poles," held rallies, and canvassed voters, and through a sudden flood of partisan newspapers that made cheap print the main medium of a new style of bare-knuckled electioneering.

Van Buren's Bucktails had demonstrated the efficacy of a partisan press by subsidizing some fifty village weeklies to echo their authoritative Albany *Argus* in every corner of New York. With the post office carrying newspapers at a cut rate and "exchange" subscriptions between editors free, village weeklies now sprang up everywhere marching to the daily Jacksonian drum of Duff Green's *United States Telegraph* from Washington, as modulated to regional sensibilities by Jacksonian triweeklies or dailies in the state capitals and principal cities. The mails groaned, too, under speeches and committee reports denouncing Adams/Clay bargain or administration extravagance carried free under the franks, or signatures, of Jacksonian congressmen.

Where genteel editors had addressed elaborately reasoned arguments to elites through a handful of traditional organs such as Washington's *National Intelligencer* or Richmond's *Enquirer,* the plebeian printer/editors of the new partisan press touched the popular pulse in the popular vernacular of ad hominem sensationalism. Extolling Jackson's Republican nobility, they seized every pretext to vilify Adams's aristocratic mendacity. In Kentucky Amos Kendall's Frankfort *Argus of Western America* denounced the President for installing a billiard table in the White House. While minister to Russia, charged Isaac Hill's Concord *Patriot* in New Hampshire, Adams had procured a young American girl for the lustful Czar.[45] This ad hominem crudity focused popular anger at the promoters and beneficiaries of market dislocation, intrusive government, and Moderate-Light cultural imperialism. "The clergy and village aristocrats" backing Adams, as a Vermont editor summarized the Jacksonian indictment, were bent on establishing "an order of nobility, a standing clergy, and the full exercise of civil and religious power."[46]

Privately the President's leading backers gave color to Jacksonian suspicion by claiming to "Constitute the Talent, wealth & influence of the State." The only public opinion that should count, said one, was "the aggregate of property and talent." And the only issue, said another, was Clay's American System of fostering capitalist development through "Internal Improvements, and Such other objects as will encourage national industry." Echoing this disdain for majority sentiment, Mrs. Adams told her son that "our tastes, our temper, our habits vary so much from those of the herd that we can never be beloved or admired."[47]

While pro-Adams editors emphasized developmental issues, they could not resist exploiting the rich material afforded by Jackson's turbulent career to return the opposition's ad hominem fire. And the two-party dynamic attracted to the President's cause some who could match the Jacksonians in plebeian crudity. Charles Hammond, Clay's editorial confidant in Cincinnati, pronounced the general a bastard and his mother a prostitute. Philadelphia editor John Binns, discovering Jackson's wartime execution of six mutinous militiamen, issued a lurid handbill embellishing the grisly details with six coffins. When the administration press exposed the adulterous beginning of the hero's relationship with Rachel, John Overton's Nashville Jackson committee issued a torrent of obfuscating testimony that has fooled even historians into thinking the episode a misunderstanding about the timing of her divorce.

Unparalleled mudslinging expressed, in the personalist idiom of popular culture, the bitterness engendering the demand for an unprecedented shift in social power. The revolutionary character of the contest is more evident in its result than its rhetoric. A doubled turnout delivered a resounding Jackson mandate. Outside New England, Old Hickory lost only Delaware (where the legislature still chose electors), New Jersey (by 2 percent), and Maryland (by 1 percent). He got 68 percent of the electoral vote, and his 56 percent of the popular vote would not be equaled until the twentieth century.

The Jackson vote, as its distribution reveals, was forcing a politics of polarizing classes and cultures on a politics of polarizing sections.

	Jackson	Adams
New England	30%	70%
Mid-Atlantic, N.Y. to Md.	57%	43%
Northwest, with Ky., Mo.	55%	45%
Southeast	76%	24%
Southwest	82%	18%

County-level distributions, especially in the middle tier of states where the contest was closest, mirror the clash of land and invading market, of contrasting modes and relations of production, and of consequent cultural dispositions. Jackson ran strongest in isolated areas of small farms and Baptist/Methodist evangelicalism—western Pennsylvania, Kentucky's Green River country, southern Ohio, Indiana and Illinois, and the upland South—and his majorities got bigger as they moved west, reaching 67 percent in Illinois and 71 percent in Missouri. By contrast, Adams's strength was concentrated along major transportation routes and in areas of market production and Moderate Light—lower New England, New York's burnt-over district, the Great Lakes region, and Kentucky's Bluegrass. In New York City, Philadelphia, Baltimore, and Cincinnati, working-class Jacksonism prevailed over bourgeois/middle-class Adamsism. These alignments of class and culture were skewed by the southern cross-class consensus for Jackson and by Yankee tribal loyalty to Adams, as heightened on each side by contrasting attitudes toward slavery. But even where distorted by the great contradiction of racist slavery, an enduring class/cultural pattern of political struggle was emerging. Adams's southern support was concentrated in towns and along routes of transportation projects, while Jackson got a substantial vote in small-farming northern New England, 40 percent in Maine and 47 percent in New Hampshire, which would soon be the country's banner Democratic state.

Ethnicity mainly reinforced these alignments of linked class and culture. Jackson's class appeal to farmers and workers was especially strong for Germans clannishly attached to their peasant tradition, and for Scotch-Irish farmers and Catholic Irish laborers as a compatriot who had humiliated their British oppressors. The universal Yankee nation gave Adams strong support, not because they were "English" and not just out of sectional loyalty, but also because agrarian crisis and capitalist transformation had pressed them most relentlessly into the cultural/political accommodation he represented.

Religion was more salient than ethnicity for most voters, and the political division coincided with the arminian/antinomian division in pervasive evangelicalism. The electoral map roots National Republicanism in the territories and classes of the Presbygational Moderate Light. Against these political/cultural agencies of capitalist transformation, Jacksonism rose from Baptist/Methodist New-Light soil to force democracy into presidential politics.[48]

Chapter 10

Millennial Democracy

JACKSONIANS hailed the "triumph of the great principle of self government over the intrigues of aristocracy" as ushering in a democratic Millennium. Jubilant multitudes turned out in homage along the hero's route to Washington and, "like the inundation of the northern barbarians into Rome," flooded the capital from five hundred miles around for his inauguration. *"They really seem to think,"* marveled Daniel Webster, *"that the country is rescued from some dreadful danger."* Huzzas from fifteen thousand throats drowned out the new President's inaugural promise of vaguely specified *"reform."* Then the sovereign people thronged the White House in such a "Saturnalia . . . of mud and filth" that tubs of punch had to be carried outside to save the furnishings from destruction and the President from suffocation. To Justice Story "the reign of King 'Mob' seemed triumphant."[1]

Yet the democratic Millennium got off to an inauspicious start. A capital seething with Calhoun/Van Buren rivalry and the importunities of office-seeking politicians greeted a bereaved President-elect seething with anger. Several weeks before Jackson left home, he had buried his beloved Rachel in the Hermitage garden. "This dear saint" had long since retreated from the scandal of their adulterous beginning into pious self-effacement. Distraught over its revival in the recent campaign, she had expired in dread of the public ordeal awaiting her in the White House. "Those vile wretches who have slandered her," the general rasped at her grave, "must look to God for mercy."[2]

By the light of Old Hickory's personalism, Rachel's persecution proved the wildest electioneering charges against the Adams men. His first order of business was to "cleanse the Augean stable" of every federal employee who had prostituted office to support these vile wretches in stealing the presidency, plundering the Treasury, and slandering the innocent. His resolve was applauded by the swarm of vulgar office-seekers riding the crest of the democratic tide, by upstart editors demanding "A CLEAN SWEEP," and by Bucktails brazenly proclaiming the New

York doctrine that "to the victor belong the spoils." The new President's inaugural call for *"reform"* focused on "those abuses that have brought the patronage of the Federal Government into conflict with the freedom of elections" and "placed or continued power in unfaithful or incompetent hands."

Ever since Jefferson discharged enough Federalist officeholders to establish a partisan balance, the tradition of a genteel, nonpartisan civil service had protected bureaucrats from dismissal except for gross misconduct. Enjoying a security of income and tenure elsewhere unknown, many had fallen into haughtiness, laxity, or alcoholism, and some into peculation. Yet higher functionaries were pillars of official society personifying the ideal of genteel government, and Jacksonian reform alarmed traditionalists of both parties.

Undaunted by an uproar against "proscription," Jackson launched his administration by ordering a "strict examination" to eliminate unnecessary expenses and positions. In addition, department heads were directed to dismiss all subordinates found lax in "private or public relations," or "who were appointed against the manifest will of the people or whose station . . . was made to operate against the freedom of elections." Within eighteen months some 10 percent of the ten-thousand-odd federal employees were replaced. Jackson himself removed 121 incumbents and reappointed 62 in bestowing on political supporters most of the 319 higher positions.[3]

Yet Jackson's removals were far from a clean sweep at the lower levels, and his higher appointments were only somewhat less genteel than his predecessors'. What transformed them into a long-lived "spoils system" was the democratic rationale he supplied for the "rotation in office" demanded by a regalvanized party system. "Office is considered as a species of property," he complained to his first Congress, making government "an engine for the support of the few at the expense of the many." Public officials should periodically be returned to "the same means of obtaining a living that are enjoyed by the millions who never held office," he argued, and public service should be made "so plain and simple" that the experienced could be replaced by ordinary "men of intelligence."

By proclaiming rotation "a leading principle in the republican system," Jackson was able to reward the new class of pragmatic politicians for mobilizing a democratic electorate while at the same time holding them to democratic accountability. In the long run, however, without an Old Hickory at the helm, the spoils system would fulfill critics' warnings by entrenching pragmatists against any accountability.

Aside from purging unworthy officeholders, Jackson's bold agenda was muted in the inaugural address he had drafted under the nervous eye of Judge Overton back in Tennessee. Reassuringly the "Napoleon of the woods" promised to respect the limits of executive power, to subordinate the military to civil authority, and to conduct foreign relations with "the forbearance becoming a powerful nation rather than the sensibility belonging to a gallant people." Reassurance became disingenuous rationalization in his pledge of "a just and liberal policy" toward the Indians and a "humane and considerate attention to their rights and their wants."

The new President implicitly challenged National Republicanism by promising to respect the powers the states "have reserved to themselves" as "sovereign members of our Union" and by insisting on "a strict and faithful economy," so as to retire the national debt and counteract the "public and private profligacy which a profuse expenditure of money by the Government is but too apt to engender." On the most controversial questions, however, the inaugural was at best ambiguous. Internal improvements were "of high importance," Jackson said, but only "so far as they can be promoted by the constitutional acts of the Federal Government." Tariff rates should be decided in "the spirit of equity, caution, and compromise," with "peculiar encouragement" for products "essential to our national independence." Muffled for the moment was the politics of popular outrage that would culminate in the Bank War. Astute management had made the national Bank a sacred cow of respectable opinion, and the alarm of Old Hickory's Tennessee counselors dissuaded him from assailing it until his heterogeneous coalition was solidified.[4]

The new Cabinet did not reassure the dismayed. Only Van Buren's appointment to the State Department commanded respect. With Calhoun reelected to the vice presidency, even his friends had to concede that the Little Magician was both worthy and deserving of the first Cabinet position. But Jackson resented the assumption that he must fall under the tutelage of one or both of these powerful rivals. Rejecting their suggestions for the remaining positions, he chose obscure men he could dominate—Samuel D. Ingham of Pennsylvania for the Treasury, John Branch of North Carolina for Navy, John M. Berrien of Georgia for Attorney General, William T. Barry of Kentucky for Postmaster General, and his undistinguished Tennessee protégé John H. Eaton for War. Eaton's scandalous recent marriage darkened the cloud over these appointments.

Yet this Cabinet manifested considerable canniness on the part of a President determined to be master of his own house. By appointing a New York Bucktail, a Pennsylvania New Schooler, two southerners, and two westerners, he recognized the factions and sections that had given him strongest support while denying predominance to any. Although Van Buren got the top spot, Jackson managed, by appointing obscure men of Radical antecedents from North Carolina and Georgia, to exclude not only the Little Magicians's South Carolina foes but also his potent Radical allies in Virginia. Never before had the Old Dominion been banished from the highest executive levels.

The Cabinet appointments also prefigured some controversial policies as yet unannounced. The westerner Eaton was positioned in the War Department and the Georgian Berrien as Attorney General to execute a final solution of the Indian problem. Branch had denounced banks, and Barry had been chief justice of Kentucky's antibank New Court. The most ingenious selection was Ingham, a paper manufacturer loyal to Pennsylvania protectionism but also a veteran Calhounite. Having resolved his conflicting loyalties by abstaining on the Tariff of Abominations, he was placed at the Treasury to compromise the most dangerous impending issue.

Calhounites were stunned. Confident of controlling the administration and eliminating protective tariffs, they were abruptly confronted by a Van Buren-headed Cabinet aligned almost solidly against them, with their only ally stymied on the question nearest their hearts. They were further appalled by the political upstarts who influenced these selections. Jackson was ignoring all political notables to counsel with his Tennessee cronies Eaton and Lewis and the vitriolic office-seeking editors Isaac Hill and Amos Kendall, who had no use for imperious Carolina gentlemen. With Eaton in the Cabinet, Lewis, Hill, and Kendall were given high sub-Cabinet appointments, and Lewis took up residence in the White House. Eaton and Lewis had recommended the two southern Radicals for the Cabinet; and Kendall sponsored his Kentucky ally Judge Barry.[5]

Until Congress reconvened in December 1829, the new administration's public image would be shaped by an ambiguous program, fierce infighting, a lackluster Cabinet, a backstairs "Kitchen Cabinet," an extensive proscription of experienced officeholders, and a tempest over the morals of Mrs. Secretary Eaton. To genteel friend and foe alike, the millennium of democracy seemed "the Millennium of the Minnows!"[6]

Haggard from grief and infirmities, the new President was reinvigorated by criticism to execute his radical mandate. "You know when I am excited all my energies come forth," he told an old friend. "If my constitution will bear me up for one year . . . have no fear."[7] A bold new politics was implicit from the start in his choice of advisers. Seeking out Isaac Hill and Amos Kendall, whom he knew only from their notoriously polemical campaign editorials, he appointed them to high federal offices and relied increasingly on their counsel about translating his unfocused mandate into rhetoric and policy.

The editors—both Yankee farm boys set adrift by agrarian crisis—epitomized the threatening new politics of appeal to popular anger against aristocrats and banks. The crippled Hill's resentment of the hale embittered his parvenu resentment of New Hampshire nabobs, against whom for a generation his choleric editorials had rallied the small-farmer Republican majority. The cadaverous Kendall had sought his fortune as a schoolteacher in Kentucky, where, in the New-Court rebellion against a banking aristocracy, he perfected the class politics that met Jackson's predilections.

Conservative Democrats took alarm at these portenders of Jacksonian radicalism. A Democratic Senate rejected Hill's appointment, and Kendall was saved only by the tiebreaking vote of a Vice President needing to demonstrate Jacksonism.

But New Hampshire sent Hill limping triumphantly back to Washington as senator; and meanwhile Jackson welcomed to his Kitchen Cabinet several of Kendall's Kentucky associates in New-Court radicalism. The Kentuckians confirmed the presidential conviction that his mandate required an ultimate assault on banking as the bastion of aristocratic privilege.

Before embarking on the new politics of class, however, Jackson had to cope with the old politics of interest and section. He had to master a following of old-style politicians divided by a dangerous North/South rift over tariffs and internal improvements. Through the Calhoun/Van Buren rivalry, the mounting bitterness of the old politics threatened his motley coalition even as it began to call itself the Democratic party.

Jackson had known Van Buren only slightly in the 1824 Senate as manager of his presidential rival Crawford, and his confidence in Calhoun was ebbing. During the 1828 campaign he had been shown a stolen letter suggesting that Calhoun had wanted him punished for his 1818 Florida invasion, rather than defending him as he had been led to believe. Although he curbed his suspicions until the election was over, a zealous Nashville Van Burenite harped on the revelation to convince Majors Eaton and Lewis that "the little Dutchman will outwit the Southron." On a campaign excursion to New Orleans to celebrate the 1828 anniversary of Jackson's victory, Lewis was further "filled with suspicions and projected injuries" by a Van Buren emissary from New York, who returned home by way of Georgia to secure corroborating evidence from Crawford. By the time Jackson's Cabinet was being selected, his closest advisers had cast their lot with Van Buren, and Nashville newspapers were insinuating Calhoun's perfidy.[8]

South Carolina's violent reaction to the Tariff of Abominations deepened Jackson's distrust of the Vice President. Although trying to restrain extremists until Jackson was elected, the Calhounites were themselves swept into the rage of a rice/cotton slavocracy habituated to total mastery. While privately canvassing the state's resources for military resistance, they harangued protest meetings with demands for boycotting and taxing northern goods, and Calhoun himself toasted "The Congress of '76—They taught the world how oppression could be successfully resisted." As soon as the presidential voting was over, the state nullification preached by lowcountry zealots was publicly endorsed by the Calhounites' leader in state politics, James Hamilton, Jr., a flamboyant planter/lawyer who had married the state's richest rice heiress. Shortly thereafter the legislature issued an official *Exposition* of the new doctrine, coupled with a *Protest* against protective tariffs as unconstitutional.

The *Exposition*'s secret author, Vice President Calhoun, was completing his breathtaking somersault from hypernationalism to hyperlocalism. While he denied the slightest change of principle, his penchant for abstraction and the political imperatives of a fevered slavocracy pushed to absurdity the state-rights orthodoxy of the hallowed Virginia and Kentucky Resolutions of 1798–1799. In declaring the Alien and Sedition Acts unconstitutional, these two sovereign states had claimed the right as contracting parties to determine when the powers delegated by the Constitution were exceeded. The more radical resolutions Jefferson drafted for the Kentucky legislature in 1799, claiming a state's right to "interpose" between its citizens and unconstitutional federal oppression, declared that such *"nullification is the rightful remedy."* But Madison's Virginia Resolutions merely called for repeal, and the Kentuckians only threatened to nullify. Deriving nullification from the "natural" right of secession, Jefferson regarded it as a final revolutionary resort.

Now as Carolina's imperious gentry pushed Jefferson's implication to its revolutionary conclusion, Calhoun advanced the arresting doctrine that nullification was a peaceable and constitutional remedy within the Union. Any state could veto any federal law it thought unconstitutional, the *Exposition* argued, and a federal function thus nullified could not be exercised constitutionally until three-fourths of the states amended the Constitution to authorize it.

The very absurdity of this blueprint for anarchy made the Carolinians' utter seriousness more ominous. Nullification was the defiance of a febrile ruling class that felt its "character for chivalry and honor to be tarnished by degenerating into abject servitude." Their leader Hamilton, legendary for a perfect record of wounding without killing all his fourteen dueling opponents, personified the hotspur temperament. Principle would compel Carolina to nullify an unreformed tariff, he punctiliously informed a presidential confidant, and "If this be treason, then make the most of it."

The agitation backfired with the Revolutionary veteran in the White House. Still smarting, perhaps, from boyhood encounters with lowcountry hauteur, he saw at once that nullification portended both a resort to force and the corollary of secession. Unmatched political antennae alerted him to a dangerous stress in the national fabric, and patriotic arousal filled his public and private discourse with fears for "the Union." As he girded himself to defend it from the nullifiers, their demands for "unconditional repeal" of protective tariffs stiffened his back against concession to disunionists. The Carolinians' "ultra-tariff violence," he told Hamilton, cost them a place in the Cabinet.[9]

The Carolina agitation prepared Jackson to recognize his affinity with Van Buren. A temperamentally improbable entente between the dapper Little Magician and the rough-hewn Old Hickory was latent in their shared neo-Jeffersonianism, embarrassed as it was for both by the tariff question. Drastic tariff reduction would alienate Jackson's cherished Pennsylvania constituency and delay his cherished retirement of the national debt while disrupting Van Buren's cherished alliance between southern planters and northern plain republicans. Van Buren's strategy was to play down the tariff and cement his neo-Jeffersonian alliance by attacking internal improvements, which were opposed both by strict-constructionist southerners and by New Yorkers and Pennsylvanians disinclined to subsidize other states' roads and canals after paying for their own.

Moreover Van Buren had positioned himself in New York to move against the national Bank, which Calhoun still supported. In the Empire City, the country's leading capital market resented the regulation and competition of the Philadelphia-headquartered and politically privileged national Bank, and working people were growing more suspicious of banks in general. As governor, Van Buren had just gotten a Safety Fund System enacted to curb the speculative excesses of New York banks. By requiring the strong city banks to stand behind the notes of the more daring upstate banks—to their mutual benefit, as the more prudent of both soon recognized—he prepared his core constituency to reject the Philadelphia "Monster" for state regulation.

Van Buren's legendary tact made the most of his affinities with the President. While Vice President Calhoun had no excuse for remaining in Washington once Congress adjourned following the inauguration, the Secretary of State found a residence on Lafayette Square where he could stroll across frequently to the White House for dinner and took up horseback riding to accompany Jackson on his daily canters. No one was more solicitous of the precarious presidential health, and no one tempered advice more cautiously to strongly held presidential views. He acquiesced gracefully when Jackson rejected his warnings and bestowed the lucrative Collectorship of Customs in New York on an engaging Tammany hack who ultimately embezzled over a million dollars. The President had "his own wishes and favorite views," Van Buren told dismayed Bucktails, "upon points which it is not my province to attempt to controul."[10]

The Eaton scandal was a fortuitous godsend for the Little Magician. While a Senator, the widower Eaton had become involved with his Washington innkeeper's lively daughter Mrs. Margaret (Peggy) O'Neal Timberlake, who was reputed to "dispense her favors wherever she took a fancy" during her husband's extended absences as a purser in the navy. When Jackson boarded briefly at the O'Neal establishment as a Senator, he reported to Rachel that the charming Peggy "plays on the Piano delightfully, and every Sunday evening entertains her pious mother with sacred music, to which we are invited." Star boarder Eaton rescued Peggy's father from bankruptcy and her husband from a shortage in his Navy accounts so he could be assigned to a four-year cruise aboard the *U.S.S. Constitution*.

Gossips had a field day when word reached Washington in 1828 that jealousy had driven Lieutenant Timberlake to suicide in a Mediterranean port. To "shut their mouths" before the new administration took office, Eaton yielded to Jackson's demand that he marry Peggy "forthwith." But marriage did not save the bride from the gathering bourgeois purity crusade. Ostracized by the capital's anti-Jackson social establishment, Mrs. Secretary Eaton was also snubbed by Mrs. Vice President Calhoun, the Cabinet Mesdames Berrien, Branch, and Ingham, and Jackson's favorite niece and White House hostess Emily Tennessee Donelson, wife of his ward and secretary Andrew Jackson Donelson. Even some who sympathized with Peggy on the ground that "women are the greatest persecutors of their own sex" felt compelled to conform to "the arbitrary decrees of the society here."

All Jackson's rage at Rachel's traducers was poured out against the traducers of his surrogate daughter-in-law. "She is as chaste as a virgin!" he stormed, precipitating a "petticoat war" that banished the Donelsons to Tennessee, forced a Cabinet reorganization, and aligned the administration against the repressive moralism of the swelling Benevolent Empire. The Kentucky Jacksonian Richard M. Johnson would be carried into the vice presidency by the popularity of his recent congressional report defending Sunday mails from the moralists; and many a farmer and worker applauded Jackson's tirades at anti-Peggy clerics as defending patriarchal independence and honor against church as well as state.

The "Eaton Malaria" enabled widower Van Buren to win the presidential heart through assiduous courtesies to Peggy. The Secretary of State was "true, harmonious, and faithful," Jackson enthused, and did everything to "render my situation, *personally,* as pleasant and comfortable as the nature of my public duties will admit." By contrast, the strong-minded Mrs. Calhoun's adamancy against Peggy focused presidential suspicion on the Vice President. Originally blaming Clay for organizing the anti-Peggy campaign to embarrass the administration, the President increasingly blamed Calhoun.

Worried by poor health in December 1829, Jackson designated his heir apparent. Van Buren was not "selfish and intriguing as has been represented by some of his enemies," he wrote in a letter to be made public by Major Lewis if circumstances required. He was instead "frank, open, candid, and manly . . . *able and prudent,* Republican in his principles and one of the most pleasant men to do business with I ever saw." The New Yorker was "not only well qualified, but desires to fill the highest office in the gift of the people who, in him, will find a true friend and safe depository of their rights and liberties." The President regretted that he could not "say as much for Mr. Calhoun," who was rumored to be involved in South Carolina's nullifying gasconade, who was silent on the national Bank, and whose friends had caused "most of the troubles, vexations, and difficulties I have had to encounter."[11]

While making Mrs. Eaton's virtue a cardinal article of Democratic faith during the summer and fall of 1829, Jackson was piecing together other elements of a politically coherent program on morning rides with Van Buren and in conversations with the Kitchen Cabinet. Stuffing the band of his big white planter hat with notes and memoranda for his first state of the union message to Congress in December, he meanwhile moved vigorously on matters not requiring immediate congressional cooperation. Tragically the first democratic fruits to ripen were racist. By removing federal barriers to total Indian expropriation, the new administration would enlist land-hungry farmers in claiming state-rights ground against the heresy of nullification.

Implicit hypocrisy had brought federal Indian policy to an impasse. Theoretically, voluntary treaties protected the tribes from state authority and white intrusion while they were being "civilized" for eventual incorporation in the body politic. Actually, the treaty/civilization policy operated as an efficient system of expropriation. Civilizing subsidies fostered a mixed-blood elite and concentrated in it the formerly diffuse tribal decision-making. These descendants of intermarried white traders were readiest to abandon hunting for merchandizing and plantation agriculture, to acquire black slaves and the white man's racism, to learn English and send their children to the white missionaries' schools, and to meet white demands for tribal land. Periodically mixed-blood chiefs were bribed into ceding by treaty enough tribal domain to satisfy white land hunger.

But bloody frontier warfare and patriarchal afflatus disposed Andrew Jackson to treat Indians more summarily, as both treacherous foes and wayward children. Empowered after the War of 1812 by military glory, the cotton boom, and farmers' hunger for land, he had pushed the treaty/civilization policy to new levels of ruthlessness. The Monroe administration could maintain the paternalist facade only by promising ultimate removal of all Indians by treaty beyond the Mississippi, where the civilizing process could be given more time. Pursuing this policy, the Adams administration learned from McIntosh's Creek treaty that "voluntary" treaties could no longer be extorted without fraud too egregious to sustain liberal pretensions.

Relentless expropriation of Creeks and Cherokees had by now stirred up fierce tribal nationalism on the most coveted lands, and civilizing paternalism had produced a self-confident and politically sophisticated generation of mixed-blood tribal patriots. With tribal survival at stake, the traditionalist majority backed mixed-blood patriots in ousting the whites' mixed-blood pawns and centralizing leadership to counter the whites' divide-and-conquer strategy. In 1827 the Cherokees adopted a United States-style constitution with bicameral legislature, three-tiered judicial system, county administrations, and tribal police. Utilizing a Cherokee alphabet devised by the self-taught Sequoyah, leaders communicated with the non-English-speaking majority through a tribal newspaper. The strengthened polities of both Creeks and Cherokees decreed death for any chief assenting to a land cession.

A perverse fate set these two progressive tribes in the path of the state of Georgia, where the paternalist treaty system was compromised by a federal commitment to extinguish Indian titles as soon as possible, and where the threat of white democracy fueled planter aggression against Indians. By intimidating President Adams into the terms of the McIntosh treaty, Governor Troup expelled Georgia's thousands of Creeks into the crowded remnant of their tribal homeland in Alabama.

The Cherokees' fiercer resistance under their new constitution was doomed by Jackson's election. The Georgia legislature now felt free to nullify their federal treaty guarantees by outlawing their constitution and subjecting them to white officials for whom they could not vote and white courts in which they could not testify. State jurisdiction invited white intruders to seize their lands and improvements with impunity.

Fatefully a gold discovery accelerated the flood of white "gamblers, swindlers, and profane Blackguards" into Cherokee northwestern Georgia, "without either law or any other power to prevent them from giving full vent to their vicious propensities." Rapid expropriation and demoralization of Georgia's proud Cherokees inspired Alabama to similarly extend state jurisdiction over its Creeks, and Mississippi over its Choctaws and Chickasaws.[12]

The Indian haters were counting on Jackson to force the tribes' removal beyond the Mississippi by repudiating the federal treaty obligation to protect them against state sovereignty and white intruders. He was not found wanting. A "talk" sent to his Creek "children" on his third day in office warned that "my white children in Alabama have extended their law over your country," and "you must be subject to that law." Only by removing across the Mississippi could they "be subject to your own laws, and the care of your father, the President."

A few weeks later Secretary Eaton bluntly made things clear to a Cherokee delegation imploring the federal protection against Georgia promised them by treaty. Their fatherly President "cannot and will not beguile you," they learned, with any expectation that he would "step forward to arrest the constitutional act of an independent State exercised within her own limits." Soon afterward Jackson sent an agent to tell "my red Choctaw children, and my Chickasaw children" that "their father cannot prevent them from being subject to the laws of the state of Mississippi" but would instead "sustain the States in the exercise of their right." Red children "must" move beyond the states, where they would be guaranteed "land of their own . . . as long as the Grass grows or water runs." There the President would protect them and "be their friend and father." Jackson's old Alabama friend John Coffee and Tennessee's popular Governor William Carroll were appointed secret agents to bribe the chiefs into removal treaties with extensive personal reservations and "other rewards."[13]

But final expropriation of the cis-Mississippi tribes required congressional approval; and the northeastern Benevolent Empire was being mobilized in opposition by the Indians' missionary friends and their sponsoring agency, the American Board of Commissioners for Foreign Missions. Therefore the administration organized an ostensibly benevolent society to campaign for removal as the only way to save the Indians. Stephen Van Rensselaer, grand old man of the benevolent movement and political ally of Van Buren, was persuaded to head this Board for the Emigration, Preservation, and Improvement of the Aborigines of America. Similarly the Reverend Isaac Scott was enlisted for an eight-month tour to stir up support for removal among eastern Baptists. Thus Jackson prepared to take high benevolent ground in his December message to Congress.

The President's novel contention that the federal government could not restrain state sovereignty over Indians absolved him from the consequences and allowed him to strike a magnanimous posture. "It is too late to inquire whether it was just" to include tribes within the boundaries of sovereign states, he told the lawmakers, but not too late to ask "whether something can not be done, consistently with the rights of the States, to preserve this much-injured race." Ignoring Cherokee renascence, he warned that Indians were doomed "to weakness and decay" when surrounded by whites, and "the fate of the Mohegan, the Narragansett, and the Delaware is fast overtaking the Choctaw, the Cherokee, and the Creek." To avert "so great a calamity," he recommended giving them an ample territory beyond the Mississippi, where "the benevolent may endeavor to teach them the arts of civilization." Any pretense of voluntary removal evaporated under Jackson's insistence that Indians who refused must surrender their hunting lands and hold even their little farming plots at the tender mercy of the states. Thus he proposed "to perpetuate the race and to attest the humanity and justice of this Government."[14]

Party lines crystallized in Congress as the administration pressured Jacksonians to support its removal bill as a Democratic party measure, while Adams/Clay men capitalized on humanitarian sympathy for the Indians to build a National Republican opposition. In the House, where Davy Crockett defied frontier Indian hating and some northeastern Democrats registered Moderate-Light benevolence, removal had to be saved three times by the tiebreaking vote of the Jacksonian Speaker. Finally a close vote of 102–97 authorized the President to exchange public land beyond the Mississippi for eastern tribal domains, to reimburse removing Indians for improvements, and to pay for their transportation. Five hundred thousand dollars was appropriated to begin a long and painful process of shameless bribery and coercion.

As a last resort the desperate Cherokees appealed to the Supreme Court, which flatly rejected Jackson's novel constitutional doctrine that Georgia law superseded federal treaty obligations. Ruling in one case that the Court lacked jurisdiction, Chief Justice Marshall nevertheless resorted to his game of *obiter dictum* to declare Georgia's extension of jurisdiction over the Indians unconstitutional. Thus he encouraged Cherokee resistance and invited another case in which the Court ordered Georgia to free a white missionary imprisoned under its unconstitutional Indian laws. But Georgia refused, and with Jackson claiming the right to interpret the Constitution for himself, the Court had no way to compel either a state or a President. Gloating that the judicial pronouncement "fell still born," Old Hickory may well have scoffed, as a congressman later recalled, that "John Marshall has made his decision: *now let him enforce it!*"

Thus Jackson and the state coercion he abetted were left free to extort seventy-odd Indian treaties ceding a hundred million eastern acres. The calculable costs ran to some $68 million and thirty-two million western acres, while the human costs were incalculable. The proud Cherokees, among the last to capitulate, lost several thousand lives to official brutality and inefficiency on their Trail of Tears to the West.[15]

Around Indian removal, a historic political coalition gathered to champion the equality and independence of white male farmers, workers, and small enterprisers. Compromised by racism and patriarchy, the Democratic party's founding principles of democracy and limited government were laid down in Jackson's first annual message. *"The majority is to govern,"* as he proclaimed "the first principle of our system"; and in the populist rhetoric of Amos Kendall he recommended a constitutional amendment to guarantee that "the will of the people" prevailed in presidential elections. The other "great principle" on which he insisted was "a government of limited and specific, and not general, powers."

Adopting Van Buren's strategy for saving limited government from nullifier perversion, the President singled out for question the federal power to make internal improvements. Constitutional doubt, he maintained, imposed a "sacred" obligation to "appeal to the source of power" through constitutional amendment. But he did not follow his Republican predecessors in recommending a roads-and-canals amendment. "The great mass of legislation relating to our internal affairs," he insisted, "was intended to be left where the Federal Convention found it—in the State governments."

Instead he proposed a "distribution" amendment to "prevent that flagicious *log rolling legislation,* which must, in the end destroy everything like harmony, if not the Union itself." Once the national debt was paid, Congress should be authorized to distribute the anticipated federal surplus among the states. State appetites for the surplus would curb congressional extravagance, he argued, and states could use distributions for roads if they wished. "Earnestly" he warned "against all encroachments upon the legitimate sphere of State sovereignty."

Distribution alarmed antiprotectionists, who counted on using any surplus to reduce the tariff; and the President alarmed them more by refusing to regard protective duties as encroaching on state sovereignty and strict construction. Denying that the new Tariff of Abominations had proven as injurious as feared, he urged "utmost caution" in reducing rates. Indeed his politically appealing proposal to spread tax relief widely, by reducing duties on tea and coffee, would make tariffs more protectionist. The revenues lost by lower duties on the commonest household luxuries, which did not compete with American products, would have to be made up by high protective duties on imports that did. Thus Jackson's tariff/distribution policy threw down the gauntlet to South Carolina's nullifiers.

The full audacity of Old Hickory's strategy was revealed only at the end of the message, in a brief but sensational attack on the only bank for which he had any constitutional responsibility, however remote. Although the national Bank was chartered for seven more years, he urged Congress and country to begin considering alternatives. "Both the constitutionality and the expediency of the law creating this bank are well questioned by a large portion of our fellow-citizens," he asserted, "and it must be admitted by all that it has failed in the great end of establishing a uniform and sound currency."[16]

Most politicians were appalled, for they could not recall a currency sounder or more encouraging to business. The Bank had redeemed itself under a gifted new president, Philadelphia's wealthy young dilettante Nicholas Biddle. Orchestrating its central banking capabilities creatively and responsibly, he dispensed the almost forgotten blessings of a reliable national currency, an ample but controlled growth of credit, easier exchanges (both intersectional and international), and the security against fluctuations of a lender of last resort. Returning prosperity under Biddle's astute guidance had convinced respectable opinion that his big Bank was essential to progress. National Republican scorn for Jackson's crude fiscal prejudices fed Democratic embarrassment. Old Hickory had overridden the expostulations of Eaton, Lewis, and Van Buren in appealing to popular judgment against the whole political establishment.

With only the likes of Kendall and Hill encouraging his patriarchal afflatus, Jackson was stirring up a democratic challenge to bourgeois/middle-class hegemony that is unparalleled in presidential annals. By attacking banking as well as internal improvements and Indian rights, he would hold the state-rights ground against planter power and nullifier heresy for a democratic Union. Then, as he now gave notice, he would politicize popular resistance to capitalist transformation by mobilizing patriarchal democracy against the money power.

The President's manifesto set off a struggle to mold his party to the clashing market/sectional interests represented by Jacksonian congressmen. The era's Great Debate on the nature of the Union erupted when the Calhounites attempted coalition with Missouri's Jacksonian champion of cheap/free land, Senator Thomas Hart Benton. Northeastern opposition to both Missouri slavery and Benton's graduation bill had given his politics a southern cast. Formerly the Southeast had joined the Northeast in opposing cheap land, partly from desire for revenues and partly from fear of depopulation and falling property values. But President Adams's plan to finance a national transportation system with land revenues made southeastern state-rights men more sympathetic to cheap land. At the same time, northeasterners became more adamant against cheap land because it threatened to lure away their cheap manufacturing labor.

When Adams's Treasury Secretary argued on this ground that "the creation of capital is retarded" by lower land prices, Benton answered with a neo-Taylorite class/sectional critique of the whole American System. Tariffs, banks, high land prices, perhaps even internal improvements, were all parts of a northeastern plot to hog the country's wealth, he preached. By taxing the "*comforts* and *necessaries*" of the South and West, northeastern "commerce collects her accumulated treasures" and northeastern "banks diffuse an abundant paper currency."

Therefore Benton courted southern support for a Jackson party that would work "*for* the poor" instead of "against them" by taking state-rights ground against high tariffs and land prices. When he backed Georgia state rights against Indians in 1828, most southern senators reciprocated by backing his barely defeated graduation bill against an almost solid Northeast. Anticipating victory in Jackson's first Congress, Benton encountered hardening resistance to a western land grab from the market's industrializing core.

Northeasterners argued that a sacred national trust was already being squandered. The minimum auction price was rarely exceeded, they complained, because extravagant surveys had glutted the land market with four times the acreage ever sold. Connecticut's National Republican Senator Samuel A. Foot precipitated the Great Debate by proposing to suspend land surveys.

Benton's philippic in reply excoriated New England as the historic enemy of western development. Linking the Yankee policies of tariff protection and expensive land as a "most complex scheme of injustice, which taxes the South to injure the West, to pauperize the poor of the North," he proposed to ally the West with the "solid phalanx of the South" and the "scattering reinforcements" of northeastern Republicanism. Voicing a new western hostility to tariffs, he called on the South to support graduation. When South Carolina's Robert Y. Hayne endorsed cheaper lands in response, New England unlimbered its heaviest ordnance against a looming South/West coalition that could be fatal to protected manufactures.[17]

Daniel Webster, by charging South Carolina with disunion, turned an unwinnable argument about sectional affinities into an argument about nationalism that eventually proved winnable at dreadful cost. Taunting Hayne into a labored defense of nullification, the "god-like Daniel" replied with a forensic masterpiece. A "cannon loaded to the lips," as Emerson described him, discharging gorgeous rhetoric in stately cadence, he rallied patriotic emotion around the organic nationhood of Story and Marshall. In the language of *Martin* and *McCulloch,* he pronounced the federal government "emphatically and truly a government of the people," not the states. "In form and substance it emanates from them. Its powers are granted by them, and are to be exercised directly on them and for their benefit."

Endlessly reprinted and recited, Webster's *Reply to Hayne* resonated the organic nationalism spreading across the North as market needs sacralized the activist national state. Abraham Lincoln's generation of schoolboys absorbed the orator's doctrine while declaiming his thrilling peroration. He hoped his dying eyes would behold, not a shattered Union, but the gorgeous ensign of the republic, now known and honored throughout the earth, still full high advanced, its arms and trophies streaming in their original lustre, not a stripe erased or polluted, not a single star obscured, bearing for its motto, no such miserable interrogatory as "What is all this worth?" nor those other words of delusion and folly, "Liberty first and Union afterwards"; but everywhere, spread all over in characters of living light, blazing on all its ample folds, as they float over the sea and over the land, and in every wind under the whole heavens, that other sentiment, dear to every true American heart,—Liberty *and* Union, now and forever, one and inseparable.[18]

The arminian state was claiming antinomian devotion, and ultimately the mystique of sacred Union would quench secession in patriotic gore.

Websterian thunder announcing Lincolnian unionism aroused nearly every member of Congress to box the constitutional compass to constituent sensibilities. But the latent northwestern appeal of organic nationalism did not stop the South/West courtship. While disquisitions for home publication droned on for weeks in both houses, Benton and the Carolinians staged a festive Jefferson Birthday Dinner to dedicate the Democratic party to the principles of '98. At the Indian Queen Hotel on April 13, the President, the Vice President, and over a hundred congressmen were invited to respond to prepared toasts and speeches extolling the Sage of Monticello, the Virginia and Kentucky resolutions, state sovereignty, and tariff reform.

The would-be molders of the Jackson party had reckoned without Jackson. Alerted by Van Buren to the Calhounite/nullifier tone of this affair, he "saw the whole plot" and came prepared. Staring sternly across at the Vice President, he led off the volunteered toasts with "Our Union: *It must be preserved.*" As Isaac Hill gleefully reported, "an order to arrest Calhoun where he sat could not have come with more blinding, staggering force." Amid consternation the shaken Vice President rose to doggedly hold his ground by toasting "The Union: Next to our liberty, the most dear."

Public confrontation between the two highest executive officials doomed the South/West coalition. With a state-rights unionism as ardent as Webster's organic nationalism, Jackson vetoed his party's southward tilt toward planter domination and proslavery chauvinism. He "could not hear the dissolution of the Union spoken of lightly," he told Kendall, and "he meant his toast as a rebuke upon the seditious sentiments which were uttered in his presence." His insistence "that the Federal Union must be preserved, *Tariff or no Tariff,*" said Kendall, "operated as a powerful damper upon some of the Hotspurs, all of whom know that Old Hickory *means what he says.*"[19]

The intersectional courtship had been artificial all along, as became plain when the nuptial articles were put to the test of actual vote. Hayne had never promised southern support for graduation, offering instead only that the public lands might be sold to the states. The South's show of good faith was strong support for a quickly enacted "preemption" bill allowing current squatters on the public lands to buy their plots at the minimum auction price. But Benton's more radical and popular graduation bill was gutted by southern senators and tabled in the House by southern votes. Nor were Benton and other northwesterners prepared for the radical tariff reform southerners demanded, helping instead to pass the administration's moderate reduction, mainly in the nonprotectionist revenue duties on tea, coffee, and cocoa.

Northwesterners were also voting as usual for internal improvements when Andrew Jackson stepped forward to slay this developmental dragon. By threatening a veto, the President put enough pressure on congressmen to block the main project, the New Orleans/Washington/Buffalo road. But supporters of all projects, combining for a test vote, passed a stock subscription for a Maysville/Lexington turnpike in Kentucky and several other projects in its wake.

The National Republican dream of a federal transportation system died when Van Buren prompted a veto of the Maysville road bill. Couched in the Little Magician's circumlocutions, Jackson's veto message declared internal improvements constitutionally doubtful and, until the debt was paid, inexpedient as well, while the Maysville road was too local to qualify for federal support in any event. Under this doctrine the President also killed four other congressionally authorized projects—exempting only the long-sanctioned appropriation for the National Road—by simply refusing to act on them after Congress adjourned on May 31, 1830. Thus inventing the pocket veto, Jackson wielded five times in his first encounter with Congress a veto power previously exercised only nine times by all his predecessors combined.[20]

The Maysville Veto "fell upon the ears like the music of other days," said Randolph of Roanoke. In the South it inoculated Radicals and farmers against nullifier heresy, and even in Benton's Northwest it proved more palatable to voters than to politicians. To save a state-rights Union from both nullifier heresy and entrepreneurial nationalism, Old Hickory had put his own stamp on the Democratic party. Vetoing coalition with nullifiers, he instead enlisted Benton's democratic Northwest in a class/sectional coalition with Randolph's Radical/farmer South and Van Buren's "plain republican" Northeast. Randolph and Benton were the first volunteers for his Bank War.

Congress adjourned to the muffled detonation of Van Buren's secret weapon. He knew, from his Georgia visit with William H. Crawford several years before, that Calhoun had wanted General Jackson disciplined in 1818 for seizing Florida. By confirming the embittered Crawford's willingness to testify, Van Buren's campaign emissary to the Hermitage had aligned Eaton and Lewis with the Little Magician as sure winner of the coming struggle for the Jackson party. Waiting through the administration's first year for the propitious moment, the Tennessee cronies had now waved the red flag of Crawford's revelation before the predictably explosive President. A day after the Jefferson Dinner, a request went off to Crawford for the promised testimony.

On May 13 a "wrinkled and care-worn" Vice President, betraying "uneasiness, a hurried, incoherent air," opened a letter from the President enclosing Crawford's statement. Frostily expressing "great surprise," Jackson demanded an explanation. His righteous recollection had conjured up a lost letter authorizing his seizure of Florida, and he loftily reminded Calhoun that he was "but executing the *wishes* of the government."[21] Back in a fortnight came fifty-two pages of political suicide. The embattled Vice President massed evidence and inference to persuade his chief that they were being estranged by a Radical plot to advance Van Buren. By publishing this elaborate exposé if Jackson forced a break, Calhoun expected to emerge triumphant and discredit the scheming Little Magician.

Characteristically pride and logic frustrated his wishful calculations. "I cannot recognize the right on your part to call in question my conduct," he began. Refusing to explain his own conduct in 1818, he then proceeded to vindicate it indirectly by implicating Jackson's. Unable to resist the President's challenge on the historical record, he threatened to expose Jackson's Florida insubordination. The general had, in fact, exceeded orders, and Calhoun implied his readiness to prove it if pushed to publication. This veiled threat nullified in advance his labored effort to turn presidential enmity against the Little Magician's plot.

Historical fact and logic were, of course, beside the point politically. Probing Old Hickory's old sore proved even more disastrous for Calhoun than it had for Clay and Crawford eleven years before. *"Et tu Brute,"* the President curtly replied. "Understanding you now, no further communication with you on this subject, is necessary." Thus the Vice President was left twisting in a limbo of unacceptable options. Clinging for months to imaginary presidential prospects, he could neither break openly with Jackson, nor join the National Republican opposition, nor assume public leadership of the growing nullification movement in South Carolina.

Meanwhile, according to insider Amos Kendall, "Van Buren glides along as smoothly as oil and as silently as a cat." The Secretary of State had scrupulously refused to advise the President about the Vice President. "If he is managing at all," said Kendall, "it is so adroitly that nobody perceives it. . . . He has the entire confidence of the President and all his personal friends, while Calhoun is fast losing it."[22]

During the summer and fall of 1830, mere whispers from the Little Magician set off calls for Jackson's reelection from amenable Democratic newspapers and legislative caucuses. The next step in Van Buren's strategy was to supplant Duff Green's pro-Calhoun *United States Telegraph*. In December 1830 a new and pro–Van Buren administration organ appeared. Editor Francis Preston Blair, a Kentucky confederate of Kendall's, brought to the Washington *Globe* a genius for slashing popular polemic that would rally Democratic hosts for a generation under the masthead motto suggested by Kendall, *"The World Is Governed Too Much!"* Total loyalty and a stubborn western radicalism against banks and elites made "Bla-ar," as Jackson called the spindly Kentuckian, an instant White House insider. Within six weeks the *Globe* was "permitted to say" that the President would accept a second term.[23]

By February 1831 Calhoun's Jacksonian route to the White House was so definitively blocked that he finally went into open revolt by publishing his correspondence with the President. Promptly Blair's *Globe* whipped the Democratic press into assault on the apostate; and with perfect timing, in April Van Buren consolidated his triumph by dispelling the Eaton Malaria. Cabinet deliberations had become impossible as the "moral party" of Ingham, Branch, and Berrien moved into the Calhoun orbit. The Little Magician, by persuading Eaton to join him in resigning from the Cabinet, enabled the President to announce a Cabinet reorganization requiring the dissidents' resignation. With Van Buren's nominees soon heading a new Cabinet, he sailed happily away from Washington's political hazards to a safe haven as minister at the Court of St. James's.

While Calhoun's bridges burned in Washington, his lieutenants were pushing South Carolina toward a constitutional showdown with Old Hickory. Disappointment with Jackson and his first Congress enabled antitariff zealots to win the legislature in October 1830 and elect James Hamilton governer. But they lacked the two-thirds majority to call a convention embodying the sovereignty of the state; and only such a convention, Calhoun taught, could constitutionally exercise the solemn remedy of nullification.[24]

When Congress reconvened in December 1830, Jackson's lecture on the constitutionality of tariffs further enraged Carolina's hotspurs. Determined to sweep the next state election, in October 1832, by a large enough majority to call a nullifying convention, they both popularized and radicalized their crusade. While "a great talking and eating machine" of local Nullifier Clubs flattered farmer/mechanic democracy with chivalric camaraderie, harangues against "craven submission" conscripted patriarchal honor for a possible collision with federal authority. Dismayed unionists soon discovered that "the timid and the time-serving" could not endure "the finger of scorn" pointed at "submission men."

George McDuffie's tirade at Charleston in May 1831 keynoted the nullifier campaign. Scorning the Union "as the majority have made it" as a "foul monster," he hailed Carolinians' Revolutionary forebears for resisting oppression to the last extremity. "Great God! are we the descendants of those ancestors," he exclaimed; "are we freemen; are we men—grown men—to be frightened . . . by the mere nursery tales of raw-heads and bloody-bones, which even the women of our country laugh to scorn?"

The spectre of an ultimate resort to force became unmistakable at rival nullifier and unionist festivities in Charleston on the Fourth of July. A noon oration by nullifier Hayne admitted some risk of secession, and that evening unionists heard thunder from Old Hickory. Condemning "declarations inconsistent with an attachment to the Union," the President's Independence Day message to Carolinians warned that his "high and sacred duties" would "present an insurmountable barrier to the success of any plan of disorganization." And these duties, he vowed, "must and will, at all hazards, be performed."

Jackson's public challenge brought Calhoun to his personal Rubicon. He had wildly misread his published exposé as a triumph of rectitude and reason that crippled his presidential rivals. "Quite feverish under the present excitement, and his hopes,"[25] he considered Jackson's fall "almost certain" and Van Buren's prospects "hopeless." He would "in the coming contest act second to none," confidants were assured. "I never stood stronger," he boasted, only weeks before July's Jacksonian thunder stirred up nullifier rebellion against his vain hopes and noncommittal stance. Not until threatened with total isolation did he burn his last bridge to national power in order to reclaim his disaffected Carolina following. A public letter from his Fort Hill plantation in late July advocated nullification as a conservative remedy.

Calhoun's confusion of wishful logic with reality became fateful when extended from his presidential fantasy to the interlocking contradictions of market and slavery that stressed his Carolina constituents. By imagining nullification to be constitutional and peaceable, he swept the wavering into his revolutionary remedy—while managing a little longer to dream of national triumph in a "period of great confusion." His conservative illusion of orderly legality steeled both white Carolina and its manichean prophet for revolutionary resistance. "Relaxation now would be fatal," he said. Sadly an old associate concluded that "Our friend Calhoun is gone, I fear, forever."

The Carolina frenzy against protection was at bottom a frenzy about slavery. Tariff oppression, said Calhoun, was "only the occasion, not the real cause." By winning the "battle at the out-posts" of tariffs, as Governor Hamilton explained, the slaveholding *citadel would be safe.* If Congress could tax Carolina for the benefit of manufacturing sections, he argued, it could "erect the *peaceful* standard of servile revolt, by establishing colonization offices in our State, to give their bounties for emancipation." Within weeks of the Fort Hill address, preacher Nat Turner set off in Virginia's Southside American slavery's bloodiest revolt. Hysteria swept the white South, burning into nullifiers Calhoun's insistence that the "peculiar domestick institutions of the Southern States" were at stake.

White Carolina's rush to nullification prompted an overture of compromise from a President rolling in revenues. With import duties and public land sales mounting as another boom gained headway, Jackson had repaid almost $40 million of the federal debt. One more year, he proudly told his third congressional session in December 1831, would "exhibit the rare example of a great nation, abounding in all the means of happiness and security, altogether free from debt."

The time had therefore come, he declared, "to relieve the people from unnecessary taxation after the extinguishment of the public debt." Without another word about distribution, he recommended lowering tariff revenues "to the wants of the Government," but as in 1830, mainly on items not produced domestically, so as to retain high rates on protected items.[26]

This was not enough to satisfy the Carolina chivalry. By now George McDuffie's ingenious forty-bale theory had them convinced that tariffs took forty of every hundred cotton bales they produced. A germ of truth made McDuffie's caricature of international trade balances plausible. In addition to taxing the planter's purchases, tariffs somewhat reduced the prices he received, by restricting American purchases of British manufactures and therefore the American exchange available to British buyers of his cotton. Grossly exaggerating this effect, the nullifiers convinced themselves that the least taint of protection exceeded constitutional powers and affronted Carolina honor. All duties must be reduced to a uniform "revenue level" of 15 percent, they demanded.

When Congress instead followed the President's advice by tailoring another substantial reduction to injure protected interests minimally, the South Carolina delegation announced that "all hope of redress from congress is irrevocably gone." By solemn address they exhorted their constituents to decide "whether the rights and the liberties which you received as a gracious inheritance from an illustrious ancestry shall be tamely surrendered without a struggle, or transmitted undiminished to your posterity."

Nullifier intransigence against protection was frankly explained by Governor Hamilton. On the real issue of slavery "we should have few confederates abroad," he acknowledged, "whereas on the subject of free trade and constitutional rights, we should have allies throughout the civilized world." The problem came closer home, for Carolina planters were simultaneously threatened by farmer democracy. Farmer majorities, shaking planter regimes across the South, were as yet unavailable for a crusade to save planter slaveholdings. Instead a desperately audacious Carolina ruling class discovered that a gentry-led crusade to nullify tariffs could turn a menacing democratic impulse against a menacing federal authority. By implicitly linking race with rustic sensibilities about taxes, honor, and remote authority, the nullification crusade inoculated South Carolina farmers against the Jackson virus and thus preserved the last American bastion of aristocratic politics.

By stirring up constant alarm at outside menace to block internal resistance and constitutional reform, Calhoun's nullifiers ruled South Carolina unchallenged for a generation. No other state, from 1832 until the Civil War, denied its voters participation in presidential elections. Nowhere else did politicians of all stripes avow elitism so frankly. The people "expect me to think for them *here*," a leading unionist told the legislature. Not only did "the people expect that their leaders . . . will think for them," agreed nullifier Governor Hamilton, but "they will be prepared to *act* as their leaders *think*."

The aggressive nullifiers neutralized the unionism of upcountry farmers by stealing their Radical state-rights principles and leaders. Arch-Radical Dr. Cooper was an easy convert; the nullifier legislature split Radicalism into warring factions by rewarding another prominent defector with election to the federal Senate; and Judge Smith retreated to Alabama. Leadership of Carolina unionism was left to Charleston's Federalist/commercial nabobs. Denouncing the Nullifier Clubs for pandering dangerously to democracy, these patrician unionists were afraid to rally popular unionism in resistance.

While the chivalry's nullifier wing intransigently rejected tariff compromise, its unionist wing allowed a leaderless populace to be swept into revolutionary resistance. "The question is no longer one of free trade but liberty and despotism," said Calhoun at the campaign's climax in the summer of 1832. "The hope of our country now rests on our gallant little state. Let every Carolinian do his duty."

In fact, the country's hopes and fears were now focused elsewhere. Nicholas Biddle and Andrew Jackson had finally faced off over the political economy's fundamental issue. In October, as South Carolina voters gave the nullifiers an overwhelming legislative majority, a Bank War inflamed the approaching presidential referendum.

The Bank War was the acid test of American democracy. Never has the farmer/worker majority given a more radical mandate to a more indomitable President. Banks, in the insurgent consciousness, both epitomized extortionate enterprise and energized its disruptions. By doggedly assailing banking, Old Hickory gradually mobilized a seemingly invincible army of disciplined Democratic voters. Never has the majority seemed so close to actually ruling.

Yet Jackson's assault on banking was distorted from the start by a Constitution designed to frustrate majorities. Barred by the federal/state division of powers from engaging entrepreneurial excess at its source in the state-chartered banks, he could smite only the national Bank designed to restrain them from another disastrous inflation. Rapprochement between big Bank and state banks compounded the antibank dilemma. Entrepreneurial resistance to central-bank discipline was allayed by Biddle's wizardry in stabilizing the money market, easing banks through stringencies, dramatically expediting transfer of funds from place to place, and, not least, amply expanding credit. State-banking businessmen and planters embraced the national Bank as essential to sustained prosperity, bringing the paper system to a historic peak of unity and power.

Old Hickory articulated a popular consciousness too fearful of this consolidating money power to be reassured by its claims of moderation. Ever more efficiently under Biddle's leadership, it energized the market's concentration of wealth and disruption of customary ways. The national Bank's innovative bills of exchange had largely engrossed the financing of intersectional/international trade. Its notes, circulating everywhere at par as legal tender to government, were driving state bank notes out of circulation to become the national currency. Biddle's most awesome power was exercised almost invisibly through orders tightening or relaxing the twenty-five branches' demands on the state banks for specie. By thus regulating all banks' ability to make loans, issue notes, and stimulate enterprise, the big Bank regulated the volume of money, credit, and enterprise for the whole economy.

Therefore the orders that went out daily from Biddle's Philadelphia Parthenon inevitably redistributed class benefits and burdens, as between capitalists and subsistence folk, creditors and debtors, employers and workers, established wealth and aspiring enterprise. Society's most profoundly political decisions were being made out of public view, by a private, profit-making corporation that was answerable only to a paper aristocracy of stockholders and banking interests, and to no public authority. This class control of economic life—exercised today through the Federal Reserve System and hardly less vital to bourgeois hegemony than control of law and constitution—was the inevitable issue in the political showdown over the market revolution.[27]

The outcome turned heavily on constraints of the American political system. While constitutional federalism shielded the state banks from national interference, the national Bank could be attacked only through a compromising party system of uneasy coalitions and pragmatic politicians of enterprising bent. Jackson's opening salvo against the Bank met opposition not only from National Republicans but also from the Democratic congressional majority elected on his coattails. The financial committees of both houses issued reports roundly repudiating this section of his first annual message. Largely in language supplied by Nicholas Biddle, the Senate committee applauded the status quo and warned against "doubtful experiments."

The House Ways and Means Committee registered a "respectful but decided dissent" from presidential animadversions about the Bank's unconstitutionality and failure to establish "a uniform and sound currency." Declaring the constitutional question "forever settled and at rest," chairman George McDuffie took Calhoun's advanced ground that Congress "not only had the power, but the most solemn constitutional obligations, to restore the disordered currency; and the Bank of the United States was ... the only safe and effectual means." The Bank had "almost completely succeeded," McDuffie insisted. "No other human agency could have" returned state bank notes to a specie-paying basis, he argued, while its own notes "actually furnished a circulating medium more uniform than specie," given the cost of transporting specie. Predicting economic disaster if the Bank were not rechartered, the committee claimed that nearly all "the prominent men of either party ... stand committed in its favor." Thus spoke the leadership of the first Jacksonian Congress.[28]

The President was unfazed. "There will be no compromise," Amos Kendall soon reported. "It will come to this: that whoever is in favor of that Bank will be against Old Hickory."[29] While contending publicly against Indians, nullifiers, and the moral party, Jackson was filling his private memorandum book with arguments against the Bank for his next annual message. It was unconstitutional, subversive of state sovereignty, and "dangerous to Liberty," he wrote, emphasizing under the latter head that it exercised "the powers of a Sovereign upon a subject vital to the well being of the whole society," concentrating "in the hands of a few men, a power over the money of the country, which may be perverted to the oppression of the people."

[margin note: Jackson position on Bank]

The Jackson revealed by these memoranda, however casual about grammar and spelling, was neither uninformed nor unsophisticated about banking. He understood that the national Bank not only "cheapens and facilitates all the fiscal operations of the government" but also "tends in some degree to equalize domestic exchange and produce a sound and uniform currency." Aided by suggestions from John Randolph, Thomas Hart Benton, and Philadelphia's Old-School radical Stephen Simpson, he devised a substitute that would "yield all its benefits, and be obnoxious to none of its objections." A branch of the Treasury, he proposed to his second congressional session in December 1830, could hold both the public funds and private deposits. Forbidden to make loans, issue notes, or purchase property, it could earn enough by selling exchange to transfer government funds free.

For all the scorn of historians and contemporary politicians, this was essentially the independent treasury that Jacksonians eventually maintained through the country's generation of most sustained prosperity. It "would not be unconstitutional, not dangerous to liberty, and would yield to government all the facilities afforded by the present Bank," said the President, while its "incidental advantages to the country would scarcely be inferior to those afforded by the present Bank." Through private deposits and sale of exchange (which were denied the later independent treasury), it would "check the issues of the state banks by taking their notes in deposit and for exchange only so long as they continue to be redeemed in specie."[30]

When a Democratic Congress again proved deaf to criticism of Biddle's Bank, Old Hickory and his anti-Bank coterie launched a class appeal over the heads of the politicians. Jackson newspapers took up the hard-money polemic against a paper aristocracy trumpeted by Blair and Kendall in the *Globe* and Benton in the Senate. The Bank "tends to aggravate the inequality of fortunes; to make the rich richer, and the poor poorer; to multiply nabobs and paupers," thundered Missouri's Old Bullion. "Gold and silver is the best currency for a republic; it suits the men of middle property and the working people best; and if I was going to establish a working man's party, it should be on the basis of hard money; a hard money party against a paper party."[31]

Aloof from the agitation, Van Buren stood ready to wheel northern Bucktails and southern Radicals into the anti-Bank crusade. The great lesson of New York politics was never to oppose a strong current of popular feeling, and in New York he got room for anti-Bank maneuver from the Safety Fund, Wall Street jealousy of Philadelphia, and the hunger of some upstate Bucktail bankers for the federal deposits. But it was primarily to ensure his succession and reconsolidate the Jeffersonian New York/Virginia coalition that the Little Magician nervously followed popular anger and Old Hickory into the Bank War.

Late in 1829, shortly before the first presidential attack on the Bank, Van Buren had journeyed again to Richmond, where it was persistently reported that he and the Junto agreed on an anti-Bank policy for the administration. About the same time, prompted by Amos Kendall, Manhattan's leading Tammany newspaper began denouncing the Bank, joined once the *Globe* opened fire by the Bucktails' upstate organ at Albany. Van Buren's position became unmistakable in April 1831, when New York's Bucktail legislature resolved against recharter. Opposition to this resolution by the city's Tammany delegation, many of them bankers, refuted suspicions of a Wall Street plot against Philadelphia's Bank.

Yet the Little Magician embarked on the biggest risk of his career with such caution that he advised against the anti-Bank manifesto in Jackson's first annual message. When the President insisted he was "pledged against the Bank," a close Van Buren associate managed to pare a lengthy denunciation in Kendall's "loose, newspaper, slashing style" to four Delphic sentences.[32] As the anti-Bank campaign heated up in early 1831, Van Buren fled to the safety of the American mission in London, bequeathing Jackson a pro-Bank Cabinet headed by Secretary of State Edward Livingston (of the eminent New York Republican clan) and Treasury Secretary Louis McLane. Anxious himself over his chief's audacity, he could well understand why ally Ritchie "scarcely ever went to bed . . . without apprehension that he would wake up to hear of some *coup d'état* by the General."[33]

Most anxious of all was Biddle, as Jackson's chances for reelection in 1832 mounted. "I do not dislike your Bank more than all banks," the President had told him on a visit to the White House. "But ever since I read the history of the South Sea Bubble I have been afraid of banks."[34] Yet the banker was getting reassurances from Major Lewis and the new Treasury Secretary McLane that the President could be persuaded to approve recharter with only minor modifications. When a new Democratic Congress convened in December 1831, Jackson allowed McLane to argue for recharter in his annual report and contented himself in the state of the union message with reminding the country of his previously expressed views.

At this point presidential politics intervened. The Antimasons had held the first national party convention to nominate William Wirt, and the National Republicans followed their example to nominate the Bank's old friend Henry Clay for President and its counsel John Sergeant for Vice President. The Democrats also held a national convention, not because of any doubt that Jackson would be their candidate, but to unite their party on Van Buren for Vice President. The Little Magician's foes in the Senate thought they had finished him politically by rejecting his appointment as minister to England. "It will kill him, sir, kill him dead," exulted Calhoun after casting the decisive vote. "He will never kick, sir, never kick."[35] Instead martyrdom ensured the New Yorker's nomination as Jackson's heir apparent.

National Republicans pressed Biddle to request recharter before the election, arguing that Jackson would either have to acquiesce or be defeated for destroying an invaluable institution. When a careful headcount confirmed a comfortable majority in Congress, Biddle submitted a memorial for recharter. Despite Benton/Bucktail charges of Bank abuses, this Democratic Congress passed a recharter bill by large margins. Van Buren, hastening back from London, reached the White House at midnight on July 3, just after the bill's arrival, to find the President ill but resolute. "The bank, Mr. Van Buren, is trying to kill me," he said, *"but I will kill it."*[36] A week later his resounding veto message went to Congress.

Few pronouncements have had a greater impact on American politics. Astutely tailored to popular suspicions by Amos Kendall, with help on constitutional questions from Attorney General Roger B. Taney (the new Cabinet's only Bank foe), it denigrated monopolistic enrichment of the Bank's wealthy stockholders, extensive stock ownership by foreigners, and northeastern exploitation of the West and South. Flatly rejecting Chief Justice Marshall's *McCulloch* doctrine, it shocked conservatives by asserting that "the Congress, the Executive, and the Court must each for itself be guided by its own opinion of the Constitution."

Most shocking were three concluding paragraphs in which Jackson confronted class reality like no other President. "The rich and powerful too often bend the acts of government to their selfish purposes," he said. ". . . Many of our rich men have not been content with equal protection and equal benefits, but have besought us to make them richer by act of Congress. By attempting to gratify their desires we have in the results of our legislation arrayed section against section, interest against interest, and man against man, in a fearful commotion which threatens to shake the foundations of our Union."

Like Jefferson and Taylor of Caroline, Jackson blamed capitalist aggrandizement on government. Against a three-century backdrop of America's equalizing person/land ratio, the natural order seemed inherently equitable until interfered with. Like Taylor, Jackson denounced the artificial property acquired by government favor while invoking protection by law for the natural "fruits of superior industry, economy, and virtue." But "when the laws undertake to add to these natural and just advantages artificial distinctions, to grant titles, gratuities, and exclusive privileges, to make the rich richer and the potent more powerful," he argued, "the humble members of society—the farmers, mechanics, and laborers—who have neither the time nor the means of securing like favors to themselves, have a right to complain of the injustice of their Government."

Early American democracy rallied against capitalist abuse of government. "If it would confine itself to equal protection," said Jackson in laying out the democratic program of dismantling the activist state, "and, as Heaven does its rains, shower its favors alike on the high and the low, the rich and the poor, it would be an unqualified blessing." Therefore he called for "a stand against all new grants of monopolies and exclusive privileges, against any prostitution of our Government to the advancement of the few at the expense of the many, and in favor of compromise and gradual reform in our code of laws and system of political economy."[37]

Respectable opinion was aghast. The veto message "has all the fury of a chained panther biting the bars of his cage," Nicholas Biddle told Henry Clay. "It is really a manifesto of anarchy—such as Marat or Robespierre might have issued to the mob of the faubourgh St. Antoine; and my hope is that it will contribute to relieve the country from the dominion of these miserable people. You are destined to be the instrument of that deliverance." But the votes to override the veto were not available, and Congress adjourned amid noisy overtures to a presidential referendum.

The veto message seemed so patently outrageous to Biddle that the Bank reprinted it by thousands in support of Clay's election. But "contrary to all reasonable calculations," as the National Republican standard-bearer was soon hearing from alarmed supporters, the veto "to a considerable extent is popular," and the Bank, even in its Pennsylvania stronghold, was so "decidedly unpopular" that it was producing "an overwhelming majority for the President."[38] When the dust of battle settled in November, Jackson had 219 electoral votes to 40 for Clay. Vermont's 7 went to the Antimasons' Wirt.

Jackson no sooner emerged victorious from his first engagement with the money power than he was challenged by the slave power. A month before the presidential election, South Carolina voters had given the nullifiers carte blanche. An instantly assembled legislature ordered instant election of a sovereign convention, and on November 24 "the people of the State of South Carolina, in Convention assembled," pronounced all tariffs "null, void, and no law."

The convention's ordinance also nullified in advance any judicial proceeding affirming the tariff laws, absolved South Carolinians of all obligations under them, and instructed the legislature to enact any measure necessary to prevent their enforcement in the state after February 1, 1833. All residents were "required and enjoined, to Obey and give effect to this Ordinance"; appeals against it to the federal judiciary were declared contempt of court; and an oath to support it was required of judges, most other officeholders, and jurors in cases involving it. The ordinance would be enforced "at any hazard," the convention proclaimed, and South Carolina would secede if the federal government attempted "to coerce the State, shut up her ports, destroy or harass her commerce, or to enforce tariffs" except through the courts.[39] Promptly the legislature authorized military conscription and four hundred thousand dollars for a state army, whose ranks were quickly filled by twenty-five thousand volunteers.

Nullification in arms aroused all Jackson's passions as an assault on the democracy he personified. Upon receiving the ordinance, "he went to his office alone and began to dash off page after page of the memorable Proclamation which was soon to electrify the country," as Major Lewis later recalled. "With that great steel pen of his, and with such rapidity, that he was obliged to scatter the written pages all over the table to let them dry," he poured out a new reverence for a Union sanctified by majority rule.[40] Unless minority veto and planter chauvinism were nipped in the bud, he saw from the start, secession would dismember the democratic Union. "Ours is a Government of laws, and depends on a will of the majority," he had long since admonished nullifer Hayne. ". . . Oppose it . . . and revolution with all its attendant evils in the end must be looked for."

Consequently Old Hickory railed against "the absurdity" that a state had "a right to secede and destroy this union, and the liberty of our country with it, or nullify the laws of the union." This was "revolution, or rebellion," he exploded to a friend; and while conceding Carolinians' "natural right" to attempt revolution, he maintained that "the ballance of the people comp[o]sing this union have a perfect right to coerce them to obedience." Constitutionally "the people are the sovereigns," he insisted, and only "thay can altar and amend." Nullification converted a "perpetual union" into "a rope of sand; under such I would not live," he exclaimed. "I will die with the union."[41]

The President considered indicting leading "Nullies" for treason and threatened "to hang the first man of them I can get my hand on to the first tree I can find." Only Van Buren's advice to isolate the nullifiers by forcing them to make the first hostile move quelled Jackson's "passion . . . to go himself with a sufficient force . . . and arrest Messrs. Calhoun, Hayne, Hamilton, and McDuffie."[42] Meanwhile he dispatched to Charleston a spy, military and naval reinforcements, army commander Winfield Scott, and five thousand muskets to arm local unionists.

Both Jackson and the nullifiers were angling for support from the rest of the antitariff South. While the Carolina legislature's token and voluntary measures against duty payments stopped far short of the convention's directive, the President pressed Congress virtually to abandon the protective policy. Tariff protection should ultimately be limited, he said in his fourth annual message on December 4, to articles of military necessity. With great factories replacing mechanic shops as beneficiaries, he put the issue in a new class perspective. "Those who have vested their capital in manufacturing establishments," he declared, "can not expect that the people will continue permanently to pay high taxes for their benefit."[43] Promptly Treasury Secretary McLane and a reconstituted House Ways and Means Committee hammered out a proposal cutting rates in half.

Yet Jackson insisted on coupling tariff reform with repudiation of nullification. Six days after the annual message, he issued a Proclamation declaring the Carolina doctrine *"incompatible with the existence of the Union"* and *"contradicted expressly by the letter of the Constitution."* He had turned over his bundle of notes to Secretary of State Edward Livingston, a distinguished jurist, with instructions to give it "your best flight of eloquence"; and Livingston provided a searing indictment of nullifier inconsistencies.

Rhetoric and emotion peaked in a Jackson-drafted concluding appeal to "fellow-citizens of my native State." Like a father whose children were "rushing to certain ruin," Old Hickory admonished Carolinians that they had been led "to the brink of insurrection." Warning that their leaders aimed at disunion, and "disunion is *treason*," he insisted that "you can not succeed," for "the laws of the United States must be executed." Instead he implored "the descendants of the Pinckneys, the Sumters, the Rutledges," and other Revolutionary heroes to "snatch from the archives of your State the disorganizing edict of its convention" and "never take the field unless the star-spangled banner of your country shall float over you."[44]

The Proclamation's ardent nationalism alarmed the many state-rights Jacksonians who opposed nullification but affirmed the theoretical right of secession as an ultimate guarantee against consolidation. Seeing secession as the real threat, Jackson could not resist the democratic resonance of the organic and indissoluble nationhood posited by Story, Marshall, and Webster. "The people of the United States formed the Constitution," declared the Proclamation. They established "a *government*, not a league"; and no state had a right to secede "because such secession does not break a league, but destroys the unity of a nation; and any injury to that unity . . . is an offense against the whole Union."

Van Buren blamed this heresy, so distressing to his Radical southern allies, on the "federal proclivity" of Livingston and the Cabinet. The President, he explained, had "more pressing and more practical questions on his mind than speculative disquisitions." Actually Jackson rejected many warnings that his nationalism went too far. "With great decision of manner," he told Major Lewis that "those are my views, and I will not change them nor strike them out." To Van Buren's objections he replied that "preservation of the union is the supreme law." Unless the ultimate threat of secession was "met boldly at the threshold" of nullification, he insisted, "our union is gone, and our liberties with it forever."[45]

State-rights Jacksonians were further perturbed by the consolidationists' sudden enthusiasm for the President. Justice Story declared that "the Chief Justice and myself have become his warmest supporters."[46] Webster and Kent led the magnates of Boston and New York in public meetings applauding the Proclamation and pledging Jackson full support against nullification. Invited to Massachusetts by a grateful legislature, he received the Yankee bourgeoisie's ultimate accolade, a Harvard LL.D.

Although Dr. Jackson welcomed all recruits and even flirted briefly with Webster,[47] he put little reliance on gentry politicians of any stripe. The Union "will now be tested," he said, "by the support I get from the people." Again demonstrating, as in the Bank War, his extraordinary resonance with politically stifled popular attitudes, he evoked against nullifiers "the united voice of the yeomanry of the country." Remote federal authority was losing its terrors for farming and working people as a people's President wielded a democratic Union against local elites. From no other man, said a Massachusetts Democrat, could a Jeffersonian populace endure the "sentiments which they received with acclamation from General Jackson." Nor "would these Doctrines be as safe in any other hands."[48]

The popular unionism articulated by Old Hickory merged with the developmental nationalism of market elites in a general outcry against nullification. The Carolina doctrine was denounced by seventeen legislatures, north and south, and condoned by none. Only Jacksonian Virginia and New York voiced reservations about Jackson's ultranationalist heresies. The sacred doctrines of '98, declared the Old Dominion, sanctioned neither nullification nor "all the principles" of his Proclamation, "many of which are in direct conflict with them." At the other end of the old Radical axis, New York's Bucktails were embarrassed by their legislative opponents' "insidious" proposal to endorse the Proclamation as advancing "the true principles upon which only the constitution can be maintained." Van Buren himself composed the legislature's substitute resolution lauding Jackson's devotion to state rights and strict construction in practice as a better guide to his "true principles" than his controversial notions about the origin and nature of the Union.

Elsewhere it seemed that "politicians may quibble about abstract notions, but the people will stand by Andrew Jackson and save the Union." The Proclamation was explicitly endorsed by most northern states and Mississippi, while the most democratic southern and western states expressed the most fulsome devotion to "that Union," as Mississippi put it, "whose value we will never stop to calculate— holding it, as our fathers held it, precious above all price."[49]

Across the South nullification focused class conflict over democracy. The nullifiers' most militant foe in the Carolina upcountry defended the Union as only less dear than a "deep rooted love of democratic principles."[50] While southern farmer constituencies rallied in defense of a democratic Union, a planter gentility already disgruntled by democracy, tariffs, and Bank War raised the standard of revolt against Jackson's doctrinal heresies and threats to coerce a sovereign state. Georgia's farmer-based faction, taking the name Union Party, rewon the state from the planter-based Radical/Troup faction, now calling itself the States Rights Party. Even in Virginia, representatives of western farmers overwhelmed Tidewater planter dissidence to get an uncompromising foe of nullification elected senator.

Tension mounted as South Carolina's February 1 deadline for blocking tariff collections approached. While the state army drilled and mounted minutemen prepared in every district to rush to Charleston's defense from federal attack, unionists mustered under arms by thousands in upcountry farming districts. Armed Carolina unionists had an important role in Jackson's strategy for thwarting nullification with the least possible appearance of military force. Although clearly authorized to use the army and/or call out the state militia to enforce the laws when civil process failed, he preferred to forestall sympathy for the nullifiers by pushing civil process to the limit. The presidential plan was to enforce the law by court orders from the federal judge in Charleston; and if his marshal met forcible resistance, unionists would be armed as a civilian *posse commitatus* of historic proportion to enforce a lawful court order.

When the unionists' genteel leaders proved too skittish about the heroic role assigned them to assure an adequate *posse commitatus,* Jackson asked Congress for authority to stave off military confrontation by moving the Carolina customhouses to federal vessels and island forts while requiring cash payment of duties before goods were landed. And in case the state attacked federal installations, he demanded that Congress reaffirm his existing powers to use the army and militia. Carolinians facing checkmate railed so passionately at the "Bloody Bill" granting his requests that this measure designed to avoid force has been known ever since as the Force Bill.

Backed overwhelmingly by popular opinion and determined to discredit disunion once and for all, Old Hickory insisted on passage of the symbolic Force Bill while letting the administration's tariff reform bill founder under protectionist amendments and nullifier scorn. Checkmated at every point by his artful blend of menace and restraint, South Carolina had to retreat. Ten days before the "Fatal First" of February, an unofficial meeting of leading nullifiers in Charleston nullified nullification. To give congressional tariff reform a chance, they urged importers to continue paying duties rather than attempting evasion through the state's oathbound courts.

Jackson's victory over disunion was diluted when Senator Henry Clay bounced back from his recent defeat with one of those creative legislative bargains that periodically redeemed his electoral ineptitude. With nullifiers desperate for a face-saving tariff reform, with manufacturers adamant against drastic reductions, and with the anti-Jackson forces in hopeless disarray, the Great Compromiser offered Calhoun a brilliant solution. The nullifier principle of a uniform percentage rate could be honored by lowering all duties to 20 percent, he proposed, while manufacturers could be mollified by spreading reductions over nine years with sharp cuts postponed until 1841–1843. Nullifiers could claim success, and manufacturers could count on years of ample protection during which the final cuts might be blocked.

Nullifier acceptance of this proposal made it irresistible to congressional Democrats as well. With the administration abandoning its tariff bill, most politicians preferred Clay's compromise to Jackson's policy of forcing South Carolina into total surrender. Jackson's price for assent was the Force Bill. Only after the Force Bill passed in February (20–1 in the Senate, with nine unhappy southern dissidents abstaining) were Democrats free to pass Clay's Compromise Tariff. South Carolina played out its charade by reassembling in convention to rescind tariff nullification—and then defiantly nullified the now moot Force Bill.

Powerful class forces compromised Jackson's effort to crush definitively, in its initial eruption around Charleston harbor, the planter chauvinism that eventually reerupted there to rend the Union. By coalescing on the Compromise Tariff, planter capital and commercial/industrial capital were able to submerge their differences in a "Whig" opposition to the Jacksonian tyranny of their common foe democracy.

Clay's brokerage saved Calhoun's nullifiers politically. By claiming credit for tariff reform, they tightened their grip on South Carolina and even imposed an oath of primary loyalty to the state that barred their unionist foes from office. With nullification totally repudiated elsewhere, north and south, Carolina's fireating gentry launched a prolonged agitation to excite other southern whites into proslavery secession.

Yet it is hard to imagine a President who could have mobilized greater political strength against nullification than Old Hickory. Understanding that a democratic Union was at stake, he linked democracy indissolubly with American nationalism. His democratic unionism held a fracturing republic together for another thirty years before drowning slavery in fratricidal blood.

By March 4, 1833, when the people's President again took the constitutional oath from Chief Justice Marshall, he had executed his popular mandate by stopping progressive capital's ambitious developmental program in its tracks. Blocking a national transportation system, retreating from protectionism, and consolidating an insurgent majority against the Monster Bank, he gave such satisfaction that every President since has had to run the gauntlet of a mass electorate. Asserting premarket values against all respectable opinion, Jackson mustered democracy to defend patriarchal independence, equality, and therefore honor, against an activist capitalist state. Yet within days of his heartfelt plea for a "government so simple and economical as scarcely to be felt,"[51] his zeal against nullifier abuse of state power undermined constitutional defenses against abuse of federal power. As his Nullification Proclamation rallied democratic nationalism around indissoluble Union, popular devotion to state rights and strict construction eroded.

Democracy—the last restraint on a sanctified capitalist state—still had to prove itself. The Bank Veto had not tamed the paper system, and during Jackson's second term an escalating Bank War would test the majority's ability to constrain the capitalist state through democratic politics. Or would a democratic facade legitimize bourgeois hegemony?

Chapter 11

Ambiguous Democracy

As DISRUPTIVE boom brought insurgency to a crest in the mid-1830s, Old Hickory executed the Jeffersonian legacy by pushing the American political system to its democratic limits. Where Jefferson's patrician assurance had trusted farmers and workers to follow high-minded gentlemen, Jackson's patriarchal afflatus forced majority will on recalcitrant politicians. Where the philosopher/statesman conducted a Fabian defense of the yeoman republic, the soldier/tribune brought to politics the sanguinary maxims of the Roman sack of Carthage. Favoring "warr to the knife, and the knife to the hilt," he was ever ready to "carry the warr into affrica."

Consequently the President was aroused to discover, while his anti-Bank mandate was still rolling in, that "the hydra of corruption is only *scotched, not dead.*" With the Bank chartered for three more years and its nemesis reelected for four, Biddle was plunging into a desperate political struggle for a two-thirds congressional majority to override a veto. The Bank's distinguished counsel, Horace Binney, was elected from Philadelphia's silk-stocking district to lead the effort in Congress, and other lawmakers were courted with large loans and legal fees. When Senator Webster, after flirting with Jackson in the nullification crisis, complained that his princely retainer had not been "*refreshed* as usual," Biddle promised a check as soon as it could be issued without knowledge of the government directors. The Bank was already cultivating newspapers with loans and payments for favorable articles, and even the staid Washington *National Intelligencer* was paid for a special edition designed to defeat the administration's House point man, James K. Polk.[1]

Marking Biddle's every hostile move while embroiled with nullifiers during the winter of 1832–1833, Jackson unlimbered his only available weapon for throttling the Monster before it throttled the people. Its charter authorized the Treasury Secretary, for cause reported to Congress, to remove the federal deposits. With the national debt almost extinguished by soaring revenues, the federal surplus at Biddle's disposal was about to swell into millions—and with it his power to regulate credit and corrupt politics.

Jackson's determination to remove the deposits alarmed most Democrats in both Congress and Cabinet. Compelled by an aroused electorate to approve the Veto, many still hoped the President would accept a modified recharter bill, and few welcomed a further assault on business confidence. Secretary of State Livingston threatened to resign, and more troublesomely, so did the Bank's authorized executioner, Treasury Secretary McLane. Moreover an agent sent by McLane to examine Biddle's books declared the deposits safe.

Nevertheless Jackson expressed grave doubts when Congress convened in December to grapple with the nullification crisis. Demanding congressional investigation of the deposits' security, he also recommended selling the federal Bank stock. But a Democratic House rejected the stock sale and, following further investigation by its Ways and Means Committee, endorsed resoundingly, 109–46, the committee majority's conclusion that the Bank was sound and the deposits safe.

Even Van Buren backed away from removal under the dismay of businessmen and politicians, staying far from Washington to avoid responsibility and filling the presidential mail with pleas for restraint toward both Bank and nullifiers. "You will say I am on my old track—caution—caution," he wrote. "But my Dr Sir, I have always thought, that considering our respective temperaments, there was no way . . . I could better render you . . . service." The President got support only from Kendall and Blair of the Kitchen Cabinet, Attorney General Taney, and Polk's report, for a Ways and Means minority, plausibly questioning the deposits' safety.[2]

But Old Hickory was ready, once he quelled the nullifiers, to appeal to the people against all politicians. He saw his resounding reelection as a mandate to fight the Bank War to a finish along the producer-class lines of the Veto. This meant—as authoritatively interpreted by Amos Kendall at the return of Congress—opposing not only the Monster, but also state banks and other oppressors of labor. In a rare and widely reprinted speech to Washington's Central Hickory Club, the President's "chief overseer" denounced the *"Nobility Systems"* that everywhere enabled "a few rich and intelligent men" to "live upon the labor of many." Even "the United States have their young *Nobility System,*" he ominously declared. "Its head is the Bank of the United States; its right arm, a protecting Tariff and Manufacturing Monopolies; its left, growing State debts and States incorporations."[3]

On these grounds Old Hickory challenged bourgeois hegemony like no other President by assailing credit, the lifeblood of escalating enterprise. When the Monster's death-struggle in the removal crisis inflamed his hard-money majorities against the whole banking system, democracy and capitalism battled to their historic détente.

As soon as the nullification crisis eased in the spring of 1833, Jackson sent Livingston on a diplomatic mission to France, kicked the recalcitrant McLane upstairs to the vacated State Department, and replaced him at the Treasury with William J. Duane, son of Philadelphia's antibank, Old-School warhorse. On the younger Duane's first evening in office, a notorious fellow Philadelphian called unannounced at his lodgings to instruct him in his duties. Claiming presidential sanction, Reuben M. Whitney sought assent to a detailed plan for transferring the deposits from the Monster to selected state banks.

The next evening he was back, trespassing on the Sabbath and bringing to enforce his demands Duane's nominal Treasury subordinate Amos Kendall, the sickly and seldom seen "diabolical genius" who was reputed to be the administration's "*thinking* machine" and "*writing* machine," if not "*lying* machine."[4] The callers left disappointed, for their host "could not wholly conceal my mortification at an attempt . . . to reduce me to a mere cypher." The rumors of "an influence, at Washington, unknown to the constitution and the country" had proved "well founded" if not "irresistible."[5]

Bruised pride aside, Whitney himself was enough to excite all the new Secretary's Old-School suspicions. Back when Duane was leading the battle against both state and national banks in the Pennsylvania legislature and taking hard-money ground with radical Workeys, Whitney had sat on the Monster's board until ousted by Biddle. Vengefully exposing the Bank's dirty linen to Jackson's Kitchen coterie, he had now come to Washington to claim his reward as legman and coach for Biddle's assailants and interrogators.

Whitney epitomized the business fixers and influence-peddlers beginning to swarm around the capitalist state. Seeking federal deposits for a Philadelphia bank managed by his brother-in-law, he made a snug provision for himself in the administration's removal plan. He was to get commissions from the deposit banks as Treasury agent to manage them—a regulator in the pay of the regulated—and he shamelessly pressed Duane for appointment to this egregious conflict of interest. Eventually, through Kendall's veiled endorsement, he extorted enough commissions from deposit banks as *their* agent—or lobbyist with favored access to the Treasury—to become the capital's most lavish host.

The confrontation between Duane and Whitney, between hard-money egalitarianism and paper-money enterprise, brought to a head the Democratic contradiction between equality and opportunity. Both impulses could unite against the Monster, but removal forced forward deep differences about what should replace it. Jackson's hard-money preference for an independent treasury, he belatedly explained to Duane, had been so repeatedly and resoundingly rejected by Congress and respectable opinion that he had reluctantly "brought my mind" to this "Experiment" with state deposit banks as "the best if not the only practicable resort."[6]

With Whitney hovering about, however, Duane saw in removal too many indications of an "anxiety to make money" by state bankers eager to "trade upon the public money." Although state-banking interests were mainly Whiggish, prorecharter, and antiremoval, some well-connected Democratic bankers—including Whitney's Philadelphia brother-in-law, a Baltimore crony of Taney's, some of Van Buren's Bucktail/Tammanyites in New York, and Boston's Democratic boss David Henshaw—were greedy for the swelling federal deposits. Congressional adamancy against an independent treasury registered state-bank resistance to credit restraint, while leaving state banks as the only alternative depositories for federal funds. Not even Old Hickory was "strong enough to encounter all the banks of all the states at once," as Senator Benton explained. "Temporizing was indispensable—and even the conciliation of a part of them."[7]

But conciliating banks "would only increase evils, already too great," in the opinion of another Treasury Secretary turning refractory. Bad timing compounded the misunderstanding generated by his touchy insecurity and the President's officious intermediaries. Duane had assumed office with Jackson impatient to depart on his New England tour and too sure of the Old Schooler's support to bother explaining the Experiment's hard-money thrust. Indirectly through deposit banks, Old Hickory intended to force a specie currency on a state-banking system beyond his direct constitutional reach. As neither man understood, both wanted to coerce banks into eschewing small notes, Jackson by rewarding all compliant banks with deposits, and Duane by receiving only their notes at an independent treasury.

While Jackson fell ill in New England and convalesced at the Virginia shore, Duane was besieged in sweltering Washington during the summer of 1833 by those "whose intercourse with the President was clandestine," presumably Kendall, Blair, and Whitney. He found their arguments suspiciously identical with the President's, even "in the identical language"—mistaking the source, in a common underestimation of Old Hickory. Congress was corruptible, the Kitchen men urged, and would thwart and subvert the veto power unless the deposits were removed. Most appalling to the high-minded Secretary was their politically astute anxiety for "a test question, at the opening of the new congress, for party purposes."

For three months Duane stalled removal. Claiming sole statutory authority for deciding, he bombarded the President with warnings that banking's "loose corporations" were "so partial in their operations, and so liable to be perverted, as to affect seriously the morals, impair the earnings, and endanger the liberties of the people." Bank profits were "a tax mainly paid by those who labour and produce," argued this veteran of working-class politics, by those upon whom "ruin heavily falls, in the event of any catastrophe." All banks, in his Old-School view, were unconstitutional, the states having sold "to chartered companies a power to do, what they cannot lawfully do themselves, that is, issue paper as money!"

Duane blamed banks for the "rapid advances" of "inequality in condition, luxury, and vice." Without banks "there might not have been so many towns," he conceded, "or such crowds as are in them; but there would have been more men at the plough; and there would have been more integrity, frugality, and content." Instead society had been convulsed with "fluctuations, revulsions and panics, ruinous in their consequences," by the "mighty power" of nearly six hundred banks.

Jackson was stunned that a man so right in pedigree and premises could be so politically unrealistic in conclusion. "I had not the smallest notion that we could differ," he told his perplexing Secretary. Nothing had ever "given me more mortification." Focused like his public on thwarting and crushing Biddle, however, and seeing the Experiment as the only politically feasible means, he deepened Duane's misgivings by praising state banks. Never, he wrote in an extended defense of his policy, had "the prospect of their permanent success and stability" been "more cheering." Duane retorted hotly (suspecting Kendall's authorship) that banking's "stimulated system" was no "indication of social happiness or moral excellence," but "an omen of the disease and decay in both." He asked only "one more appeal to congress" for an independent treasury.

The stubborn Secretary was finally driven to his last-ditch practical objection that no bank would accept federal deposits in defiance of Biddle. But Kendall went behind his back for presidential authorization to sound out bankers in the eastern cities, and then got Duane's restrictive negotiating instructions overruled to authorize the best bargain obtainable. Although most banks demurred, Kendall found seven willing, provided they didn't have to cut in competitors. All but one of the volunteer deposit banks were controlled by such enterprising Democrats as Whitney's brother-in-law and Taney's crony, who had joined the popular party for aid against more established capital and who coveted the deposits as a source of loans and profits.

Just as Kendall's volunteers were arousing Duane's deepest fears, the maddening Whitney appeared bearing a presidential ultimatum for immediate removal. With all lost save honor, the beleaguered Secretary bristled into hopeless defiance. "I refuse," he told his formidable chief, "to carry your directions into effect." He could not consent "to foster local banks, which, in their multiplication and cupidity, derange, depreciate, and banish the only currency known to the constitution, that of gold and silver." The proposed "change to local and irresponsible banks" would "promote doubt and mischief," he predicted, when "one dollar in silver cannot be paid for six dollars of paper in circulation."[8]

Quixotically the rebel also refused to resign. With Old Hickory and his advisers impatient to provide a rallying point for his anti-Bank majority before Congress met in December, poor Duane was peremptorily dismissed and replaced by Taney. Promptly Jackson's fourth (but not last) Treasury Secretary announced that, beginning October 1, the government would confide its receipts to Kendall's volunteers while disbursements gradually withdrew its balances from the Monster.

To save "this great and valuable institution," Biddle now plunged into a desperate abuse of its economic power. Although removal required some contraction of its loans, he resolved on such a severe contraction that general prostration would stampede Congress into restoring the deposits and rechartering the Bank over Jackson's veto. Only "suffering abroad" would break "the ties of party allegiance," he said. By the time the "panic session" of Congress met in December 1833, businessmen everywhere were under heavy pressure, memorials to alleviate distress by restoring the deposits were pouring in, and the discordant elements led by Clay, Calhoun, and Webster were united in a "Whig" opposition to "executive usurpation" that controlled the Senate.

Even the solidly Democratic House gave way to panic. As Biddle tightened the screw, as mercantile houses began to fail, as delegations of desperate businessmen descended on Washington, House leaders struggled for three months to stem the flood of Whig jeremiads. Protestors who braved the President's calculated tantrums at the White House were advised to "go to Nicholas Biddle." The banker's supporters warned him against relenting under "appeals to your best feelings" and "the scenes of distress and ruin you will be called upon to witness." One assured him that "nothing will be done to save the Country unless a general Bankruptcy ensues and the '*experiment*' thus proved to have failed." They need not have worried. "My own course is decided," he remorselessly declared. "All the other Banks and all the merchants may break, but the Bank of the United States shall not break."[9]

Eventually, however, the Bank's rash irresponsibility became too egregious for even its supporters. Pro-Bank Democrats in Pennsylvania were alienated when the financial pressure sabotaged a state bond issue late in February, and in March elder statesman Albert Gallatin organized a committee of New York's most prominent financiers to demand that Biddle relax the pressure. Finally in early April, as angry comprehension of Biddle's abuse of power swept the country, House Democrats mustered a majority for resolutions upholding removal and opposing recharter. So conclusively had the big Bank convicted itself that even Whig politicians were compelled to abandon it. Except for the formalities of winding up its business, the Second Bank of the United States was dead.

If Jackson had now capped victory over the nullifiers by declaring victory in the Bank War, he might have vied with the martyred Lincoln as patron saint of democratic capitalism. Instead, with the Monster defanged and resentment of aristocratic privilege peaking, he unfurled the banner of hard money to "carry the warr" to the paper vitals of enterprise. The threat of real constraint over ebullient capital by a real democracy of effectual majorities brought the political phase of the market revolution to a showdown.

The hard-money impulse got its moral energy from an agrarian ethos wary of "money-getting and money-spending." The politics of "'better times' in the mart," said Van Buren's pious law partner, was "unsuited to a free people." In the ambiguous ambience of Tammany Hall, Benjamin F. Butler called on Democrats to save the country from the "fatal doctrine,"—Whig, of course—"that the interests of trade and other pecuniary interests are the highest interests of the nation—that nothing is to be esteemed so valuable as money—and that profit-profit-profit is the 'be all and the end all' of the social state!'"[10]

Traditional moral economy and Democratic politics were being radicalized by a resurgence of working-class militancy that brought the labor movement to its first historic peak in the mid-1830s. Although shattered organizationally by the failure of independent workingmen's parties, Workeyism survived in spirit to reignite when prices spiraled ahead of wages in another cresting boom while demand for labor increased. Strikes by Baltimore hatters and New York carpenters in 1833 inspired support and organization by other trades, and the old Workey leadership reemerged in General Trades' Unions uniting all the trades in more than a dozen cities. GTUs federated fifty-three unions in Philadelphia with over ten thousand members and fifty-two in New York with an estimated two-thirds of the city's workers. Overall a fifth to a third of urban workingmen seem to have joined a union.

A wildfire of mainly successful strikes, 172 by one count, swept the Northeast between 1833 and 1836. Mounting demands for the ten-hour day culminated in a general strike by some twenty thousand Philadelphia workers. Striking trades got substantial financial support from nonstriking trades through the GTUs; local leaders met annually in a National Trades' Union to coordinate strategy; and a new spirit of class solidarity reached beyond the established trades to back, at least sporadically, unskilled and factory labor, immigrants, and working women. By 1836 the ten-hour day had been won by much of the working class. President Jackson ordered the new norm for federal navy yards, and it was soon extended to all federal workers.[11]

Workey editors, pamphleteers, and orators proclaimed a remarkably consistent analysis and program. Invariably they started with the labor theory of value to explain how capital divided society into two classes, the producing many and the exploiting few, by expropriating the fruits of labor. Arguing that Americans' "young *Nobility*" was even more exploitative than Europe's landed aristocracy, they preached a politics of class resistance through workingmen's parties and unions. Boston strike leaders A. H. Wood and Seth Luther put the Workey creed pithily: "*Capital* which can only be made productive by *labor* is endeavoring to crush *labor* the only source of wealth." Seeing their struggle for the ten-hour day as "neither more nor less than a contest between *Money* and LABOR," Wood confessed to "arraying the poor against the *principles* of the rich, and if this be arraying the poor against the rich, I say go on with tenfold fury."[12]

In New England, a shared use-value ethic of labor united embattled urban workers with aggrieved farmers, village mechanics, and some rural notables. When Boston strikers for the ten-hour day reached out for allies, rural and urban workingmen's associations federated in the New England Association of Farmers,

Mechanics, and Other Workingmen, which was soon fielding candidates for governor and Congress in Massachusetts. Here harsh reality made the Workey indictment of capitalism persuasive even to respectables alarmed by the market's assault on ancestral ways. The indictment was most cogently drawn, in fact, in rural Massachusetts, where collapse of the Federalist/antinomian synthesis jolted Ivy-educated notables into Workey radicalism. In the fall of 1830 a pillar of Federalist/Congregational orthodoxy, distressed on retiring from Congress by the decay of his Berkshire countryside, startled the Hampshire, Franklin, and Hampden Agricultural Society with a call for political revolt. "All wealth is the product of labor and belongs of right to him who produces it," exclaimed Samuel Clesson Allen, "and yet how small a part of the products of its labor falls to the laboring class!" Insisting that "the rod of the oppressor must be broken, he will not throw it away," this old-fashioned cleric/lawyer/politician hoped that, "thanks to our free institutions, the people can now do it without violence or wrong."

To "renovate society," Allen emphasized, "you must begin with its economical relations," for economic laws shaped every society "more than government, more than morals, more than religion." Reading economic laws with John Taylor's Old Republican realism, the radicalized Old Federalist argued that increased production divided society into two classes, enabling "accumulators" to impoverish "producers." The "mighty instruments of accumulation" were "currency, and credit, and the interest of money," he said, although "they produced none of the objects of wealth." With the costs of a paper currency falling "on the productive class, and not on the capitalist," he warned, great fortunes were piling up "in stocks and bonds and notes and mortgages—in claims upon the future products of the land, and upon the future earnings of the industrious." For all the complexity of this "artificial state of society," he insisted, "the great truth cannot be concealed, that he who does not raise his own bread, eats the fruits of another man's labor."

Allen regarded "non-producers, who render no equivalent to society for what they consume," as "a new sort of aristocracy, of a more uncompromising character than the feudal, or any landed aristocracy, ever can be." Governments were "but the combinations of the rich and powerful to increase their riches and extend their power," he maintained, and labor never "had a predominating influence in any government." Yet the Bank Veto so encouraged his "hopes of an economical reform" that he ran as the Workingmen's candidate for governor in 1833, promising "the experiment of *one* administration, of which the interest of this class should be the guiding star." When the two-party dynamic aborted his third-party experiment, this Federalist/Workey urged the people "to rally around General Jackson," whose Experiment was "a question between labor and the associated wealth of the country."

Allen's lawyer friend Theodore Sedgwick made the Workey perspective compelling to other talented apostates from the elite culture of stressed western Massachusetts. Starting from the free-trade zeal of his High-Federalist father and namesake, Sedgwick came to see politics as class "war for fair Play, on the part of the *poor,* & the *Labourers*" against a class using monopolies for "getting all they can." He joined the war as a Workey candidate for Congress.[13]

Sedgwick helped the precocious young local poet William Cullen Bryant make the same intellectual transition from Federalism before sending him off to New York, where he converted the *Evening Post,* via free trade, from founder Hamilton's Federalism to laborite/hard-money (soon antislavery) Democracy. Paternal tutelage sent a third Theodore Sedgwick down from the Berkshires to join the poet/editor and another brilliant young associate editor, William Leggett, in radicalizing the *Post.*

An even more surprising recruit presented himself in a public letter to the Workingmen of Northampton, cradle of the Edwardean New Light. Denouncing "the increasing, unequal distribution of wealth," rising schoolmaster/historian George Bancroft took up arms in the eternal "feud between the house of Have and the house of Want." Although superbly educated at Harvard, Gottingen, and Berlin and married into an eminent family, this son of a Unitarian parsonage felt barred from the Brahmin establishment, which detected in his "European" manners the heretical enthusiasm for "a determined uncompromising democracy" he had once publicly expressed.[14]

Rebuffed by the Yankee elite, Bancroft was claiming a role in Massachusetts politics as leader—along with principled, unpretentious Judge Marcus Morton—of the hard-money radicals who were taking over the state Democratic party. His ambition, intellectual as well as political, responded to antinomian promptings regenerated in self and society by cultural crisis. Rebelling against Unitarian rationalism for stifling the ancestral New Light in escaping ancestral Calvinism, his generation of Harvard intellectuals found intellectual warrant in German romanticism. While the class rigidity of German university life made him a zealot for American democracy, he absorbed the romantic philosophy that inspired his conception of American history.

Bancroft came home intellectually armed to refight Northampton's Edwardean war against arminian Boston on the fields of democratic history and Jacksonian class politics. He was just embarking on a monumental *History of the United States*—"a vote for Jackson in ten volumes," one critic called it—as the upwelling of an antinomian spirit of liberty untainted by mechanistic liberalism. Tracing democracy instead to the Quaker Inner Light, he scornfully contrasted John Locke's feudal fantasy of a fundamental Constitution for the Lords Proprietors of Carolina with William Penn's idyllic republican government for Pennsylvania. "Locke kindled the torch of liberty at the fires of tradition; Penn at the living light of the soul," he wrote. His historical drama climaxed in the Declaration of Independence, where Jefferson's "sympathetic character" overcame the Lockean aberrations of his day to "read the soul of the nation, and having collected in himself its best and noblest feelings, to give them out in clear and bold words, mixed with so little of himself, that his country, as it went along with him, found nothing but what it recognized as its own."[15]

Politician Bancroft, applying this New-Light democratic faith to the crisis of capitalist transformation, channeled popular antinomianism into Jacksonian class politics. Capital was about to "swallow up the profits of labor," he warned, and the people would be "pillaged by the greedy cupidity of a privileged class." Seeing "more danger from monopolies than from combinations of workmen," he exhorted Workeys to join the Jacksonian resistance. "The merchants and the lawyers, that is the money interest, broke up feudalism," his historical politics taught, and "it is now for the yeomanry and the mechanics to march at the head of civilization." In politics as in history, he brought the authority of German romanticism to a democratic impulse fed by New-Light faith in the untutored soul. Democrats of his hard-money stripe were denounced with cause as the "new lights" of politics, whose doctrines "strike at the very root of legislation and of organized society."[16]

The historian/politician became also the philosopher of radical democracy. "There is a *spirit in man*," he told Williams students at the height of the Bank War, "an internal sense, which places us in connexion with the world of intelligence and the decrees of God." This "sentiment of truth, justice, love, and beauty exists in every one," not just "the privileged few," he insisted, and therefore "the common judgment in taste, politics, and religion, is the highest authority on earth, and the nearest possible approach to an infallible decision." As the New Light suffused American politics, the voice of the people was becoming the voice of God.[17]

Jackson had not at first stirred much enthusiasm among the hard-pressed workers who were embracing the revolutionary implications of the labor theory of value. On the eve of the 1832 election, the *New England Artisan* resigned politics to "the aristocracy, who now control all the political parties of the day." But almost immediately Workeys were enthralled by the Bank Veto, "the first measure," said one, ". . . to rouse the people on this subject."[18]

While Jackson roused Workey hopes, the analytical rigor and hard-money resolve of Workey radicalism stiffened the western radicalism of the White House. Brokering this critical confluence was Yankee-bred Amos Kendall, who registered the stresses of capitalist transformation at their most severe, both agrarian and industrial, on regular visits to his rural kin near Lowell. The Workey press avidly reprinted Kendall's Hickory Club address invoking the producer-class politics of the Bank Veto against "Manufacturing Monopolies." They "break down the independent mechanic interest," he charged, and "make large masses of people" eke out "a bare subsistence" as *slaves to a few capitalists.* Inspired by a labor-value perspective linking wage slavery with paper slavery, hard-money radicalism confronted American capitalism with its most fundamental challenge.[19]

Hard money, to be sure, could not have cured the mounting ills of capitalist transformation, even if the requisite controls over state banking and international credit flows had been attainable. Complete destruction of bank paper and corporate privilege—in condescending historical hindsight—would not have restored the patriarchal independence and equality of use-value production and the pre-market person/land ratio. Only Skidmoreite desperation had tracked the miseries of penurious dependence, competitive insecurity, and alienated inequality to their source in capitalism's exploitative relations of property and labor.

Yet by invoking yesterday's radicalism against a threatening tomorrow—like most broad-based insurgencies—Workeys and Jacksonians empowered a producer majority portending more radical medicine than its initial prescriptions. Politicizing the class conflicts of capitalist transformation, the hard-money offensive rallied farmers and workers against banking as the paper aristocracy's critical mechanism of exaction. Hard money met the bourgeoisie's fiercest resistance as not only economically cramping but politically revolutionary.

Workeys brought Jackson both welcome support and a set of practical hard-money policies, as distilled from working-class experience in 1833 by another self-taught mechanic/intellectual, Philadelphia printer William M. Gouge. His *Short History of Paper Money and Banking* combined unequaled technical grasp with vernacular cogency in showing farmers and workers how they were exploited by this "*principal* cause of social evil."[20] Frustrated like Jackson by congressional adamancy against an independent treasury, Gouge proposed an alternative mode of achieving hard money through federally regulated state deposit banks. Small notes could be eliminated by forbidding deposit banks to issue notes under five dollars, eventually twenty dollars, or to receive the notes of banks that did. Thus all banks would be constrained by constant demand for specie as the everyday currency, and honest labor would be paid in stable coin. In addition, he recommended, gold should be brought back into circulation by adjusting its 15:1 coinage ratio with silver to the approximate market ratio of 16:1, and more mints should be established to coin an ample supply of "Benton's mint drops."

With the national Bank repudiated as the panic session wound down in the spring of 1834, Secretary Taney recommended Gouge's hard-money program to Congress, and the printer/economist was soon hired by the Treasury to oversee it. "We have been providing facilities for those engaged in extensive commerce," said Taney, "and have left the mechanic and the laborer to all the hazards of an insecure and unstable circulating medium." The most depreciated small notes were "too often used in payments to the poorer and more helpless classes of society," he argued, and it was "time that the just claims of this portion of society should be regarded in our legislation." As the *Globe* explained the Jacksonian hard-money program, banking would "be permitted to exist" for large commercial transactions, but its risks would be "thrown upon that part of society that profits by it, and is most able to bear occasional losses."[21]

Congress gave Jackson's Experiment short shrift. As punishment for removal, the Senate rejected Secretary Taney's appointment, pronounced a scathing Censure on the President, and blocked the administration's House bill imposing Treasury controls on the deposit banks and banning their use of small notes. Hard money dismayed Democratic politicians almost as much as Whigs. Compelled by public opinion to repudiate the national Bank, many dug in their heels when the Experiment threatened sacred credit itself.

Congressional refusal either to regulate the deposit banks or to authorize an independent treasury left the administration to manage its deposit-bank Experiment as best it could on its own responsibility. While Jackson incited "the great body of the people" against "the moneyed interest," his Treasury struggled for hard money by assuming Biddle's discipline over the economy.

The Experiment had a rocky ride economically as well as politically. Derided as administration "pets," the deposit banks promptly demonstrated the reckless expansionism Duane had feared. Taney's Baltimore crony led them into a lending spree that squandered the Treasury reserves advanced to protect them from specie raids by Biddle; and the Secretary was desperately muzzling his pets when forced from office by the Senate.

Chastened by this near-disaster, Taney's successor Levi Woodbury resolved to manage the Treasury as "a central banking institution . . . to which the deposite Banks stand as in the relation of Branches." This canny and methodical Yankee imposed his own regulations by capitalizing on his power to bestow or withdraw the pyramiding federal deposits. Pets had to eschew notes under five dollars, report their balances twice a month, and post officers' bonds when federal deposits exceeded half their paid-in capital. By ordering pets to hold more specie, on pain of losing deposits, he struggled against a rising tide of paper and credit. Additional pets were chosen for strength and reliability and restricted to thirty-odd for close scrutiny. Although most had Democratic connections, Wall Street's reputable and Whiggish Bank of America became flagship of the system and holder of the largest deposits because its president, George Newbold, proved a staunch champion of tighter credit.[22]

Ironically, and by great bad luck, before the restriction on small notes could take hold, the hard-money Experiment was overwhelmed by a fortuitous glut of silver. While rising Mexican output boosted silver imports, external demands on the country's supply dried up. Reviving cotton prices prompted the British to lavish credit on the United States rather than demanding silver to cover trade deficits; and China's growing addiction to opium from British India enabled Americans to substitute credits on London for large silver outflows in paying for Chinese goods. Biddle's panic, by cutting imports and the exchange rate, facilitated further silver imports by state banks fortifying themselves against the big Bank.[23]

Large silver stocks cushioned Biddle's contraction and, once it eased set off an inflationary firestorm. Banks bulging with bullion multiplied it in paper to feed a clamorous demand for credit. Legislatures chartered over two hundred new banks in three years, pushing the total over six hundred. As the money supply (bank notes, deposits, and circulating specie) swelled from $172 million in 1834 to $276 million in 1836, prices shot up 50 percent. Easy credit and a renewed cotton boom touched off a land boom, pushing government land sales, which had been around $2 million a year in the 1820s, to about $5 million in 1834, $15 million in 1835, and an incredible $25 million in 1836. By the last year, with imports as well as land sales booming and the federal debt finally retired, the Treasury surplus at the disposal of the deposit banks mushroomed to $42 million.

Against the world market's mysterious but mighty tides, Jacksonians railed in vain. "The present bloat in the paper system cannot continue," Benton warned the Senate. "The revulsion will come, as surely as it did in 1819–20," and Old Bullion abjured all responsibility. "I did not join in putting down the Bank of the United States, to put up a wilderness of local banks," he protested. "I did not join in putting down the paper currency of a national bank, to put up a national paper currency of a thousand local banks. I did not strike Caesar to make Anthony master of Rome."[24] But Jacksonians were suspect on grounds of *post hoc ergo propter hoc.* They disrupted a soundly flourishing economy, in the all too plausible class view of Whig politics and liberal history, by destroying Biddle's responsible regulation and turning the federal treasure over to irresponsible state banks.

Actually, as painstaking cliometric investigation has finally revealed, Biddle himself set off the inflationary spiral that his panic interrupted only briefly. During the national Bank's eighteen-month struggle for recharter back in 1831–1832, its loans had nearly doubled from $42 million to $70 million. With this rapid monetary inflation, in Albert Gallatin's expert opinion, Biddle abdicated his regulatory responsibility. The big Bank had sealed its entente with state banks by easing its reins, thus "using its money," as Taney charged, "for the purpose of obtaining a hold upon the people."[25]

Consequently the money supply, jumping in 1831 from $114 million to $155 million, began climbing toward its 1836 peak. State banks pyramided more paper credit on their specie—driving down their specie/liabilities ratio from 23 percent to 15 percent in the first year—because the national Bank seemed to reduce risk while in fact no longer able to restrain them. The money supply kept growing and the specie ratio stayed low until Biddle's panic briefly in 1834 forced banks to protect themselves with more specie.

Jacksonian policy did not generate the runaway inflation that followed. Against pressures that could have overwhelmed a vigilant and untrammeled national Bank, in fact, Secretary Woodbury's vigilant restraint of the pets held banks' overall specie ratio at the level established under Biddle in the early thirties. The money supply mushroomed not because banks recklessly stretched their resources or overexploited the Treasury deposits as loanable reserves, but because the silver glut multiplied their specie reserves and thereby their loans and note issues.

Against inflationary gale and mutinous crew, Jackson's hard-money campaign mustered the use-value ethos of the farmer/worker majority into a formidable labor-value politics of class. "We shall whip them yet," he told Senator Benton in the face of congressional resistance. "The people will take it up after a while."[26]

A people inflamed by Biddle's panic took up the hard-money cause as astutely personalized by the President's indignant Protest against the Senate's Censure and as pushed into state and local politics by Senator Benton's resolution to "expunge" the Censure. Democratic legislatures instructed or replaced censuring senators, and local elections turned on pledges by legislative candidates to vote for expunging senators. Presidential rhetoric, reverberating from the *Globe* through the Democratic press, addressed American class reality as never before or since.

Jackson's hard-money radicalism, as articulated in this climactic struggle and his Farewell Address, saw the *"great bone and sinew of this nation"* threatened by a "gradual consuming corruption, which is spreading and carrying stockjobbing, Land jobbing, and every species of speculation." Labor coincided with morality in his ethos of class. He praised "the laboring classes" for their "independent spirit, their love of liberty, their intelligence, and their high tone of moral character." His "real working classes" were "the farmers, mechanics, and laborers" who "earn their living by the sweat of their brow," who "know that their success depends upon their own industry and economy, and that they must not expect to become suddenly rich by the fruits of their toil."

The real people were being both exploited and corrupted, Old Hickory told the country. "The *paper system* has introduced a thousand ways of robbing honest labour of its earnings to make knaves rich, powerful and dangerous," he charged. Even worse, it diverted the real people "from the sober pursuits of honest industry" by exciting "rash speculation, idleness, extravagance, and a deterioration of morals," an "eager desire to amass wealth without labor," a "spirit of speculation injurious to the habits and character of the people."

Hard money, Jackson claimed, would "do more to revive and perpetuate those habits of economy and simplicity which are so congenial to the character of republicans than all the legislation which has yet been attempted." Warning that "money is power," he called for "a metalic currency to cover the labour of our country," and to check the "spirit of monopoly and thirst for exclusive privileges." Any act that "tends in the smallest degree, to give *legal* advantages to *capital* over *labor*," as the *Globe* expounded Jacksonian class politics, ". . . must necessarily increase the natural inequality in society; and finally, make two distinct classes: namely—masters and slaves."[27]

The compelling drama of Old Hero versus monster banks, of solid coin versus mercurial paper, engaged a farmer/worker majority feeling both exploited and corrupted by the inscrutable imperatives of capitalist transformation. As the people took up the Experiment, Congress was forced into the more innocuous hard-money steps of establishing new mints and revaluing gold. By 1835, when John Marshall died, enough anti-Jackson senators had been expunged to ensure the martyred Taney's confirmation as Chief Justice; and soon thereafter the Censure was expunged. With Blair alert "to whip *in* or *out* restless men,"[28] many restless Democrats were whipped out to Whiggery. The new party alignment crystallized as the underlying conflict of classes invaded the liberal polity and burned into the electorate a pattern of party attachments that would endure for generations.

Yet flooding democracy was contained at its historic high-water mark when it dared to assail a capitalist fundament only less vital than property and law. With threatened credit in boomtime demand, the battle fronts of hard money proved too numerous, and the issues too complex and too easily obfuscated, to be policed by Jackson's majorities. With inflation neutralizing the Experiment, not even Jackson and Blair could refocus the fitful attention of antinomian voters beyond the largely symbolic federal issues to the state arenas where the Bank War was ultimately decided.

Protected by the inherent looseness of two-party coalition, therefore, "Democrats by trade" were able to cling to the popular party label, and even pay lip service to hard money, while unobtrusively supporting state-bank credit against "Democrats in principle." In the obscurity of state legislatures, Democratic defectors helped Whigs charter new banks, float extravagant bond issues for internal improvements and banking capital, and frustrate efforts to ban small notes or otherwise restrain credit.

Even the strongly Democratic new Congress produced by the expunging campaign rebuffed administration legislation for enforcing hard money through the deposit system. As speculative fever mounted, Secretary Woodbury's restrictive management of the mounting surplus stirred up howls of protest from state banks and their impatient hosts of expectant borrowers. He frustrated glittering hopes every time pets fattened their specie ratios at his behest by draining coin from other banks; and he further dampened the credit explosion by concentrating the surplus in conservative Wall-Street pets restrained by New York's Safety Fund. Whig hue-and-cry against this "union of purse and sword" seduced many Democrats into a rising clamor for distributing the surplus among the states, where legislatures would devote the people's money to a "go-ahead" credit/transport infrastructure.

Hard-money men found distribution harder to resist as the mushrooming public treasure fueled suspicion of the pets' bonanza. Anyone who defended the Experiment against distribution, worried Connecticut's hard-money Senator John M. Niles, "would be said to be against the states and *for* the banks, instead of *against* the Banks, as in 1832." Uneasy all along about their unnatural alliance, they were being taunted by southern mavericks to follow their principles by abandoning all banks for an independent treasury. Even the White House, where Jackson had Gouge at work on an independent-treasury plan, was stymied by distribution's momentum and ambiguities. At the boom's frenzied peak in 1836, a Democratic Congress passed by veto-proof majorities a Distribution/Deposit Act sabotaging Treasury restraints on the deposit banks and "depositing" the enormous federal surplus with the states.[29]

No sooner had a disgusted Secretary Woodbury disavowed further responsibility for the currency than he was countermanded by "a tremendous bomb thrown without warning."[30] Again Old Hickory stunned politicians and businessmen with the only weapon at hand. Desperate to quench the wild speculation in public lands that was leading the runaway inflation, he had Woodbury issue a Specie Circular ordering the land offices to accept only gold and silver coin. Most outraged were the enterprise-minded Democrats who had sponsored distribution to enhance credit. Emboldened by the popular hero's imminent retirement when his last Congress met in December 1836, these self-styled Conservative Democrats joined Whigs in repealing the Circular by crushing majorities (Senate 41–5, House 143–59). Jackson's last official act was a pocket veto sustaining his hard-money policy against the bipartisan dismay of politicians.

A flood of public affection for Old Hickory drowned out his handpicked successor Van Buren at the inaugural ceremonies on March 4, 1837, and made his homeward journey one long ovation. Yet his resounding majorities had met such fierce resistance when they threatened the paper vitals of enterprise that he capped his stewardship with a Farewell Address full of foreboding. "Knowing that the path of freedom is continually beset by enemies who often assume the disguise of friends," he told the people, "I have devoted the last hours of my public life to warn you of the dangers." Politicians' bipartisan adamancy against hard money had exposed the limits of majority rule.

"The agricultural, the mechanical, and the laboring classes," as the retiring President diagnosed the impasse, "from their habits and the nature of their pursuits . . . are incapable of forming extensive combinations to act together." They "have but little patronage to give to the press" and "no crowd of dependents about them who hope to grow rich without labor." By contrast, he charged, "the paper-money system and its natural associations—monopoly and exclusive privileges"—enabled "corporations," "wealthy individuals," and "designing politicians" to "move together with undivided force . . . to engross all power in the hands of the few." Constitutional federalism compounded the political problem by fostering forum-shopping, he explained, for when "defeated in the General Government, the same class of intriguers and politicians will now resort to the States."

Although having done "something, I trust," to "eradicate the evil" and "restore the constitutional currency of gold and silver," Jackson admonished the people that "enough yet remains to require all your energy and perseverance."

Because "so many interests are united to resist all reform," he warned, "you must not hope the conflict will be a short one nor success easy." In both state and federal governments, he urged, the people must "become more watchful" to "check this spirit of monopoly and special privileges." As Bank War brought *Kulturkampf* to a climax, Old Hickory's valedictory, like Jefferson's, invoked democracy. "Eternal vigilance by the people is the price of liberty," he exhorted, for "Providence has . . . chosen you as the guardians of freedom, to preserve it for the benefit of the human race."[31]

Pragmatic politicians, as the people's departing hero perceived, were neutralizing his resounding majorities through the class dynamics of two-party politics. The Constitution's framers had wrought both worse and better than they knew. Although party democracy soon breached their elaborate barricades, they had unwittingly ordained a party system that made democracy safe for capitalism.

By awarding all executive power to a bare electoral majority, the Constitution mandated close competition between two heterogeneous parties. Diverse groups had to combine for a majority, but too large a majority left the winners with no extra power to satisfy too many groups, and thus vulnerable to having some picked off by opponents. When diverse opponents of the original Federalist regime coalesced as Republicans to win the presidency, however, the Federalists proved too elitist and parochial to exploit the constitutional potential for party balance. They would not compromise their principles enough to win over disaffected Republicans; and when the first party system died in their suicidal opposition to the War of 1812, politics fell into a chaos of personal/sectional factions.

A second two-party system soon emerged from public indignation at the resulting presidential imbroglio of 1824. Forced into bipolar coalition in 1828, Jackson/Calhoun/Crawford men, calling themselves Democrats, rode the rising democratic tide to overwhelm National Republican Adams/Clay men. As a new generation of realists on both sides mastered the constitutionally prescribed zero-sum game of minimal majorities, National Republicans (renaming themselves Whigs when Calhoun switched sides) adjusted their appeals to exploit excessive Democratic majorities. As the new parties moved toward closer but sectionally skewed competition, Democrats surrendered dissident elements without complaint. "Our majority is *too large*," said Benton in explaining discord among Missouri Democrats; "we shall be much stronger when the number is reduced, and when two or three newspapers shall *openly* act with the enemy which are now secretly doing it."[32]

Gradually and unevenly, as Jackson's class politics eclipsed the sectional blocs of interest politics and pushed national divisions into state elections, party balance overcame sectional candidacies. Sections, as shown by the changing distribution of presidential votes, came up for grabs when they no longer had favorite-son candidates. The Jackson/Democratic percentage of each section's popular vote is followed below by that of the leading opposition candidate (the three Whig candidates combined in 1836); and candidates' home-section percentages are underlined.

	1824	1828	1832	1836
New England	0%/_84%_	30%/_70%_	46%/54%	51%/49%
Mid-Atlantic (N.Y. to Md.)	60%/29%	57%/43%	54%/46%	_52%_/48%
Northwest (with Ky., Mo.)	35%/_46%_	55%/45%	54%/_46%_	48%/_52%_
Southeast	46%/_47%_	76%/24%	83%/17%	53%/47%
Southwest	_84%_/9%	_82%_/18%	_91%_/9%	48%/_52%_
TOTAL	42%/32%	56%/44%	56%/44%	51%/49%

The only section without a favorite son in 1824, the mid-Atlantic, was the most divided among the other four sections' candidates (considering the Adams vote implicit in the New York legislature's choice of electors), and it resumed in 1828 the close contests it had known under the first party system. The next debatable ground was the Northwest, where Jackson trailed favorite son Clay in 1824 but outpolled Yankee Adams in 1828 and Clay himself in 1832. In New England, by contrast, favorite son Adams's lopsided majorities stifled party competition until Jackson ran close behind non-Yankee Clay in 1832. Similarly outsiders got few southern votes until Jackson was no longer a candidate in 1836, when his northern disciple Van Buren narrowly lost the Southwest to favorite son Hugh Lawson White while narrowly carrying the Southeast.[33]

By Jackson's retirement, sectionally lopsided majorities had disappeared to make the two parties competitive in almost every state. Since 1828 lopsided states won by margins over 30 percent had shrunk from fourteen to one. Debatable states with margins under 12 percent more than trebled from six to nineteen, and hard-fought states won by under 6 percent doubled from four to eight. The median state margin fell from 41 percent in 1824 to 36 percent in 1828, 23 percent in 1832, and 9 percent in 1836. Class politics and party competition pushed white male turnout in presidential elections from one-fourth in 1824 to over half in 1828–1836 and four-fifths in 1840.

This process established a two-party dynamic of "equilibrium cycles" that persisted until party identifications weakened in the late twentieth century. Periodic upheavals—capitalist transformation in the Jackson years, sectional crisis in the 1850s, the crisis of industrial consolidation in the 1890s, the Great Depression in the 1930s—congealed new patterns of party identifications strongly favoring one party. Then, as the minority party chipped away at the majority, these realignment phases were succeeded by equilibrium phases of close elections lasting until another realignment phase occurred.

Through this constitutionally structured equilibrium tendency, the pragmatism and class perspective of self-making lawyer/politicians frustrated Jackson's radical majorities. As Whigs learned from Democrats to wrap entrepreneurial intent in democratic rhetoric, the parties converged in both policy and voting strength. Two-party politics pacified the class animus of an inattentive majority on the hustings while skewing policy outcomes toward the businessmen who wanted most from government, who followed politics most avidly, and whose money, influence, and domination of cultural media far outweighed mere votes.

Pragmatic Whiggery was frankly avowed by a Kentucky congressman who resolved that *"no fellow shall out democrat me."* He had *"no faith ... in this democracy,"* he told a colleague, *"but it is the road to success."* Whigs also learned to exploit popular reliance on character and personality for protection from menacing elites and government. In Illinois, said Governor Thomas Ford, politicians of all persuasions succeeded "by a continual show of friendship and condescension, ... gaiety, cheerfulness, apparent goodness of heart, and agreeable manners." Most "have none of these gifts by nature," Ford added, but "these are talents which can be acquired by a diligent practice."[34]

Whiggery appropriated egalitarianism most flagrantly through political Antimasonry. When William Morgan's presumed murder by Masons ignited rural anger in New York's burnt-over district, defeated Clintonians in the bustling canal towns turned the "blessed spirit" against the ruling Bucktail Democrats, whose local political/banking establishments frustrated their ambitions for office and enterprise. Blaming the Bucktail judicial system for shielding Morgan's murderers, editor Thurlow Weed and lawyer/politician William H. Seward astutely weaned western New York farmers from Bucktail allegiance through third-party Antimasonry, then led the Antimasons first into uneasy coalition with the hopelessly outnumbered mainline Whigs in the rest of the state, and finally into providing the biggest voting base for an amalgamated and competitive New York Whig party. Similarly Antimasons trimmed the overwhelming Jacksonian ascendancy in Pennsylvania to create a competitive Whig opposition.

The equilibrium tendency also gave Antimasonry a role where Jacksonism was weakest. For some years the blessed spirit ruled Vermont and held the balance of power in Massachusetts and Connecticut. Such new third parties—Antimasons in the 1830s, Republicans in the 1850s, Populists in the 1890s—have often figured in realignment phases of the equilibrium cycle because they permit a voting bloc to leave the party with which it has long identified without having to embrace at once the party against which it has identified.[35]

Like Antimasonry in the North, state rights provided protective coloration for anti-Jackson politics in the South. The heterogeneous coalition-building dictated by the equilibrium tendency was demonstrated most dramatically when Calhoun and his Carolina nullifiers were forced into alliance with the consolidationist National Republicans. Outrage at democracy and the Bank War prompted broader defections of planter-oriented southern politicians, especially in reaction to Jackson's hard-money Experiment. A piebald opposition papered over its internal differences by taking the Whig label as defenders of liberty against executive usurpation, and southern Whigs disguised their entrepreneurial elitism from farmer constituencies with a rhetoric of state rights.[36]

Maturation of a sectionally balanced and competitive two-party system was curiously accelerated by the Whigs' disunity in the presidential election of 1836. With their idol Clay given no chance after his 1832 rout, they were too divided among sectional favorites to risk a nominating convention. While a Democratic convention unanimously ratified Jackson's choice of Van Buren, Whigs were left supporting Webster in New England, Hugh Lawson White in the South, and William Henry Harrison in the northwestern and mid-Atlantic states. "Judge" White was a nominally Jacksonian Senator from Tennessee, where proto-Whigs were frustrated by Old Hickory's unchallengeable popularity. A longtime banker and leader of the conservative Blount/Overton faction and just remarried to the ambitious mother-in-law of Biddle's righthand man, he was so piqued at Jackson's radical advisers and policies that pro-Bank dissidents flattered him into running for President as a better Jacksonian than Van Buren. Meanwhile Whigs had found their own military hero in the bluff and hearty "General" Harrison. Once prominent in northwestern politics, this aging scion of Virginia's planter aristocracy thrust himself back into the limelight by disputing credit for victory over the northwestern Indians at Tippecanoe in 1811 with the Democrats' flamboyant vice-presidential nominee Richard M. ("Old Dick") Johnson.

Against New York's foppish Magician, these undistinguished sectional candidates maximized favorite-son advantage for the Whigs just as party lines were stabilizing. White slashed the Democrats' southeastern margin from 66 percent in 1832 to 5 percent and converted their 81 percent southwestern margin to a 3 percent Whig margin, carrying Georgia and—despite Jackson's fulminations—his own Tennessee. Harrison defied the convention against electioneering tours to win three northwestern states, while rural Antimasons gave him Yankee Vermont and three mid-Atlantic states. The Democrats gained ground only in New England, where Webster showed little strength outside his own Massachusetts. Van Buren's razor-thin margin of 1.7 percent against his three opponents combined—averting another House runoff imbroglio—crystallized an equilibrium pattern of party preferences that would persist for a generation. Inadvertently the divided Whigs had stumbled into a strategy that almost neutralized Democratic preponderance in the South and West to make them thereafter competitive everywhere.[37]

The rising Whigs sided with "Democrats by trade" to neutralize the hard-money radicalism of "Democrats in principle" by cloaking entrepreneurial policy in democratic style and rhetoric. Even in overwhelmingly Democratic Illinois, according to Governor Ford, "the legislative acts of public officers were as likely to result in favor of one party as the other." The voters "did not want government to touch them too closely," Ford explained, and so long as it "made no encroachment upon liberty" they "asked nothing and claimed nothing but to be let alone." But Democrats who got elected by exploiting Jackson's popularity "took advantage of this lethargic state of indifference of the people" and were easily "seduced" by "the sleek, smooth, pleasant men of tact and address in the minority" to pass "special laws of all kinds of individual, not general benefit" through "bargains, intrigues, and log-rolling combinations." Whig Abraham Lincoln's political star rose in this arena when he secured the state capital for Springfield by delivering his county's big delegation for an extravagant internal-improvement program.[38]

Even for the least opportunistic Democrats, defense of unambitious equality blended all too insensibly under market pressures into self-making demand for equal entrepreneurial opportunity. The shift was clearest in the market's New York vortex, where the *Evening Post*'s laissez-faire Workeyism inspired an Equal Rights Party that developed great leverage on Democratic politics by exploiting the only weak point in the two-party barricade against insurgency. These "Locofocos"—so called after the new friction matches they ignited when outnumbered regulars doused the gaslights at a Tammany-Hall showdown—played hardball against Tammany candidates who did not toe their hard-money line by either running their own quasi-third-party candidates or backing more amenable Whigs. Systematizing a strategy pioneered by Philadelphia's Old School, Locofocos forced into the political arena their radical opposition to bank charters, limited liability, and small notes.

Yet as boom stoked enterprise, these rising young urban zealots attacked banks less for subverting the use-value ethos than for exclusive charters that blocked equal access to commodity-value competition. The panacea they increasingly embraced was equal rights to engage in banking without special legislative charters. "The humblest citizens," said their polemicist Leggett, should be allowed to "associate together, and wield . . . a vast aggregate of capital, composed of the little separate sums which they could afford to invest in such an enterprise, in competition with the capitals of the purse-proud men who now almost monopolize certain branches of business."[39] The ambiguities of laissez-faire radicalism worked themselves out in 1838 when a Whig legislature enacted free banking without the Locofocos' hard-money safeguards. Capitalism found its dynamic organizational form as New York thus inspired a wave of general incorporation laws bestowing corporate privileges and immunities on all comers meeting minimal requirements.

The crusade for entrepreneurial Equal Rights against monopolistic privilege co-opted the hard-money idealism of prospering Jacksonians like Blair, who was getting rich on government printing, and Kendall, whose genius for efficient administration brought him repute as a reforming Postmaster General and finally a fortune as organizer of the nationwide telegraph business. Jacksonian insurgency against disruptive enterprise ended up making free enterprise a constitutional principle. Chief Justice Taney's first major decision, in the 1837 Charles River Bridge case, struck down chartered monopoly for the sake of free competition.

The outcome of both Bank War and market revolution turned heavily on the boom/bust cycle. Periodic booms both spurred economic takeoff and recruited the susceptible to bourgeois/middle-class culture and politics. Succeeding busts then maximized the pressure of capitalist discipline and mythology on premarket ways by multiplying exemplars of ignoble failure, making farmers more vulnerable to debts and taxes, breaking unions, and inflaming ethnic/racial conflict among desperate competitors for the meanest work. Alternating the carrot of fortune with the stick of hunger and disgrace, capital's inexorable cycles destabilized traditional life, frustrated sustained insurgency, and reinforced bourgeois cultural hegemony.

In the midthirties boom, silver-glutted banks amplified an unprecedented flood of British credit to sweep "an all-absorbing desire for sudden and splendid wealth" all the way to the Mississippi. Cotton bonanza catapulted the Southwest into a "new era," as a literary young lawyer later described it, "an era of credit without capital, and enterprise without honesty." In this "Age of Brass," wrote Joseph G. Baldwin, enterprisers adopted a "new plan of making fortunes on the profits of what they owed." Gold and silver gave way to "Rags, a very familiar character, and very popular and easy of access," who "belonged to the school of progress" and aimed "to *democratize* capital."

> Emigrants came flocking in. Money, or what passed for money, was the only cheap thing to be had. Credit was a thing of course. To refuse it—if the thing was ever done—were an insult for which a bowie-knife were not too summary or exemplary a means of redress. The State banks were issuing their bills by the sheet, like a patent steam printing press; and no other showing was asked of the applicant for the loan than great distress for money.
>
> Under this stimulating process prices rose like smoke. Lots in obscure villages were held at city prices; lands, bought at the minimum cost of government, were sold at from thirty to forty dollars per acre, and considered dirt cheap at that. The old rules of business and the calculations of prudence were alike disregarded.
>
> Rags was treasurer. Banks did a very flourishing business on the promissory notes of the individual stockholders ingeniously substituted in lieu of cash. They issued ten for one, the *one* being fictitious. They generously loaned all the directors could not use themselves. The stampede toward the golden temple became general; the delusion prevailed far and wide that this thing was not a burlesque on commerce and finance.

Trampled in the stampede was trust. "Men dropped down into their places as from the clouds," Baldwin complained. "Nobody knew who or what they were, except as they claimed, or as a surface view of their character indicated." Larceny "grew not only respectable but genteel," and swindling "was raised to the dignity of a fine art."[40]

The Age of Brass similarly plunged the Northwest into "the great land and town lot speculation" that provoked the Specie Circular. "New towns were laid out in every direction," recalled later Illinois governor Ford. Lands and lots became "the staple of the country" and "the only articles of export." Enterprising townspeople demanded a mammoth transportation system to realize their speculative dreams through rapid development; and the legislature—unattended by "the great body of the people in the country"—authorized Abe Lincoln's enormous bond issue. Entrepreneurial frenzy for banking capital and internal improvements, while peaking in the West, was everywhere pushing states into extravagant debts and Congress into distribution.[41]

The Illinois "rage for speculation" blazed highest amid a "raw and bare" scatter of shanties at "the edge of a wild prairie" on the southern shore of Lake Michigan. In three-year-old Chicago "sudden fortunes" had excited "a general frenzy" of "insatiable greediness." Harriet Martineau found the dust-blown streets swarming with speculators, while garishly accoutered horsemen cried land sales at the corners, and every storekeeper touted get-rich deals from his door. Chicago's nonchalance about the shaky "wildcat" bank paper that made fortune possible proved unshakable. "Why, sir . . . this hotel was built with that kind of stuff," the proprietor told a skeptical guest a panic later. ". . . I will take 'wild cats' for your bill, my butcher takes them of me, and the farmer from him, and so we go, making it pleasant all around." Until "the inevitable hour of reckoning" arrived, he was investing all he could "in corner lots," he said, and meanwhile "on this kind of worthless currency . . . we are creating a great city, building up all kinds of industrial establishments, and covering the lake with vessels."[42]

The inevitable hour had first arrived as boom crested in midsummer 1836. An alarming drain of specie from the Bank of England signalled that worldwide capital had again stimulated more production than its exploited labor could afford to consume. Blaming American extravagance, the Old Lady of Threadneedle Street defended herself by raising interest rates and cutting off all credit to British firms accommodating Americans. At once New York interest rates zoomed to 24 percent, and during the winter of 1836–1837 business failures mounted. With both unemployment and food prices skyrocketing, a Locofoco protest rally in February set off riotous looting of flour dealers.[43]

When Martin Van Buren assumed the presidency under these squally skies on March 4, big cotton-trading firms were beginning to fail in New Orleans and New York. By early April, with demand and prices for cotton sagging under the British contraction, bad cotton debts had brought down 93 New York firms with over $60 million in capital. Manhattan's wealthy young diarist George Templeton Strong registered mounting bourgeois dread:

[*April 7*] Terrible state of things. . . . [*April 12*] The merchants going to the devil *en masse*. . . . [*April 21*] Failure on failure. . . . [*April 27*] Strong fears entertained for the banks, and if they go, . . . political convulsion and revolution, I think, would follow. . . . [*May 1*] Arthur Tappan has failed! Help him, ye niggers! . . . . [*May 2*] Workmen thrown out of employ by the hundred daily. Business at a stand; the coal mines in Pennsylvania stopped and no fuel in prospect for next winter.

Suddenly a collapse of world prices wreaked disaster along the New York/ New Orleans cotton axis. There was "terrible news in Wall Street" on May 4, when the president of a leading deposit bank was found dead. "Some say prussic acid," Strong noted. ". . . Anyhow there's a run on the bank—street crowded." The run spread, and on the ninth Manhattan banks were drained of $652,000 in coin "as fast as the tellers can count it." Their refusal to reopen the next morning produced an "immense crowd and excitement in Wall Street, but the military prevent any disturbance."

Anger rose as banks everywhere promptly followed New York and New Orleans into suspension. The largest assemblage in Pennsylvania history massed outside Independence Hall on May 15 to denounce banking as "a system of fraud and oppression." Mobilized "*entirely* by the working classes," twenty thousand Philadelphians pledged their votes exclusively to hard-money supporters of "the only just and legal currency." New Yorkers began to "talk ominously about rebellions," and Strong feared "we shall have a revolution here."[44]

Another young New Yorker felt the contrasting class fears of suddenly workless workers—estimated at fifty thousand locally and a half million nationally—who shivered through the following winter in total destitution. Asa Shipman was just out of apprenticeship when panic struck, he recalled in a letter years later, and was supporting his widowed mother and six young siblings.

> I was then making good wages every cent of which was spent in the family so of course I had nothing ahead. . . . After a short time work with me began to get short. First I had only half of the time and finally I was told that there was no work. Imagine my situation if you can. We had food enough in the house to last perhaps a week and my last wages lasted perhaps another week. In the meantime I spent every day in search of some kind of employment but all in vain. Nothing could be got. . . . Starvation looked us in the face. . . . We often went with one meal a day and that of the plainest kind. How we ever lived for 6 weeks that way I cannot now imagine.[45]

After partial recovery, another crisis in 1839 pushed hard times into the forties, sabotaging Van Buren's chances for reelection.

Through four frustrating years, a President proverbial for adroit maneuver essayed the bold class politics of his predecessor. The panic discredited the suspending pets and polarized the Democratic party, forcing Van Buren to choose at the outset between soft-money Conservatives and hard-money Locofocos. With Locofocos demanding an independent treasury and hailing the "opportune season for entirely eradicating the curse of paper money," enterprise-minded Democrats were alarmed for "our whole credit system, which has done so much for the prosperity of the country." Fearing that the "worst passions of the people are to be appealed to," Conservatives implored the administration to rescind the Specie Circular and stand by the deposit banks. Instead the Little Magician—stiffened by Jacksonian example and exhortation against clamor from the whole bourgeoisie—called Congress into special session and proposed an independent treasury.[46]

Ever since Jackson's opening salvo against the national Bank, an independent treasury had been the preferred alternative of hard-money men, from Jackson himself through Randolph and Benton to Duane and Gouge. By dispensing with banks and independently collecting, holding, and paying its funds in specie through Treasury offices, government could dissolve its unholy union with the market while indirectly exerting hard-money pressure on it. Not only would banks have to keep more specie on hand to meet a constant demand for government payments, but much of the economy's specie would be locked up in government vaults and unavailable for credit expansion—enough when the surplus soared to have cooled off the recent boom. Held in an independent treasury, government surpluses would moderate rather than accelerate the swings of boom-and-bust.

In proposing to "divorce" government from banks and market, the new President laid down the Locofocos' radical laissez-faire doctrine as the root principle of Democratic policy. He was not willing, as Jackson had been, to accommodate commerce by letting the independent treasury deal in exchange. It was no more the business of government to "aid individuals in transfer of their funds," Van Buren insisted, than in "transportation of their merchandise." With shattered enterprise crying out for paper relief, the President washed his hands of federal responsibility for the economy. "All communities are apt to look to government for too much," he declared. Its only duty was "to enact and enforce" a fair field for "private interest, enterprise, and competition," through "a system of general laws" that left every citizen free "to reap under its benign protection, the rewards of virtue, industry, and prudence."[47]

To ensure a fair field, the President urged one addition to the system of general laws. With broken businessmen clamoring for a voluntary bankruptcy law to escape their debts, he proposed instead an involuntary bankruptcy law to force suspending banks into liquidation. Van Buren seized on Benton's radical reading of the Constitution's bankruptcy clause, as Jackson seized on the deposit-bank Experiment, to constrain banks otherwise beyond constitutional reach.

Once again a hard-money President met fierce resistance in a Democratic Congress. While both houses quietly buried compulsory bankruptcy, the struggle for an independent treasury was complicated by Calhoun's startling return to the

Democrats. Consumed by blasted hopes, he struck Harriet Martineau as a "cast-iron man" who "had never been born and never could be extinguished."[48] Embracing the independent treasury as promising southern deliverance from financial/commercial bondage to New York, Calhoun oddly insisted it receive only gold and silver coin while issuing a paper currency to supplant bank paper. By thus straddling the hard-money/soft-money rift, he was bidding for party leadership—and eventually the presidency.

Although Calhoun's ambitions proved characteristically fatuous and his strategy too ingenious by half, he did play hob with presidential strategy by focusing contention on specie receipts. Preferring specie receipts, Van Buren nevertheless hoped to woo enough Conservatives to enact the independent treasury by letting it receive notes of specie-paying banks. But Calhoun's probing exposed the speciousness of this apparent concession. By promptly presenting bank-note receipts for specie redemption, it became clear, the administration intended to match the hard-money impact of specie receipts. Consequently when the Senate approved the independent treasury with Calhoun's specie receipts, a handful of Conservatives, disdaining both bank-note receipts and specie receipts, blocked it in the nominally Democratic House by deserting to a unanimous Whiggery.[49]

The stalemate between hard-money Democrats and the Whig/Conservative coalition hamstrung Congress in fruitless wrangling through three sessions, as Calhoun brought few recruits to balance defecting Conservatives while further disrupting party cohesion with demands for symbolic validation of slavery. Fistfights led to dirks and pistols being brought to the floor; duels were constantly threatened; and finally a slight misunderstanding provoked a Kentucky Whig to preserve his honor by killing a Maine Democrat in their fourth fire of rifles at eighty yards.

Stymied in Congress, the administration was beset on other fronts. Revenues were short. An expensive, brutal war against the Seminoles in Florida's trackless swamps bogged down in the most stubborn Indian resistance ever encountered by the army. Outbreaks of Canadian/American border violence in northern New York and Maine were quelled only by the tactful firmness of the army's able Whig general Winfield Scott. Collector Samuel Swartwout—appointed by Jackson over Van Buren's strenuous objection—raised the spectre of corruption against the independent treasury by absconding to European opulence with over a million dollars from the New York Custom House.

Meanwhile the Bank War was being finally decided in state politics, where cresting democracy surged against its final obstacle. Banking dramatized capital's ability to elude democratic scrutiny or control through the forum-shopping afforded by the federal system. Just as developmentalism had mounted its counterattack from the most commercial states when driven from Washington by Jefferson, the paper system resisted Jacksonian assault behind the slippery ramparts of twenty-six legislatures. Capital's tireless advocates could not be effectively met in every federal/state forum and on every legislative/judicial issue by a democracy only spasmodically arousable, impatient of abstractions and technicalities, and dependent on politicians. For all the fury of Jackson's Bank War, therefore, a paper system entrenched in the states survived the Experiment little tamed.

Van Buren now renewed Jackson's call for state action, and popular wrath at suspending banks pushed Democrats into a concerted hard-money offensive in Congress and every legislature. While White House and *Globe* broke out the Loco-foco banner of Specie Circular, independent treasury, and compulsory bankruptcy, Democratic legislatures took up a variety of bank reforms. Although financial crisis converted many Democratic politicians to Locofoco zeal and purged others who defied the hard-money line, most bent to popular pressure as brokers of the party cohesion and electoral viability on which their careers increasingly depended.

Having surmounted federal/state forum-shopping to confront legislatures, bank reform was stymied by capital's forum-shopping from state to state. A state could ban or unduly restrict banks only at the cost of losing capital—entrepreneurial opportunity, that is, or "jobs" in today's politic bourgeois parlance—to more hospitable states. Even if willing to pay the price, a state could not escape the paper system by stopping banks at its border, for it could not stop their notes. Every bankless state found its specie driven from circulation by an inundation of the most suspect bank notes from other states. While the federal system empowered states in highly visible ways against the federal government, it left them—invisibly but perhaps more significantly—almost defenseless against mobile capital. In the face of this political/economic reality, bank reform faltered in legislatures as in Congress, often under a similar defection of a few Conservatives from a narrow Democratic majority.

The reform most popular with Democrats was forcing specie into circulation by banning small notes, usually under $5 but ranging from a token $1 up to a quite efficacious $10, and prospectively by stages in some states to $20 or even $50. The commonest alternative was requiring banks to hold specie reserves against liabilities, usually a moderately constraining fifth of circulating notes plus deposits but rising to a quite restrictive third in Louisiana. Because note-happy hinterland banks needed more restraint than deposit-heavy city banks, reserves were often required only against note issues. Lesser remedies included requiring periodic publication of balance sheets and forbidding or taxing dividends during suspension, while zealots wanted to end limited liability and force suspending banks into liquidation until banking could be constitutionally prohibited.

Reform lost impetus when the initial financial crisis eased and specie payments resumed in August 1838. Under hopes of a returning Age of Brass, some Democrats even relapsed to bank charters and bond issues until another suspension in 1839 inaugurated a severe depression of all market production lasting through the early forties. Redoubled public fury forced a measure of hard-money reform on the states and finally pushed the independent treasury through Congress to presidential signature on the Fourth of July, 1840, as a "second declaration of independence."

Reforming legislatures in the heavily capitalized Northeast were usually content with small-note bans or specie-reserve requirements to supplement New York's Safety Fund and the banks' self-stabilizing Suffolk System in New England. Devastation by the worst bank abuses of the Age of Brass pushed the Southwest into hard-money radicalism. By the midforties, Arkansas and Louisiana constitutions prohibited banking, while Alabama and Mississippi were forcing into liquidation all but one each of their thirty-three prepanic banks. Boom/bust extremities also fostered hard-money radicalism in the Northwest for a decade, though frequently diluted by Conservative defection. Iowa outlawed banks in its first constitution, while Locofocos in Ohio, Illinois, and Michigan had to settle for a constitutional requirement of popular referendum on any bank charter. Other northwestern states resorted to a state-controlled bank for protection from inflationary borrower-controlled banks chartered through forum-shopping in neighboring states. Several states in the less volatile Southeast also resorted to state-controlled banks.

The Bank War sputtered out with returning prosperity in most states, as a patchwork of partial reform emerged from the strife of twenty-six legislatures. Chastened by another paroxysm of boom-and-bust, capitalists themselves began to see merit, up to a point, in Democratic arguments for harder money and freer competition. Entrepreneurial appropriation of laissez faire was signaled in 1838 when New York Whigs enacted their own soft-money version of the hard-money free banking preached by Locofocos. Four years later Louisiana Whigs swung over to a long reviled Democratic proposal—now celebrated by historians of banking as a model of fiscal orthodoxy—setting specie reserves at a third of both deposits and note issues.[50]

The Bank War came to the same ironic end as every insurgency against the market. Carrying patriarchal democracy to a historic peak by mobilizing the anticapitalist anger and egalitarian hopes of farmers and workers, it ended up strengthening the paper system it fought. Hard-money reform helped make a bloated and chaotic banking system sufficiently lean and careful to finance an unmatched surge of growth at midcentury, stabilized in part by the independent treasury. As prosperity again intensified the inexorable pressures of forum-shopping capital, the most adamantly hard-money states succumbed to paper and market, often through the halfway house of free banking. Market revolution, essentially completed in economy, culture, and polity, gave way to industrial revolution.

In this protracted struggle, democracy proved safe for capitalism. A mass electorate, fully mobilized by producer-class radicalism and bourgeois desperation, revealed its propensity to punish incumbents for hard times while rewarding them only modestly for prosperity. As Whigs mastered popular appeal, party strengths gyrated with the commodity-price index toward stable equilibrium.

When panic discredited not only banks but incumbents, therefore, a rising Whig vote swept Democrats from power in such disparate Jacksonian strongholds as Tennessee, New York, Mississippi, Maine, and North Carolina. Partial recovery and resumption of specie payments in the summer of 1838 stemmed the Whig tide, giving the Democrats a midterm congressional majority just sufficient to enact the independent treasury in 1840. Meanwhile, however, the second suspension of October 1839 had inaugurated deep depression and a new Whig surge that swamped Van Buren's bid for reelection.[51]

While punishing Democrats as incumbents, hard times also divided them deeply over the hard-money radicalism demanded by their constituency. A bitter hard/soft struggle for the Democratic party, embroiling some states for a decade, caught up many collateral questions. Radical Democrats split the party in Mississippi by repudiating the state bonds subscribed to defaulting banks. Softs enraged hards in Pennsylvania by helping Whigs charter Biddle's Monster as a state bank when its federal charter expired. New York Bucktails broke into warring factions when Van Buren's hard-money "Barnburners" further outraged pro-bank "Hunkers" with a laissez-faire "stop-and-tax" policy to stymie further state improvements.

Democratic disarray inspired Whigs to build on their recent success with the noncommittal popular politics of White and Harrison. A new breed of leaders preaching democratic capitalism had made the Whigs competitive nationally by enlisting northeastern Antimasons for Harrison. The club-footed Lancaster lawyer Thaddeus Stevens mobilized a gubernatorial majority for Antimasonic Whiggery in Pennsylvania, and in New York a brace of self-made printer/editors helped Governor William H. Seward drive the Bucktails from power on a platform of small notes and free banking.

Albany editor Thurlow Weed, a star pupil to rival Van Buren in New York's advanced school of democratic politics, stole Jacksonian thunder by astutely crafting Whiggery as a popular crusade against the monopolistic privilege and corruption of Bucktail banks. Manhattan editor Horace Greeley, an uprooted Yankee, assuaged antinomian anxieties by blending enthusiasm for enterprise with millennial benevolence and concern for the poor. His lively editorials and provocative columnists—ranging from Margaret Fuller to Karl Marx to Arthur Brisbane, American guru of Charles Fourier's communal utopianism—made his *Tribune* the North's most cussed-and-discussed medium of news and opinion for a generation. The democratic capitalism preached by Weed and Greeley keynoted Governor Seward's first message. Enterprise "is to be cherished rather than repressed," he declared, for wealth and knowledge would grow indefinitely if "impartially distributed." Whig majorities depended, however, as these sagacious politicians knew, on a constituency leery of Masons, national Bank, or anything else smacking of monopoly and aristocracy.[52]

Their immediate problem was Whiggery's illustrious chieftain, Clay. Mustering all his remarkable forensic powers to realize his golden opportunity for the presidency, the Kentucky senator dominated his party in Congress and press. His prescription for prosperity and Whig victory was an updated American System—sharply increased tariff protection (before the major reductions under his 1833 Compromise took effect), internal improvements financed by distribution of federal land revenues, and encouragement of bank credit. Most fatefully, he promised a new national Bank when "called for by a majority of the People." With the bourgeoisie rallying in adulation around the "Great Embodiment" of Whig principles, Whig victories following the initial panic seemed to promise him the 1840 nomination.

When temporary resumption and recovery made the Democrats more formidable, however, the Antimasonic Whigs set out to block a candidate who, as Clay himself put it, would "rather be right than be President." He was "unavailable" for three reasons, Weed bluntly told him. He was a Mason, a slaveholder, and too tied to the national Bank. The New York pragmatists, though ready to fall back on the Pennsylvania/western favorite Harrison, proposed the more prepossessing General Winfield Scott.[53]

The nomination was essentially decided by bourgeois desperation to recapture the national state. New York City's mainline Whig magnates deserted their idol Clay for the pragmatists, and Boston's Brahmins similarly doused Webster's vain hopes. By a close vote, the national convention at Harrisburg in December 1839 nominated Harrison. To conciliate the pro-Clay southern Whigs, the vice-presidential nomination fell fatefully on Senator John Tyler, a Clay man of the peculiar Virginia school.

The Democratic Whig Party, adjusting in name to the pragmatists' strategy of bourgeois/middle-class democracy, plunged the country into a legendary saturnalia of mindless pageantry. Wealth opened its purse as never before for Whig salvation, and Whig zeal attested as never before the fidelity of self-making young men to an embattled bourgeois order. The sparse Democratic convention that routinely renominated Van Buren at Baltimore in May 1840 was drowned out by a three-mile-long parade of Whig young men assembling by state and county delegations with bands, banners, and campaign songs for a Harrison "ratifying convention." Everywhere young men's energy and old men's gold poured out Harrison broadsides, cartoons, biographies, and songbooks, attracting thousands to Harrison rallies. The Whig campaign found its theme in a Democratic sneer that Harrison would be content with a log cabin and a barrel of cider. Although he lived genteelly in a fine house appropriate to his distinguished lineage and local eminence, log cabins and cider barrels soon blossomed on town squares everywhere to celebrate a plain-folks Old Tippecanoe against the dandified, effeminate Little

Magician. Whig polemic contrasted "the farmer of North Bend" at his plough with a corseted, perfumed Van Buren eating from gold spoons in the White House.

Even Webster claimed the log-cabin mystique. "I am a plain man . . . a farmer," he had told Westerners on a tour to promote his own nomination, and "many a time I have tilled my father's field, and followed my father's plough." Now loyally supporting Harrison, he told a Whig rally at Saratoga Springs that "it did not happen to me to be born in a log cabin; but my elder brothers and sisters were born in a log cabin. . . . Its remains still exist. I make to it an annual visit. I carry my children to it. . . . I love to dwell on the tender recollections of this primitive family abode."[54]

The success of this Whig dramaturgy established the middle-class mode of democratic politics that henceforth maintained bourgeois hegemony against every challenge. Harrison's modest popular margin (6.1 percent) was so evenly distributed as to tip most big states his way for an electoral landslide of 234–60 (nineteen states to six) and a strongly Whig Congress. Yet Whig humbug, far from stampeding a giddy populace, did not determine the bulk of the vote. As preceding state elections clearly reveal, most 1840 voters followed party identifications already forged in the Bank War between hard money and paper enterprise.

Indeed Democrats taunted "General Mum" himself into defining the central issue. "I am in favor of the paper system . . . because I am a democrat," Harrison told an Ohio audience. "The two systems are the only means, under Heaven," he said, "by which a poor industrious man may become a rich man." Hard money "makes the poor poorer, and the rich richer," Harrison charged, while only "a properly devised banking system" was capable of "bringing the poor to a level with the rich." Although he remained General Mum about a national Bank, approval was rightly inferred from his pledge against free use of the veto.[55]

The most striking feature of this election was a surge of new voters. Four out of five eligible white males voted, a turnout rarely equaled since; and nearly one in three, the largest proportion ever, was casting his first presidential ballot. Yet turnout rose first in state elections preceding the presidential campaign, with Democrats recruiting more new voters on upturns of the price index, while Whigs did better when prices broke. What decided the outcome was the depression that deepened as the campaign opened. The Harrison hullabaloo captured the final surge of new voters for the Whigs, and this marginal effect proved barely decisive. Despite the Democratic burdens of factional strife, hard-times incumbency, and an uncharismatic candidate, Democrats so increased their 1836 vote that a switch of only 8,086 ballots in four states would have reelected Van Buren.

Fittingly the election that crystallized bourgeois/middle-class democracy exhibited the "surge" effect that has grown in presidential elections as media have communicated candidate personalities ever more vividly. Surge elections attract an influx of weakly politicized new voters, usually poor, uninformed, and attuned by their face-to-face culture to personality rather than abstractions of party and program. Because these voters are most susceptible to candidates' personas and such immediate circumstances as hard times, they flow heavily to the side advantaged in these respects, often outweighing the competing party's advantage in the underlying pattern of party identifications that determines most votes. Such a surge seems to have elected Harrison, overcoming a slight Democratic ascendancy in party identifications that reasserted itself in subsequent elections.[56]

While Whigs celebrated, Democrats mourned that "we have taught them how to conquer us!"[57] Although the "sober second thought of the people" soon restored Congress to the Democrats, the millennial enthusiasm inspired by Jackson had been ravaged amid boom-and-bust by an obdurate polity, slippery politicians, and disappointed hard-money hopes. As Democratic laissez faire proved incapable of preserving the yeoman republic, political disillusion fed middle-class cultural accommodation. In the most commercial areas by 1840, Whig voting and the middle-class mythology of democratic capitalism cut deeply into the farming and working classes.

Thus crystallized a politics that has ever since muffled the contradiction between capitalism and democracy in a mythology of consensual and democratic enterprise. Where Whigs—like Federalists before and modern Republicans since—were unabashed champions of enterprise and the bourgeois/middle-class ethic, Democrats performed the more difficult and ethically ambiguous function—like Jeffersonian Republicans and modern Democrats—of pacifying popular discontent at the least possible cost to business. The Whigs "were sent to make the rich richer and the poor poorer, and they obeyed the will of their constituents," said a Philadelphia Workey. "But the Democrats," he lamented, "what shall we say of them?"[58]

Politicians of all parties have joined ever since in a politics of interests, repressing the Jacksonian spectre of class politics by trading instead on sectional, racial, ethnic, and religious conflict. Never again challenging bourgeois hegemony, the two-party democracy that emerged from the Bank War would endow American capitalism with unparalleled dynamism and legitimacy. Within little more than a generation, as Civil War snapped restraints on national developmentalism, the capitalist state would resume its interrupted leadership toward the bourgeois Millennium.

Chapter 12

The Bourgeois Republic

Two-party politics could tame farmer/worker radicalism because bourgeois/middle-class ethos and politics pervaded centers of enterprise to cut deeply into the producer class. Ever since the onset of market revolution, the northeastern commercial gentry had been mustering cultural authority against democratic challenge to their political authority. The American bourgeoisie enlisted conservative clerics and the emerging professional/intellectual elites of lawyers, doctors, professors, writers and artists to school all classes in a pansectarian middle-class culture of effortful "character" and self-improvement.

Cultural capital Philadelphia was hobbled in this effort by Quaker privatism and denominational/party strife, while booming but equally divided New York City neglected "elegant & useful science" for "eager cultivation & rapid increase of the arts of gain."[1] Primacy in the capitalist surge—cultural as well as entrepreneurial and technological—passed to New England, where Puritanism sanctified effort and Bible-reading literacy, while topography brought water power almost to seaboard and agrarian crisis honed both labor and enterprise for manufacturing.

Arminian/antinomian polarities energized rival wings of the Yankee cultural offensive. Boston's arminian Brahmins consolidated their commercial profits for industrialization and their Unitarian institutions for cultural preeminence through family marriage alliances, testamentary trusts, and generous endowment of Athenaeum library, Massachusetts General Hospital, Lowell Institute for public lectures, Massachusetts Historical Society, *North American Review,* and preeminently Harvard College.[2] Simultaneously Yankee notables outside Boston tamed popular antinomianism to capitalist effort through the refashioned Puritanism of the Moderate Light. Pious Yankees, infiltrating business elites in the Empire City and its far-flung trading satellites, consolidated a Presbygational alliance that spread across the North with the universal Yankee nation, and even into southern commercial centers.

This two-pronged offensive, blurring Yankee differences outside New

England, preached Moderate-Light self-improvement as measured by Brahmin Boston's capitalist success and gentility. Wherever Yankees migrated they outstripped natives in wealth and culture while pressing their example through multiplying churches, colleges, schools, libraries, voluntary associations, and a new perceptual realm of mass literacy and cheap print. Voluntary associations spread rapidly across the North to promote missions and Sunday schools, enforce morality and temperance, aid and uplift the poor, and maintain libraries and lyceum lecture series for cultural self-improvement. These potent agencies of middle-class acculturation, numbering some six hundred in Massachusetts by 1830, soon recruited half the Protestants in New York City, a quarter of the males in Cincinnati, and most adults in small towns such as Quincy, Illinois. Meanwhile Harvard, Yale, and Princeton, passing from clerical to bourgeois control, educated elites for other sections and founders and faculties for their colleges. By the 1840s an exfoliating cultural infrastructure and the powerful new medium of cheap print were carrying the American bourgeoisie to the most pervasive hegemony of any modern ruling class.[3]

Arminian capital could prevail culturally, however, only by co-opting the popular antinomianism that peaked under its stresses. Drawing upon the bourgeois romanticism generated to cope with capitalist transformation in Europe, a new class of self-making intellectuals, writers, and artists swathed arminian reality in antinomian illusion. Romanticism's loving heart, mustered in service of liberalism's selfish head, muffled calculating competition and Unitarian rationalism in spiritualized nature, domestic sentimentality, and transcendental idealism.

The cutting edge of the market's cultural conquest was a surge of literacy and schooling. Ever since alphabetic writing set off a cultural revolution in ancient Greece, literacy had fostered an analytical individualism that separated educated elites for two millennia from oral majorities attuned to communal memory. Literacy began slowly to widen only with the emergence of printing press, bourgeoisie, and Protestantism in early modern Europe.[4]

Colonial American literacy seems to have extended little beyond elites, except among Bible-reading male Yankees and self-making Ben Franklins in centers of trade. Although wider literacy has been inferred from the ratio of signatures to "marks" on wills, deeds, and petitions, such documents are biased toward the more literate. Illiterates often mastered signing to sustain patriarchal honor, and many schools taught signing and writing before reading. As late as the 1840s, two Illinois school trustees asked a prospective teacher they had examined to write out his certificate of proficiency to be signed, explaining that "one had left his spectacles at home, and the other had a bad cold, so that it was not convenient for either to write more than his name."[5]

But signature ratios do reflect the differential spread of functional literacy by area and occupation. Despite calls by Revolutionary republican elites for an educated electorate, the literacy takeoff seems to have awaited commercial boom in the 1790s. Signature ratios of army enlistees (biased toward the less literate) rose to 58 percent after 1800, 61 percent in the 1830s, 65 percent in the 1840s, and 75 percent in the 1850s. These ratios varied by locality and class in the early nineteenth century to pinpoint the Yankee/commercial sources of the literacy takeoff: New England 75 percent (Massachusetts and Connecticut 79 percent), mid-Atlantic 60 percent (New York 64 percent, Pennsylvania 54 percent), and South 50 percent. Farmers lagged behind the rising average, and laborers even farther behind.[6]

Literacy was introduced as an extension of the oral arts, learned by recitation from spellers and primers and communicating traditional culture through family reading of the Bible and a few classics of Protestant piety. But print culture became a powerful solvent of traditional culture by providing alternative perspectives and nourishing through private reading (especially in the new genre of novels) the egoistic individualism of bourgeois/middle-class culture.[7]

Literacy required schooling to supplement and increasingly supplant the traditional education of parental/craft apprenticeship, and the literacy takeoff mirrored a surge of schooling. School enrollments first reached the high plateaus of the mid-nineteenth century in the urban Northeast's public/private system of academies for elites, fee schools for the aspiring, and charity schools for the poor. A fourth of New York City's population under age twenty were enrolled by 1800 (or half those aged five to fourteen), two-fifths of Salem's by 1820, and almost half of Boston's by 1826. A greater surge in the rural Northeast pushed enrollment ratios from around 40 percent in New York in 1798 to around 70 percent in both New York and Massachusetts in the 1830s and 1840s. Ratios averaged an astonishing 82 percent in the smallest Massachusetts towns by 1826, as intensifying commitment to the Puritan tradition of community-supported schools made Yankees peculiarly susceptible to cultural transformation.[8]

The literacy/schooling takeoff got its initial impetus from parents equipping children for the chancy competition of market revolution and agrarian crisis. Urban working-class children learned reading and writing at cheap "dame schools" in the parlors of struggling women such as Sarah Osborn; masters met educational obligations to apprentices cheaply through evening schools; and mechanic families scrimped to enroll sons in more expensive "writing schools" for the ciphering and record-keeping skills demanded by the market.

Hard-pressed farmers in the northeastern countryside taxed themselves for often ramshackle one-room schools where both daughters and sons without farms to inherit prepared to fend for themselves. Elected neighborhood committees minimized costs by rotating short-term "moving schools" through adjacent districts or charging fees for longer terms. Winter classes for boys were typically taught cheaply by young men between terms at college or not yet established in other occupations, and summer classes for girls by local young women who kept school a few years at a third the pay of men. Yankee women closed the 2:1 male lead in literacy so rapidly that approximately one in five replaced more expensive men to do some teaching.

Parental initiative in schooling was soon eclipsed, however, by the cultural imperialism of a bourgeoisie alarmed over rising class division and urban disorder. In the 1790s that bellwether of Moderate-Light benevolence Dr. Benjamin Rush called for tax-supported free schools to "render the mass of people more homogeneous, and thereby fit them more easily for uniform and peaceable government." Believing that "the most useful citizens . . . have never known or felt their own wills till they were one and twenty years of age," he proposed "to convert men into republican machines" by schooling them under authority "as absolute as possible."

As a stopgap alternative to public schools, Dr. Rush enlisted lay volunteers to impart elementary literacy and "devout contentment" to Philadelphia's unchurched poor children on Sundays through Bible reading and memorization. While this expedient spread to reach thousands of urban northeastern youngsters, bourgeois reformers made such headway in promoting free public schools that Sunday schools shifted in the 1830s to nurturing the middle-class piety of churchgoers' children.

Englishman Joseph Lancaster's system of cheap mass learning through student monitors and rote memorization inspired a society of New York City businessmen in 1805 with the mission of teaching "all children who are the proper objects of a gratuitous education." Attracting enough public and private support by 1825 to operate eleven schools, through which twenty thousand students were said to have passed, this Public School Society became the city's exclusive recipient of state funding to educate all children. Thus, said the society, "the indigent may be excited to emulate the cleanliness, decorum and mental improvement of those in better circumstances."[9]

The bourgeois campaign for free public schools peaked in Massachusetts, which began supplementing local school taxes with state funds in 1834. Three years later Whig Governor Edward Everett persuaded the legislature to establish a state Board of Education and appointed as its secretary the self-made Whig/Unitarian lawyer Horace Mann. Brown University and Tapping Reeve's law school had weaned Mann from the Hopkinsian/Republican proclivities of his farm boyhood in the Reverend Nathanael Emmons's Franklin. Elected state senator from Boston, he had distinguished himself as a champion of temperance, insane asylums, prison discipline, and railroads when the governor and a wealthy manufacturer friend persuaded him to take up the educational cause.

Exploiting the mainly hortatory powers of his new position with zeal and eloquence, Mann wove the design of American public education from bourgeois panic. Tirelessly criss-crossing the state at the climax of the Bank War, he targeted nervous notables with his message that democracy gave free rein to "the powers of doing evil as much as the powers of doing good." Virtually universal suffrage established "a community of power," he said, and "nothing but mere popular inclination lies between a community of power and a community of everything else."

Pointing with alarm to "the use often made of the elective franchise, the crude, unphilosophical notions, sometimes advanced in our legislative halls on questions of political economy, the erroneous views entertained by portions of the people . . . and the revolutionary ideas of others," he warned that "if the ignorant and vicious get possession of the apparatus, the intelligent and the virtuous must take such shocks as the stupid or profligate experimenters may choose to administer." The school campaign, as parodied by Ralph Waldo Emerson, appealed to fear of a politicized majority—"you must educate them to keep them from our throats."

With "unmitigated anxiety," Mann demanded that solid citizens support free schools as a "barrier against . . . those propensities . . . which our institutions foster." Thus, and only thus, "nobler faculties can be elevated into dominion and supremacy over the appetites and passions," he insisted, for *"if this is ever done, it must be mainly done during the docile and teachable years of childhood."* Class division, Jacksonian insurgency, and mounting Irish Catholic immigration convinced Whiggish reformers that parents and local communities could no longer be trusted to discipline children for the homogeneous middle-class society that capitalism required. Parents "who refuse to train up children in the way they should go, are training up incendiaries and madmen to destroy property and life, and to invade and pollute the sanctuaries of society!" Mann preached, and "society at large,— the government . . . —is bound to step in and fill the parent's place." Immigrant children, said the *Massachusetts Teacher*, "must be gathered up and forced into school and those who resist or impede this plan, whether parents or *priests* must be held accountable and punished."[10]

Massachusetts school reform, rather than raising enrollments already high, shifted urban education from private to public schools while substantially increasing length of terms, attendance, and financial support in rural schools as well. Communities lagging in these categories were flayed annually by Mann's statistical reports of each district's record. Inspired by the industrial model, the reformers called for a new class of professional educators to intensify and standardize schooling. They were applying, said Boston's first superintendent of schools, "the principle of the division of labor, which has done so much to advance and perfect the various branches of industry." Mann persuaded the state to establish several "normal schools" to train professional teachers, and under his influence Boston led the way toward graded schools, written examinations, and a hierarchical school bureaucracy.[11]

The bourgeois educational program met strong resistance even in its Massachusetts heartland. The legislature's Committee on Education denounced it in 1840 as "a system of centralization and of monopoly of power in a few hands, contrary in every respect, to the true spirit of our democratical institutions," and questioned whether "the business of keeping these schools should become a distinct and separate profession." But a coalition of small towns, farmers, and Democrats failed, by a vote of 182–245, to abolish Mann's salary, state board, and normal schools.[12]

Although such resistance frustrated comprehensive free schooling outside New England until after the Civil War, the censuses of 1840 and 1850 revealed rapidly rising national school-enrollment ratios (for whites aged five to nineteen).

	1840	1850
New England	81.4%	76.1%
Mid-Atlantic	54.7%	61.9%
Northwest	29.1%	52.4%
South	14.5%	30.4%
TOTAL	38.4%	50.4%

While New England slipped because of multiplying workers and immigrants unable to forgo children's earnings for schooling (dropping Massachusetts behind Maine and Connecticut), enrollment ratios advanced dramatically wherever else market development and/or the universal Yankee nation reinforced Whiggish reformers inspired by Mann. By 1850 Yankee-laced New York (77 percent) was far ahead of Pennsylvania, where many communities rejected school taxes under a local-option system. Yankee migrants to the Northwest and public funding initiated by New Englanders' Northwest Ordinance had pushed enrollment ratios to 74 percent in strongly Yankee Michigan and 66 percent in Yankee/commercial Ohio, while greater southern immigration and slower development held Indiana to 42 percent and Illinois to 39 percent. Even in the South, enrollment ratios—for whites—rose substantially against farmer indifference and planter resistance to school taxes, primarily because of increased public funding in more commercialized Kentucky, Tennessee, and Louisiana, and in North Carolina after constitutional reform undermined planter power. By midcentury Americans were schooling their white children at far the highest rate in the world, over double that of France and Great Britain and barely exceeded by Denmark even when unschooled black and Indian children are included.[13]

The Benevolent Empire set off an explosion of print to feed an increasingly literate populace through technological innovation and mass distribution. Stereotyped printing plates, which saved the high costs of moveable type in long runs and of hand composition in reprinting, were used largely at first by British Bible and tract societies. The first stereotyped American book was produced from British plates by the Philadelphia Bible Society in 1812, and the country's Bible societies federated in 1816 partly to consolidate resources for stereotyping. As chief customer of the pioneer stereotypers located in its headquarters city New York, the

American Bible Society turned out ten thousand stereotyped Bibles in its first year, raised production to seventy thousand on eight hand presses in its third, and soon had twenty hand presses in constant operation. The Bible Society was also the first major customer of the Fourdrinier papermaking machine, which reached the United States in the late 1820s to more than halve paper costs by 1860.

Inspired by this example, the American Tract Society federated nationally in 1825, with a foundry in the basement of its New York headquarters that stereotyped 155 titles in its first year. Both societies pioneered in bringing to the United States the first major improvement on the hand-cranked flat-bed press since Gutenberg. In 1826 the Tract Society installed New York's first steam-powered Treadwell bed-and-platen press, the workhorse of American book publishing for a generation. It soon had nine more, and the Bible Society twenty-six. The Treadwell's leading promoter, Daniel Fanshaw, served as chief printer for both societies. Aggressive exploitation of the latest technology pushed the societies' output to over three hundred thousand Bibles and six million tracts in 1829.

They were equally insistent on "systematic organization" of distribution through traveling agents and local auxiliary societies. In the early 1830s the Bible Society mustered 645 auxiliaries in a campaign to place a Bible in every home, while the Tract Society enlisted 713 auxiliaries in an effort to deliver a tract every month to every family. By this time the American Sunday-School Union and the American Temperance Society were outstripping the older societies in disseminating the Graphic Light.[14]

The print revolution was further advanced as cheaper cloth covers replaced leather book bindings, paper mills multiplied, and expanding print shops reduced wage costs by division of labor among type-setting, presswork, and other tasks. Meanwhile the biggest newspapers achieved the fastest printing with the imported Napier press, which fed paper from an overhead cylinder to accelerate tenfold the two hundred impressions per hour of the hand press. In 1846, New York's Robert Hoe perfected a rotating-cylinder press with an automatic "fly" to remove printed sheets that soon raised output to twenty thousand per hour.[15]

Politicians exploited cheapening print to impose their two-party perspective on public affairs by adding public subsidy to their private subsidies of partisan newspapers. With newspaper postage set by law at one cent a copy up to one hundred miles (free up to thirty miles after 1845), newspapers soon made up 90 percent of the mail while paying only a ninth of postal revenues. Under this stimulus the 200 newspapers of 1801 (most published weekly and only some twenty daily) multiplied to 375 in 1810, 1,200 in 1835, and 2,526 (254 dailies) in 1850. By 1840 the United States had more newspapers than any other country and almost twice the number of slightly less populous Great Britain. New York City's daily output rose from one copy per 16 inhabitants in 1830 to one per 4.5 at mid-century.

Most of the rising tide of magazines and books shared the bourgeois/religious perspective of the benevolent-society publications. Three-fourths "of all the reading of the people," a prominent cleric testified, was "purely religious." Periodical proliferation was led by religious journals, with twenty-eight monthlies and seventy-three weeklies published in 1828 and fifty-two in New York City alone by midcentury. Other periodicals arose to target every specialized audience—literati and farmers, doctors and lawyers, women and children, Democrats and Whigs. Costly and paying full postage, however, most were unprofitable and ephemeral. Some five to six hundred lived briefly and died in raising the total from twelve in 1800 to nearly a hundred in 1825, and another four to five thousand were launched to leave some six hundred survivors at midcentury.

Most prestigious were two elite journals of opinion and literature. In Philadelphia a Tuesday Club of the Federalist gentry assisted founding editor Joseph Dennie and his successor young Nicholas Biddle in writing for the *Port Folio* (1801–1827). But the *Port Folio*'s lustre was fading by 1815, when Boston's *North American Review* claimed preeminence as Brahmin/Harvard arbiter of genteel high culture for the rest of the century.

Even the *North American*'s circulation did not exceed three thousand in its earlier years, however; and except for Hezekiah *Niles' Weekly Register* of public affairs (Baltimore, 1811–1849), few periodicals were profitable until the 1840s. Professional "magazinists," preeminently Nathaniel P. Willis and Lydia H. Sigourney, were able to make a living as writers only when the sentimentality and lavishly colored fashion plates of George Graham's *Graham's Magazine* (Philadelphia, 1839–1858) and Louis Godey's *Godey's Lady's Book* (Philadelphia, 1830–1898) attracted a broad audience of bourgeois/middle-class women. Both paid the highest fees for the best writers, including Hawthorne, Poe, and Longfellow, and able editor Sarah Josepha Hale helped Godey amass a half-million-dollar fortune by pushing circulation to forty thousand in 1849 and a hundred and fifty thousand in 1860.[16]

Magazines helped stimulate a rising appetite for books. By the 1830s Americans were matching the British output of some thousand titles annually, publishers were taking the initiative from printers in book production, and Harper Brothers became New York City's largest employer. The estimated value of American book output more than doubled from $2.5 million in 1820 to $5.5 million in 1840, and again to $12.5 million in 1850. The largest category was religious; schoolbooks followed at more than a third, with forty-seven million of the popular McGuffey readers sold between 1836 and 1870; and literary works were mainly at first pirated from British authors without royalty payments. Publishers pioneered in national advertising through magazines and newspapers and developed national marketing networks through local booksellers, lending libraries, and subscription library societies. The largest readership was reached through the circulating libraries of local school districts and the Sunday-School Union, whose selection committees ensured bourgeois/middle-class orthodoxy.[17]

Writ large in the flood of print was the cultural schizophrenia of capitalist transformation. A people competing fiercely to level a wilderness luxuriated in a literature of nature and love. A new genre, the novel, had arisen from market egotism in Europe to reassure a calculating bourgeoisie of its goodness by stimulating feeling. This art for heart's sake crossed the Atlantic with the sentimental heroines of Englishman Samuel Richardson, followed after 1800 by Sir Walter Scott's romances of sentimental chivalry amid the lochs and glens of Caledonian nature. The "Sir Walter disease" met Mark Twain's scorn only after gripping Americans for half a century.[18]

American writers were slow to compete in feeding bourgeois/middle-class hunger for the romantic literature of sentiment and nature. Philadelphia novelist Charles Brockden Brown was too gloomy about market progress to be popular; and Washington Irving's clever satires satisfied only the anachronistic gentility of his New York friends. Meanwhile British sneers goaded ambitions for a distinctive national culture. Americans "have done absolutely nothing for the Sciences, for the Arts, for Literature, or even for the statesman-like studies of Politics or Political Economy," gibed the *Edinburgh Review*'s Reverend Sydney Smith in 1820. "In the four quarters of the globe, who reads an American book? or goes to an American play? or looks at an American picture or statue?"[19]

As Smith jeered, however, Irving was shifting to the romantic mode in a *Sketch-Book* of English travel that bolstered national pride by satisfying British critics. The new American canon thus established celebrated heart as source of goodness, truth, and beauty. "Heart calleth unto heart," Irving wrote in describing Christmas as the best of times, "and we draw our pleasures from the deep wells of loving-kindness, which lie in the quiet recesses of our bosoms." He submerged traditional theological concerns in the beauty of English church services and the "holy repose" of the Sabbath, amid which "every restless passion is charmed down, and we feel the natural religion of the soul gently springing up within us." Even the sting of death he muffled in the pleasure of mournful sensation:

> The sorrow for the dead is the only sorrow from which we refuse to be divorced. . . . This affliction we cherish and brood over in solitude. . . . If it has its woes, it has likewise its delights; and when the overwhelming burst of grief is calmed into the gentle tear of recollection . . . who would root out such a sorrow from the heart? . . . No, there is a voice from the tomb sweeter than a song.

Irving moralized sentimentality for the bourgeois/middle-class market by coupling it with "natural grandeur and beauty" as "the purest and most elevating of external influences." External nature catalyzed the internal heart's natural goodness, he learned from William Wordsworth's school of poets, marveling that not an English "daisy unfolds its crimson tints to the morning, but it has been noticed by these impassioned and delicate observers, and wrought up into some beautiful morality." But Shakespeare's youthful indiscretions suggested the perils of trusting the spontaneous heart. Foreshadowing guilty fascination with Lord Byron and the Hawthorne/Melville critique of romanticism, Irving speculated that the "poetic temperament" when "left to itself" might run "loosely and wildly" to "everything eccentric and licentious."[20]

The contradictions of bourgeois romanticism soon became more troublesome when New York squire James Fenimore Cooper brought Scott's formula home to the American forest. In his popular romances pitting the natural nobility of the untutored frontier scout Leatherstocking against advancing civilization, a wilder nature sustained American moral superiority over European artificiality. Of course, Cooper's wilderness had to yield to enterprise, but he saved his compatriots' natural nobility by mythologizing America as a middle-ground "garden" of cultivated nature between untamed wilderness and artificial civilization. This central theme he wound around a sentimental cliché uniting an insipidly chaste blonde heroine with a woodenly correct hero despite complications presented by a fascinatingly passionate but flawed brunette heroine.[21]

This formula for taming American nature to a sentimental bourgeois/middle-class morality met such critical needs that it soon pervaded every arena of cultural expression. Novelist William Gilmore Simms applied it to southern settings and defense of slavery; William Cullen Bryant versified it; and playwrights J. A. Stone and Robert Montgomery Bird melodramatized it for the popular stage. In the landscape paintings of the Hudson River School, painters Thomas Cole and Asher Durand conveyed uplifting emotions of the sublime. Architects of urban landscapes and buildings, aspiring "to make the outward form of all about us express our best ideal of life," eschewed the rational symmetry of Lockean esthetics for natural spontaneity and evocative Gothic. Mount Auburn Cemetery arrayed picturesque and moral nature to sanctify the final rest of Boston Brahmins; Frederick Law Olmsted contrived the grottoes and glens of Central Park to soothe harried Manhattanites; Richard Upjohn spiritualized Wall Street with the soaring lines of Trinity Church; and Andrew Jackson Downing embowered domesticity in quaint garden cottages.[22]

All genres merged in romantic apotheosis of nature's nation. Durand painted poet Bryant and artist Cole as "Kindred Spirits" dwarfed amid the sublimity of a Catskills glen. Cole sought in painting "to walk with nature as a poet"; and when he departed for Italy to hone his technique among the old masters, friend Bryant distilled American romantic nationalism in a farewell sonnet:

> *Thine eyes shall see the light of distant skies:*
> *Yet Cole! thy heart shall bear to Europe's strand*

A living image of thy native land,
  Such as on thy own glorious canvass lies. . . .
Fair scenes shall greet thee where thou goest—fair,
  But different—everywhere the trace of men. . . .
Gaze on them, till the tears shall dim thy sight,
But keep that earlier, wilder image bright.[23]

Enterprising Americans embraced that wilder image of uplifting nature for redemption from both European condescension and market amorality. While creative men elaborated an American nature romanticism, creative women found a new authorial voice and a larger audience for a sentimental romanticism focused on such affecting subjects as motherhood, betrayed maidens, innocent babes, and death, preferably in combination. Best known was "the sweet singer of Hartford," Lydia H. Sigourney. This "great and good woman" wrote fifty-seven books and over two thousand poems for over three hundred publications, especially *Graham's* and *Godey's* magazines for women and the lavishly bound and illustrated "gift books"—with titles like *Rose of Sharon, Friendship's Offering,* and (for children) *The Pearl*—that proliferated on fashionable parlor tables in the 1840s and 1850s. Sigourney was acclaimed "the American Hemans," after her then celebrated British counterpart, for such lachrymose favorites as "Anna Playing in a Graveyard," "Widow's Charge at Her Daughter's Funeral," and "Baptism of an Infant at Its Mother's Funeral."[24]

Subliminally more critical of domestic/sentimental True Womanhood were the female novelists who delineated bourgeois/middle-class femininity to the largest antebellum audience, notably Catharine Maria Sedgwick, Caroline Howard Gilman, Sarah Parton ("Fanny Fern"), E. D. E. N. Southworth, and Harriet Beecher Stowe. Mostly reared in Yankee bourgeois families and married to college-educated professionals—Stowe was the youngest of Lyman Beecher's famous brood; Sedgwick was daughter, sister, and aunt of the three Theodores; and Gilman's husband composed "Fair Harvard" for his alma mater's bicentennial celebration—they were propelled into authorship, often through secret writing, by unusual educational preparation for forbidden male roles.

Frequently earning large incomes (Stowe from the runaway bestseller *Uncle Tom's Cabin*) and supplanting their husbands as family providers, these women guiltily played out in their own lives the self-effacing female domesticity that their novels formally advocated. Yet their frustrations generated a covert subtheme that won their large following by pitting female nobility and a sexual politics of love against unreliable males. Sensitivity to oppressive power enabled Stowe, though hardly an abolitionist, to wield this sexual politics so effectively for Uncle Tom's people that President Lincoln greeted her as "the little woman whose book made such a great war."[25]

The main medium of sentimentality, however, was a Protestantism homogenizing in the North around the adaptable Moderate Light. The psychic needs of businessmen, the sexual politics of their wives, and the aspirations of the self-making pushed insecure clerics of all denominations toward a loving Christianity of middle-class respectability and capitalist effort. Articulate laywomen collaborated in the sentimentalizing drift of the Unitarian clergy. Presbyterian ministers conciliated "the great and influential men" by condoning "the frivolous maxims and amusements of the world." Self-making Baptists discarded "odd tones, disgusting whoops, and awkward gestures" for a "more correct" style, even succumbing in Boston to formal ceremony, clerical gowns, and written sermons. Those who wished "to make our denomination respectable as well as the rest" rejected criticisms that they were "going back to the place from whence we came out."[26]

The most influential expounder of romantic Christianity was the Reverend Horace Bushnell. Intellectual doubts beset him as a Yale divinity student until he realized "I have a heart as well as a head" and decided "to hold by my heart." Encouraged by the English romantic Samuel Taylor Coleridge to abandon the whole tradition of theological analysis, he preached a salvation of loving response to a loving Heavenly Father. But love should not interfere with "the laws of trade," he reassured the bourgeois pews of Hartford's North Congregational Church, for wealth was "a reward and honor which God delights to bestow upon an upright people." None, he taught, were "more genuinely Christ-like" than Christian businessmen, who could unite enterprise with benevolence by selling their shabby or leftover goods to the poor at low prices while reserving "their charities—all their sympathies . . . for a separate chapter of life." He prayed, therefore, for "a money-loving, prosperous and diligent hearer."

Hobnobbing in Hartford's best parlors with sentimentalist Sigourney, Bushnell rejected evangelical insistence on a sinful humanity requiring cataclysmic conversion. Childish innocence should be nurtured by love, he insisted, into a mature Christianity nurtured by a loving man/god Jesus. By midcentury Protestant hymnody was nurturing children with lisping assurance that

> *Jesus loves me, this I know,*
> *For the Bible tells me so.*
> *Little ones to Him belong.*
> *They are weak, but he is strong.*

Their parents, raising rejoicing voice on Sabbath mornings to "Love Divine, all loves excelling" and "O Love that will not let me go," redeemed everyday marketplace lives with assurance of being gathered at last to the great tender heart of God.[27]

The romantic orgy of self-indulgent evasion, like all belief systems, required authoritative validation for ultimate credibility. In bourgeois culture, validating authority was passing from priesthoods to secular intellectuals; their medium from theology through literature to science and the academic disciplines; and their institutional locus from church through printed page and lecture platform to the modern university. A capitalist order requiring broad assent conferred bourgeois status on validating intellectuals, thereby disarming even the radical against its gravitational force. The pivotal exemplar was Ralph Waldo Emerson.

Emerson began voicing in the 1830s the frustration of many young Unitarians with the "pale negations" of their "corpse-cold" faith. Liberated from Puritan Calvinism by the rational "understanding" that Unitarians derived from Locke, these "transcendentalists" nevertheless hungered for the antinomian fire quenched in the process. "That crowd of upturned faces, with their look of unintelligent complacency!" sputtered brilliant Margaret Fuller's diary after a typical Unitarian sermon on the rational exercise of will. "For one I would now preach the Holy Ghost as zealously as they have been preaching Man, and faith instead of the understanding, and mysticism instead &c—." Similar feelings, along with shifting cultural authority, prompted many of Fuller's male friends to abandon the Unitarian ministry after preparation at Harvard, Emerson with a comfortable legacy in Concord to underwrite the untried career of self-made secular intellectual.

Boston's rising clerical star William Ellery Channing fed the dissidents' conviction that Unitarianism "suffered from union with a heart-withering philosophy." Reared in Newport, "our bishop," as Emerson called him, had imbibed enough New-Light benevolence directly from Samuel Hopkins to recognize that "men desire excitement." Warming the Unitarian corpse by preaching affinity between a decent humanity and a loving God, Channing taught transcendentalists to "look to other schools for the thoughts which thrill us."[28]

European literatures, brought back to Harvard by Professors Edward Everett and George Ticknor, prepared them to find their thrilling thoughts, like Horace Bushnell, in Coleridge's *Aids to Reflection.* Coleridge adumbrated the German philosophical idealism of Immanuel Kant to reconnect the rebels with their antinomian roots. Jonathan Edwards's divine idea was reborn as an intuitively apprehended higher Reason that undergirded the apparent reality of the material and transcended the sensory observation and rational analysis of Lockean understanding. Emerson Americanized transcendental Reason in his 1836 manifesto *Nature.* Drawing on Coleridge's theory of language, he argued that all natural phenomena "hint or thunder" a "Universal Spirit" that "does not act upon us from without" but "through ourselves" as prompted by nature. Living in nature as a "transparent eyeball," he announced, gave "access to the entire mind of the Creator" and made man "himself the creator in the finite." "Build therefore your own world," he preached, by conforming "your life to the pure idea in your mind."[29]

Transcendentalism, Emerson was soon telling Harvard's Phi Beta Kappa soci-

ety, promised a literature worthy of nature's nation. By embracing "the comm
. . . the meal in the firkin; the milk in the pan; the ballad in the street; the news or
the boat," American writers would reveal "the sublime presence of the highest spiritual cause." They had "listened too long to the courtly muses of Europe," he said,
and needed only to trust themselves "so that each man shall feel the world is his."
This "confidence in the unsearched might of man belongs . . . to the American
Scholar," he assured an enthusiastic audience, "and if the single man plant himself
indomitably on his instincts, and there abide, the huge world will come round to
him."

Emerson's bid for radical cultural leadership culminated in his 1838 address,
by student invitation, at Harvard's Divinity School. In this citadel of latter-day
arminianism, he sounded again the Edwardean jeremiad against "the universal
decay and now almost death of faith." What he called the "fertile forms of antinomianism among the elder puritans" echoed in his rhetoric: "the pulpit is usurped
by a formalist"—"the worshipper is defrauded and disconsolate"—"the soul is not
preached"—"the priest's Sabbath has lost the splendor of nature; it is unlovely; we
are glad when it is done; we can make, we do make, even sitting in our pews, a far
better, holier, sweeter, for ourselves."

Emerson proffered instead the transcendental ecstasy of the Newest Light. One
could "dare and live after the infinite Law that is in you, and in company with the
infinite Beauty which heaven and earth reflect to you in all lovely forms," he urged.
A man should be taught "that he is an infinite Soul; that the earth and heavens are
passing into his mind; that he is drinking forever the soul of God." Calling for
teachers to "show us that God is, not was; that He speaketh, not spake," Emerson
incited the rising cohort of Unitarian clerics to "rekindle the smouldering, nigh
quenched fire on the altar." This "latest form of infidelity," outraging the Unitarian sanhedrin and scandalizing Beacon Hill as bad manners and worse, closed Harvard platforms to the heretic for almost thirty years.

Brahmins were unduly alarmed, for this exemplary American Scholar was bred
in the bosom of Boston Federalism, and breeding told. Preaching a transcendental
Reason evoked by the beauty and metaphor of nature, he could not but see the
hard-times market as a "system of selfishness."[30] Yet imperatives of class perspective and vocation made Jacksonian insurgency abhorrent and confined his hopes
to individual regeneration within a class structure he validated as natural. Linking
individual regeneration with a nature inviting "great men to subdue and enjoy it,"
he had assured the divinity students at the outset that history honored "the planters, the mechanics, the inventors, the astronomers, the builders of cities, and the
captains."

This genteel preacher, learning with the Unitarian clergy to abandon Calvinist
syllogism for literary, even poetic, expression, found the secular audience he badly
needed by seemingly spiritualizing but actually commodifying nature. Both his

1836 manifesto and his Divinity School address began by validating nature as economically exploitable "Commodity," and his very style betrayed schizophrenia. Coleridge led him to a language of homely metaphor that vividly concretized nature's facts as commodity or beauty and fed the achievements of Thoreau, Hawthorne, Melville, and Whitman.[31] But universal Reason inspired vacuous labels—Over-Soul, Unity, eternal Centre, eternal One—and commodity was redeemed from bourgeois banality by cloudy abstractions—the "fire, vital, consecrating, celestial, which burns until it shall dissolve into the waves and surges of an ocean of light."

Emerson found his secular pulpit for this doctrine of spiritual self-making in the new role of paid lecturer to bourgeois/middle-class self-improvers; and his published oeuvre consists mainly of Unitarian-style literary sermons, delivered first in Concord and Boston, and then throughout the North and in England as he became the cultural doyen of the forties and fifties. Management of lecture series was passing from lyceums to associations of self-making young men backed by local business establishments; and communities throughout the North competed to book the celebrity lecturers touted by the New York press, especially Greeley's widely disseminated and copied *Tribune*.

Concord's genteel sophisticate became star of the lecture circuit by spiritualizing the market. In every considerable city from Portland to Baltimore to St. Louis, culturally aspiring elites attested both civic and personal worth by turning out en masse to hear him. Taking his Universal Spirit on faith to satisfy antinomian doubts, they applauded his vibrant paeans to their arminian values. For his audiences, as for mythologizers of American literature and history ever since, misty disquisitions on "The Over-Soul," "Spiritual Laws," and "Circles" validated the bourgeois individualism of "Self-Reliance," the commodified nature of "Wealth," and the capitalist millennialism of "The Young American."[32]

On grounds of spiritual autonomy, Emerson defined "Self-Reliance" for bourgeois/middle-class America as excluding charity and "lying affection." To appeals for the poor, he replied, "Are they *my* poor?" and confessed shame for the "wicked dollar" he sometimes gave to "your miscellaneous popular charities" such as "alms to sots" and "the education at college of fools." Dismissing "this bountiful cause of Abolition" as "incredible tenderness for a black folk a thousand miles off," he admonished the "angry bigot" that "thy love afar is spite at home." The only obligations he acknowledged were "to nourish my parents, to support my family, to be the chaste husband of one wife"; and even to them he would say, "I must be myself. I cannot break myself any longer for you, or you."

Radical individualism combined with nature's commodity to produce "Wealth," in Emerson's most popular lecture/essay. A beneficent market, by "bringing things from where they abound to where they are wanted," gave the farmer's peaches "a new look and a hundredfold value over the fruit which grew on the same bough and lies fulsomely on the ground." Technology galvanized the market into wealth.

A clever fellow was acquainted with the expansive force of steam; he also saw the wealth of wheat and grass rotting in Michigan. Then he cunningly screws on the steam-pipe to the wheat-crop. Puff now, O Steam! The steam puffs . . . dragging all Michigan at its back to hungry New York and hungry England.

Wealth generated the moral discipline of enterprise and emulation by requiring "that each man feed himself" and inflicting "pain and insult . . . until he has fought his way to his own loaf." Then, said Emerson, "every warehouse and shop-window . . . opens a new want," for man "is born to be rich" and will not "content himself with a hut and a handful of dried pease." The most moral, it seemed to follow, were those "men of the mine, telegraph, mill, map, and survey" who "esteem wealth to be the assimilation of nature to themselves," who "talk up their project in marts and offices and entreat men to subscribe." Their "*speculative* genius is the madness of a few for the gain of the world," he asserted, and "they should own . . . whose work carves out work for more, opens a path for all." His political economy, therefore, absolutized the market's "adjusting meter of demand and supply."

Do not legislate. . . . Give no bounties, make equal laws, secure life and property, and you need not give alms. Open the doors of opportunity to talent and virtue and . . . in a free and just commonwealth, property rushes from the idle and imbecile to the industrious, brave and persevering.

Only in closing did Emerson make the market economy "a coarse symbol of the soul's economy." As a merchant hoards and invests for economic power, he said, one should invest the spiritual "liquor of life . . . with keener avarice . . . in spiritual creation and not in augmenting animal existence." This Delphic adieu, capping a panegyric to Gradgrind capitalist liberalism, saved his transcendental consistency but left his audience believing—at some level his real meaning—that he sacralized the animal existence he claimed to transcend. Like Hopkins, Finney, and Bushnell, Emerson preached transcendental grace for bourgeois/middle-class Americans "born to be rich." "Do you complain of the laws of Property?" he asked on another occasion. ". . . Let into it the new and renewing principle of love, and property will be universality."

Transcendentalized market promised national Millennium, the sage announced in summoning "The Young American" to "a high national feeling." He saw "the anti-feudal power of Commerce" combining with "the majesty of nature" to make the United States "the home of man" and "the country of the Future." Its settlement "under the free spirit of trading communities" was "the human race, under Divine leading, going forth to receive and inhabit their patrimony." In nature's nation, he said, "an organic simplicity and liberty ... offers opportunity to the human mind not known in any other region." And here, therefore, "vast tendencies concur of a new order."

Emerson's new order was untrammeled capitalism. "Trade planted America," he asserted, and "our part is plainly not to throw ourselves across the track," but "to conspire with the new works of new days."

> This great savage country should be furrowed by the plough, and combed by the harrow; these rough Alleganies should know their master; these foaming torrents should be bestridden by proud arches of stone; these wild prairies should be loaded with wheat; the swamps with rice; the hill-tops should pasture innumerable sheep and cattle.

He exulted in "the rage for road building"—in "railroad iron" as "a magician's rod" with "power to evoke the sleeping energies of land and water"—in "agricultural chemistry, coolly ... offering, by means of a teaspoonful of artificial guano, to turn a sandbank into corn"—in the "movement which made the joint-stock companies for manufactures, mining, insurance, banking," and now "proposed to plant corn, and to bake bread by companies," which "will be tried until it is done." Equating the corporation with socialist equity under the benign principle of "association," he promised that this "country of beginnings, of projects, of vast designs and expectations" would advance "into a new and more excellent social state than history has ever recorded."

By midcentury the prophet of corporate/capitalist Millennium was "universally recognized," said the American press, as "one of the great thinkers of the age."[33] Exemplifying his advice to the American Scholar, he had planted himself indomitably on his bourgeois instincts, and the huge bourgeois/middle-class world came round to him. In the bourgeois cultural marketplace, insurgent intellectuals ended up building—as had insurgent clerics—an ever more compelling bourgeois hegemony. Concord erected a triumphal arch to welcome its sage home from a European tour, and in sweet vindication he finally became an Overseer of penitent Harvard.

Romanticism—as altruistic humanity's last desperate refuge from market ego—was too illusory to quell the cultural dissonance of capitalist transformation. Emerson's benisons did not satisfy the many transcendentalists who wrenched their lives into variously resisting the bourgeois order. George Ripley quit the pulpit for communal socialism. George Bancroft eschewed both pulpit and experimental education for Locofoco history and politics. Margaret Fuller gallantly bore the burdens of smart womanhood through schoolteaching, philosophical "conversations" for self-improving ladies, literary editorship of Greeley's *Tribune*, feminist manifesto, Italian revolution, and scandalous romance cut short by shipwreck. Henry Thoreau, retreating to Walden Pond, drew the most eloquent indictment of the market's corruption while pioneering the radical politics of civil disobedience against the coercive state. Asked by his mentor what he was doing in jail after refusing taxes for an unjust war against Mexico, he replied, "What are you doing out there, Waldo?"

Other writers joined Thoreau in generating a literary renaissance by deploying Emersonian metaphor against Emersonian evasion. Self-reliance was not enough, announced Locofoco workingman/poet Walt Whitman in the opening lines of *Leaves of Grass*.

> *One's Self I sing, a single, separate person,*
> *Yet utter the word Democratic, En-Masse.*

Sailor/novelist Herman Melville blamed Emerson's "oracular gibberish" on "self-conceit" and "a defect in the region of the heart." Locofoco/novelist Nathaniel Hawthorne satirized his Concord neighbor by updating John Bunyan's classic Protestant fable of painful *Pilgrim's Progress* from sin through adversity to heaven.[34]

"The Celestial Railroad," in Hawthorne's story, now whisked Pilgrims painlessly from Bunyan's City of Destruction to the Celestial City. A bridge over the treacherous Slough of Despond was solidly ballasted, as railroad director "Mr. Smooth-it-away" assured nervous passengers, by

> volumes of French philosophy and German rationalism; tracts, sermons and essays of modern clergymen; extracts from Plato, and various Hindoo sages, together with a few ingenious commentaries upon texts of Scripture—all of which by some scientific process have been converted into a mass like granite.

A German-born "Giant Transcendentalist" had replaced Bunyan's giants to ply travelers with "plentiful meals of smoke, mist, moonshine, raw potatoes, and sawdust," although his meaning and substance "neither he for himself, nor anybody for him, has ever been able to describe." Most Pilgrims stopped short of the Celestial City in Vanity Fair, where "a great trade" produced such "an epitome of whatever is brilliant, gay, and fascinating" that many thought it "the true and only heaven," and that only fools and dreamers sought any other. Here "almost every street has its church"; and "the reverend clergy," aided by "innumerable lecturers," offered vast erudition "without even the trouble of learning to read."[35]

Hawthorne resonated Vanity-Fair America's conflicted anxiety over eroding antinomian faith and corroding human bonds. Harvard's patrician Ticknor lamented the change since his Boston boyhood, when people had "felt involved in each other's welfare and fate as it is impossible we should now, when our numbers are trebled and our affairs complicated and extended ... too wide." He worried that "the interests of each individual are grown too separate and intense to be bound in by any general sympathy with the whole."[36]

The very manners and fashions of the bourgeoisie, along with its sentimental literature, were shaped by longings for feeling and trust, as competition among self-making strangers multiplied "confidence men and painted women." A *Godey's* writer asked "Who Is Happy?" when

> life is but a masquerade, in which we dress ourselves in the finest fashions of society, use a language suited to the characters we assume;—with smiling faces, mask aching hearts; address accents of kindness to our enemies, and often those of coldness to our friends.

Godey's answer was the obsessively "sincere" lady of its high-fashion color plates—unrouged, demurely coiffed, with simple gown following natural form——whose "body charms because the soul is seen." Sincere women enforced on the social masquerade an elaborate etiquette prescribing what historian Karen Halttunen calls "the genteel performance, a system of polite conduct that demanded a flawless self-discipline practiced within an apparently easy, natural, sincere manner."

Sentimental sincerity culminated in an extravagant cult of mourning the dead that made Lydia Sigourney far more celebrated than Emerson and the renaissance writers. A demanding etiquette focused not on the deceased but on ceremonial grief attesting the goodness of the bereaved. Formal mourning—dressing in black (gray for children), declining invitations, and avoiding levity—lasted two years for widows and six months to a year for friends and other relatives of the deceased. Cemeteries became major cultural arenas and civic monuments, whose condition was "a very good index of the character of the community." Therefore, warned a clerical guardian of *The Sepulchres of Our Departed*, "have a care about your confidence, and interest, and reputation ... where you witness an air of negligence and desolation overspreading the sacred enclosure."[37]

But sentimental ideal was too manifestly contradicted by marketplace reality to ease persistent bourgeois disquiet. Enterprising Americans were driven, unsociable, uncultivated, and unhappy, worried that oracle of bourgeois orthodoxy the *American Review*. Assessing "The Influence of the Trading Spirit," the first number of this impeccably Whiggish journal warned that if "trade is destined to free and employ the masses, it is also destined to destroy for the time much of the beauty and happiness of every land." The "anxious spirit of gain" was "not natural to the human soul," said the *Review*, and "great scrupulousness of character may be united with great selfishness." Consequently "the upright man is not benevolent, and the just man is not generous. The good man is not cheerful. The religious man is not agreeable."[38]

Similar misgivings spread through the middle class in the 1840s to multiply seekers for more satisfying spiritualities and social arrangements. Fad followed fad—mesmerism, phrenology, spirit rapping, animal magnetism, water cures. When an ingenious promoter helped the Reverend William Miller stir up a last burst of millennial frenzy by predicting the Second Coming at midnight on October 22, 1844, thousands abandoned houses and possessions to don white robes and meet disappointment in fields and on hilltops across the North. A new surge of communalism spawned forty-odd "phalansteries" practicing Frenchman Charles Fourier's blend of communal enterprise, sexual equality, and capitalist property. John Humphrey Noyes's more radical doctrines of communism and "complex marriage" inspired the most durably flourishing communal experiment at Oneida, New York.

Sexual/social radicalism dispelled middle-class mythology for Dr. Thomas Low Nichols. Agitating with wife Mary Gove for free love, he "never thought America *was* a happy country." Nowhere "are the faces of the people furrowed with harder lines of care"; nowhere was there "so much hard, toilsome, unremitting labour" and "so little of recreation and enjoyment of life." Nichols blamed "the universal and everlasting struggle for wealth."

> There is no such thing in America as being contented with one's position. . . . Everyone is tugging, trying, scheming to advance—to get ahead. . . . In Europe, the poor man, as a rule, knows that he must remain poor, and he submits to his lot, and tries to make the best of it. . . . Not so in America. Every little ragged boy dreams of being President or a John Jacob Astor. The dream may be a pleasant one while it lasts, but what of . . . the excited, restless, feverish life spent in the pursuit of phantoms?

Socialism, which Nichols saw spreading with phalansteries, was

> a protest and reaction against Mammonism and a growing and almost universal egoism or selfishness. As families were scattered, . . . as politics became more and more debased and despicable, as wealth failed to satisfy . . . , men naturally inquired if there were not some form of social life less exhausting and more satisfying.[39]

Radical indictment found a surprising echo in Manhattan's fastidious patrician George Templeton Strong. The "commercial, speculating, bank-worshipping" Whiggery of the bourgeois/middle-classes, he feared, "would make us a commercial aristocracy which is mean enough everywhere, but here 'twould be a fluctuating mushroom aristocracy and the meanest the world has seen yet." Still more frightening to Strong, however, was "the jacobinical spirit and the antipathy to law and order" of the Democratic working classes.[40] More than romantic illusion would be required to stifle the northern bourgeosie's doubts and clinch its hegemony over a solidifying coalition of embittered working people, resistant farm folk, and an increasingly assertive slavocracy.

Emersonian evasion was challenged most fundamentally in an 1840 manifesto on behalf of "The Laboring Classes" by Orestes Brownson, a Workey/cleric seeker en route from Presbyterianism to Catholicism via Universalism, Unitarianism, and transcendentalism. Heralding a terrible struggle between "wealth and labor," he had "no faith in priests and pedagogues," who "always league with the people's masters, and seek to reform without disturbing the social arrangements which render reform necessary." Their only reform was to "make the individual . . . truly religious," he snorted, whereupon "all evils will either disappear, or be sanctified to the spiritual growth of the soul." This was "a capital theory" for "all who fatten on the toil and blood of their fellows," but it had been preached for millennia while the human condition grew "worse and worse."

The wage system was destroying the old republic of patriarchal equality by "repartition of the fruits of industry," Brownson lamented, and "the only way to get rid of its evils is to change the system, not its managers." Where formerly "almost any man might aspire to competence and independence," he said, under wages "one half of the human race must forever be the virtual slaves of the other." Warning that the Bank War could be "paving the way for" class war over property, he saw "hereditary descent of property" as "an anomaly in our American system, which must be removed, or the system will go down." But because "the rich, the business community, will never voluntarily consent," he grimly predicted, equality would be restored "only by the strong arm of physical force" in a "war, the like of which the world as yet has never witnessed."[41]

Ministering amid deep depression to victims of accelerating proletarianization, Brownson absorbed a working-class desperation incomprehensible to the comfortable classes. Old Workey George Henry Evans feared that "the triumph of machine labor, and ultimate prostration of human labor, cannot . . . be averted." The laborer was "degenerating into a mere machine," protested Philadelphia cotton-mill workers, "producing wealth by perpetual exertion, yet living a life of unceasing anxiety and want," with only "compensation enough to keep him in profitable working order and economical repair."

But the formidable working-class militancy of the midthirties crumbled in depression under hungry competition for any wage. When panic doomed economic struggle, the old Workey leadership had been moving toward a fundamental challenge to capitalist wage exploitation through worker cooperatives. Retreating to a radical Locofoco politics soon frustrated by the two-party dynamic, they had fallen back on Evans's scheme for a "true American party" to campaign for free land under the slogan "Vote Yourself a Farm." Meanwhile their once mighty following had been splintered by middle-class evangelicalism and ethnic strife.[42]

Hard-times desperation for self-repressive discipline opened a hitherto resistant working class to substantial penetration by the Moderate-Light Awakening. Evangelical churches grew at doubled or tripled rates in Philadelphia; Baptist congregations and chiliastic sects sprouted in New York; and everywhere multiplying Methodists hardened their polemic against liquor and sin. The confessional temperance societies and devoted female auxiliaries of the Washingtonian movement mushroomed alongside plebeian churches, as many working people disdained the bourgeois condescension of the Benevolent Empire to muster communally their own discipline of survival.[43]

Plebeian evangelicalism shattered the old mechanic culture, as Irish Catholic immigrants reinforced a worker majority resisting bourgeois/middle-class norms through new urban patterns of lower-class culture. Camaraderie of boardinghouse, street, stand-up saloon, and fiercely competitive volunteer fire companies bolstered unsuccessful manhood. Youth gangs defiantly affected the foppish attire of "Bowery B'hoys" to contest turf and intimidate genteel intruders. Costumed street parades and satirical street theater mocked elite pretensions. Mass commercial entertainment offered escape from alienated labor and straitened lives in dancehalls, the rowdy new ambience of spectator sport at racetrack and boxing match, P. T. Barnum's Broadway Museum of wonders, and especially theaters, where prostitutes prowled the upper galleries and horny-handed audiences championed favorite American actors by pelting and mobbing imported English rivals.[44]

Plebeian culture fostered a sensational subliterature. Broadsides, cheap weeklies, pamphlets, and serially published fiction expressed democratic anger at bourgeois corruption, hypocrisy, and oppression through ballads, gallows confessions, and tales of gore, wild adventure, impiety, social outcasts, and prurience. Refined for national consumption as filler for William T. Porter's New York racing sheet, *The Spirit of the Times,* this earthy genre merged Bowery boy with Mississippi boatman in braggadocio humor and punctured genteel pretension in plain-folk vernacular.

The plebeian audience made George Lippard's lurid *Quaker City* the most widely read American novel before *Uncle Tom's Cabin.* Denouncing clergymen who "preach to the Poor a Bestial submission to the Rich," Lippard chronicled a conspiracy of rich Philadelphians to enslave poor men while debauching poor women in a luxurious and dungeoned Monk's Hall. He spent his royalties and the rest of his life recruiting a conspiratorial Brotherhood to resist "degradation of the Workers of America" by conspiratorial capital.[45]

Plebeian culture found a validating public mirror in the penny press. Conventional "blanket" dailies—enormous sheets sold over the counter for six cents or by annual subscription for ten dollars, a week's wage—were first challenged in 1833 when twenty-three-year-old Workey printer Benjamin Day began vending his letter-size *Sun* on Manhattan streets for a penny. The *Sun* rose so radiantly that it soon had two local competitors and flourishing imitators in Philadelphia, Baltimore, and Boston. Within three years New York's three penny dailies had twice the circulation of all eleven blanket dailies at the *Sun's* rising. Surviving hard times, the penny press invaded smaller cities in the 1840s to accelerate the explosion of newspaper circulation.

Published mainly at first by mechanic printers of Workey antecedents, penny papers flourished by shaping content to their working-class readership. While targeting bourgeois pretension, favoritism, and hypocrisy in vivid police-court reportage of violence, sexuality, and scandal, they backed unions, strikes, and the ten-hour cause. The *Sun,* claimed founder Day, produced a "decided change in the condition of the laboring classes" by enabling them to "understand their own interest, and feel that they have numbers and strength to pursue it."

Although subordinating electoral politics to the cultural politics of the police court, penny publishers resented the Whiggery of leading blanket papers, particularly in New York the Tappan brothers' aggressively antilabor *Journal of Commerce* and James Watson Webb's *Courier and Enquirer,* which Biddle had seduced from Tammany with a fifty-thousand-dollar loan while denying credit to small printers. By professing nonpartisan, working-class skepticism about politicians and the partisan blanket press, the penny press gained credibility for its consistent endorsement of Locofoco Democratic policies, from Bank War to territorial expansion.

Soon requiring too much capital for mechanic printers, the lucrative penny field was invaded by bourgeois capital, personified in New York by the *Herald*'s shrewdly apolitical James Gordon Bennett, the *Tribune*'s Whig-financed Greeley, and the *Times*'s well-heeled Henry Raymond. As the penny press lost touch with its Workey roots, police-court sensationalism lost its antibourgeois edge. Increasingly the popular dailies pandered to the crippling contradictions of working-class egalitarianism—jingoism, nativism, and the racism of "nigger" story, blackface minstrelsy, and marauding mob.[46]

Capitalism disarmed opposition by setting the most exploited at each other's throats. Phobic contempt for failure both energized effort and turned the shame of proletarianized whites against even more vulnerable blacks and immigrants. Establishment preachers and politicians, stirring plebeian racism and nativism to virulence during the Jackson years, diverted cresting plebeian anger from a frightened bourgeoisie.

The most grievous of the hidden injuries of class inflamed endemic white racism to bolster shattered patriarchal pride. Both the job insecurity and psychosocial pain of white failure found surcease in dehumanizing "niggers"—as stupid, lazy, obsequious, larcenous, and immoral, albeit amusing in childish abandon of dance and song—and driving them from all but the most servile work. Against this vicious tide, blacks were stubbornly building supportive communities in the most squalid neighborhoods of northern cities around their own churches, schools, lodges, and a precarious middle class of ghetto preachers and tradesmen. Yet white retribution threatened the most circumspect black aspirations to dignity, let alone the black militancy of parading in celebration of West Indian emancipation, denouncing colonization as racist, and rescuing runaway slaves from the authorities. Sporadically white mobs targeted "uppity" blacks who blurred the caste boundary sustaining shaky white pride, especially when prostitution or miscegenation raised the dread spectre of "amalgamation."

The crowd in the streets was the ultimate working-class weapon. Traditionally enforcing the preindustrial moral economy, it was invoked more frequently and coercively in strikes as unskilled trades dependent on intimidation and popular support joined the skilled in Workey militancy. While strikes proliferated in the midthirties, Workeys and Locofocos were turning out ever more militant crowds for elections and political demonstrations, thirty thousand New Yorkers against a union-busting conspiracy conviction and twenty thousand Philadelphians against suspending banks. With bosses yielding the ten-hour day, Old Hickory preaching Bank War, and the penny press validating plebeian anger, a crescendo of street militancy threatened every object of plebeian ire.

Niles' Weekly Register reported civil disorders jumping from four in 1833 to twenty in 1834 and suppressed further reports when the 1835 total reached fifty-three. Gamblers were lynched in Vicksburg, Mormons were mobbed in Missouri, cheering thousands burned Catholic nuns out of their Charlestown convent school for girls across the bay from Boston, and a fraudulent bank failure plunged Baltimore into four days of savage pillage. As the death toll passed sixty, many thought "we are in the midst of a revolution." With "society shaken to its foundations," in the opinion of Dr. Channing, class crisis shocked Horace Mann's Yankee bourgeoisie into the public-school campaign.[47]

The main victims, however, were blacks and abolitionists. Sporadic black/white unity against bosses had disappeared as white attacks on black neighborhoods increased in the 1820s, igniting Providence twice and terrorizing half Cincinnati's blacks into flight. Racist terror crested when peaking street militancy collided with peaking antislavery militancy in the mid-1830s crisis. While the black indictment of colonization's racism reverberated through the polemical abolitionism of William Lloyd Garrison's Boston *Liberator,* the deep pockets, organizational genius, and evangelical zeal of New York's Tappan coterie pushed auxiliaries of the new American Anti-Slavery Society into many northern communities. Simultaneously the abolitionists' high-speed presses were loading the mails north and south with luridly illustrated exposes of slavery's horrors. Panicked slaveholders, still reeling from Nat Turner's bloody rebellion as they forced an aggressive new proslavery orthodoxy on the white South, demanded northern suppression of abolitionism as constitutional obligation and price of Union.

The white North obliged. Most northern plebeians saw abolitionists as fomenting the terrors of amalgamation. Most northern businessmen saw fanatics endangering the slave-grown exports and ever holier Union on which national prosperity depended. Most northern politicians, with the election of President Jackson's successor at hand, saw a threat to their intersectional party coalitions. Democrats depending on the white South for a Van Buren majority were especially anxious to demonstrate racial orthodoxy, while Whigs saw a chance to blunt menacing insurgency. Across the political spectrum, northern elites felt their moral integrity and authority threatened by abolitionist attack on their liberal fig-leaf colonization.

The politics of race, class, and section converged as the northern bourgeoisie aroused plebeian racism to satisfy the South. Bipartisan arrays of notables in scores of northern communities, backed by an almost unanimous press, not only denounced abolitionism in speeches and resolutions but also sanctioned or incited the mobbing of abolitionists and looting and burning of black neighborhoods. A Van Burenite congressman was rewarded with the New York attorney generalship after inciting a mob to drive the abolitionists' state convention from Utica and sack an antislavery newspaper.

Egging on Utica's Democratic incendiaries was New York City's James Watson Webb, Whig editor of the leading blanket daily and champion of colonization. Alarmed by rising insurgency in 1833, Webb had orchestrated mob disruption of the city antislavery society's organizing meeting. Then, with his *Courier and Enquirer* beset by the penny press, his financial angel Biddle under heavy assault, and colonizationists demoralized by abolitionist attack, he mounted a racist polemic against abolitionist "amalgamators." While troops were called out to curb Locofocoism in the streets at the critical Bank-War election of April 1834 and strikers in November, Webb cried on an escalating terrorism against abolitionists and blacks—meetings broken up, Finney's Broadway Tabernacle burned, and Arthur Tappan's house looted. At its climax in September, troops stood by while whites rampaged unchecked through black neighborhoods for three days, destroying over sixty houses and six churches and wrecking many more. Christian businessmen's connivance in this racist rage shocked the disillusioned Finney into exile.

Elsewhere mobs dragged Garrison by halter through the streets of Boston, demolished an abolitionist newspaper office in Cincinnati, killed abolitionist editor Elijah Lovejoy in Alton, Illinois, and razed an abolitionist meeting hall in Philadelphia. Everywhere black neighborhoods were assaulted, even in sight of the Capitol, and the abolitionist press reported 165 racist mobbings between 1835 and 1838. Authorities left blacks to the fury of mobs while defending bourgeois property with troops and shooting down antibank rioters in Baltimore. In effect if not by design, the northern bourgeoisie deflected working-class anger from bosses, banks, and aristocrats onto defenseless blacks.[48]

Abolitionism stirred up virulent racism more readily because the Tappans already personified for white workers an oppressive Whiggery of union-busting and coercive morality. Negrophobia, therefore, sealed the plebeian white North's

Democratic-party coalition with the slaveholding South. Flamboyant Congressman Mike Walsh, leader of a rowdy street-gang insurgency against well-fed Tammany regulars and tyrannical capital, thought northern workers differed from southern bondsmen only in having "to beg for the privilege" of becoming slaves. Heirs of the Workey tradition supported Calhoun against Tammany's Van Buren for the 1844 Democratic presidential nomination, and Walsh sided with the slaveholders in Congress.[49]

Consolidating the Democratic entente culturally, northern urban racism nationalized slavery by honing the blackface minstrel show into midcentury white America's favorite entertainment. The infectious music and dance of Afro/America became enormously popular when brought back from southern tours in the 1840s by white entertainers who "jumped Jim Crow" in blackface on northeastern stages. The demeaningly caricatured "Sambo" who justified racist slavery was also sufficiently disreputable to voice repressed social meanings. The minstrel show's adaptable and entertaining venue not only inculcated racism but also appropriated the vitality of black expression to other white needs.

Lowly "end man" and pompous "straight man," shaping humorous repartee to audience response, mixed plebeian racism with sexual innuendo and plebeian critique of the bourgeoisie. Stephen F. Foster's minstrel-show hits—"Carry Me Back to Old Virginny," "My Old Kentucky Home," "Old Black Joe"—appropriated the pathos of black song to plebeian white angst for farm and childhood, inspiring a plaintive balladry of pure nostalgia—"The Old Oaken Bucket" and "Home, Sweet Home"—that dominated popular music for the rest of the century. Minstrelsy "burst upon us as a glad and stunning surprise," Mark Twain recalled from his boyhood Hannibal, Missouri. Although his *Huckleberry Finn* transcended racism impressively, his autobiography confessed that "if I could have the nigger show back, . . . I should have but little further use for opera."[50]

The proletarian white trauma that ravaged blacks found white victims in a swelling influx of immigrants, especially Catholic Irish. Depression following the Napoleonic wars had brought to a crisis the long agony of Ireland's communal/subsistence Gaelic peasantry under English/Protestant oppression and the market disruption of enclosing, rack-renting landlords. In three decades after 1815 almost a million desperate Irish departed for North America, with uprooted Catholic peasants from southern Ireland replacing earlier Protestant "Scotch-Irish" migrants from Ulster. Arriving destitute, unused to market ways, and often speaking only Gaelic, they crowded the meanest neighborhoods of Atlantic ports and took over the meanest work for the meanest wages. Penetrating the interior as gang labor, Irish immigrants dug the canals and built the railroads of the transportation revolution.[51]

Heretofore American working people, in the Paine/Duane/Heighton tradition of immigrant artisan radicalism, had seen their country as a haven for

Europe's oppressed. By 1830, however, as multiplying immigrants became more Catholic, Protestant clerics were able to revive Reformation hatreds to reinforce their millennial crusade for Moderate-Light conformity. Popery was assailed—by sermons, a swarm of anti-Catholic periodicals, the Benevolent Empire's Protestant Reformation Society, and lewd exposés fabricated in collusion with pious clergymen—as unscriptural, despotic, and cloaking priestly prurience in pretense of celibacy. Lyman Beecher led the attack from his pulpit in Boston, where mobs sacked Irish neighborhoods twice in four years before a particularly lurid Beecher sermon helped spark the 1834 burning of the Charlestown convent.

Amid the turmoil of 1835, New York's Whig bellwether James Watson Webb broadened his insurgency-blunting strategy from inciting plebeian racism to politicizing plebeian nativism. Attacking immigrant competition for jobs and the patronage appointments that clinched Irish votes for the Democrats, Webb promoted a local Native American party opposing citizenship, voting, and officeholding for immigrants. Tammany quelled this first outburst of political nativism, and the labor movement maintained native/immigrant solidarity through the climactic struggles of the mid-1830s. But economic disaster and multiplying immigrants—from 38,914 in 1838 to 104,565 in 1842—soon brought plebeian nativism to a boil in the northeastern port cities.

When New York City's largest employer, Methodist publisher James Harper, was elected mayor by a nativist/Whig coalition in 1838, alien vice proved unamenable to his three rules for happiness—"Trust in God, pay your bills, and keep your bowels open." Tammany no sooner retired the ineffectual Harper than nativism was reignited in both New York and Philadelphia by Irish protests against Protestant indoctrination in the public schools, particularly use of the Protestant Bible. Street hostilities culminated in 1844 when nativist American Republican parties coalesced with the Whigs to sweep elections in both cities.

This campaign plunged Philadelphia into a summer of violence. Nativist mobs invaded Irish working-class districts, the Irish armed in self-defense, and blood was shed. As fighting engulfed the city, inflamed nativists burned three Catholic churches and blocks of Irish houses. In the bloodiest clash—13 killed and 50 wounded—nativists firing cannon attacked troops guarding a Catholic church. All that prevented nativist rage from ravaging New York as well was Bishop John Hughes's declaration—backed by a thousand armed Irishmen at each of his churches—that "if a single Catholic Church were burned in New York, the city would become a second Moscow." The bourgeoisie hastened to muzzle their nativist dogs.

Plebeian nativism registered both immigrant competition for hard-times jobs and the hard-times compulsions of middle-class culture. Most susceptible were small masters and aspiring journeymen in traditional trades where skills were least eroded and evangelical temperance sustained shrinking respectability. Fleeing a Democratic working-class identity that seemed degraded by the Irish, they fumbled toward a Whig middle-class identity through the nativist halfway house astutely crafted by Moderate-Light preachers and Whig politicians. Nativism was sporadically formidable, in fact, only when embraced by desperate Whiggery against Locofoco insurgency.[52]

Immigrant capital joined native capital in fostering interclass ethnic militancy to subvert interethnic class militancy. Many of Philadelphia's Irish worked as hand-loom weavers for putting-out Irish bosses, who had provoked a bitter three-year strike by rolling back wage gains won by interethnic Workeyism before hard times struck. The leading boss was also the leading Irish politician, whose Catholic militancy in the schools controversy triggered the ethnic carnage of 1844. Estranged from working-class allies, the Irish weavers returned to their looms on the Irish bosses' terms.[53]

Confined to the biggest cities, this first surge of political nativism subsided when an enormous Irish vote provided the Democrats' 1844 margin of presidential victory and helped pragmatists like Seward dissuade Whigs from further alienating this swelling constituency. By then, however, nativism had drowned the mid thirties dream of working-class solidarity in ethnic/religious bitterness. As returning prosperity allowed unions to build toward a new peak of militancy at midcentury, Irish potato famine turned the immigrant tide into a flood—369,980 in 1850—dooming worker unity and pushing nativism to the center of American politics. Meanwhile Irish/Americans assuaged the pain of degradation in the only way a self-making capitalist society permitted, by leading the racist assault on still more vulnerable Afro/Americans.

This era of struggle in the streets energized not only the bourgeois school campaign but also a campaign to impose bourgeois order on the streets by substituting professional police for politicized constables and night watches. The struggle for the streets raged for a generation, with conservative legislatures often forcing state-controlled police on city halls responsive to plebeian resistance. Working-class militancy in the streets—tarnished by the racist Irish violence of Civil-War Manhattan's Draft Riots and weakened by mounting immigration and multiplying ethnic divisions—finally succumbed to the brutal repression of Haymarket Square, Pullman, and Homestead.

The bourgeois/middle-class cultural offensive peaked when returning prosperity in the early 1840s brought market revolution to culmination in a generation of staggering growth. Internal trade, multiplying thirteenfold over the Erie Canal between the 1820s and 1850s and twelvefold down the Mississippi to New Orleans, registered a spectacular advance of territorial specialization in production for market.[54]

Seizing on Britain's new railroad technology to both galvanize and symbolize the market's climactic surge, Americans built nearly twice the trackage of all Europe by 1840. The first major railroads sought to capture inland trade for Baltimore, Charleston, and Boston. In 1830 the Baltimore and Ohio opened the first thirteen miles of its line up the Potomac and over the Appalachians to Wheeling. Three years later, the world's longest railroad extended 136 miles from Charleston to the cotton-rich Savannah valley. By 1835 Boston had railroad connections north to Lowell, south to Providence, and west to Worcester. In the 1840s the United States almost trebled its railway network to 8,879 miles. Local lines cross-hatched the Northeast from lower New England through Pennsylvania, and major East-West links were completed. Boston was connected with Albany in 1841, New York City with Buffalo in 1842, and Savannah with Chattanooga in 1849. Almost finished by midcentury were connections between Philadelphia and Pittsburgh, Baltimore and the Ohio River, and a second line from New York City to Lake Erie. Completing a process begun by canals and steamboats, railroads extended market production where water transport could not reach.[55]

The railroad conveyed more than commodities, for nothing so enthralled the bourgeois imagination. It was, said Emerson, a "work of art which agitates and drives mad the whole people; as music, sculpture, and picture have done on their great days respectively." Manhattan sophisticate George Templeton Strong rhapsodized over the nighttime spectacle of a locomotive

whizzing and rattling and panting, with its fiery furnace gleaming in front, its chimney vomiting fiery smoke above, and its long train of cars rushing along behind like the body and tail of a gigantic dragon—or the d——l himself—and all darting forward at the rate of twenty miles an hour. Whew!

Emerson even thought railroads "introduced a multitude of picturesque traits into our pastoral scenery," substantiating his dictum "Machinery and Transcendentalism agree well."[56]

Machinery agreed less well with slavery. While subsistence farming sustained southern resistance to market culture, scattered one-crop plantations generated much less year-round railroad freight than diversified northern production. Consequently trackage averaged only 112 miles per slave state at midcentury, compared with 442 miles per free state. Northeastern trunkline canals and railroads across the Appalachians stimulated northwestern railroad construction averaging 240 miles per state, compared with only 37 miles per southwestern state. North/South trade lagged as a sectionally skewed transportation revolution multiplied Northeast/Northwest trade. The original flow of western commodities down the Mississippi to New Orleans reversed. Wheat and flour shipped east via the Erie Canal alone rose from the equivalent of 268,000 barrels of flour in 1835 to 1,000,000 in 1840, exceeding shipments south via New Orleans after 1838. Flooding west in return, along with northeastern manufactures and imports, were Yankee immigrants and agencies of cultural transformation. Spreading over the Great Lakes plains and prairies, the universal Yankee nation challenged an older population of mainly southern origin farming the forested hills drained by the Ohio.[57]

"The conflict which is to decide the destiny of the West," preached Yankee bellwether Lyman Beecher, would determine "the moral destiny of our nation, and all our institutions and hopes, and the world's hopes." Warning that Catholic immigrants were swelling an uneducated western electorate "without intelligence, or conscience, or patriotism, or property, and driven on by demagogues," he maintained that only "schools, and colleges, and libraries, and literary enterprise, . . . pastors and churches," could reconcile "our republican institutions . . . with universal suffrage." Only conquest of the West by "those institutions which discipline the mind, and arm the conscience," Beecher insisted, could insure millennial "emancipation of the world" by American "pecuniary and moral power."[58]

The economic/cultural contest for the West culminated in Illinois when Baptist/Methodist/Democratic old-timers of the subsistence-farming southern hills were confronted in the 1830s by Presbygational/Whig Yankees invading the northern prairies with market ways acquired farther east. The old-timers were a "hospitable people, unambitious of wealth and great lovers of social enjoyment," said Governor Thomas Ford, while the "enterprising" Yankees "made farms, built mills, churches, school-houses, towns, and cities; and made roads and bridges as if by magic."

Old residents saw the Yankee newcomer as "a close, miserly, dishonest, selfish getter of money, void of generosity, hospitality, or any of the kindlier feelings."[59] One old timer said she was "getting skiery about them 'ere Yankees; there is such a power of them coming in that they and the Injuns will squatch out all the white folks." Yankees, in turn, tended to view the native as "a long, lank, lean, lazy, and ignorant animal . . . who was content to squat in a log-cabin with a large family of ill-fed and ill-clothed, idle, ignorant children."[60]

Yankee enterprise affronted the easygoing farmer who was "getting on right smart" when his hogs came "out of the wood fat enough" that he could "sit by his fire most of the time." The newcomers, complained one old-timer, worked too hard,

> jes' fer the fun o' ploughin' en reapin'. . . . Ez fer me, I kin shoot en trap all I kin eat, jes' plantin' 'nough corn fer hoecakes en a leetle fodder, en some taters en turnips en pum'kins . . . en I 'low I kin give a traveler hoe-cakes en fried chicken all he wants to fill up on.

Whereas old timers used uncultivated lands as open range, lent each other tools and livestock, and settled neighborhood disputes collectively, the newcomers insisted on fences, "Yankeed" neighbors in sharp bargaining, and resorted to law against trespassers.

Inevitably clashing modes of production and their associated cultures restructured Illinois politics. Old-timers never "dreamed that government might be made the instrument to accomplish a higher destiny," said Governor Ford. Where they opposed every measure allowing "demagogues to finger the taxpayer's money" or "swell-headed aristocrats" to act as "censors of the morals of the community," Yankees were ever ready for "a school-house, a bridge, or a church to be built, a road to be made, a school or minister to be maintained or taxes to be paid." These contrasting attitudes toward government and civic institutions structured conflicts over banking and the state's ambitious internal-improvement program, usually along Whig/Democratic lines.

Most revealing was a protracted struggle over public schools. Old-timers typically opposed public schools as requiring taxes and making their children "wholly unfitted for work on the farm." There wasn't "any use to be allus reading," thought many in this oral culture, for books didn't "do much good for a man" compared with "handy use of a rifle." Arithmetic "was quite unnecessary for farmers," and "what was the use of grammar to a person who could talk so as to be understood by everybody?" According to one critic of education,

> Cipherin's a drefful load on the mind. Thar's Si Jordan yaner; he sets figurin' o'nights, en calculatin' to see jes' how he'll come out at the end o' the year; but I allers say to myself he's like the groun'hog, he won't come out. . . . Book-larnin' don't make a man no better than he war in a state o' natur'. Them as read newspapers knows too much 'bout other folks's sins en not 'nough 'bout thar own.

When Jefferson's protégé Edward Coles and other genteel southerners got a public school system enacted in 1825 on Jeffersonian grounds, it was promptly killed by a backlash so powerful that the legislature declared: "No person shall hereafter be taxed for the support of any free school in this state unless by his own free will and consent, first had and obtained in writing." Soon, however, the towns and northern prairies began to fill with Yankees who valued schools "in dollars and cents" as preparation for "the business transactions of life." Because schools implant "early habits of industry, temperance, neatness, and regularity," they insisted, the state should educate all children. "If parents will not voluntarily cause them to be instructed," the Yankee element demanded, "the legislature in the exercise of its parental authority, must look to it."

A local-option law allowing counties to tax themselves for schools failed in 1843 but passed two years later in a legislature closely divided along north/south lines. Within four years school taxes were being levied by thirty northern and only six southern counties. Support for this policy was highly correlated with county land value (per improved acre), capital intensity (machine and implements value per improved acre), and wheat production. Repeal of the British corn laws was making northwestern wheat a profitable export rival to southern cotton, and conversion of Illinois farmers to market production was accelerated in the fifties by railroads and Cyrus McCormick's mechanical reaper.

In 1854–1855 the legislature mandated a state school tax, six months of public schooling by every district, standards for teacher certification and curriculum, and election of a state superintendent of public instruction. By this time southern Illinois was feeling the market's influence, Methodists and Baptists were aspiring to respectability and educated ministers, and Protestant divisions were being healed by nativist alarm at growing Catholic immigration.

Personifying the market's stubbornly contested conquest of Illinois was Abraham Lincoln. Old-timer southern pedigree camouflaged Honest Abe to lead the moralizing, institutionalizing offensive of bourgeois/middle-class Yankees, as his Yankee rival Stephen A. Douglas led old-timer democracy in anti-institutional resistance. While logrolling bourgeois projects for economic growth, Lincoln preached "a *political* religion" of "reverence for the laws," through education for "morality, sobriety, enterprise, and industry," and through a temperance "revolution" promising the "perfect liberty" of "all appetites controlled, all passions subdued, all matter subjected."[61] Claiming a historic national role in the Lincoln/Douglas debates of 1858, this rustic convert to bourgeois orthodoxy led progressive American capitalism beyond romantic illusion, to consolidate its political, cultural, and moral hegemony by confronting its great contradiction.

Chapter 13

The Great Contradiction

THE CAPITALIST market took off for global conquest by first propagating and then repudiating slavery. Enslaving some ten million Africans, racist mercantile capital extorted by shackle and whip the New World riches that prepared it for industrial wage-labor exploitation. "Slavery is the pivot of our industrialism today as much as machinery, credit, etc.," Karl Marx observed in the 1840s. "Without slavery you have no cotton, without cotton you have no modern industry." But because industry also required free labor and juridical equality, he understood, "*liberty* and *slavery* constitute an antagonism."[1]

Consequently market revolution made slavery the great contradiction of the liberal American republic. Northern liberal capital turned against the anachronistic planter capital impeding its political economy, and the antinomian doubts impeding its cultural hegemony were quelled by vanguard abolitionism. Yet only by enlisting free-soil Negrophobia would the northern bourgeoisie finally sanctify in fratricidal blood a racist bourgeois republic.

Capitalism inflicted ancient slavery's "social death" on unprecedented numbers with unprecedented severity. The freedom of slaves was most totally denied when capitalist liberalism absolutized masters' freedom of property and labor exploitation. Moreover, as Marx understood, slave production "for a world market dominated by the capitalist mode of production" was "conducted by *capitalists*" and rigorized by capitalist competition. Even though "the labor of Negroes precludes free wage labor," he maintained, "the capitalist mode of production exists," and "the civilized horrors of over-work are grafted onto the barbaric horrors of slavery" by "the competition between capitals."[2]

The rigors of capitalist slavery were most fully rationalized when the American cottonocracy utilized history's fullest freedoms of property and labor exploitation in harnessing human property to the industrial revolution's most dynamic sector. By dehumanizing black chattels most systematically as market commodities, a slave regime less brutal than some in other respects poisoned the liberal republic indefinitely with the most virulent white racism.

The logic of the South's law of bondage was delineated most unblushingly by the North Carolina supreme court in *State v. Mann* (1829). Because slavery existed for "the profit of the master, his security, and the public safety," Judge Thomas Ruffin declared for the court, the slave was

> doomed in his own person and posterity, to live without knowledge, and without the capacity to make any thing his own, and to toil that another may reap the fruits. . . . Such services can only be expected from one . . . who surrenders his will in implicit obedience. . . . The power of the master must be absolute to render the slave's submission perfect.

The court felt "as deeply as any man can," Ruffin added,

> the harshness of this proposition. . . . As a principle of moral rights, every person in his retirement must repudiate it. . . . It constitutes the curse of slavery to both the bond and the free portions of our population. But it is inherent in the relation of masters and slaves.[3]

Slaves' submission was rendered perfect by an elaborate machinery of domination and humiliation. While routine whipping extorted their labor and underscored the violence enforcing their subjection, the auction blocks and shackled coffles of the internal slave trade underscored their commodification. Barred from testifying against whites, they were socially protected only from sadism sufficiently egregious to shock the white community. Mounting prohibitions of manumission, literacy, and religious autonomy denied them hope or dignity.

The humanity of slaves was most cruelly denied by disruption of their most intimate relationships to ensure their multiplication and marketability as property. Law neither recognized nor protected their marriages. Masters decided who could "jump the broomstick" to cohabit, and some six hundred thousand broomstick families—nearly one in every three—were broken up by sale between 1820 and 1860. Sexual exploitation of slave women was common, and rape was a crime only against white women. "Under slavery we live surrounded by prostitutes," a planter wife lamented. ". . . Any lady is ready to tell you who is the father of all the mulatto children in everybody's household but her own."[4]

While degrading the Old South's slaves, human commodification paradoxically enabled them to multiply spectacularly by contrast with Latin American slaves. The Civil War freed ten times the number of Afro/Americans landed in North America by slave ships, whereas those delivered to tropical America outnumbered survivors at emancipation. The difference arose partly because the foreign slave trade continued almost to the end of slavery in Latin America while terminated by the United States in 1808, several generations before emancipation.

Thereafter North American cotton planters could reproduce and augment their labor force only through natural increase, whereas tropical planters of sugar and coffee found it cheaper to keep importing fresh supplies of brutally driven Africans. Consequently Latin American slaves—despite a nominally more benevolent state and church, less racism, and more chance for manumission and equality—suffered such high mortality, skewed sex ratios, and low fertility that they could not even reproduce themselves.[5]

In the Old South, by contrast, increasingly expensive slave property was managed for both production and reproduction. With the price of a "prime field hand" rising from three hundred dollars in the 1790s to nearly two thousand dollars by 1860, females were valued almost as much for offspring as males for labor. Owners relieved pregnant and nursing mothers of work, encouraged stable families, and made food and shelter at least minimally adequate. "My little negroes are consequently very healthy," boasted a disciple of this common policy, and "I am confident that I raise more of them, than where a different system is followed." Although little evidence survives of egregiously callous slave breeding, black women were auctioned as "good breeders"; sale of their progeny staved off masters' bankruptcy in the moribund Chesapeake tobacco economy; and even on the booming cotton frontier, a planter gave this advice in urging an Alabama nephew to follow him to Texas:

> Get as many young negro women as you can. Get as many cows as you can. . . . It is the greatest country for an increase that I have ever saw in my life. I have been hear six years and I have had fifteen negro children born and last year three more young negro women commenced breeding which added seven born last year. . . . Attend to the foregoing instructions and in ten or fifteen or twenty years you will do as well as any other man in this or any other country.[6]

Slavery's victims resisted its pervasive dehumanization by building their own culture. Most masters owned only a few slaves living under constant surveillance, but most slaves escaped white eyes after work in a "quarter" of cabins at some remove from the "big house" of a large plantation. Here self-esteem and an autonomous perspective were communally nurtured by strong family attachments, distinctive and vibrant religiosity, and a folk culture resonating African patterns of song, dance, storytelling, proverbs, and conjure.

Slaves expressed the less constrained sexuality of African cultures freely before marriage and less monogamously than whites—or less hypocritically—after marriage. Couples married for love, children were adored, and child-naming practices registered the strong and widely extended family ties of African kinship as people's primary refuge from severe psychic stress. But children had to be left at a tender age in the care of women too old for field work; and the family time available was often made bittersweet by parental discipline of impulses too dangerous for slave adulthood.

Planter morality coincided with self-interest in fostering stable families, which produced more babies while reducing strife and runaways. Some masters punished adultery and sponsored clergy-performed weddings before the traditional broom-jumping, especially for familiar house servants. Most masters also reinforced traditional African patriarchy by dealing with families through husbands and promoting only males as skilled artisans and drivers of the work gangs. But patriarchal authority was tenuous where women valued for fertility and muscled by field labor against abusive husbands could be defended from white sexual aggression only at the risk of life.[7]

Slave religion was a major battleground of resistance to a plantation regime demanding, through violence and humiliation, infantilized and obsequious "Sambos" who internalized their degradation. Ripped from the animistic soil of Africa where spirit possession linked people with the powers of a High God and lesser deities, slaves were powerfully drawn to the antinomian Christianity of the evangelical Awakening. Embracing with African expressiveness a Christian God who was "no respecter of persons," they were enthralled by his deliverance of the Israelites from Egyptian bondage and his promise of heavenly equality.

In the turn-of-the-century Great Revival, slaves flocked to camp meetings along with whites and often outnumbered whites as full members of Baptist and Methodist churches. While earnest white evangelicals exhorted many black congregations, some predominantly white congregations clung for years to magnetic black preachers, and blacks predominated in some of the largest churches accorded full denominational fellowship. The enthusiastic style of southern white evangelicalism was infused with African patterns of shout-and-response, rhythmic song, vocal improvisation, and hypnotic body movement. Indeed African influence on southern whites extended far beyond religion into speech, diet, housing, and patterns of work and leisure.[8]

Planter fears of Christianity's subversive effect on slaves were only briefly surmounted by the Awakening's evangelical zeal. Slave preaching and access to the Bible through literacy were soon interdicted, and the only gospel allowed to reach black ears from white evangelicals harped on obedience and hard work. But while Christian masters consigned their slaves to the segregated galleries of white churches, a vibrant underground religion of divine favor, heavenly liberation, and ecstatic song and dance flourished at night in plantation forests and slave cabins. A gospel subversive of slavery resonated through spirituals, and resentment of oppressors through secular songs and tales.[9]

This rich oral creativity sustained the integrity of Afro/American personality against a system as dehumanizing as any people have ever survived. Some managed to avoid public compromise of pride and dignity by impassive avoidance of contact and conflict with whites while meeting inescapable demands for labor and deference. But most slaves, as indicated by pervasive trickster tales of guile outwitting power, presented to whites a mask of the obsequious Sambo while venting anger among themselves through a richly creative culture of songs and stories satirizing and vilifying whites, and through the day-to-day resistance of malingering, stealing, tool breaking, and arson. When this emotionally demanding strategy generated more anger than could be contained, some turned it on whites, often suicidally, as rebels, while the weakest or most isolated turned it on themselves to internalize the Sambo role.[10]

The commonest form of rebellion was running away, singly or in small groups, for there were too many armed whites and too few remote refuges to permit the large and frequent slave revolts that occurred in Latin America. The biggest North American uprising occasioned little excitement in 1811, when Louisiana troops crushed three to five hundred slaves marching on New Orleans with flags flying and drums beating. But within a decade the white South was unnerved by a North invoking against slavery in the Missouri controversy their common heritage of Revolutionary liberalism and evangelical Christianity. Mere discovery of Denmark Vesey's insurrection plot at Charleston in 1822 plunged South Carolina into a frenzy of repression and ideological mobilization. Hysteria swept the entire white South nine years later, after some seventy slaves inspired by Nat Turner killed fifty-odd whites in a two-day rampage through Southampton County, Virginia.[11]

Although no threat so credible as Vesey and Turner ever recurred, slave-insurrection panics blazed up periodically in vigilantism against suspected blacks and Yankees to belie planter claims of confidence that their slaves were contented.[12] A white South made vulnerable by its own liberalism and Christianity was being driven into paranoia by mounting antislavery attacks. The North's first alarming challenge in the Missouri debate nourished the Vesey plot among leaders of Charleston's African Methodist Church; and Baptist visions of Apocalypse inspired Turner as the first tocsin of militant abolitionism reverberated through the outraged southern press from William Lloyd Garrison's Boston *Liberator*. Although Garrison abjured violence, he had published a month before the Southampton uprising a "Song, Supposed to be Sung by Slaves in Insurrection," which urged them to "strike for God and vengeance now."[13]

The Great Fear of 1831 revealed the depth of slaveholder misgivings by shocking the Virginia legislature into the Old South's only free and open debate over slavery. "I will not rest until slavery is abolished in Virginia," vowed Governor John Floyd; and Thomas Ritchie's Richmond *Enquirer* caught the mood of that historic moment by quoting a South Carolinian as exclaiming,

> We may shut our eyes and avert our faces, if we please, but there it is, the dark and growing evil at our doors; and meet the question we must, at no distant day. . . .
> What is to be done? Oh! my God, I do not know, but something must be done.

For two weeks that winter a score of Virginia legislators, backed by both the Democratic *Enquirer* and the state's leading Whig newspaper, invoked the whole range of antislavery argument in urging what had to be done. Although not a voice defended slavery on other than pragmatic grounds, gradual abolition failed by a lower-house vote of 73–58. "A further action for the removal of slaves," the house then resolved, "should await a more definite development of public opinion."[14]

Public opinion developed throughout the white South from recognition that a fateful choice had been made. At this critical turning point, slaveholders faced the fact that things could not go on as before if slavery were to be retained. The slaves were restive, a powerful antislavery sentiment was spreading from the British Parliament into the North, and southern minds were not yet nerved to defend the peculiar institution to which they now seemed irrevocably committed. Masters could no longer ease conscience with hopes for slavery's eventual disappearance, nor tolerate such hopes in other southerners. "It is not enough," proclaimed Calhoun's national newspaper organ,

> for them to believe that slavery has been entailed upon us by our forefathers. We must satisfy the consciences, we must allay the fears of our own people. We must satisfy them that slavery is of itself right—that it is not a sin against God—that it is not an evil, moral or political. . . . In this way, and this way only, can we prepare our own people to defend their institutions.[15]

While southern leaders of the Calhoun school began trying to convince themselves and others that slavery was a "positive good," southern legislatures followed the earlier lead of South Carolina in abridging freedom of speech and press, making manumission difficult or impossible, and imposing tighter restrictions on both slaves and free blacks. With the northern antislavery campaign gathering momentum in the midthirties, southern politicians bullied their northern colleagues into mobbing abolitionists, barring abolitionist literature from the mails, and enacting a "gag rule" barring congressional consideration of abolitionist petitions. As the white South's tormented effort to repress its own liberalism fed northern abolitionism, the great contradiction set the republic on the road to Civil War.[16]

While alarming southern whites by demanding freedom for slaves, militant abolitionists first summoned the republic to a vision of full equality for all human beings. The gradual abolitionism that drove slavery from the North had foundered under cotton boom and retreated to the project of colonizing free blacks in Africa. This covertly racist evasion, which satisfied the consciences of both northern respectables and southern slaveholders, also at first attracted rising evangelical benevolence. But around 1830, as British evangelicals pushed Parliament toward immediate abolition of colonial West Indian slavery, both gradualism and colonization became suspect to the most fervent American seekers of the teetotal benevolence preached by Finney. When black indictment of colonization opened their eyes to the sin of racism, a vision of human brotherhood committed them to immediate abolitionism as the acid test of antinomian righteousness.

The slight, balding Yankee printer William Lloyd Garrison was abolitionism's indispensably uncompromising conscience. Pushed with peculiar intensity into self-making rectitude and effort by his alcoholic father's desertion in childhood, he was equally impelled by the Baptist antinomianism of his working-class foster family to redeem the egoistic striving of middle-class mythology through selfless benevolence. After completing his apprenticeship to a Newburyport printer, he struggled for a journalistic foothold by adapting the Federalist/Whig invective of failing weeklies to various benevolent causes, including temperance, peace, and colonization.

Garrison found his consuming cause when Quaker gradualist Benjamin Lundy invited him to help edit an antislavery newspaper in Baltimore. Baltimore blacks opened his eyes to the enormity of racism by shattering his illusions about colonization, and he mounted such a scathing polemic for immediate abolition that he was jailed for libel. Bailed out by a check from Arthur Tappan, the twenty-six-year-old agitator fled to Boston, where on the first day of 1831 a militant manifesto introduced his weekly *Liberator*:

> I *will be* as harsh as truth, and as uncompromising as justice. On this subject I do not wish to think, or speak, or write, with moderation. . . . I am in earnest—I will not equivocate—I will not excuse—I will not retreat a single inch—AND I WILL BE HEARD.[17]

Garrison was heard mainly at first by northeastern blacks. Black enthusiasm for a white critique of slavery's racist roots reinforced his militancy, and black subscriptions kept his paper afloat. While southern editors soon made him nationally notorious by quoting the *Liberator* in alarm over northern fanaticism, he collected a devoted white coterie of reforming clerics, activist women, and such rebel Brahmins as lawyer/orator Wendell Phillips. Radicalized by the novel white experience of listening to what blacks were saying, Garrisonians saw southern slavery's brutality as epitomizing the national sin of racism. "Nothing can be done for the improvement of the Slaves," they insisted, "until their *rights as men* are recognized." Philadelphia's most benevolent Quakers were being similarly radicalized by persuasive blacks, and New York's Tappan coterie by Finneyite revival.[18]

In 1833 these groups capitalized on British West Indian emancipation to launch the American Anti-Slavery Society. Advocating *"immediate abandonment"* of slavery, "without expatriation," they also insisted on "equality . . . of civil and religious privileges" for blacks.[19] The Tappan group brought to abolition the impressive skills and resources they had utilized in fashioning the Benevolent Empire's awesome machinery for mass communication and organization. While high-speed presses flooded the mails north and south with vivid depictions of slavery's dehumanizing horrors—evoking such a roar of southern rage that postmasters impounded them—the Society's itinerant agents fanned out across the North to mobilize the reborn benevolence of Finneyite revival into auxiliary societies.

The soul of the campaign was Finney convert Theodore Dwight Weld. Pushed to immediatism by intimacy with an eccentric British abolitionist, the eloquent but self-effacing Weld stood out for saintly devotion among the "Holy Band" of youthful aspiring ministers who assisted in Finney's revivals. To train them for evangelizing the West, Arthur Tappan financed Lane Seminary at Cincinnati with Lyman Beecher as president; and in the eighteen-day Lane Debate of 1834, Weld convinced the Holy Band that immediate abolition was the supreme imperative of antinomian benevolence. Finding affirmation of their radical egalitarianism in Cincinnati's large black community, the students soon stirred up the racism endemic only a river's width from slavery by teaching in black schools, worshiping in black churches, visiting in black homes, and fraternizing in public with blacks. When Beecher (who professed to be both an abolitionist and a colonizationist) backed Lane's outraged trustees in banning antislavery activity, virtually the whole student body transferred to Finney's rustic Oberlin.

Promptly the Anti-Slavery Society recruited Weld's Lane rebels to proselytize the North for immediatism. Over the next several years these earnest young evangelists, expanded to "the Seventy Apostles," braved peaking racist rage and conservative alarm to preach the equal humanity of enslaved blacks. Persisting night after night in hostile communities until harassment subsided, they reaped an impressive harvest. By 1838 the Anti-Slavery Society had 1,350 auxiliaries with some quarter-million members.

When moral suasion via cheap print foundered under postal embargo, this growing movement shifted to flooding Congress with petitions for abolishing slavery in the District of Columbia, where congressional jurisdiction was most widely acknowledged. Legislative business ground to a halt as Calhoun fulminated against receiving any petition concerning slavery, and southern hotspurs exploded into violent harangues every time one was presented. To quell an agitation that threatened Van Buren's North/South coalition on the eve of the 1836 election, the Democratic House leadership pushed through a rule tabling petitions about slavery after presentation by title alone.[20]

This "gag rule" incensed the most illustrious member of Congress as denying the constitutionally guaranteed right of petition. John Quincy Adams had accepted election to the House after presidential defeat, as Mrs. Adams ruefully explained, because he could not give up his "insatiable passion" for political combat "without risking a total extinction of life." Fantasizing since the Missouri crisis about a life "nobly spent or sacrificed" in the "sublime and beautiful cause" of abolition,[21] he now struck back at the slaveholders and Jacksonians who had blasted his hopes by launching a one-man crusade against the gag rule. Infuriating most of his colleagues by circumventing the rules to foment angry discussion of the forbidden subject, "Old Man Eloquent" redeemed a ruined career by arousing much of the North against a slaveocracy threatening the civil liberties of all citizens.

While Adams galvanized the petition campaign, abolitionists broadened their appeal by circulating petitions against both the gag rule and slaveholding Texas, which was applying for annexation after throwing off Mexican rule. As thousands of volunteers plied neighbors with abolitionist argument while collecting signatures door-to-door, petitions flooded the Capitol "by waggon loads," filling a twenty-by-thirty-foot room to its fourteen-foot ceiling.[22]

The antislavery constituency mobilized by the petition campaign—extending with the universal Yankee nation from New England through burnt-over upstate New York and northern Ohio's Western Reserve—began electing congressmen and legislators (mainly Whigs) pledged to antislavery measures. In the 1840 presidential election, an abolitionist Liberty party ran James G. Birney, a onetime Alabama slaveholder converted to immediatism by Weld. Although Birney got only a modest protest vote, the Liberty party soon gained a balance-of-power influence in the critical states of New York and Ohio that sensitized the major parties to antislavery voters. In less than a decade, abolitionism had executed its historic mission by compelling a racist white North to confront the great American contradiction.[23]

Abolitionism burgeoned especially among people trying, like Garrison, to reconcile self-making egotism with ancestral altruism through the intense Christian piety of Finneyite benevolence. Mustering effort, moreover, by embracing the middle-class mythology that ascribed success or failure wholly to character, they could protect their motivational system from Workey claims of wage slavery by focusing altruistic indignation on chattel slavery. The Tappans' *Journal of Commerce* led the bourgeois assault on Workeyism, and the first issue of the *Liberator* coupled declaration of war against chattel slavery with denunciation of "efforts to enflame the minds of our working classes against the more opulent." If free workers suffered, Garrison declared, "theirs is the fault." The Workey doctrine "that man is the creature of circumstances" was "absurd and demoralizing," he insisted, because the remedy for evil was "an internal rather than an outward reorganization."[24]

When Workey/poet/abolitionist John Greenleaf Whittier protested this denigration of free workers who were also commodified and exploited, Garrison conceded the existence of abused wealth, employers who needed watching, inadequate wages, and big factories that overworked labor and neglected children's education; and he eventually endorsed the ten-hour day. But he persistently ascribed the problems of free labor to defects of character, only occasionally including those of bosses. This meant, as his close associate Wendell Phillips argued, that only "economy, self-denial, temperance, education, and moral and religious character" could improve free workers' lot.

Does legislation bear hard upon them?—their votes can alter it. Does capital wrong them?—economy will make them capitalists. Does the crowded competition of cities reduce their wages?—they have only to stay at home, devoted to other pursuits, and soon diminished supply will bring the remedy.[25]

This middle-class mythology made abolitionism appealing to upwardly mobile mechanics like Garrison and the boss shoemakers of Lynn, while even wage slaves drew sympathetic analogies from their own experience with the oppression of chattel slaves. Lynn became a Garrisonian stronghold, and everywhere mechanics were the most numerous signers of abolitionist petitions. Yet Lynn's wage-worker movement was vociferous against bosses "professing to be abolitionists . . . and making slaves at home." They were enslaving northern workers, charged the constitution of the journeyman shoemakers' union, "to a greater degree (in one sense) for the poor negro has a master, both in sickness and health; while the poor white man is a slave as long as he is able to toil, and a pauper when he can toil no more." Elsewhere some organized workers arrayed themselves against "the entire system of American slavery, black and white"; and others resolved "to abolish Wages Slavery before we meddle with Chattel Slavery"; while the least skilled and organized too often found solace in vicious racism and antiabolitionism.[26]

Abolitionism, although resisted by much of the bourgeoisie, muted class conflict over wage slavery to become the vanguard of capitalist liberalism. Rising from the middle-class soil of Moderate Light, temperance, and Antimasonic Whiggery, it satisfied antinomian doubts as romanticism could not. Suffusing free-labor enterprise with antislavery altruism, it would eventually endow the bourgeois state with hegemonic sanctity. Yet an antislavery altruism blinded to capitalist commodification of free labor and human relationships would be further compromised through politics by the racism capitalism fed.

The Anti-Slavery Society was splintered in the early 1840s by internal contradictions and supplanted by the grass-roots political abolitionism it had spawned. Fearing any departure from pure principle, Garrison excoriated politics for expedient compromise, the mainstream church (a "synagogue of Satan") for resisting abolition, and the Constitution ("A COVENANT WITH DEATH, AN AGREEMENT WITH HELL") for condoning slavery.[27] This militant perfectionism, while estranging Garrisonians from the abolitionist mainstream, first developed for Americans the full meaning of human equality. It was the Garrisonians who fought the racist condescension (including their own) that made token blacks uncomfortable in the movement. Garrisonian fears would be realized when political antislavery prevailed in concert with a racism of free soil for whites whose tragic legacy still disfigures American life.

Pure principle shattered the Anti-Slavery Society by carrying Garrisonians prophetically to the radical new ground of women's rights. Garrison had recruited a remarkable group of women—Bostonians imbued with Unitarian liberalism and Philadelphians habituated to speaking and preaching in Quaker meetings—who felt keenly the widening female discontent resonated by women's novels. Drawn to abolitionism by sensitivity to oppressive inequality, they were segregated, like women in temperance and other benevolent movements, into female auxiliaries for fund-raising and circulating petitions. At the organizing convention of the Anti-Slavery Society, one participant recalled, "we *men* were so blind, so obtuse, that we did not recognize these women as members."[28]

Inevitably abolitionist women's resentment of their own oppression was sharpened by outrage at the slave's oppression. "In striving to strike his irons off," said feisty Quaker Abby Kelley, "we found most surely that we were manacled ourselves." By enlisting women, said Boston matron Lydia Maria Child, benevolent causes "have changed the household utensil to a living, energetic being, and they have no spell to turn it into a broom again."[29]

Clerical patriarchy forced the issue in 1837, when New England women's groups heard a firsthand account of slavery's evils from two daughters of South Carolina's planter aristocracy, Sarah and Angelina Grimké, who had moved to Philadelphia after becoming Quakers. Because men were attracted to their lectures, the Grimké sisters were publicly denounced for addressing "promiscuous assemblies" by the Massachusetts association of Congregational clergy. "My womanhood is insulted, my moral feelings outraged," Angelina exclaimed to Weld, whom she would shortly marry. Now she knew "*just* how the free colored people feel towards the whites." A discussion with Boston's abolitionist women on the eve of the sisters' tour had revealed "a very general sentiment prevailing that it is time our fetters are broken"; and now finding themselves "very unexpectedly . . . in the forefront of . . . a contest for the rights of *woman*," they insisted that "this question must be met."[30]

"Men and women are CREATED EQUAL!" Sarah proclaimed in a public reply to the clergy. "They are both moral and accountable beings and whatever is right for man to do is right for woman." Claiming equal citizenship in presenting an antislavery petition from twenty thousand women to a Massachusetts legislative committee, Angelina exulted that "we Abolition Women are turning the world upside down." An Anti-Slavery Convention of American Women assembled to urge every sister "no longer to rest satisfied with the circumscribed limits in which corrupt custom and a perverted application of the Scriptures had encircled her."[31]

Most male abolitionists were appalled by the assault on patriarchy, and even the sympathetic Weld feared that the unpopular cause of the slave would be doomed if linked with the even more unpopular cause of women's rights. But Garrison stood on principle, agreeing with Angelina that the two "moral reformations . . . are bound together in . . . [one] glorious whole and that whole is Christianity, pure practical christianity." As he later told a women's rights convention, "I have been derisively called a '*Woman's Rights Man.*' I know no such distinction. I claim to be a HUMAN RIGHTS MAN, and wherever there is a human being, I see God-given rights inherent in that being whatever may be the sex or complexion."[32]

Supported by Garrison, women were admitted to the annual New England antislavery conventions and, after bitter debate in 1839, to the Society's national convention. More pragmatic abolitionists, already anxious to dissociate the movement from Garrison's antipolitics, antigovernment, antichurch purism, abandoned the national Society when Garrison—chartering a steamboat to transport "a large portion of the town of Lynn"[33] to New York for the 1840 convention—got Abby Kelley elected to the business committee. Mainstream abolitionism moved into politics, leaving the Society to articulate Garrisonian pure principle.

A militant women's-rights movement was inspired when the 1841 world anti-slavery convention in London refused to seat two Garrisonian women, Lucretia Mott and Elizabeth Cady Stanton. The diminutive Quaker dynamo Mott had enshrined at the center of her home for forty years the trailblazing feminist manifesto by Englishwoman Mary Wollstonecraft; but Stanton had just married into abolitionism and was still "slowly sawing off the chains of my spiritual bondage" when she first met Garrison in London. "A few bold strokes from the hammer of his truth, I was free!" she exclaimed.

Seven years later Mott and Stanton convened militant women and their male sympathizers at Seneca Falls, New York. Their mission, said keynoter Stanton, was to

> declare our right to be free as man is free, to be represented in the government which we are taxed to support, to have [no] such disgraceful laws as give the man the power to chastise and imprison his wife, to take the wages which she earns, the property which she inherits, and, in case of separation, the children of her love; laws which make her the mere dependent on his bounty . . . And, strange as it may seem to many, we now demand our right to vote according to the declaration of the government under which we live.

Revising the liberal republic's founding declaration, the Seneca Falls feminists held "these truths to be self-evident: that all men and women are created equal." Reciting patriarchy's "long train of abuses," they demanded for women not only the vote, but "equal participation with men in the various trades, professions and commerce." At Seneca Falls, Garrisonian principle first translated Jefferson's declaration into a vision of full human equality.[34]

While Garrisonian women opened the long struggle against patriarchy in the 1840s, political abolitionism pushed the struggle against slavery to an ultimately bloody showdown over westward expansion. Galvanized by returning prosperity, the rival capitalisms of slave-labor and free-labor exploitation locked in combat for the trans-Mississippi domain stretching to the Pacific.

The South was entering a cotton boom that by 1860 doubled the price of slaves and gave it the country's twelve wealthiest counties. With capital concentrated in expensive but portable slaves, profit-maximizing planters responded so eagerly to cheaper western lands that hardly one in five stayed in place more than twenty years. "It is useless to seek to excite patriotic emotions in behalf of the land of birth," observed a prominent Georgian, "when self-interest speaks so loudly." A sophisticated literature of plantation management inculcated greater operational rationality and labor discipline than northern factories had achieved; and plantation ledgers provided for daily, quarterly, and annual accounting of yields, costs, profits, and individual worker productivity.

Cotton capitalism bourgeoisified planter society, as shrinking families helped planter children reproduce parental status. Although the eldest son usually inherited the big house and adjacent acreage, slaves were often divided equally—at tragic cost to disrupted families—as starting capital for younger children's plantations, often on cheaper western land. Self-reliant individualism was fostered by idealizing marriage as affectionate companionship, sentimentalizing children, designing houses for individual privacy, and instilling the bourgeois virtues. "Without prudence, industry and a close attention to business," a typical father advised his son, "you cannot hope to be successful."[35]

While enriching individuals, however, the cotton bonanza inhibited the more diversified development that was industrializing the North, by monopolizing capital and entrepreneurship and by keeping land cheap relative to slaves.[36] It also sharpened conflict between planter elites and the white South's small-farmer majority.

Plantations eventually invaded every small-farming area that met cotton's requirements for fertile soil, an adequate frost-free growing season, well-timed rains, and transportation to market. Every extension of the "black belt" raised land prices and taxes to drive farmers into "white belts" where plantations could not follow—not only the great upland salient swinging southward around the Appalachian massif from western Maryland through northern Georgia and Alabama and up into central Tennessee and eastern Kentucky, but also the piney woods of the Gulf coast and hilly or isolated areas throughout the South. Here subsistence farmers could sustain patriarchal honor and equality despite insufficient capital to buy slaves and reluctance to risk farms through borrowing.

In gentrifying black belts, by contrast, traditional farm labor was denigrated as "nigger work." "Without slaves," complained an antislavery Baptist, "a man's children stand but a poor chance to marry in reputation." Under this "custom of the country," ownership of fewer than five slaves sustained patriarchal honor for half the South's slaveholders. Where planters supplemented cotton production for market with corn and hogs for plantation subsistence, these small slaveholders supplemented production for subsistence with a few bales of cotton for taxes and modest store purchases.

But the late antebellum cotton boom made slaves so prohibitively expensive for most farmers that the slaveless proportion of the free population climbed from less than two-thirds in 1830 to almost three-fourths by 1860. As farmer opportunity shrank, Jacksonian backlash against planter banks and transportation projects escalated into white-belt/black-belt conflict over suffrage, legislative apportionment, and taxation.[37]

Under abolitionist assault, class tension combined with misgiving over slavery and fear of slaves to plunge an entrepreneurial cottonocracy into desperate contention with its liberal self. The search for a convincing proslavery argument, argues liberalism's interpreter Louis Hartz, revealed "a mass of agonies and contradictions in the dream world of southern thought." The very effort affronted cherished southern commitments. When Calhoun announced to the Senate in the midthirties that slavery was "a good—a great good," a Jefferson protégé was present to protest "the obsolete and revolting theory of human rights" lately advanced by defenders of bondage. Never, said Virginia Senator William C. Rives, would he "deny, as has been done by this new school, the natural freedom and equality of man, to contend that slavery is a positive good."[38]

Slaves, as slaveholding congressman James K. Polk put the fundamental problem, "were a species of property that differed from all others; they were rational; they were human beings." Their undeniable humanity forced the southern judiciary into frequent contortions of the legal logic reducing them to freely exploitable commodities. "A slave is not in the condition of a horse," protested a Tennessee judge. "He has mental capacities, and an immortal principle in his nature"; and law should not "deprive him of many rights which are inherent in men."[39]

No theory could be found, however, that reconciled the slave's humanity with both slavery for blacks and democratic liberalism for whites. The religious defense of slavery as a great missionary institution for the conversion and uplift of blacks implied an ultimate change in their status. The most logical alternative sacrificed liberalism to glorify slavery as a neofeudal system of interdependent ranks and orders that saved the South from the corruption and turbulence of northern free society. The only proslavery doctrine that proved compatible with democratic liberalism for whites, and therefore widely acceptable to them, was black racial inferiority. Dehumanization of blacks, moreover, staved off the class shame of inequality for poor whites, justified ruthless exploitation of black labor, and muted class conflict to enlist the farmer majority in defense of the planters' imperiled labor system. Southern intellectuals were noticeably reluctant to avow publicly the white South's de facto proslavery ideology of race, and many religionists and neofeudalists defended the slave's humanity against it. The doctrine of racial inferiority, argued the intellectually impressive neofeudalist George Fitzhugh,

encourages and incites brutal masters to treat negroes, not as weak, ignorant and dependent brethren, but as wicked beasts, without the pale of humanity.... The

Southerner is the negro's friend, his only friend. Let no intermeddling abolitionist, no refined philosophy dissolve this friendship.[40]

Slavery's contradictions with liberalism and humanity, while fueling northern abolitionism, riddled the white South with inconsistencies and doubts. "I assure you, Sir," Fitzhugh confessed privately, "I see great evils in Slavery, but in a controversial work I ought not to admit them." A fire-eating South Carolinian complained in 1844 that most slaveholders in other states were "mere negro-drivers believing themselves wrong and only holding on to their negroes as something to make money out of." Even South Carolinians, he feared, had "retrograded, and must soon fall into the same category."[41]

Planter/farmer insecurities and appetites for cheap land sharpened in the 1840s to focus a desperate southern chauvinism on the New Eldorado of Texas. Slavery had figured prominently in Texas history ever since John Quincy Adams's Transcontinental Treaty with Spain surrendered imaginary American claims to the vast Gulf plains west of Louisiana. Adams's treaty was no sooner ratified in 1821 than Mexico threw off Spanish rule and allowed *empresario* Stephen F. Austin to introduce a large colony of Anglo/American immigrants. Austin was at first "compelled to hold out the idea that slavery would be tolerated," he said, "for I had to draw on Louisiana and Mississippi," but "the idea of seeing such a country as this overrun by a slave population almost makes me weep." Only some thousand slaves had been introduced by 1830, when a Mexican law prohibiting further importations bolstered his hopes for a slave-free Texas.

But Austin found that Anglo/Texans' "horrible *Mania* for speculation" squelched all consideration of "the justice of slavery, or its demoralizing effects on society." By 1835 some thirty thousand American immigrants had flooded into Texas, mainly from the South and including small slaveholders bringing some five thousand slaves. Austin had to concede that "Texas must be a slave country." When the antislavery Mexican government tried to tighten its control, slaveholder alarm helped propel Anglo/Texans into revolution. In 1836, led by Jackson's Tennessee protégé Sam Houston, they defeated a Mexican army at San Jacinto near present Houston, declared themselves an independent republic, and applied for annexation to the United States. Annexation stalled because President Jackson (who had been trying to bully Mexico into selling Texas) now saw that it would endanger Van Buren's chances in the impending presidential election; and Van Buren, once elected, deferred to the flood of antislavery petitions against Texas. It was 1843 before a more receptive President evoked a public clamor for annexation.[42]

By then northern interest in the distant Oregon country was being excited as the first large wagon train of pioneers trekked across the inhospitable Plains and Rockies to the waters of the Pacific. Although Yankee mariners had braved Cape

Horn to reap a rich harvest of sea otter furs on the northwest coast in the 1790s, wide curiosity about the exotic Far West was first aroused in 1806, when Jefferson's pathfinders Meriwether Lewis and William Clark returned from a two-year expedition up the Missouri, across the mountains, and down the Columbia to the western ocean.

Their revelation of access to abundant beaver via the Missouri set off a rush of hardy trappers and traders up the Big Muddy and inspired John Jacob Astor's American Fur Company to tap the largesse at the other end by establishing a trading post, Astoria, at the mouth of the Columbia in 1811. Although Indian resistance impeded this advance and the War of 1812 forced abandonment of Astoria, by the 1820s a swarm of fearless mountain men were trapping beaver streams through the Rockies, exploring the forbidding Great Basin beyond, and penetrating the final mountain barriers guarding the balmy valleys of Mexican California.

Simultaneously wagon trains of Missouri traders capitalized on Mexican independence to cross the southwestern plains for silver and furs from Santa Fe, New Mexico. By the 1830s, annual expeditions from St. Louis resupplied the mountain men at orgiastic rendezvous along the Green River in present western Wyoming, and Rocky Mountain beaver were being trapped out as the American Fur Company's superior capital prevailed in fierce competition with rivals.

The fur traders paved the way for the next great surge of American expansionism by thoroughly exploring the Far West. Discovering the easiest crossing of the Rockies through South Pass at the head of Wyoming's Sweetwater River, they located through it a wagonable Oregon Trail that diverged from the Missouri route's long northward detour and difficult mountain crossings via the North Platte to reach the Columbia via the Snake. Over this route the first American Indian agent for the Oregon country led 120 male settlers in 1842, followed a year later by a wagon train of a thousand men, women, and children with five thousand oxen and cattle. The area was dominated by the British Hudson's Bay Company from Fort Vancouver on the north bank of the lower Columbia, the boundary on which Britain had always insisted in fruitless negotiations with the United States. Therefore the American newcomers concentrated in the fertile Willamette valley south of Fort Vancouver, around the most durable of several American missionary outposts established in the 1830s.

For several years smaller parties had been turning off the Oregon Trail short of the Columbia to cross deserts and the lofty Sierra Nevada into California, where they joined a miscellany of retirees from pursuit of beaver and sea otter in settling interior valleys and taking over trade with the scattered *ranchero* populace along the coast. Meanwhile, with sea otters decimated like beavers by overexploitation, Yankee merchants had discovered a new source of profit in supplying the New England shoe industry with hides from the enormous herds of California missions and *ranchos*. Crowding California anchorages along with hide "droghers" were

Yankee whalers reprovisioning during four-year voyages to scour the North Pacific.

A fascinated American public was learning of these developments in the romantic Far West from travel accounts, promotional tracts, and works of such literary quality as Washington Irving's *Astoria* (1838) on Oregon and Richard Henry Dana's *Two Years before the Mast* (1840) on the hide trade. In 1843, as an American diplomat departed to negotiate a treaty removing onerous restrictions on trade with China, northeastern commercial men dreamed of a fabulous Pacific commerce and avidly eyed the magnificent harborage of San Francisco Bay as its base. With the Anglo/American population of Texas simultaneously passing one hundred thousand and bringing more slaves, expansionism was about to plunge American politics into intractable sectional conflict over slavery.[43]

Expansionism carried passions of race and section into politics more easily because stalemate in the Bank War left both parties demoralized and split into warring factions. Particularly destabilizing was the Whigs' frustration following their 1840 victory. Two weeks after inauguration, President Harrison had set his administration on a collision course with Antimasonic Whigs as well as the latent Democratic majority. Yielding to the imperious Clay, he summoned a special session of Congress to enact the bourgeoisie's updated developmental program— higher tariffs, distribution of land revenues to fund state transportation projects, voluntary bankruptcy, and a national Bank. Harrison's stunning victory was nullified by Clay's headstrong insistence on claiming it as a mandate for a new Bank. The new President's death two weeks later was less fatal to his party than his surrender to Clay's demands.[44]

Clay's arrogance, fortified by bourgeois insistence on the full fruits of victory, now encountered instead of the pliable Harrison the touchy pride and Virginia scruples of ascending Vice President John Tyler. Although a Whig Congress passed Clay's whole program, all that survived presidential veto and voter rebellion was the sharply protectionist Tariff of 1842 and repeal of the independent treasury without a national Bank to replace it. After "His Accidency" vetoed three different Bank bills, Clay's congressional Whigs formally read him out of the party, and his Cabinet resigned.

Tyler proved righter politically than the Great Embodiment and his insulated congressional following. The voluntary bankruptcy law stirred up such a storm that the Whigs themselves hastened to repeal it—but not before an estimated twenty-eight thousand broken venturers escaped nearly $500 million in debt at an average cost of little more than 10 percent in assets surrendered.[45] With Tyler's vetoes underscoring the Whigs' reemergence as the Bank party, the midterm elections produced the greatest congressional turnover since the 1816 uprising against the Salary Act. The Democratic sweep seemed to manifest "the sober second thought of the people" on which Van Buren pinned his hopes for vindication in the 1844 presidential race.

The proud but politically inept Tyler, now totally isolated, embarked on a desperate effort to win reelection by either forcing a nomination from the Democrats or running as a third-party candidate. Lavishing patronage on sycophantic opportunists (who in fact exploited it mainly on behalf of Calhoun or other anti–Van Buren Democrats), His Accidency seized on the cresting enthusiasm for territorial expansion. First he offered the British concessions on the Oregon boundary if they would coerce Mexico into ceding California to the United States. Secretary of State Webster delayed his resignation long enough to complete negotiations in which Britain's Lord Ashburton rejected the Oregon/California deal, but did agree to a treaty (1842) settling disputes over the Canadian boundary west to the Rockies.

Thwarted on the Pacific front, Tyler then threw down the gauntlet to the antislavery North by launching a propaganda campaign for annexing Texas. Promptly thirteen northern Whig congressmen, headed by John Quincy Adams, issued a manifesto denouncing annexation as "an attempt to eternize an institution" so "abhorrent to the feelings of the people of the free states" as "inevitably to result in a dissolution of the union." The North, they warned, "WOULD NOT SUBMIT TO IT."[46]

The President was staking his hopes on the South, however, and replaced Webster at the State Department with a Virginia Calhounite, Abel P. Upshur, who thought annexation "the only matter, that will take sufficient hold of the South to rally it on a southern candidate and weaken Clay & Van Buren so much there as to bring the election into the House." Although Tyler aimed to be the southern candidate, a confidential intermediary informed Calhoun that the new Secretary "considers you as the only one that can be taken up."[47] Upshur's secretly negotiated annexation treaty with Texas was almost ready for Senate ratification when he was killed by an exploding cannon while inspecting a new naval vessel. To succeed him Tyler chose Calhoun.

Although most state Democratic conventions in both South and North had by now endorsed Van Buren for President, the Carolinian entered the State Department still yearning for the Democratic nomination and equally obsessed with forcing the party into a proslavery posture. Just as he was about to send the Texas treaty to the Senate in April 1844, he learned that Frank Blair's Van Burenite *Globe* was about to endorse annexation. Fearing that Van Buren would enhance his southern popularity by coming out for Texas, Calhoun held up the treaty almost a week to make it so overtly proslavery that no northern candidate could support it. He found his opportunity in replying to a long unanswered communication from British minister Richard Pakenham.[48]

The British were trying to prevent annexation by securing Mexican recognition of Texas independence in return for Texas abolition of slavery; and Pakenham, although avowing their desire for "the general abolition of slavery through-out the world," had denied any intention of disturbing "the internal tranquility of the slave-holding States." Calhoun asserted in reply that the federal government was pursuing annexation "as the most effectual, if not the only, means" of fulfill-ing its obligation to protect the slave states from the danger of British interference with slavery in Texas. Moreover he cited census statistics of insanity and crimi-nality to argue that blacks in the free states "have invariably sunk into vice and pauperism" while attaining in the slave states a higher "elevation in morals, intel-ligence, or civilization" than "in any other age or country." Appending his Pak-enham letter to the treaty, Calhoun tossed this "Texas bombshell," as Benton called it, into the Senate.[49]

The Pakenham letter cost the Texas treaty enough northern votes to defeat ratification, and promptly the Whigs' foreordained nominee Clay announced his opposition to annexation. One day after Clay's declaration appeared, the Demo-cratic party was plunged into turmoil by a similar announcement from Van Buren.

The Texas agitation had swept expansionist fervor through the Democratic rank-and-file, not only in the South but across much of the North as well. North-western Democrats had held an Oregon convention at Cincinnati to neutralize antislavery objections to Texas by claiming leadership of the rising excitement over the 1843 migration to the Willamette valley. But Texas was now "more exciting and more absorbing than the Oregon question," they reported. "It is becoming a passion."[50]

The country's most extravagant expansionism was being trumpeted from the northeastern cities. Here the penny press and a new school of Democratic politi-cians calling themselves "Young America" were preaching jingoistic patriotism to the plebeian masses. Under titles like "More! More! More!" in the New York *Morning News,* gifted wordsmith John L. O'Sullivan proclaimed that the republ-ic's "manifest destiny" would not be fulfilled until "the whole boundless continent is ours." The New York *Herald*'s James Gordon Bennett was telling the country's largest readership that "the arms of the republic . . . must soon embrace the whole hemisphere, from the icy wilderness of the North to the most prolific regions of the smiling and prolific South." Similar proclamations filled the New York *Sun,* Brooklyn *Eagle,* Boston *Times,* Philadelphia *Public Ledger,* and Baltimore *Sun.*[51]

This historic upwelling of a new American jingoism satisfied many needs. In a painfully fracturing society, it conferred civic dignity and social inclusion on patri-otic working people. For the bourgeoisie, it quelled the class conflict of labor mil-itancy and Bank War. For the rising editors and politicians of Young America, it provided an appealing posture. Democrats were its main inciters because it muted the mounting native/Irish conflict in their working-class constituency. Most of all, perhaps, both Democrats and others embraced expansionist jingoism to mute mounting sectional conflict.

Young America preached that a democracy of state rights and limited federal powers could harmonize local differences and extend indefinitely the area of freedom. Expansionism defined a Democratic mass culture racially to include the Irish and exclude blacks by making Great Britain the nemesis of American destiny and accepting slavery as a constitutionally protected local institution. The penny press, particularly Bennett's *Herald,* treated southern interests as American interests and harped endlessly on John Bull's abolitionist meddling in Texas.[52]

The racist core of popular expansionism made a pamphlet by Senator Robert J. Walker the most influential argument for annexation in every part of the country. This Pennsylvania-reared Mississippi Democrat predicted that slavery would be ameliorated and eventually eliminated from the country by diffusion. Citing the experience of Maryland, Delaware, and Virginia, he argued that black population diminishes to the north and east as slavery extends to the south and west. His ingenious and subtly racist analysis concluded, therefore, that extension of slavery into Texas would hasten the eventual dispersal of American blacks through Latin America.[53]

The leading presidential candidates' opposition to annexation earned Clay a nomination by acclamation at the Whig national convention while provoking a mighty Democratic rebellion against Van Buren. Democratic (and democratic) identity was consolidating so strongly around race that the Little Magician's announcement dashed hopes for a signal triumph on the Texas issue. But he had devoted a long career to containing dangerous sectional conflict over slavery, and New York politics sensitized him to a further conflict between the city's plebeian racism and the growing antislavery sentiment upstate. Such considerations induced this prototype of the scheming politician to risk his chances for the Presidency by telling his party two weeks before its nominating convention:

> We have a character among the nations of the earth to maintain. . . . It has hitherto been our pride and our boast, that, whilst the lust of power, with fraud and violence in the train, has led other and differently constituted governments to aggression and conquest, our movements in these respects have always been regulated by reason and justice.

As long as war technically existed between Mexico and its rebel province, annexation of Texas would be aggression.[54]

When the Democrats assembled at Baltimore a few weeks later, annexationists, softs, and Calhounites mounted a desperate struggle to block Van Buren. Although a majority of delegates arrived under instructions to support the ex-President, enough defected to pass a rule requiring a two-thirds majority that made his nomination impossible. In angry tumult a splintering Democracy saved itself by finding the Presidency's first dark-horse candidate in James K. Polk, a slaveholding annexationist from Tennessee who was also a Jackson protégé, Van Buren loyalist, and minor hero of the Bank War. Seeking to drown dangerous sectional differences in jingoistic enthusiasm for territorial expansion on both northern and southern frontiers, the convention resolved:

> That our title to the whole of the Territory of Oregon is clear and unquestionable ... and that the reoccupation of Oregon and the reannexation of Texas, at the earliest practicable period, are great American measures.

Oregon had been "wrapped round" Texas, the Whig press complained, "just as a nurse disguises a nauseous dose in honey"; but as soon as Texas was annexed, "we venture to predict that the Oregon fever will straightway subside."[55]

"Who is James K. Polk?" Whigs jeered, for against the most illustrious leader of the day, the Tennessee politician seemed a ludicrous mismatch. After faithful service in the Bank War won him two terms as Speaker of the House, he had redeemed Jackson's state from the Whigs by winning the governorship in 1839. But he had lost two elections since, and only his obstinate contention for the vice-presidential nomination, which the party had denied him in 1840, kept him available for consideration by the 1844 convention. By this time, however, the party allegiances that determined most votes were almost evenly divided, and "Young Hickory" proved astute and indefatigable in guaranteeing a maximum Democratic turnout.

Skillfully conciliating Van Burenites, Calhounites, and Tylerites—in part by pledging to serve only one term—Polk dealt adroitly with the tariff issue that most threatened Democratic unity. His antiprotectionist record produced particular alarm in electorally powerful Pennsylvania, which the Democrats had to carry. Imploring Polk for a reassuring statement, his Pennsylvania supporters insisted that better times following the Whigs' Tariff of 1842 made antiprotectionism politically suicidal. In his only public statement on the campaign issues, he gave the Pennsylvanians what they wanted: "In adjusting the details of a revenue tariff, I have heretofore sanctioned such moderate discriminating duties, as would produce the amount of revenue needed, and at the same time afford reasonable incidental protection to home industry." This was enough to enable Pennsylvania Democrats to advertise their ticket as "POLK, DALLAS, SHUNK, and the DEMOCRATIC TARIFF OF 1842." And sometimes, "as if to show how far impudence and audacity could go," they added, "WE DARE THE WHIGS TO REPEAL IT."[56]

Clay was contrastingly maladroit in trying to stem southern Whig defections over Texas. First the Whig candidate announced that although he had no personal objection to annexation, it might destroy the Union. When this did not satisfy southerners, he issued a further declaration: "Far from having any personal objection to the annexation of Texas, I should be glad to see it, without dishonor, without war, with the common consent of the union, and upon just and fair terms." Now northern Whigs cried out in alarm, evoking still another statement: "I am decidedly opposed to the immediate annexation of Texas." The Democratic press pounced on these vacillations to undermine Clay's credibility with both sides:

> He wires in and wires out,
> And leaves the people still in doubt,
> Whether the snake that made the track,
> Was going south or coming back.[57]

Polk won by a whisker, losing his own state by 113 votes but squeezing out a national margin of 1.4 percent. The outcome turned on a scant Democratic plurality of some five thousand in New York, where the recent eruption of nativism inspired an enormous turnout of Irish Democrats, while Clay's Texas tergiversation alienated antislavery Whigs and drew off sixteen thousand votes to James G. Birney, running again as the Liberty candidate. Elsewhere the only unlikely states swung to the Democrats by the Texas issue were Georgia, perhaps Indiana, and possibly (aided by fraud) Louisiana, totaling twenty-eight electoral votes; whereas it may have lost them Ohio with twenty-three. Probably more voters favored annexation because they were Democrats than voted Democratic because they favored annexation.

Claiming this ambiguous result as a mandate, annexationists pushed through Congress on the eve of Polk's inauguration a joint resolution admitting Texas as a state. Opposition by fourteen New York Democrats was portentous. To Democratic criticism, a Connecticut Van Burenite replied, "Do you think the N York members have no sagacity, no instinct to discover public sentiment in their Districts?" The Texas controversy, they had discovered, gave the balance of power in ten upstate districts to the abolitionists, who could make the state Whig by weaning away 1 percent of the Democratic vote. "Would you have our friends there give them a new and powerful impulse?" asked the defectors' defender.[58]

Polk took office inspired by Jacksonian example, resentful of condescension by more celebrated politicians, and determined "to be *myself* President of the United States." In a rare burst of euphoric candor upon reaching the political pinnacle, this self-contained, hard-driving little man revealed to his Navy Secretary George Bancroft a remarkable agenda. The Locofoco historian long recalled how his new chief "raised his hand high in the air and bringing it down with force on his thigh, he said, there are to be four great measures of my administration"—the independent treasury, a sharply reduced revenue tariff, British acknowledgment of an American Oregon, and acquisition of Mexican California.[59]

Accomplishing all four in the single term he allotted himself, he almost doubled the republic's territory and committed the federal government to the whole Jacksonian program for almost a generation. By thus rescuing the republic from sectional disruption, he longed to prove himself another Hickory and satisfy his frustrated hunger for distinction. But his tactics alienated friend and foe alike, and his strategy brought the great contradiction to irreversible crisis.

Polk's inaugural address summoned both North and South to a unifying new mission of territorial expansion. Decrying "any narrow spirit of sectional policy," he justified Texas annexation "on the broad principle which formed . . . our Constitution." Slavery would still exist in a rejected Texas, he argued, and on this principle "our forefathers would have been prevented from forming our present Union."

Balancing Texas in his vision was the free soil of Oregon. "Our people," he exulted, "increasing to many millions, have filled the eastern valley of the Mississippi, adventurously ascended the Missouri to its headsprings, and are already engaged in establishing the blessings of self-government" on waters that "flow to the Pacific." Insisting that these brave pioneers must be protected "wherever they may be upon our soil," he sensationally defied British power by asserting, in the language of the Democratic platform, that "our title to the country of Oregon is 'clear and unquestionable.'"[60]

The new President could not yet publicly avow the most glittering objective of his continental vision—California. Within days of taking office, Young Hickory launched an Old-Hickory-style offensive to parley annexation of Texas into an extended Pacific domain embracing the magnificent harbor of San Francisco. Mexico was unreconciled to losing Texas, and just before his inauguration Polk had secured passage of the annexation resolution by convincing the most dubious Democrats that he would complete annexation by negotiating assent and boundary with Mexico. Instead, as Texans assembled a convention to approve annexation, he promised to maintain their extravagant territorial claims, extending some hundred miles west of their last straggling settlements along the Nueces, traditional boundary of Mexican Texas, to the Mexican settlements along the Rio Grande, and far up that river to include half the ancient and populous Mexican department of New Mexico, over a thousand miles from any Texas settlement.

The close-mouthed President's strategy, it is apparent in retrospect, was to bully Mexico into ceding the territory he wanted by military occupation of her Texas-claimed territory and, if this did not avail, to find a pretext for war. His agents in Texas were soon stirring up alarm over imaginary Mexican invasions, inciting Texas attacks on Mexico, and badgering the Texas authorities to request American military protection. When the Texas President refused "to assist Mr. Polk in manufacturing a war with Mexico," General Zachary Taylor's American army was ordered into Texas uninvited and crossed the Nueces. At the same time orders went out for the American naval commander in the distant Pacific to seize San Francisco in the event of war with Mexico. As soon as the Texas convention approved annexation on July 4, 1845, General Taylor was ordered "to approach as near the boundary line, the Rio Grande, as prudence will permit."[61]

But presidential prudence stalled General Taylor's advance for months on the west bank of the Nueces, for Polk's audacious continental strategy threatened simultaneous wars with both Mexico and Great Britian. His inaugural belligerence about Oregon had provoked a menacing response from the British Prime Minister. "We, too, my lords, have rights which are 'clear and unquestionable,'" Sir Robert Peel told Parliament, "and these rights . . . we are ready to maintain."[62] As Britain dispatched fortification engineers and a frigate to Oregon, the American President faced up to diplomatic/military reality.

The United States had long since retreated from the boundary of Russian Alaska at 54°40'. While the British stood adamantly on a Columbia River boundary, American negotiators had repeatedly proposed extending the 49° boundary west to the Pacific, and only a stopgap agreement for joint occupation had been possible. This left in dispute most of present Washington, the southern tip of Vancouver Island, and between them the real prize, access to splendid harbors and the interior through the Strait of San Juan de Fuca. Now Polk learned that the first break in this twenty-seven-year impasse had been imminent when he assumed office. Tyler's London minister Edward Everett had proposed to Peel's Foreign Secretary Lord Aberdeen a small deviation in the 49° boundary south around the tip of Vancouver Island and west through the strait thus opened to both countries. This Everett line was a compromise Aberdeen thought his more intransigent Prime Minister might accept.

Alarmed by Polk's inaugural provocation, Aberdeen persuaded him through unofficial channels that war could be averted by another American proposal leading, through a face-saving minuet of counterproposals, to agreement on the Everett line. Accordingly in July 1845 the United States renewed the often rejected proposal of 49°. But instead of referring it to London for a counterproposal as Aberdeen expected, the insufficiently instructed British minister at Washington summarily and rudely rejected it. Furious at what he thought British trickery, Polk withdrew the proposal, reasserted the claim to all of Oregon, and asked Congress, when it met in December, to authorize the treaty-stipulated year's notice for terminating joint occupation. His suspicions were not unfounded, for only his renewed threat of war reconciled Prime Minister Peel to eventual acceptance of the Everett line.

Businessman/planter fears of war delayed a settlement, as Calhoun returned to the Senate to lead a peace coalition of Whigs and southern Democrats that demanded compromise, blocked passage of the notice measure for five months, and encouraged the British to hold out for better terms. Although Polk's apparent intransigence for all of Oregon was driving the British from their entrenchment on the Columbia to 49°, it was also committing northwestern Democrats to 54°40' and embittering them against southern insistence on doubling the domain of slaveholding Texas while sacrificing half the free soil of Oregon.

When Congress finally approved notice in April 1846, Aberdeen promptly proposed the Everett line, with the face-saving proviso of free navigation on the

Columbia for the British Hudson's Bay Company. Polk covered his retreat from 54° 40′ by invoking the Constitution's advise-and-consent clause to refer the proposal to the Senate, which advised acceptance. A treaty was signed on June 15 and ratified by the Senate three days later. This diplomatic triumph was won, however, by a disingenuousness that fed mounting sectional bitterness.

While the sabre-rattling struggle over Oregon delayed for months General Taylor's advance from the Nueces, it did not slow the frustrated President's diplomatic offensive intended either to bully Mexico into cessions or to demonstrate the necessity for war. The Mexicans had broken diplomatic relations when Congress authorized annexation, and three weeks into the new administration an unsavory secret agent, William S. Parrott, was dispatched to Mexico City to learn whether an American minister would be received for negotiations. By thus reopening diplomatic relations, Mexico would be acquiescing in annexation and opening itself to Polk's further territorial demands.

Polk's diplomatic club was the claims issue originally wielded by Jackson. The leading capitalist nations were laying down an "international law" that demanded for their citizens the same juridical and property rights abroad they enjoyed at home; and compensation for mistreatment had been claimed on a large scale by American businessmen who rushed in amid political chaos to profit hugely from the opportunities first opened to outsiders by Mexican independence. A Mexican government crippled by coups and revolutions had already been compelled to satisfy European claims by French bombardment of Vera Cruz and a menacing demonstration of British naval power.

Polk's administration organ left the Mexicans no doubt about the territorial concessions required to satisfy American claims. Frank Blair's *Globe* had been forced to make way for a new Washington *Union* edited by Thomas Ritchie; and as Parrott demanded negotiations in Mexico City, the *Union* warned that "a corps of properly organized volunteers . . . would enable us not only to take California, but to keep it." Under this pressure a desperate Mexican regime, already facing overthrow by its most powerful general, nervously consented to receive a commissioner (not a minister) to negotiate "the present dispute" over Texas (not territorial cessions). Fearing overthrow by patriotic indignation, the Mexican government pleaded for a conciliatory commissioner and explicitly ruled out the offensive Parrott, who was pressing his own egregiously inflated claim.[63]

Instead Polk dispatched the Louisiana politician John Slidell as a regular minister, with Parrott as his secretary and with instructions to inform Mexico that American forbearance over "the injuries and outrages committed by the authorities of Mexico on American citizens . . . cannot be expected to endure much longer." Recognizing that Mexico could not pay, Slidell's instructions offered American assumption of the claims in return for a Rio Grande boundary including eastern New Mexico, $5 million in addition for the rest of New Mexico, and $25 million if California were thrown in. The alternative of congressionally declared war was publicly trumpeted by Polk's *Union:*

> Does Mexico prefer war? We are ready to wage it. Does she desire peace? She must be the first to seek it ... It is for her to say whether she will ... open the door for negotiation ... or whether she will ... wait the decisive action of the Congress of the United States.[64]

Polk was ruthlessly exploiting Mexico's political instability. Slidell's mere arrival at Vera Cruz destabilized the Mexican government, and his insistence on proceeding to the capital against its entreaties sparked its overthrow, despite its rejection of his insulting demand for reception as regular minister. At this point, in early 1846, General Taylor was finally ordered to advance to the east bank of the Rio Grande. Slidell's rejection was to be the *casus belli,* and he was told not to leave Mexico until rejected also by the new regime, so as to "satisfy the American people that all had been done which ought to have been done to avoid the necessity of resorting to hostilities." His return was not desired, he was also told, until resolution of the Oregon dispute, now "approaching a crisis," cleared the way for war on Mexico.[65]

Meanwhile the administration had responded to misleading reports of British and French interest in California by rushing two agents to assist its consul at Monterey in encouraging the Mexican *californios* to revolt against their central government, with assurance of being welcomed as "one of the free and independent States of this Union." Polk's opening message to Congress in December 1845 reinvoked the almost forgotten Monroe Doctrine to forestall interference with his plans for California. "No future European colony or dominion shall with our consent be planted or established on any part of the North American continent," he warned. Should any people on this continent "propose to unite themselves with our Confederacy, this will be a question for them and us to determine without any foreign interposition."[66]

Slidell was finally rejected by the new Mexican government on March 12, and in accordance with administration strategy he dawdled on his return to Washington until Congress passed the Oregon notice on April 23. Five days later Polk had his Secretary of State begin drafting a message calling on Congress for war to avenge Slidell's rejection. He paused over a week, however, in hope of a justifying clash on the Rio Grande, where General Taylor's cannon were aimed across the river at the plaza of Mexican Matamoras.

Slidell's perfectly timed arrival on May 8 persuaded the President to wait no longer. By now—as he no doubt calculated—the British had dispatched beyond recall a response to the Oregon notice ensuring peaceful agreement. The next day, Saturday, Polk obtained Cabinet assent for sending the war message to Congress the following Tuesday. Four hours after the Cabinet adjourned, the White House learned that an American patrol had suffered sixteen casualties in a clash with a Mexican patrol east of the Rio Grande.

Therefore at noon on Monday, May 11, Congress was presented with a war it had not authorized. The Mexicans had "violated their plighted faith" by refusing "upon the most frivolous pretexts" to receive peacemaker Slidell, the President declared, "and now, after reiterated menaces, Mexico has passed the boundary of the United States, has invaded our territory, and shed American blood upon the American soil." Since "war exists . . . by the act of Mexico herself," he called on Congress to "recognize the existence of the war" and authorize "a large and overpowering force."[67]

A disciplined Democratic majority allowed the House only two hours to debate a bill authorizing $10 million and fifty thousand volunteers; and only at the end did the leadership attach a preamble to serve in lieu of the constitutionally required declaration of war: "Whereas, by the act of the Republic of Mexico, a state of war exists between that government and the United States." Compelled either to endorse the administration's interpretation of events on the Rio Grande or oppose resources to rescue Taylor's imperiled army, members passed it 174–14, with ex-President Adams heading the little band of Whigs who dared to vote nay.[68]

The war bill was stalled briefly in the Senate by a startling congruence in outrage at the preamble between Benton, leading critic of the Texas boundary claim, and his longtime bête noire Calhoun, who thought it "monstrous" to "make war on Mexico by making war on the Constitution." But overnight friends convinced Benton "that he was bound to stick to the War party or he was a ruined man"; and the next day the Senators gave the President his war by a vote of 40–2.

Polk would not be the last President to circumvent the Constitution by contriving a confrontation that forced Congress to bow to jingoistic patriotism. Many who voted for the war bill were "as sick a set of fellows as you ever saw." "While we must all stand by our country," said one, "it is grievous to know that when we pray 'God defend the right' our prayers are not for our own country." A popular outburst of martial ardor underscored the political courage of the handful who opposed "this illegal, unrighteous, and damnable war." Adams hoped Taylor's officers would resign and his soldiers desert rather than fight such a war, and another member of his little band publicly "honored and applauded" the Mexicans for their "manly resistance." A "mushroom President" had plotted war on Mexico because "we wanted to get her territory," still another told the House. With no right "to enter a country which did not belong to us, and point his cannon at a Mexican town," he dared to send "a bill into this House, commencing with a falsehood, and couched under a shameful whereas."[69]

Polk's aggressive expansionism rode a peaking tide of racist Anglo-Saxonism in North and South alike. In celebrating Texas annexation, Locofoco editor John

L. O'Sullivan of the *Democratic Review* coined the popular label for the "manifest destiny" of Anglo-Saxon America "to overspread and to possess the whole of the continent which Providence had given us for the development of the great experiment of liberty." California was next, he proclaimed, for "already the advance guard of the irresistible army of Anglo-Saxon emigration has begun to pour down upon it." Senator Benton hailed "the arrival of the van of the Caucasian race (the Celtic-Anglo-Saxon division)" in Oregon. Reaching across the Pacific, he predicted, it would regenerate "the Yellow race," which he ranked far above the black, brown, and red races,

> but still, far below the White; and, like all the rest, must receive an impression from the superior race whenever they come in contact. It would seem that the White race alone received the divine command, to subdue and replenish the earth! . . . Civilization, or extinction, has been the fate of all people who have found themselves in the track of the advancing Whites.[70]

While respect for Anglo-Saxon British adversaries compelled compromise of the republic's substantial claim to Oregon, racist contempt for Mexicans both animated the Anglo/Texan revolution and enforced the Polk administration's unfounded claims by sword. Robert J. Walker was rewarded with the Treasury secretaryship for cheering on the Anglo/Texans against an "ignorant and fanatical colored race" that was "composed of every poisonous compound of blood and color." The Mexican race, said the leading Democratic newspaper in Illinois, was "but little removed above the negro." Secretary of State James Buchanan paved the way for conquest through "negotiations" with "the imbecile and indolent Mexican race." His bullying demands were first conveyed by the offensive Parrott, who was "fully persuaded that they can never love or respect us, as we should be loved and respected by them, until after we shall have given them a positive proof of our superiority."[71]

Consequently arrogant assumptions of Mexican cowardice and venality persuaded the administration it could "conquer a peace" in three or four months by occupying Mexico's northern provinces and bribing the central government. To the latter end it connived in bringing back from exile the most effective Mexican leader, Antonio López de Santa Anna. While intrigue with Santa Anna and seizure of undefended California and New Mexico preoccupied Washington during the early months of war, General Taylor was left without instructions on the Rio Grande.

But Santa Anna, upon seizing power, organized a stubborn resistance that held out almost two years against overwhelming American superiority in manpower and resources. A peace was finally achieved—at a cost in lives of some thirteen thousand *norteamericanos* and many more Mexicans[72]—by the professional skill of an American officer corps schooled at Calhoun's West Point and honed in Mexico to the distinguished generalship that would be displayed on both sides in the Civil War. The success of American arms owed much to generals Winfield Scott and Zachary Taylor, whose relations with their Democratic commander-in-chief were poisoned by a popularity that carried Taylor into the presidency as Polk's Whig successor and Scott into the next Whig nomination.

Taylor's two quick victories on the Rio Grande made Old Rough and Ready a national hero, ever more admired for gallantry and unpretentious forthrightness as he led his army into northeastern Mexico to take strongly defended Monterrey by storm and rout Santa Anna's larger army at Buena Vista. Polk had denied command of this initial campaign to the more senior Scott because he was at first more threatening politically. But Taylor was denied further opportunities for glory as his popularity mounted, and many of his troops were shifted to Scott for an invasion of central Mexico. Scott's swift ascent from Vera Cruz through forbidding terrain and determined resistance to occupy Mexico City was a logistical and tactical masterpiece.

Once military resistance was crushed, the American problem was to find a Mexican government sufficiently legitimate and amenable to yield the territory demanded. With the war becoming more unpopular as its Whig generals became more popular, Polk finally accepted a treaty audaciously negotiated in February 1848 by Nicholas P. Trist, a diplomatic agent he had already recalled for insubordinate connivance with the distrusted Scott. Under this Treaty of Guadelupe Hidalgo, the United States assumed its citizens' claims and paid Mexico $15 million for a Rio Grande boundary, New Mexico, and California. Racist opposition to annexing Mexican people restrained temptations to extort more or all of Mexico's territory.[73]

While President Polk's aggressive foreign policy was almost doubling the republic's territory, he had also effected a momentous and durable shift in its domestic policy. Young Hickory's first annual message to Congress in December 1845 adopted Old Hickory's populist tone in calling for consummation of every Jacksonian tendency. To protect "the hardy and brave men of the frontier . . . from the grasping speculator" and to secure "the humble homes which they have improved by their labor," he advocated preemption of public lands by settlers at the minimum price and graduation (periodic reduction) of land prices. Next he urged restoration of the independent treasury, which the Whigs had repealed in 1841, on the pure Jacksonian basis of specie receipts and disbursements. Finally he wanted the Whig Tariff of 1842 reduced to a "revenue standard." A high tariff bears hardest "on labor and the poorer classes," he charged, while it increases the profits "of wealthy manufacturers, . . . protects capital and exempts the rich from paying their just proportion." The minimum valuations and specific duties that disguised high rates should be eliminated, he said, and all duties reduced to the varying ad valorem rates at which each article produced the most revenue. The revenue standard permitted some "incidental protection," the President added, and articles of necessity "consumed by the laborer and poor" could be exempted from taxation.[74]

For six months Polk's domestic recommendations languished in a Congress distracted by Oregon crisis and Mexican War; and once the war measures were enacted, most members wanted to adjourn. But for two more months an insistent President kept them at work legislating a major turning point in federal policy. Asserting forcefully Jackson's conception that the President represents "the whole people of the United States, as each member of the legislative branch represents portions of them," he precociously seized for the executive the role of legislative initiator, leaving Congress "their veto upon his recommendation" with appeal "to the people at the ballot box." His annual message drafted in this spirit was a potent instrument of public appeal and party discipline.[75]

The message was powerfully reinforced by Ritchie's *Union*, which Polk supervised closely in defining the party line and excoriating both apostasy and individual apostates. Democratic deviants were denied patronage, called in for presidential lectures, or threatened with exposure to their constituents. When a critical vote impended, the whole Cabinet was sent to buttonhole members on Capital Hill. The President's influence was amplified at the critical juncture by the initial war fever and, especially, by his power to bestow army commands on hundreds of prominent Democrats who were militia officers.

As a result this session did not adjourn until it had passed the independent treasury by a straight party vote, and the sharply lower "Walker tariff" applying the President's revenue standard as specified in an elaborately researched report from his diligent Treasury Secretary Walker. Protectionism was further eroded by a Warehouse Act allowing importers to store goods without duty payment until the market was most favorable. The only presidential recommendation that failed (by disagreement between the houses on amendments) was graduation of land prices. Polk blocked a threatened revival of internal improvements, moreover, by vetoing an extravagant rivers-and-harbors bill for improved navigation and Great Lakes ports, which incurable presidential fantasy prompted Calhoun to support.

But the President's triumphs came at a fearful cost, and the last act of this Congress put the republic irreversibly on the road to Civil War. Behind the facade of party discipline, irrepressible differences over slavery were rising. Northern Democrats had joined in rejecting the gag rule at the previous session and again at the opening of this one. Massachusetts "Conscience" Whigs were attacking "Cotton" Whigs, and as Congress moved toward adjournment, a Whig/antislavery coalition won the banner Democratic state of New Hampshire.

Northern Democrats were on the brink of revolt against Polk's manipulative control and disingenuousness on Texas annexation, Oregon, war bill preamble, and war aims. The Van Burenites were kept in line by the President's solemn assurance to Senator John A. Dix that he "had no schemes of conquest in view in respect to Mexico," and "no intention to take possession of any portion of her territory, with a view to hold it." Northwesterners felt betrayed by the Oregon compromise and the rivers-and-harbors veto. Pennsylvania protectionists felt politically doomed by the Walker tariff. New York Van Burenites, already embittered by the Baltimore convention, saw Polk's attempt at factional impartiality in appointments as building up their "Hunker" rivals. "Tyler was bad enough," complained a veteran Bucktail, "but he had this advantage—there was no . . . genuine duplicity."[76]

These combustible materials burst into flame on Saturday afternoon, August 8, 1846, when the last-minute business of the House was interrupted by a presidential message asking $2 million to buy peace and territory through what was patently bribery. Excitedly a little group of northern Democrats selected an obscure Pennsylvanian to introduce a momentous antislavery amendment. David Wilmot, whose name would soon be a household word, probably led off as the only dissident who could get the floor, given the constituent ire he had risked to support the prosouthern party line on the gag rule and tariff.

Wilmot's amendment applied Jefferson's language from the Northwest Ordinance to any territory acquired from Mexico:

> *Provided*, That . . . neither slavery nor involuntary servitude shall ever exist in any part of said territory, except for crime, whereof the party shall first be duly convicted.

Supported 54–4 by free-state Democrats against the unanimous opposition of slave-state Democrats, the Wilmot Proviso passed the House to meet defeat from the South's disproportionate representation in the Senate. Defeat was not final, however, for reasons suggested by another Jeffersonian text resonating from the Missouri crisis:

> A geographical line, coinciding with a marked principle, moral and political, once conceived and held up to the angry passions of men, will never be obliterated; and every new irritation will mark it deeper and deeper.

Intractable differences over confining slavery, breaking through a quarter century of bipartisan suppression and held up to the angry passions of midcentury Americans, would break through every new compromise and evasion until blood was shed.[77]

What Wilmot called the "White Man's Proviso" signaled a fusion of antislavery with racism that proved unstoppable. Reintroducing it at the next session, he declared:

I have no squeamish sensitiveness upon the subject of slavery, nor morbid sympathy for the slave. I plead the cause of the rights of white freemen. I would preserve for free white labor a fair country, a rich inheritance, where the sons of toil, of my own race and own color, can live without the disgrace which association with negro slavery brings upon free labor.

In less than a generation, the vision of vastly expanded federal territories as free soil reserved for the free labor of free white men weaned enough northern racism from the Democrats to empower a Republican antislavery coalition and alarm slaveholding insecurity into suicidal rebellion.[78]

Abraham Lincoln perfected in heterogeneous Illinois the synthesis that carried the Republicans to victory. Genuinely abhorring slavery, the canny prairie lawyer inspired Yankee moralists by opposing its further advance, reassured conservatives by acknowledging its constitutional right to exist where it was, and appealed to old-timer racism by endorsing white supremacy, black colonization, and reservation of the territories "for the homes of free white people." Republicans sought, in historian James Rawley's apt summary, "to arrest the advance of slavery, subdue southern influence in the nation, secure their own rights, and defer indefinitely decisions on the dread questions of emancipation and equalitarianism."[79]

When the Civil War's unforeseen imperatives of military/ideological mobilization destroyed both slavery and slavocracy's coalition with farmer/worker democracy, market revolution culminated in unchallengeable bourgeois hegemony, moral and political. But liberal capitalism still had to confront a great contradiction in the racism it rode to power.

The long struggle for Garrisonian equality—joined ambiguously on the battlefields of Civil War, impelled slowly but inexorably by the capitalist ideal of competitive juridical equality, and gathering strength after more than a century from Garrisonian militancy against inequalities of ethnicity, gender, and sexuality—may yet empower democracy as capitalism's ultimate contradiction. A democracy purged by liberalism of racist and patriarchal contradictions may yet realize its Jacksonian promise by confronting arminian capital on behalf of antinomian humanity and ravaged land.

Bibliographical Essay

Scholarship proliferating under the meritocratic competition of the academic market-place has pushed historians into ever narrower chronological/topical fields, where special-ized literatures and methodologies inhibit integrative analysis and deviation from ortho-doxy. Even for the limited period of this volume, a comprehensive bibliography would be overwhelming while soon outdated. Consequently many works valuable for data or cited in the footnotes are omitted here to focus on those most critical for interpretation.

The Land

Environmental crisis underscores history's foundation in human adaptions to, and impacts on, the land. The ecological perspective of Carolyn Merchant, *Ecological Revolutions: Nature, Gender, and Science in New England* (Chapel Hill, 1989), illuminates nature's complex interactions with every aspect of human society, ranging from mode of production to gender. Human impacts on the same region are further delineated by William Cronon, Jr., *Changes in the Land: Indians, Colonists, and the Ecology of New England* (New York, 1983).

American Indians

The Americans who lived most harmoniously with the land are well surveyed in Wil-comb E. Washburn, *The Indian in America* (New York, 1975).For the impact of European invasion and the fur trade: Francis Jennings, *The Invasion of America: Indians, Colonialism, and the Cant of Conquest* (Chapel Hill, 1975); Harold Hickerson, "Fur Trade Colonialism and the North American Indians," *Journal of Ethnic Studies* 1 (1973): 15–44; Calvin Martin, *Keepers of the Game: Indian-Animal Relationships and the Fur Trade* (Berkeley, 1978); and Shepard Krech III, ed., *Indians, Animals, and the Fur Trade: A Critique of Keepers of the Game* (Athens, Ga., 1981).

For white attitudes and white/Indian relations: Roy Harvey Pearce, *Savagism and Civilization: A Study of the Indian and the American Mind* (Baltimore, 1967); James Axtell, *The Invasion Within: The Contest of Cultures in Colonial North America* (New York, 1985); and James Axtell, *After Columbus: Essays in the Ethnohistory of Colonial North America* (New York, 1988).

For the southeastern tribes under heaviest white pressure during this period: Peter H.

429

Wood, Gregory A. Waselkov, and M. Thomas Hatley, *Powhatan's Mantle: Indians in the Colonial Southeast* (Lincoln, 1989); James H. Merrell, *The Indians' New World: Catawbas and Their Neighbors from European Contact through the Era of Removal* (Chapel Hill, 1989); William G. McLoughlin, *Cherokee Renascence in the New Republic* (Princeton, 1987); J. Leitch Wright, Jr., *Creeks and Seminoles: Destruction and Regeneration of the Muscogulge People* (Lincoln, 1986); and Michael D. Green, *The Politics of Indian Removal: Creek Government and Society in Crisis* (Lincoln, 1982).

For federal Indian policy and Jacksonian aggression: Francis Paul Prucha, *The Great Father: The United States Government and the American Indians* (2 vols., Lincoln, 1984); Ronald N. Satz, *American Indian Policy in the Jacksonian Era* (Lincoln, 1975); Robert V. Remini, *Andrew Jackson* (3 vols., New York, 1977–1984); Michael P. Rogin, *Fathers and Children: Andrew Jackson and the Subjugation of the American Indian* (New York, 1975); and Mary Young, "The Exercise of Sovereignty in Cherokee Georgia," *Journal of the Early Republic* 10 (Spring 1990): 43–63

Agriculture

This basic human/land relationship is well surveyed by Paul W. Gates, *The Farmer's Age: Agriculture, 1815–1860* (New York, 1960). For the North: Clarence H. Danhof, *Change in Agriculture: The Northern United States, 1820–1870* (Cambridge, Mass., 1969); and Jeremy Atack and Fred Bateman, *To Their Own Soil: Agriculture in the Antebellum North* (Chicago, 1987). For the South: Lewis C. Gray's encyclopedic *History of Agriculture in the Southern United States to 1860* (2 vols., Washington, 1933); and Gavin Wright's more analytical *The Political Economy of the Cotton South: Households, Markets, and Wealth in the Nineteenth Century* (New York, 1978).

Subsistence Farming

Our historical mythology of pervasive enterprise long blinded scholars to the extent of subsistence farming revealed by Percy W. Bidwell's richly documented "Rural Economy in New England at the Beginning of the Nineteenth Century," Connecticut Academy of Arts and Sciences, *Transactions* 20 (New Haven, 1916): 241–399. The issue was not squarely joined until James T. Lemon, *The Best Poor Man's Country: A Geographical Study of Early Southeastern Pennsylvania* (Baltimore, 1972), essayed an empirical demonstration of farmer eagerness for markets. A counterview of early rural culture as familial, cooperative, and self-sufficient was presented by Michael Merrill, "Cash is Good to Eat: Self-Sufficiency and Exchange in the Rural Economy of the United States," *Radical History Review* 4 (Winter 1977): 42–71; and James A. Henretta, "Families and Farms: *Mentalite* in Pre-Industrial America," *William and Mary Quarterly* 25 (Jan. 1978): 3–32. For a review of the ensuing debate: Allan Kulikoff, "The Transition to Capitalism in Rural America," *William and Mary Quarterly* 46 (Jan. 1989): 120–44.

Extensive persistence of subsistence farming is documented by the rural community studies in the following section and by the previously cited agricultural historians Atack, Bateman, Danhof, and Wright. Advocates of a commercial orientation, on the other hand, while often overgeneralizing from ambiguous evidence, have illuminated when and how commercialization occurred. Extension of market production along the seaboard in response to European demand for wheat in the late eighteenth and early nineteenth centuries accounts for the findings of Lemon; Robert D. Mitchell, *Commercialism and Frontier: Perspectives on the Early Shenandoah Valley* (Charlottesville, 1977); and Joyce Appleby, "Commercial Farming and the 'Agrarian Myth' in the Early Republic," *Journal of American History* 68 (Mar. 1982): 831–48.

Another factor felt first in lower New England was an agrarian crisis of land scarcity, as delineated in the rural community studies for the region and in Kenneth Lockridge, "Land, Population, and the Evolution of New England Society 1630–1790," *Past and Present* 39 (April 1968): 62–80. This helps explain the evidence for commercialization reported in Bettye Hobbs Pruitt, "Self-Sufficiency and the Agricultural Economy of Eighteenth-Century Massachusetts," *William and Mary Quarterly* 41 (July 1984): 333–64, and a series of articles (*Journal of Economic History*) by Winifred B. Rothenberg: "The Market and Massachusetts Farmers, 1750–1855," 11 (June 1981): 183–314, "Markets, Values, and Capitalism: A Discourse on Method," 44 (June 1984): 171–78, "The Emergence of a Capital Market in Rural Massachusetts, 1730–1838," 45 (Dec. 1985): 781–808, and "The Emergence of Farm Labor Markets and the Transformation of the Rural Economy: Massachusetts, 1750–1855," 48 (Sept. 1988): 537–66. The New England transition to commercial production is superbly delineated in Christopher Clark, *The Roots of Rural Capitalism: Western Massachusetts, 1780–1860* (Ithica, 1990).

Rural Community Studies

The best sources for rural culture, agrarian crisis, the transition to market production, and associated social/demographic change are such closely focused studies as Hal Barron, *Those Who Stayed Behind: Rural Society in Nineteenth Century New England* (New York, 1984); John L. Brooke, *The Heart of the Commonwealth: Society and Political Culture in Worcester County, Massachusetts, 1713–1861* (New York, 1990); Robert Doherty, *Society and Power: Five New England Towns, 1800–1860* (Amherst, 1977); Christopher M. Jedrey, *The World of John Cleaveland: Family and Community in Eighteenth-Century New England* (New York, 1979); John Mack Faragher, *Sugar Creek: Life on the Illinois Prairie* (New Haven, 1986); Robert A. Gross, "Culture and Cultivation: Agriculture and Society in Thoreau's Concord," *Journal of American History* 69 (June 1982): 42–61; Richard Holmes, *Bedford and Lincoln, Massachusetts, 1729–1850* (Ann Arbor, 1980); Jonathan Prude, *The Coming of Industrial Order: Town and Factory Life in Rural Massachusetts, 1810–1860* (New York, 1983); Randolph A. Roth, *The Democratic Dilemma: Religion, Reform, and the Social Order in the Connecticut Valley of Vermont, 1791–1850* (Cambridge, England, 1987); and the citations below under "The South and the Great Contradiction: Local Studies."

The Market

The accelerating growth of a capitalist market economy in the early nineteenth century has been illuminated by "cliometricians" trained in economic theory and quantitative analysis. Their findings are lucidly synthesized for noneconomists in Susan Previant Lee and Peter Passell, *A New Economic View of American History* (New York, 1979). For the crucial role of the northeastern port/hinterland economies: Diane Lindstrom, *Economic Development in the Philadelphia Region, 1810–1850* (New York, 1978), 1–21; and Diane Lindstrom, "American Economic Growth before 1840: New Evidence and New Directions," *Journal of Economic History* 39 (Mar. 1979): 289–301. For the importance of exports: Douglass C. North, *The Economic Growth of the United States, 1790–1860* (New York, 1961).

Transportation

The indispensability of transportation improvements is made clear in George Rogers Taylor, *The Transportation Revolution 1815–1860* (New York, 1951), and amplified in

Albert Fishlow, *American Railroads and the Transformation of the Antebellum Economy* (Cambridge, Mass., 1965); Carter Goodrich et al., *Canals and American Economic Development* (New York, 1961); Erik F. Haites, James Mak, and Gary M. Walton, *Western River Transportation: The Era of Early Internal Improvement Development, 1810–1860* (Baltimore, 1975); and Louis C. Hunter, *Steamboats on the Western Rivers* (Cambridge, Mass., 1949).

Urbanization

For the pivotal role of cities in economic growth: Allan R. Pred, *Urban Growth and the Circulation of Information: The United States System of Cities, 1790–1840* (Cambridge, Mass., 1973). For the special importance of New York City: Robert G. Albion, *The Rise of New York Port [1815-1860]* (New York, 1939).

Other valuable studies include Henry C. Binford, *The First Suburbs: Residential Communities on the Boston Periphery, 1815–1860* (Chicago, 1985); Elizabeth Blackmar, *Manhattan for Rent, 1785–1850* (Ithaca, 1989); Gary L. Browne, *Baltimore in the Nation, 1789–1861* (Chapel Hill, 1980); David T. Gilchrist, ed., *The Growth of the Seaport Cities, 1790–1825* (Charlottesville, 1967); Timothy R. Mahoney, *River Towns in the Great West: The Structure of Provincial Urbanization in the American Midwest, 1820–1870* (New York, 1989); and Sam Bass Warner, Jr., *The Private City: Philadelphia in Three Periods of Its Growth* (Philadelphia, 1968).

Manufacturing

The most comprehensive account is Victor S. Clark, *History of Manufactures in the United States* (3 vols., Washington, 1916–1928). Valuable on the crucial textile industry are Robert F. Dalzell, Jr., *Enterprising Elite: The Boston Associates and the World They Made* (Cambridge, Mass., 1987); Philip B. Scranton, *Proprietary Capitalism: The Textile Manufacture at Philadelphia, 1800–1885* (New York, 1984); Barbara M. Tucker, *Samuel Slater and the Origins of the American Textile Industry, 1790–1860* (Ithaca, 1984); and Anthony F. C. Wallace, *Rockdale: The Growth of an American Village in the Early Industrial Revolution* (New York, 1972). For other industries: Thomas C. Cochran, *Frontiers of Change: Early Industrialism in America* (New York, 1981); Louis C. Hunter, *A History of Industrial Power in the United States, 1780–1930* (2 vols., Charlottesville, 1979–1985); Peter Temin, *Iron and Steel in Nineteenth-Century America: An Economic Inquiry* (Cambridge, Mass., 1974); and Robert Brooke Zevin, *The Growth of Manufacturing in Early Nineteenth Century New England* (New York, 1975).

For the role of technology: H. J. Habakkuk, *American and British Technology in the Nineteenth Century* (Cambridge, England, 1962); Donald Hoke, *Ingenious Yankees: The Rise of the American System of Manufactures in the Private Sector* (New York, 1989); David J. Jeremy, *Transatlantic Industrial Revolution: The Diffusion of Textile Technologies between Britain and America, 1790–1830s* (Cambridge, Mass., 1981); Merritt Roe Smith, *Harpers Ferry Armory and the New Technology: The Challenge of Change* (Ithaca, 1977); and Darwin H. Stapleton, *The Transfer of Early Industrial Technologies to America* (Philadelphia, 1987).

Labor

A good overview is Bruce Laurie, *Artisans into Workers: Labor in Nineteenth-Century America* (New York, 1989). Particularly illuminating are studies of working people in various cities. New York is splendidly served by Howard B. Rock, *Artisans of the Young Republic: The Tradesmen of New York City in the Age of Jefferson* (New York, 1979); Richard B.

Stott, *Workers in the Metropolis: Class, Ethnicity, and Youth in Antebellum New York City* (Ithaca, 1990); and Sean Wilentz, *Chants Democratic: New York City & the Rise of the American Working Class, 1788–1850* (New York, 1984). For other cities: Paul G. Faler, *Mechanics and Manufacturers in the Early Industrial Revolution: Lynn, Massachusetts, 1780–1860* (Albany, 1981); Susan E. Hirsch, *Roots of the American Working Class: The Industrialization of Crafts in Newark, 1800–1860* (Philadelphia, 1978); Bruce Laurie, *Working People of Philadelphia, 1800–1850* (Philadelphia, 1980); and Charles G. Steffen, "Changes in the Organization of Artisan Production in Baltimore, 1790 to 1820," *William and Mary Quarterly* 36 (Jan. 1979): 101–17. Particularly illuminating on the cultural adaptations of working people are Faler, Laurie, Stott, and Wilentz.

For working women: Mary H. Blewett, *Men, Women, and Work: Class, Gender, and Protest in the New England Shoe Industry, 1789–1910* (Champaign, 1988); Thomas Dublin, *Women at Work: The Transformation of Work and Community in Lowell, Massachusetts, 1820–1860* (New York, 1979); and Christine Stansell, *City of Women: Sex and Class in New York, 1787–1860* (New York, 1986).

For labor in the pioneering textile industry: Dublin (cited above); Gary Kulik, "Pawtucket Village and the Strike of 1824: The Origin of Class Conflict in Rhode Island," *Radical History Review* 17 (Spring 1978): 4–37; Jonathan Prude, "The Social System of Early New England Textile Mills: A Case Study, 1812–40," in Michael H. Frisch and Daniel J. Walkowitz, eds., *Working-Class America: Essays on Labor, Community, and American Society* (Urbana, 1983), 1–36; and Cynthia J. Shelton, *The Mills of Manayunk: Industrialization and Social Conflict in the Philadelphia Region, 1787–1837* (Baltimore, 1986).

Labor organization is most fully treated in John R. Commons et al., *History of Labour in the United States* (2 vols., New York, 1918). Edward Pessen delineates *Most Uncommon Jacksonians: The Radical Leaders of the Early Labor Movement* (Albany, 1967).

The South and the Great Contradiction

Market revolution drove the slaveholding South into irreconcilable conflict with the North as cotton boom reinvigorated its brutal labor system. The capitalist realities of this American tragedy have been hidden by the Old-South mythology of an aristocratic and paternalistic planter class. An excellent general account of this period of southern history is Charles S. Sydnor, *The Development of Southern Sectionalism, 1819–1848* (Baton Rouge, 1948).

Slavery

The racist nostalgia of Ulrich B. Phillips's *American Negro Slavery* (New York, 1929) has been superbly corrected by Kenneth M. Stampp, *The Peculiar Institution: Slavery in the Ante-Bellum South* (New York, 1956).

Two works of comparative perspective highlight critical features of North American slavery: its capitalist character in James Oakes, *Slavery and Freedom: An Interpretation of the Old South* (New York, 1990); and its high rate of slave reproduction in C. Vann Woodward, "Southern Slaves in the World of Thomas Malthus," in *American Counterpoint: Slavery and Racism in the North/South Dialogue* (New York, 1971), 78–106.

For the white South's internal conflicts over slavery: Clement Eaton, *The Freedom-of-Thought Struggle in the Old South* (New York, 1964); Kenneth S. Greenberg, *The Political Culture of American Slavery* (Baltimore, 1985); William S. Jenkins, *Pro-Slavery Thought in the Old South* (Chapel Hill, 1935); Charles Sellers, "The Travail of Slavery," in Charles Sellers, ed., *The Southerner as American* (Chapel Hill, 1960), 40–71; and Laurence Shore, *Southern Capitalists: The Ideological Leadership of an Elite, 1832–1885* (Chapel Hill, 1986). For the national impact of the white South's divided but escalating perturbations over slavery: William W. Freehling, *The Road to Disunion: Secessionists at Bay, 1776–1854* (New York, 1990).

Slave Culture

The autonomous culture constructed by slaves has been richly discovered in a series of works: John W. Blassingame, *The Slave Community: Plantation Life in the Antebellum South* (rev. ed., New York, 1979); Eugene Genovese, *From Rebellion to Revolution: Afro-American Slave Revolts in the Making of the Modern World* (Baton Rouge, 1979); Eugene D. Genovese, *Roll, Jordan, Roll: The World the Slaves Made* (New York, 1974); Herbert G. Gutman, *The Black Family in Slavery and Freedom, 1750–1925* (New York, 1976); Charles Joyner, *Down by the Riverside: A South Carolina Slave Community* (Urbana, 1984); Lawrence W. Levine, *Black Culture and Black Consciousness: Afro-American Folk Thought from Slavery to Freedom* (New York, 1977); Albert J. Raboteau, *Slave Religion: The 'Invisible Institution' in the Antebellum South* (New York, 1978); and Sterling Stuckey, *Slave Culture: Nationalist Theory and the Foundations of Black America* (New York, 1987).

How slaves coped psychologically is discussed insightfully by Kenneth M. Stampp, "Rebels and Sambos: The Search for the Negro's Personality in Slavery," in *The Imperiled Union: Essays on the Background of the Civil War* (New York, 1980), 39–71; and the effect of slave culture on white culture by Mechal Sobel, *The World They Made Together: Black and White Values in Eighteenth-Century Virginia* (Princeton, 1987).

Planters

James Oakes, *The Ruling Race: A History of American Slaveholders* (New York, 1982), is a long overdue corrective to a planter myth persisting in the odd Marxism of Eugene D. Genovese, *The World the Slaveholders Made: Two Essays in Interpretation* (New York, 1969), and in the otherwise illuminating treatment of *Southern Honor: Ethics and Behavior in the Old South* (New York, 1982) by Bertram Wyatt-Brown.

For a new realism about the bourgeois quality of planter family life: Jane Turner Censer, *North Carolina Planters and Their Children, 1800–1860* (Chapel Hill, 1984); and Jan Lewis, *The Pursuit of Happiness: Family and Values in Jefferson's Virginia* (New York, 1983). For planter wives: Catherine Clinton, *The Plantation Mistress: Woman's World in the Old South* (New York, 1982).

Plain Folk

Old-South mythology long blinded scholars to the small-farmer majority revealed by Frank L. Owsley, *Plain Folk of the Old South* (Baton Rouge, 1949). Harbingers of a more realistic picture of antebellum southern society include Steven Hahn, "The Yeomanry of the Non-Plantation South: Upper Piedmont Georgia, 1850–1860," in Robert C. McMath, Jr., and Vernon Burton, eds., *Class, Conflict, and Consensus: Antebellum Southern Community Studies* (Westport, 1982); Forrest McDonald and Grady McWhiney, "The Antebellum Southern Herdsman: A Reinterpretation," *Journal of Southern History* 41 (1975): 156–58; Grady McWhiney, *Cracker Culture: Celtic Ways in the Old South* (Tuscaloosa, 1988); and David F. Weiman, "the Economic Emancipation of the Non-Slaveholding Class: Upcountry Farmers in the Georgia Cotton Economy," *Journal of Economic History* 45 (Mar. 1985): 71–93.

Particularly important are economic explanations for the persistence of a small-farming mode of production alongside a planting mode: Morton Rothstein, "The Antebellum South as a Dual Economy: A Tentative Hypothesis," *Agricultural History* 41 (Oct. 1967): 373–82; and Gavin Wright and Howard Kunreuther, "Cotton, Corn, and Risk in the Nineteenth Century," *Journal of Economic History* 35 (Sept. 1975): 526–51. A more realistic understanding of planter/farmer relations is promised by Harry L. Watson, "Conflict and Collaboration: Yeomen, Slaveholders, and Politics in the Antebellum South," *Social History* 10 (Oct. 1985): 273–98.

Local Studies

The new understanding of the Old South is most solidly grounded in close analyses of localities: the studies by Hahn and Weiman cited above; Richard R. Beeman, *The Evolution of the Southern Backcountry: A Case Study of Lunenberg County, Virginia, 1746–1832* (Philadelphia, 1984); Orville Vernon Butler, *In My Father's House Are Many Mansions: Family and Community in Edgefield, South Carolina* (Chapel Hill, 1985); Peter Coclanis, *The Shadow of a Dream: Economic Life and Death in the South Carolina Low Country, 1670–1920* (New York, 1988); Lacy K. Ford, Jr., *Origins of Southern Radicalism: The South Carolina Upcountry, 1800–1860* (New York, 1988); J. William Harris, *Plain Folk and Gentry in a Slave Society: White Liberty and Black Slavery in Augusta's Hinterlands* (Middletown, Conn., 1985); Suzanne Lebsock, *The Free Women of Petersburg: Status and Culture in a Southern Town* (New York, 1983); and Frederick F. Siegel, *The Roots of Southern Distinctiveness: Tobacco and Society in Danville, Virginia, 1780–1865* (Chapel Hill, 1987).

Political Economy

Public policy was an indispensable generator of market revolution. For the intimate relationship between economic growth and state policy: Oscar and Mary Flug Handlin, *Commonwealth: A Study of the Role of Government in the American Economy: Massachusetts, 1774–1861* (rev. ed., Cambridge, Mass., 1969); Louis Hartz, *Economic Policy and Democratic Thought: Pennsylvania, 1776–1860* (Cambridge, Mass., 1948); and Nathan Miller, *The Enterprise of a Free People: Aspects of Economic Development in New York State during the Canal Period, 1792–1838* (Ithaca, 1962).

For contemporary writers on political economy: Paul K. Conkin, *Prophets of Prosperity: America's First Political Economists* (Bloomington, 1980); and Joseph Dorfman, *The Economic Mind in American Civilization, 1606–1865* (2 vols., New York, 1946).

Law

Lawrence M. Friedman, *A History of American Law* (New York, 1973), provides an excellent overview of the state's primary instrument for economic promotion. The profound transformation of law by state courts in the early nineteenth century is revealed most importantly by Morton J. Horwitz, *The Transformation of American Law, 1780–1860* (Cambridge, Mass., 1977); and William E. Nelson, *Americanization of the Common Law: The Impact of Legal Change on Massachusetts Society, 1760–1830* (Cambridge, Mass., 1975). Two prominent architects of legal change are well treated in Leonard W. Levy, *The Law of the Commonwealth and Chief Justice Shaw* (Cambridge, Mass., 1957); and R. Kent Newmyer, *Supreme Court Justice Joseph Story, Statesman of the Old Republic* (Chapel Hill, 1985).

Charles Warren, *The Supreme Court in United States History* (2 vols., Boston, 1926), remains the best account of developments in federal/constitutional law, supplemented by Charles G. Haines, *The Role of the Supreme Court in American Government and Politics, 1789–1835* (New York, 1960); and G. Edward White (with Gerald Gunther), *The Marshall Court and Cultural Change, 1816–1835* (vols. 3 and 4 of *The Oliver Wendell Holmes Devise History of the Supreme Court of the United States,* New York, 1988). For further information on major decisions: Maurice G. Baxter, *Daniel Webster & the Supreme Court* (Amherst, 1966); Maurice G. Baxter, *The Steamboat Monopoly: Gibbons v. Ogden, 1824* (New York, 1970); Stanley I. Kutler, *Privilege and Creative Destruction: The Charles River Bridge Case* (Philadelphia, 1971); and Francis N. Stites, *Private Interest and Public Gains: The Dartmouth College Case* (Amherst, 1972).

Internal Improvements

For the major role of government in the critical development of transportation facilities: Albert Fishlow, "Internal Transportation," in Lance Davis et al., *American Economic Growth: An Economist's History of the United States* (New York, 1972), 468–547; Carter Goodrich, *Government Promotion of American Canals and Railroads, 1800–1890* (New York, 1960); and Carter Goodrich, "Internal Improvements Reconsidered," *Journal of Economic History* 30 (June 1970): 289–311.

For particular developments: Carter Goodrich et al., *Canals and American Economic Development* (New York, 1961), 15–66; Forest G. Hill, *Roads, Rails & Waterways: The Army Engineers and Early Transportation* (Norman, 1957), 33–36; Harry H. Pierce, *The Railroads of New York: A Study of Government Aid, 1826–1875* (Cambridge, Mass., 1955); Julius Rubin, *Canal or Railroad? Imitation and Innovation in Response to the Erie Canal in Philadelphia, Boston, and Baltimore,* American Philosophical Society, *Transactions* 51, part 7 (Philadelphia, 1961): 15–62; Harry N. Scheiber, *The Ohio Canal Era: A Case Study of Government and the Economy, 1820–60* (Athens, Ohio, 1969); and Ronald E. Shaw, *Erie Water West: A History of the Erie Canal, 1792–1854* (Lexington, Ky., 1966).

Debtors and Creditors

Struggles over public enforcement of private debt, especially in the 1820s, are insufficiently understood. For what is known: Peter J. Coleman, *Debtors and Creditors in America: Insolvency, Imprisonment for Debt, and Bankruptcy, 1607–1900* (Madison, 1974); Samuel H. Rezneck, "The Depression of 1819–1822: A Social History," *American Historical Review* 39 (Oct. 1933): 28–47; Murray N. Rothbard, *The Panic of 1819: Reactions and Policies* (New York, 1962); Charles G. Sellers, Jr., "Banking and Politics in Jackson's Tennessee, 1817–1827," *Mississippi Valley Historical Review* 41 (June 1954): 61–84; and Arndt M. Stickles, *The Critical Court Struggle in Kentucky, 1819–1829* (Bloomington, Ind., 1929).

Corporations and Banking

The origins and development of private business corporations are delineated in E. Merrick Dodd, *American Business Corporations until 1860, with Special Reference to Massachusetts* (Cambridge, Mass., 1954); and Ronald E. Seavoy, *The Origins of the American Business Corporation, 1784–1855: The Concept of Public Service during Industrialization* (Westport, 1982).

The classic work on the rise of banking corporations, and controversies over them, is Bray Hammond, *Banks and Politics in America: From the Revolution to the Civil War* (Princeton, 1957). For state-chartered banks: J. Van Fenstermaker, *The Development of American Commercial Banking: 1782–1837* (Kent, Ohio, 1965); and Fritz Redlich, *The*

Molding of American Banking: Men and Ideas (2 vols., New York, 1947–1951). For the second national bank: Ralph C. H. Catterall, *The Second Bank of the United States* (Chicago, 1903); Thomas P. Govan, *Nicholas Biddle, Nationalist and Public Banker, 1786–1844* (Chicago, 1959); and Walter B. Smith, *Economic Aspects of the Second Bank of the United States* (Cambridge, Mass., 1953). For the Jacksonian controversies over banking, see the citations below under "Politics: The Jacksonian Regime."

Diplomacy

For the Treaty of Ghent and Anglo/American rapprochement: Samuel Flagg Bemis, *John Quincy Adams and the Foundations of American Foreign Policy* (New York, 1949); and Bradford Perkins, *Castlereagh and Adams: England and the United States 1812–1823* (Berkeley and Los Angeles, 1964).

Ernest R. May exaggerates political motives in the best account of *The Making of the Monroe Doctrine* (Cambridge, Mass., 1975).

David M. Pletcher has written the fullest if not the most insightful account of *The Diplomacy of Annexation: Texas, Oregon, and the Mexican War* (Columbia, Mo., 1973). See also: Norman A. Graebner, *Empire on the Pacific: A Study in American Continental Expansion* (New York, 1955); Frederick Merk, *Manifest Destiny and Mission in American History: A Reinterpretation* (New York, 1963); Frederick Merk, *The Oregon Question: Essays in Anglo-American Diplomacy and Politics* (Cambridge, Mass., 1967); George L. Rives, *The United States and Mexico, 1821–1848* (2 vols., New York, 1913); and Charles Sellers, *James K. Polk* (2 vols., Princeton, 1957–1966), II.

Politics

The political economy of capitalist development prevailed through a two-party political system, whose sources and dynamics are analyzed in: William H. Riker, *The Theory of Political Coalitions* (New Haven, 1962); and Charles Sellers, "The Equilibrium Cycle in Two-Party Politics," *Public Opinion Quarterly* 29 (Spring 1965): 16–38.

Most of our vast political historiography focuses narrowly on the abundant correspondence, newspapers, and legislative proceedings of politicians while slighting the constituent interests and classes to which they responded. Studies targeting constituency/issue relationships are badly needed, especially for such bellwethers of political change as New York and Pennsylvania.

Ambiguous Republicanism

For clashing attitudes toward democracy and developmentalism among Republicans of the first party system: Joyce Appleby, *Capitalism and a New Social Order: The Republican Vision of the 1790s* (New York, 1983); Richard Buel, Jr., *Securing the Revolution: Ideology in American Politics, 1789–1815* (Ithaca, 1972); Richard E. Ellis, *The Jeffersonian Crisis: Courts and Politics in the Young Republic* (New York, 1971); Paul Goodman, *The Democratic Republicans of Massachusetts: Politics in a Young Republic* (Cambridge, Mass., 1964); A. Whitney Griswold, *Farming and Democracy* (New York, 1948); Richard K. Matthews, *The Radical Politics of Thomas Jefferson* (Lawrence, Kans., 1985); Drew R. McCoy, *The Elusive Republic: Political Economy in Jeffersonian America* (Chapel Hill, 1980); John R. Nelson, Jr., *Liberty and Property: Political Economy and Policymaking in the New Nation, 1789–1812* (Baltimore, 1987); Kim T. Phillips, "William Duane, Philadelphia's Democratic Republicans, and the Origins of Modern Politics," *Pennsylvania Magazine of History and Biography* 101 (July 1977): 365–87; Steven Watts, *The Republic Reborn: War and the Making of Liberal America* (Baltimore, 1987); and Alfred F. Young, *The Democratic Republicans of New York: The Origins, 1763–1797* (Chapel Hill, 1967).

Political Realignment

Scholarship is uneven on the multiple sources of reaction against National Republicanism that produced a second party system. Excellent on the eruption of slavery controversy and its political consequences are Glover Moore, *The Missouri Controversy, 1819–1821* (Lexington, Ky. 1953); and Richard H. Brown, "The Missouri Crisis, Slavery, and the Politics of Jacksonianism," *South Atlantic Quarterly* 65 (Winter 1966): 55–72. The related resurgence of Jeffersonian antidevelopmentalism is less adequately treated in Norman K. Risjord, *The Old Republicans: Southern Conservatives in the Age of Jefferson* (New York, 1965).

Strangely neglected by historians is the rising democratic impulse visible in the extension of voting rights reported by Chilton Williamson, *American Suffrage: From Property to Democracy, 1760–1860* (Princeton, 1960); in the constitutional reforms reported by Fletcher M. Green, *Constitutional Development in the South Atlantic States, 1776–1860: A Study in the Evolution of Democracy* (Chapel Hill, 1930); and in the rising voter turnouts reported by J. R. Pole, *Political Representation in England and the Origins of the American Revolution* (Berkeley, 1971); Richard P. McCormick, "New Perspectives on Jacksonian Politics," *American Historical Review* 65 (Jan. 1960): 288–301; and Harvey Strum, "Property Qualifications and Voting Behavior in New York, 1807–1816," *Journal of the Early Republic* 1 (Winter 1981): 347–71. The first dramatic manifestation of the democratic impulse in national politics is described by C. Edward Skeen, "*Vox Populi, Vox Dei:* The Compensation Act of 1816 and the Rise of Popular Politics," *Journal of the Early Republic* 6 (Fall 1986): 253–74.

The high politics and diplomacy of the National Republican regime are splendidly narrated in George Dangerfield, *The Era of Good Feelings* (New York, 1952). For efforts by New York's Albany Regency and Virginia's Richmond Junto to link the democratic impulse with defense of slavery through a revival of two-party politics: Joseph H. Harrison, Jr., "Oligarchs and Democrats, The Richmond Junto," *Virginia Magazine of History and Biography* 78 (April 1970): 184–98; Richard Hofstadter, *The Idea of a Party System: The Rise of Legitimate Opposition in the United States, 1780–1840* (Berkeley, 1969); J. R. Pole, "Representation and Authority in Virginia from the Revolution to Reform," *Journal of Southern History* 24 (Feb. 1958): 16–50; Robert V. Remini, *Martin Van Buren and the Making of the Democratic Party* (New York, 1959); and Michael Wallace, "Changing Concepts of Party in the United States: New York, 1815–1828," *American Historical Review* 74 (Dec. 1968): 453–91.

Appropriation of this "Radical" political movement by popular enthusiasm for Andrew Jackson in the presidential elections of 1824 and 1828 is illuminated by Albert Ray Newsome, *The Presidential Election of 1824 in North Carolina* (Chapel Hill, 1939); Kim T. Phillips, "The Pennsylvania Origins of the Jackson Movement," *Political Science Quarterly* 91 (Fall 1976): 489–508; Robert V. Remini, *The Election of Andrew Jackson* (Philadelphia, 1963); and Charles Sellers, "Jackson Men with Feet of Clay," *American Historical Review* 62 (April 1957): 537–51.

The Jacksonian Regime

Jacksonian politics has been the bugbear of academic historians, whose rawest nerve was touched by Arthur M. Schlesinger, Jr., *The Age of Jackson* (Boston, 1946). Discovering a class politics of hard money, Schlesinger described the Jackson movement as a labor/farmer coalition against an oppressive "business community." Roundly crying him down, a generation of scholarship labored for an alternative interpretation consistent with the mythology of consensual capitalist enterprise. Richard Hofstadter focused on politicians rather than voters to proclaim the Jacksonians "expectant capitalists" in *The American Political Tradition and the Men Who Made It* (New York, 1948). Forced into greater complexity by discovery of the Jacksonians' antientrepreneurial rhetoric, Marvin Meyers in *The Jacksonian Persuasion: Politics and Belief* (Stanford, Calif., 1957) ingeniously declared it a way of appeasing precapitalist conscience (by destroying the national bank) while satisfying capitalist appetite (by unleashing state banks). Richard P. McCormick, *The Second American Party System: Party Formation in the Jacksonian Era* (Chapel Hill, 1966), while greatly illuminating the importance of party structure, seemed to divorce constituency from policy. Lee Benson, *The Concept of Jacksonian Democracy: New York as a Test Case* (Princeton, 1961), pioneered multivariate analysis of voters to emphasize ethnocultural influence on voting. Ronald P. Formisano reached similar conclusions about *The Birth of Mass Political Parties: Michigan, 1827–1861* (Princeton, 1971) and related ethnocultural factors to *The Transformation of Political Culture: Massachusetts Parties, 1790s–1840s* (New York, 1983).

Although each of these interpretations illuminated an aspect of the Jacksonian reality, they could not account for the popular invasion and transformation of politics. A real contest between elites and nonelites is being found by other scholars: John Ashworth, *'Agrarians' & 'Aristocrats': Party Ideology in the United States, 1837–1846* (London, 1983); Donald J. Ratcliffe, "Politics in Jacksonian Ohio: Reflections on the Ethnocultural Interpretation," *Ohio History* 88 (Winter 1979): 5–36; J. Mills Thornton, *Politics and Power in a Slave Society: Alabama, 1800–1860* (Baton Rouge, 1978); Harry L. Watson, Jr., *Jacksonian Politics and Community Conflict: The Emergence of the Second Party System in Cumberland County, North Carolina* (Baton Rouge, 1981); and Harry L. Watson, *Liberty and Power: The Politics of Jacksonian America* (New York 1990). Schlesinger may yet be judged more nearly right than his critics.

Richard B. Latner provides the best internal account of *The Presidency of Andrew Jackson: White House Politics, 1829–1837* (Athens, Ga., 1979). For the nullification controversy: Richard E. Ellis, *The Union at Risk: Jacksonian Democracy, States' Rights, and the Nullification Crisis* (New York, 1987); and William W. Freehling, *Prelude to Civil War: The Nullification Controversy in South Carolina, 1816–1836* (New York, 1965).

The most useful studies of the Bank War include Frank O. Gatell, "Sober Second Thoughts on Van Buren, the Albany Regency, and the Wall Street Conspiracy," *Journal of American History* 53 (June 1966): 19–40; Herbert Ershkowitz and William G. Shade, "Consensus or Conflict? Political Behavior in the State Legislatures during the Jacksonian Era," *Journal of American History* 58 (Dec. 1971): 591–621; John M. McFaul, *The Politics of Jacksonian Finance* (Ithaca, 1972); Harry N. Scheiber, "The Pet Banks in Jacksonian Politics and Finance, 1833–1841," *Journal of Economic History* 23 (June 1963): 196–214; William G. Shade, *Banks or No Banks: The Money Issue in Western Politics, 1832–1865* (Detroit, 1972); James Roger Sharp, *The Jacksonians versus the Banks: Politics in the States after the Panic of 1837* (New York, 1970); Peter Temin, *The Jacksonian Economy* (New York, 1969); and Jean Alexander Wilburn, *Biddle's Bank: The Crucial Years* (New York, 1967).

Parties and Elections

For the Antimasonic party: Paul Goodman, *Towards a Christian Republic: Antimasonry and the Great Transition in New England, 1826–1836* (New York, 1988); and William

Preston Vaughn, *The Antimasonic Party in the United States, 1826–1842* (Lexington, Ky., 1982). For the Whig party: Daniel Walker Howe, *The Political Culture of the American Whigs* (Chicago, 1980); and Charles Sellers, "Who Were the Southern Whigs?" *American Historical Review* 54 (Jan. 1954): 335–46.

For elections: Richard P. McCormick, *The Presidential Game: The Origins of American Presidential Politics* (New York, 1982); Richard P. McCormick, "Was There a 'Whig Strategy' in 1836?" *Journal of the Early Republic* 4 (Spring 1984): 47–70; and Michael F. Holt, "The Election of 1840, Voter Mobilization, and the Emergence of the Second American Party System: A Reappraisal of Jacksonian Voting Behavior," in William J. Cooper, Jr., et al., eds., *A Master's Due: Essays in Honor of David Herbert Donald* (Baton Rouge, 1985), 16–58.

Expansionism and Sectionalism

For expansionism: Ray Allen Billington, *Westward Expansion: A History of the American Frontier* (3rd ed., New York, 1967); and the citations above under "Political Economy: Diplomacy." The best sources for the Tyler and Polk administrations are biographies: Robert Seagar II, *And Tyler Too: A Biography of John & Julia Gardiner Tyler* (New York, 1963); and Charles Sellers, *James K. Polk* (2 vols., Princeton, 1957–1966), II. Important for the politics of the 1840s is George R. Poage, *Henry Clay and the Whig Party* (Chapel Hill, 1936). Eric Foner, "The Wilmot Proviso Revisited," *Journal of American History* 56 (Sept. 1969): 262–79, is definitive.

Political Biography

Charles M. Wiltse, *John C. Calhoun* (3 vols., Indianapolis, 1944–1951), is among the richest sources for the inner high politics of the whole period; but its partisanship for its subject should be tempered by Gerald M. Capers, *John C. Calhoun, Opportunist: A Reappraisal* (Gainesville, Fla., 1960). Important for the National Republican regime are Harry Ammon, *James Monroe: The Quest for National Identity* (New York, 1971); Samuel Flagg Bemis, *John Quincy Adams and the Union* (New York, 1956); and Raymond Walters, Jr., *Alexander James Dallas: Lawyer-Politician-Financier, 1759–1817* (Philadelphia, 1943).

Three biographies of Jackson merit mention: Robert V. Remini, *Andrew Jackson* (3 vols., New York, 1977–1984), the most detailed, breaks new ground on his importance for Indian expropriation after the War of 1812 but is not perceptive about politics; Marquis James, *The Life of Andrew Jackson* (Indianapolis, 1938), is fascinatingly informative about his character; and James C. Curtis, *Andrew Jackson and the Search for Vindication* (Boston, 1976), is concisely insightful about the sources of his personality.

Other biographies that particularly illuminate the political process include Maurice G. Baxter, *One and Indivisible: Daniel Webster and the Union* (Cambridge, Mass., 1984); William N. Chambers, *Old Bullion Benton, Senator from the New West: Thomas Hart Benton, 1782–1858* (Boston, 1956); John A. Garraty, *Silas Wright* (New York, 1949); John Niven, *Martin Van Buren: The Romantic Age of American Politics* (New York, 1983); and Merrill D. Peterson, *The Great Triumvirate: Webster, Clay, and Calhoun* (New York, 1987).

Society

The social dimension of market revolution is elucidated from one perspective by Eli Zaretsky, *Capitalism, the Family, and Personal Life* (New York, 1976), and from another by

Richard D. Brown, *Modernization: The Transformation of American Life, 1600–1865* (New York, 1976).

Family

For the family as crucible of transformation: Philip Greven, *The Protestant Temperament: Patterns of Child-Rearing, Religious Experience, and the Self in Early America* (New York, 1977); and Mary P. Ryan, *Cradle of the Middle Class: The Family in Oneida County, New York, 1790–1865* (Cambridge, England, 1981). For a critical dimension of family change: Toby L. Ditz, *Property and Kinship: Inheritance in Early Connecticut, 1750–1820* (Princeton, 1986); and Carole Shammas, Marylynn Salmon, and Michael Dahlen, *Inheritance in America: From Colonial Times to the Present* (New Brunswick, 1987). For child-rearing and youth: Philip Greven, Jr., *Child-Rearing Concepts, 1628–1861* (Ithaca, 1973); Oscar and Mary F. Handlin, *Facing Life: Youth and the Family in American History* (Boston, 1971); and Joseph F. Kett, *Rites of Passage: Adolescence in America, 1790 to the Present* (New York, 1977).

Gender and Sexuality

A generation of enriching feminist scholarship points to gender and sexuality as fundamental loci of historical change. The dynamic interplay of market discipline, sexual repression, and male domination is explored with pioneering insight and exaggeration by G. J. Barker-Benfield, *The Horrors of the Half-Known Life: Male Attitudes toward Women and Sexuality in Nineteenth-Century America* (New York, 1976). For an emerging scholarship on bourgeois/middle-class manhood: David G. Pugh, *Sons of Liberty: The Masculine Mind in Nineteenth-Century America* (Westport, 1983); and E. Anthony Rotundo, "Body and Soul: Changing Ideals of American Middle-Class Manhood, 1770–1920," *Journal of Social History* 16 (Summer 1983): 23–38.

Scholarship on female gender roles is extensive. For bourgeois/middle-class orthodoxy: Carroll Smith-Rosenberg and Charles Rosenberg, "The Female Animal: Medical and Biological Views of Woman and Her Role in Nineteenth-Century America," *Journal of American History* 60 (Sept. 1973): 332–56; and Barbara Welter, "The Cult of True Womanhood," *American Quarterly* 18 (Summer 1966): 151–74. For a more complacent view of middle-class femininity: Carl W. Degler, *At Odds: Women and the Family in America from the Revolution to the Present* (New York, 1980). For the sexual politics of female autonomy and power within "separate spheres": Barbara J. Berg, *The Remembered Gate: Origins of American Feminism: The Woman and the City, 1800–1860* (New York, 1978); Nancy F. Cott, *The Bonds of Womanhood: Woman's Sphere in New England, 1780–1835* (New Haven, 1977); Barbara Epstein, *The Politics of Domesticity: Women, Evangelism, and Temperance in Nineteenth-Century America* (Middletown, Conn., 1981); Carroll Smith-Rosenberg, *Disorderly Conduct: Visions of Gender in Victorian America* (New York, 1985); and Carroll Smith-Rosenberg, *Religion and the Rise of the American City: The New York City Mission Movement, 1812–1870* (Ithaca, 1971).

The patriarchy of traditional rural culture is strikingly delineated in John Mack Faragher, *Women and Men on the Overland Trail* (New Haven, 1979). For aspects of bourgeois/middle-class male domination: Barker-Benfield, cited above; Catherine M. Scholten, *Childbearing in American Society, 1650–1850* (New York, 1987); and James C. Mohr, *Abortion in America: The Origins and Evolution of National Policy* (New York, 1978).

For the bourgeois/middle-class ideology of sexual repression: Nancy F. Cott, "Passionless: An Interpretation of Victorian Sexual Ideology, 1790–1850," *Signs* 4 (Winter 1978): 219–36; Stephen Nissenbaum, *Sex, Diet, and Debility in Jacksonian America: Sylvester Gra-*

ham and Health Reform (Westport, 1980); Gail Pat Parsons, "Equal Treatment for All: American Medical Remedies for Male Sexual Problems, 1850–1900," *Journal of the History of Medicine and Allied Sciences* 32 (Jan. 1977): 55–71; Carroll Smith-Rosenberg, "Sex As Symbol in Victorian Purity: An Ethnohistorical Analysis of Jacksonian America," *American Journal of Sociology* 84, Supplement (1984): S212–47; and Jayme A. Sokolow, *Eros and Modernization: Sylvester Graham, Health Reform, and the Origins of Victorian Sexuality in America* (Rutherford, 1983).

Sexual behavior is dealt with cautiously in the pioneering survey, John D'Emilio and Estelle B. Freedman, *Intimate Matters: A History of Sexuality in America* (New York, 1988). Carl Degler, "What Ought to and What Was: Women's Sexuality in the 19th Century," *American Historical Review* 79 (Dec. 1974): 1467–901, argues that sexual repression has been exaggerated; and a contrary view is taken in Carol Z. Stearns and Peter N. Stearns, "Victorian Sexuality: Can Historians Do It Better?" *Journal of Social History* 18 (Spring 1985): 623–33.

The historical study of American homosexuality is opened in Martin Bauml Duberman, *About Time: Exploring the Gay Past* (New York, 1986). For sexual radicals: John C. Spurlock, *Free Love: Marriage and Middle-Class Radicalism in America, 1825–1860* (New York, 1988). For urban prostitution: Marcia Carlisle, "Disorderly City, Disorderly Women: Prostitution in Ante-Bellum Philadelphia," *Pennsylvania Magazine of History and Biography* 110 (Oct. 1986): 549–68; and two articles by Timothy J. Gilfoyle: "Strumpets and Mysogynists: Brothel 'Riots' and the Transformation of Prostitution in Antebellum New York City," *New York History* 68 (Jan. 1987): 45–65; and "The Urban Geography of Commercial Sex: Prostitution in New York City, 1790–1860," *Journal of Urban History* 13 (Aug. 1987): 371–93.

Demography

An extensive literature ascribing declining fertility to land scarcity is summarized in two works by Robert V. Wells: *Revolutions in Americans' Lives: A Demographic Perspective on the History of Americans, Their Families, and Their Society* (Westport, 1982); and *Uncle Sam's Family: Issues and Perspectives in American Demographic History* (Albany, 1985). For the increasing influence of urban/industrial culture on fertility: Maris A. Vinovskis, *Fertility in Massachusetts from the Revolution to the Civil War* (New York, 1981).

For the impressive geographical mobility of antebellum Americans: Peter D. McClelland and Richard J. Zeckhauser, *Demographic Dimensions of the New Rupublic: American Interregional Migration, Vital Statistics, and Manumissions, 1800–1860* (Cambridge, England, 1982); and Stephan Thernstrom and Peter R. Knights, "Men in Motion: Some Data and Speculations about Urban Population Mobility in Nineteenth-Century America," *Journal of Interdisciplinary History* 1 (Autumn 1970): 7–35.

Class

Sharply widening disparities of wealth in antebellum America are demonstrated by Edward Pessen, *Riches, Class, and Power before the Civil War* (Lexington, Mass., 1973); and Jeffrey G. Williamson and Peter H. Lindert, *American Inequality: A Macroeconomic History* (New York, 1980). Yet except for historians of labor, most scholars have ignored or denied the importance of class. Similarly the mythology of extensive opportunity and upward mobility continues to be asserted on faith, although contradicted by the most careful empirical study: Stuart M. Blumin, "Mobility and Change in Ante-Bellum Philadelphia," in Stephan Thernstrom and Richard Sennett, eds., *Nineteenth-Century Cities: Essays in the New Urban History* (New Haven, 1969), 165–208.

Even Blumin mystifies "middle class" as a category of structure rather than consciousness in his otherwise illuminating study of *The Emergence of the Middle Class: Social Experience in the American City, 1760–1900* (Cambridge, England, 1989). Two studies of elites, however, are sensitive to the class dynamics of power: Peter Dobkin Hall, *The Organization of American Culture, 1700–1900: Private Institutions, Elites, and the Origins of American Nationality* (New York, 1982); and Ronald Story, *The Forging of an Aristocracy: Harvard and the Boston Upper Class, 1800–1870* (Middletown, Conn., 1980).

Ethnicity

Ethnic conflict displaces class conflict in liberal historiography. For ethnic immigration: Robert Ernst, *Immigrant Life in New York City, 1825–1863* (New York, 1949); Oscar Handlin, *Boston's Immigrants 1790–1865: A Study in Acculturation* (Cambridge, Mass., 1941); and Kerby A. Miller, *Emigrants and Exiles: Ireland and the Irish Exodus to North America* (New York, 1985), 193–279. For nativism and anti-Catholicism: Ray Allen Billington, *The Protestant Crusade: A Study of the Origins of American Nativism* (New York, 1938); David Knobel, *Paddy and the Republic: Ethnicity and Nationality in Antebellum America* (Middletown, Conn., 1986); David Montgomery, "The Shuttle and the Cross: Weavers and Artisans in the Kensington Riots of 1844," *Journal of Social History* 5 (Summer 1972): 411–46; and Louis D. Scisco, *Political Nativism in New York State* (New York, 1901).

For the group most vulnerable to ethnic conflict: Ira Berlin, *Slaves without Masters: The Free Negro in the Antebellum South* (New York); and Leon F. Litwack, *North of Slavery: The Negro in the Free States, 1790–1860* (Chicago, 1961). For white racism: Jean H. Baker, *Affairs of Party: The Political Culture of Northern Democrats in the Mid-Nineteenth Century* (Ithaca, 1983); Eugene H. Berwanger, *The Frontier against Slavery: Western Anti-Negro Prejudice and the Slavery Extension Controversy* (Urbana, 1967); George M. Fredrickson, *The Black Image in the White Mind: The Debate on Afro-American Character and Destiny, 1817–1914* (New York, 1971); Reginald Horsman, *Race and Manifest Destiny: The Origins of American Racial Anglo-Saxonism* (Cambridge, Mass. 1981); Alexander Saxton, "Blackface Minstrelsy and Jacksonian Ideology," *American Quarterly* 27 (Mar. 1975): 3–28; William Stanton, *The Leopard's Spots: Scientific Attitudes toward Race in America, 1815–59* (Chicago, 1960); and Ronald Takaki, *Iron Cages: Race and Culture in Nineteenth-Century America* (New York, 1979).

Disorder and Police

For the crescendo of class/ethnic conflict in the 1830s: Michael Feldberg, *The Turbulent Era: Riot and Disorder in Jacksonian America* (New York, 1980); Paul A. Gilje, *The Road to Mobocracy: Popular Disorder in New York City, 1763–1834* (Chapel Hill, 1987); David Grimsted, "Rioting in Its Jacksonian Setting," *American Historical Review* 37 (Apr. 1972): 361–97; and Leonard L. Richards, *"Gentlemen of Property and Standing": Anti-Abolition Mobs in Jacksonian America* (New York, 1970).

Peaking class conflict inspired a campaign for bourgeois control of the streets through professional police forces, which is described with little sensitivity to class forces by David R. Johnson, *Policing the Urban Underworld: The Impact of Crime on the Development of the American Police, 1800–1887* (Philadelphia, 1979); Roger Lane, *Policing the City: Boston 1822–1885* (Cambridge, Mass., 1967); and James F. Richardson, *The New York Police: Colonial Times to 1901* (New York, 1970).

Culture

Pervasive and boundless optimism has been inferred from genteel sources by most historians of antebellum religion, literature, the arts, education, and reform. Millennial enthusiasm for economic/technological progress is reported, for example, by John F. Kasson, *Civilizing the Machine: Technology and Republican Values in America, 1776–1900* (New York, 1976). Suggesting a more complex cultural situation, however, is the mood of pious resignation found in the diaries and letters of ordinary folk by Lewis O. Saum, *The Popular Mood of Pre-Civil War America* (Westport, 1980).

Some scholars are beginning to understand culture as the medium through which people managed the wrenching transformation of personality, values, and behavior required by market revolution, particularly Michael T. Gilmore, *American Romanticism and the Marketplace* (Chicago, 1985); Donald G. Mathews, "The Second Great Awakening as an Organizing Process, 1780–1830: An Hypothesis," *American Quarterly* 21 (Spring 1969): 23–43; William G. McLoughlin, *Revivals, Awakenings, and Reform: An Essay on Religion and Social Change in America, 1607–1977* (Chicago, 1978); and George H. Thomas, *Revivalism and Cultural Change: Christianity, Nation Building, and the Market in the Nineteenth-Century United States* (Chicago, 1989).

Only a few scholars, however, have sufficiently transcended our historical mythology to recognize culture as a major, if not decisive, arena of class struggle and hegemony. See especially: Paul E. Johnson, *A Shopkeeper's Millennium: Society and Revivals in Rochester, New York, 1815–1817* (New York, 1978); Peter Dobkin Hall and Ronald Story as cited above under "Society: Class"; and Charles I. Foster and Clifford S. Griffin as cited below under "'Reform.'"

Religion

The most comprehensive survey is Sydney E. Ahlstrom, *A Religious History of the American People* (New Haven, 1972). For the arminian strain that eventuated in Unitarianism: Conrad Wright, *The Beginnings of Unitarianism in America* (Boston, 1955).

The magical substratum of the antinomian strain is delineated by Jon Butler, *Awash in a Sea of Faith: Christianizing the American People* (Cambridge, Mass., 1990); and Alan Taylor, "The Early Republic's Supernatural Economy: Treasure Seeking in the American Northeast, 1780–1830," *American Quarterly* 38 (Spring 1986): 6–34. For antinomian revivalism and the popular denominations: Terry D. Bilhartz, *Urban Religion and the Second Great Awakening: Church and Society in Early National Baltimore* (Rutherford, N.J., 1986); John B. Boles, *The Great Revival, 1787–1805: The Origins of the Southern Evangelical Mind* (Lexington, KY., 1972); Dickson D. Bruce, Jr., *And They All Sang Hallelujah: Plain-Folk Camp-Meeting Religion, 1800–1845* (Knoxville, 1974); Richard Carwardine, "The Second Great Awakening in the Urban Centers: An Examination of Methodism and the 'New Measures,'" *Journal of American History* 59 (Sept. 1972): 327–40; Richard Carwardine, *Transatlantic Revivalism: Popular Evangelicalism in Britain and America, 1790–1865* (Westport, 1978); Nathan O. Hatch, *The Democratization of American Christianity* (New Haven, 1989); Stephen A. Marini, *Radical Sects of Revolutionary New England* (Cambridge, Mass., 1982); and Donald G. Mathews, *Religion in the Old South* (Chicago, 1977).

The theological roots of Moderate-Light compromise are traced in Joseph Haroutunian, *Piety versus Moralism: The Passing of the New England Theology* (New York, 1932). A pivotal figure is treated insightfully by Joseph A. Conforti, *Samuel Hopkins and the New Divinity Movement: Calvinism, the Congregational Ministry, and Reform in New England between the Great Awakenings* (Grand Rapids, 1981). For the conservatizing and arminianizing of the Moderate Light: Charles R. Keller, *The Second Great Awakening in Connecticut* (New Haven, 1942); George W. Marsden, *The Evangelical Mind and the New School Presbyterian Experience* (New Haven, 1970); and Sidney E. Mead, *Nathaniel William Taylor, 1786–1853: A Connecticut Liberal* (Chicago, 1942). The best treatment of Finney is William G. McLoughlin, *Modern Revivalism: Charles Grandison Finney to Billy Graham* (New York 1959); while the fullest biography is Keith J. Hardman, *Charles Grandison Finney, 1792–1875: Revivalist and Reformer* (Syracuse, 1987).

For Mormonism: Fawn M. Brodie, *No Man Knows My Name: The Life of Joseph Smith, the Mormon Prophet* (rev. ed., New York, 1982); Richard L. Bushman, *Joseph Smith and the Beginnings of Mormonism* (Urbana, 1984); Mario S. DePillis, "The Quest for Religious Authority and the Rise of Mormonism," *Dialogue* 1 (Spring 1966): 68–88; J. Klaus Hansen, *Mormonism and the American Experience* (Chicago, 1981); and Jan Shipps, *Mormonism: The Story of a New Religious Tradition* (Urbana, 1985).

For the romanticizing of mainline Protestantism: Barbara M. Cross, *Horace Bushnell: Minister to a Changing America* (Chicago, 1958); Ann Douglas, *The Feminization of American Culture* (New York, 1977); William G. McLoughlin, *The Meaning of Henry Ward Beecher: An Essay on the Shifting Values of Mid-Victorian America* (New York, 1970); and Sandra S. Sizer, *Gospel Hymns and Social Religions: The Rhetoric of Nineteenth-Century Revivalism* (Philadelphia, 1978).

Literacy and Education

For scholars' less than definitive findings about early American literacy: William J. Gilmore, *Reading Becomes a Necessity of Life: Material and Cultural Life in Rural New England, 1780–1835* (Knoxville, 1989); William T. Gilmore, "Elementary Literacy on the Eve of the Industrial Revolution: Trends in Rural New England, 1760–1830," American Antiquarian Society, *Proceedings* 92 (1982): 87–171; Kenneth A. Lockridge, *Literacy in Colonial New England: An Enquiry into the Social Context of Literacy in the Early Modern West* (New York, 1974); and Lee Soltow and Edward Stevens, *The Rise of Literacy and the Common School in the United States: A Socioeconomic Analysis to 1870* (Chicago, 1981). For the striking advance in numerical literacy: Patricia Cline Cohen, *A Calculating People: The Spread of Numeracy in Early America* (Chicago, 1982).

Education is surveyed with admirable breadth in Lawrence A. Cremin, *American Education: The National Experience, 1783–1876* (New York, 1980). For the rise in schooling, both before and during the common-school campaign: Albert Fishlow, "The American Common School Revival: Fact or Fancy?" in Henry Rosovsky, ed., *Industrialization in Two Systems: Essays in Honor of Alexander Gerschenkron* (New York, 1966), 40–67; Carl F. Kaestle, *The Evolution of an Urban School System: New York City, 1750–1850* (Cambridge, Mass., 1973); Carl F. Kaestle, *Pillars of the Republic: Common Schools and American Society, 1780–1860* (New York, 1983); Carl F. Kaestle and Maris A. Vinovskis, *Education and Social Change in Nineteenth-Century Massachusetts* (Cambridge, England, 1980); and Stanley K. Schultz, *The Culture Factory: Boston Public Schools, 1789–1860* (New York, 1973).

Print Media

For the rising flood of print and its impact: David D. Hall and John B. Hench, eds., *Needs and Opportunities in the History of the Book* (Worcester, 1987); David Jaffee, "The Village Enlightenment in New England, 1760–1820," *William and Mary Quarterly* 47 (July 1990): 327–46; Frank L. Mott, *Golden Multitudes: The Story of Best Sellers in the United States* (New York, 1947); Frank L. Mott, *A History of American Journalism* (4 vols., New

York and Cambridge, Mass., 1930–1957)d David Paul Nord, "The Evangelical Origins of Mass Media in America, 1815–1835," *Journalism Monographs* 84 (1984). For the penny press: Alexander Saxton, "Problems of Class and Race in the Origins of the Mass Circulation Press," *American Quarterly* 36 (Summer 1984): 211–34; and Dan Schiller, *Objectivity and the News: The Public and the Rise of Commercial Journalism* (Philadelphia, 1981).

Bourgeois/Middle-Class Culture

The romantic quest for feeling and interpersonal authenticity is skillfully elucidated from bourgeois social ritual by Karen Halttunen, *Confidence Men and Painted Women: A Study of Middle-class Culture in America, 1830–1870* (New Haven, 1982).

Indicative of the extensive scholarship on the romantic fusion of sentimentality, nature, and middle-class morality in literature and the arts are David Grimsted, *Melodrama Unveiled: American Theater and Culture, 1800–1850* (Chicago, 1968); James Early, *Romanticism and American Architecture* (New York, 1965); Barbara Novak, *Nature and Culture:American Landscape and Painting, 1825–1875* (New York, 1980); Henry Nash Smith, *Virgin Land: The American West as Symbol and Myth* (Cambridge, Mass., 1950); and John William Ward, "The Politics of Design," *Massachusetts Review* 6 (Autumn 1965): 661–88. For the sentimentality and covert feminism of women's fiction: Nina Baym, *Woman's Fiction: A Guide to Novels by and about Women in America, 1820–1870* (Ithaca, 1978); and Mary Kelley, *Private Woman, Public Stage: Literary Domesticity in Nineteenth-Century America* (New York, 1984).

For transcendentalism's roots in Edwardean antinomianism: Perry Miller, "From Edwards to Emerson," in *Errand into the Wilderness* (Cambridge, Mass., 1956), 184–203. For Emerson's artistic achievement: F. O. Mathiessen, *American Rennaissance: Art and Expression in the Age of Emerson and Whitman* (New York, 1941). For his roots in Boston Federalism and accommodation to a bourgeois/middle-class audience: Mary Kupiec Cayton, *Emerson's Emergence: Self and Society in the Transformation of New England, 1800–1845* (Chapel Hill, 1989); and Mary Kupiec Cayton, "The Making of an American Prophet: Emerson, His Audiences, and the Rise of the Culture Industry in Nineteenth-Century America," *American Historical Review* 92 (June 1987): 597–620.

Plebeian Culture

For the class animus and masculine assertiveness of plebeian manners: Susan G. Davis, *Parades and Power: Street Theatre in Nineteenth-Century Philadelphia* (Philadelphia, 1986); Elliott J. Gorn, *The Manly Art: Bare-Knuckle Prize Fighting in America* (Ithaca, 1989); Alexander Saxton as cited under "Culture: Print Media"; and Richard B. Stott as cited under "The Market:Labor." For discovery of the rich subliterature expressing plebeian values: David S. Reynolds, *Beneath the American Renaissance: The Subversive Imagination in the Age of Emerson and Melville* (New York, 1988); and Larzer Ziff, *Literary Democracy: The Declaration of Cultural Independence in America* (New York, 1981).

"Reform"

Academic historians have emphasized the humanitarian professions of the Benevolent Empire while discounting its main thrust of capitalist discipline and bourgeois hegemony, as revealed by Charles I. Foster, *An Errand of Mercy: The Evangelical United Front, 1790–1837* (Chapel Hill, 1960); Clifford S. Griffin, *Their Brothers' Keepers: Moral Stewardship in the United States, 1800–1865* (New Brunswick, 1960); and David J. Rothman, *The Discovery of the Asylum: Social Order and Disorder in the New Republic* (Boston, 1971). The appeal of this kind of reform for the middle classes is illuminated by Paul Boyer, *Urban Masses and Moral Order in America, 1820–1920* (Cambridge, Mass., 1978); and for the bourgeoisie by Thomas L. Haskell, "Capitalism and the Origins of the Humanitarian Sensibility," *American Historical Review* 90 (Apr., June 1985): 339–61, 547–66.

For the crusade to repress rising alcoholism that epitomized benevolent reform: Joel C. Bernard, "From Theodicy to Ideology: The Origins of the American Temperance Movement" (Ph.D. dissertation, Yale University, 1983); W. J. Rorabaugh, *The Alcoholic Republic: An American Tradition* (New York, 1979); and Ian R. Tyrrell, *Sobering Up: From Temperance to Prohibition in Antebellum America, 1800–1860* (Westport, 1979). Badly needed is a study of the Washingtonian movement that elucidates the working-class response suggested by Ruth M. Alexander, " 'We are Engaged as a Band of Sisters': Class and Domesticity in the Washingtonian Temperance Movement, 1840–1850," *Journal of American History* 75 (Dec. 1988): 763–85.

A superb overview of humanitarian abolitionism and its rejection by most of the benevolent movement is James Brewer Stewart, *Holy Warriors: The Abolitionists and American Slavery* (New York, 1976). Arthur Zilversmit describes *The First Emancipation: The Abolition of Slavery in the North* (Chicago, 1967); and this movement's appeal for the most intensely benevolent businessmen is explained by David Brion Davis, *The Problem of Slavery in the Age of Revolution, 1770–1823* (Ithaca, 1975).

The evangelical mainstream of immediate abolitionism in the 1830s and 1840s is described by Robert H. Abzug, *Passionate Liberator: Theodore Dwight Weld and the Dilemma of Reform* (New York, 1981); Gilbert H. Barnes, *The Anti-Slavery Impulse, 1830–1844* (New York, 1933); and Bertram Wyatt-Brown, *Lewis Tappan and the Evangelical War against Slavery* (Cleveland, 1969). For the special contribution of William Lloyd Garrison and his disciples: Aileen S. Kraditor, *Means and Ends in American Abolitionism: Garrison and His Critics on Strategy and Tactics* (New York, 1967). The class dynamics of Garrison's abolitionism are slighted in two biographies that richly illuminate his career: Walter M. Merrill, *Against Wind and Tide: A Biography of Wm. Lloyd Garrison* (Cambridge, Mass., 1963); and John L. Thomas, *The Liberator: A Biography of William Lloyd Garrison* (Boston, 1963).

Abolitionism's relationship to capitalist transformation is addressed by Ronald G. Walters, *The Antislavery Appeal: American Abolitionism after 1830* (New York, 1978). For its impact on the churches: Donald G. Mathews, *Slavery and Methodism: A Chapter in American Morality, 1780–1845* (Princeton, 1965); and John R. McKivigan, *The War against Proslavery Religion: Abolitionism and the Northern Churches, 1830–1865* (Ithaca, 1984). The role of blacks in the movement is inadequately treated by Benjamin Quarles, *Black Abolitionists* (New York, 1969); and Jane H. Pease and William H. Pease, *They Who Would Be Free: Blacks' Search for Freedom, 1830–1861* (New York, 1974). For working-class abolitionism: Edward Magdol, *The Antislavery Rank and File: A Social Profile of the Abolitionists' Constituency* (Westport, 1986). For the move into antislavery politics: Richard H. Sewell, *Ballots for Freedom: Antislavery Politics in the United States, 1837–1860* (New York, 1976).

Emergence of the women's rights movement from abolitionism is treated in Ellen Carol DuBois, *Feminism and Suffrage: The Emergence of an Independent Women's Movement in America, 1848–1869* (Ithaca, 1978); Blanche Glassman Hersh, *The Slavery of Sex: Feminist-Abolitionists in America* (Champaign, 1978); Katherine Du Pre Lumpkin, *The Emancipation of Angelina Grimké* (Chapel Hill, 1974); Keith E. Melder, *Beginnings of Sisterhood: The American Woman's Rights Movement* (New York, 1977); and Jean Fagan Yellin, *Women and Sisters: Antislavery Feminists in American Culture* (New Haven, 1990).

Notes

Chapter 1. Land and Market

1. Marshall Sahlins, *Stone Age Economics* (Chicago, 1972), especially 41–99, 185–230; Wilcomb E. Washburn, *The Indian in America* (New York, 1975), 11–65; Francis Jennings, *The Invasion of America: Indians, Colonialism, and the Cant of Conquest* (Chapel Hill, 1975), especially 58–73.

2. Jedidiah Morse, *A Report to the Secretary of War of the United States, on Indian Affairs*... (New Haven, 1822), 375.

3. James H. Merrell, "The Indians' New World: The Catawba Experience," *William and Mary Quarterly* 41 (Oct. 1984): 537–65, quotation 543.

4. Calvin Martin, *Keepers of the Game: Indian-Animal Relationships and the Fur Trade* (Berkeley, 1978); Shepard Krech III, ed., *Indians, Animals, and the Fur Trade: A Critique of Keepers of the Game* (Athens, Ga., 1981); Harold Hickerson, "Fur Trade Colonialism and the North American Indians," *Journal of Ethnic Studies* I (1973): 15–44.

5. James Axtell, *The European and the Indian: Essays in the Ethnohistory of Colonial North America* (New York, 1981), quotations 161, 166, 206.

6. Peter A. Thomas, "Contrastive Subsistence Strategies and Land Use as Factors for Understanding Indian-White Relations in New England," *Ethnohistory* 23 (Winter 1976): 1–18.

7. Charles S. Watson, "Jeffersonian Republicanism in William Ioor's *Independence,* the First Play of South Carolina," *South Carolina Historical Magazine* 69 (July 1968): 194–203; Bertram Wyatt-Brown, *Southern Honor: Ethics and Behavior in the Old South* (New York, 1982).

8. T. H. Breen, *Puritans and Adventurers: Change and Persistence in Early America* (New York, 1980); Forrest McDonald and Grady McWhiney, "The Antebellum Southern Herdsman: A Reinterpretation," *Journal of Southern History* 41 (1975): 156–58; Steven Hahn, "Hunting, Fishing, and Foraging: Common Rights and Class Relations in the Postbellum South," *Radical History Review* 26 (1982): 37–64, especially 38–43.

9. John Mack Faragher, *Women and Men on the Overland Trail* (New Haven, 1979), passim for patriarchy, quotation 155.

10. Robert E. Gallman, "The Agricultural Sector and the Pace of Economic Growth: U.S. Experience in the Nineteenth Century," in David C. Klingman and Richard K. Vedder, eds., *Essays in Nineteenth Century Economic History: The Old Northwest* (Athens, Ohio, 1975), 35–76.

11. The pathbreaking analysis of the subsistence farming family is James A. Henretta, "Families and Farms: *Mentalite* in Pre-Industrial America," *William and Mary Quarterly* 25 (Jan. 1978): 3–32. Other studies illuminating early American demography and family history are indicated in the bibliographical essay.

12. James Haines, "Social Life and Scenes in the Early Settlement of Central Illinois," *Transactions of the Illinois State Historical Society for the Year 1905* (Springfield, Ill., 1906), 39–40; William Cooper Howells, *Recollections of Life in Ohio, from 1813 to 1849* (Cincinnati, 1895), 146.

13. Haines, "Social Life," 40.

14. Michael Merrill, "Cash Is Good to Eat: Self-Sufficiency and Exchange in the Rural Economy of the United States," *Radical History Review* 4 (Winter 1977): 42–71.

15. Howells, *Recollections*, 146–47.

16. Haines, "Social Life," 54; Robert B. Duncan, "Old Settlers," *Indiana Historical Society Publications*, 2 (Indianapolis, 1895), 396; Howells, *Recollections*, 145. The richest delineation of the subsistence culture is John Mack Faragher, *Sugar Creek: Life on the Illinois Prairie* (New Haven, 1986).

17. Joyce Appleby, "Commercial Farming and the 'Agrarian Myth' in the Early Republic," *Journal of American History* 68 (Mar. 1982): 831–48; James T. Lemon, "Household Consumption in Eighteenth-Century America and Its Relationship to Production and Trade: The Situation among Farmers in Southeastern Pennsylvania," *Agricultural History* 41 (1967): 59–70; James T. Lemon, *The Best Poor Man's Country: A Geographical Study of Early Southeastern Pennsylvania* (Baltimore, 1972), especially 27, 180–81; Robert D. Mitchell, *Commercialism and Frontier: Perspectives on the Early Shenandoah Valley* (Charlottesville, 1977).

18. Morton Rothstein, "The Antebellum South as a Dual Economy: A Tentative Hypothesis," *Agricultural History* 41 (Oct. 1967): 373–82; Gavin Wright and Howard Kunreuther, "Cotton, Corn, and Risk in the Nineteenth Century," *Journal of Economic History* 35 (Sept. 1975): 526–51; Gavin Wright, *The Political Economy of the Cotton South: Households, Markets, and Wealth in the Nineteenth Century* (New York, 1978), ch. 3; Steven Hahn, "The Yeomanry of the Non-Plantation South: Upper Piedmont Georgia, 1850–1860," in Robert C. McMath, Jr., and Vernon Burton, eds., *Class, Conflict, and Consensus: Antebellum Southern Community Studies* (Westport, 1982).

19. E. Estyn Evans, "The Scotch-Irish: Their Cultural Adaptation and Heritage in the American Old West," in E. R. R. Green, ed., *Essays in Scotch-Irish History* (London, 1969), 69–86; Arthur C. Lord, "Architectural Characteristics of Houses: Lancaster County, 1798," *Journal of the Lancaster County Historical Society* 85 (1981): 132–51.

20. The general pattern of agrarian crisis is confirmed by many of the community studies listed in the bibliographical essay, especially James T. Lemon's on southeastern Pennsylvania and those on Massachusetts towns by Christopher M. Jedrey, Robert A. Gross, Richard Holmes, and Jonathan Prude. See also: Duane E. Bell, "Dynamics of Population and Wealth in Eighteenth-Century Chester County, Pennsylvania," *Journal of Interdisciplinary History* 6 (Spring 1976): 621–44; Paul G. E. Clemens and Lucy Simler, "Rural Labor and the Farm Household in Chester County, Pennsylvania, 1750–1820," in Stephen Innes, ed., *Work and Labor in Early America* (Chapel Hill, 1988), 106–43.

21. For the agrarian crisis in New England: Kenneth Lockridge, "Land, Population and the Evolution of New England Society 1630–1790," *Past and Present* 39 (April 1968): 62–80. For the pressure of land-hungry Yankees on New York: Dixon Ryan Fox, *Yorkers and Yankees* (New York, 1940), 117–75.

22. Robert A. Gross, "Culture and Cultivation: Agriculture and Society in Thoreau's Concord," *Journal of American History* 69 (June 1982): 42–61, quotation 51; Douglas Lamar Jones, "The Strolling Poor: Transiency in Eighteenth-Century Massachusetts," *Journal of Social History* 8 (Spring 1975): 28–54; Gregory H. Nobles, "Commerce and Community: A Case Study of the Rural Broommaking Business in Antebellum Massachusetts," *Journal of the Early Republic* 4 (Fall 1984): 287–308.

23. Richard D. Birdsall, "The Second Great Awakening and the New England Social Order," *Church History* 39 (Sept. 1970): 345–64, quotation 346–47. For the rural transition from subsistence to capitalist production: Christopher Clark, "Household Economy, Market Exchange, and the Rise of Capitalism in the Connecticut Valley, 1800–1860," *Journal of Social History* 13 (Winter 1979): 169–89, quotation 175.

24. New York *Evening Post,* Feb. 13–Mar. 2, 1815.

25. The extensive and technical cliometric literature, including the national income studies by Paul A. David, Robert Gallman, and others, is lucidly synthesized for noneconomists in Susan Previant Lee and Peter Passell, *A New Economic View of American History* (New York, 1979), 19–22, 53–59. For the crucial role of the northeastern port/hinterland economies, see Diane Lindstrom, *Economic Development in the Philadelphia Region, 1810–1850* (New York, 1978), 1–21; and Diane Lindstrom, "American Economic Growth before 1840: New Evidence and New Directions," *Journal of Economic History* 39 (Mar. 1979): 289–301.

26. Thomas C. Cochran, *Business in American Life: A History* (New York, 1972), 20–25, 53; Philip Greven, *The Protestant Temperament: Patterns of Child-Rearing, Religious Experience, and the Self in Early America* (New York, 1977); Samuel Eliot Morison, *The Maritime History of Massachusetts, 1783–1860* (Boston, 1921), 41–99, 155–59.

27. Adam Seybert, *Statistical Annals . . . of the United States of America* (Philadelphia, 1818), 59–60.

28. Douglass C. North, *The Economic Growth of the United States, 1790–1860* (Englewood Cliffs, N.J., 1961), 25, 28, 41.

29. Howard B. Rock, *Artisans of the Young Republic: The Tradesmen of New York City in the Age of Jefferson* (New York, 1979), 13–16; Billy G. Smith, "The Material Lives of Laboring Philadelphians, 1750 to 1800," *William and Mary Quarterly* 38 (Apr. 1981): 163–202; Billy G. Smith, "The Vicissitudes of Fortune: The Careers of Laboring Men in Philadelphia, 1750–1800," in Stephen Innes, ed., *Work and Labor in Early America* (Chapel Hill, 1988), 221–51; Christine Stansell, *City of Women: Sex and Class in New York, 1789–1860* (New York, 1986), 3–18.

30. Sean Wilentz, *Chants Democratic: New York City & the Rise of the American Working Class, 1788–1850* (New York, 1984), 3–103, quotations 89, 91; Rock, *Artisans,* 1–147, quotation 131; Susan E. Hirsch, *Roots of the American Working Class: The Industrialization of Crafts in Newark, 1800–1860* (Philadelphia, 1978), 3–13; Charles G. Steffen, *The Mechanics of Baltimore: Workers and Politics in the Age of Revolution, 1763–1812* (Champaign, 1984), 3–190.

31. Stansell, *City of Women,* 105–29; Rock, *Artisans,* 235–63, quotation 268; Charles G. Steffen, "Changes in the Organization of Artisan Production in Baltimore, 1790 to 1820," *William and Mary Quarterly* 36 (Jan. 1979): 101–17.

32. Rock, *Artisans,* 237–88. New York's journeyman shoemakers remained strong enough to win acquittal on another conspiracy indictment in 1811; see Sean Wilentz, "Conspiracy, Power and the Early Labor Movement: *The People v. James Melvin et al.,* 1811," *Labor History* 24 (Fall 1983): 572–79.

33. Rock, *Artisans,* 184–97, quotations 189, 193.

34. Rock, *Artisans,* 104, 152–78, 246–47, quotations 153, 312; New York *Evening Post,* Feb. 28, 1815.

35. Rock, Artisans, 295–316, quotations 138, 314.

36. Alan Dawley, *Class and Community: The Industrial Revolution in Lynn* (Cambridge, Mass., 1976); Paul G. Faler, *Mechanics and Manufacturers in the Early Industrial Revolution: Lynn, Massachusetts, 1780–1860* (Albany, 1981); Mary H. Blewett, *Men, Women, and Work: Class, Gender, and Protest in the New England Shoe Industry, 1789–1910* (Champaign, 1988).

37. Jonathan Prude, "The Social System of Early New England Textile Mills: A Case Study, 1812–40," in Michael H. Frisch and Daniel J. Walkowitz, eds., *Working-Class America: Essays on Labor, Community, and American Society* (Urbana, 1983), 1–36; Jonathan Prude, *The Coming of Industrial Order: Town and Factory Life in Rural Massachusetts, 1810–1860* (New York, 1983); Anthony F. C. Wallace, *Rockdale: The Growth of an American Village in the Early Industrial Revolution* (New York, 1972).

38. Nathan Appleton, *Introduction of the Power Loom and the Origin of Lowell* (Lowell, Mass., 1858), 7–16; Rolla M. Tryon, *Household Manufactures in the United States, 1640–1860* (New York, 1917), 303–76; Percy W. Bidwell and John I. Falconer, *History of Agriculture in the Northern United States, 1620–1860* (New York, 1941), 250–53, quotation (Bushnell's punctuation edited for clarity) 252.

39. For the late survival of magical attitudes even among educated elites: Herbert Leventhal, *In the Shadow of the Enlightenment: Occultism and Renaissance Science in Eighteenth-Century America* (New York, 1976). For folk animism: Jon Butler, *Awash in a Sea of Faith: Christianizing the American People* (Cambridge, Mass., 1990), 67–97, 225–56; David D. Hall, *Worlds of Wonder, Days of Judgment: Popular Religious Beliefs in Early New England* (New York, 1989); and Alan Taylor, "The Early Republic's Supernatural Economy: Treasure Seeking in the American Northeast, 1780–1830," *American Quarterly* 38 (Spring 1986): 6–34.

40. Conrad Wright, *The Beginnings of Unitarianism in America* (Boston, 1955).

41. For the Awakening's social provenance: William G. McLoughlin, *Revivals, Awakenings, and Reform: An Essay on Religion and Social Change in America, 1607–1977* (Chicago, 1978); Donald G. Mathews, "The Second Great Awakening as an Organizing Process, 1780–1830: An Hypothesis," *American Quarterly* 21 (Spring 1969): 23–43; and George H. Thomas, *Revivalism and Cultural Change: Christianity, Nation Building, and the Market in the Nineteenth-Century United States* (Chicago, 1989). Historians confusingly apply the labels Great Revival and Second Great Awakening indiscriminately to the last two ebuillitions of the New Light, or to both combined. I use the contemporarly label Great Revival for the turn-of-the century epiphany and the historians' label for the culminating Second Great Awakening.

42. David S. Lovejoy, *Religious Enthusiasm in the New World: Heresy to Revolution* (Cambridge, Mass., 1985); Dickson D. Bruce, Jr., *And They All Sang Hallelujah: Plain-Folk Camp-Meeting Religion, 1800–1845* (Knoxville, 1974), 64, 86–87, 132; John Mack Faragher, *Women and Men on the Overland Trail* (New Haven, 1979), especially 46–47, 110–22, 145–57, quotation 155.

43. Harry S. Stout, "Religion, Communications, and the Ideological Origins of the American Revolution," *William and Mary Quarterly* 34 (Oct. 1977): 519–41; Rhys Isaac, *The Transformation of Virginia, 1740–1790* (Chapel Hill, 1982).

44. Joseph Haroutunian, *Piety versus Moralism: The Passing of the New England Theology* (New York, 1932). "Antinomian" and "arminian" refer herein to the clashing cos-

mologies symbolized by narrower theological distinctions. The evangelical movement galvanized by the antinomian New Light also contained doctrines susceptible to arminian drift
under market pressures, especially the moralism of the Methodist *Discipline,* and the free
grace for all believers of Methodists, Free-Will Baptists, and Universalists.

45. J. R. Pole, "Historians and the Problem of Early American Democracy," *American
Historical Review* 67 (April 1962): 626–46.

46. For the Awakening as rebellion against traditional authority: Alan Heimert, *Religion and the American Mind: From the Great Awakening to the Revolution* (Cambridge,
Mass., 1966). For its broader rejection of elite culture, two essays by Rhys Isaac: "Evangelical Revolt: The Nature of the Baptist Challenge to the Traditional Order in Virginia,
1765–1775," *William and Mary Quarterly* 31 (July 1974): 345–68; and "Preachers and
Patriots: Popular Culture and the Revolution in Virginia," in Alfred F. Young, ed., *The
American Revolution: Explorations in the History of American Radicalism* (DeKalb, Ill.,
1976), 125–56. For the cultural division in a Virginia county: Richard R. Beeman, "Social
Change and Cultural Conflict in Virginia: Lunenburg County, 1746–1774," *William and
Mary Quarterly* 35 (July 1978): 455–76.

47. Richard J. Hooker, ed., *The Carolina Backcountry on the Eve of the Revolution: The
Journal and Other Writings of Charles Woodmason, Anglican Itinerant* (Chapel Hill, 1953),
quotations 240–41.

48. R. R. Palmer, "Notes on the Use of the Word 'Democracy,' 1789–1799," *Political
Science Quarterly* 68 (June 1953): 203–26.

49. Elisha P. Douglass, *Rebels and Democrats: The Struggle for Equal Political Rights
and Majority Rule during the American Revolution* (Chapel Hill, 1955).

Chapter 2. Ambiguous Republicanism

1. Bray Hammond, *Banks and Politics in America: From the Revolution to the Civil War*
(Princeton, 1957), quotation, 232; T.H. Breen, *Tabacco Culture: The Mentality of the Great
Planters on the Eve of Revolution* (Princeton, 1985); Henry Mayer, *A Son of Thunder: Pat-
rick Henry and the American Republic* (New York, 1986); Bernard Mayo, *Henry Clay,
Spokesman of the New West* (Boston, 1937), quotations 9, 24.

2. Edmund S. Morgan, *American Slavery, American Freedom: The Ordeal of Colonial
Virginia* (New York, 1975), 363–87.

3. Drew R. McCoy, *The Elusive Republic: Political Economy in Jeffersonian America*
(Chapel Hill, 1980), especially 76–104.

4. Charles Warren, *The Supreme Court in United States History* (2 vols., Boston, 1926),
quotation I, 561; Richard Buel, Jr., *Securing the Revolution: Ideology in American Politics,
1789–1815* (Ithaca, 1972).

5. Paul Leicester Ford, ed., *The Writings of Thomas Jefferson* (10 vols., New York,
1899), III, 268–69; A. Whitney Griswold, *Farming and Democracy* (New York, 1948),
18–46, quotations 44–45; Richard K. Matthews, *The Radical Politics of Thomas Jefferson*
(Lawrence, Kans., 1985).

6. James Sterling Young, *The Washington Community, 1800–1828* (New York, 1966,
23–32, 41–57.

7. J. R. Pole, *Political Representation in England and the Origins of the American Revolution* (Berkeley, 1971), 544–63; Richard P. McCormick, "New Perspectives on Jacksonian Politics," *American Historical Review* 65 (Jan. 1960): 292.

8. Alvin Kass, *Politics in New York State, 1800–1828* (Syracuse, 1965), 66–67.

9. For the decisive importance of the constitutional framework in mandating a political system of two competing coalitions: William H. Riker, *The Theory of Political Coalitions* (New Haven, 1962).

10. McCoy, *Elusive Republic*, especially 120–45. For the Madisonian strain: Joyce Appleby, *Capitalism and a New Social Order: The Republican Vision of the 1790s* (New York, 1983); John R. Nelson, Jr., *Liberty and Property: Political Economy and Policymaking in the New Nation, 1789–1812* (Baltimore, 1987).

11. Paul Goodman, *The Democratic Republicans of Massachusetts: Politics in a Young Republic* (Cambridge, Mass., 1964); Louis Hartz, *Economic Policy and Democratic Thought: Pennsylvania, 1776–1860* (Cambridge, Mass., 1948), 56–57; Nathan Miller, *The Enterprise of a Free People: Aspects of Economic Development in New York State during the Canal Period, 1792–1838* (Ithaca, 1962), 12–14; Oscar and Mary Flug Handlin, *Commonwealth: A Study of the Role of Government in the American Economy: Massachusetts, 1774–1861* (rev. ed., Cambridge, Mass., 1969), 76–79.

12. Robert Greenhalgh Albion, *The Rise of New York Port (1815–1860)* (New York, 1939), 38–63, 143–64; Allan R. Pred, *Urban Growth and the Circulation of Information: The United States System of Cities, 1790–1840* (Cambridge, Mass., 1973), 123–31.

13. Julius Rubin, *Canal or Railroad? Imitation and Innovation in Response to the Erie Canal in Philadelphia, Boston, and Baltimore*, American Philosophical Society, *Transactions*, 51, Part 7 (Philadelphia, 1961), quotations 6; Nathan Miller, *Enterprise of a Free People*, 20–39; Julius Rubin, "An Innovating Public Improvement: The Erie Canal," in Carter Goodrich et al., *Canals and American Economic Development* (New York, 1961), 15–66; George R. Taylor, *The Transportation Revolution, 1815–1860* (New York, 1951), 34, 137, 173.

14. Diane Lindstrom, *Economic Development in the Philadelphia Region, 1810–1850* (New York, 1978), 40–54, 93–112, 121–51; Diane Lindstrom, "American Economic Growth before 1840: New Evidence and New Directions," *Journal of Economic History* 39 (Mar. 1979): 289–301.

15. Albert Fishlow, "Internal Transportation," in Lance Davis et al., *American Economic Growth: An Economist's History of the United States* (New York, 1972), 473–74, 482, 496.

16. Harry H. Pierce, *The Railroads of New York: A Study of Government Aid, 1826–1875* (Cambridge, Mass., 1955), 53.

17. Carter Goodrich, "Internal Improvements Reconsidered," *Journal of Economic History* 30 (June 1970): 289–311.

18. Hammond, *Banks and Politics in America*, 144–71, quotations 53, 63, 196.

19. Morton J. Horwitz, *The Transformation of American Law, 1780–1860* (Cambridge, Mass., 1977), 112; Oscar Handlin and Mary F. Handlin, "Origins of the American Business Corporation," *Journal of Economic History* 5 (May 1945): 1–23.

20. Horwitz, *American Law*, 140–59; William E. Nelson, *Americanization of the Common Law: The Impact of Legal Change on Massachusetts Society, 1760–1830* (Cambridge, 1975), 117–18.

21. Perry Miller, *Life of the Mind in America, from the Revolution to the Civil War* (New York, 1965), 223–30; Lawrence M. Friedman, *A History of American Law* (New York, 1973), 267.

22. Alexis de Tocqueville (Phillips Bradley, ed.), *Democracy in America* (2 vols., New York, 1945), I, 288–89.

23. Warren, *Supreme Court*, I, 612; A. G. Roeber, *Faithful Magistrates and Republican Lawyers: Creators of Virginia's Legal Culture, 1680–1810* (Chapel Hill, 1981), 107–8.

24. Noble E. Cunningham, Jr., ed., *Circular Letters of Congressmen to Their Constituents, 1789–1829* (3 vols., Chapel Hill, 1977), III, 1076.

25. Young, *Washington Community*, 92; Herbert Ershkowitz, *The Origins of the Whig and Democratic Parties: New Jersey Politics, 1820–1837* (Washington, 1982), 8.

26. Horwitz, *American Law*; Nelson, *Common Law*.

27. Friedman, *American Law*; 127–28.

28. Friedman, *American Law*; 96–98; Nelson, *Common Law*, 70.

29. Horwitz, *American Law*, quotation 28; Nelson, *Common Law*, 165–71.

30. Nelson, *Common Law*, 171–72.

31. Francis H. Ammann, *The Changing American Legal System: Some Selected Phases* (Columbus, Ohio, 1940), 75–77.

32. Bernard Schwartz, *The Law in America: A History* (New York, 1974), 13.

33. Horwitz, *American Law*, 23, 26.

34. Nelson, *Common Law*, 172.

35. Horwitz, *American Law*, 28, 125, 144; R. Kent Newmyer, *Supreme Court Justice Joseph Story, Statesman of the Old Republic* (Chapel Hill, 1985), 86, 118, 262–63.

36. Friedman, *American Law*, 206–7; Nelson, *Common Law*, 159.

37. Horwitz, *American Law*, 32–40, quotation 37.

38. Horwitz, *American Law*, 74.

39. Horwitz, *American Law*, 75.

40. Roscoe Pound, quoted in Schwartz, *Law in America*, 55–58.

41. Harry N. Scheiber, "The Road to *Munn*: Eminent Domain and the Concept of Public Purpose in the State Courts," *Perspectives in American History* 5 (1971): 360–66, quotation 366n.; Harry N. Scheiber, "Property Law, Expropriation, and Resource Allocation by Government, 1789–1910," *Journal of Economic History* 33 (Mar. 1973): 234–42.

42. Scheiber, "Property Law," 242.

43. Horwitz, *American Law*, 208–10; Nelson, *Common Law*, 133–36.

44. Friedman, *American Law*, 233–37, 262–64, quotation 234.

45. Nelson, *Common Law*, 143, 174.

46. Sir Henry Sumner Maine, *Popular Government* (Indianapolis, 1976), quotation 70–71; Horwitz, *American Law*, 71.

47. Warren, *Supreme Court*, I, 60.

48. Warren, *Supreme Court*, I, 62–82, 91–104, 144–49, 158–67, 367–92.

49. Warren, *Supreme Court*, I, 62–167, quotation 162; James Morton Smith, *Freedom's Fetters: The Alien and Sedition Laws and American Civil Liberties* (Ithaca, 1956), 188–220.

50. Warren, *Supreme Court*, I, 228–29.

51. Warren, *Supreme Court*, I, 179–80.

52. Warren, *Supreme Court*, I, 182, 473; G. Edward White (with Gerald Gunther), *The Marshall Court and Cultural Change, 1816–1835* (vols. 3 and 4 of *The Oliver Wendell Holmes Devise History of the Supreme Court of the United States*, New York, 1988), 622n.

53. 6 Cranch 87.

54. James McClellan, *Joseph Story and the American Constitution: A Study in Political and Legal Thought with Selected Writings* (Norman, 1971), 3–45, quotations 15, 39–40, 196; Warren, *Supreme Court*, I, 418.

55. Warren, *Supreme Court*, I, 401, 417; Ford, *Writings of Jefferson*, X, 376.

56. Warren, *Supreme Court*, I, 400–416.

57. Warren, *Supreme Court*, I, 424, 426–27; McClellan, *Story*, 4.

58. Warren, *Supreme Court*, I, 452.

59. Hammond, *Banks and Politics*, 222–32; Raymond Walters, Jr., *Alexander James Dallas: Lawyer-Politician-Financier, 1759–1817* (Philadelphia, 1943), 170–200; Raymond Walters, Jr., *Albert Gallatin, Jeffersonian Financier and Diplomat* (New York, 1957), 254–60; Charles M. Wiltse, *John C. Calhoun* (3 vols., Indianapolis, 1944–1951), I, 94–100.

60. Kim T. Phillips, "William Duane, Philadelphia's Democratic Republicans, and the Origins of Modern Politics," *Pennsylvania Magazine of History and Biography* 101 (July 1977): 370.

61. Walters, *Dallas*, especially 27, 46, 62–73, 116–18, 123–25, 128–32, 160.

62. Walters, *Gallatin*, especially 16–21, 41–44, 125, 133–39.

63. Richard E. Ellis, *The Jeffersonian Crisis: Courts and Politics in the Young Republic* (New York, 1971), especially 48–49, 157–83.

64. *American State Papers, Miscellaneous*, I, 724–41; *American State Papers, Finance*, II, 425–31; Walters, *Gallatin*, 171–73.

65. Hammond, *Banks and Politics*, 205–26, quotation 206.

66. Mayo, *Clay*, 374–77.

67. Mayo, *Clay*, 64–69, 76–79, 150–51, 158–67, 170–77, quotation 96; Ellis, *Jeffersonian Crisis*, 123–56, quotation 153.

68. Mayo, *Clay*, 334–35.

69. Wiltse, *Calhoun*, I, 11–66; Robert L. Meriwether et al., eds., *The Papers of John C. Calhoun* (Columbia, S.C., 1959–), I, 53, quotation 8.

70. Wiltse, *Calhoun*, quotation I, 105; Hammond, *Banks and Politics*, quotation 245.

71. Margaret Kinard Latimer, "South Carolina—A Protagonist of the War of 1812," *American Historical Review* 61 (July 1956): 914–29; Douglass C. North, *The Economic Growth of the United States, 1790–1860* (Englewood Cliffs, N.J., 1961), 231; George Rogers Taylor, "Agrarian Discontent in the Mississippi Valley Preceding the War of 1812," *Journal of Political Economy* 39 (Aug. 1931): 471–505.

72. Hammond, *Banks and Politics*, 213, 226–32, 253–54; Walters, *Gallatin*, 215–16, 219, 254–58, 260, 294–95, 327, 347; Walters, *Dallas*, 170–74, 177–87, 191–200; Philip G. Walters and Raymond Walters Jr., "The American Career of David Parish," *Journal of Economic History* 4 (Nov. 1944): 149–66; Wiltse, *Calhoun*, I, 94–100.

Chapter 3. "Let Us Conquer Space"

1. Edward Everett, *Orations and Speeches on Various Occasions* (Boston, 1850), 49–54.

2. *Niles' Weekly Register*, 2 Sept. 1815.

3. James D. Richardson, comp., *A Compilation of the Messages and Papers of the Presidents, 1789–1902* (10 vols., Washington, 1905), I, 562–69.

4. Richardson, *Messages of the Presidents*, I, 562–69; Bray Hammond, *Banks and Politics in America: From the Revolution to the Civil War* (Princeton, 1957), 233–41, quotation 233–34; *American State Papers: Finance*, III, 18.

5. Hammond, *Banks and Politics*, quotations 236, 243.

6. Glover Moore, *The Missouri Controversy, 1819–1821* (Lexington, Ky., 1953), 246.

7. Noble E. Cunningham, Jr., ed., *Circular Letters of Congressmen to Their Constituents, 1789–1829* (3 vols., Chapel Hill, 1977), II, 823.

8. Manning J. Dauer, *The Adams Federalists* (Baltimore, 1953), 256–57.

9. Bernard Mayo, *Henry Clay, Spokesman of the New West* (Boston, 1937), 167–68.

10. Raymond Walters, Jr., *Alexander James Dallas: Lawyer-Politician-Financier, 1759–1817* (Philadelphia, 1943), 206; *Annals of Congress,* 14th Congress, 1st Session, 431, 728–29, 829–40.

11. Walters, *Dallas,* 207–09; *Annals of Congress,* 14th Congress, 1st Session, 1329–36.

12. Charles M. Wiltse, *John C. Calhoun* (3 vols., Indianapolis, 1944–1951), I, 115–24, 403.

13. Craig L. Symonds, *Navalists and Antinavalists: The Naval Policy Debate in the United States, 1785–1827* (Newark, Del., 1980), 194–216.

14. Robert Greenhalgh Albion (Rowena Reed, ed.), *Makers of Naval Policy, 1798–1947* (Annapolis, 1980), 186–88.

15. Chase C. Mooney, *William H. Crawford, 1772–1834* (Lexington, Ky., 1974), 80–82.

16. Richardson, *Messages of the Presidents,* I, 576, 578, 584–85; Mrs. St. Julien Ravenel, *Life and Times of William Lowndes of South Carolina, 1782–1822* (Boston, 1901), 131–32.

17. J. C. Hamilton, ed., *The Works of Alexander Hamilton* (7 vols., New York, 1850–1851), IV, 104 ff.; A. A. Lipscomb and H. E. Bergh, eds., *The Writings of Thomas Jefferson* (20 vols., Washington, 1903), III, 145 ff.

18. *Annals of Congress,* 14th Congress, 2nd Session, 851–58.

19. Wiltse, *Calhoun,* I, 132–37, 403.

20. Harry Ammon, *James Monroe: The Quest for National Identity* (New York, 1971), 320, 341, 396–405, 557; Charles Francis Adams, ed., *Memoirs of John Quincy Adams, Comprising Portions of His Diary from 1795 to 1848* (Philadelphia, 1874–1877), IV, 17.

21. Richardson, *Messages of the Presidents,* II, 8, 17–18, 20, 45, 48, 61, 80, 91, 106–8, 191, 215. Monroe articulated his political economy most fully in the constitutional treatise that accompanied his 1822 veto of the act to repair the Cumberland (National) Road, especially 175–79.

22. Richard Hofstadter, *The Idea of a Party System: The Rise of Legitimate Opposition in the United States, 1780–1840* (Berkeley, 1969), 11–73, quotations 194, 196, 200; Richardson, *Messages of the Presidents,* quotation II, 145.

23. James F. Hopkins et al., eds., *The Papers of Henry Clay* (Lexington, Ky., 1959–), II, 446–51.

24. Forest G. Hill, *Roads, Rails & Waterways: The Army Engineers and Early Transportation* (Norman, 1957), 33–36; Hudson Strode, *Jefferson Davis* (3 vols., New York, 1955–1964), I, 33–45.

25. *American State Papers: Miscellaneous,* II, 533–36. Calhoun's grand design was inspired by France, where a national system of great canals was being projected by a central bureaucracy of scientifically trained engineers nurtured in the military and the Ecole Polytechnique. See Cecil O. Smith, Jr., "The Longest Run: Public Engineers and Planning in France," *American Historical Review* 95 (June 1990): 657–92.

26. Charles Warren, *The Supreme Court in United States History* (2 vols., Boston, 1926), I, 442–55, quotation 453; 1 Wheaton 304–51.

27. For the personalities and internal dynamics of the Marshall Court: G. Edward

White (assisted by Gerald Gunther), *The Marshall Court and Cultural Change, 1815–35* (vols. 3 and 4 of *The Oliver Wendell Holmes Devise History of the Supreme Court of the United States,* New York, 1988), 157–383.

28. White, *Marshall Court,* 615–18.

29. Maurice G. Baxter, *Daniel Webster & the Supreme Court* (Amherst, 1966), 80–85, 89–98.

30. Warren, *Supreme Court,* I, 476n., 485–92; James McClellan, *Joseph Story and the American Constitution: A Study in Political and Legal Thought with Selected Writings* (Norman, 1971), 240–46; Baxter, *Webster & Supreme Court,* 80–85, 89–98; R. Kent Newmyer, "A Note on the Whig Politics of Justice Joseph Story," *Mississippi Valley Historical Review* 48 (Dec. 1961): 488, 490; White, *Marshall Court,* 612–28.

31. 4 Wheaton 122 ff.

32. Warren, *Supreme Court,* I, 487, 490; Francis N. Stites, *John Marshall, Defender of the Constitution* (Boston, 1981), 125.

33. Peter J. Coleman, *Debtors and Creditors in America: Isolvency, Imprisonment for Debt, and Bankruptcy, 1607–1900* (Madison, 1974), 42–45, 116–18, 187–88, 287, quotations 271.

34. Norman K. Risjord, *The Old Republicans: Southern Conservatives in the Age of Jefferson* (New York, 1965), 211–13.

35. 4 Wheaton 518 ff.; Coleman, *Debtors and Creditors,* 32–34; White, *Marshall Court,* 628–40.

36. 4 Wheaton 624 ff.; White, *Marshall Court,* 541–67; Baxter, *Webster & Supreme Court,* 170–78.

37. Risjord, *Old Republicans,* 235–36.

38. Robert V. Remini, *Andrew Jackson* (3 vols., New York, 1977–1984), I, especially 219–32, 300–6, 322–40, 392–98.

39. Wiltse, *Calhoun,* I, 149–50, 165–68, 182–86, 198–99, 296; William H. Goetzmann, *Army Exploration in the American West, 1803–1863* (New Haven, 1959), 39–44.

40. Richardson, *Messages of the Presidents,* II, 16, 46, 235–36, 261. For additional expressions of Monroe's views: 9, 79–80, 92, 234–37, 256–57, 261, 280–83.

41. Robert L. Meriwether et al., *The Papers of John C. Calhoun* (Columbia, S.C., 1959–), III, 350; William G. McLoughlin, *Cherokee Renascence in the New Republic* (Princeton, 1987), 255.

42. Bradford Perkins, *Castlereagh and Adams: England and the United States 1812–1823* (Berkeley and Los Angeles, 1964), 39–127, 221–22.

43. Samuel Flagg Bemis, *John Quincy Adams and the Foundations of American Foreign Policy* (New York, 1949), passim, quotations 28, 31; Worthington C. Ford, ed., *Writings of John Quincy Adams* (7 vols., New York, 1913–1917), VII, 298–99.

44. Bemis, *Adams and Foreign Policy,* quotations 18, 23–24.

45. Adams, *Memoirs,* IV, 388; Bemis, *Adams and Foreign Policy,* 80, 250–51, 275–76, quotation 250; Samuel Flagg Bemis, *John Quincy Adams and the Union* (New York, 1956), 94–95, 114–18, 178–80.

46. Perkins, *Castlereagh and Adams,* 88–89, 156–72, 220–82; Bemis, *Adams and Foreign Policy,* 224–36, 278–99, 457–61; Walter LaFeber, ed., *John Quincy Adams and American Continental Empire: Letters, Papers and Speeches* (Chicago, 1965), quotations 48–51.

47. Perkins, *Castlereagh and Adams,* 220–82.

48. Remini, *Jackson,* I, 344–69; Bemis, *Adams and Foreign Policy,* 300–340; Perkins,

Castlereagh and Adams, 283–90; Adams, *Memoirs,* IV, 437–39, V, 243–53; *Writings of J. Q. Adams,* IV, 437–39.

49. Bemis, *Adams and Foreign Policy,* 300–340; Perkins, *Castlereagh and Adams,* 283–90; Adams, *Memoirs,* IV, 437–39, V, 243–53; *Writings of J. Q. Adams,* IV, 437–39.

50. Harry Ammon, "James Monroe and the Era of Good Feelings," *Virginia Magazine of History and Biography* 66 (Oct. 1958): quotation 388–89; Shaw Livermore, Jr., *The Twilight of Federalism: The Disintegration of the Federalist Party, 1815–1830* (Princeton, 1962), quotations 16; Symonds, *Navalists,* quotation 211.

Chapter 4. The Crisis of 1819

1. Richmond *Enquirer,* 14 April 1818; Harry Ammon, *James Monroe: The Quest for National Identity* (New York, 1971), 394; Charles Francis Adams, ed., *Memoirs of John Quincy Adams, Comprising Portions of His Diary from 1795 to 1848* (Philadelphia, 1874–1877), IV, 119.

2. Charles M. Wiltse, *John C. Calhoun* (3 vols., Indianapolis, 1944–1951), I, 166–68, 182–85.

3. Robert V. Remini, *Andrew Jackson* (3 vols., New York, 1977–1984), I, 370–77.

4. Glover Moore, *The Missouri Controversy, 1819–1821* (Lexington, Ky., 1953), 50.

5. C. Edward Skeen, "*Vox Populi, Vox Dei:* The Compensation Act of 1816 and the Rise of Popular Politics," *Journal of the Early Republic* 6 (Fall 1986): 253–74, quotations 261–65, 269; John Bach McMaster, *A History of the People of the United States, from the Revolution to the Civil War* (8 vols., New York, 1907–1914), IV, 357–62; Wiltse, *Calhoun,* I, 112–13, 124–25; James Sterling Young, *The Washington Community, 1800–1828* (New York, 1956), 90.

6. Noble E. Cunningham, Jr., ed., *Circular Letters of Congressmen to Their Constituents, 1789–1829* (3 vols., Chapel Hill, 1977), II, 823.

7. *Annals of Congress,* 14th Congress, 2nd Session, 576–80.

8. Paul Leicester Ford, ed., *The Writings of Thomas Jefferson* (10 vols., New York, 1899), X, 90, 170, 356–57.

9. Chilton Williamson, *American Suffrage: From Property to Democracy, 1760–1860* (Princeton, 1960), especially 169–70, 296; Fletcher M. Green, *Constitutional Development in the South Atlantic States, 1776–1860: A Study in the Evolution of Democracy* (Chapel Hill, 1930), especially 174–77, 196–97, 243; Charles S. Sydnor, *The Development of Southern Sectionalism, 1819–1848* (Baton Rouge, 1948), 33–53; Richard P. McCormick, *The Second American Party System: Party Formation in the Jacksonian Era* (Chapel Hill, 1966), especially 311–12; Richard P. McCormick, "Suffrage Classes and Party Alignments: A Study in Voter Behavior," *Mississippi Valley Historical Review* 46 (Dec. 1959): 400, 405; Ford, *Writings of Jefferson,* X, 303; William A. Schaper, "Sectionalism and Representation in South Carolina," American Historical Association, *Annual Report 1900,* 441–43.

10. Harvey Strum, "Property Qualifications and Voting Behavior in New York, 1807–1816," *Journal of the Early Republic* 1 (Winter 1981): 347–71.

11. Dixon Ryan Fox, *The Decline of Aristocracy in the Politics of New York* (New York, 1919), quotation 200; Jerome Mushkat, *Tammany: The Evolution of a Political Machine, 1789–1865* (Syracuse, 1971), 32–39.

12. Michael Wallace, "Changing Concepts of Party in the United States: New York, 1815–1828," *American Historical Review* 74 (Dec. 1968): 453–91, quotations 458, 483.

13. Robert V. Remini, *Martin Van Buren and the Making of the Democratic Party* (New York, 1959), 11; Wallace, "Changing Concepts of Party," 460–71.

14. John C. Spencer to Albert H. Tracy, 28 May 1821, Albert H. Tracy Papers (New York State Library); Alvin W. Kass, *Politics in New York State, 1800–1830* (Syracuse, 1965), 103.

15. Merrill D. Peterson, ed., *Democracy, Liberty, and Property: The State Constitutional Conventions of the 1820's* (Indianapolis, 1966), 125–42, quotations 183, 191.

16. Moore, *Missouri Controversy,* 305.

17. Joyce Appleby, "Commercial Farming and the 'Agrarian Myth' in the Early Republic," *Journal of American History* 68 (Mar. 1982): 839–44; Robert D. Mitchell, *Commercialism and Frontier: Perspectives on the Early Shenandoah Valley* (Charlottesville, 1977).

18. J. R. Pole, "Representation and Authority in Virginia from the Revolution to Reform," *Journal of Southern History* 24 (Feb. 1958): 16–50, quotation 36.

19. Ford, *Writings of Jefferson,* X, 29–30, 37–41, 45.

20. Sydnor, *Southern Sectionalism,* 33–44.

21. Harry Ammon, "The Jeffersonian Republicans in Virginia: An Interpretation," *Virginia Magazine of History and Biography* 71 (April 1963): 153–67; Harry Ammon, "The Richmond Junto, 1800–1824," *Virginia Magazine of History and Biography* 61 (Oct. 1953): 395–418, quotation 400; Joseph H. Harrison, Jr., "Oligarchs and Democrats, The Richmond Junto," *Virginia Magazine of History and Biography* 78 (Apr. 1970): 184–98; Morton J. Horwitz, *The Transformation of American Law, 1780–1860* (Cambridge, 1977), 112.

22. Harrison, "Oligarchs," 188.

23. James Roger Sharp, *The Jacksonians versus the Banks: Politics in the States after the Panic of 1837* (New York, 1970), 230–31.

24. Ammon, "Jeffersonian Republicans," quotations 164–67; *Annals of Congress,* 14th Congress, 1st Session, quotation 839.

25. Charles H. Ambler, *Sectionalism in Virginia from 1776 to 1861* (New York, 1910), 93–96; Ford, *Writings of Jefferson,* X, 41.

26. Norman K. Risjord, *The Old Republicans: Southern Conservatism in the Age of Jefferson* (New York, 1965), 209–13; Noble E. Cunningham, Jr., ed., *Circular Letters of Congressmen to Their Constituents, 1789–1829* (3 vols., Chapel Hill, 1977), quotation III, 1040.

27. Bertram Wyatt-Brown, *Southern Honor: Ethics anf Behavior in the Old South* (New York, 1982), quotation 178.

28. Adams, *Memoirs,* V, 40, 204.

29. Harry L. Watson, "Squire Oldway and His Friends: Opposition to Internal Improvements in Antebellum North Carolina," *North Carolina Historical Review* 54 (Apr. 1977): quotations 116–18; Albert Ray Newsome, *The Presidential Election of 1824 in North Carolina* (Chapel Hill, 1939), quotation 15.

30. William W. Freehling, *Prelude to Civil War: The Nullification Controversy in South Carolina, 1816–1836* (New York, 1965), 97–98; Cleveland (Ohio) *Register,* 13 Oct. 1818; Cunningham, *Circular Letters,* quotation III, 1068–69.

31. Robert E. Shalhope, *John Taylor of Caroline, Pastoral Republican* (Columbia, S.C., 1980), passim, quotation 133. For other Taylor quotations in this section: ibid., 128–29, 131–35, 138–39, 218–21; John Taylor, *An Inquiry into the Principles and Policy of the Government of the United States* (Fredericksburg, 1814), 22, 31, 202, 255, 262–63, 280, 297, 559, 562–64, 568; Paul K. Conkin, *Prophets of Prosperity: America's First Political*

Economists (Bloomington, 1980), 61; and Eugene T. Mudge, *The Social Philosophy of John Taylor of Caroline: A Study in Jeffersonian Democracy* (New York, 1959), 124–26, 161.

32. Thomas Hart Benton, *Thirty Years' View* . . . (2 vols., New York, 1854–1856), quotation I, 45; Shalhope, *Taylor*, quotation 206.

33. Kim T. Phillips, "William Duane, Philadelphia's Democratic Republicans, and the Origins of Modern Politics," *Pennsylvania Magazine of History and Biography* 101 (July 1977): 365–87, quotations 368–69, 371, 379–80. Essential for understanding Pennsylvania politics are Phillips's regrettably unpublished Ph.D. dissertation, "William Duane, Revolutionary Editor" (University of California, Berkeley, 1968), and two other articles, "Democrats of the Old School in the Era of Good Feelings," *Pennsylvania Magazine of History and Biography* 95 (July 1971): 363–82; and "The Pennsylvania Origins of the Jackson Movement," *Political Science Quarterly* 91 (Fall 1976): 489–508.

34. David Brion Davis, *The Problem of Slavery in the Age of Revolution, 1770–1823* (Ithaca, 1975), 87–89.

35. Ira Berlin, *Slaves without Masters: The Free Negro in the Antebellum South* (New York), 24–29, 79–102, 136; Leon F. Litwack, *North of Slavery: The Negro in the Free States, 1790–1860* (Chicago, 1961), 74–92.

36. Sydnor, *Southern Sectionalism*, 95; Addison Coffin, "Emigration from North Carolina," *Guilford Collegian* 4 (1891): quotation 9–11.

37. John Spencer Bassett, "Anti-Slavery Leaders of North Carolina," *Johns Hopkins University Studies*, 16, no. 6 (June 1898): 30; Walter B. Posey, "The Slavery Question in the Presbyterian Church in the Old Southwest," *Journal of Southern History* 9 (Feb. 1943): 319.

38. Davis, *Problem of Slavery*, 251–54.

39. Arthur Zilversmit, *The First Emancipation: The Abolition of Slavery in the North* (Chicago, 1967), 224, 139–229.

40. Dixon Ryan Fox, "The Negro Vote in Old New York," *Political Science Quarterly* 32 (June 1917), 252–75.

41. Glover Moore, *The Missouri Controversy, 1819–1821* (Lexington, Ky., 1953), 10–21.

42. Moore, *Missouri Controversy*, 52–59; Sydnor, *Southern Sectionalism*, 127–28.

43. Adams, *Memoirs*, IV, 529.

44. George R. Taylor, *The Transportation Revolution, 1815–1860* (New York, 1951), 32–33, 63–67, 135–36, 143; Albert Fishlow, "Internal Transportation," in Lance E. Davis et al., *American Economic Growth: An Economist's History of the United States* (New York, 1972), 472–75.

45. Murray N. Rothbard, *The Panic of 1819: Reactions and Policies* (New York, 1962), 1–10; U.S. Bureau of the Census, *Historical Statistics of the United States: Colonial Times to 1970* (2 vols., Washington, 1975), I, 430.

46. Ford, *Writings of Jefferson*, X, 2–4, 28, 31, 122; *Niles' Weekly Register*, 26 Oct. 1816.

47. *American State Papers: Finance*, III, 494–95.

48. Hammond, *Banks and Politics*, 252–62, 274–76.

49. Raymond Walters, Jr., *Albert Gallatin: Jeffersonian Financier and Diplomat* (New York, 1957), 296–97; Thomas P. Govan, *Nicholas Biddle, Nationalist and Public Banker, 1786–1844* (Chicago, 1959), quotation 51.

50. Adams, *Memoirs*, IV, 382–83; Gary L. Browne, *Baltimore in the Nation, 1789–1861* (Chapel Hill, 1980), 74–76.

51. Hammond, *Banks and Politics*, 259; Sydnor, *Southern Sectionalism*, quotation 116; Samuel H. Reznek, "The Depression of 1819–1822: A Social History," *American Historical Review* 39 (Oct. 1933): 28–47, quotation 34; James A Kehl, *Ill Feeling in the Era of Good Feeling: Western Pennsylvania Political Battles, 1815–1825* (Pittsburgh, 1956), 85.

52. U.S. Bureau of the Census, *Historical Statistics of the United States: Colonial Times to 1970* (2 vols., Washington, 1975), I, 209.

Chapter 5. Hard Times, Hard Feelings, Hard Money

1. Samuel H. Reznck, "The Depression of 1819–1822: A Social History," *American Historical Review* 39 (Oct, 1933): 28–47; Paul Leicester Ford, ed., *The Writings of Thomas Jefferson* (10 vols., New York, 1899), X, 156n–57n.

2. Charles Francis Adams, ed., *Memoirs of John Quincy Adams. Comprising Portions of His Diary from 1795 to 1848* (Philadelphia, 1884–1887), IV, 382–83; Gary L. Browne, *Baltimore in the Nation, 1789–1861* (Chapel Hill, 1980), 75–76.

3. Ford, *Writings of Jefferson*, X, 86.

4. Thomas H. Greer, "Economic and Social Effects of the Depression of 1819 in the Old Northwest," *Indiana Magazine of History* 44 (Sept. 1948): 229; Murray N. Rothbard, *The Panic of 1819: Reactions and Policies* (New York, 1962), 10–13; Glover Moore, *The Missouri Controversy, 1819–1821* (Lexington, Ky., 1953), 172–73; Charles S. Sydnor, *The Development of Southern Sectionalism, 1819–1848* (Baton Rouge, 1948), 112, quotation 113; Harry R. Stevens, "Henry Clay, the Bank, and the West in 1824," *American Historical Review* 60 (July 1955): 843–48.

5. William S. Jenkins, *Pro-Slavery Thought in the Old South* (Chapel Hill, 1937), 37–38.

6. Sydnor, *Southern Sectionalism*, 122–23.

7. Shaw Livermore, Jr., *The Twilight of Federalism: The Disintegration of the Federalist Party, 1815–1830* (Princeton, 1962), 89.

8. Livermore, *Twilight of Federalism*, 90.

9. Sydnor, *Southern Sectionalism*, quotation 96; Ford, *Writings of Jefferson*, X, 157–58, 177–78, 362.

10. Moore, *Missouri Controversy*, 65–83, 92–104, 107–13, 209–17; Adams, *Memoirs*, IV, 531, V, 210.

11. "Letters from John C. Calhoun to Charles Tait," *Gulf States Historical Magazine* 1 (Sept. 1902): 99–104.

12. Albert Ray Newsome, *The Presidential Election of 1824 in North Carolina* (Chapel Hill, 1939), 15.

13. Ford, *Writings of Jefferson*, X, 140, 171, 184; Charles Warren, *The Supreme Court in United States History* (2 vols., Boston, 1926), I, 546.

14. Robert V. Remini, *The Election of Andrew Jackson* (Philadelphia, 1963), 24; Clement Eaton, *A History of the Old South* (New York, 1966), 422, 432.

15. Moore, *Missouri Controversy*, 217–57; William W. Freehling, *Prelude to Civil War: The Nullification Controversy in South Carolina, 1816–1836* (New York, 1965), 89–116.

16. *National and State Rights, Considered by the Hon. George McDuffie . . .* [Charleston, 1830].

17. Warren, *Supreme Court*, I, 561–62.

18. G. Edward White, *The Marshall Court and Cultural Change, 1815-35* (vols. 3 and 4 of *The Oliver Wendell Holmes Devise History of the Supreme Court of the United States,* New York, 1988), 504-35.

19. Maurice G. Baxter, *Daniel Webster & the Supreme Court* (Amherst, 1966), 196-206; 9 Wheaton 1 ff.; Warren, *Supreme Court,* I, 615, quotation 606n; White, *Marshall Court,* 567-80.

20. Ford, *Writings of Jefferson,* X, 354-55.

21. Noble E. Cunningham, Jr., ed., *Circular Letters of Congressmen to Their Constituents, 1789-1829* (3 vols., Chapel Hill, 1977), III, 1138.

22. Moore, *Missouri Controversy,* 320-32; James A. Kehl, *Ill Feeling in the Era of Good Feeling: Western Pennsylvania Political Battles, 1815-1825* (Pittsburgh, 1956), quotation 203.

23. James D. Richardson, comp., *A Compilation of the Messages and Papers of the Presidents, 1789-1902* (10 vols., Washington, 1905), II, 144-83. Monroe's last-minute about-face and its significance have not been sufficiently understood. The hasty composition of the addendum and its incongruity with the rest of the document are apparent to the attentive reader; Monroe told John Quincy Adams that the National Road toll bill had been passed so "suddenly" that he had not had time to consult the Cabinet about it, and Adams expected only "his long dissertation against the Constitutional power of Congress to make internal improvements." Adams, *Memoirs,* V, 516-17.

24. *House Journal,* 15th Congress, 1st Session, 334-41.

25. Ford, *Writings of Jefferson,* X, 354-55.

26. Forest G. Hill, *Roads, Rails & Waterways: The Army Engineers and Early Transportation* (Norman, 1957), 37-70.

27. Robert E. Gallman, "The Agricultural Sector and the Pace of Economic Growth: U.S. Experience in the Nineteenth Century," in David C. Klingman and Richard K. Vedder, eds., *Essays in Nineteenth Century Economic History: The Old Northwest* (Athens, Ohio, 1975), 35-76, quotation 56.

28. For the overall deskilling of labor: Alexander James Field, "Educational Reform and Manufacturing Development in Mid-Nineteenth Century Massachusetts," *Journal of Economic History* 31 (Mar. 1976): 263-66; Richard B. Stott, *Workers in the Metropolis: Class, Ethnicity, and Youth in Antebellum New York City* (Ithaca, 1990), 65-66.

29. Patricia Cline Cohen, *A Calculating People: The Spread of Numeracy in Early America* (Chicago, 1982), passim, quotations 3-4.

30. Richard D. Brown, *Modernization: The Transformation of American Life, 1600-1865* (New York, 1976), 129, quotations 134-35.

31. Brown, *Modernization,* 151.

32. Harriet A. Weed, ed., *The Autobiography of Thurlow Weed* (New York, 1884), 17.

33. Peter Cartwright, *The Backwoods Preacher: Being the Autobiography of Peter Cartwright, an American Methodist Traveling Preacher* (London [1856]), 122-23.

34. Gov. Thomas Ford, *A History of Illinois from Its Commencement as a State in 1818 to 1847* (2 vols., Chicago, 1945), I, 129-32.

35. Harriet Martineau (S. M. Lipset, ed.), *Society in America* (New Brunswick, 1981), 167-71.

36. Clarence H. Danhof, *Change in Agriculture: The Northern United States, 1820-1870* (Cambridge, 1969), 2-23, quotations 23, 133.

37. Diane Lindstrom, *Economic Development of the Philadelphia Region, 1810-1850* (New York, 1978), 181.

38. Nathan O. Hatch, *The Democratization of American Christianity* (New Haven, 1989).

39. David M. Ludlum, *Social Ferment in Vermont, 1791–1850* (New York, 1939), 239–44, quotation 239; Stephen A. Marini, *Radical Sects of Revolutionary New England* (Cambridge, Mass., 1982), especially 40–59, 75–96, quotation 40; John B. Boles, *The Great Revival, 1787–1805: The Origins of the Southern Evangelical Mind* (Lexington, Ky., 1972); Sydney E. Ahlstrom, *A Religious History of the American People* (New Haven, 1972), 429–54; Richard Carwardine, *Transatlantic Revivalism: Popular Evangelicalism in Britain and America, 1790–1865* (Westport, 1978), 10, 46–47.

40. Harry L. Watson, Jr., *Jacksonian Politics and Community Conflict: The Emergence of the Second Party System in Cumberland County, North Carolina* (Baton Rouge, 1981), quotations 57–58.

41. Paul Goodman, *Towards a Christian Republic: Antimasonry and the Great Transition in New England, 1826–1836* (New York, 1988), quotation 77.

42. Wesley M. Gewehr, *The Great Awakening in Virginia* (Durham, N.C., 1930), 109n.

43. Donald G. Mathews, *Religion in the Old South* (Chicago, 1977), 22–35, 42–50, quotations 24, 62.

44. Boles, *Great Revival*, 103–9.

45. John Scott Strickland, "The Great Revival and Insurrectionary Fears in North Carolina: An Examination of Antebellum Southern Society and Slave Revolt Panics," in Orville V. Burton and Robert C. McMath, Jr., eds., *Class, Conflict and Consensus: Antebellum Southern Community Studies* (Westport, 1982), 77.

46. Richmond *Enquirer*, quoted in Chilicothe *Scioto Gazette*, 6 Nov. 1818; Moore, *Missouri Controversy*, 21–22, 35–36; Sydnor, *Southern Sectionalism*, 113–18, quotation 114; Newsome, *Election of 1824*, quotation 27–29.

47. Cunningham, *Circular Letters*, III, 1073.

48. Kim T. Phillips, "William Duane, Revolutionary Editor" (Ph.D. dissertation, University of California, Berkeley, 1968), 435–86, quotation 486; Kim T. Phillips, "Democrats of the Old School in the Era of Good Feelings," *Pennsylvania Magazine of History and Biography* 95 (July 1971): 363–82.

49. Unless otherwise noted, information on the little-studied struggles over debtor relief and banking legislation is derived from Rothbard, *Panic of 1819*, 32–111, 136–58.

50. James Campbell to David Campbell, 18 May 1825, David Campbell Papers (Duke University Library).

51. Ford, *History of Illinois*, I, 74–75.

52. Charles Sellers, *James K. Polk* (2 vols., Princeton, 1957–1966), I, 58.

53. William B. Campbell to David Campbell, 28 May 1835, Campbell Papers.

54. Sellers, *Polk*, quotation I, 123; Jackson (Tenn.) *Gazette*, 5 July 1828.

55. R. Carlyle Buley, *The Old Northwest: Pioneer Period, 1815–1840* (2 vols., Indianapolis, 1950), I, 589–92; Harry R. Stevens, *The Early Jackson Party in Ohio* (Durham, N.C., 1957), 20–27.

56. Bayard Rush Hall (James A. Woodburn, ed.), *The New Purchase* (Princeton, 1916), 177, 200–1; Buley, *Old Northwest*, I, 597; James N. Primm, *Economic Policy in the Development of a Western State: Missouri, 1820–1860* (Cambridge, Mass., 1954), 1–15. In Missouri, when the farmer-dominated legislature refused to prop up the banks, even large-debtor entrepreneurial interests, centering in St. Louis and led by Duff Green, supported state paper money as the only available form of relief.

57. Thomas P. Abernethy, *The Formative Period in Alabama, 1815–1828* (University,

Ala., 1965), 111–28; J. Mills Thornton, *Politics and Power in a Slave Society: Alabama, 1800–1860* (Baton Rouge, 1978), 5–20.

58. Arndt M. Stickles, *The Critical Court Struggle in Kentucky, 1819–1829* (Bloomington, Ind., 1929); Lynn L. Marshall, "The Genesis of Grass-roots Democracy in Kentucky," *Mid-America* 47 (Oct. 1965): 269–87.

59. Charles Sellers, "Banking and Politics in Jackson's Tennessee, 1817–1827," *Mississippi Valley Historical Review* 41 (June 1954): 62–74.

Chapter 6. "A General Mass of Disaffection"

1. Charles Francis Adams, ed., *Memoirs of John Quincy Adams, Comprising Portions of His Diary from 1795 to 1848* (Philadelphia, 1884–1887), IV, 128.

2. Charles Sellers, "Jackson Men with Feet of Clay," *American Historical Review* 62 (Apr. 1957), 537–51; Charles Sellers, "Banking and Politics in Jackson's Tennessee, 1817–1827," *Mississippi Valley Historical Review* 41 (June 1954): 79–81.

3. The facts of Jackson's life are most fully presented in Marquis James, *The Life of Andrew Jackson* (Indianapolis, 1938), and Robert V. Remini, *Andrew Jackson* (3 vols., New York, 1977–1984). Although most recent writers follow James (*Jackson*, 789–90) in arguing that the Jacksons took the route of their kin south from Pennsylvania and Maryland, I find more persuasive the statement in an early biography written under Jackson's supervision that this household, arriving after the others were already settled in the Waxhaws, came directly from Ireland by way of Charleston. For the Scotch-Irish migration to the Carolinas, see Robert W. Ramsey, *Carolina Cradle: Settlement of the Northwest Carolina Frontier, 1747–1762* (Chapel Hill, 1964).

4. James C. Curtis, *Andrew Jackson and the Search for Vindication* (Boston, 1976), 12.

5. Michael Paul Rogin, *Fathers and Children: Andrew Jackson and the Subjugation of the American Indian* (New York, 1975), 42.

6. Remini, *Jackson*, I, 11.

7. My understanding of Jackson's personality owes much to Curtis, *Jackson*, and Rogin, *Fathers and Children*, though I am not wholly persuaded by Rogin's Freudian emphasis on Jackson's relationship with his mother. Bertram Wyatt-Brown, *Southern Honor: Ethics and Behavior in the Old South* (New York, 1982), especially chapters 2, 3, 5, and 6, presents an illuminating treatment of the subsistence culture's code of patriarchal honor, blurred by a rather romanticized interpretation of the derivative code of the pre–Civil War slaveholding gentry.

8. Remini, *Jackson*, I, 35–164.

9. Rogin, *Fathers and Children*, 136, 142; Curtis, *Jackson*, 39, 65.

10. John William Ward, *Andrew Jackson, Symbol for an Age* (New York, 1955), 3–78; quotations 7–8, 43–44, 46.

11. James, *Jackson*, 349.

12. Sellers, "Banking and Politics," 76–77.

13. Remini, *Jackson*, quotations I, 420; II, 12, 15, 30, 32, 34, 36, 39; Jackson to William B. Lewis, 21 Sept. 1821, photostat, Jackson-Lewis Letters, Ford Collection, New York Public Library.

14. Robert V. Remini, *Martin Van Buren and the Making of the Democratic Party* (New York, 1959), 11–29, quotations 11, 23, 24; Richard Hofstadter, *The Idea of a Party System: The Rise of Legitimate Opposition in the United States, 1780–1840* (Berkeley, 1969), 212–31.

15. Adams, *Memoirs*, VI, 56.

16. Samuel Flagg Bemis, *John Quincy Adams and the Foundations of American Foreign Policy* (New York, 1949), 341–62, 384–88; Bradford Perkins, *Castlereagh and Adams: England and the United States, 1812–1823* (Berkeley, 1964), 142, 283–328, 308–11; Ernest R. May, *The Making of the Monroe Doctrine* (Cambridge, Mass., 1975), 190–200; James D. Richardson, comp., *A Compilation of the Messages and Papers of the Presidents, 1789–1902* (10 vols., Washington, 1905), II, 209, 217–19. Although May's emphasis on the personal political ambitions of the actors seems excessive, his analysis of the evolution of the Monroe Doctrine is otherwise circumstantial and acute. Cf. Harry Ammon, "The Monroe Doctrine: Domestic Politics or National Decision?" *Diplomatic History* 5 (Winter 1981): 53–70; and Ernest R. May, "Response to Harry Ammon," ibid., 71–73.

17. "Letters from John C. Calhoun to Charles Tait," *Gulf States Historical Magazine* 1 (Sept. 1902): 102–3.

18. Adams, *Memoirs*, V, 361.

19. Charles M. Wiltse, *John C. Calhoun* (3 vols., Indianapolis, 1944–1951), I, 225–54; Gerald M. Capers, *John C. Calhoun, Opportunist: A Reappraisal* (Gainesville, Fla., 1960), 55, 82–85.

20. Glover Moore, *The Missouri Controversy, 1819–1821* (Lexington, Ky., 1953), 246; Shaw Livermore, Jr., *The Twilight of Federalism: The Disintegration of the Federalist Party, 1815–1830* (Princeton, 1962), 151–53.

21. Thomas P. Abernethy, *The Formative Period in Alabama, 1815–1828* (University, Ala., 1965), 124–34; Edwin A. Miles, *Jacksonian Democracy in Mississippi* (Chapel Hill, 1960), 6–9.

22. James, *Jackson*, 336–37, 354, 370; Kim T. Phillips, "The Pennsylvania Origins of the Jackson Movement," *Political Science Quarterly* 91 (Fall 1976): 495–507; Arthur M. Schlesinger, Jr., and Fred L. Israel, eds., *History of American Presidential Elections, 1789–1968* (2 vols., New York, 1971), I, 399.

23. Harry L. Watson, *Jacksonian Politics and Community Conflict: The Emergence of the Second American Party System in Cumberland County, North Carolina* (Baton Rouge, 1981), 101–2.

24. Albert Ray Newsome, *The Presidential Election of 1824 in North Carolina* (Chapel Hill, 1939), quotations 92, 94, 137–40.

25. James, *Jackson*, 362–64, 372–73.

26. James, *Jackson*, quotations 378–95.

27. Sellers, "Banking and Politics," quotations 79.

28. In the absence of an adequate account of New York politics, developments must be pieced together from Dixon Ryan Fox, *The Decline of Aristocracy in the Politics of New York* (New York, 1919); John A. Garraty, *Silas Wright* (New York, 1949); John Niven, *Martin Van Buren: The Romantic Age of American Politics* (New York, 1983); and Robert V. Remini, *Martin Van Buren and the Making of the Democratic Party* (New York, 1959).

29. Quotations from John C. Spencer to Albert H. Tracy, 28 May 1821, Tracy Papers (New York State Library); and Fox, *Decline of Aristocracy*, 273.

30. James, *Jackson*, 414–45; Remini, *Election of Jackson*, 11–29.

31. Richard P. McCormick, "New Perspectives on Jacksonian Politics," *American Historical Review* 65 (Jan. 1960): 287–301, delineates presidential turnout; the gloss is my own.

Chapter 7. God and Mammon

1. Paul E. Johnson, *A Shopkeeper's Millennium: Society and Revivals in Rochester, New York, 1815–1817* (New York, 1978), 4; Lewis O. Saum, *The Popular Mood of Pre–Civil War America* (Westport, 1980).

2. Conrad Wright, *The Beginnings of Unitarianism in America* (Boston, 1955); Sydney E. Ahlstrom, *A Religious History of the American People* (New Haven, 1972), quotation 407.

3. Joseph A. Conforti, *Samuel Hopkins and the New Divinity Movement: Calvinism, the Congregational Ministry, and Reform in New England between the Great Awakenings* (Grand Rapids, 1981), quotations 2, 10, 117, 195.

4. Ahlstrom, *Religious History*, quotation 407.

5. Mary Beth Norton, "'My Resting Reaping Time': Sarah Osborn's Defense of Her 'Unfeminine' Activities, 1767," *Signs*, 2 (Winter 1976), 515–29, quotations 522–29.

6. Paul Goodman, *Towards a Christian Republic: Antimasonry and the Great Transition in New England, 1826–1836* (New York, 1988), quotation 93; Richard D. Birdsall, "Ezra Stiles and the New Divinity Men," *American Quarterly* 17 (Summer 1965): 248–58, especially 249.

7. James D. Essig, *The Bonds of Wickedness: American Evangelicals against Slavery, 1770–1808* (Philadelphia, 1982), quotation 90.

8. Conforti, *Hopkins;* James M. Banner, Jr., *To the Hartford Convention: The Federalists and the Origins of Party Politics in Massachusetts, 1789–1815* (New York, 1970), quotation 203.

9. Samuel Hopkins, *The Life of Mrs. Sarah Osborn . . .* (Catskill, 1814).

10. *The Works of Samuel Hopkins, D.D. . . .* (3 vols., Boston, 1852), II, 273–87.

11. John B. Boles, *The Great Revival, 1787–1805, The Origins of the Southern Evangelical Mind* (Lexington, Ky., 1972), 107–9.

12. Donald M. Scott, *From Office to Profession: The New England Ministry, 1750–1850* (Philadelphia, 1978).

13. Banner, *Hartford Convention*.

14. Sidney E. Mead, *Nathaniel William Taylor, 1786–1853: A Connecticut Liberal* (Chicago, 1942), quotation 51.

15. Essig, *Bonds of Wickedness*, 97, 107–8.

16. Timothy Dwight, *Travels in New England and New York* (4 vols., New Haven 1821–22), I, 193–94, II, 458.

17. Richard D. Birdsall, "The Second Great Awakening and the New England Social Order," *Church History* 39 (Sept. 1970), 345–64, quotations 346; Charles R. Keller, *The Second Great Awakening in Connecticut* (New Haven, 1942), quotation 152. These valuable studies need some adjustment in the new light of Conforti, *Hopkins*.

18. George W. Marsden, *The Evangelical Mind and the New School Presbyterian Experience* (New Haven, 1970).

19. Goodman, *Christian Republic*, 73–74.

20. Charles I. Foster, *An Errand of Mercy: The Evangelical United Front, 1790–1837* (Chapel Hill, 1960), especially 105–78, quotations 56, 110, 155; Paul Boyer, *Urban Masses and Moral Order in America, 1820–1920* (Cambridge, Mass., 1978), 3–64; Clifford S. Griffin, *Their Brothers' Keepers: Moral Stewardship in the United States, 1800–1865* (New Brunswick, 1960), 23–98, quotation 28.

21. Gilbert H. Barnes, *The Anti-Slavery Impulse, 1830–1844* (New York, 1964, first pub. 1933), 3–28, quotation 17; Thomas L. Haskell, "Capitalism and the Origins of the

Humanitarian Sensibility," *American Historical Review* 90 (Apr., June 1985), 339–61, 547–66; Whitney R. Cross, *The Burned-over District: The Social and Intellectual History of Enthusiastic Religion in Western New York, 1800–1850* (Ithaca, 1950), 25.

22. Cross, *Burned-over District*, especially 9–13, 22–26, 33–47, 127, 252–53,quotation 34; Mario S. DePillis, "The Quest for Religious Authority and the Rise of Mormonism," *Dialogue* 1 (Spring 1966): 68–88, quotation 72–73; Richard L. Bushman, *Joseph Smith and the Beginnings of Mormonism* (Urbana, 1984), 9–42, quotations 12, 25, 32; Fawn M. Brodie, *No Man Knows My Name: The Life of Joseph Smith, the Mormon Prophet* (rev. ed., New York, 1982), quotation 18: Ahlstrom, *Religious History*, 492–94.

23. Bushman, *Joseph Smith*, 43–188, quotation 75; Brodie, *Joseph Smith*, especially 16–97, 405–41, quotations 52, 418; David M. Ludlum, *Social Ferment in Vermont, 1791–1850* (New York, 1939), 240–44; Jan Shipps, *Mormonism: The Story of a New Religious Tradition* (Urbana, 1985), 21, 37, 173.

24. Carol McKibben, "Cities and Saints: The Relationship between Mormonism and the Growth of Metropolis in Jacksonian America" (unpublished paper), quoting Elizabeth B. Tanner and Eliza M. Partridge from Kate B. Carter, ed., *Our Pioneer Heritage* (10 vols., Salt Lake City, 1966).

25. J. Klaus Hansen, *Mormonism and the American Experience* (Chicago, 1981), especially 113–78, quotation 124; DePillis, "Quest for Religious Authority."

26 *Memoirs of Reverend Charles G. Finney* (New York, 1876), passim, quotations 24, 42, 50, 60, 81, 83, 89, 90.

27. Nancy F. Cott, *The Bonds of Womanhood: Woman's Sphere in New England, 1780–1835* (New Haven, 1977), 101–3, 132–35, quotation 131–32.

28. Mary P. Ryan, *Cradle of the Middle Class: The Family in Oneida County, New York, 1790–1865* (Cambridge, 1981), 60–104, quotations 76–78.

29. Finney, *Memoirs*, passim, quotations 24, 42, 50, 60, 81, 83, 89, 90; William G. McLoughlin, *Modern Revivalism: Charles Grandison Finney to Billy Graham* (New York, 1959), 14–64, quotation 14.

30. McLoughlin, *Modern Revivalism*, 65–120, quotations 14, 113–16, 118–20; Ryan, *Cradle of the Middle Class*, 60–104.

31. Johnson, *Shopkeeper's Millennium*, 95–109, quotation 5.

32. Barnes, *Anti-Slavery Impulse*, quotations 20–21, 23; Bertram Wyatt-Brown, *Lewis Tappan and the Evangelical War against Slavery* (Cleveland, 1969), 1–94, quotations, 5, 6, 11–12.

33. Charles Grandison Finney (William G. McLoughlin, ed.), *Lectures on Revivals of Religion* (Cambridge, 1960), quotations xlix–l; Bernard A. Weisberger, *They Gathered at the River: The Story of the Great Revivalists and Their Impact upon Religion in America* (Boston, 1958), quotations 158.

34. McLoughlin, *Modern Revivalism*, quotations 53, 76, 79, 87, 89, 105; Finney, *Memoirs*, 320–51, quotations 315–16, 321, 328, 331, 334, 340.

Chapter 8. Ethos vs. Eros

1. Stuart M. Blumin, *The Emergence of the Middle Class: Social Experience in the American City, 1760–1900* (Cambridge, England, 1989). Blumin's fine delineation emphasizes the new white-collar class rather than the cross-class ideology that seems to me fundamental.

2. Calvin Colton, *Junius Tracts, VII: Capital and Labor* (New York, 1844), 15.

3. Jeffrey G. Williamson and Peter H. Lindert, *American Inequality: A Macroeconomic History* (New York, 1980), especially 36–46, 65–75, 97–102, quotation 37–38.

4. Edward Pessen, *Riches, Class, and Power before the Civil War* (Lexington, Mass., 1973), especially 77–91; Stuart M. Blumin, "Mobility and Change in Ante-Bellum Philadelphia," in Stephan Thernstrom and Richard Sennett, eds., *Nineteenth-Century Cities: Essays in the New Urban History* (New Haven, 1969), 165–208.

5. Stephan Thernstrom and Peter R. Knights, "Men in Motion: Some Data and Speculations about Urban Population Mobility in Nineteenth-Century America," *Journal of Interdisciplinary History* 1 (Autumn 1970): 7–35.

6. Robert V. Wells, *Uncle Sam's Family: Issues and Perspectives in American Demographic History* (Albany, 1985), 28–56; Robert V. Wells, *Revolution in Americans' Lives: A Demographic Perspective on the History of Americans, Their Families, and Their Society* (Westport, 1982), 93; Maris A. Vinovskis, *Fertility in Massachusetts from the Revolution to the Civil War* (New York, 1981); Morton O. Schapiro, "Land Availability and Fertility in the United States, 1760–1870," *Journal of Economic History* 42 (Sept. 1982): 577–600.

7. Paul G. Faler, *Mechanics and Manufacturers in the Early Industrial Revolution: Lynn, Massachusetts, 1780–1860* (Albany, 1981), 126.

8. Carroll Smith-Rosenberg, "Sex As Symbol in Victorian Purity: An Ethnohistorical Analysis of Jacksonian America," *American Journal of Sociology* 84, Supplement (1984): S212–47; Angus McLaren, *Reproductive Rituals: The Perception of Fertility in England from the Sixteenth Century to the Nineteenth Century* (London, 1984); Kathleen Verduin, "'Our Cursed Natures': Sexuality and the Puritan Conscience," *New England Quarterly* 56 (June 1983): 220–37; R. W. Roetger, "The Transformation of Sexual Morality in 'Puritan' New England: Evidence from New Haven Court Records, 1639–1698," *Canadian Journal of American Studies* 15 (Fall 1984): 243–57.For a cautious synthesis of scholarship on the nineteenth-century transformation of dauntingly inscrutable sexuality; John D'Emilio and estelle B. Freedman, *Intimate Matters: A History of Sexuality in America* (New York, 1988), 3–167.

9. Philip Greven, *The Protestant Temperament: Patterns of Child-Rearing, Religious Experience, and the Self in Early America* (New York, 1977), delineates the middle-class family as the Evangelical family, while distinguishing two forms of the elite family, the Genteel (planters) and the Moderate.

10. Barbara Welter, "The Cult of True Womanhood," *American Quarterly* 18 (Summer 1966): 151–74, quotations passim; Carroll Smith-Rosenberg and Charles Rosenberg, "The Female Animal: Medical and Biological Views of Woman and Her Role in Nineteenth-Century America," *Journal of American History* 60 (Sept. 1973): 332–56, quotation 335.

11. Carroll Smith-Rosenberg, *Disorderly Conduct: Visions of Gender in Victorian America* (New York, 1985), especially 109–64.

12. Carroll Smith-Rosenberg, *Religion and the Rise of the American City: The New York City Mission Movement, 1812–1870* (Ithaca, 1971), 70–124, quotations 121–23; Barbara J. Berg, *The Remembered Gate: Origins of American Feminism: The Woman and the City, 1800–1860* (New York, 1978), 176–222, quotations 80, 153, 181–82, 190.

13. Berg, *Remembered Gate*, 84; Nancy F. Cott, "Passionless: An Interpretation of Victorian Sexual Ideology, 1790–1850," *Signs* 4 (Winter 1978): 219–36, quotation 234.

14. Berg, *Remembered Gate*, 78, 80.

15. The deep psychodynamics and sexual politics of antebellum manhood are discovered—although overinterpreted and misattributed to Tocqueville's "democracy"—in G. J.

Barker-Benfield, *The Horrors of the Half-Known Life: Male Attitudes toward Women and Sexuality in Nineteenth-Century America* (New York, 1976), especially 135–214; quotations 136, 140, 146, 157–58, 170.

16. Stephen Nissenbaum, *Sex, Diet, and Debility in Jacksonian America: Sylvester Graham and Health Reform* (Westport, 1980), especially 9–15, 25–38, 105–24; quotations 11–12, 25, 30, 32, 112–13, 117–19.

17. Barker-Benfield, *Half-Known Life,* 173–75.

18. Jayme A. Sokolow, *Eros and Modernization: Sylvester Graham, Health Reform, and the Origins of Victorian Sexuality in America* (Rutherford, 1983), especially 55–99, quotations 87–88, 91.

19. Barker-Benfield, *Half-Known Life,* 145–48, 156, 162.

20. Barker-Benfield, *Half-Known Life,* 206, 210.

21. Robert L. Meriwether et al., eds., *The Papers of John C. Calhoun* (Columbia, S.C., 1959–), I, 53.

22. Edward Livingston, *A System of Penal Law for the State of Louisiana* (Pittsburgh, 1833), 17.

23. Barker-Benfield, *Half-Known Life,* 207.

24. Ronald Takaki, *Iron Cages: Race and Culture in Nineteenth-Century America* (New York, 1979), 16–35, quotations 22–24, 26; Charles Dickens, *American Notes for General Circulation* (London, 1850), 68–77; Joel C. Bernard, "From Theodicy to Ideology: The Origins of the American Temperance Movement" (Ph.D. dissertation, Yale University, 1983), quotation 153.

25. Sokolow, *Eros and Modernization,* 59–65, 143–52, quotations 64, 65, 87, 147.

26. David J. Rothman, *The Discovery of the Asylum: Social Order and Disorder in the New Republic* (Boston, 1971), especially 109–54, quotations 112–13, 115–17, 120.

27. Catherine M. Scholten, " 'On the Importance of the Obsetrick Art': Changing Customs of Childbirth in America, 1760–1825," *William and Mary Quarterly* 34 (July 1977), 426–45, quotations 431, 438, 441.

28. Barker-Benfield, *Half-Known Life,* 31–32.

29. Barker-Benfield, *Half-Known Life,* 93–105, quotations 93–95, 106, 110–13, 118. For orthodox medicine's continuing repressiveness toward male sexuality, see Gail Pat Parsons, "Equal Treatment for All: American Medical Remedies for Male Sexual Problems, 1850–1900," *Journal of the History of Medicine and Allied Sciences* 32 (Jan. 1977), 55–71.

30. Takaki, *Iron Cages,* quotations 139–43.

31. Sokolow, *Eros and Modernization,* 19–35; James C. Mohr, *Abortion in America: The Origins and Evolution of National Policy* (New York, 1978), ch. 1; Carol Z. Stearns and Peter N. Stearns, "Victorian Sexuality: Can Historians Do It Better?" *Journal of Social History* 18 (1985): 623–33.

32. W. J. Rorabaugh, *The Alcoholic Republic: An American Tradition* (New York, 1979), especially 5–32, 149–83, 233, quotation 3; Bernard, "From Theodicy to Ideology," quotation ii; Ian R. Tyrrell, *Sobering Up: From Temperance to Prohibition in Antebellum America, 1800–1860* (Westport, 1979), ch. 1.

33. James F. Hopkins et al., eds., *The papers of Henry Clay* (Lexington, Ky., 1957–), VIII, 213, 231, 254, 330, 600–1, 778.

34. Faler, *Mechanics and Manufacturers,* 111; Charles Sellers, *James K. Polk* (2 vols., Princeton, 1957–1965), quotations I, 115–16, 185.

35. Bernard, "From Theodicy to Ideology," especially 163–210, 310–37, 387, 398–99, 416, quotations 150, 209, 220, 222, 316, 347–48, 433; Tyrell, *Sobering Up,* espe-

cially 33–86, quotations 55, 75, 77; Rorabaugh, *Alcoholic Republic,* 35–57, 196, quotation 44.

36. Rorabaugh, *Alcoholic Republic,* 202, 233; Bernard, "From Theodicy to Ideology," quotations 253; especially Tyrell, *Sobering Up.*

37. For the class dynamics of Moderate-Light teetotalism: Tyrrell, *Sobering Up,* 87–124; Faler, *Mechanics and Manufacturers,* 100–38; and Paul E. Johnson, *A Shopkeeper's Millennium: Society and Revivals in Rochester, New York, 1815–1837* (New York, 1978), 116–41.

38. Bertram Wyatt-Brown, *Lewis Tappan and the Evangelical War against Slavery* (Cleveland, 1969), 54, 226–47.

39. Mary F. Ryan, *Cradle of the Middle Class: The Family in Oneida County, New York, 1790–1865* (Cambridge, 1981), quotations 141–42, 154, 176, 180–82.

Chapter 9. Politicians "Reapply Principles"

1. L. H. Butterfield, "The Jubilee of Independence: July 4, 1826," *Virginia Magazine of History and Biography* 61 (Apr. 1953): 119–40, quotations 124, 134–35.

2. Paul Leicester Ford, ed., *The Writings of Thomas Jefferson* (10 vols., New York, 1899), X, 317–18, 331n.

3. James D. Richardson, comp., *A Compilation of the Messages and Papers of the Presidents, 1789–1902* (10 vols., Washington, 1905), II, 294–317; Charles Francis Adams, ed., *The Memoirs of John Quincy Adams Comprising Portions of His Diary from 1795 to 1848* (Philadelphia, 1874–1877), quotations IV, 32; VI, 474; VII, 359; Mary W. M. Hargreaves, *The Presidency of John Quincy Adams* (Lawrence, Kans., 1985), especially 41–66, 247–80, quotation 166.

4. James F. Hopkins et al., eds., *The Papers of Henry Clay* (Lexington, Ky., 1959–), quotations IV, 119, 226–27, 301, 895.

5. Robert L. Meriwether et al., eds., *The Papers of John C. Calhoun* (Columbia, S.C., 1959–), quotations X, 10, 23, 39–40, 47, 128–29, 132.

6. J. Hector St. John de Crevecoeur, *Letters from an American Farmer* (New York, 1957), 167–68.

7. This section is based mainly on William W. Freehling, *Prelude to Civil War: The Nullification Controversy in South Carolina, 1816–1836* (New York, 1965), 7–121, with quotations drawn, except where otherwise indicated, from 14–15, 53, 62, 66–68, 77–81, 115–16.

8. Norma L. Peterson, *Littleton Waller Tazewell* (Charlottesville, 1983), 31–32.

9. Charles Sellers, "The Travail of Slavery," in Charles Sellers, ed., *The Southerner as American* (Chapel Hill, 1960), 40–71, quotation 58.

10. Mark Bils, "Tariff Protection and Production in the Early U.S. Cotton Textile Industry," *Journal of Economic History* 44 (Dec. 1984): 1033–45.

11. U.S. Department of Commerce, Bureau of the Census, *Historical Statistics of the United States: Colonial Times to 1970* (2 vols., Washington, 1975), I, 209.

12. Merrill D. Peterson, ed., *Democracy, Liberty, and Property: the State Constitutional Conventions of the 1820s* (Indianapolis, 1966), 271–85, quotations 281.

13. Freehling, *Prelude to Civil War,* 96, 106–7, quotation 119.

14. Ulrich B. Phillips, "Georgia and State Rights," American Historical Association, *Annual Report* (1901), 3–224, especially 53–65, 99–119, quotation 63; Paul Murray, "Economic Sectionalism in Georgia Politics, 1825–1855," *Journal of Southern History* 10

(Aug. 1944): 293–307; William G. McLoughlin, *Cherokee Renascence in the New Republic* (Princeton, 1987), quotation 449.

15. Harry L. Watson, "Conflict and Collaboration: Yeomen, Slaveholders, and Politics in the Antebellum South," *Social History* 10 (Oct. 1985): 273–98, especially 274; James Oakes, *The Ruling Race: A History of American Slaveholders* (New York, 1982), especially 37–40, 67–87, 96–122; Harriet Martineau, *Society in America* (New Brunswick, 1981), quotation 153. The antebellum class realities revealed by Frank L. Owsley, *Plain Folk of the Old South* (Baton Rouge, 1949) are confirmed and elaborated by the local studies (see bibliographical essay) of Richard R. Beeman, Orville V. Burton, Lacy K. Ford, Steven Hahn, J. William Harris, and John T. Schlotterbeck. Liberal historiography embraces both southern romantics and the odd Marxism of Eugene Genovese to sustain a myth exculpating capitalism from black enslavement. While greatly illuminating the slave experience, Genovese imagines an Old South kept precapitalist by the dominance of "seigneurial" planters.

16. Peter D. McClelland and Richard J. Zeckhauser, *Demographic Dimensions of the New Republic: American Interregional Migration, Vital Statistics, and Manumissions, 1800–1860* (Cambridge, England, 1982), 6–7, 18, 51–52; Gregory S. Ross, "Hoosier Origins: The Nativity of Indiana's United States Born Population in 1850," *Indiana Magazine of History* 81 (1985): 201–32.

17. Sellers, "Travail of Slavery," 42, 64.

18. Donald G. Mathews, *Slavery and Methodism: A Chapter in American Morality, 1780–1845* (Princeton, 1965); Oakes, *Ruling Race*, ch. 4.

19. Frances Trollope, *Domestic Manners of the Americans* (New York, 1832), quotations 93–95, 108–9; Richard Flower, *Letters from Lexington and the Illinois* (London, 1819), quotation 10; James Flint, *Letters from America* (Edinburgh, 1882), quotation 142–43; Isaac Holmes, *An Account of the United States of America . . .* (London [1823]), quotations 343–44, 359–60, 375–76; James Stuart, *Three Years in North America* (2 vols., Edinburgh, 1833), II, quotation 428–30.

20. Steven C. Bullock, "A Pure and Sublime System: The Appeal of Post-Revolutionary Freemasonry," *Journal of the Early Republic* 9 (Fall 1989): 359–73, quotation 367.

21. Ronald P. Formisano with Kathleen Smith Kutolowski, "Antimasonry and Masonry: The Genesis of Protest, 1826–1827," *American Quarterly* 29 (Summer 1977): 139–65, quotation 144.

22. Paul Goodman, *Towards a Christian Republic: Antimasonry and the Great Transition, in New England, 1826–1836* (New York, 1988), quotation 25.

23. Betsy Blackmar, "Re-walking the 'Walking City': Housing and Property Relations in New York City, 1780–1840," *Radical History Review* 21 (Fall 1979), 131–48; Tom W. Smith, "The Dawn of the Urban-Industrial Era: The Social Structure of Philadelphia, 1790–1830" (Ph.D. dissertation, University of Chicago, 1980).

24. Sean Wilentz, *Chants Democratic: New York City & the Rise of the American Working Class, 1788–1850* (New York, 1984), quotations 62, 82; Allan R. Pred, *The Spatial Dynamics of U.S. Urban-Industrial Growth, 1800–1914: Interpretive and Theoretical Essays* (Cambridge, Mass., 1966), 159.

25. Stuart M. Blumin, *The Emergence of the Middle Class: Social Experience in the American City, 1760–1900* (Cambridge, England, 1989), especially 30–38.

26. Andrew R. L. Cayton, "The Fragmentation of 'a Great Family': The Panic of 1819 and the Rise of the Middling Interest in Boston, 1818–1822," *Journal of the Early Republic* 2 (Summer 1982): 143–67, quotations 147–50, 154, 157, 159–60, 162; Gary L. Browne, *Baltimore in the Nation, 1789–1861* (Chapel Hill, 1980), 97, 103–11, quotation 111.

27. Wilentz, *Chants Democratic*, 40, 145–50; Howard B. Rock, *Artisans of the New Republic: The Tradesmen of New York City in the Age of Jefferson* (New York, 1979), 316–19; Richard Carwardine, "The Second Great Awakening in the Urban Centers: An Examination of Methodism and the 'New Measures,'" *Journal of American History* 59 (Sept. 1972): 327–40; Terry D. Bilhartz, *Urban Religion and the Second Great Awakening: Church and Society in Early National Baltimore* (Rutherford, N.J., 1986).

28. Wilentz, *Chants Democratic*, 168–71.

29. Wilentz, *Chants Democratic*, 153–64, quotations 159, 161; Bruce Laurie, *Working People of Philadelphia, 1800–1850* (Philadelphia, 1980), 67–74.

30. Wilentz, *Chants Democratic*, 165–67.

31. Laurie, *Working People*, 75–79, quotation 76; Bruce Laurie, *Artisans into Workers: Labor in Nineteenth-Century America* (New York, 1989), 67–72.

32. Wilentz, *Chants Democratic*, 172–216, quotations 183, 186–87, 194.

33. Laurie, *Artisans into Workers*, 79–83; Edward Pessen, *Most Uncommon Jacksonians: The Radical Leaders of the Early Labor Movement* (Albany, N.Y., 1967), especially 3–33; Arthur M. Schlesinger, Jr., *The Age of Jackson* (Boston, 1946), quotation 133.

34. Gary Kulik, "Pawtucket Village and the Strike of 1824: The Origin of Class Conflict in Rhode Island," *Radical History Review* 17 (Spring 1978): 4–37.

35. Thomas Dublin, *Women at Work: The Transformation of Work and Community in Lowell, Massachusetts, 1820–1860* (New York, 1979).

36. Charles M. Wiltse, *John C. Calhoun* (3 vols., Indianapolis, 1944–1951), I, 404; Daniel Feller, *The Public Lands in Jacksonian Politics* (Madison, 1984), 59–67, 82–85, 96–101; Frederick Jackson Turner, *Rise of the New West, 1819–1829* (New York, 1906), 199; Hargreaves, *Presidency of Adams*, 173–80.

37. Charles Sellers, *James K. Polk* (2 vols., Princeton, 1957–1966), I, 153.

38. William N. Chambers, *Old Bullion Benton, Senator from the New West: Thomas Hart Benton, 1782–1858* (Boston, 1956), 3–131, quotations 84, 87, 89.

39. Wiltse, *Calhoun*, I, 315–98; Sellers, *Polk*, I, 102–10, quotation 106.

40. Robert V. Remini, *Martin Van Buren and the Making of the Democratic Party* (New York, 1959), 93–185, quotations 113, 151–52; John Niven, *Martin Van Buren: The Romantic Age of American Politics* (New York, 1983), 165–214; Richard H. Brown, "The Missouri Crisis, Slavery, and the Politics of Jacksonianism," *South Atlantic Quarterly* 65 (Winter 1966): 55–72, quotations 62–63, 66, 69–70.

41. Hopkins, *Clay Papers*, VII, 263–64.

42. Feller, *Public Lands*, quotation 233.

43. Charles Sellers, "The Equilibrium Cycle in Two-Party Politics," *Public Opinion Quarterly* 29 (Spring 1965): 16–38.

44. Remini, *Van Buren*, 130.

45. Robert V. Remini, *The Election of Andrew Jackson* (Philadelphia, 1963), especially 76–80, 102–8, 117–18, 151–62.

46. Randolph A. Roth, *The Democratic Dilemma: Religion, Reform, and the Social Order in the Connecticut River Valley of Vermont, 1791–1850* (Cambridge, England, 1987), 143.

47. Hopkins, *Clay Papers*, VI, 569; VII, 243; Hargreaves, *Presidency of Adams*, 253.

48. Edward Stanwood, *A History of the Presidency* (rev. ed., 2 vols., Boston, 1928), election statistics, I, 136, 146; Frederick Jackson Turner, *The United States, 1830–1850: The Nation and Its Sections* (New York, 1935), election map 29; Donald J. Ratcliffe, "Politics in Jacksonian Ohio: Reflections on the Ethnocultural Interpretation," *Ohio History* 88 (Winter 1979): 5–36.

Chapter 10. Millennial Democracy

1. Robert V. Remini, *The Election of Andrew Jackson* (Philadelphia, 1963), quotations 199, 202; Arthur M. Schlesinger, Jr., *The Age of Jackson* (Boston, 1945), quotation 6.

2. Marquis James, *The Life of Andrew Jackson* (2 vols. in 1, Indianapolis, 1938), quotation 482.

3. James, *Jackson*, quotation 500; Eric M. Ericsson, "The Federal Civil Service under President Jackson," *Mississippi Valley Historical Review* 13 (March 1927): 517–40; Sidney H. Aronson, *Status and Kinship in the Higher Civil Service: Standards of Selection in the Administrations of John Adams, Thomas Jefferson, and Andrew Jackson* (Cambridge, Mass., 1964).

4. James D. Richardson, comp., *A Compilation of the Messages and Papers of the Presidents, 1789–1902* (10 vols., Washington, 1905), quotations II, 437–38, 448–49.

5. Richard B. Latner, *The Presidency of Andrew Jackson: White House Politics, 1829–1837* (Athens, Ga., 1979), 31–57.

6. James, *Jackson*, quotation 491.

7. James, *Jackson*, 496.

8. Charles Sellers, *James K. Polk* (2 vols., Princeton, 1957–1966), quotations I, 138.

9. Charles M. Wiltse, *John C. Calhoun* (3 vols., Indianapolis, 1944–1951), I, 362–64, quotation 380; William W. Freehling, *Prelude to Civil War: The Nullification Controversy in South Carolina, 1816–1836* (New York, 1965), 143–54, 205–13, quotations 149, 152–53, 234.

10. Latner, *Presidency of Jackson*, 52–73, quotation 72.

11. James, *Jackson*, quotations 508–9; Robert V. Remini, *Andrew Jackson* (3 vols., New York, 1977–1984), II, 192–216, quotations 62, 164–65, 209, 214; James F. Hopkins et al., eds., *The Papers of Henry Clay* (Lexington, Ky., 1959–), quotation VIII, 135.

12. William G. McLoughlin, *Cherokee Renascence in the New Republic* (Princeton, 1986), quotations 431n, 425, 427; Michael D. Green, *The Politics of Indian Removal: Creek Government and Society in Crisis* (Lincoln, Neb., 1982); Mary Young, "The Exercise of Sovereignty in Cherokee Georgia," *Journal of the Early Republic* 10 (Spring 1990): 43–63.

13. Michael P. Rogin, *Fathers and Children: Andrew Jackson and the Subjugation of the American Indian* (New York, 1975), 206–48, quotations 216–17.

14. Richardson, *Messages of the Presidents*, II, 456–59.

15. Ronald N. Satz, *American Indian Policy in the Jacksonian Era* (Lincoln, Neb., 1975), 9–125.

16. Richardson, *Messages of the Presidents*, II, 441–62, quotations 447–48, 450, 452, 462; Richard E. Ellis, *The Union at Risk: Jacksonian Democracy, States' Rights, and the Nullification Crisis* (New York, 1987), quotation 54.

17. Ellis, *Union at Risk*, 41–73, quotation 184; Daniel Feller, *The Public Lands in Jacksonian Politics* (Madison, 1984), 68–142, quotations 77–78, 92, 113; William N. Chambers, *Old Bullion Benton, Senator from the New West: Thomas Hart Benton, 1782–1858* (Boston, 1956), 132–70, quotations 134–35; Wiltse, *Calhoun*, II, 54.

18. Wiltse, *Calhoun*, II, 64.

19. James, *Jackson*, quotation 539; Sellers, *Polk*, quotation I, 147; quotation from Kendall to F. P. Blair, 25 Apr. 1830, Blair-Lee Papers (Princeton University Library); Remini, *Jackson*, quotation II, 254.

20. Richardson, *Messages of the Presidents*, II, 483–94.

21. James, *Jackson,* quotations 540–41; Wiltse, *Calhoun,* II, 73–109, quotations 76.

22. Remini, *Jackson,* II, quotations 237, 245, 247.

23. Wiltse, *Calhoun,* quotation II, 93.

24. This section mainly follows Freehling, *Prelude to Civil War,* 192–250, with quotations, unless otherwise ascribed, from pp. 89, 221–27, 234–35, 241, 248–49, 257.

25. Merrill D. Peterson, *The Great Triumvirate: Webster, Clay, and Calhoun* (New York, 1987), 191.

26. Richardson, *Messages of the Presidents,* II, 544–58, quotations 556.

27. For an illuminating account of the Bank War from the Bank's perspective: Bray Hammond, *Banks and Politics in America: From the Revolution to the Civil War* (Princeton, 1957), 369–410.

28. Hammond, *Banks and Politics,* 376–78; *Register of Debates,* 22nd Congress, 1st Session, Appendix, 128–32.

29. Sellers, *Polk,* I, 177.

30. "Andrew Jackson's Memorandum Book 1829–32," Andrew Jackson Papers (Library of Congress).

31. Schlesinger, *Age of Jackson,* 81.

32. Hammond, *Banks and Politics,* 375n.

33. Schlesinger, *Age of Jackson,* 37; Frank O. Gatell, "Sober Second Thoughts on Van Buren, the Albany Regency, and the Wall Street Conspiracy," *Journal of American History* 53 (June 1966): 19–40.

34. Hammond, *Banks and Politics,* 373.

35. Schlesinger, *Age of Jackson,* 55.

36. Schlesinger, *Age of Jackson,* 89.

37. Richardson, *Messages of the Presidents,* II, 576–91, quotations 590–91.

38. Hopkins, *Clay Papers,* quotations VIII, 556, 577, 596.

39. Thomas Cooper, ed., *Statutes at Large of South Carolina* (Columbia, S.C., 1836), quotations I, 329–31. The best accounts of the nullification crisis are Freehling, *Prelude to Civil War,* 252–97, and Ellis, *Union at Risk,* 74–198, quotations 78–85.

40. James Parton, *Life of Andrew Jackson* (3 vols., New York, 1861), III, 466.

41. John Spencer Bassett, ed., *Correspondence of Andrew Jackson* (7 vols., Washington, 1926–1935), quotations IV, 141–42, 449–50.

42. Ellis, *Union at Risk,* 78.

43. Richardson, *Messages of the Presidents,* II, 597–99.

44. Richardson, *Messages of the Presidents,* II, 641–56.

45. Parton, *Jackson,* III, 467; John C. Fitzpatrick, ed., *The Autobiography of Martin Van Buren,* American Historical Association, *Annual Report* (1918), II, 545–46; Bassett, *Correspondence of Jackson,* V, 11–12.

46. Ellis, *Union at Risk,* 85.

47. Sydney Nathans, *Daniel Webster and Jacksonian Democracy* (Baltimore, 1973), 48–73.

48. Bassett, *Correspondence of Jackson,* IV, 504–6; Schlesinger, *Age of Jackson,* 96.

49. *State Papers on Nullification . . . Published by Order of the General Court of Massachusetts . . .* [Boston, 1834], quotations 138, 197, 229; Fitzpatrick, *Autobiography of Van Buren,* 549–52.

50. Lillian F. Kibler, *Benjamin F. Perry, South Carolina Unionist* [Durham, N. C., 1946], 93.

51. Richardson, *Messages of the Presidents,* II, 606.

Chapter 11. Ambiguous Democracy

1. Charles Sellers, *James K. Polk* (2 vols., Princeton. 1957–1966), I, 186–232, for the removal struggle, quotation 190; Thomas P. Govan, *Nicholas Biddle: Nationalist and Public Banker, 1786–1844* (Chicago, 1959), 205–36, quotation 262.

2. Richard B. Latner, "A New Look at Jacksonian Politics," *Journal of American History* 61 (Mar. 1975): 943–69, quotation 959; Ari Hogenboom and Herbert Ershkowitz, eds., "Levi Woodbury's 'Intimate Memoranda' of the Jackson Administration," *Pennsylvania Magazine of History and Biography* 92 (Oct. 1968): 507–15, especially 513.

3. Arthur M. Schlesinger, Jr., *The Age of Jackson* (Boston, 1945), 97.

4. Schlesinger, *Age of Jackson*, 72–73.

5. For the roles of Duane and Whitney: [William J. Duane,] *Narrative and Correspondence Concerning the Removal of the Deposites and Occurrences Connected Therewith* (Philadelphia, 1838), especially 5, 12–14, 74, 104–5, 168–74, quotation 5; John M. McFaul, *The Politics of Jacksonian Finance* (Ithaca, 1972), 16–81.

6. Sellers, *Polk*, I, 224.

7. [Duane,] *Narrative*, quotation 48; Jean Alexander Wilburn, *Biddle's Bank: The Crucial Years* (New York, 1967), 31–45; Sellers, *Polk*, quotation I, 223.

8. [Duane,] *Narrative*, quotations 9–10, 48–50, 58, 65, 79, 103, 168–69; Bray Hammond, *Banks and Politics in America: From the Revolution to the Civil War* (Princeton, 1957), 411–38, quotations 417–18.

9. Hammond, *Banks and Politics*, quotation 431; Sellers, *Polk*, I, quotations 214, 218–19.

10. Sydney Nathans, *Daniel Webster and Jacksonian Democracy* (Baltimore, 1973), 143–44.

11. Bruce Laurie, *Artisans and Workers: Labor in Nineteenth-Century America* (New York, 1989), 83–91; Bruce Laurie, *Working People of Philadelphia, 1800–1850* (Philadelphia, 1980), 85–104; Sean Wilentz, *Chants Democratic: New York City & the Rise of the American Working Class, 1788–1850* (New York, 1984), 219–96.

12. Schlesinger, *Age of Jackson*, 166–67.

13. Schlesinger, *Age of Jackson*, 148–58.

14. Schlesinger, *Age of Jackson*, quotations 159, 162–63.

15. George Bancroft, *History of the United States* (10 vols., Boston, 1834–74), II, ch. 16, VIII, ch. 70.

16. Schlesinger, *Age of Jackson*, 162–63; Joseph Dorfman, *The Economic Mind in American Civilization, 1606–1865* (2 vols., New York, 1946), II, 601–61, quotation 612; John Ashworth, *'Agrarians' & 'Aristocrats': Party Ideology in the United States, 1837–1846* (London, 1983), quotation 118.

17. George Bancroft, *Literary and Historical Miscellanies* (New York, 1855), 409, 415.

18. Schlesinger, *Age of Jackson*, 151, 156.

19. Schlesinger, *Age of Jackson*, 156.

20. Hammond, *Banks and Politics*, 37.

21. Quotation, *House Committee Reports*, 23d Congress, 1st Session, no. 422; McFaul, *Jacksonian Finance*, passim, quotation 75.

22. Harry N. Scheiber, "The Pet Banks in Jacksonian Politics and Finance, 1833–1841," *Journal of Economic History* 23 (June 1963), 197–214, quotation 208; McFaul, *Jacksonian Finance*, 143–77.

23. Peter Temin, *The Jacksonian Economy* (New York, 1969), especially 59–112 for causes of the inflation.

24. Thomas Hart Benton, *Thirty Years' View* . . . (2 vols., New York, 1854), I, 703.

25. Hammond, *Banks and Politics*, 423–24, 438–39, quotation 424.

26. Robert V. Remini, *Andrew Jackson* (3 vols., New York, 1977–1984), III, 150.

27. Marvin Meyers, *The Jacksonian Persuasion: Politics and Belief* (Stanford, Calif., 1957), 11–23, quotations 15–16, 19–20; Remini, *Jackson*, quotations III, 341, 345, 417, 431.

28. F. P. Blair to A. Jackson, 24 Mar. 1845, Andrew Jackson Papers (Library of Congress).

29. McFaul, *Jacksonian Finance*, 82–142, 178–85, quotation 138.

30. Remini, *Jackson*, III, 328.

31. James D. Richardson, comp., *A Compilation of the Messages and Papers of the Presidents, 1789–1902* (10 vols., Washington, 1905), III, 304–7.

32. Charles Sellers, "The Equilibrium Cycle in Two-Party Politics," *Public Opinion Quarterly* 29 (Spring 1965), 16–38, quotation 30; William H. Riker, *The Theory of Political Coalitions* (New Haven, 1962).

33. Richard P. McCormick, *The Second American Party System: Party Formation in the Jacksonian Era* (Chapel Hill, 1966), especially 3–31, 329–56; Richard P. McCormick, *The Presidential Game: The Origins of American Presidential Politics* (New York, 1982).

34. Harry L. Watson, *Liberty and Power: The Politics of Jacksonian America* (New York 1990), quotation 201; Thomas Ford, *A History of Illinois from Its Commencement as a State in 1818 to 1847* (2 vols., Chicago, 1945), II, 93–94.

35. William Preston Vaughn, *The Antimasonic Party in the United States, 1826–1842* (Lexington, Ky., 1982); Paul Goodman, *Towards a Christian Republic: Antimasonry and the Great Transition in New England, 1826–1836* (New York, 1988).

36. Charles Sellers, "Who Were the Southern Whigs?" *American Historical Review* 54 (Jan. 1954): 335–46.

37. Richard P. McCormick, "Was There a 'Whig Strategy' in 1836?" *Journal of the Early Republic* 4 (Spring 1984): 47–70.

38. Ford, *History of Illinois*, I, 120–23, 143–44.

39. Theodore Sedgwick, ed., *A Collection of the Political Writings of William Leggett* (2 vols., New York, 1839), I, 143.

40. Joseph G. Baldwin, *The Flush Times of Alabama and Mississippi* (New York, 1957), 59–63 (paragraphing supplied and ellipses elided).

41. Ford, *History of Illinois*, I, 279–83.

42. Harriet Martineau, *Society in America* (New York, 1962), 164–65; Meyers, *Jacksonian Persuasion*, 104.

43. Temin, *Jacksonian Economy*, 113–77.

44. Allan Nevins and Milton H. Thomas, eds., *The Diary of George Templeton Strong: Young Man in New York, 1835–1849* (4 vols., New York, 1952), I, 55–65; James Roger Sharp, *The Jacksonians versus the Banks: Politics in the States after the Panic of 1837* (New York, 1970), 287; Major L. Wilson, *The Presidency of Martin Van Buren* (Lawrence, Kans., 1984), 54.

45. William H. Siles, ed., "Quiet Desperation: A Personal View of the Panic of 1837," *New York History* 67 (Jan. 1986): 89–92; Samuel Rezneck, "The Social History of an American Depression, 1837–1843," *American Historical Review* 40 (July 1935): 662–87.

46. Sharp, *Jacksonians versus the Banks*, 12, 300.

47. Wilson, *Presidency of Van Buren*, passim, quotations 72–74.

48. Harriet Martineau, *Retrospect of Western Travel* (2 vols., London, 1838), I, 144.

49. McFaul, *Jacksonian Finance*, 178–209.

50. Sharp, *Jacksonians versus the Banks,* passim; William G. Shade, *Banks or No Banks: The Money Issue in Western Politics, 1832–1865* (Detroit, 1972), 20–174.

51. Michael F. Holt, "The Election of 1840, Voter Mobilization, and the Emergence of the Second American Party System: A Reappraisal of Jacksonian Voting Behavior," in William J. Cooper, Jr., et al., eds., *A Master's Due: Essays in Honor of David Herbert Donald* (Baton Rouge, 1985), 16–58.

52. Wilson, *Presidency of Van Buren,* passim, quotation 125.

53. James F. Hopkins et al., eds., *The Papers of Henry Clay* (Lexington, Ky., 1959–), IX, 283, 323.

54. Nathans, *Webster,* 113; *The Writings and Speeches of Daniel Webster* (18 vols., Boston, 1903), III, 30.

55. William Nisbet Chambers, "The Election of 1840," in Arthur M. Schlesinger, Jr., and Fred L. Israel, eds., *History of American Elections, 1789–1968* (2 vols., New York, 1971), I, 641–744, quotation 741.

56. Sellers, "Equilibrium Cycle."

57. *United States Magazine and Democratic Review* 7 (1840): 486.

58. Pessen, *Most Uncommon Jacksonians,* 123.

Chapter 12. The Bourgeois Republic

1. E. Digby Baltzell, *Puritan Boston and Quaker Philadelphia: Two Protestant Ethics and the Spirit of Class Authority and Leadership* (New York, 1979); Thomas Bender, *New York Intellect: A History of Intellectual Life in New York City, from 1750 to the Beginnings of Our Own Time* (New York, 1987), 9–88, quotation 34.

2. Ronald Story, *The Forging of an Aristocracy: Harvard and the Boston Upper Class, 1800–1870* (Middletown, 1980).

3. Peter Dobkin Hall, *The Organization of American Culture, 1700–1900: Private Institutions, Elites, and the Origins of American Nationality* (New York, 1982), especially 55–94, 151–206; Richard D. Brown, "The Emergence of Urban Society in Rural Massachusetts, 1760–1820," *Journal of American History* 61 (June 1974): 29–51, especially 40–41; Lawrence A. Cremin, *American Education: The National Experience, 1783–1876* (New York, 1980), 212–13, 312–18.

4. Walter J. Ong, *Orality and Literacy: The Technologizing of the Word* (London, 1982); Jack Goody, ed., *Literacy in Traditional Societies* (Cambridge, England, 1968).

5. William T. Gilmore, "Elementary Literacy on the Eve of the Industrial Revolution: Trends in Rural New England, 1760–1830," American Antiquarian Society, *Proceedings* 92 (1982): 87–171; Kenneth A. Lockridge, *Literacy in Colonial New England: An Enquiry into the Social Context of Literacy in the Early Modern West* (New York, 1974); Caroline M. Kirkland, *Western Clearings* (New York, 1845), quotation 157.

6. Lee Soltow and Edward Stevens, *The Rise of Literacy and the Common School in the United States: A Socioeconomic Analysis to 1870* (Chicago, 1981), especially 34, 50–53, 155. The self-reported high rates of literacy among respondents to mid-nineteenth century census takers are suspect.

7. David Jaffee, "The Village Enlightenment in New England, 1760–1820," *William and Mary Quarterly* 47 (July 1990): 327–46; William J. Gilmore, *Reading Becomes a Necessity of Life: Material and Cultural Life in Rural New England, 1780–1835* (Knoxville, 1989). Gilmore's suggestive insights are inadequately supported by his evidence of books recorded in surviving estate inventories.

8. Carl F. Kaestle and Maris A. Vinovskis, *Education and Social Change in Nineteenth-Century Massachusetts* (Cambridge, England, 1980), especially 9–45; Albert Fishlow, "The American Common School Revival: Fact or Fancy?" in Henry Rosovsky, ed., *Industrialization in Two Systems: Essays in Honor of Alexander Gerschenkron* (New York, 1966), 40–67.

9. Carl F. Kaestle, *Pillars of the Republic: Common Schools and American Society, 1780–1860* (New York, 1983), quotation 7; Carl F. Kaestle, *The Evolution of an Urban School System: New York City, 1750–1850* (Cambridge, Mass., 1973), quotations 83, 85, 123.

10. Quotations from: Cremin, *National Experience,* 117; Mary Mann, ed., *Life and Works of Horace Mann* (3 vols., Cambridge, Mass., 1867), II, 143–88; [Horace Mann,] *Tenth Annual Report of the Board of Education, Together with the Tenth Annual Report of the Secretary of the Board* (Boston, 1846), 235; Brooks Atkinson, ed., *The Complete Essays and Other Writings of Ralph Waldo Emerson* (New York, 1940), 458–59; and Anne Norton, *Alternative Americas: A Reading of Antebellum Political Culture* (Chicago, 1986), 82.

11. Stanley K. Schultz, *The Culture Factory: Boston Public Schools, 1789–1860* (New York, 1973), quotation 131.

12. Kaestle and Vinovskis, *Education and Social Change,* 217–18.

13. Fishlow, "Common School Revival"; Cremin, *National Experience,* 182–83, 488.

14. David Paul Nord, "The Evangelical Origins of Mass Media in America, 1815–1835," *Journalism Monographs,* no. 84 (1984), especially 8–17; Cremin, *National Experience,* 69, 188–91.

15. David D. Hall and John B. Hench, eds., *Needs and Opportunities in the History of the Book* (Worcester, 1987), 17–29; Alexander Saxton, "Problems of Class and Race in the Origins of the Mass Circulation Press," *American Quarterly* 36 (Summer 1984): 211–34.

16. Frank L. Mott, *A History of American Magazines* (4 vols., New York and Cambridge, Mass., 1930–1957), I, especially 120–23, 341, 370, 494–99, 506, 514, 517, 581, quotation 370.

17. Cremin, *National Experience,* 301–10, 488–90.

18. Frank L. Mott, *Golden Multitudes: The Story of Best Sellers in the United States* (New York, 1947), 35–79.

19. Mott, *Golden Multitudes,* 70.

20. Washington Irving, *The Sketch-Book of Geoffrey Crayon, Gent.* (New York, [1819–20] 1897), quotations 56, 84, 116–17, 144, 207.

21. Henry Nash Smith, *Virgin Land: The American West as Symbol and Myth* (Cambridge, Mass., 1950), especially 59–70.

22. David Grimsted, *Melodrama Unveiled: American Theater and Culture, 1800–1850* (Chicago, 1968); Barbara Novak, *Nature and Culture: American Landscape and Painting, 1825–1875* (New York, 1980); Thomas Bender, "The 'Rural' Cemetery Movement: Urban Travail and the Appeal to Nature," *New England Quarterly* 47 (June 1974): 196–211; Ross L. Miller, "The Landscaper's Utopia versus the City: A Mismatch," *New England Quarterly* 59 (June 1976), 179–93; James Early, *Romanticism and American Architecture* (New York, 1965); John William Ward, "The Politics of Design," *Massachusetts Review* 6 (Autumn 1965): 661–88, quotation 666.

23. W. L. Nathan, "Thomas Cole and the Romantic Landscape," in George Boas, ed., *Romanticism in America* (Baltimore, 1940), 24–62, quotation 34; William Cullen Bryant, *Poetical Works* (New York, 1854), 181.

24. Mott, *American Magazines,* I, 494–99; Mrs. L. H. Sigourney, *Select Poems* (Philadelphia, 1856).

25. Mary Kelley, *Private Woman, Public Stage: Literary Domesticity in Nineteenth-Century America* (New York, 1984); Nina Baym, *Woman's Fiction: A Guide to Novels by and about Women in America, 1820–1870* (Ithaca, 1978); Mott, *Golden Multitudes*, quotation 121.

26. James D. Essig, *The Bonds of Wickedness: American Evangelicals against Slavery, 1770–1808* (Philadelphia, 1983), quotations 58; Ann Douglas, *The Feminization of American Culture* (New York, 1977); Nathan O. Hatch, *The Democratization of American Christianity* (New Haven, 1989), 193–94, 201–6.

27. Barbara M. Cross, *Horace Bushnell: Minister to a Changing America* (Chicago, 1958), quotations 36–37, 45–46; Theodore T. Munger, *Horace Bushnell: Preacher and Theologian* (Boston, 1890), quotation 25.

28. Perry Miller, *Errand into the Wilderness* (Cambridge, Mass., 1956), 184–203, quotations 199–200; *The Works of William E. Channing, D.D.* (Boston, 1891), quotations 272.

29. Emerson quotations in this section are from Atkinson, *Complete Writings of Emerson*, 6, 23, 25, 35–36, 42, 61–63, 67, 73–80, 148–49, 160, 450, 455, 694–716; and R. W. Emerson, "The Young American," *Dial* 4 (April 1844): 484–507. For Emerson's social context and intellectual development: Mary Kupiec Cayton, *Emerson's Emergence: Self and Society in the Transformation of New England, 1800–1845* (Chapel Hill, 1989).

30. Michael T. Gilmore, *American Romanticism and the Marketplace* (Chicago, 1985), 1–34, quotations 19–21.

31. F. O. Mathiessen, *American Renaissance: Art and Expression in the Age of Emerson and Whitman* (New York, 1941).

32. Mary Kupiec Cayton, "The Making of an American Prophet: Emerson, His Audiences, and the Rise of the Culture Industry in Nineteenth-Century America," *American Historical Review* 92 (June 1987): 597–620.

33. Cayton, "American Prophet," 617.

34. Mathiessen, *American Renaissance*, quotations 185; Walt Whitman, *Leaves of Grass* (New York, 1931), 1.

35. *The Works of Nathaniel Hawthorne* (Boston, 1882), V., 212–34.

36. Schultz, *Culture Factory*, 73.

37. Karen Halttunen, *Confidence Men and Painted Women: A Study of Middle-class Culture in America, 1830–1870* (New Haven, 1982), 66, 71, 93, 134.

38. *The American Review: A Whig Journal of Politics, Literature, Art and Science* 1 (Jan. 1845): 95–98.

39. Dr. Thomas Low Nichols, *Forty Years of American Life, 1821–1861* (2 vols., New York, 1869), I, 401–7.

40. Allan Nevins and Milton H. Thomas, eds. (abridged by Thomas J. Pressly), *The Diary of George Templeton Strong* (Seattle, 1988), 34.

41. Orestes A. Brownson, "The Laboring Classes," *Boston Quarterly Review* 3 (July 1840): 366–95.

42. Anthony F. C. Wallace, *Rockdale: The Growth of an American Village in the Early Industrial Revolution* (New York, 1972), quotation 389; John R. Commons, ed., *Documentary History of American Industrial Society* (Cleveland, 1910–1911), quotations VIII, part 1, pp. 305–7, part 2, p. 194; Bruce Laurie, *Artisans into Workers: Labor in Nineteenth-Century America* (New York, 1989), 89–91, 99–101.

43. Bruce Laurie, *Working People of Philadelphia, 1800–1850* (Philadelphia, 1980), 115–24, 140–47; Sean Wilentz, *Chants Democratic: New York City & the Rise of the American Working Class, 1788–1850* (New York, 1984), 306–14; Ruth M. Alexander,

"'We Are Engaged as a Band of Sisters': Class and Domesticity in the Washingtonian Temperance Movement, 1840–1850," *Journal of American History* 75 (Dec. 1988): 763–85.

44. Richard B. Stott, *Workers in the Metropolis: Class, Ethnicity, and Youth in Antebellum New York City* (Ithaca, 1990), 212–76; Wilentz, *Chants Democratic*, 255–389; Susan G. Davis, *Parades and Power: Street Theatre in Nineteenth-Century Philadelphia* (Philadelphia, 1986).

45. David S. Reynolds, *Beneath the American Renaissance: The Subversive Imagination in the Age of Emerson and Melville* (New York, 1988), 198–224; Larzer Ziff, *Literary Democracy: The Declaration of Cultural Independence in America* (New York, 1981), 87–107, quotations 92, 94.

46. Saxton, "Mass-Circulation Press," passim, quotation 224; Dan Schiller, *Objectivity and the News: The Public and the Rise of Commercial Journalism* (Philadelphia, 1981), 12–75.

47. Paul A. Gilje, *The Road to Mobocracy: Popular Disorder in New York City, 1763–1834* (Chapel Hill, 1987), especially 145–202; Michael Feldberg, *The Turbulent Era: Riot and Disorder in Jacksonian America* (New York, 1980); David Grimsted, "Rioting in Its Jacksonian Setting," *American Historical Review* 37 (Apr. 1972): 361–97; Carl E. Prince, "The Great 'Riot Year': Jacksonian Democracy and Patterns of Violence in 1834," *Journal of the Early Republic* 5 (Spring 1985): 1–19, quotation 3; Michel Chevalier, (John W. Ward, ed.,) *Society, Manners, and Politics in the United States* (New York, 1961), quotation 371.

48. Leonard L. Richards, *"Gentlemen of Property and Standing": Anti-Abolition Mobs in Jacksonian America* (New York, 1970); Emma Jones Lapsansky, "'Since They Got Those Separate Churches': Afro-Americans and Racism in Jacksonian Philadelphia," *American Quarterly* 32 (Spring 1980): 54–78.

49. Wilentz, *Chants Democratic*, 326–35, quotation 333.

50. Alexander Saxton, "Blackface Minstrelsy and Jacksonian Ideology," *American Quarterly* 27 (Mar. 1975), 3–28, quotation 3; Jean Baker, *Affairs of Party: The Political Culture of Northern Democrats in the Mid-Nineteenth Century* (Ithaca, 1983), 212–58.

51. Kerby A. Miller, *Emigrants and Exiles: Ireland and the Irish Exodus to North America* (New York, 1985), 193–279.

52. Ray Allen Billington, *The Protestant Crusade: A Study of the Origins of American Nativism* (New York, 1938), 32–237, quotation 231; Wilentz, *Chants Democratic*, 85–86, 222–23, 263–69, 315–25, 356–59, quotation 319; U.S. Department of Commerce, Bureau of the Census, *Historical Statistics of the United States: Colonial Times to 1957* (Washington, 1960), 57; Laurie, *Working People*, 124–33.

53. David Montgomery, "The Shuttle and the Cross: Weavers and Artisans in the Kensington Riots of 1844," *Journal of Social History* 5 (Summer 1972): 411–46.

54. George Rogers Taylor, *The Transportation Revolution, 1815–1860* (New York, 1951), 153–76, especially 173.

55. Taylor, *Transportation Revolution*, 74–103.

56. John F. Kasson, *Civilizing the Machine: Technology and Republican Values in America, 1776–1900* (New York, 1976), 172–80, quotations 117, 119, 172, 179–80.

57. Taylor, *Transportation Revolution*, 79, 161; Albert Fishlow, *American Railroads and the Transformation of the Ante-Bellum Economy* (Cambridge, Mass., 1965).

58. David L. Weddle, "The Law and the Revival: A 'New Divinity' for the Settlements," *Church History* 47 (June 1978): 196–214, quotation 203; Lyman Beecher, *A Plea for the West* (Cincinnati, 1835).

59. Thomas Ford, *A History of Illinois from Its Commencement as a State in 1818 to*

1847 (2 vols., Chicago, 1945), quotations II, 89–91. For a superb account of rural Illinois culture and its transformation in one community: John Mack Faragher, *Sugar Creek: Life on the Illinois Prairie* (New Haven, 1986).

60. This account draws heavily upon Lizabeth A. Cohen, "Yankees, Yeomen, and the Battle over School Reform in Antebellum Illinois" (unpublished paper, 1981). Remaining quotations in this section are drawn, unless otherwise indicated, from Cohen, pp. 9, 24–25, 30, 33, 39–41, 44, citing Christiana H. Tillson (Milo M. Quaife ed.), *A Woman's Story of Pioneer Illinois* (Chicago, 1919), 15, 81–82; Francis Grierson, *The Valley of Shadows: Recollections of the Lincoln Country, 1858–1863* (Boston, 1909), 42–43; Ford, *History of Illinois*, I, 121–22; John Pulliam, "Changing Attitudes toward Free Public Schools in Illinois," *History of Education Quarterly* 7 (Summer 1967): 193–94; Don Harrison Doyle, *The Social Order of a Frontier Community: Jacksonville, Illinois, 1825–1870* (Urbana, 1978), 220; Richard J. Jensen, *Illinois: A Bicentennial History* (Nashville, 1978), 52–53; Robert W. Patterson, *Early Society in Southern Illinois* (Chicago, 1881), 24; Paul Belting, *The Development of the Free Public High School in Illinois to 1860* (Springfield, 1919), 24; and William L. Pillsbury, "Early Education in Illinois," in Illinois Superintendent of Public Instruction, *Sixteenth Biennial Report* (Springfield, 1886), cix, cxvii.

61. Don E. Fehrenbacher, ed., *Abraham Lincoln: A Documentary Portrait through His Speeches and Writings* (Stanford, 1977), 39; Norton, *Alternative Americas*, 77.

Chapter 13. The Great Contradiction

1. Karl Marx (Saul K. Padover, ed.), *On America and the Civil War* (New York, 1972), 36.

2. Orlando Patterson, *Slavery and Social Death* (Cambridge, Mass., 1982); James Oakes, *Slavery and Freedom: An Interpretation of the Old South* (New York, 1990), 3–79, quotation 55; Marx, *On America*, quotation 29. Cf. Elizabeth Fox-Genovese and Eugene D. Genovese, *Fruits of Merchant Capital: Slavery and Bourgeois Property in the Rise and Expansion of Capitalism* (New York, 1983), especially 16–25, which dismisses Marx's "lapses" to cite Lenin and even Stalin as authorities for seeing southern planters as "prebourgeois."

3. Eugene D. Genovese, *Roll, Jordan, Roll: The World the Slaves Made* (New York, 1974), 35.

4. Oakes, *Slavery and Freedom*, 9, 137–94; Kenneth M. Stampp, *The Peculiar Institution: Slavery in the Ante-Bellum South* (New York, 1956), 192–236, quotation 356.

5. C. Vann Woodward, "Southern Slaves in the World of Thomas Malthus," in *American Counterpoint: Slavery and Racism in the North/South Dialogue* (New York, 1971), 78–106.

6. Oakes, *Slavery and Freedom*, 103, 143.

7. John W. Blassingame, *The Slave Community: Plantation Life in the Antebellum South* (rev. ed., New York, 1979); Genovese, *Roll, Jordan, Roll*; Herbert G. Gutman, *The Black Family in Slavery and Freedom, 1750–1925* (New York, 1976).

8. Albert J. Raboteau, *Slave Religion: The 'Invisible Institution' in the Antebellum South* (New York, 1978); Mechal Sobel, *Trabelin' On: The Slave Journey to an Anglo-Baptist Faith* (Westport, Conn., 1979); Blassingame, *Slave Community*, 99; Mechal Sobel, *The World They Made Together: Black and White Values in Eighteenth-Century Virginia* (Princeton, 1987).

9. Lawrence W. Levine, *Black Culture and Black Consciousness: Afro-American Folk Thought from Slavery to Freedom* (New York, 1977), 3–135.

10. Kenneth M. Stampp, "Rebels and Sambos: The Search for the Negro's Personality in Slavery," in *The Imperiled Union: Essays on the Background of the Civil War* (New York, 1980), 39–71.

11. Eugene Genovese, *From Rebellion to Revolution: Afro-American Slave Revolts in the Making of the Modern World* (Baton Rouge, 1979).

12. Clement Eaton, *The Freedom-of-Thought Struggle in the Old South* (New York, 1964), 89–117.

13. Charles S. Sydnor, *The Development of Southern Sectionalism, 1819–1848* (Baton Rouge, 1948), 225.

14. Charles Sellers, "The Travail of Slavery," in Sellers, ed., *The Southerner as American* (Chapel Hill, 1960), 40–71, quotations 49–50; Sydnor, *Southern Sectionalism*, 227–28.

15. Washington *United States Telegraph*, 5 Dec. 1835.

16. Eaton, *Freedom-of-Thought Struggle*, 120–237. The white South's complex politics of slavery is most fully delineated in William W. Freehling, *The Road to Disunion: Secessionists at Bay, 1776–1854* (New York, 1990).

17. John L. Thomas, *The Liberator: A Biography of William Lloyd Garrison* (Boston, 1963); Boston *Liberator*, 1 Jan. 1831.

18. Aileen S. Kraditor, *Means and Ends in American Abolitionism: Garrison and His Critics on Strategy and Tactics* (New York, 1967), quotation 27. For militant black opposition to colonization and black influence on white abolitionists: Benjamin Quarles, *Black Abolitionists* (New York, 1969); Jane H. Pease and William H. Pease, *They Who Would Be Free: Blacks' Search for Freedom, 1830–1861* (New York, 1974).

19. Kraditor, *Means and Ends*, 5.

20. Gilbert H. Barnes, *The Anti-Slavery Impulse, 1830–1844* (New York, 1933), 38–120.

21. Leonard L. Richards, *The Life and Times of Congressman John Quincy Adams* (New York, 1986), 7; Charles Francis Adams, ed., *Memoirs of John Quincy Adams, Comprising Portions of His Diary from 1795 to 1848* (Philadelphia, 1884–1887), IV, 531.

22. Barnes, *Anti-Slavery Impulse*, 121–45, quotation 144.

23. Richard H. Sewell, *Ballots for Freedom: Antislavery Politics in the United States, 1837–1860* (New York, 1976).

24. Ronald G. Walters, *The Antislavery Appeal: American Abolitionism after 1830* (New York, 1978), especially 111–28; Walter M. Merrill, *Against Wind and Tide: A Biography of Wm. Lloyd Garrison* (Cambridge, Mass., 1963), quotations 47, 132; Kraditor, *Means and Ends*, quotation 268–69.

25. I am indebted to Paul Goodman for references to treatments of the labor question in the *Liberator*, 29 Jan., 5 Feb., 3 Sept., 24 Sept., 1 Oct. 1831; 14 Apr., 1 Sept., 13 Oct. 1832; 20 Dec. 1834; 7 Jan., 31 Mar. 1837; and 28 Sept. 1838; Kraditor, *Means and Ends*, quotation 250.

26. Edward Magdol, *The Antislavery Rank and File: A Social Profile of the Abolitionists' Constituency* (Westport, 1986); Paul G. Faler, *Mechanics and Manufacturers in the Early Industrial Revolution: Lynn, Massachusetts, 1760–1860* (Albany, 1981), quotations 212–14; Sean Wilentz, *Chants Democratic: New York City & the Rise of the American Working Class, 1788–1850* (New York, 1984), 263–64, quotations 382.

27. Kraditor, *Means and Ends*, 200.

28. For the emergence of feminism from abolitionism: Blanche Glassman Hersh, *The Slavery of Sex: Feminist-Abolitionists in America* (Champaign, 1978), quotation 14.

29. Ellen Carol DuBois, *Feminism and Suffrage: The Emergence of an Independent*

Women's Movement in America, 1848–1869 (Ithaca, 1978), 34; Kraditor, *Means and Ends*, 47.

30. Gilbert H. Barnes and Dwight L. Dumond, eds., *Letters of Theodore Dwight Weld, Angelina Grimké Weld, and Sarah Grimké* (2 vols., New York, 1934), I, 414–16; Hersh, *Slavery of Sex*, 20.

31. DuBois, *Feminism and Suffrage*, 36; Hersh, *Slavery of Sex*, 16.

32. *Weld-Grimké Letters*, I, 436; Kraditor, *Means and Ends*, 73.

33. Barnes, *Anti-Slavery Impulse*, 169.

34. *Address of Mrs. Elizabeth Cady Stanton, Delivered at Seneca Falls & Rochester, N.Y., July 19th & August 2d, 1848* (New York, 1870); Susan B. Anthony, Elizabeth Cady Stanton, and Matilda Gage, *History of Woman Suffrage* (Rochester, N.Y.), quotation I, 70–73.

35. James Oakes, *The Ruling Race: A History of American Slaveholders* (New York, 1983), 39, 69–95; Oakes, *Slavery and Freedom*, 84–103, quotations, 92, 100; Michael Mullin, ed., *American Negro Slavery: A Documentary History* (New York, 1976), 23–24.

36. Gavin Wright, *The Political Economy of the Cotton South: Households, Markets, and Wealth in the Nineteenth Century* (New York, 1978), especially 116–25.

37. Oakes, *Slavery and Freedom*, 104–36; James D. Essig, *The Bonds of Wickedness: American Evangelicals against Slavery, 1707–1808* (Philadelphia, 1983), quotation 62; Oakes, *Ruling Race*, 358.

38. Louis Hartz, *The Liberal Tradition in America: An Interpretation of American Political Thought since the Revolution* (New York, 1955), 145–200, quotation 194; *Register of Debates*, 24th Congress, 2nd Session, 719–23. For the white South's inner contradictions: Sellers, "Travail of Slavery"; and Ralph E. Morrow, "The Proslavery Argument Revisited," *Mississippi Valley Historical Review* 48 (June 1961): 79–94.

39. *Register of Debates*, 19th Congress, 1st Session, 1649; Sellers, "Travail of Slavery," 57–58.

40. Harvey Wish, *George Fitzhugh: Propagandist of the Old South* (Baton Rouge, 1943), 111.

41. Wish, *Fitzhugh*, 111; R. W. Barnwell to R. B. Rhett, 1 Nov. 1844, Robert Barnwell Rhett Papers (Southern Historical Collection, University of North Carolina).

42. Leland D. Baldwin, ed., *The Flavor of the Past: Readings in American Social and Political Portraiture* (2 vols., New York, 1968), quotations I, 407–8. Scholarship on preannexation Texas is distilled in Ray Allen Billington, *Westward Expansion: A History of the American Frontier* (3rd ed., New York, 1967), 483–508.

43. Billington, *Westward Expansion*, 444–65, 509–33, 552–66; Norman A. Graebner, *Empire on the Pacific: A Study in American Continental Expansion* (New York, 1955), 1–82.

44. For the politics of the Harrison/Tyler administration: George R. Poage, *Henry Clay and the Whig Party* (Chapel Hill, 1936); and Robert Seagar II, *And Tyler Too: A Biography of John & Julia Gardiner Tyler* (New York, 1963).

45. Samuel Rezneck, "The Social History of an American Depression, 1837–1843," *American Historical Review* 40 (July 1935): 682.

46. *Niles' Register*, 13 May 1843, 175.

47. Virgil Maxcy to J. C. Calhoun, 10 Dec. 1843, John C. Calhoun Papers (Clemson University Library).

48. Charles Sellers, *James K. Polk* (2 vols., Princeton, 1957–1966), II, 29–31, 57–58.

49. William R. Manning, ed., *The Diplomatic Correspondence of the United States: Inter-American Affairs, 1831–1860* (Washington, 1936), VI, 18–25.

50. James Shields to Sidney Breese, 12 Apr. 1844, Sidney Breese Papers (Illinois State Library). For the Texas issue and the presidential election of 1844: Sellers, *Polk*, II, 3–212.

51. Frederick Merk, *Manifest Destiny and Mission in American History: A Reinterpretation* (New York, 1963), 24–60, quotations 46.

52. Jean Baker, *Affairs of Party: The Political Culture of Northern Democrats in the Mid-Nineteenth Century* (Ithaca, 1983).

53. Thomas R. Hietala, *Manifest Design: Anxious Aggrandizement in Late Jacksonian America* (Ithaca, 1985), 26–54.

54. Washington *Globe*, 27 Apr. 1844.

55. Washington *Globe*, 30 May 1844; Montpelier *Watchman and Journal*, 28 June 1844, in Edwin A. Miles, "'Fifty-four Forty or Fight'—An American Political Legend," *Mississippi Valley Historical Review* 44 (Sept. 1957): 298.

56. J. K. Polk to J. K. Kane, copy, 19 June 1844, James K. Polk Papers (Library of Congress); Nathan Sargent, *Public Men and Events from . . . 1817, to . . . 1853* (2 vols., Philadelphia, 1875), II, 235.

57. Poage, *Clay and the Whig Party*, 143–47; Washington *Madisonian*, 29 Aug. 1844.

58. J. M. Niles to Gideon Welles, 31 Jan. 1845, Gideon Welles Papers (Library of Congress).

59. For Polk's expansionism: Sellers, *Polk*, II, 205–66, 323–444, quotations 164–65, 213.

60. James D. Richardson, comp., *A Compilation of the Messages and Papers of the Presidents, 1789–1902* (10 vols., Washington, 1905), IV, 373–82.

61. Anson Jones, *Memoranda and Official Correspondence Relating to the Republic of Texas, Its History and Annexation, with a Brief Autobiography of the Author* (New York, 1859), 96; *House Executive Documents*, 30th Congress, 1st Session, no. 60, pp. 82–83.

62. *Parliamentary Debates*, 3rd. Ser., 178.

63. Washington *Union*, 6 June 1845; Manning, *Diplomatic Correspondence*, VIII, 763–64.

64. Manning, *Diplomatic Correspondence*, VIII, 172–82; Washington *Union*, 2 Oct. 1845.

65. Manning, *Diplomatic Correspondence*, VIII, 189–92.

66. Manning, *Diplomatic Correspondence*, VIII, 169–71; Richardson, *Messages of the Presidents*, IV, 398.

67. Richardson, *Messages of the Presidents*, IV, 449–50.

68. *Congressional Globe*, 29th Congress, 1st Session, 791–95.

69. *Congressional Globe*, 29th Congress, 1st Session, 796, 815, 977–78; E. B. Lee to S. P. Lee, 12 May 1846, and Montgomery Blair to S. P. Lee, 13 May 1846, Blair-Lee Papers (Princeton University Library); R. C. Winthrop to Clifford, 15 May 1846, Robert C. Winthrop Papers (Massachusetts Historical Society); J. R. Giddings to J. A. Giddings, 13 May 1846, Joshua R. Giddings Papers (Ohio State Archaeological and Historical Society); J. H. Henry to J. J. Hardin, 12 May 1846, John J. Hardin Papers (Chicago Historical Society); letter of Luther Severance, 12 May 1846, Washington *Union*, 22 May 1846.

70. *United States Magazine and Democratic Review*, 17 (July-August 1845): 5–10; *Congressional Globe*, 29th Congress, 1st Session, 917–18; Reginald Horsman, *Race and Manifest Destiny: The Origins of American Racial Anglo-Saxonism* (Cambridge, Mass. 1981), especially 208–48.

71. Horsman, *Race and Manifest Destiny*, 215–20; Merk, *Manifest Destiny*, 39n; Manning, *Diplomatic Correspondence*, VIII, 760.

72. Justin H. Smith, *The War with Mexico* (2 vols., New York, 1919), II, 319.

73. Sellers, *Polk,* II, 421–44.

74. Richardson, *Messages of the Presidents,* IV, 385–416. For Polk's domestic program: Sellers, *Polk,* II, 324–30, 343–46, 445–76.

75. Richardson, *Messages of the Presidents,* IV, 662–70.

76. J. A. Dix to Silas Wright, 10 July 1846, in Morgan Dix, *Memoirs of John Adams Dix* (2 vols., New York, 1883), I, 202; C. C. Cambreleng to Martin Van Buren, Martin Van Buren Papers (Library of Congress).

77. *Congressional Globe,* 29th Congress, 1st Session, 1210–15; Paul Leicester Ford, ed., *The Writings of Thomas Jefferson* (10 vols., New York, 1892–1899), X, 157; Eric Foner, "The Wilmot Proviso Revisted," *Journal of American History* 56 (Sept. 1969): 262–79.

78. *Congressional Globe,* 29th Congress, 2nd Session, Appendix, 317; Eugene H. Berwanger, *The Frontier against Slavery: Western Anti-Negro Prejudice and the Slavery Extension Controversy* (Urbana, 1967), especially 123–37.

79. James A. Rawley, *Race and Politics: "Bleeding Kansas" and the Coming of the Civil War* (Philadelphia, 1969), quotations 151, 268–69.

Index